Value-Driven Operations Management: An Integrated Modular Approach

Instructor's Evaluation Sampler

Series Editors
Steven A. Melnyk
Morgan Swink
both of Michigan State University

McGraw-Hill Irwin

Boston Burr Ridge, IL Dubuque, IA Madison, WI New York San Francisco St. Louis
Bangkok Bogotá Caracas Kuala Lumpur Lisbon London Madrid Mexico City
Milan Montreal New Delhi Santiago Seoul Singapore Sydney Taipei Toronto

McGraw-Hill Higher Education
A Division of The McGraw-Hill Companies

VALUE-DRIVEN OPERATIONS MANAGEMENT: AN INTEGRATED MODULAR APPROACH
Instructor's Evaluation Sampler

Published by McGraw-Hill/Irwin, an imprint of The McGraw-Hill Companies, Inc., 1221 Avenue of the Americas, New York, NY, 10020.

This book is printed on acid-free paper.

1 2 3 4 5 6 7 8 9 0 QPD QPD 0 9 8 7 6 5 4 3 2

ISBN 0-07-253383-8

Publisher: Brent Gordon
Senior sponsoring editor: Scott Isenberg
Developmental editor: Christina A. Sanders
Senior marketing manager: Zina Craft
Senior project manager: Kimberly D. Hooker
Cover design: Adam Rooke

Table of Contents

The Value-Driven Approach to Operations Management

Steven A. Melnyk
Michigan State University

Morgan Swink
Michigan State University

McGraw-Hill Irwin

Boston Burr Ridge, IL Dubuque, IA Madison, WI New York San Francisco St. Louis
Bangkok Bogotá Caracas Kuala Lumpur Lisbon London Madrid Mexico City
Milan Montreal New Delhi Santiago Seoul Singapore Sydney Taipei Toronto

The Value-Driven Approach to Operations Management

Module Objectives

By the end of this module, you should be able to

- Understand what the operations management system is and the role that it plays in the modern firm.
- Recognize how the operations management system and its capabilities are shaped by certain decisions taken by management.
- Identify the major partners that influence the activities of the operations management system.
- Explain the notion of value and the relationship between value and the effective and efficient operations management system.
- Understand fundamental changes in the operations management system and in concepts of value over the years.
- Explain why operations management is an inherently dynamic system and identify the factors that contribute to this dynamic character.

Audi Reinvents Itself by Discovering Value

Audi has long been a manufacturer of top quality cars—cars designed and built for the discriminating buyer. As such, Audi competes with the likes of BMW and Mercedes. However, in 1986 Audi experienced a crisis that almost drove it out of the North American market. In that year, a TV consumers' program reported several cases in which Audi 5000 model cars equipped with automatic transmissions (an option preferred by most American buyers) allegedly accelerated by themselves, causing damage and injury. The problem and negative publicity became so bad that many parking garages and valet services refused to accept Audi 5000s because they saw them as dangerous.

Audi's response to the situation did not help matters. They flatly denied that any problem existed. Customers who brought their cars to dealers to have them checked were turned away, after simply being told that there was nothing wrong. The customers reacted angrily. After all, they had paid a premium price for a premium product, yet they weren't receiving "premium treatment." Predictably, they refused to buy Audis in the future. The results were disastrous for Audi. Its total US sales fell from 74,000 cars in 1985 to 12,000 cars in 1991—a drop of 83.8%. A decision had to be made—to stay in the American market or to leave it completely and focus on the European market. Audi's managers decided that it had to stay in the American market, since it is the largest market for prestige cars. Leaving the American market would greatly harm Audi's reputation not only in the United States but also everywhere else in the world.

In 1994, Audi began a "comeback," using a system-wide overhaul ultimately driven by a rediscovered and enlarged understanding of value. The three-pronged strategy included three elements: (1) a superior product; (2) superior support; and, (3) superior dealer service.

Audi recognized that it had to design and build cars that were every bit as good and in some ways better than the cars produced by BMW and Mercedes. Product design and development processes were re-engineered, and operations managers focused on driving out waste, reducing product introduction lead times, and improving product conformance quality. By 2001, the fit and finish of Audi's cars was considered the best in the auto industry. Audi also worked on designing cars that were "right"—everything was where it should be in order to make the car a seamless extension of the driver. As a result, the new "A" series cars won many awards for superior handling, quality, and performance.

In the area of product support, Audi reduced the risk associated with buying a new car. They were the first to offer a program in which every scheduled maintenance and repair needed within the first three years (including oil changes and wiper blade replacement) were covered at no cost to the buyer. The only item not covered was tires.

Finally, Audi overhauled its dealer network. It recognized that the Audi buyer wanted more than simply to buy a car from a dealer. Instead, customers wanted a relationship with their dealers, service representatives, and mechanics. Audi buyers liked to talk about their cars, and they wanted personalized service. Audi recruited new dealers and workers whose psychological characteristics matched and supported those of Audi and its customers. In the resulting new dealer network, a salesperson is more inclined to become personally involved with customers, learning things about them such as where they go on vacation.

As a result of this new strategy, Audi customers have become "married" to their Audis, and Audi's staff has excelled at selling cars. The results have been impressive. Audi's position in the American market is now solid. By the end of 2000, Audi sales had reached an all-time high of 650,000 cars. Thanks to a more complete understanding of value from the customer's point of view, Audi has thrived.

There is no doubt about it, in the 1980s and 90s Audi reinvented and transformed itself. Why did Audi undertake such a radical transformation? The crisis in 1986 served as a wake-up call, sparking a recognition that the automotive business is about much more than simply designing and manufacturing cars that look good and perform reliably. These attributes alone are no longer enough to provide a competitive advantage; they are now expected. Product loyalty is a thing of the past. Today, consumers have much more information, and they will buy what they believe to be the best "overall product." This overall product concept goes beyond the physical product to include convenience, fast and responsive support, and relationships, all provided at reasonably low costs.

Today, business is about designing and delivering value. When superior value is offered, customers buy. When they buy, market share and profits naturally increase. The auto industry is certainly not unique. Most industries have or will experience similar fundamental changes in the ways firms sell to customers and the ways they must design, build and deliver products and services. To succeed in this new market, a different type of operations management system is needed. In this module, we introduce the field of operations management and the basics of an emerging value-based and value-driven view of the field.

Operations management includes the theory and practice of managing goods-and service-transformation processes. For many students, operations management implies factories, heavy machinery, assembly lines, and dull, repetitive tasks, all of which are misconceptions. If these are the elements of operations management, what does it have to do with the revolution at Audi? The answer is: everything. Just as Audi changed, so has the field of operations management. Many of the themes introduced in this opening story—themes of value, customer focus, the importance of product design, the increasing role of service offerings and the emergence of the supply chain—reflect the changing scope of today's operations management system. Operations management is no longer something that takes place within the walls of a factory. Today's operations management systems are dynamic, highly varied, and inexorably linked with other functions inside and outside the firm.

The following statements help define and describe operations management:

- Operations management is a business function concerning how firms design, make, and deliver goods and services to their customers.
- A value-based operations management model has important implications for analysis, management, design, control, and evaluation of the operations management system.
- To be effective, operations management must be consistent with the strategic goals of the firm.
- The operations management system brings together four major sets of players:—the firm, its suppliers, its customers, and stakeholders.

- Operations management systems consist of flows (movements) and storages of goods, people, money, and information.
- Operations management systems consist of processes, including product design/redesign, process design/redesign, performance measurement, planning, acquiring, making, and delivering.
- Operations management is fundamentally dynamic because of changes in technologies, resources, customers' desires, and strategic paradigms.

These ideas promote a better understanding of "new" operations management systems. The study of operations management is not simply the study of making things; rather, it is the study of how managers can generate better value for customers.

What Is Operations Management?

Operations management (OM) is a *field of management* that attempts to understand, explain, predict, and change the organizational and strategic effects of the transformation process. In other words, operations management deals with the effective and efficient management of the transformation process. **Effectiveness** is *doing the right things;* **efficiency** is *doing things right.* Effective operations satisfy the needs and expectations of customers in ways that contribute to the overall objectives and goals of the company. To evaluate effectiveness, managers ask, "Did we build something that the customer really wanted and deliver that product or service in a way that helped the firm to compete in the marketplace?" Efficiency minimizes the costs incurred to deliver outputs. Managers ask, "How does the cost of the inputs we consume compare with the value of the outputs we produce?" Effectiveness deals with issues of customer satisfaction and strategic positioning. It is evaluated by customers, both current and potential. Efficiency concerns matters such as productivity, cost control, and variance analysis. It is measured internally in units such as dollars or labor hours. Effectiveness is necessary for long-term survival; efficiency is important for short-term survival.

Critical Decisions in Operations Management

The scope of an operations management system can be established by answering certain critical questions, namely

- **What?** What type of activities and what types of goods or services are to be delivered by the system? What types of value are to be offered?
- **What resources?** What resources are needed, and how should they be developed, allocated, and controlled?
- **How?** How is the good or service to be designed, made, and delivered?
- **How much?** How much should our transformation process be able to deliver (and under what conditions)?
- **When?** When should the products be made, activities carried out, services delivered, or capacities/facilities come on line?
- **Where and who?** Where should the work be done and who should do it? Which activities should be the responsibility of suppliers, of partners, or of the firm?
- **For whom?** Who are the intended or targeted consumers of the goods and services produced by a firm's processes.
- **What measures?** How should we assess performance?

These questions are addressed by decisions in 9 critical areas of operations management (see Exhibit 1). Taken together, these decisions define the operations management system of the firm, how it is structured, how it operates, and how it is evaluated.

EXHIBIT 1
Critical Operations Management Decisions

Source: Adapted from Robert H. Hayes and Steven C. Wheelwright, *Restoring Our Competitive Edge: Competing through Manufacturing* (New York: John Wiley & Sons, 1984), p. 31.

Type of Decision	Operations Management Decision Area	Issues Considered
Structural	Capacity	Amount of capacity, timing of changes in capacity, type of capacity used
	Facilities	Size of facilities, location of facilities, specialization of what the facilities do
	Technology	Hardware: equipment, automation, linkages Information systems and software: equipment, type, purpose of packages, interfaces/linkages Process knowledge: generation, retention, application
	Supply chain	Direction, extent, responsibilities, types of relationships across resources
Tactical	Workforce	Skill level, wage policies, employment security
	Production planning and materials control	Sourcing policies, centralization, decision rules, span of control
	Performance measurement	Defect/problem detection, monitoring, feedback, intervention, focus of performance measurement
	Organization	Authority hierarchy, control/reward systems, roles of staff people, intrafirm relationships
	Renewal/improvement	When to revisit or change actions previously taken in the preceding decisions; what type of actions to take (and under what conditions)

The first four decision categories presented in Exhibit 1—**capacity, facilities, technology,** and **supply chain**—are **structural** in nature. They affect strategy and the physical operations management system. Once made, decisions in these areas act as constraints, determining what the operations management system can and cannot do well. Altering these decisions often requires significant investment and time—often years.

The remaining five decision areas—**workforce, production planning and materials control, performance measurement, organization,** and **renewal/improvement,** are **tactical** in nature. These determine what is done, when it is done, who does it, and how it is done.

The 9 decision categories are closely interrelated. For example, decisions regarding the supply chain also affect the type of information technology that must be in place, how production is scheduled and how people are recruited and evaluated. Because these categories are interrelated, it is not wise to look at a single decision in isolation.

Processes and Operations Management

Operations management is activity/decision oriented. Operations management is also ***process*** oriented. The operations management system is made up of many processes that span many organizational subunits. However, these can be grouped into three major subprocesses (see Exhibit 2 page 6): product/process design, planning/scheduling/execution, and performance measurements and improvement. To manage operations management effectively, one must think in terms of processes and subprocesses and understand their interrelationships and linkages.

What, then, is a process? A **process** is defined by a sequence and organization (either formal or informal) of all activities needed to convert inputs into outputs. If we want to change the outcomes, then we must change the process.

A process draws together inputs, transformation activities, and outputs into a unified system (see Exhibit 3 page 6). It identifies the resources needed, for example, machines, material, labor, energy, and information. A process also describes the activities needed to convert inputs into outputs. For example, one uses a grill and heat to convert a raw hamburger patty (an input) into a cooked hamburger (an output). Other activities transport or move items from one area to another. Still other activities store raw materials, work-in-

EXHIBIT 2
Three Basic Operations Management Processes

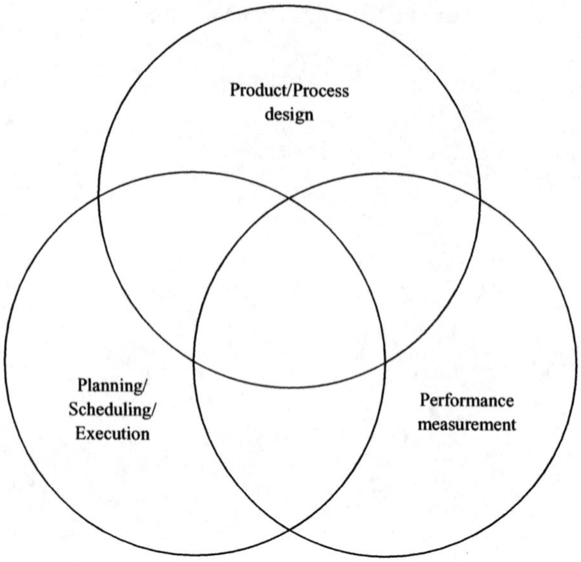

process (begun but unfinished outputs), or completed work. Finally, some activities check or inspect work to make sure that it meets standards for quality, quantity, lead time, or timing.

Operations management processes involve the production of a physical good, information, a service, or all three. Some processes generate goods and services that firms sell to customers (resource management processes); others plan the next generation of goods and services or their associated processes (innovation processes) or plan where the firm as a whole should go (strategic management processes). Still others measure resources (measurement processes) or coordinate activities between a firm and its suppliers (supply-chain management processes).

The structure of operations processes influences the ability of the firm to serve its customers. We all have experienced organizations with complex, bureaucratic processes that seem incapable of providing a desired service in a timely manner. The design of a process should reflect what customers want. If customers prize quick response, for example, then the process should be designed to be fast and flexible. Managers must identify and eliminate unnecessary or redundant steps, reduce distances between steps or activities, and diminish the time needed to complete each step.

This connection between the process and the customer must be maintained. If the customer changes, then the process may also have to change.

EXHIBIT 3 **The Process and Its Major Components**

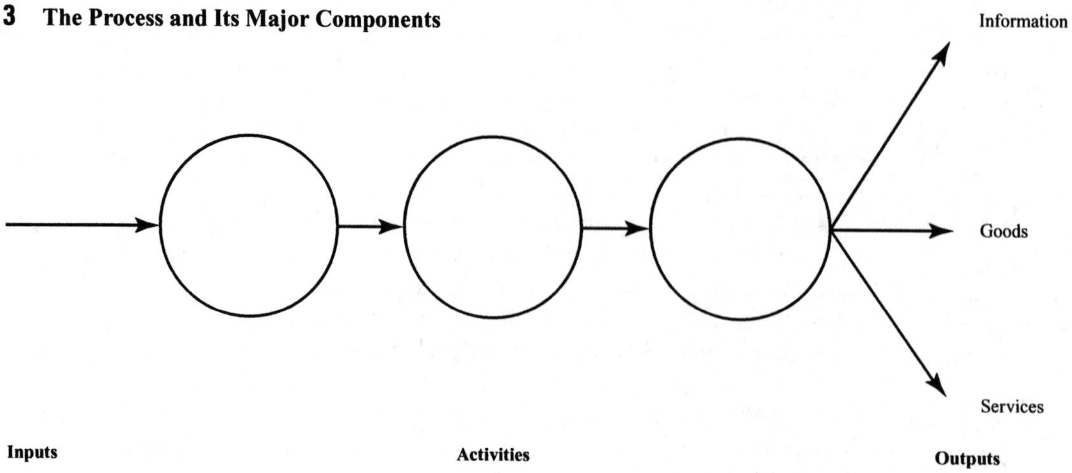

Physical Goods versus Services

Traditionally, the output of the operations management process has been described as either a good or a service. These two types of outputs are differentiated by the product's tangible or intangible nature. Exhibit 4 summarizes the differences between goods and services.

EXHIBIT 4
Characteristics of Goods and Services

Physical Goods	Services
Tangible	Intangible
Can be inventoried	Cannot be inventoried
Little customer contact (consumption is separate from production)	Extensive customer contact (simultaneous consumption and production)
Long lead times	Short lead times
Capital intensive	Labor intensive
Quality easily assessed	Quality very difficult to assess (more perceptual)
Material is transformed	Customer is transformed

Goods

A **good** has a definite physical presence; it can be touched and stored (inventoried), and the firm can produce it in advance of customer demand. The module you are now reading, your car, the television that you watch at night after you finish studying are all goods. The decision to produce goods affects the design and implementation of the operations management system in several ways.

First, because they can inventory goods, operations managers can separate the product's consumer from the place where the firm produces it. This allows firms to locate manufacturing plants where it makes economical sense. For example, the first steel plants were located near Pittsburgh, Pennsylvania, for proximity to sources of iron ore and coal, two critical ingredients in steel.

The production of goods, as compared with that of services, requires little contact with the customer. Firms often produce fairly standardized goods in advance of customer orders so they can respond quickly to those orders. Customer contacts are greatest during the design of the product, when the customer places the order, and when the product is delivered.

Manufacturing processes for goods typically are capital intensive, with machines working to make products. For example, in an auto assembly plant, robots attach windows to cars, and transfer lines move cars from one operation to another. The combination of a capital-intensive process and physical separation between the customer and the manufacturing process often results in long lead times.

Finally, operations managers can relatively easily establish quality standards for tangible goods and measure the products against these standards. For example, they can objectively evaluate whether the good works (functionality), how long it works (reliability), how it operates under adverse conditions (durability), whether is it safe to use (safety), and how it appears (aesthetics).

Services

In contrast to goods, **services** are largely intangible and experiential. For example, at a restaurant, you buy not only food but also the atmosphere in which you eat. Since services are intangible, they cannot be stored. While goods manufacturing systems can accumulate and distribute inventory to smooth out imbalances between supply and demand, a producer of services must maintain enough production capacity to meet demand during peak periods; otherwise, it must backlog the demand. When you go into a restaurant during its busy time and the greeter asks you to wait in the lounge, you become part of a backlog of demand.

Since producers cannot inventory services, the production and consumption of the service must occur at the same time. In addition, the production process is often very visible to the customer. Customers observe the operation of the process and its structure because it routes them from one operation to another until they are served and sent on their way. The link between consumption and production tends to keep lead times shorter than those for tangible goods. If the lead times are long, customers are likely to leave the process without consuming the service.

Furthermore, customers play a very important role in the delivery of a service, telling servers what they want, when they want it, and how they want the service delivered. In some cases, as with an automated teller machine (ATM), the customer may even perform the service. As a result, production systems for services tend to be more flexible than for manufacturing systems.

Quality control is more difficult for services than for goods. Managers cannot easily and objectively measure a service product and its attributes. Rather than evaluating products, service providers tend to evaluate methods of delivery. Since services are very labor intensive, managers evaluate how workers deliver the service to the customer. For example, a quality control inspector for McDonald's studies how counter workers greet customers who arrive to place orders, how they take orders, how they fill orders, and how they close out transactions, that is, what they say when they give food to customers.

Because service quality lies in the labor-intensive process, it becomes important to train workers in people skills, that is, how to interact with customers and how to deliver the service to customers.

Total Product Experience

Increasingly, the distinction between goods and services is blurring. This is due to the recognition by managers of the importance of the **total product experience.** For this reason, we will refer to the combined outputs of a process as a **product.** This term covers both goods and all its related services, including all aspects of the consumption experience.

In reality, the marketplace includes very few pure goods and pure services. Most products are hybrids, mixtures of goods and services. When you buy a new car, for example, you want to know not only whether the car is well built but also what services the dealer offers for financing, maintenance, and repairs. You do not simply buy a car; you also buy the support that comes with that car. Furthermore, many services also include tangible products. A hospital, for example, provides medicines and bandages along with intangible diagnostic and treatment services.

Understanding hybrid products leads managers to think in terms of the total product experience, the combination of tangibles (goods) and the intangibles (services and experiences) designed to win the customer's approval.[1] Customers do not think of services and goods separately; both are parts of the entire product package.

Provide examples of (a) pure goods, (b) pure services, and (3) hybrids. How many products are either pure goods or pure services?

Operations Management's Partners

Operations management processes combine the actions and activities of four major partners: (1) the customer, (2) stakeholders, (3) suppliers, and (4) the firm. It is important to have a working understanding of these partners.

Customers

Customers include anyone who consumes the outputs of the operations management system. Unless the firm has clearly identified its customers, it cannot structure an effective or efficient operations management function. Knowledge of the customer allows a manager to accurately describe the customers' wishes, what they are willing to pay, what they do not consider acceptable, and what they view as minimum acceptable levels of performance. This information helps the operations management manager to design and run the operations management system by identifying[2]

[1] Karl Albrecht, *The Only Thing That Matters* (New York: Harper Business, 1992), p. 13.
[2] Terry Hill, *Manufacturing Strategy: Text and Cases* (New York: McGraw-Hill/Irwin, 2000).

- **Order winners.** These are the product traits that are likely to cause customers to choose one product over a competing product, for example, better performance, lower cost. These are traits on which the operations management system must excel.
- **Order qualifiers.** These are the product traits such as lead times, cost, or quality that must meet a certain level in order for the product to even be considered by customers. The firm must perform acceptably on these traits. In many cases, the customer may not be aware of any level of performance in excess of those minimum levels that they have established.
- **Order losers.** Poor performance on these traits can cause the loss of either current or future business.

Order winners and order qualifiers form the basis for customers' expectations. Order losers, in contrast, result from customers' actual experiences with the firm and its operations management process. They represent the gap between what the firm delivers and what customers expect.

Any firm has at least three different categories of customers: internal customers, for example, manufacturing is an internal customer of the product design process at Ford; intermediate customers, for example, a car dealership or rental company; and final customers, the ultimate users who actually use the product, such as the person who actually buys and drives the car off the dealer's lot. While each customer group is important, it is beneficial for a firm to identify critical customers. Critical customers are the ones who have the greatest impact on products, sales, and future growth opportunities.

Stakeholders

A **stakeholder,** in contrast to a customer, is any person or group of people with an interest in the functions of an operations management system or firm and its well-being (financial and otherwise). Stakeholders include unions/employees, the local community, social groups (such as those who are against the unnecessary suffering of animals used in testing or who are concerned about pollution and the state of the environment), government, and financial investors. Why differentiate between customers and stakeholders? Stakeholders' demands of the operations management system often differ from the demands of customers. For example, customers might care most about the price and quality of products; some stakeholders might care most about environmental waste. Like customers, stakeholders can significantly affect how a firm operates.

Suppliers

Suppliers are firms for which our operations management system is itself a customer. Suppliers are becoming increasingly important because they can help a firm react quickly to changes in customer demand by providing capacity (volume), expertise, and resources. Increasingly, the operations manager is being called on to manage both the corporate operations management system and the operations management systems of its suppliers.

The Firm

The operations management system needs to interact closely and in a consistent manner with other functions in the firm. Operations management strategies cannot be developed in isolation. Instead any operating decision should take into account its effects on finance, marketing, research and development, and other key functions.

Value: The Driver of the Operations Management System

In the past, operations managers tended to focus on cost as the key driver of decisions. Since pricing decisions are frequently divorced from operating decisions, operations managers have long worked under the premise that they can improve corporate performance directly only by reducing costs and improving productivity. However, mainly focusing on cost can create problems. Suppose that in order to reduce costs, a manager decides not to spend money on preventive maintenance. As the condition of the equipment inevitably deteriorates, quality problems arise, overall costs increase, and lead times grow. To reduce costs further, the manager might invest less money in employee training and education, causing workers to be less effective at dealing with the problems they encounter on the shop floor. To save still more money, the firm may employ fewer workers, leaving remaining workers to cover the same amount of work. Workers rush to finish, reducing quality even further. This sequence degenerates into a vicious, cost-driven cycle.

In moving away from a myopic focus on costs and prices, it is incumbent upon the firm to understand what elements of value are important for different customer segments. We define **value** as

> the customer's subjective evaluation, adjusted for cost, of how well a product meets or exceeds his or her expectations.

Customers enter purchase decisions with a set of expectations. The firm's operating system possesses a set of capabilities—what the transformation process can and cannot do. If a customer's expectations are consistent with the capabilities of the transformation process, then value is likely to be delivered.

A focus on value leads to a more strategic and complete management approach. We identified some of the dangers of a cost-focused management approach earlier. Similar problems may arise when any single performance objective, for example, quality, is pursued in isolation. In order for an operating system to be effective, it must address all aspects of customers' expectations. It must deliver value as the customer defines it.

The Importance of Operations Management: A Value-Based History

One way to understand the importance of operations management is to comprehend the role that operations management has had in determining the economic destiny of people around the world. It can be argued that differences in operations management account for differences in the quality of life enjoyed across various countries. In the modern and post-modern eras, shifts in economic power can be traced to the industrial and technological revolutions whose roots lie in operations management.

Recognizing changes in value over time provides another perspective that is important for a full understanding of operations management. As industrialized people have gained the ability to provide goods and services beyond their basic needs, that is, food, shelter, and clothing, their expectations and concepts of value also have grown. The following sections trace the major developments in operations management with an emphasis on changes in the notions of value.

Modern operations management, as we know it now, is relatively young. It is usually associated with the Industrial Revolution, which took place in Great Britain between 1765 and 1815. Yet, as a management field of study, operations management is much older. Until recently, it was natural to associate operations management with manufacturing. The origins of operations management can be traced through history as far back as ancient Greece, Rome, or Egypt. For example, in ancient Rome, there were factories that specialized in making olive oil jars, food oils, cloth, weapons, and the like (more examples of early factories are found in the In Practice box). These factories were driven then, as now, by the need to deliver higher value for their customers. Initially, the goal of these factories was to reduce costs, improve quality, and increase output so that products could be made available to more and more people.

Evolution of Modern Operations Management

Until the start of the Industrial Revolution, machinery and power were very limited. For the most part, power was provided by humans, animals, or water. In addition, most factories were small in size. All of this changed with the emergence of the Industrial Revolution in Britain and its spread throughout the rest of Europe. Since then, modern operations management has evolved at different rates throughout the world. As an example, we trace

In Practice

MANUFACTURING IN THE RENAISSANCE

Operations management was a key influence even during the Renaissance. For example, a primitive form of an assembly line existed in Venice during this time period. A major sea-trading power, Venice made much of its wealth not only by trading with other areas using Venice-based ships but also by outfitting ships going out to trade. A ship that was preparing for a trading voyage would enter a canal lined with shops that sold rope, barrels, canvas, deck hardware, and food provisions. As the ship proceeded down the canal, employees located in the various shops on the top floors would toss down supplies. By the time a ship left the canal, it would be completely outfitted.

During this period, many of the practices that we consider to be part of modern operations management were introduced, including the division of labor and specialization. These practices permeated throughout business establishments as well as the studios of Italy, which were responsible for creating many of our current masterpieces.

seven major stages in the evolution of North American practices.[3] Other countries also have experienced and are today experiencing similar stages of evolution.

- 1800–1850: Age of technical capitalists
- 1850–1890: Introduction of mass production
- 1890–1920: Scientific management in operations management
- 1920–1960 Golden age of American manufacturing
- 1960–1980: Decline of American industry
- 1980–1995: World-class operations
- 1995–present: E-Business—operations management meets the Internet.

Ultimately, these changes have all been driven by value. The concept of value is not new; it has always been a driving force that motivated and shaped the developing practices in operations management. These seven stages identify responses to evolving technologies, changing markets, increasing competition, and product developments. At each stage, there was a unique value-related challenge that operations management had to address with a set of technological and/or managerial innovations that precipitated advances in operations management.

1800–1850: Age of the Technical Capitalists

Beginning in the 1800s, demand was high as the United States grew. The problem was a lack of capacity. Value was based first on availability and secondly on price. Most Americans bought from producers in New England—if the product was available—or from Britain. However, in the early 1800s, this situation began to change thanks to one of the greatest acts of industrial espionage ever committed. In 1800, Francis Cabot Lowell visited the great manufacturing centers of Great Britain, where he memorized the technical features of all of the great technological innovations introduced by the British. On returning to Boston, he worked with community leaders to establish the revolutionary town of Lowell. The town's infrastructure was organized around the principles of production. Mr. Lowell conceived a new internal organizational structure consisting of three major divisions of labor: (1) management, (2) sales, and (3) labor. In addition, this period witnessed the introduction of interchangeable parts (a critical component of mass production), as well as the emergence of the transportation network.

1850–1890: Introduction of Mass Production

During this period, value was still about availability and price. The task of the operations manager was to expand production (demand still greatly exceeded capacity) while reducing the costs of production. The emergence of steam and electrical power made it possible for factories to move from locations near water, which was needed to generate power, to urban

[3] The material for the first five stages is taken from Romeyn Everdell, "From Lowell to Sunnyvale," in *Leading Manufacturing Excellence,* ed. Patricia E. Moody (New York: John Wiley & Sons, 1997), pp.18–44.

centers—areas of low labor cost. As a result, a large-scale, permanent labor force emerged. Increasing demand for products was fueled by the growth of the United States and the impact of the Civil War. Higher volumes of production led to the discovery of the economy-of-scale effect: as size of a plant grew, the unit costs of production fell. Further fueling the growth of the factory was technological innovation—this was the time of Alexander Graham Bell and Thomas Edison—leading to increased automation.

1890–1920: Scientific Management in Operations Management

At the turn of the century, management scientists such as Frederick Taylor and Frank Gilbreth began to systematically address problems involving personnel, hiring, training; manufacturing/design engineering, design of equipment and processes; rate setting, level of output; and material control. This period saw the growth of the production staff, which was the starting point for operations management as a business profession. In the marketplace, customers not only wanted more new products, they wanted more variety. This value-based change produced new operations management challenges associated with managing product change, changeovers, and product proliferation.

1920–1960: Golden Age of American Manufacturing

In this period, American industry dominated the global market. This was due in part to the effects of two world wars, which effectively crippled much of the manufacturing capacity in Europe and the Far East. During this time, the goal of operations management was simple: stretch capacity to meet demands that greatly exceeded supply (capacity). This period was characterized by labor/management power struggles in the United States. Automation continued to increase, and overhead mounted as material handlers, equipment maintenance, inspectors, planners, and schedulers were added. This period also saw the simultaneous introduction of computers and quantitative methods, both of which were aimed at improving efficiency and increasing output.

1960–1980: Decline of American Industry

Changes abounded for the operations manager during these two decades. The economy began to slow down, and, as many of the manufacturing systems crippled by World War II were rebuilt, worldwide capacity soon met and then exceeded demand. While there was abundant capacity in many industries, especially the automotive industry, there was not enough of the specific type of capacity demanded by the customer. Customers sought more customized products, but the existing capacity was designed to build standard products. In response, Japanese manufacturing firms grew in prominence, aided by just-in-time (JIT) systems, which allowed firms to simultaneously reduce costs, reduce lead times, improve quality, and enhance flexibility. Rather than relying on automation, JIT extensively used detailed studies of processes—how activities were carried out—and the abilities of employees.

1980–1995: World-Class Operations

By the start of the 1980s, American firms recognized serious threats from foreign competitors and increasingly demanding customers. This new environment raised the standard of expected basic performance. The phrase "world-class manufacturing" (WCM) came to denote a firm whose practices were so good that it could compete with anyone in the world. Operations management became a central focus of competition, spawning initiatives such as time-based competition, mass customization, and total quality management.[4] Each of these initiatives spawned operating improvements by focusing on specific types of value desired by the customer. By this time computers had become widely used to control equipment, for example, flexible manufacturing systems (FMS); to collect data, for example, bar coding; and to plan and schedule production. Also during this period, managers became very aware of the unexploited power of the supply chain. The emphasis of operations management shifted from managing resources to managing relationships (linking the firm to its suppliers on one side

[4] These value-based initiatives are discussed in greater detail in the "Value-Driven Operations Strategy" module by Steven A. Melnyk, Morgan Swink (New York: McGraw-Hill/Irwin 2002)

and to its customers on the other side). Operations management principles and process-focused improvements [lead by initiatives such as business process reengineering (BPR)] were increasingly applied to services as well as manufacturing.

Just as the scope of operations management was expanding, so was the scope of value. Products took on a larger meaning to include services as well as tangible goods. Firms sought to increase product value by offering more services and more problem-solving capabilities. By the end of this period, some American firms disappeared. Those that were left were leaner, more aggressive, and more value-oriented.

1995–Present: E-Business—Operations Management Meets the Internet

The power of the Internet is radically transforming business today. This system of communication has revolutionized not only how people shop and search for products; it also has significantly influenced operations management. The Internet gives customers more information, greater choice, lower costs, and speed. It has forced management to rethink its channels for accessing and serving customers. In addition, it has enabled firms to reorganize their internal systems and external relationships with suppliers and partners in order to achieve greater delivery speed and flexibility, reduce inventory, and, ultimately, increase profits. The concept of value has continued to expand. One important dimension of growth fostered by the Internet is value through networking. Manufacturers are now viewing the sales of their tangible goods as opportunities for establishing ongoing relationships with customers.

Summary

As we can see from this brief history, operations management is fundamentally dynamic. What works in one period might not work in another. We also see that operations management has always been value driven. These traits and developments are summarized in Exhibit 5.

EXHIBIT 5 **Evolution of Operations Management: A Value-Driven Perspective**

	1800–1850 Age of Technical Capitalists	1850–1890 Introduction of Mass Production	1890–1920 Scientific Management	1920–1960 Golden Age	1960–1980 Decline of American Industry	1980–1995 World-Class Manufacturing	1995–Present E-Commerce
Value challenge	Increase availability; reduce cost	Increase availability; reduce cost	Reduce cost; increase variety	Reduce cost; increase variety	Reduce waste; enhance quality	Improve quality; reduce cost; reduce lead times; enhance responsiveness	Increase information to customer; increase choice; reduce costs; reduce lead times
Technical advances	Improved manufacturing technology; interchangeable parts; locating factories on waterways and in industrial centers; emerging transportation network	Emergence of local factory; movement to urban areas; introduction of steam and electrical power; new machines; economies of scale	More systematic approaches to operations management; moving assembly line	Increased automation; introduction of computers and quantitative methods	Just-in-time systems; emergence of process control	Increased role of computers on the shop floor; emergence of world-class practices and benchmarks; business process reengineering; enhanced information systems; greater awareness of need for supply chain coordination	Internet; enhanced information systems and communications technologies

continued

EXHIBIT 5 **Evolution of Operations Management: A Value-Driven Perspective** *continued*

	1800–1850 Age of Technical Capitalists	1850–1890 Introduction of Mass Production	1890–1920 Scientific Management	1920–1960 Golden Age	1960–1980 Decline of American Industry	1980–1995 World-Class Manufacturing	1995–Present E-Commerce
Labor	Recruited women; increased formal training; company-owned housing	Large-scale, permanent labor force (recruited from low labor-cost areas)	Large-scale permanent labor force	Labor/management power struggles; increased indirect labor due to need for activities such as material handling and inspection	Women re-enter workforce; shift in focus from workers being part of the process to being problem solvers; increased labor–management cooperation	Reduction in direct labor; greater emphasis on core competencies	Continued reduction in direct labor
Structure	Division of labor in management: (1) plant management, (2) sales, and (3) labor.	Plant management refined; introduction of foreman to control day-to-day operations	Increased labor specialization; growth of production staff; vertical integration	Increased specialization; new management categories such as planners and schedulers	Reduction in staff; more responsibility given to line workers	Internal teams: collaborative relationships involving suppliers and customers	Redesign of the supply chain; blurring boundaries between suppliers; customers, and firm
Operations span of focus	Internal factory	Internal factory	Internal factory	Internal factory	Internal factory	Internal factory plus R&D Outsourcing	Internal factory and supply chain
Capacity versus demand	D > C	D > C	D > C	D > C	D <= C	D < C	D < C

Operations Management Dynamics: The Product Life Cycle and the Value Cycle

Operations management is involved in the design and delivery of products that are always changing. One popular way of thinking about product changes is the **product life cycle (PLC)**. The PLC is a graphical representation (see Exhibit 6) of the various stages that a product goes through from birth to death.

The product life cycle identifies four stages through which most products progress. Underlying the product life cycle model are some very important assumptions, namely

- All products have a limited life.
- All products pass through distinct phases.
- Profits rise and fall at different rates throughout the phases.
- Different strategies are required at each of the four stages.

If you think about it, there is logic to the product life cycle concept. We all know of products that have gone from one stage to the next. However, there is something disturbing about the product life cycle. It assumes that a product that enters the maturity stage is doomed eventually to decline, which is not always the case. Consider the story of the 35mm SLR (single-lens reflex) camera.

EXHIBIT 6 The Product Life Cycle

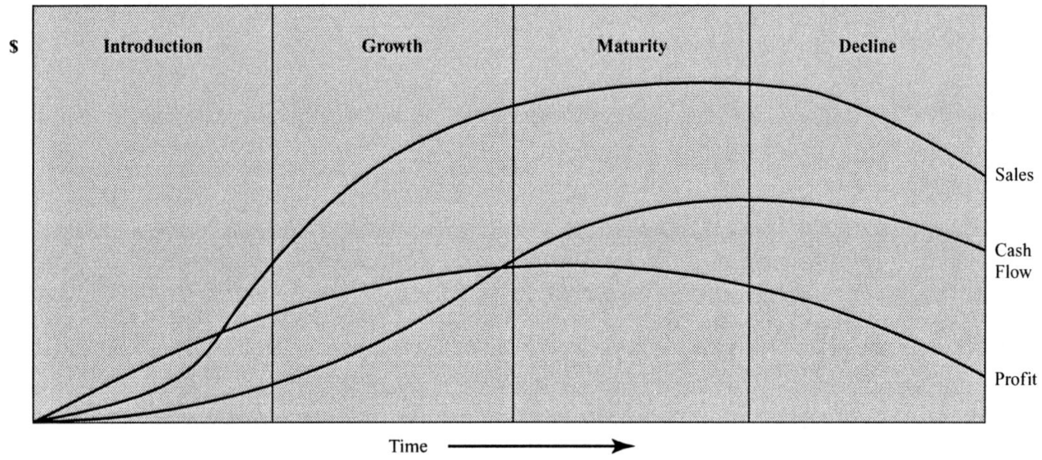

The Value Cycle

One method of managing the dynamic nature of products is to think in terms of a **value cycle** (see Exhibit 7). This cycle consists of four stages: (1) value indentification, (2) value design, (3) value execution, and (4) value renewal. Any product or process will go through all four stages. Some of a firm's products will be in the first stage, some in the second, some in the third, and the remainder in the fourth.

The first stage, **value identification,** focuses on the process of creating customers. Here, the firm targets specific customer segments, examines their needs, and develops value-based statements aimed at fulfilling these needs. In the second stage, **value design,** the firm focuses on the design of the products and their supporting processes. It is here that the firm ensures that what it can deliver is consistent with what it has promised. Value design seeks to balance demand articulation with demand fulfillment. Demand articulation is a statement of customer expectation, which may or may not be formed by the firm. Demand fulfillment defines the way the firm plans to satisfy the demands placed on it by its customers and is influenced by the scope of products and services offered

EXHIBIT 7
The Value Cycle

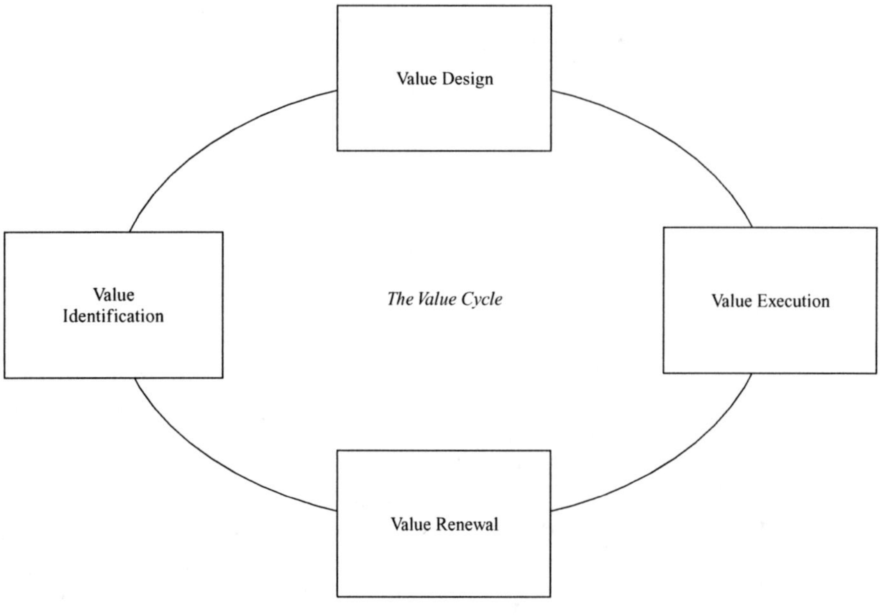

In Practice

THE RENEWAL OF THE 35mm SLR CAMERA

In the early 1980s, the 35mm single-lens reflex camera was considered a maturity product heading into decline. While it produced great pictures—since one could look through the lens and see the picture that one was about to take before it was taken—it was considered difficult to use by the average photographer. Taking a "great" picture required setting the shutter speed and the aperture (the size of the lens opening) while simultaneously focusing on the subject. This was hard enough for a professional; it was horrible for an amateur who just wanted to pick up the camera, aim, and take a picture. In 1986, Minolta looked at this situation and saw a solution. If it could marry the easy use of point-and-shoot cameras with the quality of the 35mm SLR, it could reinvent the camera market. The vehicle for this marriage was computer technology, and from this marriage was born the Maxxum line of cameras. In one step, Minolta made existing 35mm cameras obsolete while creating a new and higher demand for a new generation of 35mm cameras. Minolta recognized that the value cycle offers an ever-present opportunity for renewal. In the Maxxum, Minolta renewed the demand for 35mm cameras by augmenting the value that the camera provided. Currently, the 35mm SLR is experiencing another rejuvenation due to digital technology.

by the firm and by the various processes used in designing, planning, creating, and delivering them. It is here that the firm deals with issues of capacity as volume (output) and capacity as capability (what the firm can and cannot do). Value design also deals with supply chain decisions affecting what is done in **internal** versus **external factories,** how the work stages are structured, and how they are interrelated. The third stage is **value execution.** Here the firm delivers the products using the processes given to it by the previous stage. Thus, value execution is constrained by actions taken in the previous two stages. Value execution involves managing capacity, schedules, physical flows, information flows, technology, and resources.

The fourth and final stage is **value renewal.** Once a firm has defined a specific type of value, designed the products and processes to deliver that version of value, and delivered it, the firm must expect that the level of value experienced by the customer will deteriorate over time. There are several reasons for this. Customers view something that is initially exciting as something old and expected over time; competitors attack the firm; new products or substitutes appear. Irrespective of the reasons, the firm must eventually rethink and redefine the type of value that it offers its customers.

Decisions made in value renewal lead back to the first stage of the value cycle, value identification. It is this cycling that makes the value concept so dynamic and attractive. Cycling causes a product currently in the maturity or decline stage of its life cycle to gain new life, returning to either the introduction or growth stage. With the value cycle, it is important to recognize that there is no such thing as a permanent solution or answer. Firms are constantly moving through the cycle, revisiting decisions previously made. As a consequence, an operations management system needs to recognize the phases and changes that its products are experiencing and position itself to meet the changing demands of value over time.

Value as the Constant in an Ever-Changing Field

Just as products and firms experience dynamics, so too do the study and practice of operations management. In recent times, operations management as a field has exploded in knowledge and content. Twenty years ago, operations management was mostly about inventory planning and control, capacity, scheduling, workflow design, facility location, facility layout, work design, and aggregate planning. Teachers delivered this body of knowledge using a "problem-solving" perspective. Today, things have changed. Just as the practice of operations management has experienced a revolution—thanks to the emergence of new initiatives such as world-class manufacturing and e-commerce—so has the theory of operations management. The body of knowledge now includes topics such as lean manufacturing, knowledge management, supply-chain management, and global operations management. Furthermore, a variety of different approaches to the teaching of operations management have developed. Some emphasize the quantitative tools of operations management; others present perspectives of operations management, such as the theory of constraints, total quality management, or just-in-time operations.

As illustrated by the history of operations management, the one thing that remains constant is value. Value drives decisions in all areas of management, but it is an especially salient force in the area of operations because operational activities are where transformation takes place. Thus, operational activities embody the primary value-creating processes in a firm. Since value is so fundamental, it serves as an effective lens through which to view the many content areas of operations management.

Module Summary

This module has provided a broad overview and introduction to operations management. In discussing the scope and complexity of operations management, we have made the following points:

1. The goal of the modern firm is to develop and run an operations management system able to deliver superior value to the firm's targeted consumers.
2. Operations management deals with the effective and efficient management of the transformation process. This focus covers not only the activity of making goods and services but also includes the design of these goods and services (and the processes needed to make them) and the eventual revising and updating of these products and processes. As a system, operations management consists of three major subsystems and their interactions: (1) product/process design, (2) planning/scheduling/execution, and (3) performance measurement and improvement.
3. The capabilities of the operations management system are determined by how the firm's management addresses the 10 critical operations management decisions.
4. The operations management system involves four major partners: (1) customers, (2) suppliers, (3) various stakeholders, and (4) the firm. The varying needs of the customer are described using the traits of order winners, order qualifiers, and order losers.
5. Operations management is fundamentally dynamic; it is ever changing. A review of the historical evolution of this field shows that most of these changes can be ultimately traced back to value and changes in what constitutes value.

We began this module by studying a revolution now taking place at Audi. We now see that this revolution can trace its roots ultimately to a corporate need for Audi to generate more value for its customers. The theme of value is one that repeatedly influences and shapes the theory, practice, and development of operations management.

Key Terms

capacity, *5*
customers, *8*
effectiveness, *4*
efficiency, *4*
external factory, *16*
facilities, *5*
goods, *7*
internal factory, *16*
operations management, *4*
order losers, *9*
order qualifiers, *9*
order winners, *9*
organization, *5*
performance measurement, *5*
production planning and materials control, *5*
process, *5*
product, *8*
product life cycle (PLC), *14*
renewal/improvement, *5*
services, *7*
stakeholders, *9*
structural decision, *4*
suppliers, *9*
supply chain, *5*
tactical decision, *5*
technology, *5*
total product experience, *8*
value, *10*
value cycle, *15*
value design, *15*
value execution, *15*
value identification, *15*
value renewal, *16*
workforce, *5*

Discussion Questions

1. Explain what the operations management function does and how it relates to your academic major. Then pick a company to illustrate your response.
2. Review *Fortune* magazine's "Most Admired" American companies for 1959, 1979, and the most current year. The issue normally appears in August of the year. Which companies remained on the top throughout this period. Which ones disappeared? What do you think led to the survival and demise of these companies?
3. Select two products that you have recently purchased; one should be a service and the other a manufactured good. Review the process that you used to make the decision to purchase each

item. Then identify your order winners, order qualifiers, and order losers for products in each of these two areas.

4. How would you define the operations management function in each of the following corporations?
   a. Marriott hotels.
   b. Private golf and tennis club.
   c. Ben & Jerry's ice cream.
   d. Exxon Corp.
5. Use the university environment to illustrate how your school's dean might define efficiency and effectiveness. Now use a student perspective to illustrate these differences. What might explain the differences?
6. Consider the following processes that you frequently encounter as a college student:
   a. Enrolling in college.
   b. Taking a class.
   c. Buying a ticket for a play, concert, or basketball game.

   Describe each process and its input, activities, and outputs. What is being converted or transformed in each process? Identify the forms of capacity that you might expect to encounter in each process. Identify the customers and any stakeholders for each. Finally, for each process, identify a set of appropriate measures of performance.
7. Describe a paradigm shift that has happened in your life. Can you cite one that has occurred in the business world? In world affairs?
8. Consider the following situations:
   a. You can buy and receive prescription eyeglasses in one hour.
   b. You can buy a personal computer containing a self-diagnostic program.
   c. You can communicate with your relatives in Peoria, Illinois, via the Internet.

   Each case presents a possible paradigm shift. Describe the underlying nature of the paradigm shift. What are the implications of each shift for the customer, the operations management process, and the appropriate measures of performance? If you were a competitor dealing with these paradigm shifts, how could you respond?
9. Recall the last time you went to a fast-food restaurant such as McDonald's. Use this visit to illustrate the term *total product experience.*
10. The following firms have long been seen as having sustainable competitive advantages.
    a. Hewlett-Packard
    b. Coca-Cola
    c. Xerox
    d. Wal-Mart

    Go to the library and read about one of these companies. Also draw from your experience with that company to identify that company's competitive advantage. What about the company has given it a competitive advantage? Discuss how operations management relates to the company's competitive advantage.
11. Why should a firm consider the position of stakeholders when evaluating alternatives or considering what actions it should implement in its operations management system? Consider the role of government and its impact. (Hint: Consider working conditions and pollution.)
12. In the computer industry, the product life cycle is becoming increasingly shorter. For example, IBM now estimates that most of its products have an effective product life cycle of nine months or less. In this environment, consider the role of the value cycle. What happens when we get to the end of one generation of computer chips? Why do we move to the next generation of chips? What advantages (value) do these new generations of chips offer?

Cases

THE BOOK RETAILING INDUSTRY

Consider the following changes in how we buy books. Initially, we went out to the small bookstore to buy our books. There, we were faced with a limited selection. However, the people were friendly and they knew the types of books that they had in stock. Then mega-bookstores such as Barnes and Noble and Borders came along, offering larger selections, often at lower prices. They also encouraged browsing by locating coffee/cappuccino shops either inside the stores or next to them. The latest development is Amazon.com. This Internet-based store offers none of amenities of a Barnes and Noble. However, Amazon.com does offer an extremely large selection, combined with prices that are on average 10 to 30 percent lower than those found in a typical bookstore.

QUESTIONS

1. Using the value cycle, explain the changes that each development (Barnes and Noble and Amazon.com) had on independent bookstores. How could the independent bookstores have effectively reacted to these changes?
2. What type of operations management systems did each development have to have in place to be successful?
3. What do you see as being the next stage after Amazon.com? Why? What type of operations management system will this stage require?

Internet Activity

Wal-Mart and Dell have revolutionized the retail and computer industries respectively. In each case, they relied extensively on their suppliers. Read about these firms. You can find numerous articles about them on the Internet. What advantages did their supplier base provide these firms?

Related Modules of Interest

- Foundations of Value
- Value-Driven Operations Strategy
- Foundations of Process Management

Selected Readings

Albrecht, Karl. *The Only Thing That Matters.* New York: Harper Business, 1992.

Barker, Joel Arthur. *Paradigms: The Business of Discovering the Future.* New York: Harper Business, 1992.

Everdell, Romeyn. "From Lowell to Sunnyvale." In *Leading Manufacturing Excellence,* ed. Patricia E. Moody. New York: John Wiley & Sons, 1997, pp. 18–44.

Garwood, Dave, and Michael Bane. *Shifting Paradigms: Reshaping the Future of Industry.* Marietta, GA: Dogwood Publishing, 1990.

Giffi, Craig, Aleda V. Roth, and Gregory M. Seal. *Competing in World Class Manufacturing: America's 21st Century Challenge.* New York: McGraw-Hill/Irwin, 1990.

Hill, Terry. *Manufacturing Strategy: Text and Cases.* New York: McGraw-Hill/Irwin, 2000.

Imai, Masaaki. *Gemba Kaizen.* New York: McGraw-Hill, 1997.

Pine, B. Joseph, II. *Mass Customization: The New Frontier in Business Competition.* Cambridge, MA: Harvard Business School Press, 1993.

Schonberger, Richard J. *World Class Manufacturing: The Next Decade.* New York: Free Press, 1996.

Womack, James P., and Daniel T. Jones. *Lean Thinking.* New York: Simon & Schuster, 1996.

Foundations of Value

Steven A. Melnyk
Michigan State University

Morgan Swink
Michigan State University

McGraw-Hill Irwin

Boston Burr Ridge, IL Dubuque, IA Madison, WI New York San Francisco St. Louis
Bangkok Bogotá Caracas Kuala Lumpur Lisbon London Madrid Mexico City
Milan Montreal New Delhi Santiago Seoul Singapore Sydney Taipei Toronto

Foundations of Value

Module Objectives

By the end of this module, you should be able to

- Identify and understand value and its various elements including quality, timeliness, and total cost.
- Understand the basic value-adding functions a firm can provide.
- Explain the differences between value through design and value through execution and understand the roles of operations managers in affecting both.
- Understand the relationship of value to waste.
- Understand the meaning of the value chain and its various components.

The Decline and Rebirth of Schwinn

For almost a hundred years, the name Schwinn was synonymous with bicycles and quality. A good bike enters the life of a child like a good friend, and generations of kids learned how to ride on Schwinn's sturdy, brightly colored bikes. Many of these kids grew up to be parents, parents who wanted their kids to ride Schwinns.

In the early 1970s, markets began to change, but Schwinn seemingly did not quite understand what was happening. Out in California, a loose fraternity of gearheads and hippies was converting Schwinn's single-speed, coaster-braked clunkers into a new vehicle capable of screaming down Mount Tamalpais. A dirt trail with a 1,300-foot drop and breath-snatching switchbacks was not for the timid, but the five-minute ride yielded what these hippies called a lifetime buzz.

One of these early gearheads was Gary Fisher. Fisher selected a Schwinn frame for its sturdiness and added newly engineered parts from around the world to make a revolutionary bike that was capable of pedaling up a hill with sufficient braking to survive the test of the Mount Tamalpais downhill run. Fisher had become a local cult hero by inventing a new type of bicycle, the mountain bike, which generated instant demand, because they were comfortable and fun to ride.

Soon, Schwinn executives dispatched a team of engineers to visit Fisher's new company. Fisher recalls, "This guy in his fifties was looking down at me like I was some jerk kid who didn't know anything." One snickered, "This wasn't a bicycle; it was a mongrel." As you might have expected, the Schwinn team returned to Chicago with the firm conviction that this amateur was no threat given their firm's collective knowledge of the bicycle market.

As a result, Schwinn was slow to respond to the craze for mountain bikes. When the company finally came out with subsequent versions, it always seemed to be "not as good." Schwinn was seen as stodgy and behind the times. Increasingly, consumers looked to the firms founded by gearheads for the best in mountain bikes. Demand for Schwinns fell rapidly. By the summer of 1992, the family-dominated board of directors was forced to declare bankruptcy. The great grandchildren of founder Ignaz Schwinn tearfully watched as their dividends, corporate perks, and children's birthrights were slowly lost. Thus ended a 100-year chapter in one of America's great companies.

Yet, Schwinn's story does not end here. In 1993, the company emerged from bankruptcy with a completely new image. A group of investors, named the Scott Sports Group, bought all of the rights to Schwinn, its name, and its assets. Scott moved Schwinn's operations to Colorado, the capital of mountain biking, then proceeded to completely reinvent the company, its operations management system, its products, and its image. Instead of being a laggard, Schwinn became a leader in bicycle design. By heightening its sensitivity to its customers and by rediscovering how to design and deliver products of fantastic value, the firm revitalized itself and introduced new products that wowed mountain bike enthusiasts.

Source: Gary Strauss, "Schwinn Files for Chapter 11," *USA Today,* October 9, 1992, p. 1B; Judith Crown and Glenn Coleman, *No Hands* (New York: Henry Holt, 1996); Zapata Espinosa, "The Comeback Rig—Schwinn Bounces Back with a Hot, New Suspension Bike," *Mountain Bike,* February 1995, pp. 50–52.

This module begins with the death and rebirth of an American icon—the Schwinn Bicycle Company. How could a company that once symbolized the epitome of the bicycle for almost every child in America fail and die? And how did it reemerge? The answer to both of these questions is the same: value. Schwinn died in 1992 because it no longer offered value to its customers. The new customer wanted mountain bikes that were light, fast, and comfortable to ride, that is, suspended. The old Schwinn could not or would not deliver this type of bike as quickly as its competitors did, but the new Schwinn can. This story highlights the importance and dynamic nature of value. This module explores how concepts of value from design and value from execution both shape and are shaped by the operations management system.

Value, Customers, and Operations Management

To survive and prosper in today's dynamic and demanding economy, every company, be it Compaq, Burger King, FedEx, or BankOne, needs to excel in attracting customers and keeping them. The most effective way of doing this is to provide value. Value is not a new concept, but successful firms are continually discovering new ways to create value for their customers. The possibilities are numerous. Firms can offer lower prices. They can offer higher-quality products in terms of superior performing goods or in the form of goods-service bundles that more fully meet customers' specific needs and expectations. Firms can deliver products faster or more reliably. A comprehensive approach is to seek to improve customers' entire consumption experiences, including all the aspects of the customer's product search, purchase, use, and disposal. Whatever strategies they choose, firms can only create and keep customers when they offer levels of value greater than those offered by their competitors.

Value Added

In business, processes are used to transfer value to customers in the form of products. A *product* could involve delivering a tangible good to customers, it could involve performing a service for customers, or it could be and usually is a combination of the two. Throughout this module, products will be discussed as the conveyances of value from value-creating firms to value-consuming customers. We define a product as the sum of all its associated goods and services.

Product: The output of a process, including the sum of all its associated goods and services.

Exhibit 1 on page 4 provides a framework that identifies basic value-adding activities. Value involves change and exchange. It might be a product, information, or the customer herself or himself who is changed. In many firms, the primary aspects of value come from *transformation,* for example, transforming raw materials and components into finished goods. Other firms might add value by transporting goods to needed locations, or by storing goods for future use. Transformations in form, location, and time are basic types of substantive transformation that add value to products, to information, or to customers.

It is important to realize that other types of transformation also add value. Experiential transformations that provide value include things such as entertainment, knowledge transfer, and changes in status. Firms add value by creating settings and delivering information that is useful or enjoyable. Operations managers often find that there are many linkages between substantive and experiential aspects of value. In a theme park such as Disney World, substantive transformations—for example, the ways information is transformed and delivered, the ways people are moved, and the ways they are stored in waiting lines—have a lot to do with customers' perceptions of their experience. Traditional brick-and-mortar firms are now giving more attention to the experiential aspects of their businesses. Witness the growth of theme retailers such as the Hard Rock Cafe, NikeTown, and the like. In reaction to the tremendous growth of Web-based retailing, traditional retailers are offering product demonstrations, training, and other experiences not available via the Internet. Even pure manufacturing firms are getting into the act. As Intel Chairman Andy Grove remarked at the a recent Comdex computer show, "We need to look at our business as more than simply

EXHIBIT 1 Basic Value-Adding Activities—Example of an Auto Manufacturer

Basic Technology	Example Type of Value Added	What Is Changed or Exchanged in the Value Process: Tangible Item	Information	Customer
Transformation	Changes in physical form or orientation	• Parts and components fabrication and assembly	• Creation of an owner's manual	
	Changes in physical location	• Delivery of purchased car	• Communicating car availability/delivery data	• Providing means of transportation
	Changes in time and availability	• Storing cars on a dealer's lot	• Placing owner's manual on the Web	
	Changes in status, experience, and/or knowledge	• Branding	• Advertising or other ways of informing potential customers	• Enabling personal distinction via car ownership • Providing training videos/plant tours
Problem solving	Technical support	• Repair services	• Customers' online help/onboard diagnostics	
	Decision support and consulting		• Sales support online or through salesperson • Global positioning system (GPS) and network	
Mediation/ networking	Pooling of risks or resources			• Financing • Roadside service insurance
	Enhanced communication/ transactions/ ownership transfer	• Maintaining a dealer network		• Establishing owners' clubs

the building and selling of personal computers [that is, goods]. Our business is the delivery of information [services] and lifelike interactive experiences."

The lower portions of Exhibit 1 identify two additional value-adding activities: *problem solving* and *mediation/networking*.[1] Firms that offer professional or technical services provide value by solving specific problems for customers. These firms use resources in different ways depending on the diagnosis of the problems at hand. For example, a physician suggests customized treatments for ailing patients depending on his understanding of the root problems that are involved.

Can you name other types of value not listed in Exhibit 1? Pick a firm that interests you and identify all of the aspects of value the firm delivers. What dimensions of value does a school deliver? A hospital? A social club?

Telephone companies, banks, distributors, and insurance firms create value primarily through mediation and the creation of networks. These firms essentially provide ways to link together customers who wish to be interdependent. Membership in networks provided

[1] Sources of value are discussed in C. B. Sabell and Ø. D. Fjeldstad, "Configuring Value for Competitive Advantage: On Chains, Shops, and Networks," *Strategic Management Journal* 19 (1998), pp. 413–37.

by banks and insurance firms provides substantial advantages such as greater returns on investment and reduced risk. Online auctions (ebay.com), brokers (schwab.com), and portals (skymall.com, taxi-online.com) also provide good examples of value through networking. These Web-based firms enable points of contact between buyers and sellers of goods and services. The value of such networks is said to increase as a function of the square of the number of network users.

The framework in Exhibit 1 can be used to specify and analyze the fundamental dimensions of value in a product as well as how these dimensions relate to one another. For example, a car company not only delivers the value of transforming raw materials into automobiles, it also delivers to customers a driving experience plus the ability to engage in future experiences. This example suggests the complex nature of value and the fact that multiple aspects of value provided by a given product are interdependent.

A firm's conceptualization of its value-adding activities is an important aspect of its strategy. For example, Federal Express is a well-known shipper of packaged items. Much of its business has to do with delivering letters and business documents. What is the value added in this business? Is it changing the location of customers' tangible items, or is it changing the location of *information* that is really the value added? Could Federal Express add even more value by addressing problem solving or networking aspects of its service? The way that Federal Express answers these questions could be important for identifying operational improvements and new market opportunities.

Value Defined

Value is a concept that appeals to everyone. The concept itself has been around for a long time. More than two hundred years ago, Adam Smith[2] defined two types of value: *value in exchange,* an economic concept in which value depends on the attributes and options associated with a good or service, and *value in use,* an intrinsic measure of absolute worth. From this we can glean that product value has to do with rarity and usefulness. What makes value difficult to define is the fact that estimates of rarity and usefulness are judgments made by individual customers based on their own points of view.

Customers determine value using both experiential (subjective) and logical (objective) assessments. That which is valuable to one person is not necessarily valuable to someone else. (One man's junk is another man's treasure.) For example, one person may enjoy listening to country and western music while another may find classic rock more to his or her taste. On the other hand, there are usually objective aspects of goods and services that are evaluated fairly consistently by customers, for example, whether or not the CD player plays the music flawlessly. In addition, value involves *expectations.* Customers routinely compare a product against its anticipated benefit. Nearly everyone has returned to a restaurant he or she remembered as being wonderful, only to be disappointed. The restaurant may have been just as good or even better, but the expectation that we had far exceeded what the restaurant could do consistently.

We define value as

> **Value:** A customer's subjective evaluation, adjusted for cost, of how well a product meets or exceeds expectations.

Putting this definition in the form of an equation helps us to acquire a better understanding of the value concept.

$$\text{Value} = \text{Customer's evaluation of (benefits/total cost)}$$

In this **value equation,** benefits can include many product aspects, but operations managers tend to focus on two primary elements: quality and timeliness. Both of these elements have several manifestations that will be discussed later. For now, we can broadly define each performance element as follows:

[2] Adam Smith, *An Inquiry into the Nature and Causes of the Wealth of Nations* (London: W. Strahan and T. Cadell, 1776).

Quality: How fit a product is for customer use. This includes how well the designed functionality and performance of the entire product-consumption experience meet the customer's specific needs and expectations, and how well the actual functionality and performance of the product match its design specifications.

Timeliness: Availability of the product. The degree to which a product is delivered where the customer needs it exactly when the customer needs it, not before or after the customer needs it.

Total cost: The sum of all costs incurred by the customer during the consumption experience. This includes all costs associated with the product, beginning with its acquisition and including its use, maintenance, and disposal.

Value through Design and Value through Execution

The activities that create value can be grouped into two major categories: (1) product-and-process design activities that establish what value is and how it should be delivered and (2) execution activities that fulfill the potential value of the design. The relationships of design and execution to the basic elements of value are illustrated in Exhibit 2.

Value is created **through design** activities that specify levels of product function and service performance. What a good or service can or cannot do and the needs that it addresses (or does not address) are determined during the design phase. Fundamentally, product and process design specifications determine the level of value offered. Setting these specifications first involves understanding customers' needs and expectations. Moreover, firms often seek to shape customers' expectations through marketing communications. Through communications and through design, the firm affects customers' perceptions of product quality and timeliness. If the product design offers little value, then the execution activities have little value. Through pricing and promotion strategies and through managing design, development, and sales costs, organizational functions such as research and development, marketing, and sales contribute to the product pricing aspects of value. Greater productivity and effectiveness in these activities enable more competitive pricing strategies.

Value through execution describes value that results from how the product is made, how the good or service is delivered, and how the good or service is supported after the sale. Operations managers exert a great deal of influence on value through execution by virtue of process designs, training, capacity planning and management, scheduling, materials management, and supply-chain design and management. For example, operations managers affect product quality by consistently delivering goods and services that conform to design specifications. Improved product conformance raises customer satisfaction and product reliability. In addition, operations-based value added services have become an increasingly important source of product differentiation. One way the operations function plays a stronger

EXHIBIT 2
Relationships of Design and Execution to Value

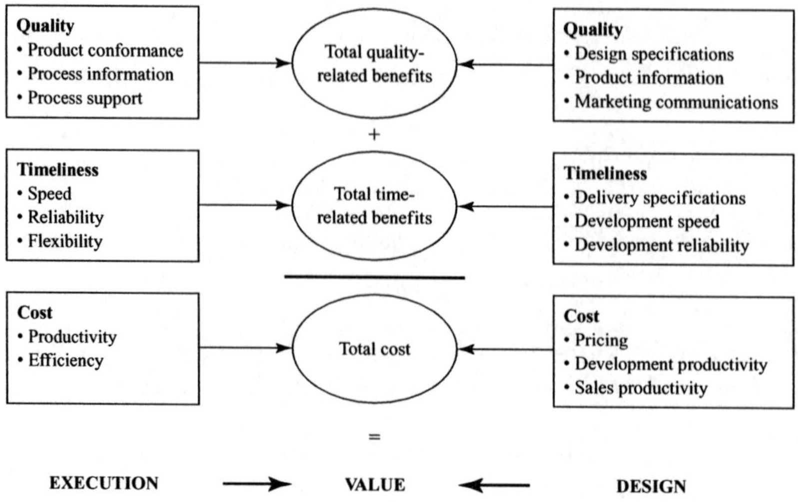

EXHIBIT 3
Fundamental Value-Adding Interfaces

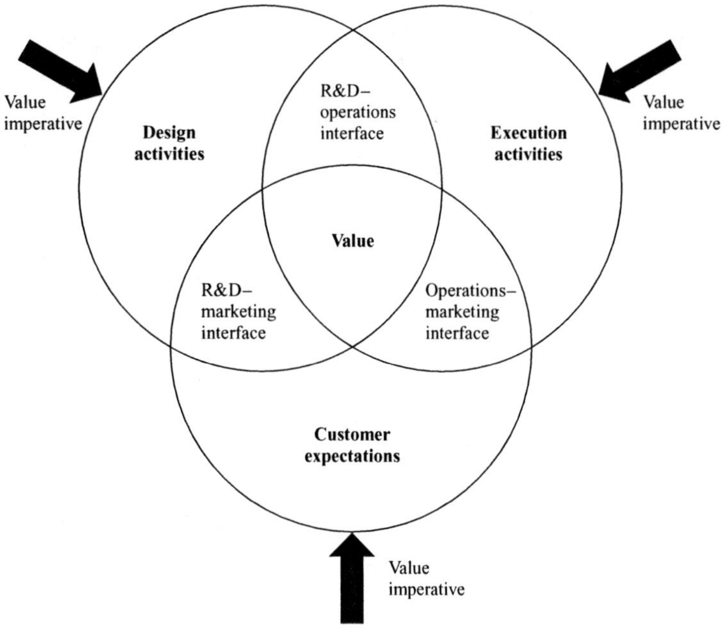

value added role is by providing superior production and service information and support to customers. Flexibility also has become a prominent strategic operations capability in recent times. By building flexible and speedy operating processes, operations managers enable the firm to deliver a wide range of products in a timely manner while maintaining low operating costs. Further, delivering these capabilities in a productive, cost-efficient manner allows competitive pricing.

While most operations managers focus on adding value through execution, they cannot ignore value through design. The fit between product design specifications and the capabilities of the execution system is extremely important. Design greatly influences the costs incurred in execution. For example, some researchers estimate that about 80 percent of a product's manufacturing cost is affected by decisions made during the design stage.[3] Similarly, traits such as flexibility, quality, and speed also are significantly affected by decisions made during the design phase. Looking at it the other way, the capabilities of the execution system greatly constrain the possibilities that can feasibly be considered in design.

Exhibit 3 illustrates the interplay of design activities, execution activities, and customer expectations in relation to value. As noted above, the fit between design specifications and the execution system's capabilities defines the value experienced by the customer. Operations managers need to work closely with research and development personnel to ensure design specifications are feasible, that is, they can be consistently and efficiently executed. A high frequency of product defects is one indication that the design–execution interface is lacking. The interface between research and development and marketing personnel is no less important. Customers' expectations should drive product design specifications, and marketing personnel are usually in the best position to learn about and influence customers' expectations. There is no sense in designing product features that customers do not want or need. Finally, strong interactions between marketing and operations functions are needed to ensure that marketing communications fit well with what the execution system can handle. If marketing and advertising communications promise customers more than the system can deliver, customer-perceived value will suffer. This is often the case in services, for example, a hotel, partly because customers' expectations of service vary widely.

Clarifying value and making it an important objective in a firm motivates closer connections among design activities, execution activities, and activities that shape customer

[3] H.W. Stoll, "Design for Manufacture: An Overview," *Applied Mechanics Reviews* 39, no. 9 (1986), pp. 1356–64.

In Practice

THE APPLE III COMPUTER

The development of the Apple III computer provides a good example of poor linkage between design and execution. Apple assigned two separate teams to design the computer: one team for the case and externals and another for the internal aspects, motherboard, and so on. The teams designed a very precise fit between the internal system and the outside casing. This required very close tolerances, that is, very little allowed variation, on the dimensions of the mating parts. When the new product was released for production, outgoing quality suffered. Customers received many computers in a nonworking state. The reason: components were damaged when the internal system was inserted into the case. Poor design was the ultimate cause of the quality problem.

expectations. This **value imperative** drives decision makers to consider how their decisions affect other players in the overall scheme. In effect, this imperative creates greater alignment and fit across value-based activities and customer expectations, which would be represented in Exhibit 3 by closer and closer alignment of the three circles. In order to make the circles more concentric, the interfaces among research and development, marketing, and operations personnel must grow. As a result, value also grows.

Solving Value-Related Problems

Operations management is problem solving in action. Through problem solving, operations managers strive to reduce waste or enhance value by changing how the operations management system is designed, structured, managed, and evaluated. Value-related problems usually result from a lack of fit among customer expectations, product design, and operations execution. When a problem occurs, it is important to attack it at the right level.

One source of problems is a lack of fit between a customer's expectations and what a firm can economically do with its existing processes and capabilities. A problem of this type frequently occurs when customers and their tastes/expectations have changed or when the firm is trying to serve two or more customer segments that are too diverse. Suppose we serve two basic customer segments. The first segment gives us orders with plenty of lead time. They want low-cost and on-time delivery. The second segment consists of customers who place emergency orders. Order arrival is difficult to predict. These customers want immediate service, and cost is no object. One system cannot serve both customers effectively, leaving the firm three options: (1) change to other customers, (2) change the firm's capabilities, or (3) try to change the customer's tastes/expectations. All three options are attempts to align the customer's perceptions of value with the firm's abilities to deliver value. All three options take time, money, and effort.

Design-related problems occur when the functionality of the product does not provide value to the targeted market segment. Again, the firm can respond by changing its design, by looking for a more appropriate market, or by changing the customers' expectations. Design-related problems also include instances where the product design does not match up well with the operating system's capabilities. Consider the story of the Apple III computer.

Most operations managers tend to concentrate on value problems that stem from difficulties with execution processes. The process may have missing steps or too many steps, or the structure of the process may be wrong. For example, a major manufacturer of outboard marine engines recently found it was unable to meet the needs of a market that wanted short lead times, consistent quality, and low cost. An analysis of the firm's production process showed that out of 122 process steps, only 27 actually added value to the product. Obviously, the reason that costs were high and lead times were long was due to inefficiencies in the firm's process.

Execution-related problems also occur when operations systems use the wrong set of measures. For example, consider a firm that wants to deliver a high-quality service very quickly, yet its performance is assessed only using cost-based measures. Over time, such a performance measurement system will motivate workers to shift their emphasis from quality and lead time to cost. With this shift comes a value problem.

Understanding the Elements of Value

It is important to clearly understand how operations processes contribute to the elements of value. Precision and clarity are important. For example, it is not enough to simply say that quality is the company's most important element of value. Many firms emphasize quality. However, different aspects of quality may be more or less important depending on customer and competitor issues. Clearly defining aspects of quality, timeliness, and cost gives the firm a better picture of how operational elements support value. The concepts of quality, timeliness, and cost are multifaceted. Similarly, operations terms such as *flexibility* also have multiple meanings.

Specificity and precision in the use of these terms help operations managers avoid confusion that often leads to inappropriate decisions and investments. Precise definitions also facilitate better and more useful measures.

Understanding Aspects of Quality

Since the mid-1980s, quality has become the defining component of value in the view of many managers and customers. Over the past two decades, companies have made huge investments in quality-improvement initiatives. Many have realized sizable returns on these investments. For example, Stanley, a 140-year-old manufacturer of hand tools, more than doubled its profits by reducing product scrap from 15 to 3 percent. Similar stories filled the popular press in the years ending the twentieth century.

Today, quality management has moved beyond an initiative to become a way of life in most firms. Even so, quality is frequently a poorly understood concept. Some managers see quality as nothing more than conformance to product specifications, while others take a much broader view.

Earlier we broadly defined quality as fitness for the customer's use. Thus, the customer's evaluation of quality depends on the match between his/her expectations and his/her perceptions of what is actually delivered. Customer expectations vary according to circumstances. For example, a trip to McDonald's may represent a quality meal for a spouse on February 15, but not on February 14, Valentine's Day. All other things being equal, however, customer expectations tend to rise over time and through experience.

In order to successfully comprehend and meet customer expectations, firms must describe and understand multiple dimensions of product quality that people might assess. If someone were to ask you to judge the quality of a microcomputer, you might reply by talking about how long the computer would run before needing repair or whether it would run every time that you turned on the power switch. These descriptions identify dimensions of quality that can be measured. Other dimensions are not as easy to quantify. In a classic article on quality, David Garvin defined eight primary dimensions of quality.[4] We have adapted them slightly and present them as follows:

- **Performance:** The degree to which a product meets or exceeds certain operating characteristics. For an automobile, this would include traits such as acceleration, handling, speed, and safety.
- **Features:** Characteristics that supplement basic functions. For some customers, the presence of unique features or the total number of options available is an important aspect of quality.
- **Reliability:** A measure of how long a product performs before it fails. Alternatively, it is the probability that a product will malfunction or fail within a certain time period or number of uses.

[4] David A. Garvin, "Competing on the Eight Dimensions of Quality," *Harvard Business Review,* November–December 1987, pp. 101–109.

- **Conformance:** The degree to which a product meets established standards, that is, specifications. This is a dimension that is often emphasized in operations management.
- **Durability:** A measure of product life or the amount of use one gets before a product deteriorates. Durability may be shorter or longer depending on the operating environment.
- **Support:** A measure of the competence of product support in terms of information, maintenance, or repair. Consumers frequently equate rapid repair and reduced downtime with higher quality.
- **Aesthetics:** A subjective assessment of a product's look, feel, sound, taste, or smell. Aesthetics differ from performance in that aesthetics are not universal. What feels like high quality to one customer may not feel that way to another.
- **Perceived quality:** An assessment of quality based on images, advertising, brand names, the reputation of the firm, or other information that is not directly associated with a product's attributes.

These eight dimensions of quality help managers identify ways their companies can compete. In the microcomputer market, for example, Dell competes on support while Hewlett-Packard and IBM compete on durability and perceived quality. By stressing dimensions of quality different from those offered by competitors, provided that customers value the differences, a firm can differentiate its products and make them unique. Note that these quality dimensions can also be applied to service products. A more focused discussion of quality in services is provided in the "Service Operations Management" module.

Quality as a Source of Value

Since many customers regard quality as an important source of value, some dimensions of quality are treated as minimum requirements for a customer to even consider purchasing a good or service. For example, poor conformance quality, that is, many defects, is not tolerated in most markets. At the same time, superior quality can serve as a basis of product and company differentiation. Firms that produce high-quality products have many advantages including improved company reputation and easier selling, the elimination of time-consuming activities and costly resources required to correct quality-related problems, and employees who are motivated by the knowledge they produce great products.

Understanding Aspects of Timeliness

Recall that timeliness refers to the degree to which a product is delivered where the customer needs it, exactly when the customer needs it. Two operational aspects of timeliness are speed and reliability. **Speed** has to do with how quickly activities are executed. **Reliability** is a measure of how close an activity's completion time is to its expected completion time.

Within the operations management function, many use the term **lead time** to describe both operational aspects of timeliness. Lead time is simply a term that describes the amount of time that passes between the beginning and the ending of an activity or a set of activities. Managers study lead times in two ways. They look at lead time as an individual event, perhaps evaluating how long it takes the operations management system to fill a specific order or to design a specific product. Alternatively, managers look at distributions of lead times (see Exhibit 4 page 11). Both perspectives offer valuable insights into the performance of the operations management system. For example, a scheduler working for an airline may want to know how long it took a specific flight to go from Houston, Texas, to Cleveland, Ohio. In this case, the scheduler is interested in the speed with which the flight was completed. Over time, the same manager may collect the same information from numerous flights, each going from Houston to Cleveland. With this information, the manager can estimate the reliability of the flights on this route, that is, what percentage of the flights will arrive on time. He can determine the extent to which flights might be early or late. If the distribution of lead times is unacceptable, then managers seek ways to change the activities associated with the flight.

Value tends to be enhanced when lead time and lead time variability are reduced. Operations managers often focus efforts first on reducing average lead time and then on reducing lead time variance.

In Exhibit 4, the average flight time for the Houston–Cleveland flight is 3.4 hours. Which aspect of timeliness, speed or reliability, do you think is the most valuable to customers in this case? On which aspect of lead time should operations managers focus first?

Lead Time Categories

Operations managers concern themselves with lead times associated with many different activities that may be grouped into five major categories. These categories cover all stages of planning and execution in the value-driven operations management system:

Product design and development lead time is the total time interval needed to conceptualize, design, test, and launch a new product into full-scale production.

Order lead time includes the time that passes from the moment a customer recognizes his or her product need to the instant that production operations begin to work on that order, including time required to place the order, schedule it, and so forth.

Procurement lead time is the lead time associated with obtaining (through purchases) the inputs for the operations process.

Production lead time (throughput time) begins at the moment the production or service system begins working on an order. It ends when the completed order is transferred to the distribution system for delivery.

Delivery lead time measures the time consumed by the distribution system, including warehousing and transportation. It ends the moment that the product reaches the customer.

These lead time elements can be combined to estimate the customer's experienced **order-to-delivery** (OTD) **lead time** for a product, as defined below; OTD is an important concept because it forms the focus of many lead time reduction activities. A major issue is that of who—the customer, the firm, or the supplier—will bear what portions of the total product fulfillment lead time and at what cost.

Order-to-delivery lead time = *f*(design lead time, order lead time, procurement lead time, production lead time, delivery lead time)

Note that OTD lead time is defined as a function of the various individual lead time components. OTD lead time is not simply the sum of these components in all cases. For some

EXHIBIT 4
Distribution of Lead Time for Houston–Cleveland Flights

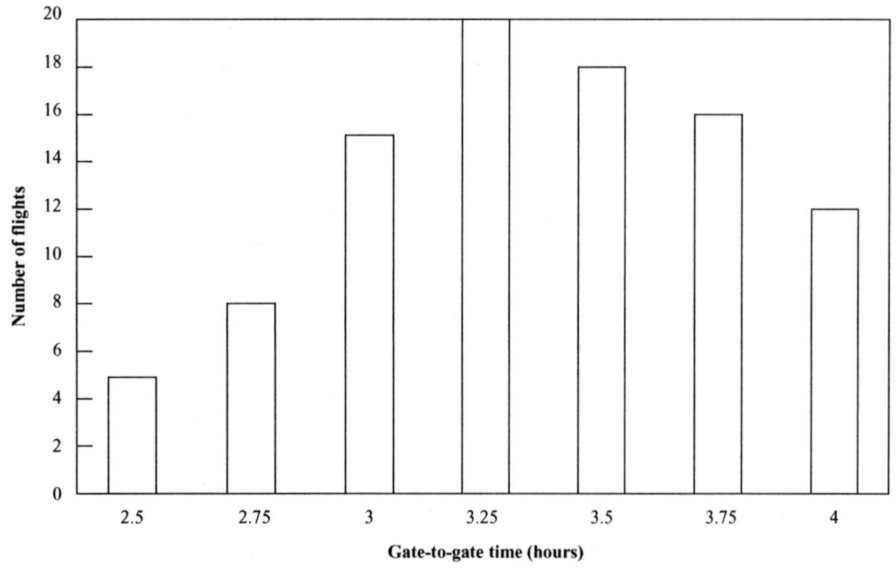

businesses, only certain lead time elements apply. Customers who get a haircut, for example, only experience order and production lead time. On the other hand, customers who purchase highly customized goods will probably experience all five elements of lead time. The next section discusses differences in OTD lead time across various business contexts.

Market Orientation and Order-to-Delivery Lead Time

Whether a customer or a firm bears the brunt of the **total fulfillment lead time** depends on the market orientation of the product. In general, any product has one of four **market orientations:**

- Engineer to order (ETO).
- Make to order (MTO).
- Assemble to order (ATO).
- Make to stock (MTS).

These four categories describe how a firm processes customer orders as well as who bears the cost of lead time. They also determine how the operations management system can enhance value for both the firm and the customer. In the following discussion, please note that the lead time elements in the total fulfillment lead time chain can occur in a different sequence depending on the market orientation. Exhibit 5 illustrates differences in lead time according to market orientation.

EXHIBIT 5 Market Orientation and Customer Experienced OTD Lead Time

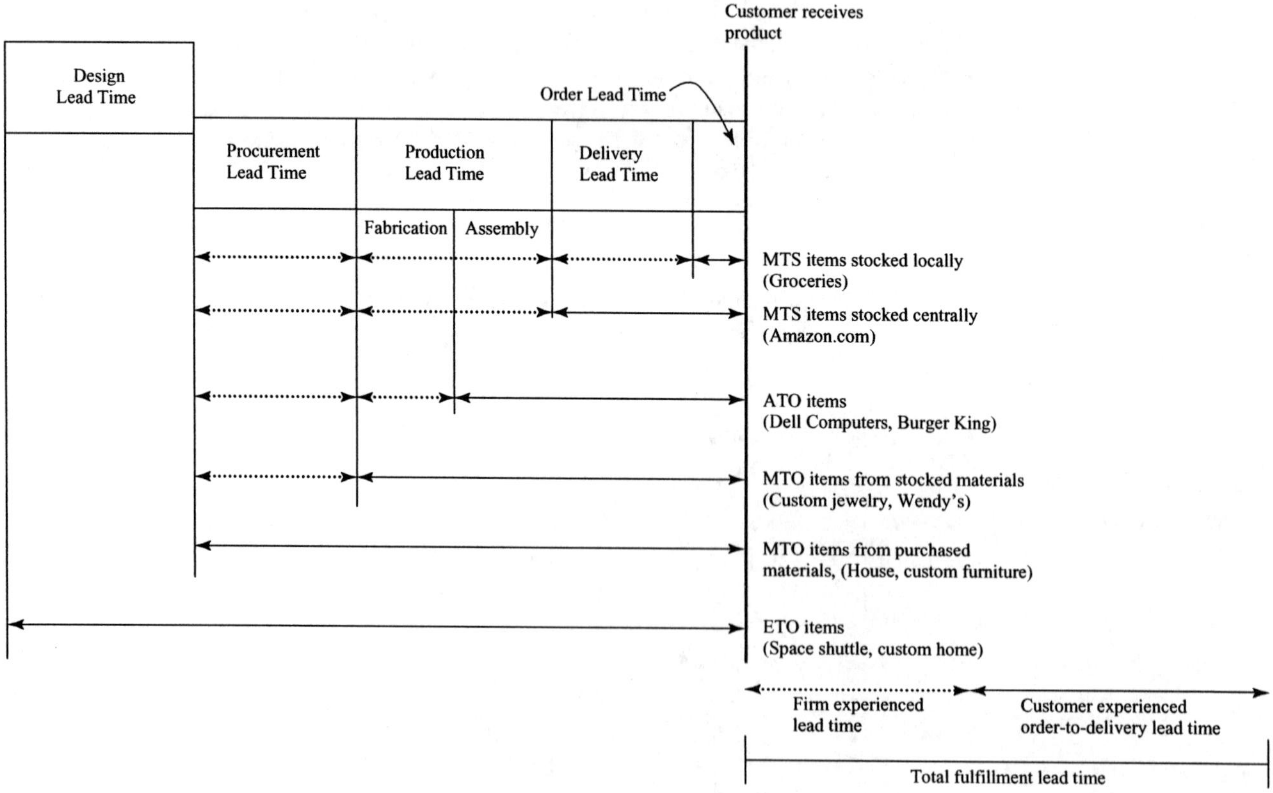

Engineer to Order (ETO)

Products that firms engineer to order are unique and extensively customized for the specific needs of individual customers. Examples of ETO products include a custom-built house, an oil tanker, specialized industrial equipment, and a hand-built bicycle. A highly customized training program is an example of an ETO service.

Since each ETO product requires an entirely new design, it is difficult to reduce lead times by carrying inventory, though some firms do carry raw materials in anticipation of product needs. For example, Cannondale Bicycle, a major American manufacturer of customized road and mountain bicycles, stocks specialized steel blanks, but it does not keep stocks of components such as assembled, unpainted frames. A producer of ETO products must wait for a customer's order before beginning any activity. As a result, the customer bears the entire cost of the total product fulfillment lead time.

Make to Order (MTO)

Make-to-order products follow standard designs, but they cannot be stored economically. Such products may be too big or too expensive to store, such as a jet airplane or a boat, or they may be perishable, for example, a meal at an elegant restaurant. Moreover, a manufacturing firm sometimes cannot hold inventories of MTO products because they are subject to extensive user customization. All pure services are in essence MTO operations because the service cannot be stored.

Production of MTO items closely resembles that of ETO items in that a customer order triggers activities at the very elementary stages of the production process. If one or more of the raw materials for an MTO product are not stocked, then the customer must bear the entire cost of the lead time as shown in Exhibit 5. If, however, the firm stocks all of the raw materials and components needed to make a unique order, then procurement lead time is avoided. In either case, design lead time is avoided.

Like ETO products, MTO products compete on the basis of flexibility, responsiveness, and capacity. Make to order differs from engineer to order primarily in the importance of the producer's engineering capability. A firm that sells ETO products must have the capability to clearly understand, capture, and communicate each individual customer's unique needs. MTO products are designed for broad groups of customers.

Assemble to Order (ATO)

Assemble-to-order products are produced in wide varieties by combining standard inventoried components in different ways. For example, you can buy paint in many different shades and colors. It would be very difficult and expensive for a paint store to carry sufficient stocks of all colors to meet unpredictable customer demand. Furthermore, once a dealer mixes a specific color, it cannot reverse the process; if a store mixes a color that no one wants, it is stuck with the paint. The answer to this problem is to mix (assemble) the base paint and coloring agents after the order is placed. In the same manner, many firms assemble end products to order. Raw materials and components are produced and stocked, but no finished product is created until a customer places an order. By postponing final assembly operations, manufacturers avoid having to hold large amounts and varieties of finished goods. Unfortunately, this means that the customer must bear the cost of the assembly portion of production lead time. Successful sellers of ATO products must keep their assembly lead times as short as possible.

Another important objective in ATO products is ensuring compatibility across modules and components in the delivered product. Certain combinations of modules in products may not work together well. For example, in computers, a certain video memory card may not function properly with certain monitor sizes or DVD players. It is important that these product combinations be identified and avoided, especially when customers are the ones making product configuration choices. The process of ensuring product integrity in this way is sometimes called *configure to order (CTO).* Dell's Web-based ordering system provides a good example of CTO. Incompatible module combinations are immediately flagged when they are selected (see www.dell.com).

Make to Stock (MTS)

Make to stock is the market orientation consumers most often experience. As the name implies, a seller keeps inventories in stock in order to have the product immediately available for purchase. To meet this requirement for availability, firms produce items based on forecasts rather than known orders. Make-to-stock items are typically standardized, fairly mature products. Firms that produce MTS products absorb nearly all of the costs of lead time. The customer bears the order lead time and, if the item is not stocked locally, delivery lead time. Interestingly, the rise of the World Wide Web has offered customers the opportunity to trade off order lead time for delivery lead time. Consider these options: (1) drive to a local bookstore, find the book you want, purchase it, and return home or (2) find the book using Amazon.com or some other Web-based retailer, place the order, and have the book delivered to your home within two days. Option two essentially sacrifices speed of delivery in favor of ease and speed of ordering. Your preference between the two options may depend on a number of things, but it is likely that this trade-off will be at the forefront of your decision.

In general, make-to-stock products compete primarily based on cost and availability. Examples of such products include most retail goods, such as breakfast cereals, milk, shirts, jeans, and office desks.

As we move from ETO to MTS, the OTD lead time goes from 100 percent to nearly 0 percent of the total fulfillment lead time. For each type of product, lead times affect value. With ETO products, there is a strong incentive to reduce lead times because shorter OTD lead times are often very attractive to customers. Reducing lead times for MTS products often translates into lower costs, higher quality, and enhanced flexibility. Again, these changes produce positive impacts on the value equation. However, lead time reliability is usually most important for MTS products.

Timeliness as a Source of Value

Managers increase value when they reduce and/or make more reliable one of the following two types of lead times: **time to market** and **OTD lead time.** Time to market measures the total time that a firm takes to conceive, design, test, and ramp up a new or revised product for the market. This lead time is a once-in-product-life-cycle event. That is, a firm may spend 18 months designing a car and getting the supply chain ready for production of the first car, but once that first car has been made, there is no significant design product lead time needed to make subsequent copies of that car.

In service systems, many customers judge the quality of a service largely on the firm's OTD lead time performance. For example, a dining experience is marred by slow service. Or consider the situation where a shoe salesperson seems to have gotten lost in the back room. The operations manager thinks of this gap as an OTD lead time problem. Customers often call it poor service.

Fast to Market (FTM)

Fast-to-market firms gain a competitive advantage by getting their new products to market more quickly than their competitors do. Examples of such companies include Chrysler and Toyota (automotive), Intel and Hewlett-Packard (electronics), and the Gap (retail clothing). Some success stories are summarized in Exhibit 6. By shortening product development and launch times, fast-to-market firms are able to produce a continuous stream of new product introductions that capture market share and create greater market awareness.

Experience has shown that consistently introducing new products faster than competitors can allow a firm to dominate the marketplace. For example, Honda won the war with Yamaha for dominance of Japan's motorcycle market in the late 1970s and early 1980s by maintaining better product variety.

EXHIBIT 6
Fast-to-Market Competitors

	Product	Old Time	New Time
Honda	Autos	5.0 years	2.0 years
AT&T	Phones	2.0 years	1.0 year
Navistar	Trucks	5.0 years	2.5 years
Hewlett-Packard	Printers	4.5 years	22.0 months

In Practice

HONDA VERSUS YAMAHA

In 18 months, Honda introduced 81 new motorcycle models in Japan. Yamaha was able to introduce only 34. This difference is even more startling when one considers that both competitors had only 60 models each in their entire product lines in the late 1970s. Yet taking these figures alone understates their effect on the market. Honda also discontinued 32 models for a total of 113 changes in its product line. Yamaha retired only 3 models and introduced 34 new models for a total of 37 changes. The consumer was seeing fresh Hondas and increasingly stale Yamahas.

Source: Jame C. Abegglen & George Stalk, Jr., *Kaisha: The Japanese Corporation*, New York, Basic Books, 1985 pp. 49–50.

A fast-to-market strategy is most attractive to companies that deal with products in the introduction or growth stages of the product life cycle and to companies that stress continuous innovation. For example, a designer of fashion clothing might pursue a fast-to-market strategy, as might a computer hardware or software manufacturer. These companies have found lead time reductions very profitable. A McKinsey study found that introducing a product on-time but 50 percent over budget generated higher profits than a product introduced on budget but six months late.[5]

To understand how advantages can be gained from fast to market, consider the following example. Both Company ABC and Company XYZ design a new cellular telephone. Company ABC introduces its new line in 8 months while Company XYZ takes 12 months. Company ABC's four-month lead time advantage over XYZ allows it to command a premium for its new cellular telephone (since for four months it is the only new product available) that helps to cover its development costs. Furthermore, Company ABC has a four-month head start in developing the next-generation product and is able to quickly exploit any new technologies that have emerged since the start of development on the first-generation cellular telephone.

In contrast, Company XYZ enters the market with a cellular telephone based on almost the same technology as the products of Company ABC. Unable to offer any performance advantage to its customers, Company XYZ must offer lower prices in order to gain market share. Unfortunately, Company ABC already has four months of production experience and associated cost improvements. Like ABC, Company XYZ begins working on the next generation immediately after it introduces the new line, but ABC started four months earlier. As XYZ completes about one-third of its design process, ABC introduces its new-generation product, and XYZ has nothing comparable to offer. Customers see ABC offering newer and better products faster, while they see XYZ offering stale technology.

Other advantages offered by being fast to market include increased visibility in the marketplace, greater name recognition, and greater interest from those customers who want the newest and the best. In short, being fast to market creates greater value. This, in turn, translates into increased market share and higher profitability.

Fast Order-to-Delivery Fulfillment

Companies also compete by quickly responding to customer orders for existing products. Many firms are now actively competing on this basis, as Exhibit 7 illustrates. These firms work to reduce the interval from the time a customer places an order until that order reaches the customer. Like fast-to-market competition, a number of factors make fast fulfillment very attractive.

First, many customers are willing to pay premium prices to get their purchases sooner, increasing profits for the fast-fulfillment supplier. Second, managers of fast-fulfillment firms have found strong relationships between lead time and the other dimensions of value. They

[5] Cited in J. T. Vessey, "The New Competitors: They Think in Terms of Speed to Market," *Academy of Management Executive* 5, no. 2 (1991), pp. 23–33.

EXHIBIT 7
Reducing Order-to-Delivery Lead Time

	Product	Old Time	New Time
General Electric	Circuit breaker boxes	3 weeks	3 days
Motorola	Pagers	3 weeks	2 hours
Hewlett-Packard	Test equipment	4 weeks	5 days
Brunswick	Fishing reels	3 weeks	1 week
Matsushita	Washing machines	360 hours	2 hours
Harley-Davidson	Motorcycles	360 days	< 3 days
Zaring National	Homes	160 days	90 days
Cast-Fab	Metal parts	12 weeks	5 days
Grote Industries	Safety lighting systems	55 days	34 days
Forethought	Insurance policies	90 days	1 day

have found that reductions in lead time are correlated with

- **Increases in quality.** Reducing lead times requires the operations management system to do things right the first time, every time. With shorter lead times, the firm tends to build products according to the latest specifications, so obsolete parts or out-of-date specifications cause fewer quality problems.
- **Reductions in inventory.** Shorter lead times allow firms to carry less work-in-process inventory because products pass through the operations management system to customers more quickly, so the firm needs less storage space. For the same level of output, fast-fulfillment firms can operate physically smaller plants than slower competitors.
- **Improvements in flexibility.** As lead times fall, the firm can wait longer to start building a product, which enhances its scheduling flexibility. Furthermore, with shorter lead times, the firm tends to build in smaller lot sizes, so it can afford to build products in the exact quantities and to the specifications demanded by customers.
- **Reductions in cost.** Altogether, reductions in lead time, inventory, and physical space requirements combine with improvements in quality—less scrap, salvage, and rework—to lower operating costs.

Consider Motorola's Florida-based pocket pager plant, which was seeking an advantage over Japanese competitors such as NEC, Hitachi, and Fujitsu. Conformance quality was not an option since Japanese firms produced products with near-perfect quality. Motorola was hesitant to add product features as a source of differentiation because it feared that the pagers would become too complex for customers to operate. Price differences did not seem to be sufficiently important. Fast OTD fulfillment seemed to offer the only basis for sustainable competitive advantage. U.S.-based Motorola was much closer to customers than the Japanese firms. Motorola seized this advantage by designing and building an extremely fast fulfillment system. Customers place orders via a toll-free number. Within 20 minutes of placing the order, workers gather the necessary parts and send them to the production line. A customized pager can be built within two hours, and it is usually shipped the same day. Customers appreciate this convenience and speed. Motorola also gains significant internal advantages from fast OTD fulfillment: less inventory, less physical space required, fewer quality problems, and lower costs.

Reliable OTD Lead Time

In some business settings, being on time is even more important than being fast. Reliable product delivery is usually of great value to customers when they absorb costs due to delays or early delivery. For example, consider a components supplier to a manufacturing plant. If the supplier delivers components to the plant before they are needed, the customer incurs inventory costs, including costs of capital, storage, damage, and so forth. If the supplier delivers components late, the customer's operating lines may be starved or even shut down, potentially costing the customer thousands of dollars per hour. You can probably imagine similar situations in a service setting. For example, imagine a construction crew sitting idle while it waits for a building inspector to issue required building permits.

In many industries, reliable delivery is a minimum requirement for doing business. Just-in-time manufacturing philosophies have become the norm over the past two decades. And suppliers are expected to deliver materials and components within tight time windows. In warehousing it is not uncommon for customers to require that delivery trucks arrive within 30-minute windows of time. If manufacturers can count on consistent and timely deliveries, they can hold less raw materials inventories and experience less variation in production schedules. Due to these advantages, reliable delivery is a source of value to them. Common carriers such as Federal Express have formed their entire business strategies around reliable delivery.

Flexibility and Its Impact on the Elements of Value

Flexibility represents a relatively new strategic emphasis in many firms as they seek to enhance value and find competitive advantage in the marketplace. Customers do not evaluate flexibility directly, because flexibility is an internal operating capability. As such, flexibility is not considered to be a basic element of value. However, a more flexible firm can generally offer a wider variety of high-quality goods and services more quickly, more reliably, and at lower costs than nonflexible firms can. Consequently, many Japanese, European, and American firms now view flexibility as an important strategic weapon.

Many managers and students have formed only vague notions of flexibility, describing it with terms such as responsiveness, speed of response, and adaptability. For the purposes of this module, **flexibility** is the ability of an operations management system to respond to changes in demand, in supply, or in processes with little cost or time penalty. These changes can be generated externally, as when the market begins demanding a different mix of products and a firm changes its schedule to provide the desired product mix. Change also can be generated internally, as when a machine breaks down and operations managers rearrange the flow of products through the system to avoid disappointing customers.

The flexibility of the operations management system can be described in terms of the number of different possibilities the operations management system can handle. For example, early on in the growth of the fast-food industry, McDonald's production process allowed it to offer a more flexible breakfast menu than Burger King, because Burger King built its process around a flame-broiling cooking method while McDonald's relied on a flat grill. A person can cook pancakes, omelets, and eggs on a grill; it is far more difficult to flame-broil eggs.

Flexibility attracts customers because it helps them and the firm itself deal with uncertainty. Competitors' actions can cause uncertainty, as when a competitor introduces a new product. To remain competitive, other firms must either match or beat this new product. Uncertainty can result when a customer wants a firm to accommodate changes in product mix or volume. Uncertainty also can stem from internal causes, such as variability in material or in equipment availability.

Dimensions of Flexibility

David Upton, a Harvard professor who has studied flexibility in factories extensively, identifies three basic aspects of flexibility:[6]

- **Range:** The variety of operating states and outputs that an operations manager can produce.
- **Mobility:** The ability of the operations management system to move from one operating state to another quickly or with little cost, for example, time to change over production from one product to another.
- **Uniformity of performance:** The ability of the operations management system to produce a variety of outputs or volumes without loss in operating performance.

[6] D. M. Upton, "What Really Makes Factories Flexible?" *Harvard Business Review,* July–August 1995, pp. 74–84.

Different range, mobility, and uniformity-of-performance characteristics create various types of flexibility. A firm's consideration of the different types of flexibility should emphasize these critical points:

1. *The specific methods chosen to improve flexibility should reflect how the firm competes.* For example, a firm that competes on the basis of reliable deliveries should identify rerouting/program flexibility as critical to its success. Other firms need mix flexibility to respond to an unpredictable flow of customer needs such as a home appliance repair shop.
2. *Enhancing flexibility requires cooperation both inside and outside the firm.* For example, a suitably designed product greatly enhances the ability of the operations manager to implement and compete on modification flexibility. To emphasize volume flexibility, a firm needs the support of suppliers. Success in enhancing mix or changeover flexibility depends on strong links with the internal marketing function and with customers.
3. *Improving flexibility affects all elements of value.* Flexibility relates aspects of quality (such as product variety) and timeliness (responsiveness) to aspects of cost (eg., non-value added time, labor costs, and so on). Flexibility is improved when the cost or time required to make changes is reduced. In general, reductions in lead times enable greater flexibility, and improvements in quality reduce costs and lead times, which also enhance flexibility.

Today's market links flexibility with value. Firms have experienced beneficial effects from enhancing flexibility, including

- *Consistency with shorter product life cycles.* Product life cycles are compressed, making all products increasingly like fashion goods that survive only for short times. Flexibility helps a firm to cope with short and shrinking product life cycles.
- *Niche marketing opportunities.* The fundamental shift from producing for broad-based markets to producing for individuals is called niche marketing. Success in niche marketing is strongly linked to flexibility that allows the firm to produce in small lots, perhaps even to build each item to a customer's unique specifications.
- *Premium prices for flexibility.* Flexibility allows a firm to fine-tune products to meet specific needs, justifying premium prices. Also, a flexible supplier helps customers cope with uncertainty, for which customers are willing to pay premium prices.
- *Reductions in lead time.* Flexibility optimizes both range and time. Enhanced flexibility often translates directly into reduced lead time, thus improving the firm's ability to make timely deliveries to customers.
- *Reductions in cost.* Flexibility reduces the need for inventory. Also, worker productivity improves as employees spend less time in non-value added activities, such as setting up and tearing down machines for product changeovers. Improved productivity, together with shorter lead times and higher quality, translates into lower costs.

Understanding Aspects of Total Cost

Having explored the numerator of the value equation, we now turn to the denominator, total **cost.** There are a number of different types of costs that customers must bear in order to acquire and utilize goods and services. Consider the following costs of owning and operating an automobile:

- **Acquisition costs:** The purchase price of a car, for example.
- **Repair costs:** The cost of replacing a broken part.
- **Maintenance costs:** The cost of oil changes and tune-ups.
- **Operating costs:** The cost of gas and tires.

- **Salvage/resale costs:** The cost recovered upon selling a car.
- **Disposal costs:** The cost of disposing of a wrecked car.

Most of these costs to the customer are a direct reflection of the firm's operating costs plus a profit margin. Consequently, operations managers are very concerned with internal costs of materials, production, and service operations. In addition to tracking costs directly, operations managers measure other indicators of cost effectiveness, such as yield, efficiency, utilization, and productivity. These cost-oriented measures have clear links to profitability. For example, productivity and profitability are linked in the following way:

$$\text{Profitability} = \text{Sales/Costs} = \text{Output quantity} \times \text{Unit price/Input quantity} \times \text{Unit cost}$$
$$= (\text{Output quantity/Input quantity})/(\text{Unit price/Unit cost})$$
$$= \text{Productivity} \times \text{Price recovery factor}$$

Perhaps more importantly, productivity and cost-related factors in operations affect long-term profitability because they greatly influence the pricing competitiveness of the firm. This, in turn, is related to market share, growth, and other aspects of firm performance.

Low Cost as a Source of Value

Marketers know well that people like to buy things cheaply, but they do not like cheap things. This statement describes both the major attraction and the problem of emphasizing cost as the firm's major source of value. Customers want at least the same performance for a lower cost, not simply less for less. A cost-driven approach to value treats performance as given and focuses on reducing cost.

To achieve this objective, the operations management system must reexamine both the product (good and service) it offers and the processes by which it delivers the product. This reexamination seeks to identify product features that customers do not value highly or process traits that contribute unnecessarily to cost. These product and process features become candidates for elimination since the value they add does not justify their costs.

The danger of short-term, cost-driven value enhancement lies in the potential for abuse and an excessive emphasis on cost reduction. Such an approach ignores long-term implications that often directly and negatively affect timeliness and quality. For example, to lower cost, a firm might use a cheaper material that reduces quality. To save costs, management may decide to devote less time and resources to preventive maintenance of equipment and safety management. In the short term, these changes do save costs. However, in the long run, they reduce the availability of equipment and increase the burden of lost time due to on-the-job accidents.

Managing the Value Equation

To succeed, managers must put the value equation to work, which requires deciding how much emphasis is placed on each of the components of value. To understand and manage the value equation, managers need to keep a few key points in mind. First, while the three major elements of value are interrelated, they focus on different activities. As the value-enhancement orientation shifts, perhaps from quality to timeliness, the underlying processes must also change. This critical orientation toward process management and its link to a specific type of value is a basic requirement of a strong operations strategy.

At the same time, timeliness, quality, and total cost are clearly interdependent. Quality focuses on activities that make a product better, though they also seem to improve timeliness. Improving timeliness seems to require its own focused efforts, although improvements in timeliness also seem to boost quality. Both elements of performance significantly affect costs. Improvements in quality and timeliness produce cost reductions as by-products or residual effects. In the short term, value-enhancement actions may increase costs. In the long term, however, they reduce costs by eliminating problems that cause long lead times, limited flexibility, and poor quality. Conversely, a focus on costs often erodes quality and increases lead times.

Value improvement is a simple concept to discuss but a very difficult one to implement. Effective value-driven management requires extreme precision. When asked, managers at most firms will tell you that their firm produces high-quality goods and services. However, they might say something different if asked what are the most important points of competitive differentiation. One cannot simply say, for example, that the firm will compete based on quality. From the earlier discussion we know that there are many different dimensions of quality. A decision to compete on quality defines an overall orientation and focus, but it demands elaboration to specify the types of quality on which to base competition. Only by specifying these dimensions precisely can the operations manager and the operations management system deliver the product promised by the firm and desired by the customer. A firm's definition of value influences the types of processes it builds, the investments it makes, the control systems it implements, and the way it measures performance. Without clear and detailed definitions, the operations manager runs a very real risk of investing in unsuitable systems and processes that fail to fulfill the dimensions of value desired by the customer.

Waste, the Antithesis of Value

It is impossible to talk about value without also talking about waste. **Waste** is the antithesis of value. Value and waste define the two primary challenges facing the modern operations manager. The first is to enhance the level of value fulfilled by the operations management system; the second is to eliminate or reduce the level of waste within the system. Waste exists at two levels: at the effectiveness (strategic) level and the efficiency (tactical) level.[7]

Effectiveness deals with *doing the right things* for the customer. Waste, in this case, is any activity that adversely affects the value equation for the customer. Of course, wasteful activities for one customer may be valuable for another customer. Consider inventory, for example. In general, operations managers view inventory as wasteful, because it consumes resources such as storage space, capital, and people who count and manage it. If customers don't value these activities, the inventory is indeed wasteful. However, there may be circumstances where inventory, say, of finished goods, is the most economical way to provide the level of product availability that the customer demands. Customers expect to find inventory at a grocery store, for example. In this scenario, inventory is not wasteful because it increases the effectiveness of the system.

Efficiency deals with *doing things right.* Waste, then, is anything that causes an excess of the minimum amounts of materials, parts, equipment, facilities, labor, and time essential to produce and deliver the desired product and service to the customer.[8] Returning to our example of inventory, any amount of inventory in the operations system beyond the minimum level required to provide acceptable product availability would be considered waste. Many "continuous improvement" approaches to operations management focus on this aspect of waste. They seek to change *how* things are done in order to operate the system with maximum efficiency. Strategic initiatives, on the other hand, seek to change *what* things are done in order to improve effectiveness.

Many firms use labor content as a metric for estimating value in a product. Whenever you add labor, you correspondingly add value. Do you agree with this practice? How might you fundamentally challenge this view?

[7] Types of waste are discussed in detail in the module "Lean/Just-in-Time Systems"; Steven A. Melnyk, Lawrence D. Fredendall (New York: McGraw-Hill/Irwin, 2002).

[8] Mokshagundam L. Srikanth and M. Michael Umble, *Synchronous Management: Profit-Based Manufacturing for the 21st Century,* Vol. 1 (Guilford, CT: The Spectrum Publishing Company, 1997), p. 5.

Value and waste are hard taskmasters. They drive and motivate the operations manager; they shape and influence the operations management system, its structure, its processes, and the resources it consumes. The work of reducing waste and increasing value never ends.

Pollution is considered a form of waste. Why is it so considered? What makes pollution different from other forms of waste encountered within the Operations Management system?

The Value Chain

We have discussed value in terms of operating objectives and performance outcomes. In order to reach these objectives, a host of resources must be brought together. Designing and delivering value is a corporate activity usually involving many different organizations and functions. Each of these value partners adds value in specialized ways as the product, information, or customer passes through the entire processing system. The term **value chain** describes the connections among various value-adding organizations and functions. The operations management system is the heart of the value chain. Typically, marketing managers and product designers play leadership roles in determining the aspects of value that customers desire. Operations managers then take the lead in fulfilling those value aspects reliably.

As Exhibit 8 suggests, there are four primary operations management activities represented in the value chain: planning, sourcing, making, and delivery. Every firm involved in the value chain procures resources, makes some type of transformations, and fulfills requirements for downstream partners or customers. Sourcing involves all the activities required to identify sources of raw materials and supplies, negotiate terms of supply, and secure the timely delivery of high-quality supplies. Supplier relationship management is crucial in accomplishing sourcing activities. Decisions such as the number and types of suppliers selected and the types of relationships fostered have large impacts on the capabilities of the sourcing function. Making involves all the processes required to transform raw materials and components (or customers) into finished products. This includes managing facilities, technologies, and people; scheduling and allocating orders among production facilities; processing the orders; and ensuring quality. Delivery comprises all the activities required to anticipate, gather, and communicate customer orders; store and transport products; and close the sale. Delivery processes touch customers directly. As such, the management of customer relationships has great impact on

EXHIBIT 8
Basic Activities in the Value Chain

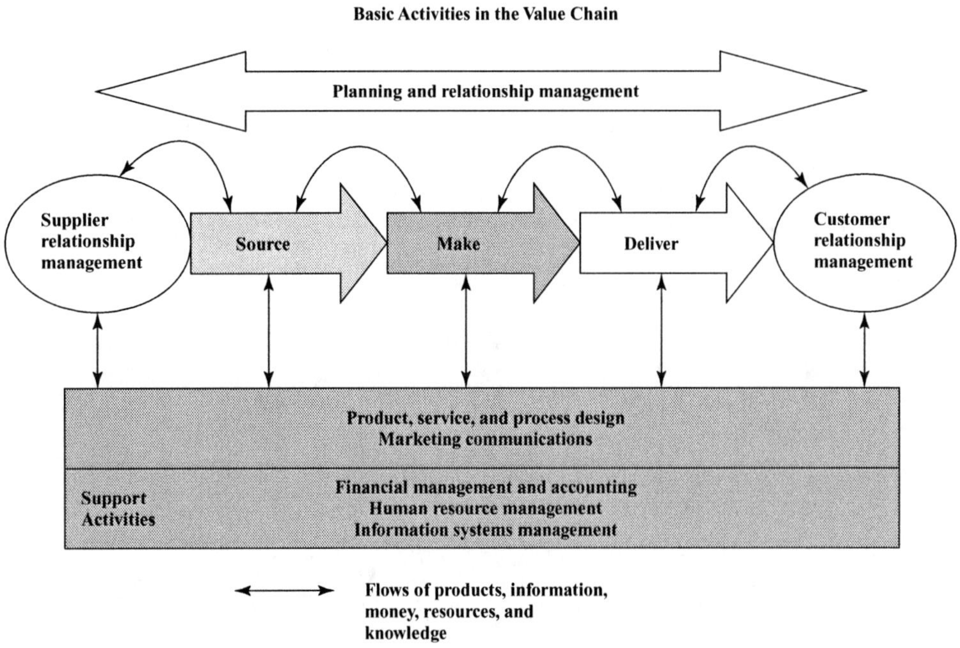

delivery, creating effects that ripple throughout the rest of the supply chain. Aspects such as the types of customers a firm chooses to serve and the characteristics of orders—for example, size and timing characteristics—determine to a great degree the locations and configuration of facilities networks, the information systems required, transportation resources needed, and a host of other issues.

Other primary activities in the value chain are product design and marketing communications. Product design creates value by transferring and transforming information in ways that capture and meet customer needs. Marketing communications add value by shaping customers' expectations. While these activities mainly exist outside the realm of normal operations functions, and perhaps *because* they do, it is very important that the decisions and plans made in these areas are highly integrated with the primary operating activities.

While these functions are presented as separate links in the value chain, they should be thought of as highly integrated activities. Decisions made in one stage of the chain have serious effects on the capabilities of another stage of the chain. For example, the inventory management policies chosen by managers in the delivery part of the chain can either help or hinder production managers' abilities to operate a stable, high-quality process. During the past decade, managers have come to realize that many, if not most, of the opportunities to improve value added capabilities come from better coordination and integration of the basic value-chain functions.

Accordingly, determining value-chain structure and managing interfirm and interfunctional relationships have become very important processes. Many firms have considered adding or dropping partners in order to restructure their value chains more effectively. Some are considering new partnership arrangements, sometimes even with competitors. For example, IBM and Xerox are sharing physical storage facilities for some spare parts and other products in order to reap the advantages of pooled stocks and economies of scale. Firms also are designing new ways to communicate across corporate and functional boundaries, including the use of new information and communication technologies, teaming arrangements, and alliances. These changes are creating a very exciting and dynamic environment for operations managers.

A Typical Structure

The basic value chain functions depicted in Exhibit 8 are fleshed out in many different forms depending on the nature of the good or service offered as well as industry and market conditions. Exhibit 9 shows a typical value chain for a manufactured product, including all

EXHIBIT 9 Physical Value Chain for a Manufactured Product

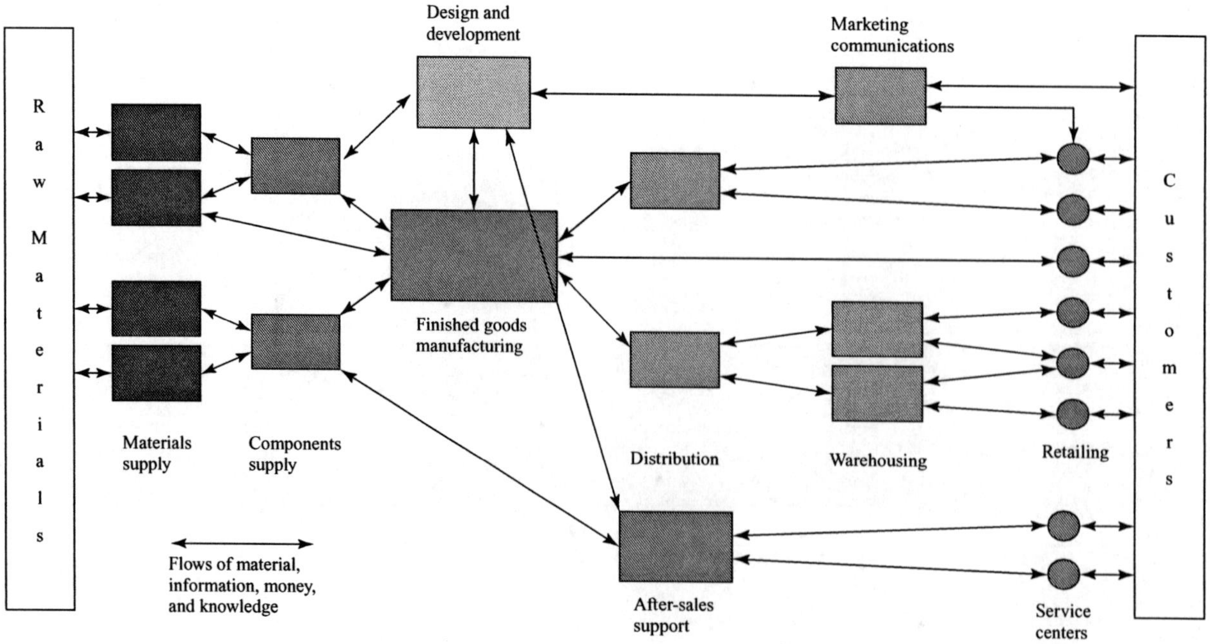

aspects of product and service design and delivery. Note that the value chain includes customer information and support activities, for example, marketing communications, such as promotion and after-sales service, as well as manufacturing and transportation.

Cycles of sourcing, making, and delivery occur over and over at each stage of the value chain. Delivery activities at one stage of the value chain are closely associated with the downstream stage's sourcing activities. Also note that a single firm usually maintains multiple channels of supply and distribution. For example, each personal computer manufacturer serves its customer segments in different ways by including direct sales over the phone or through the Web, sales through mass retailers, and sales through value added resellers (VARs). Establishing and managing new connections and channels within the value chain is itself a key value-adding activity.

A single firm might control within its corporate boundaries any number of the value-adding activities. Vertically integrated firms contain and control many of the stages. For example, early in its corporate life, Ford represented the ultimate in vertical integration. Henry Ford owned the forests that supplied the wood that formed the spokes in the wheels of Model T automobiles. He also owned the transportation, distribution, and retailing facilities used to deliver cars from factories to customers. Ford controlled all the essential stages of the value chain from raw-earth materials to the final product.

Today few firms are so highly integrated. In fact, there has been more of a move toward vertical disintegration—or outsourcing—in many industries. Many computer manufacturers, for example, do not own any of the component manufacturing, distribution, retailing, or after-sales service operations. Instead, they rely on close partnerships with suppliers to manage these activities. Even so, companies are increasingly recognizing that it is important to consider the effects of their decisions on both the upstream and downstream stages of the value chain.

The value-chain concept is powerful because it prompts operations managers to consider all of the aspects of value added that are, or could be, provided to the end customer. Firms that consider all stages of the value chain when they design and develop new products are more likely to introduce products that meet customers' needs more effectively and at lower cost. End-use customers are not the only customers who benefit. Rather, the value chain should be viewed as a chain of customers. At each stage of the chain, all the involved partners share improvements and cost savings achieved at that stage.

Module Summary

As we can see from the discussion presented in this module, value is critical to the survival of the firm. It also can seem to be a complex concept. However, certain critical truths capture most of the essential features of value.

1. **Value begins and ends with the customer.** The effectiveness of any firm's value definition is ultimately assessed by the customer through that person's purchases.
2. **Value and waste are closely related.** Whenever one defines value, one also has defined the conditions for waste since whatever does not add value must ultimately result in waste.
3. **Value is relative.** Since it is difficult to perfectly satisfy each customer's expectations, value is usually judged against prior experiences, competitor's offerings, or an established goal.
4. **Value is dynamic.** Thanks to changes in capabilities, customers, environment (technology, competition, and the government), and the corporate vision, value is always changing and evolving.
5. **Value is created through the coordinated efforts of many functions within and across a business's value chain.** Operations management must understand and interact with other organizational functions in order to deliver value successfully.

This module has provided an introduction to the concept of value as a driver for operations management system design. By now, you should understand the meaning behind the following statements:

- The basic operational elements of value are quality, timeliness, and total cost.
- Deficiencies in value usually occur from a lack of fit between value design, value fulfillment, and/or customer expectations.

- Timeliness and time-based competition have many aspects including fast to market, fast fulfillment, and reliable delivery strategies.
- Different market orientations regarding timeliness include engineer-to-order, make-to-order, assemble-to-order, and make-to-stock products.
- The concept of quality is multidimensional in nature.
- Cost, the denominator of the value equation, performs major roles in reporting performance, aiding in the management and evaluation of operations, and providing a source of value.
- Flexibility is in essence an ability of the operations management system to respond quickly, in terms of range and time, to externally and internally generated changes.
- Waste is a natural complement to value. Waste describes anything within the operations environment that is in excess of the minimum amounts of materials, parts, equipment, facilities, labor, and time that are essential to produce and deliver the desired product and service to the customer.

Key Terms

Cost, *18*
Flexibility, *17*
Lead-time categories, *11*
Market orientations, *12*
Order to delivery lead time, *11*
Product, *3*
Quality, *6*
Reliability, *10*
Speed/lead time, *10*
Time to market, *14*
Timeliness, *14*
Total fulfillment lead time, *12*
Value, *5*
Value added, *3*
Value chain, *21*
Value equation, *5*
Value imperative, *8*
Value through design, *6*
Value through execution, *6*
Waste, *20*

Discussion Questions

1. Review the marketplace and find three instances in which competitors are working in a collaborative manner.
2. Review the events of your daily life. Then identify activities in which you have experienced the following types of lead time:
   a. Production lead time.
   b. Delivery lead time.
   c. Product design lead time.
3. For question 2, would you value the goods or services provided in each case if the lead time had been significantly reduced? Why?
4. How might system variance have been a cause of lengthy lead time for your responses to questions 2 and 3?
5. Consider products you consume. Identify purchases you have made from firms with the following market orientations:
   a. Make to stock.
   b. Make to order.
   c. Assemble to order.
   d. Engineer to order.

   In each case, what are the conditions that enable or require a firm to adopt this market orientation?
6. Discuss how a firm's market orientation influences the following aspects of value:
   a. Delivery speed, that is, how quickly a customer gets the product.
   b. Variety of the product offerings.
   c. Design quality.
   d. Cost of the good or service.
7. Which market orientation would you consider for a standard product that has low, infrequent demand? What are the trade-offs you would consider in making this decision?
8. For each of the following service operations, develop a lead time taxonomy identifying all the lead times involved. In each case, start with the customer's decision that he or she wants something, such as a pizza, and end with the service-rendering transaction:
   a. Delivering a pizza.
   b. Installing a second telephone line.
   c. Securing a home mortgage.
   d. Burying a much-loved individual.

9. Think of items you have purchased over the past year from firms competing on the basis of time. How did time influence your decision to buy that product?
10. Explain how flexibility can be used to create a broader range of products or to produce and deliver goods or services more quickly. Give examples.
11. Discuss instances where you or your family has paid a premium for products purchased from a flexible source. What were the trade-offs involved?
12. Discuss the differences between design quality and quality of conformance.
13. Review your monthly household budget, and then try to identify expenditures that seem to represent waste. Would all members of your household agree?
14. Why does improving a process in most cases result in reduced costs, reduced lead time, improved quality, and enhanced flexibility, while focusing on the costs alone tends to reduce quality, increase lead time, and reduce flexibility?

Cases

The Personal Computer Industry

Personal computers are now integral to our daily lives. While this technological revolution may have seemed to happen flawlessly, for companies in this fast-paced industry it has been a rough ride. With the increasing number of different possible channels for sales, it has become important to identify which are appropriate for the customer base that a firm wants to attract.

Three of the more successful PC companies are Dell, Gateway, and Compaq. Each of these firms has chosen a different approach to customer service, employing different operations techniques.

DELL

Dell Corporation has embraced the technological revolution to its fullest. Not only has it been able to keep up with the changes in computer technologies, it is one of most successful retailers on the Internet. From the start, it was Dell's intent to produce computers only as customers requested them. Currently Dell holds only six days' worth of inventory in its entire manufacturing and distribution system. Its product is delivered directly to customers by one of the parcel services, for example, UPS.

Dell's website has been a major sales tool for the company; however, it also has a large sales force to serve corporate clients. Personal attention is important for corporate customers. In addition, Dell has established a sales tool on its website where each company has its own personalized space that provides information on previously purchased computers by that company. This capability allows the purchasing personnel of the corporation to see what equipment was purchased in the past and helps determine what they might need in the future. Recently Dell has extended its services to help corporations determine their needs for networking. Dell has established a consulting division to provide customers with additional help, and at this point in time it is not charging extra for its consulting work.

Not only has Dell been a frontrunner in utilizing the Internet to its advantage, it has optimized its supply-chain capabilities. Some of Dell's system components may never come to its facilities but are delivered directly to customers. All of Dell's suppliers have direct connections to Dell via Valuechain.Dell.com, which allows suppliers to deliver the parts necessary to complete any order on time and with great efficiency.

GATEWAY

Gateway, just like Dell, has been very effective in utilizing the Internet to help its sales soar ahead of many of its competitors. However, Gateway has decided to extend its operations to the retail side by opening small stores called Gateway Country, where customers can come in and try out a computer system. The stores also provide an opportunity for consumers who are unfamiliar with computer terminology to learn more about computers before they make a purchase. Gateway Country stores hold training sessions for people who are not computer literate.

Each Gateway computer system is personalized for an individual customer, which means Gateway has no finished-goods inventory. The firm turns inventory over 40 times per year, which has cut the cost of computers. However, it also has made Gateway highly dependent on its suppliers. Furthermore, since each computer has to be specially made for a client, lead times have increased. Even if a computer is purchased through a Gateway Country store, the system is delivered to the customer by one of the parcel service companies.

In reaction to strong competition, Gateway decided to establish a packaged purchase option, allowing customers to purchase software, peripherals, and Internet access all in one location. This strategy makes Gateway a one-stop-shop for any computer needs. Gateway was also the first company to provide financing for customers to purchase a new computer system, and now the company has even allowed consumers to lease a computer system and exchange it for a new one in three or more years. This service has made computer purchasing easier and provides a valuable service to the customers who are worried about their computer becoming obsolete in six months after they purchased it.

COMPAQ

Compaq has made its name selling computer systems through retail outlets such as Best Buy and Circuit City. Since Compaq builds computer systems to stock, their customers receive the computer at the time of purchase. Recently, Compaq has worked with value added resellers (VARs) such as Inacom Corp. to configure customized Compaq systems for corporate clients. And Compaq has created its own Internet site where customers can choose the computer system they want to buy. To receive the system, however, customers must go to a retail store.

To increase its sales, Compaq has recently acquired Digital Equipment Corp. (DEC), a consulting company. DEC's business is to provide consulting services for corporations about their network needs. Since DEC is now a part of the Compaq, it often suggests installing Compaq equipment to fulfill any networking need a company may have. The acquisition of DEC should help Compaq compete with Dell's consulting services as they try to secure customers at an early stage of the purchasing process.

QUESTIONS

1. What primary market segments make up the PC customer bases for Dell, Gateway, and Compaq?
2. How does each firm serve each of these market segments? What supply-chain channels are used?
3. What aspects of value are provided by these firms? Which aspects does each supply-chain channel emphasize?
4. Are any of the three companies better suited to serve all market segments?

Related Modules of Interest

- Foundations of Process Management
- Value-Driven Operations Strategy
- Lean/Just-in-Time Systems

Selected Readings

Abegglen, James C., and George Stalk Jr. *Kaisha: The Japanese Corporation.* New York: Basic Books, 1985.

Bethune, Gordon (with Scott Huler). *From Worst to First.* New York: John Wiley & Sons, 1998.

Blackburn, Joseph D. *Time-Based Competition: The Next Battleground in American Manufacturing.* New York: McGraw-Hill/Irwin, 1991.

Bower, Joseph L., and Thomas Hout. "Fast-Cycle Capability for Competitive Power." *Harvard Business Review,* November–December 1988.

Clark, Kim B., and Takahiro Fujimoto. *Product Development Performance.* Cambridge, MA: Harvard Business School Press, 1991.

Garvin, David A. *Managing Quality.* New York: Free Press, 1988.

Hall, Robert. *The Soul of the Enterprise.* New York: Harper Business, 1993.

Normann, Richard, and Rafael Ramirez. "From Value Chain to Value Constellation: Designing an Interactive Strategy." *Harvard Business Review,* July–August 1993.

Slack, Nigel. "Flexibility as a Manufacturing Objective." *International Journal of Operations and Production Management* 3, no. 3 (1983), pp. 4–13.

Srikanth, Mokshagundam L., and M. Michael Umble. *Synchronous Management: Profit-Based Manufacturing for the 21st Century,* Vol. 1. Guilford, CT: Spectrum Publishing Company, 1997.

Stabell, Charles B., and Oystein D. Fjeldstad. "Configuring Value for Competitive Advantage: On Chains, Shops, and Networks." *Strategic Management Journal* 19 (1998), pp. 413–37.

Value-Driven Operations Strategy

Steven A. Melnyk
Michigan State University

Morgan Swink
Michigan State University

McGraw-Hill Irwin

Boston Burr Ridge, IL Dubuque, IA Madison, WI New York San Francisco St. Louis
Bangkok Bogotá Caracas Kuala Lumpur Lisbon London Madrid Mexico City
Milan Montreal New Delhi Santiago Seoul Singapore Sydney Taipei Toronto

Value-Driven Operations Strategy

Module objectives

By the end of this module, you should be able to

- Understand the importance of and need for an operations strategy within the value-driven operations management system.
- Recognize the different levels of strategic planning found in most firms.
- Identify the various factors affecting value within the strategic planning process.
- Describe the strategic planning process that converts value into action.
- Recognize various value-based strategic initiatives and describe their linkage to the value proposition.

Steve Jobs's Apple Gets Way Cooler

Steve Jobs, the personal-computer industry's chief aesthetic officer, is in his element. Here in the boardroom at Apple Computer's Cupertino, California, headquarters, he's the only person seated. Reclining, actually. Hands clasped behind his head, he stares pokerfaced at a couple of web pages displayed side by side on an outsized 22-inch-wide Apple Cinema flat-panel monitor. Twelve weary-looking men—programmers, marketers, graphic designers, and Web experts—stand in pensive poses, forming an arc behind him.

"The icon for 'real estate' doesn't do anything for me at all," announces Jobs. He points at a Web-link button on the mocked-up home page for iReviews, Apple's new Website-rating service. "That's not what a 'for sale' sign looks like. And I don't much like this 'investing' icon either. I can't tell if it's supposed to look like a dollar bill or a stock certificate. But this old-fashioned highway sign for 'cars'—now that's cool. I love it! You instantly know exactly what it means."

Jobs has been presiding over secret meetings like this several hours a day, three or four times a week, throughout most of November and December. No detail was too trivial to escape his scrutiny as he passed final judgment on the look and feel—or what he calls the fit and finish—of a series of ambitious Apple software products and Internet initiatives that he would announce in early January (2000) at the annual MacWorld trade show in San Francisco. These surprise announcements would be his way of drawing a new line in the sand and daring Microsoft or Compaq or AOL or Sun or any other competitor to cross it.

Everyone expected him to unveil a new computer or two. Instead, Jobs showed off a flashy, completely redesigned Macintosh operating system called Mac OS X [ten], which, when it's delivered this summer, will put a glossy new face on the Mac. "We made the buttons on the screen so good you'll want to lick them," he says. Just as provocative was a set of jazzy and useful free Internet services available immediately—online data-storage space, build-'em-yourself personal home pages and websites, and a new kind of Web content, to name just a few. These Web services, which Apple calls iTools, are designed to work exclusively with Macintosh computers, not PCs or any other kind of Internet device. Jobs' goal: to use the Internet to make Apple's computers show up Wintel PCs rather than merely stay even.

Once again Steve Jobs is trying to win by design—to use aesthetics and finesse instead of brute force to change the rules of the computing game. That's what he did when he rolled out the first Macintosh in 1984. He did it again upon returning to Apple in 1997, when he coaxed engineers to come up with the sleek, colorful iMacs and iBooks, winsome machines that consumers are buying hand over fist. Now he has turned his connoisseur's eye beyond the box, hoping that a fresh approach to system software and especially to the Internet will further fuel demand for Apple products.

Most of the software and Web innovations spring from the technologies and engineers that Apple acquired in 1997 when it bought Next, the company Jobs started in 1985. These capabilities added to Apple and combined with Jobs' leadership have helped to turn Apple around. Since 1998, profits have grown and stock prices have increased. In early December 1999, Apple's stock price set an all-time high of $118 and has been hovering around $100 ever since, eight times the price at its nadir, shortly after Jobs took over. This success is a sure sign that Apple and Steve Jobs must be doing something right—something that makes Apple once again different in the marketplace and something that the customer wants and is willing to pay for.

Source: Brent Schlender, "Steve Jobs' Apple Gets Way Cooler," *Fortune*, January 24, 2000, pp. 66–71.

What a turnaround Apple Computers has experienced! In 1996 to 1997, the computing community effectively wrote off Apple Computers. Articles were written about the impending demise of Apple and about the legacy that Apple would leave to the computer world. To most of the "experts," Apple was another victim of the Wintel[1] Gargantua. However, the rumors of its demise were greatly exaggerated. By 2000, Apple had undergone a complete transformation. It had become leaner and more entrepreneurial in nature. Instead of trying to be all things to all people and markets, Apple had decided to focus on certain critical markets and on developing certain types of products and services. Apple is now profitable, growing, and considered an innovative force in the personal computer market.

The revival of Apple is due to several factors. These include a loyal, even fanatical, user base, attractive and well-designed products; and the presence at Apple's helm of a well-respected and highly credible leader who is considered to be thoroughly familiar with the computer industry, Steve Jobs. However, a large reason for Apple's revival lies in its *strategy*.

Strategy is a critical element in the value-driven operations management system. Strategy provides the bridge between the theory of value and the way that it is made real at firms such as Apple Computers. Without a sound, value-linked strategy, a firm such as Apple cannot hope to survive in the long term. The process of developing and articulating strategy contributes to firm performance in the following ways:

- Strategy defines the specific types of value the firm seeks to deliver to its customers.
- Strategy involves identifying specific target customers that it will pursue through its design activities and through the management of its transformation system.
- Strategy shapes the investments that the firm makes in its plants, equipment, information systems, and people (how they are recruited and trained).
- Strategy acts as the basis on which various plans and timetables are developed and implemented.
- Strategy communicates corporate goals and expectations both internally (to its employees) and externally (to stakeholders such as the investor).
- Strategy helps to integrate and coordinate planning and activities at the various levels of the firm (corporate, strategic business unit, and functional).
- Strategy seeks to create balance through value among four major factors: operations capabilities, corporate vision, customers, and the competitive environment.

As we will see in this module, various dimensions of value are associated with specific operational business strategies. We begin by reviewing the elements of Apple's current strategy. Then we examine the various types of planning (and plans) that must be considered when developing and implementing a strategy. The rest of this module deals with the strategic planning process and its interrelationships with value.

[1] "Wintel" is a word that is based on Microsoft *Win*dows and In*tel*. It describes a computer that uses the Intel microprocessor and the Microsoft Windows operating system.

Examining Apple's Strategy for Survival and Growth

As previously noted, much of the reason for Apple's survival and growth can be traced to its strategy. This strategy embodies the following critical decisions:

- *Apple will focus its attention on two critical customers: consumers and program developers.* The computer marketplace consists of many different segments including enterprise users (i.e., businesses), graphic artists, consumers (home computer users), Internet users, schools, and programmer developers (to name a few). In the past, Apple has tried to provide a product for every segment. This strategy has resulted in a proliferation of models and product confusion among its customers. Today Apple recognizes that it cannot be "all things to all people." As a result, it has targeted two segments: the home user (who wants a computer that is stable and easy to use) and the program developer. Program developers are critical because they develop the programs that make computers useful. The more programs present for a computer platform such as the Apple, the easier that it is to sell that computer. Apple has targeted the developer by building for them a set of development tools and procedures called "Cocoa." These tools allow programmers to build brand new programs in about a tenth the time it would take to develop them for any other operating system.
- *Apple will emphasize speed, quality, and innovation.* Apple cannot offer the low-cost computer systems provided by other "generic" computer companies. To successfully demand a premium price, Apple must be able to quickly offer the customer the latest and best hardware and software, before they are offered on the Microsoft Windows platform. Apple also now emphasizes superior quality in terms of ease of use and reliability (i.e., a system not subject to random crashes). As Steve Jobs put it,[2] "This is what customers pay us for—to sweat all these details so it's easy and pleasant for them to use our computers. We're supposed to be really good at this."
- *Apple will focus on its core competencies.* Apple's core competency is its ability to design software with features that focus on latent demand (i.e., customer needs that are not obvious). For example, Apple introduced digital movie editing—the ability to import and edit film from digital camcorders. Customers did not demand this feature initially. However, once they saw it, they wanted it. A second core competency is the ability to design and deliver innovative, highly stylized products. This ability is very evident in both the iMac and iBook computers now offered by Apple. Apple's focus on these core competencies means they will avoid doing things they are not particularly good at. For example, Apple recently turned down an opportunity to start its own ISP (Internet service provider) company, because they realized that this was not something they could do better than competitors. Instead, they partnered with Earthlink, an existing ISP, to create an exclusive ISP for Apple.
- *Apple will offer features unique to the Macintosh.* In the past, Apple offered many of its software utilities (e.g., Apple QuickTime) for both the Macintosh and Windows environments. This was done in part because Apple wanted to have a presence in the business world (where Windows is the de facto standard). However, Apple now plans to offer software and hardware capabilities unique to its own platform—capabilities that will make people buy these machines if they want to have access to these capabilities.
- *Apple will act like a small entrepreneurial company.* If Apple is to compete as a fast innovator, then it must think and act like a small entrepreneurial firm where cross-functional work is the norm.

[2] Steve Jobs, "Apple's One-Dollar-a-Year Man," *Fortune,* January 24, 2000, pp. 71–76.

From this strategy, we can see the value concept that Apple is trying to generate in the marketplace and the specific type of customers that it is trying to attract. While the long-term viability of Apple is still questionable, the evidence now available, as measured in terms of speed of new product introduction, profitability, sales, and stock prices, indicates that this strategy is working.

Implications for the Operations Management System

Apple's strategy has major implications for the design, management, and evaluation of the operations management function:

- *Flexibility and responsiveness must drive the operations management system.* In Apple's new corporate strategy, operations will no longer have the luxury of building long runs of the same product. Long runs (while cost efficient) are inconsistent with Apple's emphasis on continual innovation and speed. Rather, operations must efficiently execute short runs. This means that it must reduce changeover costs and be flexible in production scheduling. The operations management system must be able to quickly and efficiently incorporate product and software design changes into manufacturing. Further, it must be able to track the specific computers with the changes that were made to them (important for warranty and customer service purposes).
- *Close cooperation with product design personnel is critical.* Apple lives in an environment where there is little tolerance for a poorly designed or built product. Given short new-product lead times and limited production runs, there is little opportunity to "debug" a design once it has been released. As a result, product design people need to work closely with operations managers during the design phase. Product designers must know the technical limitations of the operations management system, and operations managers need to expand these limitations. Operations managers must understand the key features and performance objectives of the product design so that they can help ensure that these objectives are met.
- *Close cooperation with suppliers in the supply chain is necessary.* Within this dynamic environment, operations managers must develop new and changing capabilities. The traditional approach for developing these capabilities through internal investments in plant capacity has limits. It simply takes too long for the resulting capacity to come "on line." As a result, operations management must depend on closer ties with its suppliers to provide these changing capabilities as they are needed. In addition, operations must be able to quickly forge new relationships to gain access to new capabilities as they are needed. This ability involves learning and knowledge of the capabilities of each partner in the supply chain—information that is needed to ensure that the "right" capabilities are in place at the "right" time to meet strategic and corporate needs.
- *Consistent metrics must be in place.* The performance of the operations management system cannot be measured using cost-based metrics. Reducing cost, while important, is not enough to meet Apple's strategic objectives. Rather, operations management must be measured on its ability to reduce lead time, improve responsiveness and flexibility, and enhance quality. The critical metrics used must capture and report these dimensions of performance.

As can be seen from this brief discussion, Apple's strategy strongly impacts the operations management system. At the same time, it also should be recognized that Apple's strategy could not be effectively formed without considering the capabilities of its operations management system. This interaction between operations capabilities and strategic objectives is explored in greater detail later on in this module.

Strategic Planning—The Different Levels

Within most modern firms, planning processes take place at several different levels. Internally, there is a hierarchy of strategic plans, consisting of (1) corporate planning, (2) strategic business unit (SBU) planning, and (3) functional planning. These three levels should be closely linked and interdependent (as shown in Exhibit 1). What happens at one level, under the appropriate set of conditions, should influence the planning at the other two levels. Furthermore, all three sets of plans must be consistent with and supportive of each other. In this section, we examine in detail these three planning levels. We conclude by introducing a relatively new type of strategic consideration: external integration (or consideration of strategic planning within the context of the supply chain).

EXHIBIT 1
The Hierarchy of Strategic Planning within the Firm

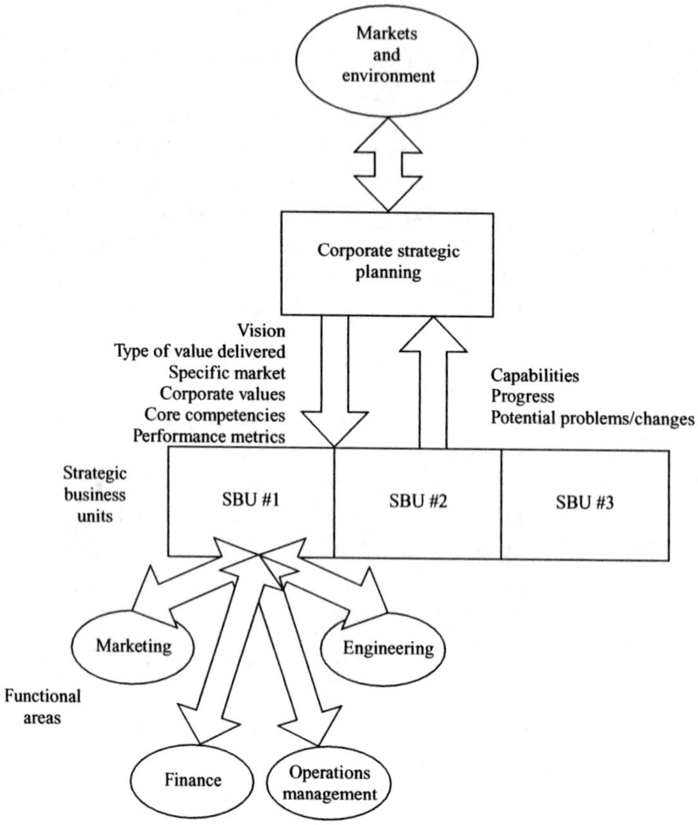

Corporate Planning

Of the three sets of strategic plans, the **corporate strategic plan** is the broadest in scope. It covers the longest time horizon and sets the tone, direction, and goals of the firm as a whole. The corporate plan also addresses the most critical decisions that must be answered either explicitly or implicitly within every firm, if it is to survive and grow, namely:

- What business(es) should we be in, and how do they interrelate?
- How do we, as a firm, generate value for our customers?
- What are our target markets now? Five years from now?
- What is the nature of the competitive environment in which we operate?
- What are the basic values and the vision that drive our firm?

- How do we judge/measure the success of our businesses?
- What should be our core competencies if we are to thrive?
- Do we have the resources and competencies in place to achieve these objectives?

Of the three levels of planning, corporate strategic planning is the least constrained. However, the decisions made at this level (i.e., how the preceding questions are answered) are critical because they constrain (limit) the type of decisions that can be made at the subsequent two planning levels.

Planning at the Strategic Business Unit Level

Many firms are involved in more than one business. For example, General Electric operates businesses in more than 20 primary areas from aircraft engines to vendor financial services. Because products and markets differ, a separate management team (usually headed by a president or vice president) runs each of these semi-independent organizations, known as **strategic business units** (SBUs). Each team is responsible for the performance of its unit, as measured in terms of growth, market share, and profitability. An SBU can be organized along product, market, or geographic dimensions. The critical feature of an SBU is that within the SBU, products have similar sets of order winners, order qualifiers, and order losers.[3]

Order winners: These are product value traits that are likely to cause customers to choose one product over a competing product (e.g., better performance, lower cost). These are traits on which the OM system must excel.

Order qualifiers: These are product value traits that must meet a certain level in order for the product even to be considered by the customer. The firm must perform acceptably (at a par with competitors) on these traits.

Order losers: Poor performance on these traits can cause the loss of current business or customer relationships.

SBU planning essentially deals with the question, "How should our business unit compete?" How this question is answered is shaped by the corporate strategy, the specific requirements of the SBU's products and market, and the SBU's operating capabilities.

Planning at the SBU level differs from corporate planning in several ways. First, it is constrained by decisions made at the corporate level. Second, it tends to be more detailed, with a shorter time horizon (the number of time periods covered by the plan). Finally, the SBU plan tends to be more action oriented in that it contains specific product and market-based initiatives and goals.

Go to the homepage for General Electric (www.GE.com) and, using the information provided there, determine

- The corporate vision and values.
- The major features of the corporate strategy.
- The number and composition of the major SBUs.
- How the SBUs compete in their specific markets.

Functional Planning

Every SBU consists of many functional groups, such as operations management, marketing, accounting, engineering, purchasing, logistics, and finance (to name a few). Each of these functions has to generate a strategic plan—one that is coordinated with and supportive of the SBU plan. To that extent, the **functional plan** must address certain critical questions:

[3] Terry Hill, *Manufacturing Strategy: Text and Cases, 2nd ed.* (New York: McGraw-Hill/Irwin, 1994).

- What specifically do we have to do to support the corporate and SBU strategies?
- What are the critical resources that we have to manage carefully if we are to achieve the corporate/SBU objectives?
- What metrics should we have in place to ensure we are making progress on these plans?
- What capabilities found in our function should be considered or recognized by the two higher stages of strategy?
- How should we coordinate our activities with those of the other functional areas within the firm to reduce friction and to enhance the ability of the firm/SBU to attain its overall objectives?

Of the three levels of planning, the functional plan is the most detailed, as well as the most constrained, as it must operate within a set of constraints set by decisions made within the corporate and SBU strategic plans. Most functional plans are organized around a critical plan. In marketing, this plan often is the "sales plan." For the operations management system, this plan is the "production plan." The production plan typically focuses on capacity, which is a critical resource since it determines how much (what volume) the function can produce. More importantly, it determines what the operations management system and the SBU can and cannot do. Capacity is also critical because of the time lag between the time when the decision is made to add (or change) the capacity of the operations management system and when the capacity comes "on line" and becomes available for use.

Before leaving this discussion of the three levels of planning, we offer some comments on the relationships between these three levels. First, it is important to remember the principle that planning is done from the top down, while execution takes place from the bottom up. That is, management begins with the corporate plan, then proceeds to the SBU plan, and finally ends with the functional plan. However, execution begins with the functional plans and then moves up to ultimately execute the corporate plan. Second, this planning process cannot proceed from one stage to the next in this hierarchy until those responsible for the planning at the higher level have ensured that the plan is feasible. That is, an SBU plan should not be formulated until top management has ensured that the corporate strategy is not only well articulated but also feasible. As a result, planning tends to be iterative. Planning problems at lower levels (such as at the functional planning level) may cause a revision of a higher-level plan; for example, when planning at the operations management level identifies insufficient capacity to meet the SBU and corporate strategic objectives. This lack of capacity may force a reevaluation (and change) of both the SBU and corporate strategic plans.

Finally, the corporate and SBU plans should not be formulated without first considering and recognizing the capabilities and core competencies emerging from the functional areas (this point is discussed in greater detail later on in this module). This last point deals with the critical concern of **consistency.** Consistency describes the extent to which the actions and plans developed in one area are in line with or supportive of the actions and plans made elsewhere. Consistency operates at three levels:

- **Hierarchical consistency:** This is consistency between corporate, SBU, and functional strategic plans. How the firm plans to compete (a decision made at the corporate level) must be consistent with the actions and the capabilities of the operations management for hierarchical consistency to exist.
- **Cross-functional consistency:** This form of consistency deals with how well the plans and actions of the operations management system are aligned with the plans and actions of the other functional areas. Exhibit 2 illustrates this concept. In this exhibit, the operations management system is surrounded by various functional groups. The outer circle consists of critical activities or decisions. For a given decision, the exhibit identifies functional areas with which the operations management system must interact. Consistency is critical across these functions. For example, decisions affecting product quality require consistency across operations management, marketing, and sales functions. Marketing

EXHIBIT 2
Cross-Functional Consistency Illustrated

Source: C. H. Fine and A. C. Hax, "Manufacturing Strategy: A Methodology and an Illustration," *Interfaces* 15, no. 6 (1985).

and sales personnel understand customers' needs, while operations personnel understand process capabilities related to quality. It is critical that these two sets of information are combined when plans or promises are made that pertain to product quality.

- **Internal consistency:** All planning and actions within a functional area should be mutually supportive and internally aligned. This means that decisions made in all areas of operations management should be in line with each other and with the goals and intent of the overall plans for the operations management system.

Developing and maintaining consistency are not easy. They require awareness by the operations manager not only of what is going on in operations management, but also what is taking place in the other functional areas as well as at the strategic level.

Strategic Planning within the Supply-Chain Context

The preceding discussion has focused attention on strategic planning within the corporation. This discussion overlooks the increasingly important role played by the supply chain. The supply chain involves not only the firm but also its upstream and downstream suppliers, partners, and customers. More and more, firms are relying on these members of the supply chain to provide needed capabilities in order to better respond to a more demanding marketplace.[4] Consequently, strategic planning must now expand to encompass these supply-chain constituents. There should be **vertical consistency** between the firm's decisions and those made in other supply-chain organizations. That is, the strategic goals of the critical suppliers should be in sync with those of the firm. Furthermore, the strategic goals of the firm should be in sync with the needs and demands of its critical customers. For example, if the firm decides to compete on the basis of quality (i.e., it focuses on designing and delivering the finest quality of products), then it only makes sense for that firm to seek out and work with suppliers that also emphasize quality products and to sell to customers who place a premium on seeking out and buying quality products.

What would the implications be for a firm where vertical consistency is lacking? Consider a situation where a supplier who is focused on quality deals with a firm that is emphasizing cost and, in turn, deals with customers that are time-sensitive.

[4] This point is explored in greater detail in the "Supply Chain Structure and Strategy" module by Steven A. Melnyk and Morgan Swink (New York: McGraw-Hill/Irwin 2002).

In Practice

HUFFY AND SEROTTA: TWO VERY DIFFERENT BICYCLE MANUFACTURERS

Huffy

Huffy primarily builds bicycles that are found at the low end of the price range (i.e., in the $100 to $250 price range). Sold primarily through toy and department stores, the typical Huffy bicycle is purchased either for a child or for someone who wants a bike for an occasional ride. These customers want low-cost, durable, no-frills transportation; that is, they want a bicycle that is not too heavy (an order qualifier) and that will not break when roughly handled (what happens when a child gets a bicycle). In sum, Huffy customers want low price and durability.

Huffy's transformation process excels at producing durable bicycles at a low cost. The system doesn't produce a wide variety. To reduce costs, the number of models and the component options are greatly reduced. Each bicycle comes in a limited number of frame sizes. This allows Huffy to use extensive automation. Robots weld bike frames, so labor costs are reduced. Huffy's manufacturing approach results in a large fixed-cost base and relatively low variable costs, an approach that is well suited to large volume production.

Huffy's bikes are designed with an eye to cost reduction. Instead of using high-quality, extremely durable metals such as chromolloy steel, Huffy makes extensive use of lower-grade, softer steel. (Most bicycle riders are not really aware of these differences in steel.) Cables are held in place using plastic fasteners (not the metal guides found on most medium and high-end bicycles). Quick release wheel fasteners are dropped in favor of simpler, more secure, and cheaper nut-and-bolt wheel fasteners.

The product design and manufacturing processes support a low-cost, durable bicycle produced in large quantities. However, these same factors also limit the transformation process at Huffy. Huffy could not use this same process to meet the demands of those buyers who want custom-built, performance bicycles.

Serotta Competition Bicycles

To build a performance bicycle requires a different set of skills (and a correspondingly different transformation process). A performance bicycle such as a Serotta Competition bicycle is lighter and has more demanding specifications. In addition, performance bike customers have stronger preferences and want more choices in terms of options (components), sizes, and colors. These customers look for craftsmanship in the bike's construction. They are not particularly price sensitive. Where Huffy bicycles sell for prices in hundreds of dollars, Serotta bicycles sell for thousands (the starting price for a Serotta Legend TG, the lowest-priced bicycle, is about $1,850).

Serotta employs a transformation process that is quite different from Huffy's. To reduce weight in a bicycle requires the skill of a craftsman—someone who has the time and knowledge to remove excess weight through filing. Performance bicycles also require the use of lighter and stronger materials (e.g., steel, carbon fiber, aluminum, titanium, or metal matrix materials). Serotta offers a large number of different bikes, with its primary specialty being road bicycles (especially those for road racing). Serotta's operations emphasize high performance quality and flexibility in terms of wide product variety. The company uses only premium bicycle components, and it continually tests its bicycles in high-stress situations such as long stage bike races. Unlike Huffy, which is organized around large runs of a fairly standardized bicycle, Serotta is organized around small production batches in which each bicycle often has a different paint scheme and different components. Instead of making extensive use of automation, Serotta has highly skilled craftsmen who use manually operated, general-purpose machines. Each bicycle requires extensive labor-intensive operations such as hand brazing and filing.

Both Huffy and Serotta Competition Bicycles have developed transformation processes well suited to their respective markets. Each system has inherent limitations. Huffy would have a difficult time building a high-performance bicycle; and Serotta Competition Bicycles would have a difficult time building a department store bicycle that could be sold for less than $200.

Components of a Value-Based Strategy

Value, while critical to operations management, is not determined by the operations management function alone. Rather, the process of defining and establishing value is a central part of the strategic planning process at all levels. How a firm defines value drives its conceptualizations of four other elements of strategy: (1) operations capabilities, (2) corporate vision, (3) customers, and (4) the competitive environment. Together, these five interdependent elements form the **value wheel** (see Exhibit 3).

Operations Capabilities

When we talk about **operations capabilities,** we are looking at both the internal (our own) OM system and the external OM system (our suppliers and their capabilities). Operations capability consists of two critical attributes of the transformation process: capacity (the volume of output it can build) and competencies (technological and organizational abilities).

Each transformation process bundles together a limited set of operations capabilities. Simply stated, no system can be all things to all people; no system can excel at all tasks or dimensions of value (i.e., timeliness, cost, and quality). Each system is uniquely suited to

EXHIBIT 3
The Value Wheel and Its Components

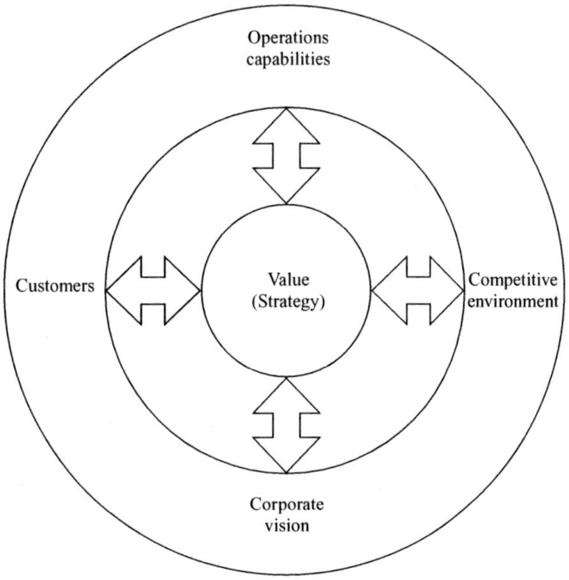

certain types of activities and each excels in satisfying or exceeding the needs of certain types of customers. To better understand this concept, consider the differences between the capabilities offered by Huffy bicycles and Serotta Competition bicycles.

The specific capabilities of a transformation process are the result of numerous decisions affecting technology, manufacturing process structure (e.g., whether we use an assembly line or a job shop), information systems, people (number, training, skills), location of facilities, planning systems, and execution systems.[5] These factors define what the transformation system can and cannot do, and related decisions should be tightly interrelated with the types of value offered by the firm.

Corporate Vision

Every firm, irrespective of its size, market, or orientation (service or manufacturing), has a vision of its culture and values, its businesses, and what it wants to be. This **corporate vision** can be implicit (held internally by the management and the people of the firm) or explicit. Some examples of explicit vision statements are provided in Exhibit 4 on page 12. Each of these statements defines the company's business.

Each of these mission statements states the "who" or the "what the firm will be" part of a corporate strategy. While mission statements often state or imply certain goals, they usually only allude vaguely to the means that the firm will use to reach them. For example, FedEx uses the term "information-rich" and Callaway declares that "technology" will be the means to the desired end state. Cannondale describes the shape of the value chain and the organizational environment within it. Boeing is a tad more specific in terms of what means it would use to gain a competitive advantage, that is, by being "short to market," have "short cycle times," and so on. Boeing recognizes in its mission statement that its competitive advantage rests in its ability to manage a very complex product and a very complex process—that of designing and delivering aircraft and their associated support systems. This means that Boeing must excel at knowing its customers (critical in the design process), at integrating all of the various components and systems into a seamless whole and at reducing and eliminating waste. This last requirement reflects the more competitive market that now exists in the aircraft market.

Corporate vision determines how the firm and its managers will identify opportunities and react to them. This reaction determines the type of value offered. For example, Hewlett-Packard was once presented the opportunity to produce a line of low-cost calculators. Management declined because this opportunity was not consistent with the corporate vision,

[5] These factors are discussed in "The Value-Driven Approach to Operations Management" module by Steven A. Melnyk and Morgan Swink (New York: McGraw-Hill/Irwin 2002).

EXHIBIT 4
Examples of Corporate Vision Statements

FedEx's Vision

To connect the global marketplace via an integrated information-rich distribution network that lets shippers transport time-sensitive, high-value cargo to virtually any destination in the world within 24 to 48 hours.

Callaway Golf Company

Callaway Golf Company, through the use of technology, designs and manufactures premium, innovative golf clubs that are demonstrably superior to, and pleasingly different from, its competition.

Boeing's Vision 2016

Vision 2016 calls for Boeing to be a global enterprise for aerospace leadership by designing, producing, and supporting commercial airplanes, defense systems, and defense and civil space systems by relying on four major elements: (1) people working together; (2) detailed customer knowledge and focus; (3) large-scale system integration; and, (4) a lean enterprise. The result is a system that will design and deliver better products in less time.

Cannondale 's Philosophy

Our passion is to be the best cycling company in the world. We will succeed because:
We care about our customers, suppliers, and each other.
We design and deliver a stream of innovative products.
We continuously improve
We concentrate on detail.
We limit our distribution to the best bicycle retailers in the world.
We govern our every deed by what is just and right.

which was to be a provider of leading-edge technology provided in an easy-to-use form and at a fair price. In contrast, Cannondale has recently begun developing a motorcycle. This activity is consistent with Cannondale's vision of itself as the best cycling company in the world. In short, vision defines the specific dimensions and traits of value that the firm plans to offer its customers. In turn, the firm's vision affects the types of capabilities that will be developed within its supply chain and transformation processes and will influence the type and size of investments made by the firm in its operations management system.

What type of operations management system would you develop if you worked for (1) Callaway Golf, (2) Boeing, or (3) Cannondale?

Customers[6]

At first blush, the concept of a **customer** seems intuitively simple and self-evident. Every business must serve a customer. Customers determine the ultimate acceptability of the firm's value proposition. However, the customer concept is muddied by the fact that a firm actually has many different customers. We describe customers using three critical dimensions:

- Chains of customers.
- Critical customers.
- Nature of demand.

Chains of Customers

A **chain of customers** (see Exhibit 5) often extends from inside the firm through multiple levels of sales and distribution to the ultimate consumers of the product. This is an important concept because it reminds us of the number and variety of the customers that are

[6] The concept of the customer was introduced in "The Value-Driven Approach to Operations Management" module by Steven A. Melnyk and Morgan Swink (New York: McGraw-Hill/Irwin 2002).

EXHIBIT 5 **The Chain of Customers for an Integrated Manufacturing Firm**

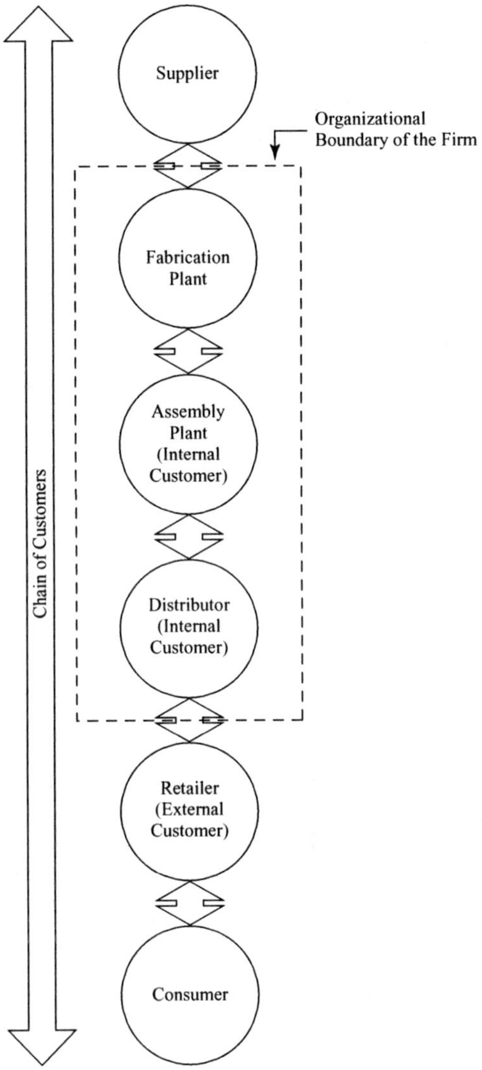

potentially served by any firm. This diversity makes defining value a complex and difficult task. Within a chain of customers there are three major groups: (1) **internal customers,** (2) **external customers,** and (3) **consumers.** In addition, the firm is responsible to its stakeholders.

Stakeholders include any person or group of people with an interest in the function and operation of the operations management system or the firm, and its well-being (financial and otherwise). Typically, the most important stakeholders are

- Financial stakeholders: stockholders, banks, and investment firms.
- *Resource stakeholders:* employees, suppliers, and labor unions.
- *Community stakeholders:* surrounding towns and social and religious groups.
- *Societal stakeholders:* groups such as the Consumers Union (the publishers of *Consumer Reports*).
- *Governmental stakeholders:* government groups at the local, state/provincial, or federal level.

Stakeholders also can be customers. Their presence must be recognized because they can and do affect the specific ways the firm can and will define value.

Critical Customers

The presence of so many different customers complicates the task of defining value. Each customer group has its own set of requirements and expectations. Many times, these demands are in conflict. The child wants a bicycle that is "cool" to ride and easy to pedal; the parent wants a bicycle that is inexpensive, safe to ride, and durable (so that it can be handed down to another sibling); the bicycle mechanic wants a bicycle that is easy to assemble and service; the purchasing agent wants bicycles that are well built (to reduce warranty costs) and delivered on time and at good terms. Management faces the challenge of rationalizing these multiple and often conflicting requirements. The answer is to identify the **critical customers**—those customers who determine the availability of our products in the marketplace, who are opinion leaders, or who are responsible for a bulk of our business. Identifying critical customers gives strategic plans focus.

Different firms target different customers as critical customers. For example, Huffy has targeted the purchasing agent and the store managers as critical customers. It has determined that these two customers determine product availability, and it is product availability that affects the consumers' purchasing decision (i.e., the consumers will make their decision from what is available on the store floor). In contrast, Schwinn, during the 1950s and 1960s, targeted consumers (children and their parents). They sponsored children's shows such as *Captain Kangaroo,* where the children were told repeatedly about the advantages of owning a Schwinn. Schwinn also paid for advertising campaigns targeted at parents. These ads argued that Schwinn bicycles cost a bit more but were far better built. The goal for critical customers is to profitably delight them. The goal for other customers is to avoid upsetting them.

Nature of Demand

Once the firm has identified its customers and market segment, it must begin to understand what value means to them. This isn't always easy. Customers usually have **articulated (or explicit) demands**—needs that they can describe. However, value often depends on **latent demands**—problem or needs that they are unable to describe. Firms are often fairly effective

In Practice

XEROX LEARNS TO TAP LATENT DEMAND . . . AND GROWS

When Xerox management conceived the idea of a photocopier, they first offered it to IBM, which dismissed the concept, seeing no apparent need for it. Xerox had difficulty selling its photocopiers to other firms as well. It managed to gain a foothold in the business market only by placing the photocopiers free of charge and collecting fees solely on the number of copies made at 5 cents each. Managers accepted this option since it wouldn't really cost them anything, they reasoned, because no one would use a Xerox machine when carbon paper seemed just as easy.

Xerox succeeded because its process and product met the needs of some real customers, secretaries. After secretaries learned how to operate the new photocopiers, they used them extensively. Compared with carbon copies, they found the Xerox process to be easier, less prone to error, quicker, and cleaner. Correcting an error on a carbon copy was a dirty, time-consuming, and frustrating experience. In contrast, they could correct errors on photocopies simply by running the corrected sheet through the machine again. Xerox turned an idea that IBM didn't want into a success because it identified and satisfied a latent desire.

in reacting to articulated demands. However, in order to meet latent demands, the firm must commit to knowing its customers so well that it can determine what the customers want almost before they know themselves. Firms such as Nucor Steel, Landmark Graphics, and Schneider Nation Trucking are experts at anticipating and meeting latent desires. History is also filled with examples of products such as Xerox's photocopier and the Sony Walkman that initially satisfied latent desires. This point is clearly illustrated in the "In Practice" vignette above.

Competitive Environment

The **competitive environment** consists of at least three major components. The first is the competition. Competitors are important because their actions can change the nature of value. For example, in the automotive industry, the traditional new car warranty was 12 months/12,000 miles. However, in the mid 1980s, when a 36-month/36,000-mile warranty was offered by one competitor, it quickly became the standard for every car company. Today, even more extensive warranties are offered. When developing a value statement, we must be aware of the potential disruptive efforts exercised by our competitors.

The second element involves changes in technology. Technology affects what we can do, the costs and lead time we incur, and the type of markets we can serve. Technology changes also affect investments in capabilities. These changes can take the form of hard technology changes, where the change focuses on how products are built (the hardware side). For example, in the 1980s investments in computerized word processors made the typewriter obsolete. These changes also can take the form of soft technology changes, where the changes involve the methods, organizations, and communications networks. The current Internet explosion is an example of this latter type of change.

The experiences of Chelsea Milling Company, the maker of Jiffy Corn Muffin Mix, provide a good example of a type of soft technology change that forced a hard technology change. For decades, Chelsea competed against the giants, such as General Mills and Pillsbury, mostly on the basis of cost. Then the distribution system changed. A significant proportion of Jiffy's customers started to buy from outlets that sold multipacks of products, that is, warehouse-like outlets such as Costco, Price Club, and Sam's Club. As the low-cost producer, Chelsea lacked the packaging capability to make multiple packs of its mix products. This environmental shift required Chelsea to make substantial investments in packaging technology.

The third and final element consists of macro-environmental issues. These issues involve changes in customer tastes and in economic conditions. Changes in fashion can rapidly alter the demands for numerous products. Similarly, economic conditions have major effects on consumer spending, especially for expensive discretionary purchases and durable goods.

Each of the elements of a value-based strategy must be addressed in order for that strategy to be complete. In addition, strategy makers should comprehend the intertwined relationships among the various elements and the core dimensions of value that the firm seeks to deliver.

The Strategic Planning Process

The challenge facing management is achieving consistency and competitive advantage through the elements of the value wheel. The **strategic planning process** is designed to meet this challenge. The output of this process is the definition of value developed by the firm, implemented in its OM system (and its supply chain), and offered to the critical customers.

While there are many approaches to strategic planning, we briefly illustrate the basic approach first developed and presented by Mintzberg.[7] This basic approach is sufficiently market driven to be consistent with the value-driven approach. Mintzberg's "basic plan format" consists of the following steps:

1. Mission statement
   a. Business definition: What business are we in?
   b. Long-term objectives: What would we want it to be by 20?
2. Scan the external environment
   a. Industry environment analysis: Who are we up against?
   b. Macro-environment analysis (social, technical, economic, political)
   c. Assessment of opportunities and threats
3. Scan the internal environment
   a. Value-chain analysis
   b. Financial analysis
   c. Assessment of internal strengths and weaknesses
4. Formulate corporate or business unit strategic plan
5. Implement programs

In the first step, we are interested in defining the firm's vision. In the second, we focus on the customer and the environment. The third deals with an assessment of the firm's capabilities. In the fourth step we generate a strategic plan that is built around the form of value we will offer our customers.

Once a corporation or business unit has formulated a strategic plan, it then must implement it. The corporate strategy must be transformed into meaningful goals and initiatives for the functional areas. In the OM case, the operations strategy should guide those within the function regarding how best to support the corporation's efforts to realize its long-term goals.

For some companies, performing this transformation task has proved difficult. A major part of the problem is that people in marketing and elsewhere in top management seemingly speak a different language than the top people in operations. Worse yet, people in operations all too often take pride in being able to accomplish "the impossible," but often at the expense of efficiency and, worse yet, effectiveness. A means of communication and discussion is needed.

In the 1970s, Terry Hill designed a rather straightforward approach.[8] The key is to analyze why customers purchase from your firm and why they purchase from your competitors. The order winning, order qualifying, and order losing traits serve as the basis for communication between functional groups within the firm. Exhibit 6 on the next page serves as a guide for determining the operations strategy for a business. While its terms are largely manufacturing oriented, the concept is robust enough also to work well in service system strategies.

In the leftmost column, the objectives defined by the corporate or business unit strategy are stated. Marketing then translates those goals into policies that define its functional

[7] H. Mintzberg J. B. Quinn, *Readings in the Strategy Process,* (Upper Saddle River, NJ: Prentice-Hall, 1998).
[8] Hill, *Manufacturing Strategy.*

EXHIBIT 6 Framework of Integrating Manufacturing and Marketing Strategies

Corporate Objectives	Marketing Strategy	Order Winners	Manufacturing Strategy: Process Choice	Manufacturing Strategy: Infrastructure
Growth	Product market	Price	Process choices	Functional support
Survival	and segments	Quality	Capacity	Production planning and contro
Profit	Range	Delivery speed	Facilitiesl	
ROI, ROA	Mix	Delivery reliability	Technology	Quality control
Other	Volume	Color range	Supply chain	Workforce
	Standard vs. customized	Product range		Organization
	Level of innovation	Design leadership		
	Leader vs. follower	Technical support		

strategy. The central column is critical. Marketing and operations personnel must agree upon the basic aspects of value that cause customers to buy products. The basic logic of this approach is that once operations knows what it needs to do, it can go about reconfiguring its value chain processes accordingly. If it is product variety that is needed, then a flexible process choice will be needed.

The advantage of this approach is that it forces marketing and operations to discuss the trade-offs inherent in strategic choices. For example, high degrees of product customization normally can be accomplished only at a cost. Narrowly defined standard products may not appeal to a large enough market segment. A dialogue is needed to balance functional requirements and to focus on the needs of customers.

Value-Based Strategic Initiatives

Now that we understand the basic process of strategic planning, we can look at how value is operationalized as a strategic initiative. We will do this by examining three major **value-based strategic initiatives** that have emerged and produced major impacts on operations management systems in recent times: total quality management, time-based competition, and mass customization. While broad-based initiatives such as these are not strategies per se, they are often useful for driving the firm and its operations management system in directions consistent with specific business and functional strategies.

Total Quality Management

Since the mid 1980s, the concept of quality has been recast into a broad-based corporate strategic initiative now referred to as **total quality management** (TQM). In a TQM approach, quality becomes part of the corporate fabric. It becomes an integral element of how the firm competes in the marketplace, how it generates value, and how it wins customers. As Logothesis defines it:

> Total quality management is a culture; inherent in this culture is a total commitment to quality and attitude expressed by everybody's involvement in the process of continuous improvement of products and services, through the use of innovative scientific methods.[9]

As a strategic initiative, TQM is an approach that is built on the following premises:

- It is no longer assumed that higher quality is attainable only at higher cost. When quality is improved by reducing waste, lower cost is the consequence.

[9] N. Logothetis, *Managing for Total Quality: From Deming to Taguchi and SPC* (Hertfordshire, UK: Prentice Hall International, 1992), p. 5.

- Unlike quality-control programs, quality assurance and quality improvement are not tasks for professional specialists only; they concern everyone in an organization. Management must initiate quality management, but everyone must be involved, not only on special team improvement projects but also in everyday work.
- Good managers must understand the processes of an organization; the idea that management skills are readily transferable to any kind of organization is misleading.
- Management must influence or control upstream causes in processes to influence quality, cost, or profits, which are the residuals or results of the processes.
- Tools and techniques of quality improvement are useful only if the organizational culture is sound, specifically if there is a focus on pleasing customers (especially critical customers).
- To effectively manage processes, it is necessary to understand statistical variation and to isolate the root causes of variation.[10]

One can see from this set of operating premises that quality management initiatives are aimed at improving multiple aspects of product quality (product performance, conformance, reliability) and also process quality (capability, repeatability, efficiency). Further, there is a concerted effort by the organization to drive product design and delivery processes directly by the voice of the customer, so that customer needs (in terms of product function and features) are more consistently and more completely satisfied.

Total quality management initiatives were arguably the most prevalent defining movement of the 1980s and 1990s. Some firms have reported a 10 to 1 return on their investments in TQM. These returns come from many sources: increased sales to existing customers, sales to new customers, reduced processing costs (due to less rework and lower scrap rates), fewer customer complaints (resulting in an improved corporate reputation), greater customer goodwill, lower field service costs (due to fewer breakdowns in the field and less need to repair these defective problems), and improved employee morale (everyone wants to work with a winner). Benefits such as these create compelling reasons to invest in this strategic initiative.[11]

Time-Based Competition—Competing on Time

Time has value to most customers. As mentioned earlier, customers are often willing to pay premium prices for products that are designed and delivered quickly (assuming, of course, that those products work well and satisfy real customer needs). Targeting time as a major source of value is referred to as **time-based competition (TBC).** Implementation of TBC initiatives is bringing great success to companies in the United States. To understand the importance of time as a competitive weapon, return to our discussion of Apple computers at the beginning of this module. Most of Apple's products have life cycles of less than nine months, and over 50 percent of the profit is made during the first 40 days of product life. If a company such as Apple is to succeed in the marketplace, it must bring products to market quickly while ensuring that these products are designed right and that they are built right. There is little time to go back and correct problems.

The prevalence of TBC is evident all around us. Intel has now begun to introduce electronic processing chips faster and faster (less than 18 months) at lower and lower prices—a strategy that has put some of its competitors out of business and put others on the defensive. Companies such as Honda and Toyota have reduced the time to market for new products (i.e., the time needed to go from concept to full-scale production) from over five years to less than two years now. Firms also have worked hard to reduce order-to-delivery lead times. Exhibit 7 presents some examples. For all of these firms, time has become a competitive weapon and TBC their major strategic initiative.

[10] H. V. Roberts and B. F. Sergesketter, *Quality Is Personal: A Foundation for Total Quality Management* (New York: Free Press, 1993).

[11] Total quality management is explored in greater detail in two modules focused on this topic.

EXHIBIT 7 American Firms' Experience with Time-Based Competition

Business	Delivery Time Advantage	Growth Difference	Performance Difference
Wal-Mart discount stores	80%	36% vs. 12%	19% vs. 9% profit
Century Door industrial doors	66%	15% vs. 5%	10% vs. 0.2% return on stock
Wilsonart decorative laminates	75%	9% vs. 3%	40% vs. 10% return on net assets
Thomasville Furniture	70%	12% vs. 3%	21% vs. 11% return on assets

TBC manages lead times in three major ways. First, it addresses only those lead times that the customer values most. Second, reductions in lead times must reduce both mean and variance measures. Third, lead time reductions must be achieved through system analysis and changes in underlying processes rather than product-driven changes, that is, TBC cannot rely solely on excess resources (inventory, capacity, or skilled workers) to reduce lead times. Rather, TBC must implement a broad-based strategy to reduce lead times by changing the firm's processes and structures for designing, manufacturing, and delivering products for its customers. Firms employing TBC are discovered the truth of Tom Peters' observation that "Speed is Life."

Mass Customization—Competing through Flexibility

Consider the following description of **mass customization:**

> Manufacturing used to be pretty simple. The factory manager rarely had to think about suppliers or customers. All he did was to make sure that his machinery was producing widgets at the maximum hourly rate. Once he had worked out how to stick to that "standard rate" of production, he could sit back and relax. Customer needs? Delivery times? Efficient purchasing? That was what the purchasing department and the sales department were there for. Piles of inventory lying around, both raw materials and finished goods—not his problem.
>
> Now it is. The 1980s were the decade of lean production and right-first-time quality management. Now the game has grown even tougher. Customers are more and more demanding. They increasingly want the basic product to be enhanced by some individual variations, or some special service. Companies sweat to keep up with their demands, in terms both of the actual products and of the way they are delivered. A world-wide survey of over 900 manufacturing companies by Deloitte Consulting has found that, though the companies' products seemed better than ever before, customer dissatisfaction has kept on growing.
>
> The solution lies in "mass customization." This means making basically similar products in hundreds, even thousands of variations to suit specific customers' needs. Some customers want deliveries in small lots at short order. Other will take bigger deliveries less frequently. Either way, of course, they want it at mass-production low prices.[12]

As the preceding quote shows, operations managers are seeking to cope with increasingly demanding customers through strategies that emphasize flexibility. Mass customization offers customers variety and customized products through flexibility and quick response times.[13] This approach generates value for customers by creating enough variety and opportunities for customization that nearly everyone finds almost exactly what he or she wants. Instead of forcing customers to compromise and buy products that come close enough to what they want, mass customization focuses on creating transformation and design processes that respond to the needs of the buyer. This requires an operations management system that is more productive with fewer resources than any previous type of operations

[12] "No Factory Is an Island: Meet the Global Factory," *The Economist,* June 20, 1998 (supplement), p. 8.
[13] B. Joseph Pine II, *Mass Customization: The New Frontier in Business Competition* (Cambridge, MA: Harvard Business School, 1993), p. 44.

EXHIBIT 8 **The Evolution of Operations Management**

Factory Focus	Mass Production	Flexible Production	Mass Customization
Period of history	1900–1970	1971–2000	2001–2020
Typical number of Machine Tools	150	30–50	25–30
Products made	10–15	100–1,000	Unlimited
Products reworked due to poor quality	25% or more	0.02% or less	Under 0.0005%

Source: Otis Porter, "Custom-Made, Direct from the Plant," *Business Week*, no. 3399 (November 18, 1994), p. 158.

management system (Exhibit 8). Mass customization is niche marketing taken to its ultimate extreme.

A number of manufacturing companies have adapted this relatively new approach, including AT&T, Coke, Pepsi, General Mills, McDonald's, U.S. Robotics, and Caterpillar. Mass customization also is being applied in other business contexts. Consider CitiCorp with its 15-minute mortgage program, or Procter & Gamble, who produces babies' diapers in 13 different designs, each targeted to a specific age group, sex, and weight class. One of the most successful mass customizers has been Ross Operating Valve, headquartered in Troy, Michigan:

> "I cannot train people quick enough to take care of all the potential new business," says David L. Ross, marketing director at Ross Operating Valve Company, a private 350-employee maker of pneumatic valves. At the Ross/Flex plant in Lavonia, GA, customers phone to discuss what valves they need with company engineers called integrators. The specs are entered into a CAD/CAM system to design a one-of-a-kind valve, and automated machine tools grind out the metal parts overnight. Finished valves are delivered in as little as 72 hours, at a typical cost of $3,000. That's about one-hundredth the time and one-tenth the cost of traditional methods.[14]

The effects of mass customization extend beyond the operations management system to research and development, marketing, and finance and accounting (Exhibit 9 on the next page). Success in implementing mass customization requires a change in focus from economies of scale, in which a firm builds more of a single item to reduce per-unit costs, to economies of scope, in which it tries to produce variety at almost the same cost and within almost the same time limits as building identical items. Mass customization also relies on new relationships with suppliers. Rather than simple providers of goods and services, suppliers must become sources of expertise and resources. Instead of working alone to meet the challenge of flexibility, the operations manager must work with suppliers in on-going relationships that join their expertise and resources with those of the firm.

It is easy to see that each of the initiatives described above focuses on particular aspects of value. Quality management initiatives tend to focus on improving products' consistency or performance and their relationships to customers' needs. Time-based initiatives focus on improving speed or reliability of new product introduction or order fulfillment, with an eye toward the value that customers place on improved timeliness. Mass customization initiatives are aimed at improving product variety and customization while maintaining or reducing product cost, again with ever-finer distinctions of customers' needs in mind. It is important to remember that key determinants of the success of these types of initiatives are (1) top management and employee commitment to the proposition, (2) an understanding of the ways that customers will value the improvements, and (3) structuring of product design and operations management systems to be in synch with targeted changes in performance.

[14] Otis Porter, "Custom-Made, Direct from the Plant," *Business Week*, no. 3399 (November 18, 1994),p. 158.

EXHIBIT 9 Corporate Implications of Mass Customization

	Operations Management	Research and Development	Marketing	Finance and Accounting
Focus	Total process efficiency	Continual incremental innovations	Gaining market share by fulfilling customer wants and needs—first domestically and then in export markets	Manager- and worker-useful information
Positive effects	Low overhead and bureaucracy Optimum quality Elimination of waste Continual process improvement Low inventory carrying costs High labor productivity Integration of thinking and doing High utilization of and investment in worker skills Low total costs High production flexibility Greater variety at lower costs	Continual improvements, eventual technological superiority Integration of innovation and production Frequent process innovations Low costs and short cycle times Mutually beneficial relationships with other firms Better fulfillment of customer wants and needs	Filling the niches Ability to respond quickly to changing customer needs Market takeover High sales domestically and through exports Technology-intensive products	Sound long-and short-term decisions Long-term supplier interdependence Low costs, high profits Long-term investment in capital, people, and technology Attention to core competencies
Negative effects	Demanding, stressful environment	Lack of breakthrough innovations	Too enamored of technology	Stockholders ignored

Source: B. Joseph Pine II, *Mass Customization: The New Frontier in Business Competition* (Cambridge, MA: Harvard Business School, 1993), pp. 111–22.

Module Summary

This module has introduced the details of value-based operations strategy making—a process that converts the theory of value into actions that are feasible, effective, and efficient. In discussing this process, we have made the following points:

1. Strategy and strategic planning are critical to the value-driven operations management system. Strategy defines the specific type of value that the firm will deliver to its customers. Strategic planning is a process that takes place at three levels: corporate strategic planning, planning at the SBU level, and functional planning. These three levels are integrated, with planning taking place from the top down, while execution takes place from the bottom up.

2. At the heart of the strategic planning process is the value wheel. Strategy is used to bring together five critical elements: value, operations capabilities, corporate vision, customers, and the competitive environment.

3. Strategic planning is a process that is strongly hierarchical in nature. For business strategy to be effective, it must be linked to operations management strategies.

4. Strategic initiatives often provide effective means for operationalizing value-based strategies. Three important value-based strategic initiatives in recent years include total quality management (TQM), time-based competition (TBC), and mass customization. Each of these initiatives emphasizes specific elements of value, including quality (TQM), timeliness (TBC), and flexibility (mass customization).

Key Terms

articulated/explicit demand, *13*
chain of customers, *12*
competitive environment, *14*
consistency in strategic planning, *8*
consumers, *12*
corporate strategic planning, *6*
corporate vision, *11*
critical customers, *13*
cross-functional consistency, *8*
customer, *12*
external customers, *13*
functional plan, *7*
hierarchical consistency, *8*
internal consistency, *9*
internal customers, *13*
latent demand, *13*
mass customization, *18*
operations capabilities, *10*
stakeholders, *13*
strategic business unit, *7*
strategic planning process, *15*
time-based competition (TBC), *17*
total quality management (TQM), *16*
value-based strategic initiatives, *16*
value wheel, *10*
vertical consistency, *9*

Discussion Questions

1. Apply the corporate/SBU/functional planning hierarchy introduced in this module to your university/college or business. What would be the equivalent to corporate planning? SBU planning? Functional planning?
2. Using the hierarchy of strategic planning, compare the three levels of planning in terms of their planning horizon (how far out into the future they would plan), level of detail, and extent of constraints. Which level of planning would consider the longest time horizon? Which would be the most constrained? Which would have the least amount of detail? Most amount of detail?
3. Using your school or functional area as the unit of analysis, discuss and apply the concepts of
   a. Internal consistency.
   b. Cross-functional consistency.
   c. Hierarchical consistency.
   d. Vertical consistency.
4. How would you define *capabilities* within a school of business?
5. Given that McDonald's excels at the delivery of standard products, discuss the problems created by trying to introduce a concept such as a do-it-yourself salad bar?
6. Using your business school and university/college as the basis of study, identify and discuss examples of
   a. Resource stakeholders.
   b. Community stakeholders.
   c. Societal stakeholders.
   d. Governmental stakeholders.

   How can each of these stakeholders affect the way that the university and the business school carry out their various activities.
7. When can a consumer be a critical consumer? When is the consumer not a critical consumer?
8. What is total quality management? Differentiate it from initiatives such as time-based competition and mass customization?
9. Is a company that decides to compete through TQM prevented from subsequently competing through either time-based competition or mass customization?
10. What product characteristics and market conditions favor a mass customization strategy?
11. What are the implications for both the firm and the operations management system of gaps between either of the following:
    a. The customers and value.
    b. Capabilities and value.
    c. Vision and value.
    d. The environment and value.

Cases

STEINWAY & SONS PIANO

Steinway pianos have long been the premier brand among serious pianists. Franz Liszt called his Steinway "a glorious masterpiece." Gioacchino Rossini, a 19th-century composer, described the Steinway sound as "great as thunder, sweet as the fluting of a nightingale." In short, Steinway's product is the piano of choice for the vast majority of concert artists.

From its beginning, Steinways were a work of art. Jose Feghali, a classical pianist, illustrated this point when he remarked, "With the best pianos, you can walk into a room with 10 pianos and it's like playing 10 different instruments." The prices of the 5,000 or so pianos that Steinway produces each year range from $10,000 for an upright to $62,000 for a special-order concert grand piano.

In the 1990s, Steinway & Sons encountered some problems. John and Robert Birmingham purchased the firm in a $53.5 million leverage buyout deal. John's previous experience involved making plastic windows for envelopes. Robert's most recent experience was with a mail-order business selling products with bear themes. Robert Birmingham said they were delighted with the purchase because they viewed Steinway as a "great opportunity" given that the firm had "a great name and a great tradition."

Steinway's craft-driven organization had not fared too well under its previous owner, CBS. The turmoil resulting from frequent management changes had reduced the consistency of Steinway's cherished reputation. Dealers complained that Steinways weren't of the same quality any more—they were often badly tuned and had sloppy finishes. Finally, in 1978, CBS hired a long-time piano industry executive who helped restore much of Steinway's reputation.

Now, a new set of outsiders owned them. That the owners liked classical music did not assure Steinway's 1,000 employees that they knew how to make classic quality pianos. To make matters worse, the Birmingham brothers were now talking about using their "extensive manufacturing experience" to streamline operations. One commented that the operation was "too reliant on a few craftsmen."

Soon modern manufacturing methods crept into the Steinway operation. A computer control system was introduced to keep track of parts and inventory. Eight million dollars was invested in new equipment to make the quality of small parts, such as piano hammers, more consistent. The loose-leaf binders that specified how pianos were to be built were replaced with engineering drawings. By the late 1980s, Steinway had entered the 20th century. John Birmingham lamented: "The music industry is made up largely of people enamored of music and the instruments they make, but they don't necessarily have great management skills."

As Steinway became more scientific, some stakeholders began to be concerned. Many of the older craftsmen found the new work environment not to their liking and left. Equally important, some within the industry began to be concerned that Steinway pianos were losing their personality. Some dealers and their customers even began to question the quality of Steinway's latest pianos. One classical pianist fumed that he had to use a 30-year-old Steinway because he could not find a new one he liked. Another dealer hired a consultant to review the quality of the pianos he had purchased from Steinway. He claimed that the soundboard, a key contributor to a piano's quality, had developed cracks. The consultant reported that this problem "indicated inadequate or improper controls over wood moisture content during various stages of manufacture." Subsequent study indicated that Steinway's new production quotas may have caused workers to pull wood from the conditioning rooms before it was ready to be bent, say, into a piano.

QUESTIONS

Assume that you are hired as a consultant to help Steinway deal with these latest problems. How could you use a value-driven approach to help this firm address these problems? What would you recommend?

TRAIL FRAMES CHASSIS—THE GULFSTREAM PROPOSAL

Trail Frames Chassis (TFC) of Elkhart, Indiana, is a major manufacturer of chassis for the motor home and van markets. Since it was founded in 1976 by two unemployed truck manufacturing engineers, TFC has grown into one of the major suppliers in this market. Success in the motor home and van markets is difficult because of the constant rate of change taking place. Motor homes and vans are increasingly being bought by people in their late 40s to 60s. What these people want is a motor home that rides like a car. They are willing to pay for innovations such as ABS (anti-lock breaking systems), assisted steering, and computer-balanced suspension.

TFC produces a pusher type of chassis. This is one powered by a diesel engine that is located in the rear. While expensive to build, this design offers the customer a large number of advantages (no tunnel for the transmission, reduced engine noise, better handling). However, these chassis are used in motor homes that are very expensive ($150,000 and up). TFC builds its chassis for the large manufacturers—companies such as Winnebago, Airstream, and Gulf Air. In general, these companies place orders for small quantities (5 to 10 in a batch). Many of the units in a batch are customized to a specific customer's requirements.

TFC has become successful because of its ability to develop new lines of designs in a timely fashion. These designs build on TFC's extensive experience with motor home users. They also build on TFC's knowledge of new technological advances and its ability to incorporate these advances into its designs. As a result, TFC has become the technological leader in this market. It is generally recognized that no one in the industry can match TFC's design and marketing knowledge base.

TFC is proud of its ability to design and build highly customized chassis. As John Stickley, its young and aggressive chief operating officer, is proud of pointing out, "Trail Frames has never met a customized chassis it didn't like." Complementing this focus on customization and speed, TFC has developed a culture of doing anything necessary to meet the needs of the customer. Changes often are introduced "on the fly" with an engineer taking a change down to the assembly line. In many cases, the bills of materials (the recipes for what goes into a given chassis) that were generated initially in engineering do not agree with the components and parts actually put into the chassis.

This approach has served TFC well for a number of years. However, recently sales for TFC have begun to level off. After visiting numerous customers in the field, John Stickley identified what he thought was the reason for this leveling off: the market for high-end, customized motor home chassis had been effectively saturated. There were only just so many customized motor homes that people wanted. Several of the major customers for TFC had strongly hinted that there was another market that TFC could enter that would be consistent with its design strengths and its reputation.

THE PROPOSAL

Many of TFC's customers had noticed that there was a significant gap between the high-end motor homes that TFC served and the low-end market. The high end consisted primarily of pushers and began at $150,000. On the other hand, the low end consisted of "puller"—a chassis with the engine in front. That is, a motor home manufacturer would take an existing truck body (which consisted of the front end and the cab) and mount on it a motor home body. These products sold for between $35,000 and $70,000. Clearly, there was a significant gap between the two markets. One of TFC's major customers, Gulfstream, approached TFC with an interesting proposal. It wanted TFC to design and build a low-end pusher chassis for this market. This chassis would go into a motor home that would cost between $75,000 and $90,000. In contrast to the current line of products, this chassis would not be customized. Rather, once the chassis was designed, it would not be changed. Production runs would go up from batches of five to batch runs of 100. Critical to success in this market would be cost and conformance to the schedule. If TFC could be the first to produce such a chassis, it would own the market. The financials were very attractive. Theoretically, it seemed easy for TFC to enter this market. All that had to be done was to select an existing chassis and take out the "costs" by using less expensive components. While TFC had never built such a chassis, there was no reason why it should not work. The only danger that the people at TFC could identify was that once it entered this market, it would be potentially competing with such firms as Ford, GM, and Toyota (major suppliers of the existing chassis). However, these firms supplied pullers—not pushers, like the proposed TFC product. In spite of these issues, John was not sure as to whether this was the "right" market for TFC.

QUESTIONS

1. Compare the order winner, order qualifiers, and order losers for the customized chassis and for the proposed TFC chassis. To what extent are these factors similar?

2. What type of strategic consistency would you expect to find in TFC for its existing customized chassis? Would this be the same type of consistency that you would find with the proposed chassis?

3. Evaluate the proposal for this new line of chassis using the value wheel concept introduced in this chapter. Is this a business that TFC should enter? If yes, why? If no, why not?

4. What would you recommend to John Stickley that TFC should do to increase its sales and to stimulate demand?
5. Which of the various value-based corporate initiatives discussed in this module make most sense to TFC? Why?

Internet Activity

Using Internet-based information, study the corporate vision statements of companies such as

a. Apple
b. HP
c. Procter & Gamble
d. Cannondale
e. Schwinn

What are the major similarities and differences that you can see between these vision statements?

Related Modules of Interest

- Foundations of Value
- Foundations of Process Management
- Supply Chain Structure and Strategy

Selected Readings

Blackburn, Joseph D. *Time-Based Competition: The Next Battleground in American Manufacturing.* New York: McGraw-Hill/Irwin, 1991.

Bower, Joseph L., and Thomas Hout. "Fast-Cycle Capability for Competitive Power." *Harvard Business Review,* November–December 1988.

Clark, Kim B., and Takahiro Fujimoto. *Product Development Performance*. Cambridge, MA: Harvard Business School Press, 1991.

Fine, C. H., and A. C. Hax. "Manufacturing Strategy: A Methodology and an Illustration." *Interfaces* 15, no. 6 (1985).

Garvin, David A. *Managing Quality*. New York: Free Press, 1988.

Hall, Robert. *The Soul of the Enterprise*. New York: Harper Business, 1993.

Pine, B. Joseph, II. *Mass Customization: The New Frontier in Business Competition.* Cambridge, MA: Harvard Business School Press, 1993.

Roberts, H. V., and B. F. Sergesketter. *Quality Is Personal: A Foundation for Total Quality Management.* New York: Free Press, 1993.

Foundations of Process Management

Steven A. Melnyk
Michigan State University

Morgan Swink
Michigan State University

McGraw-Hill Irwin

Boston Burr Ridge, IL Dubuque, IA Madison, WI New York San Francisco St. Louis
Bangkok Bogotá Caracas Kuala Lumpur Lisbon London Madrid Mexico City
Milan Montreal New Delhi Santiago Seoul Singapore Sydney Taipei Toronto

Foundations of Process Management

Module Objectives

By the end of this module, you should be able to

- Understand the concept of process thinking and its importance to the value-driven OM system.
- Define processes, understanding the various components of processes and types of inputs and outputs.
- Understand the impacts of bottlenecks, variance, and other drivers of process performance.
- Identify useful metrics for any process.
- Understand process improvement methodologies such as business process reengineering and kaizen events.

Putting the Sizzle Back in McDonald's

During the binge years of the mid-1990s, a new McDonald's store opened somewhere in America every few hours. The growth not only cannibalized sales at existing outlets, but it also diverted attention from a fact that was becoming very evident to the customer—the food that was now prepared and served within these stores was no longer that good. Overworked employees churned out sandwiches in large batches and let them set for 10 minutes or longer under heat lamps. Restaurants stopped toasting the buns and began nuking[1] the burgers—lettuce, tomato, and all—in commercial microwaves. At times, someone ordered a Big Mac and got a big mess instead.

This created a mess not only for the customer but also for McDonald's. After all, McDonald's is engaged in an intense food fight. Its restaurants face cutthroat competition in the domestic quick-service restaurant market against the likes of Burger King, Wendy's, and Hardee's. In an attempt to lure picky bargain-minded customers, the chains have waged destructive price wars. McDonald's attempts to attract customers by introducing new products (e.g., McDLT, the McLean, and the Arch Deluxe) have mostly failed. Recently, the managers at McDonald's recognized that the real problem was the cooking process. For the food to taste better, something had to be done.

That "something" was a five-year effort to radically renovate McDonald's kitchens. The program, marketed as "Made for You," promises to deliver hot, fresh, custom-made sandwiches. McDonald's is counting on this new system to spice up its stale menu and to avoid future stumbles. New video screens in the cooking areas display detailed orders, allowing workers to begin assembling sandwiches even before customers finish paying for their meals. No more than two sandwiches are made at once. And the buns are getting toasted again, thanks to what McDonald's calls a "revolutionary" new machine that browns bread in less than 15 seconds. McDonald's says the new system allows orders to be placed, processed, and delivered in 90 seconds or less. The greatest benefit of Made for You is its flexibility. By doing away with mass-produced hamburgers, the system allows for virtually any kind of made-to-order sandwiches. As a result, McDonald's has as many as 40 new menu items in development.

The $180 million rollout of Made for You, now in place in all 13,755 of McDonald's U.S. and Canadian units, has prompted one of the chain's biggest new product launches in recent memory. There's the Big Xtra! Sandwich, two new chicken choices, Fruit'N Yogurt Parfaits, and McSalad Shakers. In the West, the chain is testing a concept called McChoice, which lets customers slap sauces like honey mustard and garden ranch on their burgers. "We want to bring back food as the co-star of our marketing and restaurant experience," says Alan Feldman, McDonald's U.S. chief. By introducing a new process, perhaps their dream will come true.

[1] Nuking is another term for microwaving.

Source: Phat X. Chiem, "Putting the Sizzle Back in McDonald's," *Chicago Tribune*, April 16, 2000, p. Business 1, Business 2.

Recent times have not been kind to McDonald's. Ultimately, the management at McDonald's realized that the reason that the customers weren't coming in was because of the food. Simply put, the food was "bad." Why? The process. The old process encouraged the servers to "build" sandwiches in large batches (where they ultimately sat, waited, and became soggy). Since McDonald's was among the first to offer fast, low-cost food, this early process design was well suited as a means to differentiate their products. (They were fast and cheap.) In terms of value, customers were willing to trade off quality (taste) for timeliness and low cost. However, as competitors grew and eventually matched McDonald's speed and cost, McDonald's lost their advantage, and customers began seeking more.

Faced by flattening sales and falling market share, McDonald's had to do something. It did. It introduced new sandwiches; they failed. It cut prices; the competition matched the cuts (and no one won). It seemed that the only time McDonald's was able to rev up sales was during Beanie Baby promotions. The demand for these products was so high in some stores that customers would buy the Happy Meals© to get the Beanie Babies—and then throw away the meals. Why not simply sell toys and forget about selling food, asked one wag. Finally, the managers at McDonald's realized that they had to improve the taste of the food. For many customers, taste is a matter of customized ingredients. McDonald's original process approach discouraged customization. Anyone who has ever asked for a Big Mac without the sauce or without the pickle can tell you that in the past the operation slowed to a crawl when dealing with such requests. By implementing the Made for You process, McDonald's has recognized that in order to change the quality of its food, it must change the process. McDonald's has re-discovered **process thinking**—an approach to a system's improvement that focuses attention not only on the system's outputs (the sandwiches) but on the processes responsible for these outputs.

Processes and Value

Process thinking is not new; neither is it unique to McDonald's. However, a revitalized emphasis on process thinking is taking hold today in many manufacturing firms, and service-oriented firms as well. Processes play the fundamental role in determining the specific types of value that a firm and its OM system can offer. Every process has structural and resource constraints that limit the range of outputs it can produce. Thus, in order to change the type of value offered, the process must be changed. The primary task of the modern value-driven operations manager is that of managing processes. In this module, we introduce the reader to this important concept at two levels. In the first part of the module, we examine the conceptual foundations of process thinking. In the second, we look at the tools useful for applying process thinking to OM.

A **process** is a system of activities that uses resources to transform inputs into valuable outputs. Each process has a structure that defines, orders, and links the activities included in the operation. It also usually has procedures, monitoring and control structures, and feedback mechanisms. **Process thinking** is a structured approach that views a firm and its various activities and functions in terms of the underlying processes. With this approach, managers design, document, manage, and change business processes with the goal of ensuring that these processes make the "desired" results inevitable. Process thinking causes managers to address critical process elements including activities, inputs, outputs, flows, structure, resources, and metrics. This module will cover these elements, beginning with a high-level description of business processes. Certain important premises form the foundation for process thinking:

- Every firm can be defined by its various processes. These processes determine the type of product (goods or services) that the firm can provide its customers.
- Processes determine the traits and the specific type of value delivered by the firm. When viewed in this light, products can be seen as "residuals"—outputs of the process.
- To change the traits of the products, we must identify the appropriate processes and act on them.
- Capacity and processes are linked. Processes are subject to resource constraints and operating inefficiencies that serve to limit capacity.

It is important to note that the notion of "process" is much more general than the notion of "manufacturing processes." Manufacturing processes are specific types of organizational structures used to order and link production activities. When we talk about manufacturing processes, we usually talk about specific characteristics of organizational structures such as job shops, flow, manufacturing cells, or repetitive manufacturing systems. Process thinking is far broader and can be applied to any set of operations that involve transformation.

Processes in the Firm

The first premise of process thinking is that the entire firm can be viewed as nothing more than processes. To understand this notion, consider some of the major types of processes found in almost every firm, shown in Exhibit 1.

EXHIBIT 1
Major Types of Business Processes

Business Process	Inputs	Outputs
Strategic planning	Competitor data, market assessments, internal capability assessments, economic forecasts	Strategic vision, long-term objectives and plans
Innovation	Technological developments, customer needs, production capabilities	New products, new production technologies
Customer service	Customer orders and requests, complaints, demand forecasts, priorities	Entered orders, delivery commitments, resolved problems
Resource management	Strategic objectives, resource costs, availability of existing resources	Capacity plans, hiring plans, facilities plans
Supply chain	Supplier capabilities, raw materials, customer orders, demand forecasts	Fulfilled orders, production schedules, goods and services
Performance measurement	Raw information, benchmarks, standards	Performance variances, trends

These processes consist of smaller and more focused subprocesses. Between every pair of subprocesses, an interface must be maintained. Often these interfaces cross departmental boundaries. This is an important consideration since these interfaces often can become managerial "black holes." For example, orders can be lost when they move from one department to another.

As shown in Exhibit 2, every process can be described in four different ways.

The process as formally documented. Most firms attempt to document their processes (especially the critical ones). Customers or certifying authorities may require documentation (as in the case of ISO/QS 9000 quality certification).[2]

EXHIBIT 2
Gaps in Process Descriptions

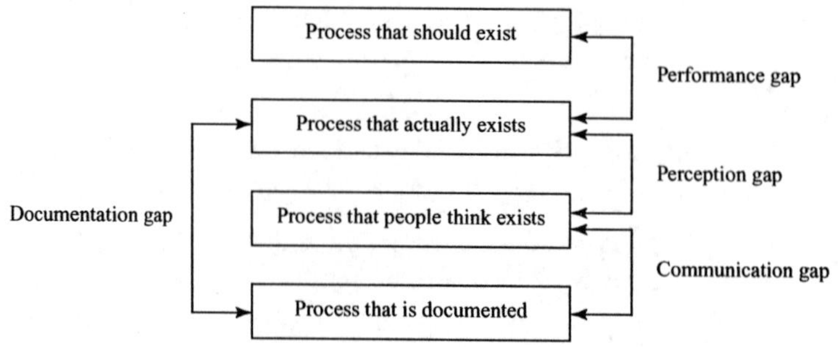

[2] The ISO/QS 9000 certification standards are discussed in Steven A. Melnyk, Lawrence D. Fredenell, "Total Quality Management" (New York: McGraw-Hill/Irwin 2002).

Documentation also helps in teaching processes to new employees, customers, or suppliers. Unfortunately, processes change over time due to changes in technologies, product designs, and methods. Unless documentation is meticulously maintained, it loses its accuracy, limiting its usefulness. This documentation gap contributes to confusion, conflict, and communication gaps since managers' perceptions of processes often are based on documentation, while workers' perceptions are based on what really goes on.

The process as people think that it exists. The process that people think exists often differs from the documented process, and also may differ from the process that actually exists. The reason is that most process workers see only a part of the entire process—the part in which they are involved. They know this one part well; they make assumptions about what takes place in the other parts of the process. This perceptual gap leads to faulty decisions and counterproductive actions.

The process as it actually exists. Often, we describe this process as the "base" or "as is" process. One of our objectives should be to reduce the gap between this and other forms of the process.

The process as it should exist. The difference between this form of the process and the actual process is one of value. In the process that should exist, all of the activities that are either inefficient or ineffective (i.e., do not add value) have been changed or eliminated.

Between these four forms, there exist gaps. These gaps are critical because they create frustration and confusion (since people do not know which process is right). Ultimately, these gaps also contribute to increased costs, increased lead time, and reduced quality—all conditions inconsistent with the value-driven approach. One of the objectives of process management is to eliminate these gaps. For the operations manager, the task of reducing these gaps is generally accomplished in two phases. The first phase involves defining the process as it actually exists and making documentation and worker perceptions consistent with this definition. In the second phase, the value perspective (as will be shown later in this module) is applied. The approach seeks to identify the value content of various activities, and to reduce activities that do not contribute to value while enhancing the effectiveness and efficiency of activities that directly contribute to value. The twin concerns of reducing waste and enhancing value underlie many of the activities of the operations manager within the value-driven firm.

Anatomy of a Process

Processes are central to a company's success. At the same time, they stir deep confusion in many managers. Processes involve activities, but they are not the same as activities. Processes draw on structures and resources, but they are not simply structures or collections of resources. Instead, a process is a system involving all these rudiments. As we said earlier, a process is a system of activities that uses resources to transform inputs into valuable outputs. A process can be fully described by the five major rudiments embedded in this definition:

1. Activities.
2. Inputs/outputs/flows.
3. Structure.
4. Resources.
5. Metrics.

Activities within a Process

A process usually consists of many different activities. For example, at McDonald's, the activity of moving buns and patties to the Made for You line is different from the activity of cooking the patties or assembling a sandwich. One of the first steps in process thinking is to recognize different types of activities in a process. Activities fall into six distinct categories:

- An **operation** is any activity that intentionally transforms an input. Operations occur when a physical change is made to an input, when information is communicated, when a transaction is made, or when planning and calculations take place. For the most part, operations are the major source of value in OM systems.
- A **decision** is a point in the process where the path that an input follows is determined by a choice or evaluation that someone in the process makes. For example, the routing of a loan application in a mortgage firm may depend on whether or not the applicant meets certain criteria.
- **Transportation** is any activity that moves an object from one place to another without transforming its other characteristics.
- An **inspection** checks or verifies the results of another activity. An inspection might examine a part to see if it is the right item or to compare it against a standard.
- A **delay** occurs when the flow of an object is unintentionally stopped as a result of interference. You experience a delay when you wait in line to check in to a hotel. Delays also take place when objects have to wait because other inputs (information or materials) or resources that are needed to execute an operation are not available. For example, delays occur because parts are missing or because machines break down.
- **Storage** is an activity where items are kept *under formal control.* Access to stored items requires authorization. For example, when you put money in a bank, you are placing money into storage. In manufacturing, storage occurs in many places, including stockrooms, warehouses, and holding/receiving areas.

To many students, there does not seem much to differentiate a storage from a delay. However, two key traits differentiate the two activity types. As previously noted, storages involve a formal control system. In contrast, there is no such control mechanism for a delay. For example, a bank provides storage for money. There is a formal control system present. You can only withdraw money if you have sufficient funds in your account and if you have the "right" authorization to do so. However, once the money goes into your wallet, it experiences a delay. No formal control mechanism is present. The second differentiating trait is that storage is a planned activity while a delay is caused by unplanned factors. Consequently, there is greater variability (and unpredictability) associated with delays.

Inputs, Outputs, and Flows

Process activities link inputs to outputs through a series of flows. Most processes involve two basic types of flows: information flows and physical flows. **Information flows** form critical links both internally (between the OM system and the other corporate functions) and externally (between the firm and its customers and suppliers). **Physical flows** are flows that you can see and touch. You can see a product van moving along an assembly line or a meal being prepared in a restaurant.

Inputs come from outside the process. They are the items acted upon by the process. Even a simple process relies on a wide range of inputs including materials, energy, information, capital, and even people (in the case of a service process).

Outputs are the products or outcomes of the process, including goods, services, and information. Intended outputs usually have value for customers. However, processes also usually produce unintended outputs that are either unexpected or natural by-products (e.g., pollution and environmental waste).

Structure

Structure deals with the organization of inputs, activities, resources, and outputs of a process. Process managers define this structure by sequencing activities, positioning them with resources, and linking them. Activities in a process do not occur randomly (at least, they aren't supposed too!). Oftentimes, the requirements of the process determine the precedence and sequence of activities. A process that can operate only in one specific sequence is subject to a **strict precedence;** for example, a cook cannot possibly make pancakes before preparing the batter. Other times activities can occur in more than one sequence. For example, a computer assembly process can insert microchips in many different sequences.

While sequencing determines the order in which activities are executed throughout the entire process, **positioning** organizes activities and resources in relation to each other. Activities are positioned either *sequentially* or *in parallel.* **Sequential positioning** places activities in series, one after another. In contrast, **parallel positioning** overlaps activities so that they can occur simultaneously. Sometimes activities must be positioned in sequence because of technological constraints (again, you can't cook pancakes until you make the batter). Other times, activities are positioned sequentially because of resource constraints. Consider a manual process that has only one worker. The single worker can't accomplish two tasks at the same time.

Activities in a process may be closely or loosely linked. The tightness of a link between activities results from the relationships created as activities are positioned. The physical distance between two activities can create a close or loose **spatial link.** Other **physical links** are created by tangible connections between related activities. For example, an automobile assembly line physically links activities by placing workstations in a specific configuration and moving cars past them in a set order on a conveyor system.

Part of structuring processes involves locating activities in functional departments. It is common for processes to involve multiple departments and for flows to frequently cross departmental boundaries. Managing these interfaces is critical for a number of reasons. As flows cross departments, an order (i.e., the item being processed) may be lost because the transfer of responsibility from one department to the next doesn't occur smoothly. Each department has its own procedures for describing problems, rewarding performance, and carrying out activities. When different departments come into contact, we have to ensure that everyone involved sees the problems and major tasks in the same way. For example, order tracking systems may need to be made consistent. Finally, the overhead costs of managing process interfaces can be quite high if high levels of coordination are required.

Resources

Since it usually isn't possible to get something for nothing, activities in processes always consume resources. For example, a storage activity requires floor space (for the inventory). It also may require a person who is responsible for managing access to the inventory. An inspection requires floor space for storing the items to be inspected and either a machine or a person to actually do the inspection. Exhibit 3 gives examples of the resource needs typically associated with the different categories of activities.

EXHIBIT 3
Resource Needs by Process Activities

Process Activity	Examples of Associated Resources
Operation	Tools, manpower, machine capacity
Decision	Management or worker brainpower, diagnostic tools, procedures, guidelines, checklists
Transportation	Pallets, carts, fork lift trucks, trucks (space inside of carrier), trains
Inspection	Inspectors, inspection stations, gauges, robots, machine vision equipment
Delay	Space on shop floor, bins, carts, racks, computer memory (information delays)
Storage	Storage space (floor space), racks, bins, stockroom clerks, database (information storage)

Metrics

Processes do not and cannot work in a vacuum. Rather, they exist to serve and meet the needs of certain customers. To ensure that processes can achieve this objective, we must establish a meaningful bridge between the customers to be served and the processes that

EXHIBIT 4 **Examples of Process Metrics**

Value Component	Metric	Rationale/Discussion
Cost	Contribution margin	The difference between revenues generated by a process and the variable cost to the firm of operating that process. Most appropriate in processes that are treated as profit centers.
	Variance from budget	Measures the difference between planned (budgeted) costs and the actual costs. An indication of how efficiently or well run the process has been.
	Ratio of direct to indirect labor	Raising indirect costs increases the fixed costs, thus raising the break-even point and reducing the flexibility of the process. A low ratio of direct to indirect labor indicates this type of inefficiency, while a higher ratio suggests more efficient cost performance.
	Inventory turnover	This metric determines how long inventory stays within the process before it is moved out. A lower value indicates more inventory staying longer within the system, thus increasing carrying costs and working capital requirements.
	Paperwork burden	Carlos del Rio of SmithKline Beecham Pharmaceuticals developed this metric (sum of steps or time devoted to completing paperwork) after observing a direct link between costs, system complexity, and paperwork.*
	Level of scrap–rejects–rework	Scrap, rejects, and rework consume process capacity and materials to correct defects within products. These activities increase costs without returning any offsetting revenues. They also reduce process efficiency.
Timeliness	Average throughput time	This measures the average time that it takes an order to move through the process.
	Dwell time	Total decision, delay, and storage time divided by the average throughput time.
	Number of steps in the process	The greater the number of steps, the longer the lead time and the more complex the process.
	Number of rings before an operator answers the phone.	This measure is frequently used in service firms. It measures the overall responsiveness of the process to a customer call.
	On-time delivery	This metric evaluates the reliability of the process, and the extent to which customers' delivery expectations are met.
	Average setup time	The ability to change from one order to another is greatly dependent on the setup time. The shorter the setup time, the shorter the lead time.
	Minimum order quantity	This is an indicator of throughput time because the smaller the quantity, the faster an order moves through the process.
	Average distance (ft) between activities	Closer activities require shorter move times and easier coordination.
	Percentage of activities organized in parallel	Sequential organization of activities requires longer lead times than parallel organization of activities.
Quality	PPM (parts defective per million)	This is a direct indicator of quality within a process. The lower the number, the higher the quality. This metric is frequently cited in industry.
	Percentage of repairs done correctly the first time	Often used in service settings such as a garage, this measures how well people diagnose and correct problems.
	C_{pk}	This measure is a ratio of product tolerance limits to the limits of process variation. It indicates how well the process is able to meet or exceed customer requirements.
Overall value	$\frac{\Sigma \text{(Value-adding activities)}}{\Sigma \text{(All activities in the process)}}$	This measure can be calculated as the ratio of the number of value generating activities or the total time spent within value generating activities to the total number of activities (or total through put time).
	$\frac{\Sigma \text{(Operations)}}{\Sigma \text{(Operations + Movements + Storages + Delays + Inspections)}}$	Since it is often difficult to determine which activities are responsible for value, a commonly used proxy is to count operations as the primary value-adding activities. This measure, like the preceding one, can count either the number of activities or the total time.

* Brian H. Maskell, *Performance Measurement for World Class Manufacturing* (Cambridge, MA: Productivity Press, 1991), pp. 280–82.

are to serve these customers. This bridge is the metric. Metrics establish quantitative and qualitative measures of performance by converting the elements of value (timeliness, cost, and quality) from vaguely and generally stated concepts into very precise operational terms. In so doing, metrics provide standards or expectations against which we can assess the performance of a specific activity or a specific process. They define what the process must do well in order to effectively and efficiently serve its customers. Metrics also act as a means of communication and feedback within the process. They are a critical element of the process because they allow managers and corporate personnel to monitor, control, and improve system performance.

Exhibit 4 provides some examples of process metrics that can be used to emphasize different elements of value.

Principles of Process Performance

The rudiments of processes—activities, inputs/outputs/flows, structure, resources, and metrics—work together to impact process performance. For a process to work well, choices in these areas need to be mutually reinforcing, as indicated in Exhibit 5. In the following sections, we discuss a number of basic principles that should guide the ways that processes are designed and operated:

- Bottleneck activities limit process capacity.
- Variability destroys capacity.
- Structure follows process priorities.
- Metrics drive the process.

EXHIBIT 5
The Factors Affecting a Process's Performance

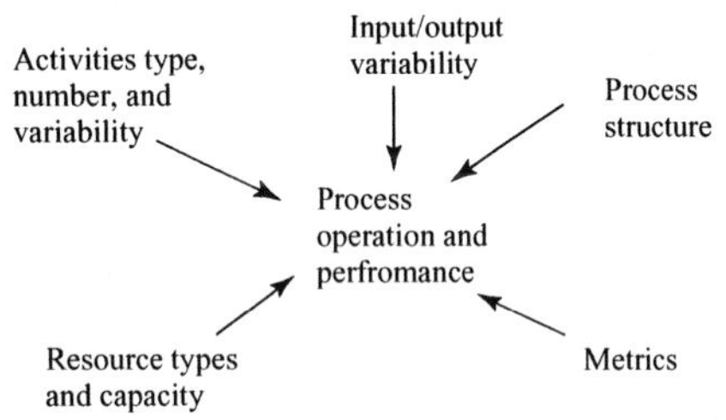

Bottleneck Activities Limit Process Capacity

Capacity can be expressed in terms of either resource availability (i.e., machine hours, labor hours, tools, or square feet of floor space available) or potential output (number of parts that the process can produce in a day, dollars' worth of products it can produce in an hour, etc.). Process capacity is usually defined as a rate describing the quantity of output generated per unit of time.[3] The inverse of this rate is known as the process's **cycle time,** which is defined as the amount of time that passes between the outputs of two successive units.

In any process, we need to deal with **maximum capacity** (otherwise referred to as **design capacity**) and **actual capacity.** Maximum capacity is the largest amount of output that a process can possibly generate. It is usually expressed as a theoretical upper limit rather than a practical level of production. Actual capacity is the output that a process truly attains in practice. Actual capacity is always less than maximum capacity because of problems and inefficiencies in the process.

It is important to realize that a process's resources limit its maximum capacity. Maximum capacity can be increased only in one of three ways. First, we can physically increase the level of resources in the process (e.g., by hiring more people). Second, we can change

[3] Other forms of capacity, such as capabilities, are discussed in the "Capacity Management" module (New York: McGraw-Hill Irwin).

how we do the various activities (reduce the resource requirements per activity). Finally, we can change the entire process by eliminating activities (thus freeing up the resources previously consumed by those activities). It is also important to realize that every process has a bottleneck activity (or activities). The **bottleneck** is the activity in the process that has the least capacity, due to the limits on its available resources. Consider the following examples.

Exhibit 6 shows a circuit board assembly process with four serially positioned operations. The maximum capacity for this process, 275 boards per hour, is based on the capacity of Operation C, which has the lowest capacity. Although Operation B can produce 125 more boards per hour, the process cannot exploit this excess capacity because Operation C can accept only 275 boards an hour.

EXHIBIT 6
Maximum Capacity in a Serially Positioned Process

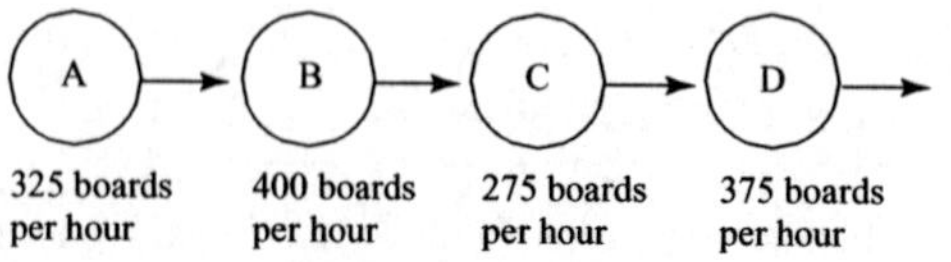

A Process for Manufacuring Circuit Boards
(all capacities listed are maximum)

The maximum process capacity changes for activities organized in parallel. If the parallel tasks represent the same type of activity, then their cumulative capacity equals the sum of their individual capacities. Exhibit 7 revises the circuit board assembly process to show a second operation made up of three parallel operations, each performing the same type of task. The total capacity for this second operation is not 90 boards (the single-operation minimum) but 400 boards (the sum of the capacities of Operations E, F, and B). The maximum capacity for the overall process remains at 275 boards per hour, however, because the work must still flow through Operation C.

EXHIBIT 7
Maximum Capacity in a Parallel Positioned Process

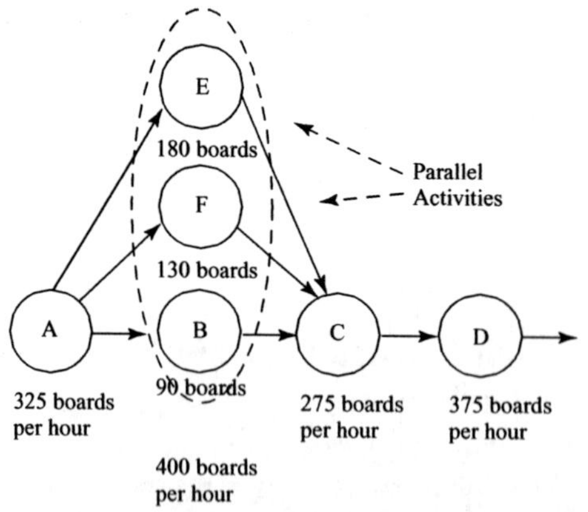

Within any process, we are typically interested in two output-related aspects. The first is the maximum output of the entire process. The second is the minimum **throughput time** for the process, that is, the time needed for a product to pass through the entire process. The bottleneck activity affects both of these aspects of performance. To improve the overall output capacity of the process, we must ensure that bottlenecks are always busy. An hour of lost output at the bottleneck equates to an hour of lost output for the entire process. This may mean that we keep extra work waiting in front of the bottleneck activity so that it always has something to work on. It also may mean that we closely monitor the operation of the bottleneck to ensure that it is working correctly. The bottleneck activity is the first place to invest in programs such as preventive maintenance. Investing in any activity other than the bottleneck would be a waste of time and money, because increasing the capacity of a nonbottleneck activity does not increase overall output.

Bottleneck capacity also determines throughput time to a great degree. The lower the capacity at a bottleneck activity, the more time that an order must spend at that activity. If there are large differences in capacity across sequential activities, work-in-process (WIP) inventory usually begins to grow. For example, if a machine that produces 30 units per hour feeds a machine that produces 20 parts per hour, then inventory grows between the two activities at the rate of 10 units per hour. As inventory grows, throughput time also grows, because orders spend more and more time waiting in inventory queues before they are processed.

It is clear that capacity affects the timeliness of outputs produced by a process, but capacity also affects other aspects of value including cost and quality. As WIP inventory grows due to bottlenecks, costs increase. More money is tied up in this inventory. Floor space is needed to store these items. Labor is needed to track and control this inventory. All of these factors increase costs. Quality also suffers. As inventory grows, more units are susceptible to damage, and problems in production are not as easily detected. In addition, insufficient capacity tends to encourage process workers to hurry, which in turn leads to mistakes. As one manager said, "Quality is the first victim of insufficient capacity."

What symptoms would you look for that would indicate the presence of a bottleneck? Consider how inventory levels and resource utilization might differ in front and behind a bottleneck.

Variability Destroys Process Capacity

The previous discussion of bottlenecks focused on assessing the effects of maximum capacity on process performance. As it was earlier stated, however, the actual capacity of a process is rarely equal to its maximum capacity. This is because processes rarely perform up to their full potential. There are always problems such as quality yields that are less than 100 percent and resources that are unavailable (e.g., machine breakdowns, absent employees). One of the greatest detriments to process capacity is variability. Variability can exist in outputs, inputs, or the process activities themselves.[4]

Exhibit 8, on page 12, summarizes the effects that different types of variability have on process capac-ity. Essentially, variability of different sorts introduces complexity and uncertainty into processes, which in turn increase the difficulty of efficiently utilizing resources so that the maximum output can be achieved. In addition, resources must be dedicated to managing complexity and uncertainty. For example, more support personnel are needed to accomplish planning and control activities that do not contribute directly to producing outputs. These activities take away from the total productive capacity of the process.

Because variability creates such dire impacts on process performance, managers spend a great deal of time and effort in managing and responding to variability. There are three basic ways to deal with variability in a process. First, and foremost, the best way to deal with variability is to *reduce it.* This means finding sources of variability in process activities and eliminating or controlling them. For example, experimentation with the settings of a production machine might uncover ways to reduce its inherent variability. The second way to deal with variation is to *buffer it.* By placing safety stock or buffer inventories before and after highly variable activities, one can reduce some of the bad effects on resource utilization. Finally, managers deal with variation by designing processes that *exibly respond to it.* By investing in flexible technologies and cross-training of labor, managers can create processes that quickly react to unplanned situations so that, once again, the detrimental effects of variation are minimized.

[4] The impact of variability on process performance also is discussed in Steven A. Melnyk, Lawrence D Fredenall, "Lean Systems Tools and Procedures" (New York: McGraw-Hill/Irwin 2002).

EXHIBIT 8 **Types and Effects of Process Variability**

Type of Variability	Effects on Capacity
Product variety	As one facility is used to produce a wider range of products, more process changeovers are required. Each changeover requires time that could otherwise be used to create output.
Schedule	As demand and production schedules vary, they become more complex and coordination becomes more difficult. Different activities become bottlenecks at different times (especially if product variety is large). This increases the potential for bottleneck activities to be poorly scheduled and left idle.
Quality (yield)	Defective product subtracts from the effective capacity of the process. In addition, productive resources are consumed by quality control and rework activities.
Resource availability	Absent employees and broken-down machines hold up production.
Processing speed	As processing speed at an activity becomes more variable, upstream activities are blocked from clearing work from their areas and downstream activities are starved for needed inputs more frequently. This increases idle time, thereby reducing output.
Quality of supplies	Poor quality results in unexpectedly insufficient quantities of needed inputs (e.g., materials, energy, information). It also introduces variance into the process that may result in poor final product quality.
Delivery of supplies	As delivery variability increases, there is greater potential for process activities to halt because they are missing needed components.

Structure Follows Process Priorities

"Form follows function" is a popular maxim that guides the design of products. In the same way, the sequencing, positioning, and linking of process activities should be closely tied to the priorities that process managers place on various performance outcomes. For example, a process designed to minimize delivery speed might be structured quite differently from a process that minimizes operating costs. There are several effects of structuring on process performance that should be considered. As we change the structure of a process, we affect the resources required to provide a given capacity. We also can affect the specific capabilities that we want from the capacity. Exhibit 9 provides some guiding rules of thumb for process structural design.

Consider the sequencing of activities required for a UPS driver to deliver packages. The order in which he makes the deliveries (i.e., his route) has a large effect on the total time (resources) required to complete the process.

EXHIBIT 9
Rules of Thumb for Process Structuring Decisions

Sequencing Activities

- Sequence activities according to technological or resource constraints.
- For each resource, sequence activities to minimize set-ups, distance, or other activity transition costs.

Positioning Resources and Activities

- Use flexible, multipurpose resources to achieve dynamic positioning when possible.
- Use redundant resources and parallel copies of activities to reduce throughout time and increase route flexibility.
- Use single resources and serial activities to minimize cost.
- Assign resources to achieve continuous flow where possible.
- Minimize cross-departmental hand-offs.
- Keep "non-value-adding but necessary" activities (e.g., measurement) off the critical (i.e. longest) path.

Linking Activities

- Co-locate activities that share resources or information.
- Use fixed physical links to pace the process and reduce variable costs if the process is balanced.
- Avoid fixed physical links if processes are variable or imbalanced.
- Reduce fixed physical links to lower fixed operating costs.

Activity and resource positioning also produce strong effects. Suppose that we add another UPS driver to serve the stations along the route and break the total delivery zone into two parts. In a purely serial process, the lead times are simply the sum of the lead times of the individual steps. In a parallel process, the lead time of the process is the lead time of the longest activity path (i.e., the longer of the two routes for our UPS drivers). Thus, parallel processes are faster than serial processes. Parallel processes also offer more flexibility than serial processes, because resources are duplicated and the number of paths that an input can take through the processes is increased (compare Exhibit 7 to Exhibit 6). On the other hand, parallel processes tend to consume more resources than serial processes. Because resources are duplicated in parallel processes, they tend to be less completely utilized, thus adding cost to the entire process. This is especially true when there is cycle time imbalance across process stages.

Linking decisions are also important for process performance. Locating two related activities closer to one another reduces the time needed to move components and tools, or to share resources between them. Dedicated physical links can be used to reduce transfer time and variability, resulting in lower material handling costs. However, building physical links requires initial investment and fixed operating costs. Physical links also limit the amount of WIP inventory that can be stored. Finally, physical links limit process flexibility. If some change requires activities to occur in a different sequence, one must change physical links, tearing up existing lines and building new ones. This consumes considerable time and money.

Over the years, a number of "classic" process structures have evolved. Each of these structures (job shop, batch shop, assembly line, continuous flow) represents a scheme of supportive choices or combinations of decisions regarding the sequencing, positioning, and linking of activities in a process.[5]

Metrics Drive the Process

"Show me how someone is measured, and I'll show you how they perform." This collective wisdom applies to all business processes that employ humans as key resources. It is the nature of human workers to maximize performance in the ways that provide them maximum rewards. Consequently it is important to make sure that process metrics and incentives are well understood and that they drive activities in the desired directions.

Several steps can be taken to ensure that metrics motivate process behaviors that increase customer value. The first is to identify and prioritize the customers served by the process. Every process serves many potential customers, some of which may be internal to the operation. For example, a school serves its students as "customers" who consume education. At the same time, the school serves many other customers including the students' parents, recruiters who hire the students, and even the community as whole. Different customer groups rarely have identical wishes, and it is rarely possible to completely satisfy all customers. Consequently, we must identify the critical (most important) customers. Second, we have to prioritize the requirements of these critical customers, while not losing sight of less critical groups. Third, we must pick a limited number of critical requirements and provide meaningful operational definitions (metrics) for them. These metrics should be consistent with the specific types of value that the firm provides within the marketplace and with the ways the firm differentiates itself from its competitors. Having established metrics, we can then assess the adequacy of the current process and establish objectives for a redesigned process as needed. These ideas are summarized in Exhibit 10.

EXHIBIT 10
The Seven "Shoulds" of Process Metrics

Source: Adapted from a list generated by Roger Schmenner, Indiana University.

Process Performance Metrics

Should be significantly nonfinancial in character.
Should be simple—and visual.
Should not necessarily be identical across locations, units, or levels.
Should provide the links between strategy and action.
Should measure only what is important.
Should make their own measurements obsolete.
Should be consistent and attuned to the critical customer.

[5] These process types are discussed fully in Kenneth K. Boyer, "Process Choices" (New York: McGraw-Hill/Irwin 2002).

Process Improvement Tactics for Enhancing Value

Research of approaches for improving processes has identified certain emergent tactics:[6]

Less of/system simplification: This tactic emphasizes documenting and analyzing processes in order to eliminate or reposition any non-value-adding activities. The goal is to generate simpler processes that focus on value. Example: Eliminate the generation of reports that no one reads.

As one/system integration: This tactic emphasizes cross-functional execution of activities. Barriers between functional areas often become black holes where items become lost or misplaced. In addition, better quality results when all of the activities in a process are understood by all of the parties involved. Example: Coordinate the planning of procurement, production, and delivery for an order.

Same as/standardization: This tactic standardizes inputs, outputs, or activities in a process. It reduces variability in processes by ensuring that activities are done exactly the same way every time. It also reduces complexity by reducing the number of unique inputs and outputs used and created by a process. Examples: Document and follow a standard procedure for a task. Replace two similar parts with one generic part.

Focus on/segment activities: This tactic attempts to parse process activities or products into "cells" or groups that have similar processing characteristics so that each cell can focus on developing the unique capabilities it needs to handle its particular demands. Example: Create two separate cells: one that processes high-volume, low-variety items and another that processes low-volume, high-variety items.

At once/parallel activities: This tactic repositions activities in a process so that the longest path of activities is minimized. Wherever possible, activities are removed from the longest (critical) path so they can be executed in parallel with the activities on the longest path. Example: Split the bottleneck task into several subtasks that can be accomplished simultaneously.

Watch it/variance control: This tactic emphasizes predictability in the process. It identifies tasks with the highest variance and examines them to uncover the reasons for the variance. Example: Conduct experiments to determine how environmental factors affect processing time.

Not here/focus on core competencies: This tactic reduces the internal process to include only those activities that we do well. Outside parties perform activities that they do better. Example: A manufacturing firm outsources its logistics operations.

Better than/automation: This tactic replaces less efficient procedures and technologies with more efficient ones. Newer technologies often automate activities, thus making them faster and less variable. Example: Replace a human painter with a robot.

More of/extra resources: This tactic simply adds resources to bottleneck activities. Example: Have two workers execute the activity instead of one.

The first six of these tactics involve fundamental changes to processes and can lead to long-term competitive advantage since they require process analysis, and improvement solutions are generated inside the firm. In contrast, the last three tactics are best described as process enhancers. They are associated more with procuring improvements from outside the firm. As such, they do not generate long-term competitive advantages since they are easily copied by competitors.

[6] Adapted from Carter, Phillip L., Melnyk, Steven A., and Handfield, Robert B., "Identifying the Basic Process Strategies for Time-Based Competition," *Production and Inventory Management Quarterly,* Vol. 36, No. 1, (1955), pp. 65-70.

Programs for Process Improvement*

Operations managers employ a number of programs or approaches to guide the systematic improvement of processes. Exhibit 11 places four types of programs in order on a spectrum representing the scope and magnitude of change. In the following paragraphs we briefly discuss two sharply contrasting approaches. Business process reengineering is an approach for radically redesigning processes, while kaizen events is an approach for making frequent, incremental improvements.

EXHIBIT 11
Spectrum of Programs for Process Improvement

	Process Reengineering	Process Renovation	Kaizen Events	Continuous Improvement
Example	Entirely new process	New equipment	New layout	Revised procedure
Scope of change	What is produced Technology used How it is done	Technology used How it is done	How it is done	How it is done
Starting point	Customer needs	Customer needs Existing process	Existing process	Existing process
Funding	Major development funds	Capital outlay	Little required	Improvement budget
Frequency	One time event	Every few years	Regularly	Continually (day-to-day)

Business Process Reengineering—Radical Process Change

As we saw from the beginning story, McDonald's has begun to rethink its process of making and delivering sandwiches to its customers. To successfully achieve this transformation, it was not enough to simply modify parts of the existing process. Instead, what was demanded was a rethinking of the entire process of taking orders, processing these orders, making the sandwiches, and delivering them to the customer quickly. This notion of radical rethinking of processes forms the foundation of **business process reengineering (BPR).**

Hammer and Champy describe business process reengineering as "the fundamental rethinking and radical redesign of business processes to achieve dramatic improvements in critical contemporary measures of performance, such as cost, quality, service, and speed."[7] Business process reengineering begins, not with the existing process, but with a precise image of the outputs that customers want. It then uses a "clean sheet" approach to develop a process that delivers those exact outputs. BPR focuses not on what is, but on what should be.

Kaizen Events—Small Process Changes Made Quickly

For most firms, BPR is a major undertaking, requiring a great deal of time, effort, and resources (McDonald's spent over two years reconfiguring their processes). This approach involves risk and requires faith that customers will accept the new process. Unfortunately, the success rate for BPR is between 10 and 15 percent. In some cases, an approach that is narrower in scope, short-term in nature, intense, and focused on certain key processes may provide better results. One such approach is the use of *kaizen events.*

*These approaches are discussed more fully in the "Process Learning and Innovation" module (New York: McGraw-Hill/Irwin).

[7] Michael Hammer and James Champy, *Reengineering the Corporation* (New York: Harper Business, 1993), p. 32.

A **kaizen event** is a process-based approach aimed at improving existing processes. It is characterized by the following traits:

- *Short-term:* Kaizen events usually take between one and four days from start to finish. During this period, the teams are introduced to the process analysis tools they will use. They then study the process, identify opportunities for improvement, implement them, assess their impact, redo the cycle, and present their results to management.
- *Team-oriented:* The responsibility for an event is placed in the hands of a cross-functional team consisting of employees from the process being studied, employees from outside of the process, management, and, in some cases, supplier representatives. The team is responsible for studying, implementing, assessing, and improving the process. As a result, the team members develop greater ownership of the changes.
- *Highly focused:* One specific process is identified and all the attention of the team is focused on studying, documenting, analyzing, and improving the performance of that process.
- *Action-Oriented:* An interesting feature of this process is the immediacy of action. Any change identified and approved by the group is immediately implemented. The only major constraint is that the changes not require any major funding or capital requests. Equipment layout is changed as required (this does dictate the involvement of facilities management). After the changes have been implemented, the new system is run and the resulting performance documented and compared with the old system. As one American manager put it, the motto of a kaizen event is "ready, fire, aim."
- *Verifiable by metrics:* Improvements in the process must be verified. Typically this is done using metrics such as floor space occupied by the process, operators required per day, distance traveled by an order within the process, work-in-process inventory (in piece count), setup time (measured in minutes), quality recommendations generated, and safety improvements implemented.
- *Repetitive:* Once begun, kaizen events are regularly repeated. Each event generates an action list or a list of opportunities for improvement identified by the team in areas that they could address within their event. These items, in turn, become the focal point for future kaizen events.

Business process engineering and kaizen events represent two ends of a spectrum of approaches for improving processes. Managers must decide where to start along this spectrum from incremental fine-tuning to dramatic changes. Much of this decision depends on the size of the gaps between the output of the current process, customers' definitions of value, and the output of competitors' processes. Substantial gaps justify business process reengineering because they indicate serious inadequacies in the current process. Small gaps between the output of the current process and customer demands encourage incremental improvements rather than highly disruptive reengineering.

Module Summary

At the heart of every OM system, processes define the firm's capabilities and the specific type of value that it can deliver to customers. The importance of processes is emphasized in the following critical lessons:

1. Every system and every firm are defined by their various processes. These processes determine what the system can and cannot do. They also define the type of product and the specific type of value that the system delivers to its customer.
2. A process is a collection of activities that convert various inputs into outputs that customers value. Inputs used by processes include materials, energy, information, management, technology, and labor. Outputs consist of products, information, and knowledge.
3. Processes are characterized by activities (i.e., operations, decisions, storage, transportation, delays, and inspections), flows (inputs and outputs), structures (organization schemes of activities), resources, and metrics.
4. The maximum level of output from any process is determined by the activity (or activities) with the lowest capacity. Attempts to increase output and decrease lead time focus on such activities, known as bottlenecks.
5. Processes can be either modified or replaced. Business process reengineering is a useful approach for replacing processes. Kaizen events are appropriate when intensive, focused modifications in the current process are desired.

The operations manager cannot underestimate the importance of the process. To compete effectively in the marketplace, a firm must always maintain a tight fit between what its process can deliver and what customers want and demand.

Key Terms

Discussion Questions

1. Define the processes that you follow from the time you decide to leave for class until you return home. Illustrate the activities in a process flow chart.
2. In what ways would a distance learning system change the process you detailed in Question 1? Prepare a process flow diagram describing the new sequence of activities and their spatial arrangement. How might the value content of this process differ from that of the process in Question 1?
3. Which of the five activity categories is most appropriate for the following actions that you observe:
   a. A person taking an order from you at a restaurant
   b. A conveyor belt carrying your order to you at a store
   c. Work waiting at a work station
   d. Parts in a bin that an operator is working on
   e. The safe at your bank
   f. The advisor at your college checking your transcripts over to make sure that you have enough credits to graduate?
4. Under what conditions would inspections, storages, and transports be considered value-adding?
5. In class, you are involved in a process—the process of learning? Who are the internal and external customers for this process? What are you within this process?
6. How would you define the capacity of your school of business? In what way does capacity influence the value of your college experience?
7. When is the capacity of a process with parallel activities defined by that parallel path with the least capacity? Give an illustration.
8. Describe the role of performance measurement in business process analysis. How does value enter into this process? Does it cause any problems?
9. Your school of business wants to dramatically enhance its reputation within its region. Create a vision statement to help all school stakeholders understand the direction of the proposed business process reengineering process. Then prepare the corresponding impact statement. Then outline the process that you think the school would need to take to implement a business process reengineering program for your school.
10. After considering a business process reengineering approach, your school's faculty decides that an incremental approach might be better. Prepare a program designed to enhance the value of your school's business degree by 50 percent five years from now.
11. Under what conditions would you use a Kaizen Event? Business Process Reengineering?
12. Why is it important to begin with the metrics first rather than starting by looking first at the process?

Solved Problem

Process Capacity at Zug Island Steel

Zug Island operates a mill that makes steel for a variety of uses. You have been hired as a consultant to evaluate the current state of operations of the coking oven, blast furnace, and basic oxygen furnace (BOF) departments. In the first stage of the process, a coking oven changes coal from a nearby coal dump into coke. The coke is left to cool in a heap and then moved to a pile near the blast furnace. Currently, the coke oven has a design capacity of 71,000 tons of coke per year.

The blast furnace converts coke from the pile and iron pellets, also from a nearby pile, into pig iron. The pig iron is moved to a staging area to cool. The blast furnace uses 1.5 tons of coke and 2.3 tons of iron pellets to make every ton of pig iron, with a design capacity of 55,000 tons of pig iron per year.

In the next step, the BOFs convert pig iron into steel, which is taken to a soaking pit to await the next stage of processing. The BOFs require 0.8 ton of pig iron and 1.2 tons of scrap and chemicals to produce a ton of steel. They have a design capacity of 68,000 tons of steel per year.

Over the last year, the plant produced 60,000 tons of steel. You have been asked to calculate the capacity of the production process at Zug Island, stating results in tons of finished product (i.e., tons of steel). Also, the company is considering increasing the capacity of the blast furnace from 55,000 tons to 70,000 tons of pig iron per year, citing two major reasons. First, managers see a need to balance capacity across processes. Second, the change seems very attractive economically, with a return on investment significantly above the firm's requirement. What is your evaluation of this proposed change?

Solution

Initially, this problem seems complex with many different activities and capacities stated in varying units such as pig iron tons, steel tons, and coke tons. The four-step procedure makes it accessible, however.

1. Exhibit 12 lays out three operations (the coking oven, the blast furnace, and the basic oxygen furnaces) and six storage activities within the steel-making process. The process is organized basically sequentially, as the coking oven feeds the blast furnace that feeds the basic oxygen furnaces. Therefore, the overall capacity for this process depends on that of the lowest-capacity activity.

EXHIBIT 12
Process Flow for Zug Island Steel

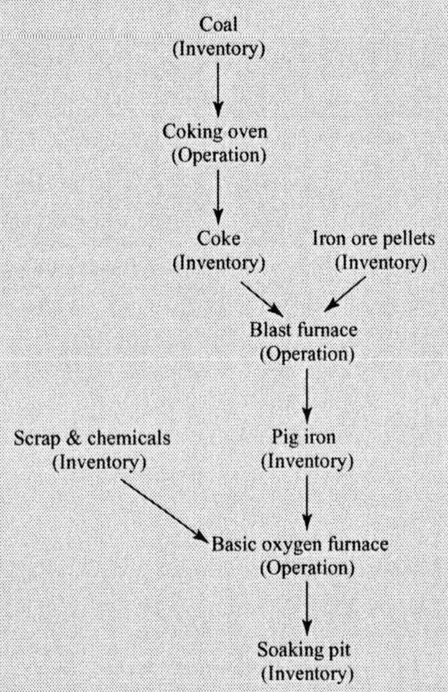

2. The most appropriate time period for the capacity calculation is one year since all data are stated in annual units.
3. To establish a common unit of measure, the calculation must convert the first two units—coke tons and pig iron tons—to steel tons to satisfy the company's requirements for the capacity data. As Exhibit 13 shows, to convert the output of the coke oven (measured in coke tons) into pig iron tons, divide the number of coke tons by 1.5 because the blast furnace needs 1.5 tons of coke to create a ton of pig iron. Similarly, to convert steel ton to coke tons, multiply the output of the BOF (in steel tons) by 0.8 (because it takes 0.8 ton of pig iron to make a ton of steel) and that result by 1.5 (because it takes 1.5 tons of coke to make a ton of pig iron).

EXHIBIT 13
Converting between Different Units of Capacity Measurement

Unit of Capacity	To Convert to Coke Tons	To Convert to Pig Iron Tons	To Convert to Steel Tons
Output of coke oven (CO)	No conversion	(CO output)/1.5	(CO output)/(1.5 × 0.8)
Output of blast furnace (BF)	BF output × 1.5	No conversion	BF output/0.8 ;
Output of basic oxygen furnace (BOF)	BOF output × 1.5 × 0.8	BOF output × 0.8	No conversion

4. Finally, Exhibit 14 calculates the maximum capacity for each operation. This shows a maximum capacity for the steel-making process of 59,166.67 steel tons per year. The coke oven is the bottleneck for the process, since it generates the lowest output, measured in any units. The coke oven cannot produce enough coke to keep the blast furnace and BOFs operating at capacity, constraining the overall output of the process. The maximum capacities of the blast furnace and the BOFs are fairly well-balanced.

This capacity calculation indicates that the blast furnace is not the bottleneck, so the proposed investment in expanding its capacity would not improve the overall capacity of the process. In fact, at the higher capacity, the blast furnace would be used only 67.6 percent of the time, found by dividing the coke oven's output of 59,166.76 steel tons by the new blast furnace output of 87,500.

EXHIBIT 14
Calculating Maximum Capacity

Unit of Capacity	Maximum Coke Tons	Maximum Pig Iron Tons	Maximum Steel Tons
Output of coke oven (CO)	71,000	47,333.33	59,166.67
Output of blast furnace (BF)	82,500	55,000	68,750
Output of basic oxygen furnace (BOF)	81,600	54,400	68,000

Problems

1. Mike operates a hair-cutting salon that specializes in providing quick walk-in service for just about any type of haircut. He deals with customers as they walk in the door. This includes writing down the customer's name and what they desire in terms of hair cut, wash, dry, and so forth. This process usually takes two minutes. If no hair stylist is available, the customer then goes to the waiting area, where he/she is processed on a first-come, first-serve basis. The salon has five hair stylists who work eight hours each day. It takes, on average, 25 minutes for a stylist to greet the customer, wash and/or cut his/her hair, and wish him/her a fond farewell. Then Mike completes the process by taking the customer's money and telling him/her about the satisfaction guarantee offered by the shop. This final set of steps takes two minutes on average.
   a. Assume that the waiting area always has at least one customer in it. How many customers on average can Mike's salon process in a day (assuming no problems in utilization, yield, or efficiency)?
   b. Suppose that you need an "average" haircut, and as you walk into the salon you see three people sitting in the waiting area. You notice that another person is just sitting down in the empty chair of one of the stylists and the other stylists are all busy with customers. Assuming you choose to wait, how long would you expect it to be before you are ready to leave the salon?
2. Cooper's Copy Shop is considering two different processes for completing copying jobs brought in by customers. Process A uses one person to set up the job and do the copying. If this approach is used, an experienced person can complete an average of 20 jobs per day. Process B uses two people. One person does the setup and the second person does the actual copying. Setup on one job can be done while copying is being completed on another, but copying must be completed on one job before the copying machine can start copying the next. After some practice, this second process can be completed with a standard time of 10 minutes for setup and 15 minutes for actual copying. In either case, assume an eight-hour day, 5 days per week, 250 days per year.
   a. Assuming ideal conditions, what is the maximum capacity of Process B?
   b. How long would it take to process 200 jobs using Process A (assume only one worker and one machine)?
   c. How long would it take to process 200 jobs using Process B (assume only one "production line")?
   d. If Cooper is primarily interested in providing low cost to customers, which process should he put in place?
   e. If Cooper is primarily interested in providing quick service to customers, which process should he put in place?

Cases

EVERGREEN PRODUCTS

The top managers of Evergreen Products of East Lansing, Michigan, have asked you to act as a consultant on a problem plaguing the entire company. Evergreen Products manufactures decorated containers and care tags for a market consisting primarily of small to medium florists and grocery stores. The containers are relatively inexpensive to make, but they are sold at a high markup (60 percent). The same is true for the tags. Because of the targeted market segment, management feels that it must be able to provide its customers with quick delivery and quality. However, this has not been happening lately.

To understand what happens, it is useful to first follow the course of an order received from the customer. Orders are placed in one of two ways at Evergreen. First, customers may notice that their stocks are getting low. They call the Evergreen sales department with an order, which is received by one of three clerks. The clerk records on a sheet the customer number, the type of product, and the quantity needed. At this point, a customer due date is set based on the customer's needs. However, the clerks try to encourage a due date that is about five working days out (there is no hard-and-fast rule for this procedure).

Once a day, the sales account manager picks up all sales orders. He is responsible for ensuring that all orders are complete and accurately entered and that the customer's credit rating is OK. If it is, the order is put into another pile where it is picked up once every morning. If the order is not acceptable or if there are errors, the order is returned to the person who took the order. That person is then responsible for correcting the problem within a reasonable period of time. When the order has been corrected, the process is repeated. It takes about half a day to move from phone order to sales account manager and about an hour to clear the sales account manager. Forty percent of the orders experience some form of error.

The second way that an order can be placed is through the company's own traveling salespersons who stop in on accounts and check their inventory stocks. When they see that an item is low, they fill out an order. They then phone the order into the plant (about once every day—this varies depending on how busy they are). Since each salesperson is rated on the total dollar sales he/she generates, there is a built-in incentive to be very concerned about clients' inventory stocks. When the order is turned over to the sales account manager, the process is identical to the one previously described. On average, the delay for entering orders through the salesperson is about half a day (but it can range up to two days).

Once the order clears the sales account manager, it goes to accounting, where it first is put into the day's pile. It is then entered into the accounting system. This step marks the beginning of the billing process. It takes an average of half a day to clear accounting (but this can range up to two days). From here, it goes to the shop floor scheduler.

The shop floor scheduler reviews all orders for accuracy and completeness. Any problem orders are set aside and returned to the sales account manager for correction. About 15 percent of the orders are typically set aside each day. The rest of the orders are released to the shop floor. It typically takes one day to clear the shop floor. The time can vary depending on the time of year. Christmas, Valentine's Day, Easter, Mother's Day, and other similar holidays put a great deal of pressure on the shop floor (which runs on average at 80 percent utilization). The shop floor is held accountable for meeting all quoted customer due dates.

Top management is concerned over the poor performance of the shop floor. Inventories are high and growing, overtime is excessive, on-time delivery performance is poor, and customer dissatisfaction is growing. The top manager has asked you if he should replace the current shop floor planner.

QUESTIONS

1. What are the desired outcomes for Evergreen? What should Evergreen wish to accomplish with its order entry system? How do we know if the order entry system is working well or poorly? How is it doing now?

2. What do the customers want from Evergreen? What type of problems do the existing customers pose for Evergreen? Why?

3. Apply the process for incorporating value through process thinking to this problem. What metrics would you apply to this process? What insights into the process did you obtain?

4. How would you improve the operation of the current order entry process at Evergreen? Be specific. Apply the strategies for enhancing value in dealing with this question (e.g., system simplification, system integration, parallel activities).

Hints: (1) Make sure that you identify and understand the various customers. (2) Bound the process by focusing only on the orders that come into the system by telephone. (3) Make sure that you establish metrics at the outset.

Related Modules of Interest

- Process Choices
- Project Management
- Total Quality Management

Selected Readings

Andrews, Dorine C., and Susan K. Stalick. *Business Reengineering: The Survival Guide.* Englewood Cliffs, NJ: Yourdon Press, 1994.

Balm, Gerald J. *Benchmarking: A Practitioner's Guide for Becoming and Staying the Best.* Schaumburg, IL: QPMA Press, 1992.

Blackstone, John H., Jr. *Capacity Management.* Cincinnati, OH: South-Western Publishing Company, 1989.

Hammer, M. "Reengineering Work: Don't Automate, Obliterate." *Harvard Business Review,* July–August 1990, pp. 104–12.

Hammer, Michael, and James Champy. *Reengineering the Corporation.* New York: Harper Business, 1993.

Harrington, H. James. *Business Process Improvement: The Breakthrough Strategy for Total Quality, Productivity and Competitiveness.* New York: McGraw-Hill, 1991.

Imai, Masaaki. *Gemba Kaizen.* New York: McGraw-Hill, 1997.

Maskell, Brian H. *Performance Measurement for World Class Manufacturing.* Cambridge, MA: Productivity Press, 1991.

Melan, Eugene H. *Process Management: Methods for Improving Products and Service.* New York: McGraw-Hill, 1993.

Melnyk, Steven A., and William R. Wassweiler. "Business Process Reengineering: Understanding the Process, Responding to the Right Needs." *APICS: 37th International Conference Proceedings.* San Diego, CA, October 30–November 4, 1994, pp. 115–20.

Raeker, Roland H. "New Times, Old Tools." *APICS: 35th International Conference Proceedings.* Montreal, Quebec, Canada, October 18–23, 1992, pp. 255–58.

Rummler, G. A., and A. P. Brache. *Improving Performance: How to Manage the White Space on the Organization Chart.* San Francisco, CA: Jossey-Bass Publishers, 1990.

Watson, Gregory H. *The Benchmarking Workbook.* Cambridge, MA: Productivity Press, 1992.

Womack, J. P., and D. T. Jones. *Lean Thinking: Banish Waste and Create Wealth in Your Corporation.* New York: Simon and Schuster, 1996.

Process Choices

Kenneth K. Boyer
Michigan State University

McGraw-Hill Irwin

Boston Burr Ridge, IL Dubuque, IA Madison, WI New York San Francisco St. Louis
Bangkok Bogotá Caracas Kuala Lumpur Lisbon London Madrid Mexico City
Milan Montreal New Delhi Santiago Seoul Singapore Sydney Taipei Toronto

Process Choices

Module Objectives

By the end of this module, you should be able to

- Understand the fundamental process choices made by both manufacturing and service organizations.
- Describe the product-process matrix for manufacturing organizations and the service-system design matrix for service organizations.
- Understand the relationships between unit cost, process flexibility, capital investment, worker skill, and technology choice that characterize different aggregate process choices.
- Match strategic goals with appropriate process choices.
- Comprehend the effects of computerized technologies, including the Internet, on traditional product-process relationships.

Baking the RIGHT Way

Baked goods represent a common product that can be produced easily using a variety of different processes. Large-volume, prepackaged consumer products such as Oreos or Wonder bread most often are produced using line processes, while smaller specialty or neighborhood bakeries typically employ batch or job shop processes.

Bama Foods opened a processing plant in Beijing in 1992 to supply apple, pineapple, and bean-curd pies for the over 200 McDonald's restaurants in China and Korea. Bama's U.S. facilities include a $32 million, 135,000-square-foot biscuit facility that is completely automated and can drop 1,600 pounds of dough every six minutes onto two parallel dough-processing lines. The dough is smoothed, stamped into round biscuits, then dropped into baking pans with an overall output of 60,000 biscuits per hour.

River City Biscotti owners Traci Soebbing and Lisa Wolfe have learned by trial and error the fine points of making biscotti since opening their business in 1998. They sell items to 15 retail businesses in the Spokane, Washington, area. The production process is batch oriented with the two women spending about five hours per batch baking, finishing, and packaging biscotti. In contrast to Bama Foods, River City Biscotti uses general-purpose equipment such as an industrial mixer and convection oven. Soebbing and Wolfe perform most of the work without specialized equipment—hauling 50-pound sacks of sugar and flour around. In fact, to give their almond-flavored biscotti that special touch, they hand scrape the outer membrane of an orange peel, called the zest, and add it to their recipe.

Cliff Simon offers a customized baked good that turns cakes into works of art that cost anywhere from $65 to $15,000. He has created a pink-painted tongue for the rock group Kiss, a New York Mets logo in chocolate for singer Billy Joel, and a Simonized butter sponge cake likeness of the composer Rossini for opera singer Marilyn Horne. His job shop processing methods allow this high level of customization but are extremely inefficient and expensive in comparison to companies such as River City Biscotti and Bama Foods. The high level of hands-on work and creative design has its risks—Simon wept when his four-foot-tall, lemon-walnut Tower of Babel wedding cake for Diana Ross nearly suffered its own biblical collapse.

Source: S. Hosking, "Fledgling River City Biscotti Looks to Expand Base," *Journal of Business* 14, no. 2 (January 14, 1999), p. A15; "Let Them Eat Cakes," *People Weekly* 49, no. 17 (May 4, 1998), pp. 152–53; and K. Thuermer, "Bama Foods Bakes in Beijing: Quality Control and Bean-Curd Pies," *World Trade* 11, no. 3 (March 1998), pp. 46–47.

Process Choice and Its Relationship to Value

"I didn't fail ten thousand times. I successfully eliminated, ten thousand times, materials and combinations which wouldn't work."

Thomas Edison

In the preceding vignette, we saw three different ways of making baked goods, be it a pie (as in the case of Bama Foods), cookies (River City Biscotti), or cakes (Cliff Simon). Each of these different process structures offers exactly the operating traits that are most desired by the target customers. Bama Foods picked a highly automated production line to produce consistent pies quickly and at low cost. Its customer, McDonald's of China PRC, wants exactly that, since it sells millions of pies to its consumers. These buyers are not interested in waiting; they probably would not appreciate the subtleties of including zest in their pies.

The process used by River City Biscotti is also well suited to its customers. Customers of River City Biscotti want quality; they do not want mass-produced goods (if they did, they would buy from a grocery store). They want products that are fresh and "good." These attributes come from making biscotti cookies in small batches and from adding such personal touches as including zest in the cookies. For Traci Soebbing and Lisa Wolfe, the small batch-oriented production process is appropriate because it delivers the type of value that their critical customers appreciate and are willing to pay for.

Finally, Cliff Simons is paid to make truly unique cakes—products that must be designed from scratch. These are products that you could not buy in a grocery store or typical bakery. The production process found in Simon's shop is very flexible. It must be so since Cliff does not build a standard product. Every day, he creates something different.

These three companies highlight the importance of the production process decision. For an operations management system to effectively and efficiently deliver value, there must be a tight fit between what the critical customer(s) wants (i.e., is willing to pay for) and what the production process can reliably deliver. If this fit is not there, then value is not realized. McDonald's would not be willing to tolerate the inefficiencies of a Cliff Simon production process. Similarly a Bama Foods type of plant would not be well suited to deliver only one unit of a pink-painted tongue cake for the rock group Kiss.

In this module, we explore the impact of the production process choice on value. We will see that process choice involves not only issues of production volume but also desired capabilities, that is, what the processes can and cannot do. Choosing the "wrong" type of process from a value perspective can be devastating to an organization's future.

Elements of Process Choice

To understand the linkage between value and process choice, it is important that we understand what the process choice affects. First, process choices impact the amount of volume (i.e., output) and product variety that can be produced efficiently. The three processes described in the opening vignette represent very different levels of volume and variety, with the Bama Foods system having the highest volume (lowest variety) and Cliff Simon's operation having the lowest volume (highest variety). Process choice also affects the capabilities of the production process, that is, the things that the process can do well and those things that the process cannot do well. Capabilities are critical from a value perspective since these must meet or exceed customer expectations and demands for value to be delivered. Consider the three processes as summarized in Exhibit 1 on page 4.

In making a process choice, we are trying to match the capabilities offered by the process with the demands of customers. When the two are in synch, value is realized; when there is a mismatch, the process is ineffective and likely to lead to customer dissatisfaction. Process capabilities stem from the overall process structure, which is a result of decisions and investments affecting

- Process layout.
- Equipment.
- Staffing and training.
- Scheduling and organization of work.
- Information systems.
- Product design (i.e., extent to which the product is standardized).

EXHIBIT 1
A Comparison of Three Processes for Baking

Company	Process	Strength	Weakness
Bama Foods	Line process	• High volume output • Consistency of product • Short lead time to produce one unit • Low cost	• Very inflexible • Difficult to do short runs • Changeovers in products require large setups • Expensive from a capital (equipment) perspective
River City Biscotti	Batch process	• Somewhat more flexible than line • Can deliver small batches quickly • Lower-cost equipment • Lower setup costs	• Cannot respond quickly to rapid upward changes in demand • Higher costs than line • Longer lead times • Less consistency of quality
Cliff Simon	Job shop	• Able to design and deliver unique product • Highly flexible • Very low setup times • Low-cost capital equipment	• Highly variable quality • Very dependent on skill of employees • Very long lead times • Very high costs • Very low total output volume

In order for the "right" choices to be made, operations managers must understand the options available to them. Sometimes, a product or service can be provided using several different process structures, but generally there is one process structure that fits best.

The Product-Process Matrix

The **product-process matrix** (see Exhibit 2) originally was developed to match different generic types of manufacturing process structures to different product types (ranging from low-volume, low-standardization products to high-volume, high-standardization commodity products). The matrix shows that there is a trade-off between high-volume standardized products that get produced for a low per-unit cost and low-volume, customized products that have a high per-unit cost. Other trade-offs exist between issues such as the degree of capitalized investment and customer involvement, and the use of generalized versus specialized equipment. Exhibit 3 gives an overview of these trade-offs and the characteristics that describe the different process types.

EXHIBIT 2
Product-Process Matrix

Source: Adapted from R. Hayes and S. Wheelwright, *Restoring Our Competitive Edge: Competing Through Manufacturing* (New York: John Wiley & Sons, 1984).

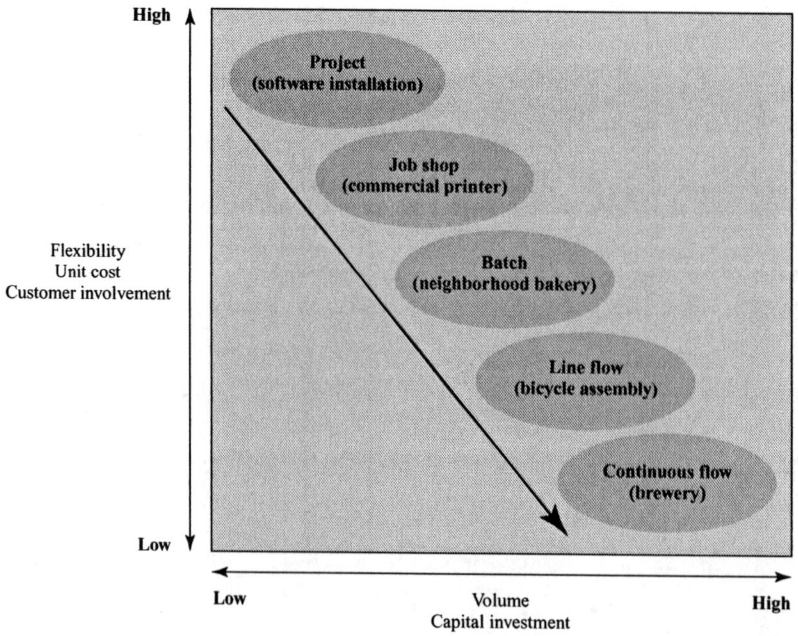

EXHIBIT 3 An Overview of Manufacturing Process Characteristics

	Project	Job Shop	Batch	Line Flow	Continuous Flow
Facility size	Located on customer site	Usually small	Moderate	Often large	Large
Process flow	Independent activities	Many patterns	Dominant patterns	Rigid pattern	Inflexible
Speed	Slow	Slow	Moderate	Fast	Very fast
Run length	Unique events	Short	Moderate	Long	Very long
Labor content	Very high	Very high	Varies	Low	Very low
Skill level	High	High	Mixed	Low	Varies
Material requirements	Somewhat predictable	Hard to predict	More predictable	Predictable	Very predictable
Scheduling	Uncertain, frequent changes	Uncertain, frequent changes	Varies, frequent expediting	Fixed	Inflexible, technology dictates
Challenges	Estimating completion time, managing critical activities	Estimating labor utilities, debottlenecking, fast response	Balancing stages, responding to diverse needs	Productivity improvement, occasional rebalancing	Avoiding downtime, expansions, cost min.

Projects

A **project** is a unique set of activities, so projects are technically different from repetitive processes. Examples of projects include constructing an office building or housing development, developing or installing a new software program, organizing a jazz festival, and developing and introducing a new product or service. A high degree of customization, a wide scope of activities, a high degree of customer involvement, and the use of primarily generalized tools and equipment characterize projects. The exact composition and sequence of tasks vary widely from project to project because of the high degree of customization. There are typically numerous inter-related tasks (often hundreds) that must be completed in a sequential order and that involve workers from very different areas of the organization. Thus, a critical characteristic of a project is the requirement for close coordination between the various people and organizations involved with the project. This coordination can be primarily within a single organization, but increasingly involves the exchange of information and resources across several different businesses.

Job Shop Process

Examples of job shop processes include a delicatessen with a large variety of sandwiches, a commercial printer, airplane manufacturers, custom furniture manufacturers, and a machine shop. A **job shop process** structure provides high flexibility to produce a variety of products in limited volumes. Customization tends to be high, although not as high as for projects, while volume per product is fairly low. Worker skills tend to be broad and equipment tends to be general purpose. For example, a commercial printer might have a printing press that can print on several different paper sizes with several different combinations of color (i.e., two-color, four-color, or six-color) and quality. Workers in this situation must have a broad variety of skills in order to set up the equipment for a variety of orders. This printing press is a good example of general-purpose equipment that has the flexibility to do many jobs, but is fairly inefficient due to the need to specifically set up the press for each new job.

Companies that use a job shop process often must bid against competitors for work, and products are typically made to order rather than produced ahead of time for inventory or based on demand forecasts. Most resources are organized around common processing characteristics rather than a given product. For example, a custom furniture manufacturer would most likely have an area for turning equipment (to turn chair or table legs), another area for varnishing, and a separate area for upholstery. This organization is appropriate because different products will flow through the system in different ways. For example, a mission-style table might not require either the turning of table legs (since they are square not round) or any upholstery. On the other hand, a Chippendale chair would require all three areas (turning, varnishing, and upholstery) and would thus follow a different path through the plant.

Batch Process

Batch process examples include a neighborhood bakery, home mortgage loan processing, production of parts or components to feed an assembly line, or the production of winter coats. A **batch process** structure is essentially a higher volume job shop, in which the same or similar products are produced repetitively. The variety of products in a batch process is significantly lower than in a job shop, with variety primarily being achieved through an assemble-to-order approach (in which components or parts are assembled from inventory in the appropriate combinations for each order). Variety remains too large for resources to be dedicated to a single product or family of products. Products are produced in moderate-size batches (typically from 10 to 1,000 units per batch) where once one batch is finished at a location, then a batch of another product is made. Flow through the plant is still jumbled with different batches requiring different processing steps, but dominant patterns begin to emerge. Batch processes span a wide range of volume and variety combinations. Not surprisingly, batch processes are the most common type of process found in manufacturing firms.

Line Flow Process

Examples of line flow processes include television assembly, food production (such as canned vegetables), book printing, or Beanie Baby production. **Line flow processes** use dedicated resources to produce high volumes of standardized products. The flow of products is organized around a single (or few) product(s). Steps are arranged in a linear sequence and broken up into the smallest steps possible. Workers specialize at a single task and equipment may be designed to perform a single action. For example, Oreos are produced at Nabisco with a dedicated set of resources that (1) shape the raw cookie dough, (2) bake the cookies, (3) apply the cream filling, (4) match the two halves of the cookie together, and (5) package the cookies, all with minimal human intervention. This equipment is specifically designed for making Oreos and represents a fairly large fixed investment of several million dollars. However, it is ideally suited for its task and can produce thousands of Oreos per hour, thus making the per-unit cost on the order of a few pennies per Oreo.

Every step in the process is performed repetitively, over and over with very little variation in the products. The advantage of this approach is that both equipment and workers can be very specialized. One major disadvantage is that workers tend to become bored or do not have a good understanding of the final product since they only perform one small step out of hundreds or thousands. Line processes typically employ a make-to-stock approach of producing items not to individual customer orders but to be held in inventory and used to fill future orders. A limited degree of variety can be introduced through careful design. For example, Oreos can be modified somewhat by having the roller cut cookies into different shapes (say squares instead of circles) or a different color of filling can be applied such as green for Christmas Oreos.

Continuous Flow Process

Examples of continuous flow processes include petroleum refining, chemical production, brewing of beer, and soda and paint production. **Continuous flow processes** produce high volumes with low flexibility. They work with nondiscrete items that are not divided into their final packages until the very end of production. For example, beer is brewed in a series of very large containers and pipes—not until the brewing process is complete is beer poured into bottles, cans or kegs for final delivery to the end consumer. Occupying an extreme on the product-process matrix, continuous processes are extremely capital intensive, very standardized, and very inflexible. They tend to be operated 24 hours a day to recoup the huge investment in equipment. Worker skills tend to be focused on maintaining the equipment and fixing problems. Tremendously efficient, the cost of any disruptions of production due to broken equipment, defective raw materials, or worker error is enormous, often running into tens of thousands of dollars per hour of lost production. Thus, worker skills tend to be focused on maintenance, repair, and the design of the system.

Service Process Matrix

Service-oriented businesses share some fundamental similarities to manufacturing, but also differ in critical ways. Two of the most fundamental differences are, first, that customers are much more involved in the service delivery process, and, second, that in most cases inventory cannot be used to buffer fluctuations in demand. The **service process matrix** shown in Exhibit 4 illustrates that service operations can be classified along the dimensions of customer involvement and labor intensity. In general, services allow greater customization and customer involvement for the consumer. While this results in better product fit, it also leads to greater inefficiencies and a greater degree of labor intensity, as human labor is required to provide the flexibility needed to increase customization. As customers become more involved with a service process, they generally receive a more customized product, but at the expense of a loss in production efficiency, thus increasing delivery costs. Thus, one of the key challenges for service processes is to retain the ability to customize and encourage customer involvement without greatly inhibiting production efficiency.

EXHIBIT 4
Service Process Matrix

Source: R.W. Schmenner, "How Can Service Businesses Survive and Prosper?" *Sloan Management Review* 27, no. 3 (1986), pp. 21–32, 1986.

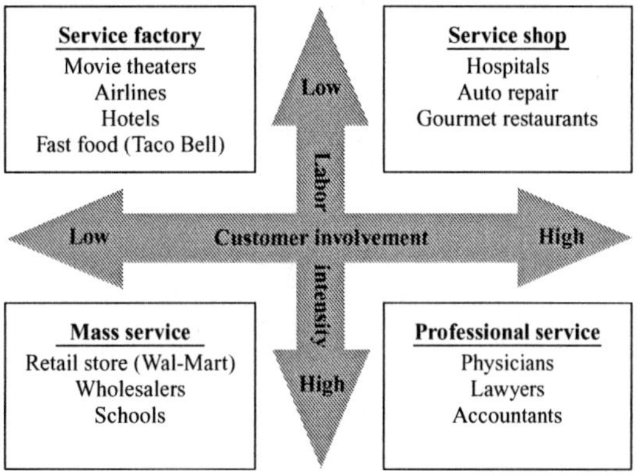

Service Factory

Services with both low customer contact/customization and a low degree of labor intensity are classified as **service factories.** Similar to continuous flow processes in manufacturing, the facilities and equipment in service factories account for a large fraction of costs. Much of the transportation industry (airlines, trucking companies), hotels, and fast-food establishments can be classified as service factories because of low customer contact, customization, and low labor intensity. Consider a major airline such as Delta. Customers tend not to be highly involved in the process of setting flight times or options. While you may be able to choose either the 8 AM flight or the 11 AM flight from Chicago to Seattle, individual customers do not have input regarding the exact time a flight will leave. Similarly, customers do not have input regarding what type of aircraft will be used, what amount of individual seat space will be provided (much to many passengers' chagrin!), or when or what meal will be served. While service factories have a fairly high amount of labor content relative to manufacturing enterprises, the degree of labor intensity is fairly low compared to other service businesses. For example, airlines average around $150,000 to $200,000 revenue per employee, a level much higher than that for Mass Services.

Service Shop

Services with low labor intensity but high customer contact/customization are classified as **Service Shops.** Similar to a job shop–process in the manufacturing industry, service shops can provide various types of customized services for their customers. Hospitals and auto and other repair services are excellent examples of service shops. Service shops tend to focus on issues such as employee scheduling, work control, and technology selection. Since the range of jobs is so variable, the control and scheduling are critical components. The degree of capital investment can be considerable. For example, the equipment in a hospital such as MRI machines, x-ray equipment, and operating rooms can cost millions of dollars.

Mass Service

Mass services have low customer contact/customization in combination with high labor intensity. Retail companies, wholesaling, and schools are examples of mass service. Consider a large retail store such as a Wal-Mart. Transactions are fairly standardized with customer contact for the most part only involving entering price/item information and ringing up a bill of sale. A primary goal in this setting is to minimize the number of exceptions such as returned items, irate customers, or out-of-stock items. These exceptions cause costly disruptions to the highly standardized business operations in mass services.

Professional Service

Professional services have both high customer contact/customization and a high degree of labor intensity. Services provided by doctors, lawyers, accountants, and architects all have very high labor costs due to the large amount of education associated with these professions. In addition, these services tend to be highly customized according to the particular situation/need of each customer. A common approach to managing these services is to separate the business into front-office operations that have close contact with customers (i.e. doctors examining patients) and back-office operations that deal with ancillary issues that do not require such high skills. For example, physicians' offices typically have a group of clerks whose primary job is to file insurance papers, send and receive patient bills, and schedule/monitor appointments. While these tasks are certainly of critical importance, they generally require less skill and are compensated at a much lower level.

Layout Types

The physical orientation, or layout, of departments or work centers within an organization are defined by the general pattern of work and material flow. The three basic **layout types** include process layouts, product layouts, and fixed-position layouts. Hybrid layouts (group technology, also known as cellular manufacturing) combine features of these basic layouts.

Process Layout

Process layouts group machines, equipment, or people with similar functions or goals together. A machine shop generally has all the presses in one area, the lathes in another, and the drills in a third area. Similarly, a copy shop might have all the copiers in one area, computers in another, and faxes and scanning machines in a third area. Parts or jobs travel from area to area, depending on what machines or work centers are required for that part/job. This type of layout is used when there is a large degree of variety in the jobs and no standard set of equipment required for each job. Since demand for each product is fairly low, it is not economically feasible to dedicate either equipment or people to a single task. The flow tends to be jumbled in a process layout because of the varied paths taken by different jobs or products.

Product Layout

Product layouts dedicate equipment and workers to specific products on a linear route. When volumes for a particular product are high, resources can be specialized and designed for a specific product. A good example is the making of lunches for a school picnic: students might be lined up at a counter and assigned repetitive tasks. The first student would apply mayonnaise or mustard to the bread, the second would add the meat, the third would add lettuce and/or tomatoes, and the fourth would put the sandwiches in bags. Product layouts can be dedicated to a single product or can be mixed-model lines (as in the case of the sandwich line, each sandwich can be a little different by adding mustard or mayonnaise at stage one; turkey, beef, or ham at stage two; and lettuce, tomato, or onions at stage 3—for a total of $2 \times 3 \times 3 = 18$ sandwich combinations). Product lines are often in a straight line, but also can follow an L, O, S, or U shape.

Exhibit 5 shows examples of process versus product layouts, while Exhibit 6 compares the advantages of each layout type.

EXHIBIT 5
Layout Types

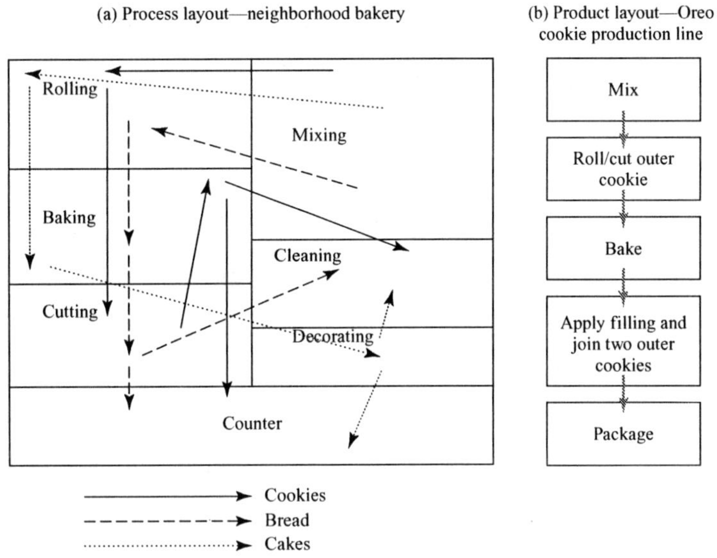

EXHIBIT 6
Comparison of Advantages and Disadvantages for Process and Product Layouts

Process Layouts	Product Layouts
Advantages	
• Resources are general purpose and less capital intensive	• Faster processing rates
• Flexibility is high—can adapt easily to changes in product mix or volume	• Lower inventories (and faster throughput)
• Capacity utilization is high because of the ability to perform multiple jobs/tasks on each piece of equipment	• Fewer changeovers, less material handling, more efficient
Disadvantages	
• Frequent changeovers result in lost production time	• Low flexibility
• High inventory levels necessary to compensate for variable output rates	• Low utlization for lower-volume products
• Product throughput time can be very long	• High risk of layout redesign for products/ services with uncertain life cycles
• Production planning and control are challenging	

Fixed-Position Layout

A **fixed-position layout** requires the product (due to its extreme weight or size) to remain at its location. The equipment required for each step must be moved to the site. Construction sites, shipyards, movie studios, airplane plants, and road construction are typical fixed-position layouts. One of the primary challenges of this layout type is scheduling workers and equipment so that they don't conflict or bump into each other. Thus, this layout type is most often associated with a project.

Hybrid Layout

Hybrid layouts include **group technology** or **cellular layouts,** which attempt to combine the advantages of process and product layouts by grouping disparate machines into work centers or cells to work on products that have similar shapes and processing requirements. Group technology groups parts or products with similar characteristics into a family and then dedicates a group of machines and persons to the production of that family. Families may be based on size, shape (all parts are round or square), demand, manufacturing, or routing requirements. A family represents a set of products with similar processing requirements. The goal is to smooth the flow of these items while minimizing the need for changeovers and setups. By locating the machines and workers close together in a cellular layout, the distance the parts must travel is shortened and the workers' experience producing the parts is focused. The production of sandwiches at a Subway is a form of group technology—the resources are devoted to producing a family of sandwiches that have a degree of variation but are fundamentally similar in the steps needed for their production. Exhibit 7 illustrates the cell development process followed by Rockwell's Telecommunication Division, maker of wave-guide parts. Part A shows the original process-oriented layout; part B, the planned relocation of process based on parts-family production requirments; and part C, an enlarged layout of the cell designed to perform all but the finishing operation. According to Schonberger, cellular organization was practical here because (1) distinct parts families existed; (2) there were several of each type of machine, so taking a machine out of a cluster did not rob the cluster of all its capacity, leaving no way to produce other products; (3) the work centers were easily moveable stand-alone machine tools—heavy, but anchored to the floor rather simply. He adds that these three features represent general guidelines for deciding where cells make sense.

Strategy and Process Choice

Matching the strategy an organization follows with an appropriate process choice is a critical decision. Typically, operations that produce a wide range of products or service choices will employ processes in the upper left quadrant of the product-process matrix such as project, job, or batch. In contrast, companies that focus on achieving the lowest possible cost per unit are more likely to standardize their operations and use either a line or continuous flow process. The vignette at the beginning of this module on baking the right way illustrates how different processes can be employed to meet different strategic objectives.

United Airlines and Southwest Airlines provide another example of differing processes. While they operate in the same industry and largely employ the same basic technologies, there are numerous areas where they have different processes to support strategic differences. Southwest Airlines focuses primarily on low cost. In order to support this focus, Southwest utilizes a single plane type (which makes maintenance, scheduling, and turnaround time easier to manage), simplifies their check-in procedure so that customers do not have assigned seats, and does not serve meals (saving on the need to schedule catering and cleaning for planes, as well as reducing the need to hire extra flight attendants and have more kitchen space on each plane). While these process choices reduce cost, they also sacrifice much of the flexibility and quality that is prized by more full-service airlines such as United. For example, United employs several plane types that provide much greater flexibility in terms of the routes they fly.

EXHIBIT 7

Developing a Cell to Produce Wave-Guide Parts

From Chase, Aquilano & Jacobs, *Operations Management for Competitive Advantage*, 9th edition, McGraw Hill

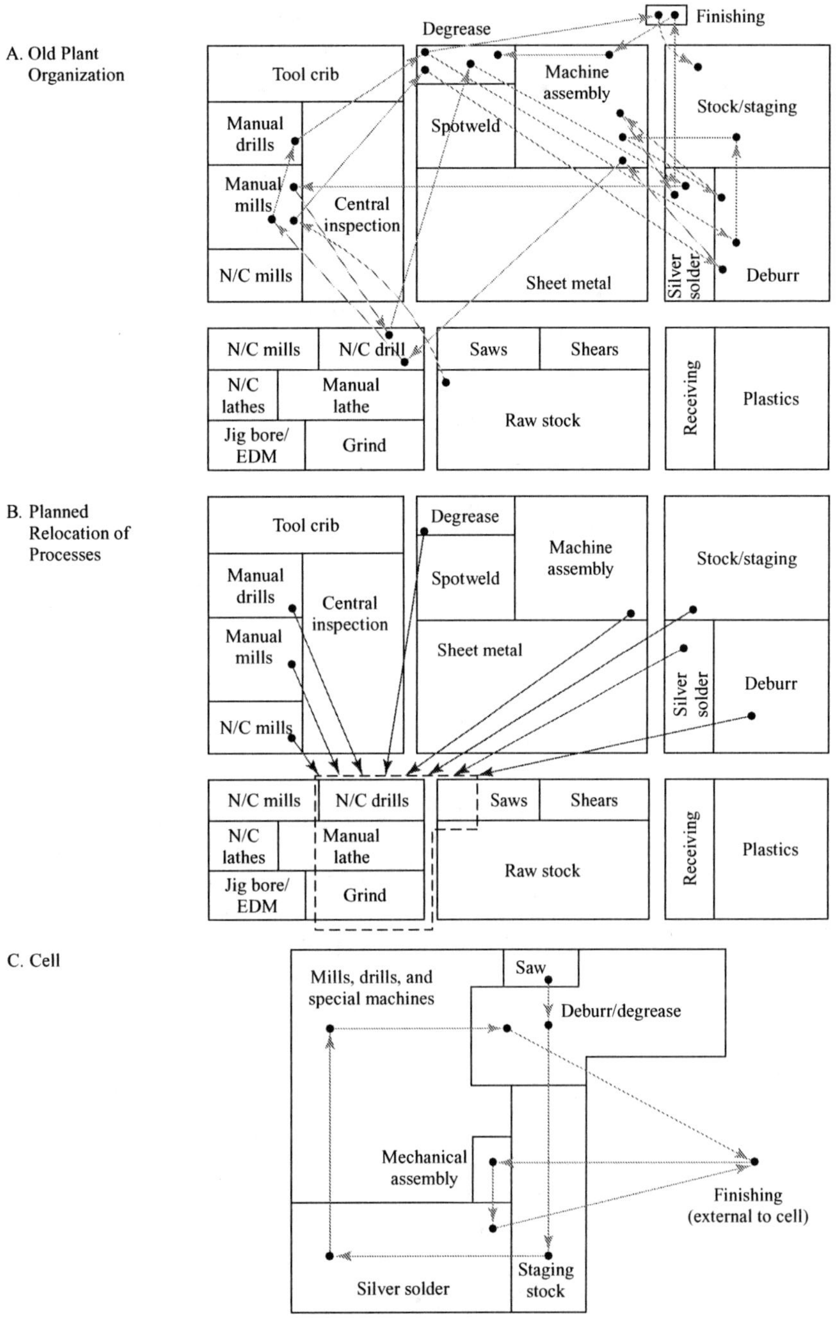

Technology Impacts

Technology was a major driver of changes in process design throughout the 20th century and will continue to have a large impact as we move into the 21st century. The foundations of mass production were laid in the early 1900s by men such as Henry Ford and Frederick Winslow Taylor based on new technologies such as standardized parts and machine tools, improved gasoline engines, assembly-line techniques, and many others. Office and service work have been similarly affected by improvements in transportation, office equipment (such as electric typewriters, photocopiers, and telephones), and construction techniques, including improved lighting and central air conditioning and heating. Numerous technologies affecting the business environment at the end of the 20th century included electronic devices such as cellular phones, personal digital assistants, and computers; genetic advances in identifying genes and related therapies; and materials advances that provide improved raw materials.

Describe three technologies that have been developed in the last five years. How does each of these change business processes?

The connection of millions of individual computers and users through the Internet has provided one of the largest process design shifts business has experienced. The Internet allows companies to market product directly to consumers, thus cutting out middlemen completely. Alternatively, the Internet allows much improved communication where businesses can more easily track their key inputs and outputs. When consumers order goods over the Internet, the business fulfilling that order does not have to have the same physical person actually answer the phone or greet the customer. While there is still a need for someone to fill the order (i.e., pick the goods or service requested and ship/deliver to the consumer), this transaction can now be more specialized and buffered. In other words, a company such as Office Depot does not need to have a large number of operators standing buy to take orders over the telephone. Instead, it can have a crew of e-mail operators—this crew can be smaller because demand does not need to be filled instantaneously (i.e., if a phone is busy, the customer may hang up rather than wait on hold). In addition, Internet transactions often have the benefit of self-sourcing, wherein some of the work of inputting data is shifted to consumers. Consider a bank that formerly had many tellers. Now that consumers can enter their own transactions via ATM or the Internet, the bank can greatly cut back on its workforce.

Designing Processes

Break-Even Analysis

Break-even analysis is a basic mathematical technique that allows a comparison of total costs for different processes such as using general-purpose equipment that can be used for multiple tasks or dedicated equipment designed for a single standardized task. This technique takes the fixed costs of buying or developing a process or technology and adds the variable costs for producing each unit and finds the break-even point for which the cost of two or more processes are equal in cost. For example, consider a small neighborhood bookstore that can buy a software package for $5,000 per year that will handle all of its sales and inventory transactions, but the software is written to be general purpose and applicable to many different businesses. Thus, the per-transaction cost (based on the labor time taken to perform each transaction) is $0.50. The bookstore also can buy a customized software package that costs $10,000 per year, but since it is designed specifically for this bookstore, it will handle each transaction for $0.20. Which software package should the store buy if it will handle 15,000 transactions per year?

The break-even point is found by setting the cost equations for each piece of software equal to each other. The cost equation is equal to the fixed cost of equipment plus the variable cost per unit times the number of units produced. Solving for the number of units produced provides the break-even quantity.

Specialized Software **General-Purpose Software**

$$\$10{,}000 + \$0.20 \times Q = \$5{,}000 + \$0.50 \times Q$$

Where Q = Number of units produced

Solve for Q:

$$\$5{,}000 = \$0.30\ Q$$

$$Q = 16{,}666.66 \text{ units}$$

Exhibit 8 illustrates the relationship between the two software packages. If the bookstore is going to have 15,000 transactions per year, it should buy the general-purpose software since the break-even point is 16,667 units. The specialized software would be cheaper if the bookstore would have more than 16,667 transactions a year.

EXHIBIT 8
Break-Even Analysis for Process Choice

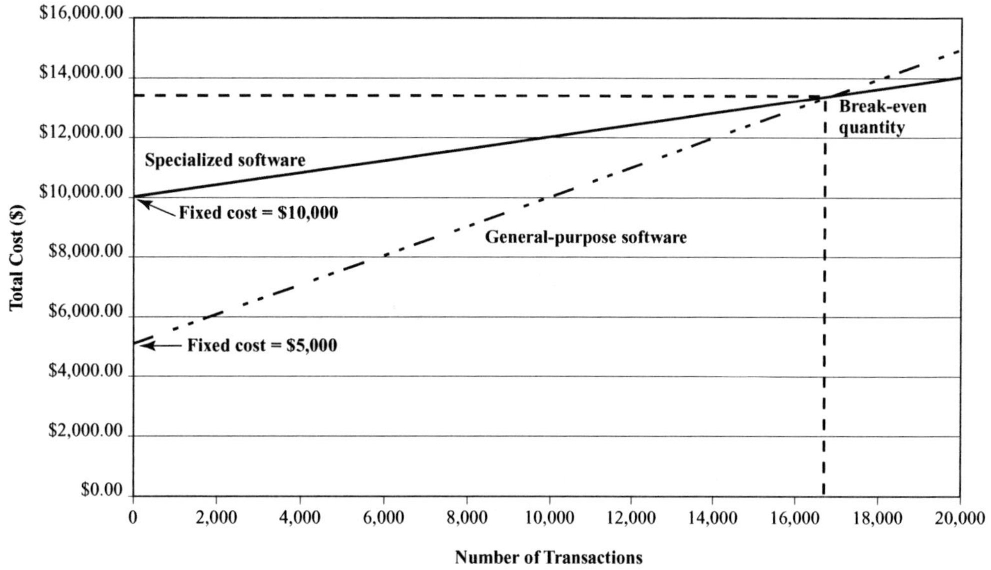

Break-even analysis can be used for a variety of basic process choices. Another example is choosing whether to manufacture a product in house or to outsource it to a subcontractor.

Reengineering

"Even when I was young I suspected that much might be done in a better way."

Henry Ford

Reengineering involves a shift from a functional perspective of the business to a process-oriented perspective. Reengineering arose as an important business initiative in the early 1990s following the lead of consultants such as Michael Hammer and James Champy (with their best-selling book *Reengineering the Corporation: A Manifesto for Business Revolution*) and James Harrington and Thomas Davenport. The goal is to identify core processes that add value to the finished product or service and eliminate steps that are inefficient or non–value adding. Many of these inefficiencies result from communications difficulties caused by the separation of functional departments into silos. A primary component of reengineering involves drawing flowcharts of processes "as is," or as they currently exist. Then, a flowchart is developed to show the process as it "should be." This ideal process is often more efficient because it sheds repetitive tasks, non–value adding tasks, and other wasteful activities that are the result of changes that have occurred over a long timespan since the original process was put into place.

Process Analysis Techniques

Flowcharting (also called Process Mapping)

Flowcharting involves graphically portraying the key elements, steps, participants, and materials of a process. Process modeling provides a means of quickly conveying the key elements of a process, or, as the saying goes, "a picture is worth a thousand words." Both current and future business processes can be diagrammed. This technique helps illustrate areas where improvements can be made and steps eliminated. In addition, the steps involved in documenting processes help develop a thorough understanding.

The goal is to reveal the departments involved and allow people to (1) see the sequence of steps, (2) draw boundaries around the process, (3) identify key players and functional groups within the bounded process, (4) identify handoffs between subprocesses, and (5) identify supplier/customer interfaces. Exhibit 9, on page 14, provides an example of a flowchart for the process of taking orders for tickets by telephone for the Chicago Symphony Orchestra.

EXHIBIT 9
Flowchart for Chicago Symphony Orchestra Telephone Ticketing

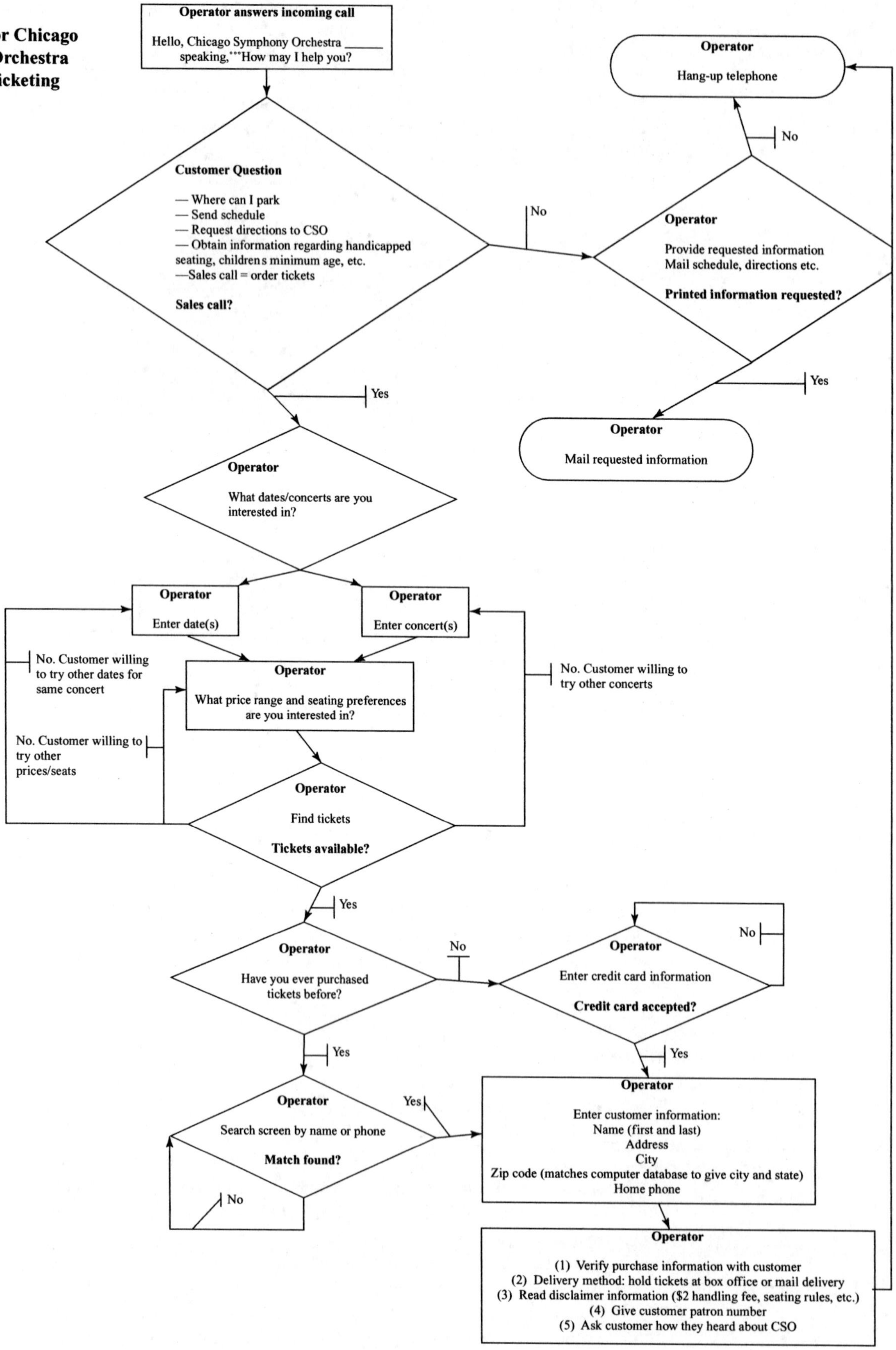

In Practice

WEBVAN AND TESCO: A NEW WAY TO SHOP FOR GROCERIES—BUT WHERE IS THE VALUE?

During the Internet frenzy of 1998–2000, several companies made huge bets that selling groceries on-line was a growth market and represented a new way of doing business. Companies such as Webvan and Peapod collected customer orders on-line and delivered groceries directly to consumer's houses. Traditional grocery stores have a very low profit margin, typically earning less than 1 percent on every dollar of sales. The key to profitability is to move groceries in large volumes. In theory, selling groceries on-line offers numerous process advantages. First, workforce costs can be lowered because there no longer is the same need to estimate how many cashiers and clerks to have working during every hour of operation—on-line grocers receive the order, then fill the order sometime during the next 24 hours according to scheduling. This ability to aggregate many orders helps reduce the need to schedule extra employees to handle fluctuations in demand. Second, on-line grocers can save on storage and display costs since the customers never see the warehouse. Third, purchasing costs should be lower since these companies are buying in very large quantities and do not have to break orders up across numerous smaller stores. In order to capitalize on these potential efficiencies, Webvan invested over a billion dollars to build automated warehouse and distribution facilities in 26 markets. Their Suwanee, Georgia, distribution center was a 350,000-square-foot warehouse the size of 18 traditional grocery stores. Automated machinery was used to assist workers in filling multiple orders fast and efficiently. Webvan made extensive use of process design tools such as simulation to maximize the efficiency of their distribution centers.[1]

However, as Webvan and other on-line grocers discovered the hard way, there are also numerous challenges and drawbacks to on-line groceries. First and foremost, the delivery of groceries to the customer presents severe logistical difficulties. Companies such as Webvan and Peapod seek to deliver groceries within either a 30-minute or 2-hour delivery window. The tighter the window, the more consumers like the service, but tight windows make deliveries difficult. It is this *last mile* that proved to be a crucial barrier to making on-line groceries a viable business model. Webvan could not make their processes cost competitive with traditional grocers such as Kroger, Meijer, or Safeway. In short, their value proposition was not matched to their process. Webvan tried to build market share by offering groceries delivered to a customer's door in a specified 30-minute window at prices comparable to what consumers get by doing the shopping themselves. Webvan's process was simply unable to meet this challenge. Hindsight being 20–20, it is possible that Webvan could have been more successful by utilizing a process that focused less on providing groceries at low cost and more on providing timely delivery. Sure, the market would not have been as large, but there are consumers that would pay more for convenience—however, this market is certainly much smaller than a majority of the market as Webvan appeared to believe. In short, Webvan went bankrupt—falling from a high market value of $1.35 billion to the $2.7 million for which Louis Borders sold his 45 million shares (at 6 cents per share) in July 2001.[2]

In contrast to Webvan, Tesco, Britain's leading grocer, has implemented a very different process for providing on-line ordering of groceries. First, Tesco is marketing on-line groceries as a convenience, not as a low price option—charging customers an $8 delivery charge in addition to the retail cost of groceries. Second, Tesco has kept the operations of grocery delivery simple by using existing assets rather than building high-tech warehouses. On-line orders are filled by Tesco employees at the nearest Tesco store, then picked up and delivered via van. This approach works much better for lower volumes of business, albeit at a high cost per order, than Webvan's high fixed-investment, low variable-cost approach—which was only viable with a very high volume of orders. The net result is that Tesco had sales of $336 million in 2000, making it the world's largest on-line grocery.[3]

[1] E. O'Briant, "Webvan Revs Up," *IIE Solutions*, September 2000, pp. 26–33.

[2] T. Rizzo, "The Death of Webvan—Rest in Peace and Good Riddance to a Value-Chain Illiterate," *Internet World*, August 1, 2001, pp. 4–5.

[3] R. Tomlinson, "A British E-Grocer Takes on Amazon," *Fortune*, June 12, 2000, pp. 246–55; and J. R. Hagerty and J. Hall "British Supermarkets Giant Cooks Up Plans to Go Global—Tesco's Move to Duplicate High Growth at Home Comes with Big Risks," *The Wall Street Journal*, July 5, 2001, p. A9.

> Webvan does have some real assets, in particular 'the state of the art' distribution centers they built. I place that phrase in quotation marks because the state of the art is only valuable *if it actually works* within the value chain of a given business.
>
> *Tony Rizzo, Internet World*

Can you make a list of the ways that processes might differ between an on-line grocer and a traditional grocery store? For example, how is the checkout process going to differ? How will an on-line grocer schedule deliveries to ensure timeliness? How should factors such as traffic, accidents, missing customers, and so forth be accounted for in order to minimize late deliveries? Finally, how can on-line grocery shopping be faster for the customer? Should it take less time total for you to enter your order and the company to pick and deliver it than if you went to a traditional grocery store?

Simulation

Process **simulation** employs computer software to develop a visual model of a process that incorporates multiple workcenters, inputs, and processing techniques as variables. Different scenarios can be evaluated without actually changing processes and disrupting business as usual. As computer power has increased over the last two decades, simulation programs have been developed that can model business processes in such detail that entire factories can be represented. While simulation has historically been used primarily in manufacturing, there is an increasing emphasis on service processes. For example, a computer simulation could be developed to show the flow of customers through the checkout line at a grocery store. Variables that could be incorporated and studied in such a model might include the number of baggers (by assisting the cashier and specializing the work each performs, customers should flow through the checkout line faster) or the time required to check each customer out (i.e., what is the effect of the person who forgets his or her checkbook or the effect of a price check?). There are numerous software programs that can be employed for simulation analysis.[1]

From-to Charts

One of the most fundamental principles for managing and designing multistep, materials-oriented processes is to minimize the distance traveled by pieces, components, and finished products. While a variety of analysis techniques exist, the most elementary involves developing **from-to charts** that show the number of trips or the amount of materials flowing between different departments or workcenters. The number of trips between departments/workcenters is measured for each pair and shown in a chart like that in Exhibit 10. These trips can be weighted according to importance, difficulty, or some other criteria. For example, a patient moving between registration and an exam room might not receive as high a weight as a specimen being sent from emergency to the laboratory, since the test to be performed on the specimen might be critically important.

When the trips in Exhibit 10(A) are weighted equally, we can compare the two alternative layouts shown in Exhibit 10(B). This is done by computing the **Load × Distance** by multiplying the number of trips in Exhibit 10(A) by the distances in Exhibit 10(C). The distances in (C) are simple distances where adjoining cells are assigned a distance of 1 (e.g., registration and the birthing center in Layout 1), while cells not directly connected are given a distance of 2 or 3 (e.g., the exam room and registration in Layout 1). The Load × Distance score for Layout 1 is calculated as

$$\mathrm{LD} = \sum_{i=1}^{N} \sum_{j=1}^{N} L_{ij} C_{ij} D_{ij}$$

where L_{ij} represents the number of trips or loads moving between department i and department j in a time period, C_{ij} represents the weight for that load (as noted earlier, lab tests moving from emergency to the laboratory might receive a higher weight than patients moving from registration to an exam room), and D_{ij} represents the distances between departments. The distance (D_{ij}) is the only variable, since it can be varied based on different assignments of departments to locations. In situations where all loads are considered to have equal weight, C_{ij} is set equal to 1 (this is the case in this problem). For example, let's compare layouts 1 and 2:

$$\begin{aligned}\text{LD (Layout 1)} &= 0 \times (1) + 20 \times (2) + 10 \times (1) + 40 \times (2) + 50 \times (3) + 20 \times (1) + \\ &\quad 10 \times (2) + 25 \times (1) + 5 \times (2) + 0 \times (3) + 15 \times (2) + 20 \times (1) + \\ &\quad 45 \times (1) + 5 \times (2) + 30 \times (1) \\ &= 510\end{aligned}$$

[1] See C. Harrell, B. Ghosh, and R. Bowden, *Simulation Using ProModel* (Boston: McGraw-Hill, 2000); or D. Kelton, R. Sadowski, and D. Sadowski, *Simulation with Arena,* 2nd ed. (New York: McGraw-Hill, 2000).

EXHIBIT 10
From-to Charts
(A) From-to chart for Southeastern Hospital

Room	Registration	Emergency	X-ray	Birthing Center	Laboratory	Exam
Registration	—					
Emergency	0	—				
X-ray	20	20	—			
Birthing Center	10	10	0	—		
Laboratory	40	25	15	45	—	
Exam Room	50	5	20	5	30	—

(B) Alternative layouts for Southeastern Hospital

Layout 1

Registration	Emergency	X-ray
Birthing Center	Laboratory	Exam Room

Revised Layout 2

X-ray	Laboratory	Birthing Center
Exam Room	Registration	Emergency

(C) Distance chart for Southeastern Hospital

[*Note:* Distances in parentheses () are for Layout 2 in (B)]

Room	Registration	Emergency	X-ray	Birthing Center	Laboratory	Exam
Registration	—					
Emergency	1 (1)	—				
X-ray	2 (2)	1 (3)	—			
Birthing Center	1 (2)	2 (1)	3 (2)	—		
Laboratory	2 (1)	1 (2)	2 (1)	1 (1)	—	
Exam room	3 (1)	2 (2)	1 (1)	2 (3)	1 (2)	—

$$\begin{aligned}\text{LD (Layout 2)} &= 0 \times (1) + 20 \times (2) + 10 \times (2) + 40 \times (1) + 50 \times (1) + 20 \times (3) + \\ &\quad 10 \times (1) + 25 \times (2) + 5 \times (2) + 0 \times (2) + 15 \times (1) + 20 \times (1) + \\ &\quad 45 \times (1) + 5 \times (3) + 30 \times (2) \\ &= 435\end{aligned}$$

Thus, based on the Load × Distance score, the second layout is more efficient. The improvement comes from moving registration closer to both the laboratory (the distance changes from 2 to 1) and the exam room (distance changes from 3 to 1). This technique, or one of several variations, can be applied to many facility layout decisions.

Is Layout 2 the optimal layout for Southeastern Hospital, or can you develop a more efficient layout?

Process Selection—The Process Swamp

The key to maximizing process value from process analysis and redesign techniques such as reengineering, flowcharting, simulation, and from-to charts is choosing processes to improve that will have the greatest impact. Business organizations have hundreds of processes including things such as purchasing, production planning, quality assessment, personnel recruiting, research and development, market research, and succession planning. Numerous examples of reengineering have been offered as both success and failure stories. While large operational improvements may seem impressive, the bottom-line profitability of the business may not improve. Numerous paradoxical outcomes have been cited, such as the insurance company that cuts claims processing time by 44 percent yet still experiences a drop in profits.[2] The difference between success and failure is often choosing the right process. It is critical that the customer be considered in every decision, since the end result must be an improvement in perceived value. For example, total quality management often

[2] G. Hall, R. Rosenthal, and J. Wade, "How to Make Reengineering Really Work," *Harvard Business Review*, November–December 1993.

simplifies processes by reducing the focus to manufacturing related or tangible-output-related processes that can be objectively measured. Yet, this approach ignores more intangible processes such as product development or customer relations. Process management must be viewed as a holistic approach involving the improvement of all processes, but with priority on the ones that *most matter to consumers.*

Self-Sourcing

Self-sourcing includes customers in the process in a way that reduces the resource demands on the organization providing the product or service while also providing the customer with improved service. Salad bars and self-service gasoline are excellent examples of well-established self-sourcing practices. Allowing customers in restaurants to make their own salads provides an increased level of choice and control of both ingredients and portions for the customer. From the restaurant's perspective, the self-serve salad bar is easier to maintain since the restaurant employees do not have to make every salad. Similarly, self-service gasoline results in a dramatic increase in productivity for gas stations since fewer employees are needed to process sales when the customers pump their own gas. Customers like this service because it is generally quicker and cheaper. However, companies must be aware that self-sourcing can lead to unforeseen changes in other components of the business. For example, salad bars require frequent restocking and cleaning, which may be hard to control because they are separated from the rest of the food preparation areas. Similarly, salad bars require measures to control customer behavior so that the food is not harmed (i.e., glass sneeze guards and signs asking that plates be used only *once*). Self-service gasoline also requires new procedures since customers have a tendency to forget to pay, forget to return the pump handle to the pump, or many other things that can be costly or dangerous.

A critical advantage of the Internet is that it provides new ways to self-source that are beneficial to both consumers and companies. The sale of airplane tickets allows customers to browse at their leisure, often quicker than if they telephone the company directly, while also offering a better view of the various flight options. Perhaps most importantly, websites such as Travelocity allow consumers to compare prices for several airlines. From the airline's perspective, sales over the Internet allow customers to connect directly into their computer system without the need to have a battery of phone operators waiting for customers to call, at which point the operators must then read the same information to the customer. Clearly, it is in the airline's advantage to cut the operator out of the process if their main role is simply to relay information. Thus, Internet ticket sales can be very cost effective while simultaneously offering more choice and better visibility. A potential drawback to the use of the Internet is that it requires greater technical knowledge on the part of the company's employees and the Internet site itself must be designed in a way that is easy to understand and navigate. In addition, there are serious challenges regarding data entry errors such as when a consumer accidentally chooses an unintended flight or destination. The best way to prevent these errors is to simplify the ordering process, but some procedures must be developed to handle the inevitable errors that result.

What other types of self-sourcing can you think of? What are the advantages and challenges this provides to consumers and companies? In particular, what are the benefits and challenges of self-sourcing on the Internet?

Outsourcing

Over the past decade, outsourcing of noncore production and service activities to external suppliers has become a common method to streamline and improve processes. **Outsourcing** involves selecting suppliers with an expertise in a particular area of business to produce and deliver a component part or service to another company. The use of outsourcing has increased for two primary reasons. First, the total quality management movement in the 1980s helped create an awareness in companies that it is difficult to be world class in multiple activities and that settling for second-best products produced in house just to maintain the work within a single organization was not the best approach. Second, the rapid increase in capabilities of information technologies and other communication devices has made it much easier to manage multitier supply chains. For example, first electronic data interchange (EDI) and now the Internet provide a quick and efficient method of communicating across organizational boundaries. Thus, many companies choose to focus on a single aspect of their business in which they are world class and then outsource many noncore activities.

As e-commerce has boomed over the last several years, numerous companies have discovered that while they are good at traditional aspects of their business, they are not skilled at developing and maintaining the complex IT infrastructure necessary to support Internet transactions. Thus, many companies are choosing to concentrate on the mortar part of their "clicks and mortar" business while outsourcing the IT responsibilities, or the clicks, to companies such as @Manage. This company offers real-time monitoring of network devices, applications, services, and URLs and allows companies to concentrate on the areas in which they are skilled. Similar applications of outsourcing can be found in South Korea, where members of the long monopolistic chaebols—Samsung, Hyundai, LG Group, and SK Group—are increasingly teaming with Internet start-up firms to share expertise. Samsung has used leading local Internet-solutions company Enet to provide back-office Internet software for use in the global business-to-business chemical site www.chemCross.com.

Module Summary

This module has summarized the basic process structures that businesses adopt. These general process types are categorized on the product-process matrix according to a basic trade-off between efficiency/volume/low unit cost and flexibility of production for manufacturing into five groups: project, job shop, batch, line flow, and continuous flow. Organizations that employ each of these general process structures share similar characteristics with respect to the type of technology, degree of human skill/involvement, volume of production, flexibility with respect to different products, types of layout, and so forth. While there are numerous types of each overall process (line process, for example), the similarities are generally more numerous than the differences. Service operations can be classified according to a similar scheme: the service process matrix that categorizes processes as service factories, service shops, mass services, or professional services. These general process types differ in terms of the degree of customer involvement versus the degree of labor intensity.

There are four general classes of layouts that are used for these process types. Product layouts where equipment is dedicated to individual products or product families are used for high-volume processes (line, continuous, service factory), while process layouts organized by equipment type are used for lower-volume processes (batch, job shop, professional service). Two special types of layouts include fixed position, for extremely large, project processes such as construction or ship building, and hybrid layouts that employ group technology to group equipment by product families in an effort to capture the best features of both process and product layouts.

Finally, this module examined some basic process analysis tools. These tools include large-scale process redesign in reengineering; basic analytical tools such as break-even, flowcharting, simulation, and from-to charts; and conceptual methods for creating new process relationships such as self-sourcing and outsourcing. Managing processes to fit the strategic objectives of the business is a fundamental facet of successful organizations. Businesses in the same industry can employ very different processes to fit widely varying strategic objectives. This module has provided an introduction to the general process types and analytical tools. The module on Process Management provides much more detailed methods and insights into this critical area.

Key Terms

Batch process, *6*
Break-even analysis, *12*
Cellular layouts, *10*
Continuous flow process, *6*
Fixed-position layout, *10*
Flowcharting, *13*
From-to charts, *16*
Group technology, *10*
Hybrid layouts *10*
Job shop process, *5*
Layout types, *8*
Line flow process, *6*
Load × Distance, *16*
Mass services, *8*
Outsourcing, *18*
Process layout, *8*
Product layout, *9*
Product-process matrix, *4*
Project, *5*
Professional services, *8*
Reengineering, *13*
Self-sourcing, *18*
Service factories, *7*
Service process matrix, *7*
Service shops, *8*
Simulation, *16*

Discussion Questions

1. What type of process does a fast-food restaurant such as Taco Bell or Burger King employ? How does this type of process differ from that used by a more upscale restaurant such as the Russian Tea Room in New York City? How does a Bennigans compare to each of these?
2. What are the key challenges in running a line process? How would you manage inventory, scheduling, workforce, and so on?
3. Describe ways in which the processes at an on-line bookseller such as Amazon.com would differ from those at a traditional bookseller such as a Little Professor. For example, how would the books be inventoried and categorized? Draw a flowchart for the process of filling one customer order for each type of bookstore. Are there different quality concerns for each type?
4. Provide three examples of self-sourcing. How do each of these examples benefit the business providing the product/service? The customer?
5. What activities should a hotel consider outsourcing? Why? What activities would you consider outsourcing in your business?
6. What are the major challenges for a professional service process such as a doctor's office? How is patient scheduling done? How is billing conducted?
7. Draw a flowchart of a process in your business or past experience. Does the flowchart of how the process is currently done exactly match how it should be done? Can you find any opportunities for improving the process?
8. Give three examples of project processes. What are the five biggest keys to running a project successfully?

Problems

1. Hank's Hamburgers can prepare its hamburger patties manually for a fixed cost of zero and a variable cost of 5 cents ($0.05) per patty. Hank's could also buy a hamburger pressing machine for an annual cost of $400 that would reduce the variable cost to make each hamburger to 3 cents ($0.03) per patty. Use break-even analysis to determine the number of hamburgers Hank's must make each year to make the hamburger-pressing machine the more attractive choice.
2. Catalyst Camcorders manufacturers combination video camera/personal digital assistants that allow videotaping and Internet access/posting of videotapes from the same piece of equipment. Catalyst is considering outsourcing the production of an internal circuit board for the camera/PDA. This component can be outsourced for an annual administrative cost of $2,000 per year and a production cost of $4 per board. Alternatively, Catalyst can lease equipment to manufacture the circuit board for $20,000 per year and produce the circuit boards for $3.50 per board. If the anticipated production in the first year is 25,000 boards, what would you recommend that Catalyst do?
3. A printing company named Speedy Printing has three choices for the process of printing promotional fliers. The first choice is to print the fliers using a basic personal computer and color printer. This method involves a start-up cost of $1,500 for equipment and the fliers would cost an additional $1.10 per unit. The second choice would be to invest in a general-purpose printing press for $2,500, in which case the fliers would cost $0.90 a piece. Finally, Speedy could invest in a specialized printing press that would cost $6,000 to buy and $0.80 per unit to operate. Graph the break-even quantities for these options.
4. The table below provides a from-to chart of the number of trips between eight departments in the corporate offices of the May-BUR-Insured company. Calculate the load distance score for the current layout given below. Is this the best possible layout based on the data given in the table? If not, develop a layout that reduces the Load × Distance score.

From-to Chart for May-BUR-Insured

Department	A	B	C	D	E	F	G	H
A	—							
B	50	—						
C	40	20	—					
D	30	70	25	—				
E	80	30	100	40	—			
F	55	40	10	20	30	—		
G	20	35	10	10	40	120	—	
H	10	15	0	50	50	40	20	—

Current Layout for May-BUR-Insured

E	B	G	A
H	F	D	C

5. Sam's Scooters is a medium-sized, batch-process producer of scooters. The table below provides a from-to chart of the number of trips between the departments in Sam's production facility. Develop a layout that minimizes the Load × Distance score.

From-to Chart for Sam's Scooters

Department	Shipping	Assembly	Painting	Parts Fabrication	Stockroom	Quality Control
Shipping	—					
Assembly	150	—				
Painting	10	100	—			
Parts Fabrication	80	120	50	—		
Stockroom	20	70	10	60	—	
Quality Control	50	90	20	0	15	—

Cases

PRINTING PARTNERS INC.

Hank Olson had worked for a major book publisher, Pony Publishing, for 20 years as a printing press operator. While Hank was very good at his job and enjoyed it, his dream had always been to open his own company. So, in 1999, after his youngest child left for college, he quit to open his own printing firm—Printing Partners Inc. He planned to hire two or three workers to help him run the company, which would specialize in printing catalogs, leaflets, brochures, and other advertising materials for local businesses. In developing his business plan, Hank was fairly confident that he had adequate knowledge of the fundamental procedure for running a printing press, but he wanted to be sure he planned for areas where processes would be different from his work at Pony Publishing.

To start, Hank drew up a plan for locating his equipment. At Pony, all the equipment was arranged in straight lines dedicated to a single product. Paperback books had a dedicated printing press that printed the black and white pages in each book, another press that printed the color pages, a third press that printed the covers, a collator that assembled and matched these three components, and finally a binder that bound the entire book together. This line flow for paperback book production was run only for large volumes, with a minimum production quantity of 5,000 books. The primary job for employees involved setting the line up, which generally took three to four hours to fine-tune the equipment and change the printing plates. Printing press operators were also responsible for watching the equipment for problems and quickly catching any breakdowns. Changeovers from one book to another happened fairly infrequently, generally about once every three or four days. Pony had two other dedicated lines: one for hardcover books with little color content and another for photograph or coffee table books. Each of these had highly specialized equipment designed for specific jobs and was very expensive, with an average investment of $250,000 per line. Since the capital investment for Pony was so high, the company typically scheduled the presses for two to three months in advance in order to minimize downtime.

Hank knew that he needed to design his layout and processes in a substantially different manner. First, he decided that since Printing Partners would be handling smaller jobs (from 500 to 5,000 units on average), his equipment would have to be more flexible. Therefore, he ordered three general-purpose printing presses: one for color pages, one for black and white pages, and one for glossy/cardboard materials. These presses were grouped together since different jobs would require different processing steps. Similarly, he ordered two pieces of binding equipment: one for spiral binding materials and one for hardbound. To develop printing plates, Hank bought a computer-controlled engraver that cost $100,000 and had the ability to download the proofs of each page directly to the engraving machine. This machine used computer technology to offer the flexibility to produce an infinite variety of printing plates, but the cost per plate was substantially higher than the more specialized technology employed at Pony. Finally, Hank knew that the range of skills for his employees needed to be much broader than that of the workers at Pony. The work at Printing Partners ranged from setting up the presses, to collating pages, running the binders, fixing any trouble spots, and so forth. Generally speaking, the workers were much more involved in each production step at Printing Partners than at Pony Printing.

QUESTIONS

1. Draw a basic flowchart for each of the printing companies. What process differences are difficult to show on a material-oriented flowchart? For example, describe the order process and production planning for each company.
2. How will workforce policies differ between the two companies? How does Pony Publishing account for a sick or missing employee? Can they afford to shut down the line for an entire day, or do they arrange for a replacement? How should Printing Partners deal with missing employees?
3. What other differences/similarities should Hank Olson consider when starting his business?
4. As Printing Partners grows (assuming they are successful), how will their process change?

Related Modules of Interest

- Foundations of Process Management
- Advanced Operations Technologies
- Service Operations Management
- Facilities Network Design
- Waiting Line Models
- Project Management
- Process Mapping and Analysis

Selected Readings

Boyer, K. "E-Operations: A Guide to How the Internet Streamlines Operations." *Business Horizons,* v. 44, no. 1, Jan-Feb 2001, pp. 1–8.

Davenport, T. H. *Process Innovation: Reengineering Work Through Information Technology.* Boston: Harvard Business School Press, 1995.

DeToro, I., and A. Tenner. *Process Redesign: The Implementation Guide for Managers.* Reading, MA: Addison-Wesley, 1997.

Hammer, M., and J. Champy. *Reengineering the Corporation: A Manifesto for Business Revolution.* New York: Harper Business, 1993.

Harrell, C., B. Ghosh, and R. Bowden. *Simulation Using ProModel.* Boston: McGraw-Hill, 2000.

Harrington, D. H. *Business Process Improvement: The Breakthrough Strategy to Total Quality, Productivity and Competitiveness.* New York: McGraw-Hill, 1991.

Hayes, R., and S. Wheelwright. *Restoring Our Competitive Edge: Competing Through Manufacturing.* New York: John Wiley & Sons, 1984.

Kelton, D., R. Sadowski, and D. Sadowski. *Simulation with Arena,* 2nd ed. New York: McGraw-Hill, 2000.

Larkin, J. "When Opposites Attract." *Far Eastern Economic Review* 163, no. 36 (September 7, 2000), pp. 34–36.

Metters, R., and V. Vargas. "A Typology of De-coupling Strategies in Mixed Services." *Journal of Operations Management* 18, no. 6 (2000), pp. 663–82.

Moore, C., and J. Jones, "Managed Services Lure Corporations." *Infoworld* 22, no. 39 (September 25, 2000), p. 14.

O'Briant, E. "Webvan Revs Up." *IIE Solutions,* September 2000, pp. 26–33.

Saccomano, A. "Virtual Supermarket." *Traffic World* 259, no. 3 (July 19, 1999), pp. 16–17.

Schmenner, R.W. "How Can Service Businesses Survive and Prosper."? *Sloan Management Review* 27, no. 3 (1986) pp. 21–32.

Verma, R., and K. Boyer. "Service Classification and Management Challenges." *Journal of Business Strategies* 17, no. 1 (2000), pp. 5–24.

Service Operations Management

William Youngdahl
Thunderbird University

McGraw-Hill Irwin

Boston Burr Ridge, IL Dubuque, IA Madison, WI New York San Francisco St. Louis
Bangkok Bogotá Caracas Kuala Lumpur Lisbon London Madrid Mexico City
Milan Montreal New Delhi Santiago Seoul Singapore Sydney Taipei Toronto

Service Operations Management

Module Objectives

By the end of this module, you should be able to

- Understand the importance of and need for a service focus within the value-driven operations management system.
- Develop and implement service delivery system designs that maximize customers' perceptions of service value.
- Assess customers' perceptions of service quality and develop action plans for closing gaps in service design and delivery.
- Develop plans for preventing poor service and for recovering from failed service encounters.
- Describe some impact of the Internet and telecommunications on e-service delivery and service globalization.

My Trip on America West

I just spent 45 minutes buying an upgrade to a roundtrip flight on America West Airlines. And, boy, do I feel like a fool!

My wife, Charlotte, and I had reservations to fly from San Jose to Phoenix and back for a computer-industry conference. We had nonrefundable coach tickets costing $295 per person. On a lark, I decided that we should upgrade to first class. Since I never fly on America West, I would have had to pay for the upgrade.

We arrived at the gate at 9:45 A.M. The flight was scheduled to depart at 10:36. We boarded the plane at 10:30 A.M.

Why the delay? Because buying a simple upgrade at a cost of $250 each way per person took 45 minutes. It required the full-time attention of one of the two gate clerks, as well as assistance from the gate supervisor. Everyone else on the plane had to check in with the one other gate attendant, a process that—of course—took twice as long as usual. As they waited in line, they all could see that I was the one holding things up. And the five other people going to the same conference, all of whom I know pretty well, could see I was holding them up to actually pay for a first-class upgrade! That's why I feel like a fool—like me, the five are frequent travelers, people who should know better than to try to upgrade at the last minute.

Source: Stewart Alsop, "My Trip on America West, or Why Customer Service Still Matters," *Fortune,* November 11, 1999, p. 359.

We begin this module with an experience one customer, Stewart Alsop, had with America West Airlines. It could have been anyone, but this particular customer happened to be a columnist for *Fortune,* a magazine with circulation in the millions and Web-based content to extend the reach even further. Each time service providers come into contact with customers, an opportunity arises to create service disciples, service rebels, or simply indifferent customers who may or may not return for service in the future. Unfortunately, service rebels tend to have a far greater impact on future sales than service disciples. In one study involving the restaurant industry, it was found that the average service disciple tells his story to about seven people, but an average service rebel tells over 50 people. Clearly, Stewart Alsop became a service rebel—spreading his tale of service woe as far and wide as possible.

What result did this customer seek? The quick answer is an upgrade. He got the upgrade. But the service process or experience has as much to do with satisfaction as it does with the outcome or product of the service encounter. Additionally, service customers often play very active roles in the production of service. As seen in this example, how well we play the service game can have a spillover impact on other customers in the service delivery system. The interplay between the psychological aspects of services and the operations in place to deliver the services places an unusual burden on service operations managers relative to those faced by manufacturing counterparts.

Delivering service value requires more than appropriate scheduling and application of quantitative or mathematical models. Defining and delivering service value require one to get into the heads, and even hearts, of customers and employees. The design of service begins with a clear understanding of what customers expect. Often these expectations are based on market research requiring operations managers to work closely with their marketing counterparts. Additionally, the selection and training of service personnel requires close attention to both task-oriented skills and personality in order to make sure that tasks do not overshadow important elements of treatment. Finally, since customers often are involved in the production of service, they require training too. Clearly, service operations managers also must work closely with human resource management counterparts to develop both employee and customer training processes.

This interdisciplinary nature of service operations management poses great challenges, but it also makes service operations stand out as a unique and rich area of operations management. In this module, we explore how to define, design, and deliver service value. We begin with an examination of service value, as it exists in different service contexts. Typical contexts identified as services include banks, airlines, insurance companies, and even Internet providers. However, services are also important in other operations management settings. We will discuss how services affect the manufacturer as well as the insurance company. Following this discussion we will examine the elements of service design and improvement, and conclude the module by taking a look at how globalization and technology changes are affecting service operations.

Service Value

Each time that a customer comes into contact with a firm's operations management system, he or she forms a perception of the value gained from this interaction. This concept is referred to as the **moment of truth.** Stewart Alsop experienced just such a moment when he requested an upgrade on American West. Unfortunately for him (and for American West), he perceived little value from the transaction. From his perspective, the costs (added time and embarrassment) probably exceeded the benefits. All the accoutrements of a great first-class passenger experience were probably lost on him, and he was clearly not satisfied with the level of value he received.

The Value Equation Applied to Services

From this scenario we see that **service value** can be defined as a subjective function of customers' perceptions of what they receive in a service encounter relative to what they give or lose in the encounter. Customers assess the outcomes or results from service encounters as well as the process of the service delivery itself. Additionally, they give their money, time, and energies as costs of service admission. The **value equation** provides a powerful tool for understanding service value:[1]

$$\text{Value} = \frac{\text{Benefits}}{\text{Total cost}}$$

This equation should be interpreted as a conceptual model of service value rather than an equation with which you would attempt to arrive at some service value index. The variables are not independent. That is, aspects of service quality and timeliness, which make up the benefits, also could impact customers' perceptions of the total costs that they have to pay.

[1] A slightly different form of this equation is presented in James L. Heskett, W. Earle Sasser Jr., and Leonard A. Schlesinger, *The Service Profit Chain* (New York: Free Press, 1997), p. 40.

EXHIBIT 1
Service Process Quality Metrics

A. Parasuraman, V. A. Zeithaml, and L. L. Berry, "SERVQUAL: A Multiple Item Scale for Measuring Customer Perceptions of Service Quality," *Journal of Retailing*, April 1992, pp. 57–71.

Service Quality Dimension	Description
Tangibles	Appearance of physical facilities, equipment, personnel, and communication materials.
Reliability	Ability to perform the promised service dependably and accurately.
Responsiveness	Willingness to help customers and provide prompt service.
Assurance	Knowledge and courtesy of employees and their ability to convey trust and confidence.
Empathy	Caring, individualized attention paid to service customers.

For example, the lack of timely response to Alsop's upgrade request was the source of two of the costs he had to pay: the costs of frustration and embarrassment. This idea will become clearer as each variable in the value equation is described.

Benefits

Customers buy beneficial results. From a product perspective, we buy a saw in order to acquire cut wood. We buy a drill to get to the result of holes. Likewise, from a service perspective, parents take their children to Disneyland to "buy" the benefits of priceless memories and true—although perhaps not everlasting—appreciation from their children. Likewise, if we fly to Disneyland, the benefit of the service of air transportation is getting from our point of departure to an airport near Disneyland relatively quickly. One way to understand results as a designer and manager of services is to ask, "What do our customers really want to achieve when purchasing our service?" **Service results** may well depend on **process quality** and process timeliness, but sound design of the service concept and delivery processes is the key initial step in guaranteeing results.

Imagine if you took your children, or someone else's, to Disneyland and Goofy was standing at the front gate smoking a cigarette. Or you stopped a street sweeper to ask him how to find Space Mountain and he ignored you and walked away. Customers' perceptions of the service delivery transactions can indeed make as much difference as the ultimate results of the service. Fortunately, Disneyland's training and fail-safes built into their service processes would never create a situation in which Goofy would act out of character in front of customers or in which any "on-stage cast member" would ignore a guest. Such breakdowns in service processes would cause immediate disappointments and dissatisfaction. Poor service quality can lead to negative service results.

Service process quality metrics—the dimensions of service process quality (SERVQUAL), a critical component of the benefits—are summarized in Exhibit 1. For manufactured products, we often conceptually separate delivery speed and reliability from quality-related elements of value. However, in services these elements are intertwined. Customers often judge the quality of services based on how long they have to wait to receive them or how willing service providers are to provide prompt service. If you have been to a Disney theme park on a busy day you have probably mentally compared the amount of time you spent waiting in lines to the amount of time you spent having fun. Speed and reliability of delivery are clearly key benefits people seek in service encounters.

Since service process quality and timeliness can either damage or enhance the results of the service encounter, service operations managers must design customer-centric service processes that begin with the end result in mind. Otherwise customers and service employees become victims of flawed service processes that simply cannot deliver desired results.

Total Costs

The "total cost" part of the value equation includes the **price** that we pay for a service. Again, this will impact our perceptions of service value. If we pay for premium service but receive less than premium benefits, we will not perceive high service value. Once again consider Disney. The company charges a premium price for admission to its theme parks. It can do so because high-level benefits are virtually guaranteed, at least from the most important customers' perspectives—children. Excellence in service design and service operations management provides opportunities for premium pricing and profitability.

In contrast, Southwest Airlines provides an example of a service firm that provides high value through a low price. By avoiding hubs, by sticking with point-to-point flights, and by flying a single type of aircraft, Southwest is able to minimize turnaround time and costs. Coupled with comprehensive employee selection and training practices, Southwest's focused service operations deliver consistently on the critical dimensions of customer delight and profitability at a relatively low price.

In addition to price, the total cost associated with services also includes other **customer acquisition costs.** These costs consist of both monetary and nonmonetary costs of accessing the service beyond the price. Monetary costs include such things as lost wages from having to take time off work to access a service (e.g., a dentist) and the costs of transportation to get to a service provider. Nonmonetary costs include a person's energy and emotions that may be offered up to the service altar.

Another way to think of nonmonetary customer acquisition costs is to ask, "What do customers do to increase the likelihood of getting the service benefits that they want?" Unlike work-in-process inventory on a manufacturing floor, customers do not sit idly waiting for desired results. Generally speaking, service customers are active contributing participants in the delivery of service. Exhibit 2 provides a list of behaviors in which customers engage to increase the likelihood of satisfaction and desired results.

By understanding the types of behaviors in which customers will engage before and during a service encounter, we can build processes into our service operations to facilitate preparation, relationship building, and information exchange and detect and respond to early signs of intervention.

EXHIBIT 2
Nonmonetary Service Acquisition Costs

Source: Adapted from William E. Youngdahl and Deborah L. Kellogg, "The Service Customer's Value Chain: A Critical Incident Study of Customers' Satisfaction-Seeking Behaviors," *Journal of Operations Management* 15, no. 1 (1997), pp. 19–32.

Nonmonetary Service Acquisition Cost	Description
Preparation	Preparing for the service by such actions as seeking referrals, researching competitors, and arriving early.
Relationship building	Building a relationship with the service provider through such actions as smiling, offering words of kindness, getting to know providers, "trying to build loyalty," and asking for servers by name.
Information exchange	Providing and seeking information to clarify service expectations and seek status.
Intervention	Providing negative performance feedback and involving oneself in problem diagnosis and resolution.

Measuring Service Value

While the conceptual elements of the service value equation are useful to understand, they are difficult to measure directly and completely. Consequently, most measurement systems concentrate on individual elements of service quality, timeliness and cost, or they assess

In Practice

SERVICE-ENHANCED MANUFACTURING

QCC Kayaks, a maker of customized kayaks, provides design services via its Internet home page and/or sales representatives. When you open up the home page (http://www.qcckayaks.com), you are asked a series of questions regarding your height/weight, type of kayaking desired, and level of experience (current and desired) and whether stability or speed is important to you. Based on your responses to these questions, a specific kayak model is recommended for you. In addition, you can configure the kayak to your specific needs based on material, colors, and whether you want a rudder, a skeg, or no rudder. The result is not only a highly configured kayak but also a very personalized ordering experience.

GE Turbines builds turbines that go into installations such as power generation stations. Buyers of a power turbine are very sensitive to on-time completion of their units, since late delivery can have major impacts on plant building costs. When a customer wants to find out about the status of their order, GE sends a person to the production floor with a video camera. The camera view is fed directly into the Internet so that the buyer has the assurance of actually seeing the order's current state of completion.

General Motors has added service-in-use to its products through the creation of the On-star system. By building communications technology and navigation systems into its cars, GM now has the capability to enhance the customer's consumption experience by providing information, emergency help, and other services.

overall aggregate measures such as customer satisfaction. The 1980s ushered in the management mantra of customer satisfaction. Companies such as Xerox, with their Leadership through Quality initiative, began systematically measuring levels of customer satisfaction through customer surveys and focus groups. Often affiliated with total quality management, customer satisfaction became job one—a rallying point for sweeping initiatives throughout both service and manufacturing industries. With the survival of Xerox at stake, and the failure of many total quality management initiatives, one cannot help but wonder whether customer satisfaction was enough. Clearly, it was not.

Perhaps *delight* was the answer? Let's not just satisfy customers; let's delight them by exceeding their expectations. Hal Mather, an operations management consultant, put it best when he said that any firm should *profitably delight the customer.* Customer delight, to this day, remains a worthy goal. After all, when service providers exceed our expectations, we are much more likely to be loyal customers than when service providers just meet our expectations. There's always another service provider waiting to meet our expectations. But service delight comes at the cost of increasing service expectations. Today's delight becomes tomorrow's expectation. The goal of service delight drives the need for continuous improvement of service delivery systems.

Service Context: Service or Manufacturing?

We previously pointed out that services involve unique operations management environments. The "pure" service context is one that you would find in a bank, a consultant's office, a travel agency, a theme park (such as Disney World), or a hairdresser's/barber shop. In these systems the customer is the product and transformations to the product are often intangible. Customers can be transformed by an experience (such as you would get from a fine restaurant), by knowledge (from a school), by status (membership in an exclusive club), and so on.

It is important to recognize, however, that services are also important in traditionally "non-service" industries, and increasingly so. Service has been and continues to be a key element of the total value package offered by many manufacturing firms. For example, many industrial equipment products are chosen by customers based primarily on the firm's after-sales service capabilities. Xerox has been known as an excellent service provider in this regard. Today many manufacturing firms are enhancing their products by adding services at various stages of customer encounters including order entry and tracking, product design, production, delivery, product use, and disposal. Some examples are provided in the In Practice box.

Making sharp distinctions between manufacturing and services, while helping to provide order to our jobs as operations managers, can nevertheless lead to counterproductive decisions in the design and performance of operations management systems. We need to recognize that the creation and consumption of almost all manufactured products also involve myriad service opportunities. In addition, operations managers in manufacturing firms often find that they are tasked with managing internal service operations. For example, purchasing managers provide technical and informational services to manufacturing, R&D, marketing, and other functional areas. Therefore, the principles of service operations management apply to service aspects of manufacturing as well as to more "pure" services, and, conversely, manufacturing principles often apply to service operations. Progressive operations managers recognize this and keep their eyes on the ball—delivering customer-centric value-added solutions to meet customers' complete service and product needs.

Elements of Service Design

Service design ranges from the creation of new service business to the addition, adaptation, or modification of new service elements within an existing business. In order to begin the design process, we must return to the value equation. By starting with an understanding of what our customers value, we can determine the service value proposition. While we are developing the service proposition, we can think through the other elements of the service including what services and resources will be included, how the services will be delivered, and how service quality will be ensured.

Service Value Proposition

A **service value proposition** is a succinct statement of the service provided and its expected value to customers. Consider the case of Cisco Systems, a dominant player in network equipment and services that enable e-business transactions. Since its customers' revenue sources often flow from the network that is being installed, Cisco offers a financing program through its Cisco Systems Finance group. The service value propositions, displayed in Exhibit 3, describe the key elements of benefits of the program from the customer's perspective.

Once we have developed a service value proposition, we need to get more specific about how to design the service concept and delivery system. The service value proposition ensures that we have created the links between customer-defined service value and what we intend to accomplish. The service package translates the service value proposition into specific components of service design.

EXHIBIT 3
Cisco Systems Finance Program Value Propositions

Source: http://www.cisco.com/warp/public/csc/explore/datasheets/proj_fin_eur.html.

- **Deferred payments**—let you borrow aggressively while matching costs to revenues.
- **Aligned with the manufacturer**—finance your network with the company who best understands your business—Cisco Systems—and tailors its financing products to conform to the unique service provider business model.
- **Full financial product suite**—Cisco is investing in your success as a business, and forging a long-term relationship with you as both a technology and financial partner, with other financing programs you can use later as your business grows.
- **One-stop shopping**—with one place to go for best-of-class technology solutions and financing, it's easier and faster to get your network built and business started.

Service Package

The **service package** describes the explicit services, implicit services, facilitating goods, supporting facility, and human resources included in the service design. Once we have designed the service package, we can budget for specific resources and begin building a service business or a new service within an existing service or manufacturing business.

Explicit services comprise the core benefits of the service. For example, Cisco's customers are able to defer payments until their networks generate revenues. For most of its customers using these financial (loan) services, deferring payments is the explicit service being provided. **Implicit services** include psychological and other tangential benefits derived from the explicit services. For example, an implicit service benefit derived from Cisco's financial services is a closer and deepened relationship with Cisco. Both Cisco and its customers benefit from this deepened relationship. Customers learn more about the benefits and use of Cisco products and services, and Cisco benefits from increased revenues.

Facilitating goods are the tangible elements of the service product. A hamburger is a facilitating good at McDonald's. This module on service operations is a facilitating good for an educational service of some type. Loan documents are facilitating goods of Cisco's finance program. Since customers actually see, touch, and even smell facilitating goods, these tangible aspects of service delivery must be managed as the physical evidence of quality service.

The **supporting facility** comprises the entire set of physical resources required to deliver the service. These resources can include buildings, information systems infrastructure, Web pages, and any other physical resources, including paper clips, that might be required to deliver the service.

Human resources, often not considered in classical definitions of the service package, are truly the most important resources to be identified and selected in the service design and delivery processes. In addition to being able to complete specific service tasks, employees also must be able to interact appropriately with customers to deliver treatment that is consistent with the service value proposition.

Types of Services

The service package and service value proposition determine to a great extent the type of service required to deliver value. Classifying services into basic types can be useful since the different types of services provide unique sets of benefits and presuppose unique operational requirements as well. However, services do not typically lend themselves to single classifications since service businesses can involve many different types and stages of service encounters to complete a given service transaction. With this reality in mind, understanding basic service types allows service designers to apply different approaches to services as required.*

Coproduction Approach

The **coproduction approach** to service delivery implies active contribution by service customers. Prototypical examples include self-service gas pumps, salad bars, and self-service soft drink dispensers at fast-food restaurants. Both customers and service providers benefit from coproduction. Customers feel that they have more control over the service encounter and service providers benefit from customers providing input to service delivery. When designing services for coproduction, clear signage and instructions must be provided to customers. When salad bars first became popular, service providers had to cheerfully walk customers through the process of helping themselves. If we expect customers to contribute to service production, we need to make it easy for them to do so.

Production-Line Approach

Theodore Levitt, the Harvard Business School professor who first conceptualized this approach, stated, "The managerial rationality embodied in the practical imagination we see exercised so effectively everywhere in manufacturing can, given the effort, be applied with similarly munificent results in the service industries."[2] Levitt viewed the **production-line approach** as one by which services could significantly improve their performance on both cost, largely through improved efficiency, as well as quality. The production-line approach

* Services can also be typed according to their process structure characteristics such as volume, variety, and capital intensity. This approach for typing services is discussed in the "Process Choices" module by Kenneth K. Boyer (New York: McGraw-Hill/Irwin 2002).

[2] Theodore Levitt, "The Industrialization of Service," *Harvard Business Review* 54, no. 5 (1976), p. 42.

In Practice

PRESIDENTIAL SUITE, THE PLAZA, NEW YORK

Guests who are rolling in the dough can check into the same digs as tycoon Alfred Vanderbilt! The 28-year-old chose to make the brand-new Plaza hotel his bachelor pad back in 1907 when an entire year's bill was only $25,000. Since then, little has changed—except the prices. Now, one night's stay is a cool $15,000, and the Plaza is still heralded as the city's most elite hotel. The two-level Presidential Suite occupies the entire 18th floor of the hotel; plus, guests have access to a rooftop area. Within the 7,800-square-foot space, there are two living rooms, a parlor, and a library. That's in addition to six bedrooms and seven—yes, seven—bathrooms. The suite also has a private wine cellar, four balconies and a staff of maids, a butler, and a chauffeur with a Rolls Royce. For those quick snacks, there's even a private chef on call at any hour of the day.

Source: http://travel.discovery.com/ideas/wbestlst/xhtsuite/xhtsuite1.html#1.

relies on basic manufacturing assembly line techniques being applied to service operations. The defining characteristics of the production-line approach include the characteristics summarized in Exhibit 4.

EXHIBIT 4
Characteristics of the Production-Line Approach to Service Delivery

Characteristic	Example
Limited discretionary action of personnel	Levitt's prototypic service example, McDonald's, is able to promise customers a consistent service package by automating most parts of the production process and clearly defining employees' tasks.
Division of labor	Cooks, take-out-window cashiers, and front-line cashiers focus on specialized tasks.
Substitution of technology for people	Lights and buzzers pace hamburger production just as the moving assembly line sets the pace of mass production of automobiles.
Service standardization	Many travelers frequent McDonald's because they know exactly what to expect.

Customized-Care Approach

Service businesses that employ the **customized-care approach** to service delivery provide highly personalized service to meet each customer's unique needs and desires. In most cases, customers are willing to pay a premium for such highly personalized attention. Complete focus on customers' needs and desires requires significant personal attention from service providers who are selected and trained for their ability to serve customers with extraordinary levels of care. Clearly, the focus has to be directed more toward effectiveness than efficiency when designing services using a customized-care approach.

Front Office and Back Office

When designing a service system, it is useful to think in terms of the extent of contact the employees have with customers. For example, employees in the check-clearing operation of a major bank perform in *back-office* roles. They perform a production function that is removed from the customer. The design focus of most back-office service tasks is on making the operations as efficient as possible. Bank tellers serve in a *front-office* capacity. Front-office service personnel have direct contact with customers and must focus on treatment as well as service tasks. The front-office and back-office distinction can be useful when considering different types of services. For example, a stay at the Presidential Suite at the Plaza is clearly a customized-care service. But elements of running the hotel such as laundry services and certain back-office aspects of food processing in the hotel's restaurants might lend themselves to the production line approach to service.

EXHIBIT 5
A Service Blueprint for Hotel Room Service

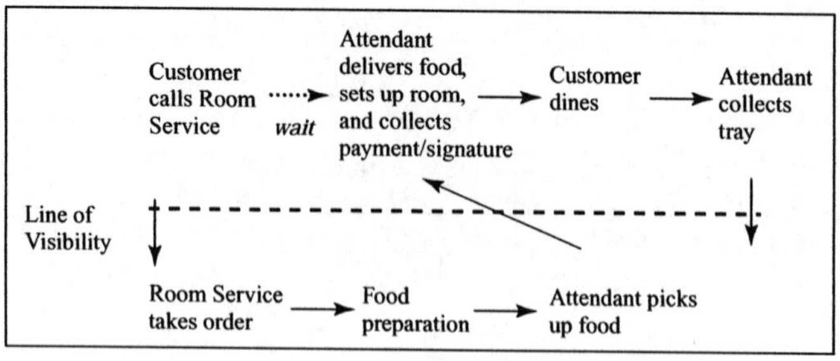

Service Blueprinting

Service blueprinting can be used to flowchart steps in service delivery processes and determine points of customer contact in order to delineate front-office from back-office service activities. Additionally, service blueprinting provides the opportunity to identify potential failure points, steps during which customers have to wait, and important decision points throughout the flow of a service encounter, or series of encounters. A line of visibility separates points of customer contact, or the front office, from back-office operations. Consider the blueprinting for hotel room service displayed in Exhibit 5.

Once the basic service blueprint has been developed, a service design team can explore potential opportunities for service failure. For example, when the customer first calls room service, it is possible that nobody answers the phone. When a room service attendant does answer the phone, politeness, promptness, and accuracy are required to meet the customer's expectations. By examining each potential failure point, service operations managers can design and implement fail-safing devices to minimize the possibility of service errors and perceived failure.

Fail-Safing Service Design and Delivery

Service fail-safing is a relatively new service design approach borrowed from manufacturing approaches that were developed to minimize the possibility of human error on the production line. The Japanese term often used to describe these approaches is "poka-yoke." In service design, we attempt to fail-safe service tasks, the treatment of customers, and the handling of tangibles which provide the physical evidence of service quality. By doing so, we will avoid the necessity of frequent service recovery. Exhibit 6 provides a summary of service fail-safing examples for tasks, treatment, and tangibles.

EXHIBIT 6
Fail-Safing Service Tasks, Treatment, and Tangibles

Source: Richard B. Chase and Douglas M. Stewart, "Making Your Service Fail-Safe," *Sloan Management Review* 35, no. 3 (1994).

Examples of Service Errors	Fail-Safing Examples
Tasks	
• Performing tasks incorrectly • Performing tasks that were not requested • Performing tasks too slowly • Performing tasks in the wrong order	• Color-coded cash register keys • Surgical trays with indentations for ensuring all instruments have been retrieved
Treatment	
• Failure to acknowledge the customer • Not listening to the customer • Reacting inappropriately	• Eye-color checklist to ensure eye contact • Employees trained to observe when customers smile to encourage employee smiling
Tangibles	
• Lack of cleanliness • Failure to control ambient conditions including light, odor, and temperature • Failure to proofread documents for accuracy	• Cleaning checklist • Mirrors to check appearance • Peer review of documents

In Practice

SERVICE GUARANTEE AT BLUE VALLEY WELDING SUPPLY, INC.

Blue Valley Welding Supply Inc., an Allentown, Pennsylvania–based distributor of industrial gases, promises on-time delivery or free gas, regardless of the size of the order. As an incentive to perform, the company's management agreed to set aside $4 per employee for each day during which no deliveries were missed.

After starting the program, Blue Valley extended it not only to late deliveries, but also to bad cylinders, where a leaky valve negates on-time delivery by forcing the customer to wait for a replacement.

Not only did the company's on-time delivery rate increase from about 96 to more than 99.8 percent, but the standard missed delivery actually costs less than what the company pays its 20-plus workers for an error-free day.

During the first six months of 1990—the second year for the program—Blue Valley shipped more than 25,000 cylinders and missed just three deliveries. The total payout to customers during that time was just $121.03. Blue Valley's parent company, New Jersey–based JWS Technologies Inc., has a similar guarantee program that has achieved equal service-delivery improvement.

"There is no question that we work harder because we want to live up to the guarantee," says Tucker Lyons, Blue Valley's vice president and general manager.

"We do things now—like checking cylinders we receive from suppliers to make sure there are no leaks—that we didn't do before, and that makes us more efficient."

"If someone is looking for free gas, they'll be pretty disappointed; we don't mess up very often. Customers come to us because they want on-time delivery, because they don't want their people standing around waiting for the gas to arrive."

Source: Dan Maher, "Service Guarantees," *Manage*, 32, no. 4(1992), pp. 22–25.

Many service managers resist notions that service can be fail-safed. Indeed, it is unlikely that the "poka yokes" presented in Exhibit 6 would ensure 100 percent satisfaction or delight. Progressive service operations managers build fail-safes into service design to *minimize* opportunities for service failures. These managers also consider service guarantees as a design tool for focusing a service organization's attention on getting things done right the first time.

Service Guarantees

"Absolutely positively overnight." This service guarantee from FedEx is easy to communicate and easy to understand. There are no hidden conditions. If the package doesn't get their overnight, there's no charge. The message sends a strong marketing signal to existing and prospective customers. From an operations standpoint, a **service guarantee** focuses attention on the details of service delivery.

The process of putting a service guarantee in writing provides the following immediate benefits:

- Service guarantee payouts receive excellent returns with respect to service improvement opportunities. When a customer invokes a service guarantee, the information can be used to improve the service delivery system.
- Meaningful compensation from a service guarantee can turn disgruntled customers into loyal ones. Customers who feel they have been treated fairly forgive quickly.
- Service guarantees focus service providers on the details of service delivery, including the development and measurement of key service quality metrics. Service blueprinting can be used to identify potential failure points that could lead to payouts. By directing fail-safing and measurement activities to these potential failure points, service operations managers ensure that service promises are kept.
- Service guarantees create a sense of urgency to live up to the promise. FedEx employees clearly understand that packages must be delivered overnight.

For a service guarantee to be effective, it must be meaningful to customers, easy for customers and employees to understand, paid out without conditions or repercussions of any kind, and consistent with the capabilities of the organization. Even after designing the service package based on a customer-centric service value proposition and promising delivery within an effective service guarantee, service operations managers still will need to plan for the unexpected, analyze service performance, and direct service improvement efforts.

Service Recovery, Analysis, and Improvement

It costs far more to attract new customers than it does to retain existing ones. Existing customers tend to spend more money over time, and since they understand the service delivery process, they tend to be less costly to serve as well. Therefore, recovering from service mishaps before customers become dissatisfied or even angry provides great financial benefits from the retention of loyal customers. In addition to recovering from service failures, service providers need to analyze their service design and delivery system in order to generate and implement improvements.

Service Recovery

Service recoveries are real-time responses to perceived service failures. Important words to remember from this definition are *real-time* and *perceived.* In order to avoid losing a customer, recovery must take place as soon as dissatisfaction has been detected. The service is failing if the customer perceives the service to be failing. Customers' perception is reality in the service business. Service recovery best practices include[3]

- Incorporating recovery into hiring, training, and empowerment.
- Establishing recovery guidelines and standards.
- Providing systems that promote easy access and effective responses.
- Maintaining customer and product databases.

Effective service recovery begins with hiring people who can be trusted and trained to make the appropriate decisions required to satisfy customers when things start to go wrong. Empowering employees with the right to make decisions that may deviate from standard operating procedures requires careful attention to selection and training processes. The Ritz-Carlton, for example, empowers all employees to spend significant resources at their discretion to satisfy disgruntled customers. Ford Motor Company uses assessment centers to evaluate the service recovery skills, among others, of prospective employees.

Service organizations must establish clear guidelines for service recovery in order to expect employees to respond autonomously. The Ritz-Carlton employs a value-driven set of "gold standards" that includes specific guidelines for service recovery. Without standards in place for service recovery, the likelihood of a bungled recovery remains high. Botched service recoveries confirm disgruntled customers' negative suspicions about a service organization.

Progressive service organizations offer multiple opportunities and channels for customer complaints. The worst thing that can happen to a service organization is to have a dissatisfied customer "defect" to the competition without ever voicing any complaint. Twenty-four-hour, seven-day-per a week (24-by-7) call centers such as GE's "Answer Center" provide around-the-clock easy access. In addition to answering questions, GE's representatives often follow up with apology letters and certificates for products or service. Ultimately, any service employee can serve as a listening post to detect early warning signs of dissatisfaction such as body language and certain types of questions such as "Will I be served soon?"

Accessing important customer information through information databases and having access to information about the company's service and product offerings empower service employees to make appropriate decisions about how to best recover. USAA, a respected insurance agency, scans all customer complaint letters into a customer information database. Service representatives can access this information to understand the history of a customer's particular situation, and scan service offerings to develop an appropriate and customized recovery.

[3] Steven W. Brown, "Best Practices in Service Recovery," *Marketing Management,* Summer 2000.

Effective service recovery can serve to increase customer loyalty by going the extra mile. It is an important part of service design and execution. However, excessive service recovery signals the need for more thoughtful analysis and service delivery system improvement.

The Service Gap Model

The **service gap model**, displayed in Exhibit 7, is a powerful tool for analyzing and improving service delivery. By identifying actual or potential gaps between different stages of the service design and delivery processes, service managers can systematically design or improve a service delivery system. This model can be applied to any service business or service components of manufacturing businesses.

EXHIBIT 7
The Service Gap Model

Adapted from V. A. Zeithaml, A. Parasuraman, and L. Berry, *Delivering Quality Service: Balancing Customer Perceptions and Expectations* (New York: Free Press, 1990).

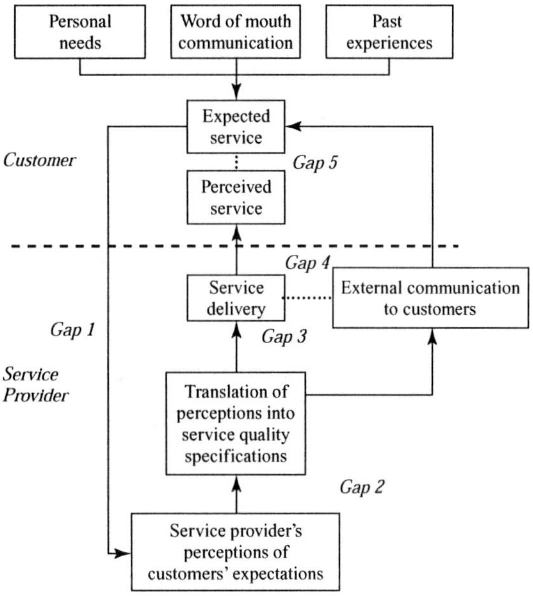

Delivering customer-centric services begins with an understanding of customers' expectations. Customers develop expectations from four sources: personal needs, word-of-mouth communication, past experiences, and communication from service providers. Personal needs will vary by customer market segment. Customers with certain physical disabilities, for example, might have unique personal needs that will impact the design of physical facilities as well as the types of customer participation available to the service designer. Word-of-mouth communications related to experiences others have had with a service provider also shape expectation. Our personal past experiences with a service provider or similar service providers shape expectations more strongly than any other influence. We tend to expect today what we received yesterday. Finally, communication from service providers in a variety of forms such as advertising, signage, and direct verbal messages influences our expectations.

Customers enter into a service encounter with certain expectations regarding the appearance of tangibles, reliability and responsiveness of the service, and other characteristics such as the attitudes and competencies of employees and the degree of attention they will receive from the service provider. By using focus groups or other survey methods, service designers can assess how important each service quality dimension is to customers during the service delivery processes (see the SERVQUAL metrics displayed in Exhibit 1). This information can be used later to guide service quality improvement efforts.

Now that we know what matters to customers in terms of their expectations, we must translate these expectations into service quality, or design, specifications—the written service procedures and processes.

The service quality specifications guide actual service delivery and the communication of service delivery capabilities to customers. The service delivery, or moment of truth, creates the opportunity for customers to evaluate whether their expectations have been met or exceeded. If service expectations were higher than the perceived delivery, dissatisfaction results. If there is a match between expectations and perceptions of service delivery, satisfaction results. Customers' delight occurs when perceptions of the service delivery exceed expectations.

Identifying and Closing the Gaps

Five potential gaps exist: (1) a failure to understand what our customers expect, (2) an inability to translate expectations into service design specifications, (3) an inability to deliver the service per the design specifications, (4) communicated expectations that do not match service delivery capabilities, and (5) dissatisfaction due to unmet expectations.

Gap 1: Failure to Understand What Our Customers Expect Many methods exist to gather information about customers' expectations. The simplest method is to ask them what they would like to experience and what outcomes they would like to receive from the service. While sophisticated survey methods can get to the information you need and provide important baseline values for your service quality metrics, consider the face-to-face discussions during service encounters as a first step in the process of understanding your customers' expectations. In this way, the actual service providers serve as listening posts gathering information and updating organizationwide understanding of customers' expectations. Additionally, this first-hand information will prove invaluable when designing more sophisticated survey approaches such as questionnaires and focus groups.

Gap 2: Inability to Translate Expectations into Service Design Specifications When closing gaps, we must start with the assumption that the preceding gaps have been closed. In other words, we need to close the gaps one at a time. Otherwise we will be unable to isolate causes for the gaps. Therefore, starting with the assumption that we do indeed understand our customers' expectations, we need to understand why a gap exists between known expectations and the design of the service, or the service quality specifications. The most common root cause for this gap is a lack of knowledge on the part of those responsible for service design. The most straightforward and lasting method for closing this gap involves education in the area of service design. This education should include knowledge of the service package, gap model analysis, service blueprinting, and examination of best practices from world-class service organizations.

Gap 3: Inability to Deliver the Service per the Design Specification This gap presents exciting opportunities for operations managers. Assuming that we have the appropriate service design in place, we need to understand why our service delivery system is unable to deliver in conformance with the design. Selection and training of service personnel deserve particular attention when attempting to close this gap since service employees need to posess the skills and knowledge to perform service tasks as well as the ability to provide the appropriate level of treatment. Operations managers work closely with their human resource management counterparts to ensure appropriate selection and training. From a process-analysis perspective, service blueprinting can be used to identify potential failure points around which employees' training programs can be developed. Finally, the potential failure points identify opportunities to improve or build new poka yokes, or service fail-safing approaches.

Gap 4: Communicated Expectations That Do Not Match Service Delivery Capabilities The situation of overpromising and underdelivering virtually guarantees dissatisfaction. Service operations managers must work closely with those in marketing or other areas who are responsible for external communication to customers. Additionally, training of employees must address this gap as well.

Alternatives to overpromising include promising exactly what can be delivered or promising somewhat less than that dictated by current capabilities. So which will it be? Promise less, or promise exactly what can be delivered? Promising less than can be delivered sets an organization up for delighting its customers, but the promise may not be enough to attract customers in the first place. Generally speaking, the best practice for external communication is to communicate expectations consistent with actual delivery capabilities. Communicating how long a customer has to wait before or during service delivery stands out as a noteworthy exception. Most automated telephone systems that indicate wait times actually present a projected wait time that is longer than the actual wait time. After all, if you wait five minutes on hold and you thought the wait would be eight minutes, you might end up feeling better about the service experience.

Gap 5: Dissatisfaction Due to Unmet Expectations The difference between what customers expect and what they perceive determines the magnitude and direction of this gap. The gap direction of concern is dissatisfaction. Dissatisfaction occurs when customers perceive they receive less than expected levels of quality (and value) from the service encounter. The only way to close the dissatisfaction gap is to first close the preceding four gaps. It's that simple, or complicated.

The Importance–Performance Matrix

Another thing to keep in mind is to focus on what matters. Recall that we ask customers which service quality dimensions are most important to them when we are assessing their expectations. After assessing their satisfaction through some form of survey during or after the service encounter, we need to react appropriately to the data. A powerful tool for directing service quality improvement efforts is an **importance–performance matrix.** Consider the results from a survey that assessed importance of service quality dimensions as well as the perceived performance on service quality dimensions for a particular service. This importance–performance matrix is displayed in Exhibit 8.

Notice that customers reported satisfaction with reliability, assurance, and tangible dimensions of the service. Responsiveness and empathy did not rate highly on satisfaction. As service operations managers, should we direct time and energy toward improving responsiveness and empathy? Since empathy was not terribly important to customers, resources should be directed to improve responsiveness, a dimension of great importance to customers. By focusing on what matters, operations managers can leverage the greatest impacts from their improvement efforts.

What about tangibles? Satisfaction is high, but importance is low. What would you do in this case? This could be an opportunity to direct resources that have been spent on relatively unimportant tangible aspects of the service toward initiatives to improve responsiveness. The key to designing and improving services is to focus on what matters to customers.

The gap model stands out as a key tool for service operations managers to ensure that each step in the service design and delivery process has been scrutinized to deliver levels of service

EXHIBIT 8
Importance–Performance Matrix

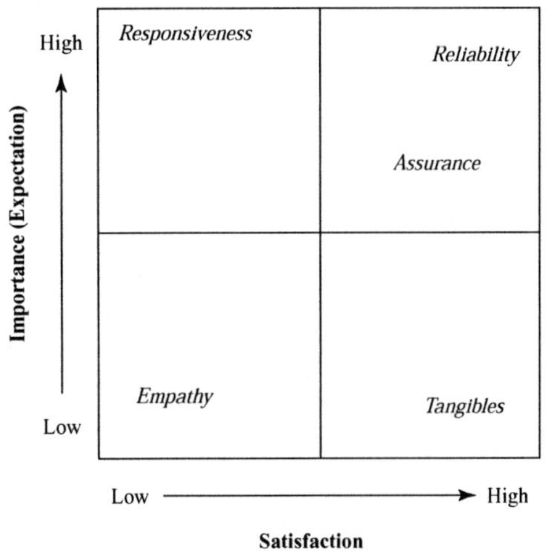

at or above customers' expectations. By focusing on what matters, scarce resources can be deployed to make the greatest impact on customers' perceptions of service quality and value. Next, we examine briefly the global context of services and e-services.

Globalization of Services and E-Service

The Internet and advanced telecommunications have opened the door to expand globalization of services and create new forms of **e-service.** Many exciting opportunities await service operations managers who choose to venture in these new directions.

Service Globalization

The **globalization** of manufacturing was driven by the availability of relatively cheap and safe transportation to take advantage of lower labor costs and proximity to markets. Advances in information technology (IT) and telecommunications provide new opportunities for the globalization of services that will extend well beyond the rapid globalization of fast food.[4]

Back-office service operations already exist throughout the world. The Philippines and Indonesia are becoming a global center for cartoon animation. Singapore is positioned as the nerve center of an economic triangle in which Malaysia supplies white-collar services and Indonesia supplies factories. IT departments from around the globe continue to outsource to India.

Customer-facing services present more challenges, but several examples exist. Dell has established a call center in Ireland for all of its European customers. Talisma, a Seattle-based software outsourcing company, manages Real Network's customer support out of Bangalore, India, by e-mail. In addition to expanding the reach and location possibilities of services through the Internet and telecommunications, service operations managers must localize services to deliver cultural-specific value to customers around the globe. In order to meet local needs, local service managers must be involved in adapting service delivery models or designs transferred from another country.

E-Service

Ron Zemke and Tom Connellan recently applied their bricks-and-mortar service expertise to the study of on-line service. They examined on-line businesses such as LandsEnd.com, Dell.com, Amazon.com, REI.com, and Gap.com to develop a list of seven best practices for on-line service.[5]

E-service principle 1: Practice easy-to-do business. The keys are to make it easy to *find* and *use* a website. The emphasis should be placed on functionality and simplicity rather than on company histories and high-bandwidth graphics. It also means that e-mails are answered in less than an hour and toll-free telephone numbers are listed on every page.

E-service principle 2: Design for distinction. Branding becomes a critical point of differentiation. A distinct look and feel translate to perceptions of trustworthiness. Consider your own favorite site for purchasing books or other items on-line. Does the site itself engender feelings of security and trust? What types of sites have made you feel insecure?

E-service principle 3: Personalize the e-experience. Sites that provide personalized information and recommendations help companies develop lasting relationships with customers. Amazon.com provides recommendations for books based on past purchase patterns. By going the extra mile, these e-tailers develop the hook to develop and

[4] Andrew Wileman, "International Service," *Management Today,* December 1999.
[5] Ron Zemke and Tom Connellan, *E-Service: 24 Ways to Keep Your Customers—When the Competition Is Just a Click Away* (Amacom, 2001); and Chris Lee, "E-Service," *Training,* January 2001.

maintain customer loyalty. The sites become "sticky," meaning that customers believe that it is more desirable and less costly to stick with a particular e-tailer than to search for suitable replacement sites.

E-service principle 4: Deliver end-to-end service. E-service masters recognize that the sale doesn't conclude with the click of a mouse. Benchmark organizations such as Dell.com send electronic order confirmations, provide on-line access to the assembly and shipping status of orders, and provide personalized Web pages for each computer to provide information about updates and upgrades.

E-service principle 5: Encourage human contact. Human contact can come in the forms of telephone contact, chat services with service representatives, exchanges of e-mail, and cobrowsing techniques that allow service reps to browse a website with a customer. Some sites also provide opportunities for community building, a process for letting customers get to know one another and in the process help build a community of loyal customers. Consider the coproduction benefits of allowing customers to share service and product knowledge with one another.

E-service principle 6: Make recovery a point of pride. Dot-com's service recovery processes must involve mechanisms such as e-mail, chat, and phone contact to encourage customer feedback and problem resolution through empowered customer service reps. E-service providers need to focus on service recovery even more so than bricks-and-mortar counterparts in order to allay customers' fears of doing business on-line. If a customer cannot resolve issues with a human service rep, her suspicions about doing business will be confirmed and she will defect to the bricks-and-mortar competition.

E-service principle 7: Build a retention strategy. Making customers stick to a site involves creative approaches to building loyalty. Loyal customers tend to buy more. They are also easier and therefore cheaper to serve. Finally, they create more word-of-mouth advertising. Cameraworld.com provides "bonus bucks" to lure customers to the next purchase. Omahasteaks.com and Amazon.com give their best customers free gifts.

One thing has become clear in recent years. While the Web has provided a new way of accessing companies' services and goods, the fundamentals of sound service operations management and need for profitable business models must not disappear as we e-enable businesses. Indeed, as evidenced in these seven principles of e-service, the basics of effective service operations management transcend business platforms from the bricks-and-mortar of "traditional" service businesses to new on-line services.

Module Summary

Service operations management provides a conceptual framework and set of tools for designing, executing, delivering, and improving services.

1. Worrying about the difference between service and manufacturing can be counterproductive. Most services contain some physical product, and most products of significance come bundled with services. Service approaches can be applied to manufacturing, and manufacturing approaches can be applied to services.
2. Effective service design begins with an understanding of customer-defined service value. Service value represents the trade-offs between what customers receive from a service in the forms of results and process quality and what customers give to the service in the forms of money and energy related to the service acquisition process.
3. By identifying potential failure points in a service delivery system, operations managers can design service fail-safing devices, or poka yokes, to minimize the possibility of future service failures. Additionally, service recovery efforts can be designed and directed around these potential failure points to retain loyal customers.
4. The service gap model can be used to analyze each step in a service delivery process to identify and close service delivery gaps. This powerful tool isolates specific causes of dissatisfaction so that service quality improvement initiatives lead to increased service value.
5. The Internet and World Wide Web will continue to influence the practice and globalization of service delivery. Exciting new challenges exist to blend traditional service operations management practices with new Web-based approaches.

The basic concepts and tools of service operations included in this module will provide opportunities for improving both internal and external customer service in both profit-seeking and not-for-profit organizations. No matter what business you are in, the service value equation and other tools will serve you well as useful starting points for providing service value to others.

Key Terms

Coproduction approach, *8*
Customized-care approach, *9*
Customer acquisition costs, *5*
E-service, *16*
Explicit service, *7*
Facilitating goods, *8*
Globalization, *16*
Human resources, *8*
Implicit service, *7*
Importance–performance matrix, *15*
Moment of truth, *3*
Price, *4*
Process quality, *4*
Production-line approach, *8*
Service blueprint, *9*
Service fail-safing, *10*
Service gap model, *13*
Service guarantee, *11*
Service package, *7*
Service process quality metrics, *4*
Service recovery, *12*
Service results, *4*
Service value, *3*
Service value equation, *3*
Service value proposition, *7*
Supporting facility, *8*

Discussion Questions

1. Consider an on-line brokerage service that you have used or would consider using. Describe the service package for the on-line service.
2. Consider a particular service for which you are a customer. Determine the elements of customer value from the standpoint of the service value equation for this service. How would you rate the value you receive from the service? Why?
3. How can you fail-safe courteous customer treatment?
4. Develop a service blueprint for a dog grooming business.
5. Apply the service gap model to some service aspect of your educational institution. Identify all five gaps and approaches for closing each gap.
6. Which of the five SERVQUAL metrics are most important to you? On what does your answer depend?
7. Consider a service experience during which a service provider recovered effectively from a nearly failed encounter. What made the recovery effective?
8. If a customer is delighted after setting extremely low expectations, was the service of high quality?
9. Explain the sequence of steps you would take in designing a new service.
10. How would you use an importance–performance matrix to guide service improvement efforts?
11. What is the significance of service customer loyalty?
12. How does coproduction differ from other service design alternatives?

Cases

NORTHWEST AIRLINES E-TICKETS[15]

Northwest Airlines e-ticket customers departing from Gerald R. Ford International Airport can look forward to faster check-ins, thanks to the airline's new E-Service center.

Northwest was the first airline at the local airport to introduce the special service for its e-ticket holders, making Gerald R. Ford International Airport only the 32nd airport in the country where the service is available.

"There's been a demand for this in Grand Rapids for some time, so we're happy to have it in by the holidays," said Matt Friedman, a spokesman for the airline.

"There's a lot of business travel in and out of Grand Rapids and a lot of business travel customers have used E-Service Centers in other airports like Detroit and Minneapolis."

With every passing year the airline sees a significant rise e-ticket sales, Friedman said.

Three years ago e-tickets were a small percentage of overall airline ticket sales, but they now surpass paper ticket sales among the 293,000 passengers flying in and out of Ford International via Northwest annually.

About 65 percent of Northwest's domestic customers travel on e-tickets these days, he noted.

"One of the things we found in doing this all over the state and all over the country is that with airline customers there are different comfort levels with technology,"" Friedman remarked.

"The key is to have systems in place so if you're very comfortable with technology, it's there for you; and if you're not comfortable with it, there is the traditional way of going through the process available to you."

The E-Service Center island has two touch-screen computers that allow e-ticket holders to check in, obtain boarding passes, and check their luggage as well.

The customer's credit card number serves as the source of identification. E-ticket passengers simply swipe their credit card through the machine, just as they do at an ATM, and the computer pulls up the reservation.

The machine asks how many pieces of luggage the customer is checking, and located just a few steps from the machine is a special bag drop counter for e-ticket holders where luggage tags are printed out and attached by an attendant.

Customers also can change seats, if additional seats are available, using the computer touch screen.

How much time a customer can save depends on the time of day and the airport, Friedman said.

If it's a busy time of day, if there are flight irregularities, or if bad weather is scrambling schedules and people are lined up at the ticket counter rebooking flights, it might take slightly longer.

But Friedman said the delays would be nowhere near the length of time paper-ticket customers are going to spend waiting in line under those same kinds of conditions.

"If your flight is on time and all you need is a boarding pass, you're going to save a lot of time," he said. "There's no question it's a time saver for everybody."

QUESTIONS

1. How does the e-ticket service contribute to customers' perceptions of service value from the standpoint of the service value equation?
2. Develop a simple service blueprint for traditional ticketing and for the e-ticket service. Comment on the differences between the two blueprints.

Related Modules of Interest

- SexProcess Choices
- Process Management
- Process Mapping and Analysis
- Total Quality Management
- Waiting-Line Models

Source: Anne B. Emrich, "Northwest Opens E-Service at Ford," *Grand Rapids Business Journal,* November 20, 2000, p. B7.

Selected Readings

Discovering the Soul of Service: The Nine Drivers of Sustainable Business Success by Leonard L. Berry, Free Press, 1999.

Driving Customer Equity: How Customer Lifetime Value is Reshaping Corporate Strategy by Roland T. Rust, Valarie A. Zeithaml, and Katherine N. Lemon, Free Press, 2000.

Loyalty Rules! How Todays Leaders Build Lasting Relationships by Frederic F. Reichheld, Harvard Business School Press, 2001.

Managing the Professional Service Firm by David H. Maister, Free Press, 1997.

The Service Profit Chain: How Leading Companies Link Profit and Growth to Loyalty, Satisfaction, and Value by James L. Heskett, W. Earl Sasser, Leonard A. Schlesinger, James L. Herskett, and Earl W. Sasser, New York: Free Press, 1997.

Service Management: Operations, Strategy, and Information Technology by James A. Fitzsimmons, Mona J. Fitzsimmons, McGraw-Hill, 1997.

Service Operations Management by Graham Clark and Robert Johnston, Financal Times Management, 2001.

Winning the Service Game by Benjamin Schneider and David E. Bowen, Harvard Business School Press, 1995.

Total Quality Management

Frameworks, Measures, and Standards

Steven A. Melnyk
Michigan State University

Lawrence D. Fredendall
Clemson University

McGraw-Hill Irwin

Boston Burr Ridge, IL Dubuque, IA Madison, WI New York San Francisco St. Louis
Bangkok Bogotá Caracas Kuala Lumpur Lisbon London Madrid Mexico City
Milan Montreal New Delhi Santiago Seoul Singapore Sydney Taipei Toronto

Total Quality Management: Frameworks, Measures, and Standards

Module Objectives

By the end of this module, you should be able to

- Trace the evolution of total quality management (TQM) beyond a simple emphasis on product conformance.
- Explain the four major axioms of TQM: commitment to quality; extensive use of scientific tools, technologies, and methods; total involvement in the quality undertaking; and continuous improvement.
- Describe the impact of TQM pioneers such as Deming, Juran, Crosby, and Imai on the development of TQM.
- Identify the various metrics used to evaluate performance on the quality dimension.
- Explain the various standards and certification programs that have been implemented at the state, national, and international levels.
- Understand new developments in quality such as six sigma.

Human Face of Quality at L.L. Bean

What's worse than being stranded in a canoe without a paddle? Being stranded without a canoe. That's what one sales representative at L.L. Bean thought when he received a complaint from a New York customer that a canoe hadn't arrived in time for a weekend trip. So the loyal employee strapped a canoe on his car and personally drove it hundreds of miles from the company's offices in Maine to save the customer's canoe trip.

This incident provided L.L. Bean executives with a dramatic good news/bad news scenario. The good news was that their employees were committed to going out of their way to provide quality customer service. The bad news was how very far this employee had to go out of his way. Far from being reassuring, the incident left management with a disturbing question: Why wasn't the canoe shipped on time in the first place?

The resultant soul-searching set L.L. Bean on the path to total quality management (TQM). An investigation revealed that, although L.L. Bean employees had the mind-set for quality, they often didn't have the authority to carry it out. They also didn't have the "big picture" and needed wider knowledge about processes throughout the company to help them prevent problems.

Rather than focus on improving processes first, as many companies might, L. L. Bean set about improving its employee training and development. But even before that, it came up with a clearly stated definition of what it wanted to achieve with its TQM system and communicated that to all of its employees.

L.L. Bean's TQM definition reads: "Total quality involves managing an enterprise to maximize customer satisfaction in the most efficient and effective way possible by totally involving people in improving the way work is done." Now in its sixth year, that emphasis on human resources has helped L.L. Bean reengineer every process in the company. The implementation of TQM has boosted profits, enhanced safety, and reduced backlogs. Best of all, customer satisfaction is up, too—and intrepid sales representatives no longer have to drive hundreds of miles to save their customers' canoe trips.

Source: Dawn Anfuso, "At L.L. Bean, Quality Starts with People," *Personnel Journal* 73, no. 1 (January 1994), p. 60.

The ability to rejuvenate itself, as L.L. Bean did, is one of the defining traits of **total quality management.** For some companies, new energy from TQM has meant the difference between survival and extinction. For example, Hyundai, a Korean-based automotive manufacturer, experienced a 26 percent one-year increase in sales in 2001[1]—a development

[1] Sholnn Freeman, "March Auto Sales Fell by 4.5%, but Pace Topped Forecasts in an Uncertain Time," *The Wall Street Journal,* April 4, 2001, p. A3.

that could be attributed to its recognition and acceptance of quality as a strategic imperative. Leading practitioners of TQM now include Motorola, Hewlett-Packard, and Stanley Tools.

Total quality management establishes an organizationwide focus on quality, merging the development of a quality-oriented corporate culture with intensive use of management and statistical tools aimed at designing and delivering quality products to customers. TQM can dramatically improve corporate practices and performance. Over a decade ago, Hewlett-Packard found defects in 4 of every 1,000 soldered computer components. While the company's goal was to cut defects in half, it was able to reduce the rate to 2 per 1 million soldered components. TQM also can impact broader areas of performance extending to customer service (as in the L.L. Bean opening vignette) and other areas of the firm.

In this module, we explore the management underpinnings of total quality management to provide a foundation for the reader's continued exploration of this fascinating and dynamic topic. The presentation begins with an overview of the historical development of the TQM movement. In a subsequent section, we then describe the strategic thrust and total corporate undertaking that characterize that movement and discuss the change in corporate culture and thinking that successful implementation produces.

Total Quality Management: An Overview

Total quality management is a multifaceted idea that takes on even philosophical proportions. As we will see, TQM addresses many dimensions of business management, especially those relating to value creation.

Total Quality and Value

Value is defined as the customer's evaluation of the quality and timeliness traits of a product, divided by the costs incurred. Therefore, quality, or *what* is delivered, is an integral part of the value equation. However, the idea of "total quality" goes beyond just what is delivered. In fact, the notions of "total quality" and value are almost synonymous, so when total quality is high, the customer's perception of value is also high. Doing things in a "total quality" way and according to the "total quality" approach means that there is high integrity and reliability in the process. Processes managed with total quality produce little waste, and therefore involve a high degree of value-adding activity.

Origins of TQM

Total quality management did not start to become the way to do business in North America and Europe until the early 1980s. However, TQM has a long history in Japan, where it was first developed, refined, and used extensively.

World War II devastated the Japanese economy. Japan had such a reputation for building inferior copies of products designed elsewhere that the phrase "Made in Japan" was synonymous with poor quality. In 1946, even making a telephone call across town could become an adventure, with unreliable equipment and uncertain coverage. After the war, Japanese managers searched for ways to restructure their firms and the country's economy as a whole. W. Edwards Deming, Joseph Juran, and many others brought the seeds of a new management theory to Japan as they worked as statisticians with the American Occupation Force. They advocated merging statistical techniques with management tools and frameworks to create the theory that would transform that nation's economy—total quality management.

Interest in this theory spread with news of Japan's success with TQM, reinforced by reports of improvements at such early North American implementers as GE, Hewlett-Packard, and Motorola. The emphasis in TQM on the basic principles of customer satisfaction, employee empowerment, powerful management, and statistical tools has dramatically reoriented firms and altered their structures.

In Practice

CORPORATE STRUCTURE AND THE MOMENT OF TRUTH

Like many service companies, Scandinavian Airlines (SAS) serves its customers through a series of interactions. For SAS managers to dedicate themselves to orienting the company toward each customer's individual needs, they had to abandon their reliance on rule books and instructions from distant corporate offices. They had to place responsibility for ideas, decisions, and actions with the people who represented SAS during the 15 seconds of customer interactions that became moments of truth. This group included ticket agents, flight attendants, baggage handlers, and all other front-line employees. If those workers had to wait for a decision on an individual problem to flow down the organizational chain of command, then those 15 golden seconds would elapse without a response, and the firm would have lost an opportunity to earn a loyal customer.

The recognition that only the line employee could provide good service to the customer was a radical change. The traditional corporate structure is a pyramid capped by the chief executive and a number of highly qualified vice presidents, all well-educated, skilled specialists in finance, production, exports, and sales, who try to make all the decisions necessary to run the company. At the bottom of the pyramid, both blue-collar and white-collar foot soldiers deal daily with the customers and have the knowledge about the company's front-line operations; they are typically powerless to respond to the individual situations that arise.

Source: Jan Carlzon, *Moments of Truth* (Cambridge, MA: Ballinger, 1987).

The image of traditional business organization resembles a pyramid (Exhibit 1). At its base, operating employees interact routinely with customers, so they see the daily problems and difficulties of the firm's system. From this close vantage point, they can offer the clearest insight into the tasks and activities that it must accomplish to produce a good or service. The employees, in turn, support progressively smaller layers of management from supervisors to lower-level managers, middle managers, and top managers. Ultimately, this entire pyramid culminates with the leader of the organization, typically the owner, president, or CEO. From this high perch, the top leader must guide the entire organization and formulate the strategic vision that drives and directs its actions.

TQM challenges this structure because it directs support in the opposite direction. Operating employees have the closest contact with customers, and they work with the details of the processes that generate the firm's goods and services. Operating employees, not top or intermediate-level managers, determine the quality level that the firm offers. They know more than anyone else about the firm's problems and the effects that the solutions must achieve. As a result, TQM advocates believe, the entire organization should support the operating employees. This view turns the traditional organization upside down (Exhibit 1), assigning managers the responsibility of supporting employees. Jan Carlzon of SAS Airlines has articulated this view, as the In Practice box reports.

EXHIBIT 1
Traditional versus TQM View of Organizational Structure

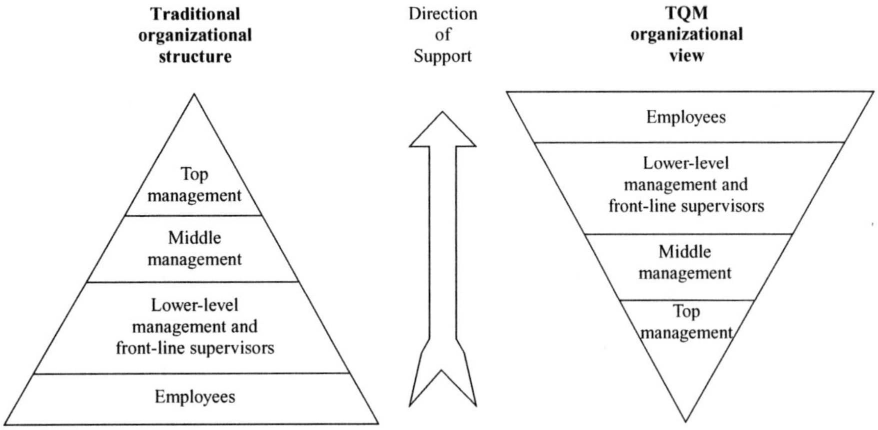

In Practice

EMPOWERMENT CURES SMALL BUSINESS WOES

Corporate America has had almost a decade to adjust to the TQM ideals of empowerment and teamwork. As these ideas filter down into smaller, family-owned businesses, the transformations are no less dramatic—or successful.

Take Growing Green, Inc., of St. Louis, for example. Teri Pesapane started the small gift shop, plantscaping, and plant care business with her husband Joel back in 1973 with just $3,200 from their savings. In the beginning, the husband-and-wife team was able to handle all aspects of the business, with Teri closing the deals and Joel making the deliveries.

As the business grew, the Pesapanes took on additional employees, and by 1988 their business boasted revenues of $700,000 and a staff of 16. But instead of enjoying the success, the Pesapanes found they had a crisis on their hands, both personally and professionally. Employee turnover was high, morale was low, and the Pesapanes felt they couldn't go anywhere for even a weekend because their business might fall apart.

"Employees couldn't make decisions," explained one long-time employee. "We had to check with Joel about every detail—from what to spray a plant with to whether a large ficus tree needed to be fertilized."

The Pesapanes realized they had to give up some control. After attending a seminar on work team management, they divided the company into small action teams. The sales team brings in new business, operations handles plant installations, service maintains plants at customer sites, and an administrative team handles billing and other financial matters. Senior-level employees from each of these teams make up a management team. Teri and Joel no longer involve themselves in the daily decision making of their work teams. Instead, they act as sounding boards and provide "big picture" leadership.

The new system works so well that the Pesapanes even venture out of the country these days. When they come back, they find that, not only has their business not fallen apart, but their sales team has brought in new contracts. With 250 clients and revenues of about $1 million, it's clear that Growing Green has benefited from implementing the same TQM culture that has rejuvenated America's larger corporations. And that's been personally satisfying to everyone involved. "We want our people to grow, just like our plants," explained Joel.

Source: Barbara Buchholz and Margaret Crane, "Nurturing the Team Spirit at Growing Green," *Your Company*, Spring 1995, p. 11.

Defining the TQM Concept

Logothetis describes total quality management as "a culture; inherent in this culture is a total commitment to quality and attitude expressed by everybody's involvement in the process of continuous improvement of products and services, through the use of innovative scientific methods."[2] This definition highlights four major TQM axioms, illustrated in Exhibit 2.

Commitment to Quality

Everyone in the organization must make a commitment to producing quality products. This springs from unquestioning acceptance that quality offers a viable focus for developing and

EXHIBIT 2
Major Axioms of TQM

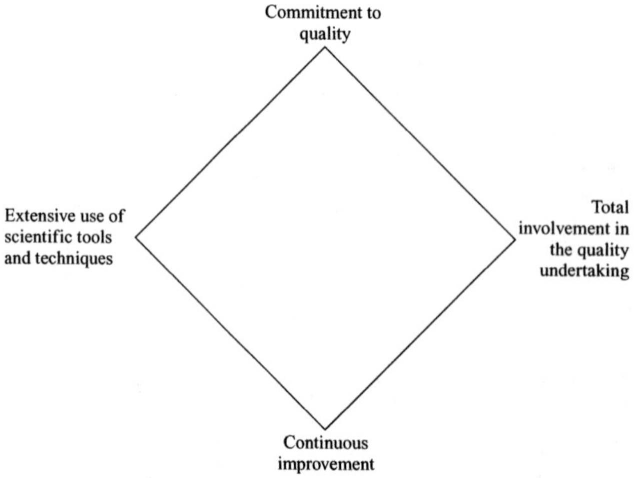

[2] Nickolas Logothetis, *Managing for Total Quality: From Deming to Taguchi and SPC.* (Hertfordshire, UK: Prentice Hall International, 1992), p. 5.

maintaining a sustainable competitive advantage in the marketplace. Everyone has to trust that customers want quality enough to buy from a firm that offers it, even at a higher price than competitors' products at a lower quality level. Second, organization members must make a commitment to customers. This commitment requires every representative of a firm to maintain and deliver quality at every interchange or transaction with either customers or suppliers. Third, TQM demands a commitment by top managers. Top managers must take actions that support the organization's move toward TQM, allocate resources to that move, and become champions of TQM within the firm. And finally, TQM requires a commitment of the firm as a whole. For TQM to work, everyone who contributes to the firm's product, including employees, managers, and suppliers, must accept quality as a critical component of both the survival of the firm and its ability to satisfy its customers.

Extensive Use of Scientific Tools, Technologies, and Methods

Total quality management requires an organization to replace subjective procedures and rules with powerful **statistical tools.** Statistics can help the TQM practitioner identify and ignore random variations to focus instead on systematic changes in the process or product. These various tools are covered in the TQM Tools module of this series.

Total Involvement in the Quality Undertaking

TQM can succeed only through teamwork and empowerment. Teamwork brings together people from different functional areas into groups that can enrich the decision-making process with information from many different perspectives. Empowerment gives both responsibility for delivering quality and authority to identify problems and then formulate and implement solutions to employees who have direct contact with a problem. Empowerment frees employees from the need to ask for permission from a manager; they simply do whatever they must to solve the problem. The In Practice box presents a good example of empowerment.

Continuous Improvement

The fourth axiom of total quality management requires never-ending improvement. TQM inspires members of an organization to improve something, no matter how small, every day. This formalized system of continuous improvement is now referred to as *kaizen*.

TQM Frameworks—The Pioneers

Total quality management draws on frameworks and tools to achieve its objectives. **TQM frameworks** are the mental models that act as magnifying glasses through which managers can examine processes that affect the firm's design and delivery of quality. These frameworks provide numerous general guidelines and rules of thumb. Management frameworks most clearly show the influence of TQM pioneers such as Deming, Juran, Crosby, and Imai.

- Dr. W. Edwards Deming articulated his 14 points for management, 5 deadly sins and diseases, the theory of variance, and the role of management.
- Dr. Joseph Juran outlined the habit of quality, the quality trilogy, and the universal breakthrough sequence.
- Philip B. Crosby enumerated the absolutes for quality management and the 14 steps for quality improvement.
- Masaaki Imai explained the principle of kaizen, or continuous improvement.

Deming—The Philosopher of TQM

To many, the name W. Edwards Deming is synonymous with quality and total quality management. Along with Juran, Deming exposed Japanese managers to the fundamental concepts of quality production. Deming first envisioned quality management as an organizationwide

In Practice

POINT 3—CEASE DEPENDENCY ON INSPECTION TO ACHIEVE QUALITY: INSPECTION AT CONSOLIDATED DIESEL CORPORATION

Consolidated Diesel Corporation of Whitakers, North Carolina, manufactured small diesel engines as a joint venture between Cummins and J. I. Case Tractor. From the outset, the plant was designed expressly to manufacture a quality diesel engine every time. The initial plant layout placed a single inspection station at the end of the final assembly line, where inspectors would hook up finished engines to a computer that would run a battery of tests. If this revealed a problem, inspectors could repair the engine and send it on its way immediately.

The plant managers discovered that inspection staff became very good at correcting symptoms. Their efforts to fix defects in the engines did nothing to eliminate the underlying problem, however. If an inspector found an improperly tightened screw in a clamp, that problem was likely to occur in the next engine as well. The person who created the problem never knew of its existence.

To remedy this process failure, the employees recommended removing any engine with a defect, no matter how small, from the line and returning it to the area that created the defect. The engine waited behind the operator until he or she corrected the defect, which had to be done before the operator could take a lunch or coffee break. A waiting engine acted as a visual signal of a process problem, and the number of defective engines indicated the severity of the problem. The system returned a defective engine to the operator quickly, helping people to determine what caused the problem before making more mistakes.

This system gave every operator an incentive to make each engine right the first time, every time.

Source: Steven A. Melnyk and Phillip L. Carter, *Shop Floor Control: Principles, Practices, and Case Studies* (Falls Church, VA: American Production and Inventory Control Society, 1987), pp. 279–323.

activity rather than a technical task for inspectors or a specialized quality-assurance group. He identified quality as a management responsibility, observing that managers must create the systems and processes that generate quality. Deming made the initial insight that a firm could never inspect quality into a product. Rather, a quality product combines a good design with effective production methods. Only by meeting both of these conditions could a firm assure quality.

Known for his strong views and opinions (see Exhibit 3), Deming created a set of guidelines for achieving quality that could change every aspect of an organization's management.

EXHIBIT 3
W. Edwards Deming on Current Management Practice

Source: Deming, W. Edwards, *Out of the Crisis*, Cambridge, Mass.: Massachusetts Institute of Technology, Center for Advanced Engineering Study, 1986.

- It would be a mistake to export American Management to a friendly country. America is the world's most underdeveloped nation!
- The wealth of a nation depends on its people, management, and government, more than its natural resources.
- The right Quality and Uniformity are foundations of commerce, prosperity, and peace.
- The workers are handicapped by the system, and the system belongs to the management.
- Defects are not free; somebody makes them and gets paid to make them!
- When will management learn that they have a moral obligation to protect investment and safeguard jobs?
- A quality program launched by ceremonies, speeches, raising of flags, beating of drums, badges, and heavy applause is a delusion and a snare!
- Management needs training to learn about their company.
- The job of management is not supervision but leadership.
- The big problem in leadership and training arises from a standard of what is acceptable work and what is not.
- Putting out fires is not improvement.
- When managers visit other companies seeking examples, one can only hope that they will enjoy the ride, because this is the only thing they will be getting out of it!
- Absenteeism is a function of poor management. If people feel important to a job, they will come to work.
- Focusing on outcome is not an effective way to improve a process or an activity.
- Slogans, exhortations, and posters with targets to be met (without providing the means to meet them) are directed to the wrong people. They take no account of the fact that most of the trouble comes from the system.

He realized that an organization's very survival depended on making such changes rather than assuming that past success assured continued operations. When someone asked Deming to justify the need for his TQM recommendations, he answered, "You do not have to do this—survival is not compulsory."[3]

Deming's 14 Points for Management

Deming succinctly summarized his views on management and its relationship with quality in his **14 points** for management (Exhibit 4). Altogether, these guidelines describe a fundamental basis for an organization's culture. They define a process by which managers actively seek out bad practices and habits and replace them with better, more effective practices.

Deming used his 14 points for management to emphasize the critical role of managers in total quality management. He saw managers rather than workers or equipment as the real obstacle to TQM, often pointing out that 85 percent of quality problems could be traced to management, while workers were responsible for the remaining 15 percent. In the mid-1980s, one analyst has claimed, the percentage of problems caused by managers increased to 94 percent.[4] To understand the power of these 14 points and the implications of not heeding their lessons, consider the lessons learned by Consolidated Diesel in the In Practice box.

1. Take one of the 14 points and demonstrate its application by using information taken from an article or story. Prove to yourself that these 14 points really do make sense.
2. Why is it important to target and get commitment from top management and superiors in a company?
3. Are there any instances under which inspection is necessary?
4. What is the difference between commitment and involvement?

Deming's Theory of Variance

Most of Deming's work revolves around his **theory of variance.** This theory views variations from standard activities as a major source of problems for all operations management (OM) processes and most firms. Variance causes unpredictability, which increases uncertainty and reduces control over the processes. TQM assigns managers the task of finding the sources of this variance and eliminating it to significantly improve OM system performance through a process of continuing improvement.

Variance can come from many sources. Activities within the OM system can disrupt standard work flows, as can the actions of such groups as marketing, engineering, purchasing, and accounting. Managers can categorize all variances as either *controlled* or *uncontrolled.*

EXHIBIT 4
Deming's 14 Points for Management

Source: Deming, W. Edwards, *Out of the Crisis,* Cambridge, Mass.: Massachusetts Institute of Technology, Center for Advanced Engineering Study, 1986.

1. Create consistency of purpose for continual improvement of product and service.
2. Adopt the new philosophy for economic stability.
3. Cease dependency on inspection to achieve quality (see In Practice box for an example of this point in action).
4. End the practice of awarding business on price tag alone.
5. Improve constantly and forever the system of production and service.
6. Institute training on the job.
7. Adopt and institute modern methods of supervision and leadership.
8. Drive out fear.
9. Break down barriers between departments and individuals.
10. Eliminate the use of slogans, posters, and exhortations.
11. Eliminate work standards and numerical quotas.
12. Remove barriers that rob the hourly worker of the right to pride in workmanship.
13. Institute a vigorous program of education and retraining.
14. Define top management's permanent commitment to ever-improving quality and productivity.

[3] Ibid., p. 61.
[4] Ibid., p. 27.

A **controlled variance** responds to efforts by a worker to correct or manage the activity; an **uncontrolled variance** reflects the impact of some factor outside the control of the employee, who cannot correct it.

Workers or managers can correct a variance by either changing its common causes or removing its special causes. **Common causes** reflect systematic problems in an OM process, including weaknesses in product design, failure to match incoming components to needs, equipment malfunctions, poor facilities maintenance, and incomplete or inaccurate routing documents and bills of material. In contrast, **special causes** reflect short-term sources of variance in an OM process that operators could correct. Special causes might include problems such as a lack of knowledge or skill, worker inattention, or a bad batch of incoming materials. Correcting common causes requires a management response, while shop-floor personnel must correct special causes.

Differentiating variances as either controlled or uncontrolled and as results of either common or special causes defines the matrix of responsibility in Exhibit 5. This table reemphasizes the pivotal role of managers in TQM since they bear responsibility for three of the four cells.

EXHIBIT 5
Categories of Variance

		Source of Variance	
		Common Cause	**Special Cause**
Type of Variance	**Controlled**	Management	Employee
	Uncontrolled	Management	Management

Deming's Deadly Diseases and Sins

Deming recognized that implementation of his 14 points would strain managers' skills and determination. Successful application of these guidelines can completely transform an OM system and even an entire firm. As an initial step toward TQM, managers can first eliminate certain bad practices, or **five deadly diseases and sins,** as Deming called them (Exhibit 6).

EXHIBIT 6
Five Deadly Sins

Source: Deming, W. Edwards, *Out of the Crisis,* Cambridge, Mass.: Massachusetts Institute of Technology, Center for Advanced Engineering Study, 1986.

- *Lack of constancy:* Once you commit to quality, you cannot allow any variations in this message.
- *Concentration on short-term profits:* A process that focuses on short-term profits encourages short-term thinking and short-term actions. Managers may cut costs in the short term while sacrificing the long-term thinking and planning that total quality management demands and raising costs overall.
- *Overreliance on performance appraisals:* A performance appraisal system or any similar program for rating the merit of individual employees can hinder the implementation of TQM by encouraging rivalry, fear, and short-term thinking. Performance appraisals tend to focus attention on outputs, not on the processes that create the outputs.
- *Job-hopping:* Excessive rotation of manager and people encourages short-term thinking and inhibits their ability to understand the long-term implications of their actions.
- *Overemphasis on visible figures:* Performance cannot be measured accurately using only quantitative information. Rather, total costs, consisting of both quantitative and qualitative information, are needed.

Juran and Total Quality Management

After Deming, Dr. Joseph Juran has had the greatest impact on the theory and practice of quality management. Besides writing 12 books on the subject, Juran has pioneered training manuals for managers and spoken across the world on quality. Juran's contribution to total quality management centers on four themes:

- Compelling definitions of *quality* and the *cost of quality* (COQ).
- Quality habit.
- Quality trilogy.
- Universal breakthrough sequence.

Quality Defined and the Cost of Quality

Rather than defining the term *quality* by references to conformance to specifications (a definition based on quality-control criteria), Juran defined quality as **"fitness for use."** This broad definition accommodates variations in levels of quality, so it does not force the same level of quality for every situation. Instead, the appropriate level of quality matches the use that customers intend for the good or service. A student who wants to travel from home to lecture halls may not need a Rolls-Royce; a Ford Focus or Honda Civic may offer adequate quality.

Fitness for use results from many product traits[5] that dictate how well the designed functionality and performance of the entire product-consumption experience meets the customer's specific needs and expectations, and how well the actual functionality and performance of the product matches its design specifications. Fitness for use requires both **quality of design** and **quality of conformance.** *Quality of design* reflects the suitability of a product's design concept and specifications for its intended use. *Quality of conformance* reflects how well an actual product achieves the intentions of its design.

To make a product with excellent designed functionality and actual performance, managers must carefully control quality over the entire product life cycle from concept to design to prototype to production to phase-out or renewal. Like Deming's methods, Juran advocated appropriate statistical tools for each quality trait.

Juran's approach to quality emphasizes active involvement in daily operations. It presents specific tests and desired outcomes, making it a valuable shop-floor tool. This may present a problem, however, since operations workers deal with issues that top managers may find mundane. To get the attention of top managers, Juran developed the concept of the **cost of quality** (COQ).

The COQ makes the costs generated by poor quality visible. These costs are usually hidden in overhead and consequently are not visible to top management. The COQ helps management quantify the impact of quality on their company performance in dollars and cents. The COQ consists of four major categories (into which all costs can be assigned):

- **Prevention costs:** Costs that result from efforts to prevent defects and limit failure and appraisal costs, including quality planning, new-product reviews, training, process control, periodic improvement projects, and continuous improvement. These are the costs of avoiding quality problems.
- **Internal failure costs:** Costs that result from detection of quality defects in products prior to shipment to customers, including scrap, salvage, rework, excess inventory, and inspection.
- **External failure costs:** Costs that result from identifying defects in products after they reach customers, including complaint adjustments, loss of goodwill, returned materials, and field service or repairs.
- **Appraisal costs:** Costs that result from examinations to assess products' quality levels, including incoming material inspections, product and process inspections, inspection staff, and maintenance of test equipment.

Prevention costs are the cost of ensuring good quality; the remaining three represent the costs of poor quality. When managers begin to track these costs, they usually find that the

[5] David A. Garvin, "Competing on the Eight Dimensions of Quality," *Harvard Business Review*, Nov–Dec, 1987, 101–109.

cost of poor quality is often surprisingly large. In some cases the cost of poor quality accounts for between 50 and 80 percent of the overall COQ. In most companies, the costs of external failure are often far greater than the costs of internal failure and the costs of internal failure are often far greater than the costs of prevention. When managers recognize this, they can use the COQ to justify investments in prevention to avoid the other quality costs. It makes sense to continue to invest in prevention until the prevention costs exceed the costs of poor quality.

Quality Habit

Like Deming, Juran saw quality as a process of continuous improvement. To formalize this process, Juran introduced the concept of the **quality habit.** This habit, while it was to become as routine as washing every morning, was developed through the use of a four-stage process:[6]

1. Establish specific goals that identify what organization members should do and why.
2. Establish plans for reaching those goals with enough detail to guide people's actions from beginning to end.
3. Assign clear responsibilities for meeting the goals.
4. Base rewards on results.

Quality Trilogy

Juran's **quality trilogy** identified the three major activities of TQM: quality planning, quality control, and quality improvement. First, managers and employees develop a plan to improve the process. They then make the improvement. Once they establish that an improvement has actually been achieved, they institute control procedures to hold the improvement. Repeating this cycle of the quality trilogy (Exhibit 7) creates a never ending process for making incremental quality improvements.

EXHIBIT 7
Quality Trilogy

Universal Breakthrough Sequence

Juran's universal breakthrough sequence identifies a set of actions directed toward achieving major leaps in quality. This sequence specifies seven general actions that can apply to any situation or organizational problem, either within or outside operations management. The seven steps of the universal breakthrough sequence are summarized in Exhibit 8. Juran believed that all breakthroughs follow this universal sequence of steps.

Juran and Deming

Juran and Deming shared similar points of view on many subjects. Both agreed on the important role of top managers in TQM, and both recognized a crisis of quality in manufacturing. They agreed that both internal and external customers, continuous improvement, and the need for effective training and tools are important to implement total quality. However, Juran and Deming differed about some aspects of TQM. Deming was more process

[6] Logothetis, *Managing for Total Quality*, p. 64.

EXHIBIT 8
The Universal Breakthrough Sequence

1. *Proof of need.* Create an awareness of the need for change. Show that the costs of not changing are greater than the costs of changing.
2. *Project identification.* Pick a specific project. Recognize that people achieve breakthroughs by working on concrete projects that can show real benefits. Also pick those projects that have highly visible payoffs. Remember—nothing succeeds like success.
3. *Organize for improvement.* Put in place the organization needed for success. This consists of resources, top management committees, assignment of employees, and the implementation of detailed work policies and procedures, with milestones and well-defined ending conditions.
4. *Diagnostic journey.* Before implementing change, identify and understand the problems and their causes.
5. *Remedial action.* Work to identify and implement necessary corrective actions. Focus on the vital few, rather than on the trivial many.
6. *Resistance to change.* Recognize that change always attracts resistance. Overcoming resistance means encouraging wide participation in TQM projects and requires that people have sufficient time to understand and accept the changes.
7. *Holding onto the gains.* Finally, we must prevent a return to the "old" ways of doing things. This is done by establishing new standards, increasing training, and developing new control systems with early warning signals, appropriate tools, and data support systems. At this point, we are ready to repeat the process again.

oriented while Juran was more concerned about the output. In many ways, Juran continued and extended traditional ways of thinking about quality while Deming advocated a break with tradition and a new approach to quality management.

Philip B. Crosby and Total Quality Management

Philip B. Crosby, the third major influence on the management tools of total quality management, started his career as a line inspector, working his way up to corporate vice president and quality director of ITT. Crosby's contribution to TQM focused on (1) absolutes for quality management and (2) 14 steps for quality improvement.

Crosby addressed his message that quality management provides a viable strategy for corporate survival and growth to top management. Further, he denied that a firm must invest large sums to improve quality. Crosby asserted that a quality management program will generate savings that ultimately will pay for itself, so that ultimately, *quality is free.*

How can quality be free? Don't you have to make investments in quality up front? Can you think of an example where "quality is free"?

Crosby also advocated the ambitious goal of **zero defects.** To accomplish this managers must ensure that they design and build products with the objective from the outset of generating products without any defects.

Absolutes for Quality Management

Crosby identified four laws, called **absolutes for quality management,** that define the fundamental elements of any effective TQM system.

1. *Quality is conformance to requirements, not goodness.* Crosby stated that the only sensible definition of quality was based on what the customer wants. A firm produces quality only when the good or service meets or exceeds customers' expectations. Managers must ensure that everyone within the firm understands these requirements. They must then provide the tools necessary to achieve those requirements.

2. *Quality systems amount to prevention.* The path to TQM must begin with a thorough study and evaluation of current processes in which managers identify every opportunity for quality problems to disrupt a process and eliminate those opportunities.

3. *Zero defects define the performance standard.* Any effective TQM system must have a goal of zero defects. More than a slogan, the call for zero defects promotes a comprehensive method for designing, producing, and delivering a good or service that tries to eliminate any possibility for defects. It also advocates a corporate environment that accepts no possibility of errors.

4. *Measurement of quality is the price of nonconformance.* To make quality a strategic issue, managers must measure it. They must continuously assess the cost of failing to achieve quality goals in dollar units. The costs of doing things wrong (rejects, inspections, warranty repairs, field service complaints, satisfying unhappy customers, salvage, rework, etc.) represent the **price of nonconformance** (PONC).

Crosby agreed with Juran that once top managers understand the high costs of poor quality, they will make the necessary investments in quality training and education, improved product and process design, and better buyer–supplier relations. The cost of these efforts is the **price of conformance** (POC).

Crosby's 14 Steps for Quality Improvement

Like Deming and Juran, Crosby viewed the march toward quality as a never-ending journey. Before beginning this journey, managers first must assess their firm's current quality culture. A firm can be positioned at one of five states of quality awareness and quality culture:

- *Uncertainty.* The firm remains unaware of the importance of quality as a strategic imperative.
- *Awakening.* Managers understand the importance of quality, but they have not yet acted to improve it.
- *Enlightenment.* Managers openly acknowledge the importance of quality and the corporate need for improvement, and they have begun to take concrete action to improve overall quality by establishing a formal program.
- *Wisdom.* Managers have established a quality management program that is working well, identifying problems early and routinely pursuing corrective actions. The program emphasizes prevention rather than appraisal.
- *Certainty.* Quality has become an unavoidable component of the current management structure. The entire system is designed to ensure that the firm can attain its goal of zero defects. Any problems are both infrequent and truly random events.

Once managers have determined their firm's current quality culture, they can begin improving quality by implementing Crosby's **14 steps for quality improvement** (Exhibit 9).

Crosby disputed Deming's Point 10 and believed that slogans, mottoes, and posters were both appropriate and useful. Crosby also recommended that companies use performance measures and performance goals, a position that contradicted Deming's Point 11.

Imai and Continuous Improvement (Kaizen)

Masaaki Imai's contribution to TQM was his recognition of the need for **kaizen,** or **continuous improvement.** Kaizen is a Japanese name for a formal system to promote continuous improvement initially developed as part of just-in-time systems.[7]

Kaizen is based on the notion that the long-term survival and success of any organization occurs only when everyone in the firm actively pursues opportunities to identify and implement improvements every day. Pursuit of small improvements keeps people thinking about the process and its current operation. They identify potential improvements by understanding the functions of the current system and its weaknesses or relative inefficiencies. Furthermore, small improvements are often gained without needing any large investments—

[7] Kaizen, and Kaizen Events, are discussed in greater detail in the "Lean Systems Tools and Procedures" module by Steven A. Melnyk, Lawrence D. Frendenall, (New York: McGraw-Hill/Irwin 2002).

EXHIBIT 9
Crosby's 14 Steps for Quality Improvement

Source: Crosby, Philip B. *Quality Is Free: the Art of Making Quality Certain*, New York: McGraw-Hill, 1979.

1. *Management commitment.* Managers, especially at the top level, make quality a high-priority item for the firm.
2. *Quality improvement teams.* Cross-functional teams are established to achieve these improvements in quality. These teams have clear access to top management and are involved in guiding the process of quality improvement.
3. *Quality measurement.* Clear measures of quality, stated in meaningful terms that relate specifically to individual activities, are established and monitored.
4. *Cost of quality evaluation.* Data are gathered to assess the cost of both conformance and, more important, nonconformance.
5. *Quality awareness.* Formal programs aimed at creating awareness through the company are established.
6. *Corrective action.* The teams previously formed identify, study, and resolve problems in the OM system. The ultimate goal is that of prevention over correction.
7. *Zero-defects planning.* The firm moves from correcting problems to totally eliminating them. This is a top management task.
8. *Employee education.* The TQM program must train managers and employees at all levels to fulfill their roles properly in quality improvement.
9. *Zero-defects day.* This day marks a major turning point in the life of the firm. It signals to everyone that their work must now meet a new, higher standard of performance and that expectations have risen significantly.
10. *Goal setting.* These goals, set by management, guide performance and keep quality in the forefront of organizational activities.
11. *Error cause removal.* The focus now moves from correcting problems to removing the underlying causes.
12. *Recognition.* The TQM should include public, nonfinancial expressions of appreciation to those employees and managers whose actions have helped the firm achieve or exceed its quality objectives.
13. *Quality council.* This is a group of quality professional and team leaders who meet regularly to share experiences and discuss quality problems and ideas.
14. *Do it all over again!* Because the march towards quality is never-ending, the final step returns the program to the beginning, to repeat the path at a higher level.

a position that is captured within the motto of "creativity before capital." Kaizen has three guiding principles:

- *Process view of the system.* The basic unit of analysis in kaizen is the process. To create continuous improvement, we first must identify the appropriate processes and focus our attentions on these processes.
- *Success comes from people.* Any successful kaizen program relies heavily on people's knowledge of their firms' processes and their insights and intuition to conceive improvements. Success requires discipline, employee participation, skill development, and effective communication. The total quality management program at L.L. Bean, described in the opening vignette, illustrates kaizen in action.
- *Constant sense of urgency.* A successful kaizen program depends on unceasing awareness of the need for change. Everyone must feel that he or she can improve his or her performance and never accept a current process, however good, as sufficient. Complacency and overconfidence drain the energy from kaizen. In response to a question about his struggles to improve late in his career, Satchel Paige, a great baseball pitcher and popular wit, replied, "Never look behind yourself. You never know what might be gaining on you."

Other TQM Pioneers

Total quality management has benefited from the insights and hard work of many managers and writers. In addition to the four mentioned above, there are other people whose contributions should be recognized and acknowledged. These include Walter Shewhart,

Taguchi, Shigeo Shingo, and Myron Tribus. It was Shewhart who recognized the presence of variability in manufacturing processes. It was also Shewhart who married the concept of quality with the language and analytical capabilities of statistics. Professor Taguchi recognized the need to describe how the presence (or lack) of quality influences costs. He also integrated product design with process management through a structured approach aimed at ensuring the firm could consistently design high-quality product designs and implement them in controlled production processes. Shigeo Shingo was a Japanese manufacturing engineer involved in the early stages of developing the Toyota production system. He engineered the development and deployment of poka-yoke. Poka-yoke, or mistake proofing, is a device to detect and warn an operator when a mistake occurs. It prevents mistakes from becoming defects. Finally, Myron Tribus, past vice president of research and development for Xerox, was one of the first successful American implementers of TQM systems and procedures.

In short, TQM has many fathers. It is their diversity that helped make TQM such a broad and all-encompassing system.

Total Quality Management—Summarizing the Management Framework

While these pioneers have disagreed on details, they offer a unified message on certain important themes, which form the basic tenets of TQM.

Quality is not a tactical tool, but a strategic goal that an organization must achieve to survive and grow. The importance of quality forces an organization to extend responsibility for quality beyond any single functional area. Since every member affects the quality that the OM system delivers to customers, everyone must be involved.

The most effective quality management programs emphasize prevention of defects over inspection to find defects before they reach customers. To continually improve quality, an organization must understand and improve the process that generates it.

Effective quality management requires the support and commitment of managers, from the top down, to inspire and direct the actions of employees who must ultimately deliver quality. Quality improves when an organization focuses its corporate culture on the goal of building quality into its most essential structures. Quality management is a continuing process. Its critical importance requires vigilant protection from compromises driven by short-term considerations or actions. Daily details can overshadow the more distant goals of TQM unless some formal system sets clear specifications for quality as a standard for routine activities and as a basis for competition. National, state, and international programs such as ISO 9000 and the Malcolm Baldrige National Quality Award define such specifications.

TQM—Measuring Quality within the Firm

Measurement and metrics are critical elements of quality management, just as they are in the entire value-driven operations management system. Quality measurements and their metrics occur at the following levels:

- Product quality traits.
- Quality performance at the corporate level.
- Quality through design.
- Vendor quality.
- Production quality.

Product Quality Traits

Quality can be characterized using measurable traits. For example, *functionality* can be measured in such simple terms as the percentage of computers that arrived at the customers' locations "dead on arrival" (i.e., the computers would not work when they were first turned on by the customers). *Reliability* can be measured in terms of length of time that a hard disk can be expected to operate before it breaks down—the "mean time to failure." *Durability* can be measured in terms of the lowest temperature at which a computer can be operated before failing (e.g., this computer can be operated at temperatures of no lower than 10 degrees Fahrenheit). *Aesthetics* can be measured in the number of blemishes noted on a computer. For each trait that we measure, the result can be expressed either in the form of "yes/no" (product is acceptable or not) or as a number.

Take a candy such as M&Ms. Identify the important traits of quality and develop measures that would help you determine the quality of the candy. Which of these measures pertain to the product itself? Which of these measures would focus on the packaging or the services surrounding the product?

Quality Performance at the Corporate Level

It is difficult to measure the overall ability of the firm to deliver quality. So often firms rely on their compliance to standards as a measure of their corporate quality. For example, the organization might become certified to either or both ISO 9000 and QS 9000 (both of these standards are discussed in greater detail later in this module) to demonstrate that the corporation has achieved a given level of quality performance. Or a firm (if it is American) might apply for the Malcolm Baldrige National Quality Award (again discussed in greater detail later on), or one of the various local and statewide quality awards to indicate its quality performance.

Quality through Design

Design quality can be measured using either external or internal measures. An example of an external measure is the annual design awards given out by *Business Week.* There are numerous examples of internal measures of design quality, including

- The number of engineering change notices (ECNs) and engineering change orders (ECOs). The larger the number of ECOs or ECNs, the greater indication that the design was not done "right" the first time.
- The number of field recalls.
- Customer satisfaction surveys.

Vendor Quality

Measuring the quality of products received from vendors is critical to the effective management of the supplier relationship. Examples include

- The number of defective items.
- The percentage of shipments received early.
- The percentage of shipments received late.

Production Quality

Measures of internal production quality include

- Level of scrap.
- Number of hours of inspection labor (relative to the total hours of labor).
- Amount of rework.
- Percentage of costs due to warranty costs.
- Yield.
- Cost of quality.

These measures provide information that allows managers to plan and evaluate the OM function.

Six Sigma—The Next Stage in the Quality Journey

By the end of the 1990s, some managers began to question how effectively TQM generated and maintained a sustainable competitive advantage. They complained that most TQM programs gave smaller and smaller improvements. They proposed improvements to TQM concepts to create what is now referred to as the **six-sigma** (6σ) **program.** In this usage, "sigma" refers to the standard deviation of a process output, an indicator of process variability. A primary objective of six-sigma programs is to design and improve products and processes so that product specifications are reliably produced. In a six-sigma approach, sources of process variability (represented as sigma) are identified and reduced, thereby lowering the process output's "sigma." Changes are made to the product design or the process operation until the width of the product specification limits (the acceptable range for output) is at least twelve times the value of the process sigma, that is, plus or minus "six sigma" from the centered process mean. This relationship between the product specifications and the process sigma ensures that the vast majority of the process output will be acceptable. The "Quality Improvement Tools and Techniques" module discusses these ideas in greater detail.

Six sigma is a relatively new development that has been adopted by firms such as Motorola, Allied Signal, and GE. Its objective is to satisfy customers by continuously improving quality. The benefits generated by its use have been both real and significant (see Exhibit 10).

EXHIBIT 10
Six Sigma in Action—Benefits Generated

Source: www.airacad.com/transact.htm.

Motorola ROI—1987–1994

- Reduced in-process defect levels by a factor of 200.
- Reduced manufacturing costs by $1.4 billion.
- Increased employee production on a dollar basis by 126 percent.
- Increased stockholders' share value fourfold.

Allied Signal ROI—1992–1996

- Reduced costs by $1.4 billion.
- Had 14 percent growth per quarter.
- Had 520 percent price/share growth.
- Reduced new product introduction time by 16 percent.
- Reduced bills/cycle by 24 percent.

General Electric ROI—1995–1998

- Produced companywide savings of over $1 billion.
- Estimated annual savings to be $6.6 billion by the year 2000.

Defining the Six-Sigma Program

Different writers have defined six sigma in different ways, but it is clear that six sigma is another step in the TQM evolution. Six sigma is a corporatewide approach to quality that integrates the business elements of the customer, metrics, strategy, value, processes, quality, and statistical tools. Six Sigma strives for breakthrough improvements.

Six sigma is based on certain critical premises and assumptions:

All processes inherently move over time. Often we treat processes as if they are stationary (i.e., they stay centered on their mean output value). Yet this is frequently not the case. Processes do "jump" around. It is this type of movement that creates quality problems. For example, imagine a grinding process that automatically grinds metal parts to a specified width. As the grinding wheel wears, we would expect the average width of the processed parts to increase. When a process is stable and centered within specification limits, a three-sigma quality level means that the firm produces defect-free products 99.74 percent of the time. A six-sigma process that is centered produces defect-free products 99.99966 percent of the time. However, as shown in Exhibit 11, if the process jumps so that its center is 1.5 sigma away from

EXHIBIT 11
Defects per Million Parts when the Process is 1.5 Sigma Off Center

Source: www.airacad.com/transact.htm.

Sigma Level	Defects per Million Parts
2 σ	308,537
3 σ	66,807
4 σ	6,210
5 σ	233
6 σ	3.4

the nominal value, then a six-sigma process produces only 3.4 defects per million parts, while a three-sigma process produces 66,807 defects per million parts. Practical examples of the differences between six sigma and three sigma are given in Exhibit 12.

To go from the traditional TQM three-sigma to six-sigma quality effort requires a more intensive approach. With three sigma, our focus is on the obvious or "low hanging" fruit. We tend to use simple statistical tools (e.g., control charts, run charts, or histograms) to identify and solve problems. To achieve six-sigma quality, we have to focus on the design of the processes using a structured approach to system improvement based on experimentation and data.

To achieve truly world-class quality and performance, we need to focus on the processes. If your task is to reduce the number of parts rejected, you cannot do so by focusing only on the rejects. Instead, you have to focus on the factors that give rise to process variability—factors such as the quality of material, the specifications, the equipment (e.g., condition), and the training of the people involved. By focusing on these causal factors, you can significantly improve quality.

Six-sigma quality is the result of a well-defined and structured process. Six-sigma quality is not something that is achieved by chance. Rather, it is the product of a process that is highly repeatable—a process with well-defined tasks and milestones. This process is discussed in the next section.

EXHIBIT 12
Comparing Sigma Quality Levels

Source: www.airacad.com/transact.htm.

The Classical View of Quality: "99.9% Good" (3.8σ)	The Six-Sigma View of Quality: "99.99966% Good" (6σ)
• 20,000 lost articles of mail per hour.	• Seven lost articles of mail per hour.
• Unsafe drinking water almost 15 minutes each day.	• One minute of unsafe drinking water every seven months.
• 5,000 incorrect surgical operations per week.	• 1.7 incorrect surgical operations per week.
• Two short or long landings at most major airports daily.	• One short or long landing at most major airports every five years.
• 200,000 wrong drug prescriptions each year.	• 68 wrong drug prescriptions each year.
• No electricity for almost seven hours each month.	• One hour without electricity every 34 years.

D-M-A-I-C—The Six-Sigma Process

At the heart of the six-sigma program, as implemented by GE, is a five-step process, **D-M-A-I-C.** Each of these letters denotes a major activity that must be completed in order for management to achieve the objectives of six sigma.

D—Define. The first step is to identify who, in general, are the customers served and who specifically are the critical or important customers. It is also at this step that answers to the following questions are provided:

- Who is the customer?
- Who is the critical or important customer?

EXHIBIT 13
Sample Customer CTQs

- Customer responsiveness/communication.
- Marketplace competitive—product/price/value.
- On-time, accurate, and complete customer deliverables.
- Product/service technical performance.
- Predictable and reliable delivery times.

- What does the customer think is critical to quality and value (i.e., what are the "critical to quality" [CTQ] measures as illustrated in Exhibit 13)?
- What is the business strategy?
- What processes are involved?
- What measures accurately reflect the interests, concerns, and expectations of the critical customer?

An important outcome of this step is the creation of the customer dashboard—the set of performance measures defined by the customer that are used to evaluate the performance of the various processes and to identify candidates for improvement. Examples of such performance measures include cost of quality, customer satisfaction, and on-time delivery.

M—Measure. Next, we must be able to answer the question, "What is the frequency of defects?" To do this requires that we measure the CTQ characteristics frequently and regularly. The information provided by these measures is used as an input into the next step.

A—Analyze. Using the information from the preceding stage, we determine when and where the defects affecting the performance of the system occur. This includes identifying the sources of unwanted variability in the system.

I—Improve. Once we have identified the source of the defects, we next develop a plan of action aimed at correcting the problems and at improving the performance of the targeted processes.

C—Control. The final step in this process focuses on institutionalizing the changes identified and implemented in the preceding step. The goal of this step is to make sure that the processes are corrected in the short term and that they remain "fixed" in the long term.

There is a sixth potential step—"Do it over again." The six-sigma program is designed to be repeatable and predictable. As can be seen from this brief description, it is evolutionary in that it builds on and extends many of the tools and themes used not only within TQM but also within the value-driven operations management system.

Formalized Process Control in ISO 9000

ISO 9000 defines a set of internationally accepted standards for business quality initially adopted in 1987 by the International Organization for Standardization (ISO).[9] This standard was subsequently revised in 1994 and most recently in 2000. The newest version of ISO 9000 is referred to as the **ISO 9000:2000 standard.** The ISO 9000 standard was initially developed to facilitate international trade. One indication of its success is that national bodies from over 120 countries now support this standard. As a standard, ISO 9000:2000 is intended to be applicable to all forms of organizations, irrespective of their size and their product offerings. It has been implemented in banks, consulting operations, manufacturing plants, software development firms, tourism operations, and even universities.

ISO 9000:2000 focuses on the processes that make up the quality management system (QMS). Its purpose is to ensure that the quality management processes needed to document, implement, monitor, and improve quality are in place.

[9] John T. Rabbit and Peter A. Bergh, *The ISO 9000 Book* (White Plains, NY: Quality Resources, 1993), p. 9.

The Process of Attaining ISO 9000:2000 Certification

ISO 9000 certification requires that a firm be audited by an external body. This certification states that the firm's QMS has been evaluated and that it meets or exceeds the requirements set down in the ISO 9000:2000 standards. The attainment of ISO 9000:2000 certification is itself the result of a process. Typically, once a firm has developed and implemented a corporate QMS consistent with the ISO 9000:2000 standards, it conducts an internal audit to determine whether its QMS is consistent with the standards. After responding to any deficiencies found in the audit, the firm contracts with a registrar (an external and independent body)[10] to audit the effectiveness of the QMS. If the firm's QMS is officially certified, it is recorded by the registrar as ISO 9000:2000 certified.

Clearly, attaining ISO 9000 certification is demanding and time-consuming. This process can take anywhere from 3 to 24 months to implement, depending on the initial level of compliance of the firm's systems.[11]

The ISO 9000:2000 Standard

As previously noted, ISO 9000 was officially revised in 2000. Prior to 2000, there were three standards: ISO 9001:1994, ISO 9002:1994, and ISO 9003:1994. There is now only one standard: ISO 9001:2000. All firms that want to retain their ISO 9000 certification are making plans to become ISO 9001:2000 certified. The new standard consists of five sections and is more logical than the old standard and more compatible with the ISO 14001 environmental management systems. The major sections of the standard are given in Exhibit 14 on page 22.

In addition to its new structure, ISO 9001:2000 has several other important changes. First, it is more customer-oriented, with a great emphasis placed on defining, meeting, and achieving customer satisfaction. Second, it emphasizes the need to make improvements on a regular basis. Third, it recognizes the importance of product design to quality by including **product realization** (i.e., all the processes and activities a firm undertakes to design, develop, and build a new product) in the standard. Fourth, it includes standards about customer requirements, statutory requirements, the quality infrastructure, and on-going improvement. Finally, the new standard was written to be more flexible and less prescriptive than the ISO 9000:1994 standard. In general, the new standards tell management what to do, not how to do it.

Benefits of ISO 9000 Certification

There are three forces creating the impetus for ISO 9000 certification:

- International competitiveness and customer demands.
- Market realities and perceptions.
- Internal organizational health.

International Competitiveness and Customer Demands Increasingly, firms recognize the need for certification to sell products to customers in Europe, including Great Britain. The European Economic Community (EC) (with a total population of over 380 million people) is establishing a single set of standards for manufacturers to simplify free trade among the member states. The EC has accepted the provisions of ISO 9000 verbatim, so a company must usually follow these standards to have any hope of selling to EC customers.

In addition, every major industrial nation in the world has accepted these standards, and the U.S. Department of Defense and NATO are incorporating them into purchasing requirements. In short, ISO 9000 certification has become a necessary condition to sell to customers in major markets. In April 1994, over 2,500 American companies and over 30,000 European firms had accepted this reality and become ISO certified. In April 2001, 35,772 firms were certified in the United States.[12] For many companies, ISO 9000 certification is a cost of doing business in today's world.

[10] It is possible to self-certify a system to be ISO 9000:2000 compliant. However, such an action does not carry the weight and credibility of external certification.
[11] Rabbit and Bergh, *ISO 9000 Book,* pp. 77–78.
[12] http://www.qsuonline.com/, June 3, 2001.

EXHIBIT 14 The ISO 9001:2000 Certification Structure

Section	Focus/Description
4	**System requirements**
4.1	Establish your quality system Develop, implement, and improve QMS
4.2	Document your quality system Develop, prepare, control, and maintain quality system documents
5	**Management requirements**
5.1	Support quality Promote the importance of quality; develop, implement, and improve the QMS
5.2	Satisfy your customer Identify, meet, and enhance customer requirements
5.3	Establish a quality policy Define and manage your organization's quality policy
5.4	Carry out quality planning Formulate your quality objectives and plan QMS
5.5	Control your quality system Define responsibilities, appoint management representatives, and support internal communications
5.6	Performance management reviews Review QMS and examine review
6	**Resource requirements**
6.1	Provide quality resources Identify and provide quality resource requirements
6.2	Provide quality personnel Use and support competent personnel
6.3	Provide quality infrastructure Identify, provide, and maintain the needed infrastructure
6.4	Provide quality environment Identify and manage the needed work environment
7	**Realization requirements**
7.1	Control realization planning Plan and develop the product realization process
7.2	Control customer processes Identify and review customers' product requirements Communicate with your customers
7.3	Control product development Plan, design, and develop product development cycle, including inputs, outputs, review process, design verification process, and the design and development change process
7.4	Control purchasing functions Control, document, and verify the purchasing process
7.5	Control operational activities Control, validate, and identify production and service provision
7.6	Control monitoring devices Identify monitoring and measuring needs, select, calibrate, protect, validate, and use monitoring and measuring devices
8	**Remedial requirements**
8.1	Perform remedial processes Plan and implement remedial processes
8.2	Monitor and measure quality Monitor and measure customer satisfaction Plan and perform regular internal audits Monitor and measure quality processes Monitor and measure product characteristics
8.3	Control nonconforming products Develop a procedure to identify, document, and control nonconforming products and verify those nonconforming products that were corrected
8.4	Analyze quality information Define quality management system, collect quality management system data, and provide quality management information
8.5	Make quality improvements Improve quality management system and correct actual nonconformities and prevent potential nonconformities.

Source: Praxion, 2001, available at www.praxion.com/iso-9000-standard.html.

Market Realities and Perceptions A noncertified company faces increasing difficulty competing against ISO 9000–certified firms. Certification makes a competitor seem like a better, more reliable vendor. Media reports in newspapers, television, and such popular business magazines as *Business Week* and *Fortune* reinforce this perception of better quality from ISO 9000–certified firms.

Internal Organizational Health Finally, ISO 9000–certified firms have benefited from improvements in their internal organizational health in the course of the process. To pass the audit, people within the firm re-examine and critically challenge their practices and weed out inefficiencies. This activity helps to relieve pent-up organizational frustration and invites employees to assume responsibility for improving both operations and the formal quality process. This empowers people and raises effectiveness. Finally, the certification process improves communication links between functional areas within the firm. It forces people to forge agreements on such important issues as the firm's definition of value and its identification of its target market. All of these activities relieve internal stress and boost morale and effect iveness.

QS-9000

QS-9000 is the acronym for "Quality System Requirements QS-9000." QS-9000 is the supplier quality standard issued jointly by Daimler Chrysler Corporation, Ford Motor Company, and General Motors Corporation. QS-9000 also has been adopted by several heavy truck companies, including Navistar International Transportation Corporation and PACCAR, Inc. These companies require that their suppliers of production materials, production and service parts, heat treating, painting and plating, and other finishing services to the automotive companies become QS-9000 certified.

The registrars who certify companies' compliance with the ISO 9000 standards reached an agreement with the automotive industry that the QS-9000 requirements are specific industry interpretations of ISO 9000. So these registrars can simultaneously certify companies to ISO 9000 and QS 9000.

Quality Awards: Formalizing the Search for Quality

The increased awareness of the importance of quality has inspired the introduction of numerous quality awards, at the city, state, and international levels. At present, some 40 states have their own quality awards programs in place. These quality programs have formalized systems for evaluating the ability of any firm to consistently design, produce, and deliver a quality product. In the process, they have established a new set of hurdles for firms to clear. For example, Motorola expects all of its North American suppliers to apply for the Malcolm Baldrige Award and to strive to meet its standards. The Malcolm Baldrige National Quality Award is the foundation on which many of the current state, national, and international awards are based.

Malcolm Baldrige National Quality Award: Recognizing Outstanding Quality

The **Malcolm Baldrige National Quality Award** (MBNQA) is presented annually to U.S. companies that best represent the successful implementation of quality in the design, production, and delivery of products for the marketplace. The Baldrige Award recognizes companies that represent the most effective pursuit and attainment of total quality. The list of past winners includes many firms from the elite of American industry. A listing of the winning websites can be found at http://www.quality.nist.gov/docs/winners/lnks8897.htm.

The Malcolm Baldrige National Quality Award emerged as a response to the competitive challenges facing U.S. businesses in the early 1980s. A bill to establish such an award passed the House of Representatives on June 8, 1987, with the strong support of Secretary of Commerce Malcolm Baldrige, confirming the strategic importance of quality to the welfare of American industry. When Malcolm Baldrige was killed in a rodeo accident, the award was renamed in his honor. (The In Practice box presents a brief biography of Baldrige.)

In Practice

MALCOLM BALDRIGE: A BRIEF BIOGRAPHY

Malcolm Baldrige was nominated as secretary of Commerce by President Reagan on December 11, 1980, and confirmed by the U.S. Senate on January 22, 1981.

During his tenure, Baldrige played a major role in developing and carrying out administration trade policy. He took the lead in resolving difficulties in technology transfers with China and India. Baldrige held the first cabinet-level talks with the Soviet Union in seven years, which paved the way for increased access by U.S. firms to the Soviet market. He was highly regarded by the world's preeminent leaders.

Leading the administration's effort to pass the Export Trading Company Act of 1982, Baldrige was named by the president to chair a cabinet-level trade strike force to search out unfair trading practices and recommend ways to end those practices. He was the leader in the reform of the nation's antitrust laws.

Baldrige's award-winning managerial excellence contributed to the long-term improvement in the economy and the efficiency and effectiveness of government. Within the Commerce Department, Baldrige reduced the budget by more than 30 percent and administrative personnel by 25 percent.

Baldrige worked during his boyhood as a ranch hand and earned several awards as a professional team roper on the rodeo circuit. He was Professional Rodeo Man of the Year in 1980 and was installed in the National Cowboy Hall of Fame in Oklahoma City in 1984.

Malcolm Baldrige died July 25, 1987, in a rodeo accident in California. His service as secretary of Commerce was one of the longest in history. He was possibly the most colorful secretary of Commerce and one of the most beloved.

Source: National Institute of Standards and Technology. www.quality.nist.gov

Goals and Procedures of the Malcolm Baldrige National Quality Award

The National Quality Award is intended to recognize and encourage improvements in quality and productivity by

- Stimulating companies to attain excellence in quality for the pride of achievement and improved profitability.
- Recognizing outstanding companies and disseminating the experiences of these firms to teach others about quality and its impact on corporate performance.
- Establishing guidelines for quality assessment by organizations in business, government, and other areas.
- Gathering detailed information from award winners about how to manage for superior quality by changing corporate cultures and practices.

There is a four-stage award evaluation process that involves independent review of the award applications by outsiders, on-site visits, and judges' reviews. The evaluators all contribute their time and are only reimbursed for their travel expenses. The review-and-evaluation process is administered by the National Institute of Standards and Technology (NIST).[13]

There are seven award examination categories that are evaluated. As shown in Exhibit 15, each applicant can have a total score of 1,000 or fewer points. The weights assigned to each category clearly demonstrate that the Baldrige award emphasizes business results. These categories have changed over time as the reviewers have become aware of the changing requirements of business. For example, the emphasis on supplier partnering is new and reflects the increasing importance of the supply chain.

Benefits of the Malcolm Baldrige National Quality Award Program

Achieving excellent scores in the Baldrige Award's numerous categories represents a significant accomplishment. Many firms apply every year, but no more than six can be recognized (at most, two each in the manufacturing, services, and small-firm divisions). Why would a firm undertake this very expensive application process with such short odds of winning?

Self-Assessment Tool The process of applying for the Baldrige Award often has results more important than the selection of the winner. As they apply the award's categories to

[13] Marion Mills Steeples, *The Corporate Guide to the Malcolm Baldrige National Quality Award* (New York: McGraw-Hill/Irwin, 1993), pp. 19–20.

EXHIBIT 15 The 2001 Examination Items and Point Values for the Malcolm Baldrige National Quality Award Program

	2001 Examination Categories/Items	Point Values	
1	Leadership	**120**	
	1.1 Organizational system		80
	1.2 Public responsibility and citizenship		40
2	Strategic planning	**85**	
	2.1 Strategy development		40
	2.2 Strategy deployment		45
3	Customer and market focus	**85**	
	3.1 Customer and Market Knowledge		40
	3.2 Customer Relationships and Satisfaction		45
4	Information and Analysis	**90**	
	4.1 Measurement and Analysis of Organizational Performance		50
	4.2 Information Management		40
5	Human resource focus	**85**	
	5.1 Work systems		35
	5.2 Employee education, training, and development		25
	5.3 Employee Well-Being and Satisfaction		25
6	Process Management	**85**	
	6.1 Product and service processes		45
	6.2 Business processes		25
	6.3 Support processes		15
7	Business results	**450**	
	7.1 Customer satisfaction results		125
	7.2 Financial and market results		125
	7.3 Human resources results		80
	7.4 Operational effectiveness results		120
	Total Points	**1000**	

Source: National Institute of Standards and Technology, *Baldrige National Quality Program 2001—Criteria for Performance Excellence* (Gaithersburg, MD: NIST, 2001).

company processes, both managers and employees learn much about their own operations and their success in serving their customers. This self-assessment can yield dramatic and important insights. As one expert in this area has noted, "When you're doing an award, you're trying to dress up an organization. When you are doing a self-assessment, you're trying to dress down an organization, to get into the core." This is also one reason why NIST distributes an average of 175,000 copies of the criteria every year.

Baldrige Effect In general, for every application received, over 2,000 firms request guidelines and applications. Many firms never really intend to apply for the award; instead, their managers use its categories and evaluation process as guidelines for improving their processes.

Sharing Information All winners of the Baldrige Award agree to actively teach others about quality and about their firms' experiences with quality. This leads to beneficial exchanges of information through war stories and through formal education and training programs.

ISO 9000 versus the Malcolm Baldrige National Quality Award

At first glance, it may seem that ISO 9000 and the Malcolm Baldrige National Quality Award are complementary. However, this is not the case, as shown in the following differences:

- The ISO 9000 program is an international program while the Malcolm Baldrige National Quality Award is targeted primarily to the American market and American firms.
- ISO 9000 is a minimum standard, while the MBNQA is a "stretch" goal.

- ISO 9000 is focused on processes, procedures, and the extent to which the firm's personnel are familiar with these aspects and their actions comply with them. In contrast, the MBNQA is far more comprehensive in the scope of topics covered.
- ISO 9000 is not extensively focused on the relationship between quality and strategic planning in any depth. It is also very internally oriented. In contrast, the MBNQA forces managers to show how their quality program has strategically affected the performance of the firm and improved the extent to which the firm is better able to satisfy the needs of its customers.

As can be seen, these two programs are very different. As a result, a firm that is ISO 9000 certified cannot count on winning, or even scoring well, in the MBNQA program.

TQEM—Marrying TQM with Environmental Concerns

TQM is fundamentally a dynamic concept. It is constantly changing and evolving. One recent development has involved managers and consultants applying the principles, tools, procedures and systems of TQM to improve corporate environmental performance and responsibility. This application of TQM principles, frameworks, and procedures to environmental problems is now referred to as **total quality environmental management,** or TQEM.

With TQEM, we recognize that quality involves more than the product and service; it also involves the impact of the firm's operations and its products on the environment. Just as TQM is concerned with product waste, TQEM is concerned with environmental pollution.

ISO 14000—Formalizing the Pursuit of TQEM

Beginning in 1996, a new certification system was introduced—the **ISO 14000** standards. This standard, which is based on the widely accepted ISO 9000 standards, focuses on environmental systems and procedures. ISO 14000 embodies a set of voluntary standards and guidelines designed to help an organization integrate environmental management into its business. This standard is not intended to replace any current regulations; rather it is a management tool to ensure environmental performance.

At present, ISO 14000 has only one standard for certification—ISO 14001, which is the standard for the environmental management system (EMS). The EMS provides and identifies the organizational structure, planning activities, responsibilities, practice, procedures, processes, and resources for developing, implementing, achieving, reviewing, and maintaining the environmental policy. The EMS consists of five major elements:

- Environmental policy.
- Planning.
- Implementation and operation.
- Checking and corrective action.
- Management review.

The ISO 14001 standard identifies what each element of the corporate EMS must contain. ISO 14001 is similar to ISO 9000 in that it focuses on procedures, metrics, systems, and employee compliance.

From 1996 to late 2000, some 18,000 plants worldwide achieved this ISO 14001 certification, but less than 1,000 were located in the United States. Some of the reported benefits are[14]

- Improved environmental performance.
- Improved internal management methods.

[14] Rainer Ochsenkuehn, *Introduction to ISO 14000 Handbook* (Fairfax, VA: The Victoria Group, 1996) p. 8.

- Improved stakeholder satisfaction.
- Avoidance of a potential nontariff barrier to certain markets.
- Competitive advantage in certain markets.
- Possibly fewer EPA inspections.
- Reduced cost of environmental, health, and safety activities.
- Probable reduction in regulatory noncompliance and associated fines.
- Improved access to capital and reduced capital costs.
- Reductions in insurance costs.
- Improved image.

TQM—A Corporate System or a People System?

Before leaving this module, it is important to address an important question: "Is TQM a corporate system or a people system?" To this point, we have spent a great deal of time focusing on the system issues needed to make TQM part of the corporate culture. However, this perspective underestimates the importance of people to TQM. For TQM to be successful, it must become a people system. That is, it must be accepted by the people involved. If the people do not "buy in" to TQM, if the people do not accept the premises of TQM or the need for TQM, then TQM will not succeed. The purpose of the systems emphasized by TQM advocates is ultimately to facilitate and enable the activities of the people.

Module Summary

We began this module by reviewing the experiences of L.L. Bean in transforming and improving its processes through total quality management. The rest of the module explored the concept of TQM and its evolution. Specifically, the following themes and issues were addressed in this chapter:

1. Total quality management strives to achieve a sustainable competitive advantage by focusing company actions on customer satisfaction, employee empowerment, and powerful management and statistical tools to achieve superior quality.
2. It is important to integrate TQM into the firm's strategic activities by ensuring that the voice of the customer is heard. The new six-sigma approach to quality is a corporatewide system to integrate the elements of the customer, strategy, value, processes, statistical tools, and metrics. This approach has been implemented successfully in firms such as Motorola and GE.
3. Formal certification to quality standards such as ISO 9000 or QS 9000 ensures that a firm has passed a rigorous audit to confirm that its major processes have been documented, that everyone associated with those processes understands correct procedures, and that people routinely follow these procedures. ISO 9000 seems likely to make certification a near-universal order qualifier in important markets in Europe and elsewhere.
4. Many firms use the Malcolm Baldrige National Quality Award guidelines to assess the performance of their quality management systems.
5. TQM is now transforming itself into TQEM. In this system, TQM is expanded to include environmental issues and concerns. This extension is being formalized in the ISO 14000 certification standards—a standard that is similar to ISO 9000, except that it focuses on environmental performance and environmental management systems.

TQM promotes a broad, cross-functional strategy for generating value through profound changes in a firm's corporate culture and management goals. Success requires a firm to carry this initiative to employees throughout the firm, arming them with the statistical tools and techniques they need to achieve the objectives of TQM. These tools and procedures are examined in another module.

Key Terms

14 steps for quality improvement, *14*
Absolutes for quality management, *13*
Appraisal costs, *11*
Common cause, *10*
Controlled variance, *10*
Cost of quality, *11*
Deming's 14 points, *7*
D-M-A-I-C, *19*
External failure costs, *11*
Fitness for use, *11*
Five deadly diseases and sins, *10*
Internal failure costs, *11*
ISO 9000, *20*
ISO 9000:2000 standard, *20*
ISO 14000, *26*
Kaizen/continuous improvement, *14*
Malcolm Baldrige National Quality Award, *23*
Prevention costs, *11*
Price of conformance, *13*
Price of nonconformance, *14*
Product realization, *21*
Quality habit, *12*
Quality of conformance, *11*
Quality of design, *11*
Quality trilogy, *12*
QS 9000, *23*
Six-sigma program, *18*
Special cause, *10*
Statistical tools for quality, *5*
Theory of variance, *9*
Total quality environmental management, *26*
Total quality management, *3*
TQM frameworks, *7*
Uncontrolled variance, *10*
Zero defects, *13*

Discussion Questions

1. A common proverb used in business is: "That which is not measured is not managed." In what ways does total quality management agree and disagree with this statement?
2. To what extent are the various measures discussed in this module process or output oriented? Given the orientation and goals of TQM, which would you expect to be more important?
3. Why is the orientation of the "Direction of support" arrow in Exhibit 1 an important element of the total quality management approach? Is the Japanese business culture more amenable to this orientation? Explain.
4. Employee empowerment is an essential element of total quality management in services. Cite instances where the service provider empowered its employee to go the extra mile to totally delight you. Then indicate an instance where the opposite happened. What programs should have been in place to prevent substandard service?
5. You have been commissioned to create a local equivalent of the Malcolm Baldridge Award for your college's campus. The winner will receive free campus parking for one academic year. Prepare a list of criteria for use in deciding who on your campus is most worthy of this award. How would you propose that these factors be measured? Should they be?
6. Take any one of Deming's 14 points and find an example of either its application or lack of application from your newspaper or a business periodical such as *Fortune* or *Business Week*.
7. The eighth of Deming's 14 Points of Management states that a firm must "drive out fear." Discuss the practicality of this tenet. Can an effective TQM program be realized in an organization in which employees experience fear?
8. Discuss the conditions under which inspecting a good or service is not waste. For what products would you be willing to pay more because their performance is assured through some inspection process? Cite a product for which this condition previously existed but that you now are willing to buy without inspection.
9. You have been appointed head of quality control for your organization (a firm at which you have worked or your college). During the first month, you interview disciples of Deming, Juran, and Crosby. Each seems to be equally affable and competent. Which consultant would you hire for your organization? Why?
10. As a star operations management student, you try to apply kaizen at your work. An experienced supervisor retorts, "kaizen—that is just another one of those Japanese fads. I'll wait for next year's." Is the supervisor's interpretation incorrect? Why do you think she might feel that way?
11. Why are export-oriented countries such as Germany and Japan on the leading edge of the quality movement?
12. Why are most quality awards based on the Malcolm Baldrige National Quality Award program? Why not the ISO 9000 standard?
13. Does achieving ISO 14000 certification mean that a firm has eliminated pollution?
14. "TQM is great, but don't try to apply it to your home life." Is there wisdom in this statement? Why?
15. Apply Juran's five dimensions of quality to the domestic use of nuclear power to electrify homes and industry. Is it a useful construct for debating the merits of this technology? Is there any other quality construct that is more useful? Why?
16. If TQM is to be a "people" system, what conditions must be in place first in the firm? What are the possible repercussions for the firm if the people don't buy in to TQM? Why?

17. It has been noted by several consultants and those familiar with the new ISO 14000 certification that selling this standard to American firms has been far harder than it was to sell the ISO 9000 standards? Why? [*Hint*: Think about the marketplace benefits to be gained by achieving this level of certification.]

Cases

ADVANCED LASER TECHNOLOGY, INC.

Punita Bigolow and her husband have a small, highly successful firm that serves a narrow niche of medical applications of laser technologies. The firm has only four customers, but each is a leading player in the emerging medical-electronics technology markets. Each firm has told Bigolow that it is pleased with her product, service, and ability to provide leading edge technology.

Bigolow's problem begins in the form of a memo. One of her major customers has just decided to seek ISO 9000 certification. As the customer has grown, it needs ISO 9000 certification to effectively compete in international markets. Bigolow understands this logic so far.

The next paragraph reads:

> As part of our ISO 9000 certification process, we will expect each of our key suppliers to become ISO 9000 certified. While we realize that this may impose some hardships on you, we are firmly convinced that the end result will be goods and services of world class quality.

What little Bigolow knows about ISO 9000 is that this new requirement would pose an enormous problem for Advanced Laser Technology. Her firm has five employees: herself, her engineer husband, two technicians, and one secretary. How will ALT be able to document all that it did?

It seems to be a catch-22 situation. If Bigolow and her husband divert all their attention to document all 20 aspects of Section 4 of ISO 9000, then the firm risks losing its competitive edge in this fast-changing technological field. If ALT hires a consultant to help with this certification process, it risks diverting both management attention and critical cash resources. As she reflects on this dilemma, Bigolow wonders, "How does this add to value?"

QUESTIONS

What would you recommend for Bigolow?

Internet Activities

1. Using information taken from the Internet and from various financial sources (such as *The Wall Street Journal*), make a decision as to whether you would invest in a firm that won the Malcolm Baldrige National Quality Award. Indicate the basis of your decision?
2. What firms have currently obtained ISO 14000 certification and what were their reasons? Use the Internet for your source of information.

Go to the web sites of 5 different companies of your choosing. Compare and contrast how these firms define quality (either implicitly or explicitly) and their quality mission. Are certain definitions more or less appropriate for a given industry?

Related Modules of Interest

- Quality Improvement Tools and Techniques
- Lean System Tools and Procedures
- Foundations of Value

Selected Readings

Bhote, Keri R. *Strategic Supplier Management: A Blueprint for Revitalizing the Manufacturer-Supplier Partnership.* New York: American Management Association, 1989.

Breen, Michael; Bob Jud; and Pablo E. Pareja. *An Introduction to ISO 9000.* Dearborn, MI: Society of Manufacturing Engineers, Reference Publication Division, 1993.

Breyfogle, Forrest W., III; James M. Cupello; and Becki Meadows. *Managing Six Sigma: A Practical Guide to Understanding, Assessing, and Implementing the Strategy That Yields Bottom-Line Success.* New York: John Wiley & Sons, 2001.

Carlzon, Jan. *Moments of Truth.* Cambridge, MA: Harper & Row, 1989.

Crosby, Philip B. *Quality Is Free.* New York: McGraw-Hill, 1979.

Dean, James W., Jr., and James R. Evans. *Total Quality: Management, Organization, and Strategy.* Minneapolis/St. Paul, MN: West, 1994.

Deming, W. Edwards. *Quality, Productivity, and Competitive Position.* Cambridge, MA: MIT Center for Advanced Engineering Study, 1982.

———. *Out of the Crisis.* Cambridge, MA: MIT Center for Advanced Engineering Study, 1986.

Garvin, David A. *Managing Quality.* New York: Free Press, 1988.

Imai, Masaaki. *Kaizen: The Key to Japan's Competitive Success.* New York: Random House, 1986.

Juran, Joseph M., and Frank M. Gryna Jr. *Quality Planning and Analysis.* New York: McGraw-Hill, 1980.

Logothetis, N. *Managing for Total Quality: From Deming to Taguchi and SPC.* Hertfordshire, UK: Prentice Hall International, 1992.

Makower, Joel. *The E Factor.* New York: Times Books, 1993.

Maskell, Brian. *Performance Measurement for World-Class Manufacturing.* Cambridge, MA: Productivity Press, 1991.

Ochsenkuehn, Rainer. *Introduction to ISO 14000 Handbook.* Fairfax, VA: The Victoria Group, 1996.

Rabbit, John T., and Peter A. Bergh. *The ISO 9000 Book.* White Plains, NY: Quality Resources, 1993.

Steeples, Marion Mills. *The Corporate Guide to the Malcolm Baldrige National Quality Award.* New York: McGraw-Hill Irwin, 1993.

Tribus, Myron, ed. *Quality First: Selected Papers on Quality and Productivity Improvements.* Washington, D.C: American Quality and Productivity Institute, 1988.

Quality Improvement Tools and Techniques

Steven A. Melnyk
Michigan State University

Lawrence D. Fredendall
Clemson University

McGraw-Hill Irwin

Boston Burr Ridge, IL Dubuque, IA Madison, WI New York San Francisco St. Louis
Bangkok Bogotá Caracas Kuala Lumpur Lisbon London Madrid Mexico City
Milan Montreal New Delhi Santiago Seoul Singapore Sydney Taipei Toronto

Quality Improvement Tools and Techniques

Module Objectives

By the end of this module, you should be able to

- Understand the role of problem solving in TQM and use the plan–do–check–act cycle.
- Explain the primal importance of data in total quality management.
- Differentiate attribute data from variable data to determine appropriate inputs for TQM statistical tools.
- Explain the principles and applications of the tools used in TQM systems.

Improving Operations at Sulzer Bingham Pumps, Inc.

When it first began its quality improvement program in 1990, Sulzer Bingham Pumps, Inc., of Portland, Oregon, had almost nowhere to go but up. The company had a long history, first as Willamette Iron and Steel, then as the corporate headquarters and primary manufacturing facility of centrifugal pumps for the Swiss-based Sulzer companies. But employee morale, product deliveries, and customer satisfaction had plummeted—along with profitability. The parent company demanded improvements and Sulzer Bingham Pumps responded with a strategic total quality management (TQM) program that required a cultural change among managers.

The company began by calling their 750 employees "co-workers" and including them in more decisions. After asking them how to improve safety programs and plant layout, the company spent $2 million upgrading facilities and equipment. They also began a continuous companywide training program and developed 14 six- to nine-member teams to assess coworker and customer satisfaction, supplier relationships, process improvements, education, cost of quality, and more.

Next they studied why they were losing customers. The reasons: poor quality and late delivery. After researching other companies' programs, Sulzer decided to adopt a formal 14-step improvement approach and hired a full-time TQM facilitator to implement it. It helped the company become a leader in both quality and on-time delivery, and earned Sulzer strategic alliances with key international customers including Dupont, Chevron Oil, and Fluor Daniel.

After applying for an Oregon Quality Award in 1995, Sulzer refined its program further, based on recommendations in the detailed feedback report. To improve and formalize customer communication, managers automatically distribute a customer survey and direct customer concerns to the appropriate teams. They also meet with cross-functional teams to upgrade their human resources policies and procedures.

Because they now understand that cultural change takes a long time, they are able to ride out performance fluctuations, and benchmark their progress in steps. "Our effort is to continually reinforce and improve our TQM process," Sulzer says.

As a result, Sulzer Bingham Pumps has

- Increased market share and profits.
- Boosted on-time delivery from 40 percent to 98 percent.
- Cut lead times by 25 percent.
- Won quality awards from customers and the Sulzer organization.

What's next? "We're headed toward self-managed work teams, an enhanced co-worker recognition process, a 'seamless supply chain' that ensures consistent communications and standards companywide, and further improvements to our human resources program," Sulzer says. "We work toward making cultural change. Now we have the people to accomplish it."

Source: "Going Beyond Good Enough," *Oregon Business* 20, no. 5 (May 1997), p. 3.

Sulzer Bingham Pumps is a success story. Here is a company that was able to transform itself from a failure in 1990 to a success in 1997. This radical transformation was due to several elements: the decision to implement a TQM system and the recognition that the real experts in identifying and correcting various problems in the company were the employees. Sulzer Bingham Pumps built upon this expertise by training employees in TQM.

Total quality management empowers both managers and employees by giving them access to the appropriate set of conceptual and analytical tools and procedures. These tools and procedures help people measure and improve processes. They also provide the means for identifying potential problems and for describing these problems to others. In this module, we discuss the TQM tools available to employees and management.

> Empowerment occurs when knowledge (of the tools and how to use them) is combined with the authority on the part of the employees to use the tools as they see fit.

Standard Problem Solving

Most of the TQM tools serve the fundamental objective of finding and solving problems. Systematically finding, analyzing, and solving problems is critical to improving operating processes. A standard problem-solving method ensures that all employees use systematic, data-driven methods during problem solving. Companies may use a wide variety of problem-solving methods. For example, some use the six-sigma approach. At Ford Motor Company employees are trained in the 8D (D stands for "discipline") problem-solving method.[1] The exact problem-solving method used is not important. What is important is that the method is systematic, data-driven, and simple to understand. The seven-step problem-solving method shown in Exhibit 1 is a common approach.

EXHIBIT 1
The Seven-Step Problem-Solving Method

Source: S. Shiba, A. Graham and D. Walden, *A New American TQM* (Portland, OR: Productivity Press, 1993); and R. M. Hodgetts, *Implementing TQM in Small & Medium-Sized Organizations* (New York, AMACOM, 1996).

1. *Identify the problem*—any deviation of the process from its expected performance.
2. *Collect and analyze data* related to the problem.
3. *Identify and explore the causes of the problem,* developing alternative explanations.
4. *Develop, plan, and implement the solution.*
5. *Evaluate the effects of the implementation.* If the problem is not completely solved, go back to step 3.
6. *Standardize the solution* to ensure that its solution is used by everyone.
7. *Review the problem-solving process* to identify how it could solve the next problem better.

Plan–Do–Check–Act Cycles (Deming Wheel)

Another popular approach to problem solving is the **plan–do–check–act cycle,** or **PDCA cycle,** which gets its name from the four major activities it embodies, as shown in Exhibit 2, page 4. This procedure is also known as the **Deming wheel** or Deming cycle (in honor of Edward Deming, the man who frequently used it). The PDCA cycle describes the sequence managers or workers use to solve problems and improve quality continuously over time.[2]

How to Implement a PDCA Cycle

The PDCA cycle consists of four separate but linked activities:

- *Plan.* Managers identify a problem by studying the current situation to detect a gap between it and the desired future situation. A large gap can create significant opportunities for improvement; a small gap represents a chance for a continuous, incremental improvement. During this stage, managers also identify actions to improve the situation (i.e., close the gap). This step ends with the formulation of a plan for closing the recognized gap (e.g., a plan for reducing the number of defects coming from a specific process).

[1] Ford Motor Company, *Team-Oriented Problem Solving,* 1987, p. I–1.

[2] Howard Gitlow, Shelley Gitlow, Alan Oppenheim, and Rosa Oppenheim, *Tools and Methods for the Improvement of Quality* (New York: McGraw-Hill/Irwin, 1989), pp. 159–60.

EXHIBIT 2
The Deming Wheel

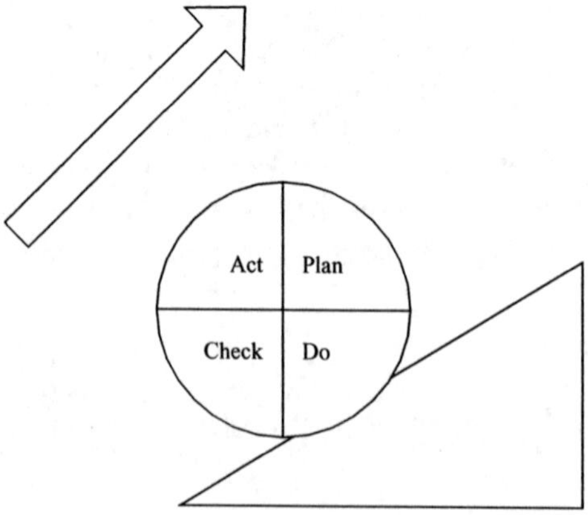

- *Do.* Having formulated the plan, managers and users next proceed to implement it. Frequently, they begin by implementing a change in a pilot project to assess its large-scale feasibility.
- *Check.* This step consists primarily of monitoring and inspecting the results. These activities are carried out to determine if the plan and its implementation have generated the desired result. In addition, the activities of this step watch for any unplanned problems elsewhere in the system or for the presence of previously hidden problems uncovered by the newly implemented changes. It is in this step that the issue of performance measurement and metrics become critical. The data that are gathered and used must be accurate.
- *Act.* In the final stage, managers and users review information collected in the check step and take appropriate corrective actions. The major intent of this step is to prevent any reoccurrence of problems identified and addressed in the previous three stages. It also institutionalizes earlier changes (through revised procedures and associated training) and forms a starting point for the next round of the PDCA cycle.

Most of the TQM tools introduced in this module deal with steps 1, 2, and 3 of the seven-step problem-solving method, or, alternatively, steps P, D, and C of the PDCA cycle. All of the tools make heavy use of data. Before examining tools to use in problem-solving analysis, we will look at characteristics of the data itself.

Data

Lear Corporation, a major supplier of automotive interiors, has the following sign posted at one of its plants for everyone to see:

> Without data, all you have is opinion.

One of the basic tenets of TQM is that decisions should be made on the basis of hard data whenever possible. The specific nature of the data determines what TQM tools we can use and what tools we cannot use. As a result, understanding data and its nature is critical.

Data falls into one of two categories: *variable data* or *attribute data.* **Variable data** measure quantifiable process outputs such as length, weight, diameter, and so on. Examples of variable data include the sizes of drilled holes in a part, the number of typographical errors per page, the hardness of steel, and the serving temperature of hamburgers in the serving bins of a fast-food restaurant.

The concept of magnitude is central to all variable data. To understand its importance, consider the example of a receiving department in a plant. Each day, shipments of parts arrive from a supplier. Each batch is checked for defective parts by sampling 50 units. If out of the 50 units, eight or more bad units are found, then the batch is rejected. Otherwise, the shipment is accepted. Exhibit 3 summarizes the data for 20 batches.

EXHIBIT 3
Variable Data for Defects per Batch

Date of Batch	Number of Defects	Action
3/7	2	Accept
3/7	4	Accept
3/7	8	Reject
3/8	12	Reject
3/8	3	Accept
3/8	7	Accept
3/8	5	Accept
3/8	10	Reject
3/9	4	Accept
3/9	4	Accept
3/9	9	Reject
3/10	0	Accept
3/11	1	Accept
3/11	2	Accept
3/11	9	Reject
3/11	2	Accept
3/14	6	Accept
3/14	3	Accept
3/14	11	Reject
3/14	7	Accept

Counting defects in each batch has led to 14 acceptances and 6 rejections (for a total acceptance rate of 70 percent). The number of defects is variable data because one can arrange the data in increasing order of magnitude, starting with 0 defects on March 10 and reaching 12 defects on March 8. Furthermore, one can make meaningful comparisons of the data. The first sample had two defects; the second had four. The first batch had half as many defects as the second. Each number has an absolute magnitude, and a relative magnitude as well.

In contrast, **attribute data** indicate only qualitative or categorical characteristics of a process output (pass/fail, go/no-go, good/bad). Exhibit 3 presents attribute data in the last column, Action, which describes the decision based on the variable data. Comparisons with attribute data yield only limited insights. If you could see only the first and last columns of Exhibit 3, you could determine that the first two batches were acceptable, but you could not say how good the samples were or make any comparisons between them. The attribute data indicate nothing about any differences between the first and second batches. Even when such data indicate a difference, as between the second and third samples, you could conclude only that the second must have had seven or fewer defects while the third must have had eight or more defects.

Variable and attribute measures are linked. An analyst can convert variable data into attribute data, as when a sample with eight defects gains the attribute of a reject while a batch with three defects gains the attribute of an acceptable batch. The relationship usually runs only one way, however; attribute data indicate little or nothing about variables. The accept/reject decision indicates only whether or not a sample included more than a set number of defects. This distinction is important. Some of the tools presented in this module need variable data while others use attribute data.

Quality Improvement Tools

Quality improvement tools are a set of fundamental techniques for capturing and analyzing data in order to identify and solve problems. They include

- Histogram.
- Process capability analysis.
- Cause-and-effect diagram.

- Check sheets.
- Process flow diagram.
- Pareto analysis.
- Process control charts.
- Acceptance sampling.
- Scatter diagram.

These tools address the fundamental aspects of processes and their outputs. As such, they can be used in almost any operating setting. Notice that some of these are actually sets of tools. For example, there are many types of control charts. In the following sections, each tool is discussed in terms of its objective, the procedure for its use, and the expected output or outcome of using it. These are simple tools, but when used in proper combination with each other, they can provide excellent insights.

Histogram

Objectives

Variability exists in every activity or process. A **histogram** graphically displays the distribution of outcomes data gathered during the operation of a process to show the extent of variability within the system. That is, it shows the frequency of occurrence of outcomes across ranges of a certain measure. Examples of histograms are shown in Exhibit 4. A histogram could be used to graphically display variations in how long donors take to give blood, the sizes of mounting holes in successive units of a part, or the weights of assembled dashboard panels. Histograms help problem solvers identify three critical traits of process output distributions:

- *Center of the distribution:* This point is located halfway between the highest and lowest values of the histogram. Process managers often desire that the mean of the distribution (often written as μ) should coincide with the center of the histogram's graphic picture of the distribution. Any gap between these two points indicates skew or bias in the distribution.
- *Width of the distribution.* The range, which is the difference between the highest and lowest values in a distribution, is shown graphically by a histogram. The width or central tendency of the distribution indicates the predictability of the process that generated the distribution. A wider distribution indicates a less predictable activity; a narrower distribution is more predictable.
- *Shape of the distribution.* The overall shape of a distribution often provides insights into different problems in the data or influences on the overall distribution.

Examine the five different distributions shown in Exhibit 4. Most students are familiar with the normal, **bell-shaped distribution.** This symmetrical distribution indicates a natural spread of data from a single stable process. In contrast, the **double-** or twin-**peaked distribution** often indicates that two normal distributions have been combined. The **plateau distribution** shows a flat region with no distinct peak. This pattern also sometimes results from combining multiple data sets, each of which may have a normal distribution. If the means of the various distributions occur evenly across a particular range, the result is a flat region. The **comb distribution** has multiple peaks and troughs, indicating wide variation. This distribution occurs if there are errors such as defects in the process, faulty measurements, errors in data collection, rounding errors, or poor grouping of data into categories for the histogram. Finally, the **skewed distribution** shows an asymmetrical pattern of data. The narrow tail of a positively skewed distribution extends to the right, as in Exhibit 4. The tail of a negatively skewed distribution extends to the left. Such patterns often suggest some limit that is restraining data on one side of the distribution. For example, a histogram of the number of defective

EXHIBIT 4
Common Histogram Shapes

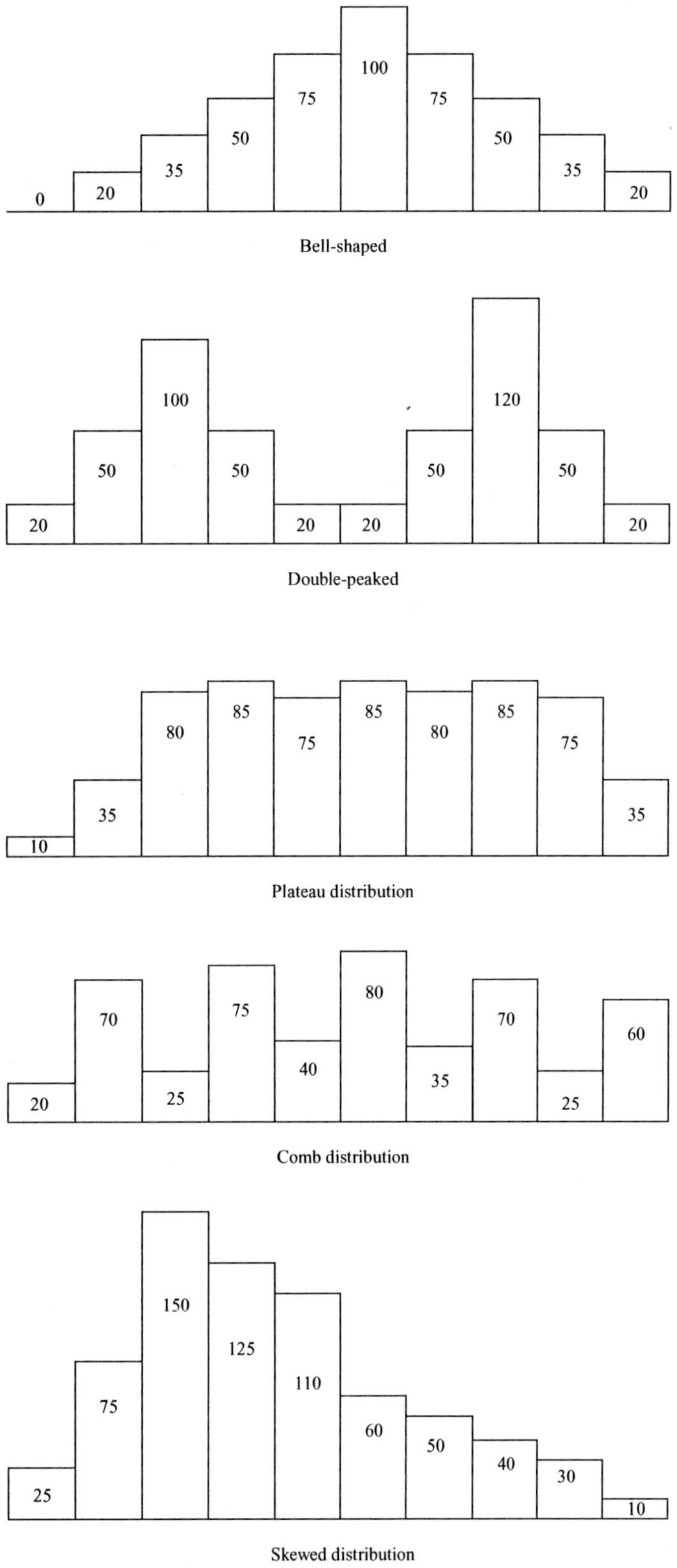

microchips per 1,000 CPUs would probably be positively skewed because zero defects is a natural lower limit near which much of the data should fall.

A critical decision in creating a histogram is to determine the number of categories into which to group the data (each of the histograms in Exhibit 4 contains 10 categories). Exhibit 5, page 8,

EXHIBIT 5
Guidelines for Histogram Categories

Source: Kaoru Ishikawa, *Guide to Quality Control* (White Plains, NY: Quality Resources, 1982), p. 8.

Number of Data Points in the Sample	Number of Categories
Less than 50	5–7
50–100	6–10
101–250	7–12
Over 250	10–20

provides some general guidelines for choosing the number of categories. A valid histogram needs at least 30 data points, but more observations are better.

Process Capability Analysis: C_p and C_{pk}

Objectives

The concept of process capability brings together two major elements: a product's design specifications and the variability present within the process used to create it. Typically, we can represent the design specifications for a product characteristic using the concept of the **specification width** (S). This width denotes the range of output variations that are acceptable. The specification width is usually determined by product functionality, or by the amount of variance that the customer is willing to tolerate and still view the product as acceptable. For example, an engineer ordering a pump from Sulzer Bingham may have some predetermined range of output that he or she will accept from the pump. Any level of output below or above this range would be unacceptable, because the pump would be unable to reliably fulfill the purpose the engineer has in mind.

While the specification width denotes the desired range of outcomes, **process width** (P) denotes the actual range of outcomes. Process width indicates the interval between the lower and upper ends of the distribution of process output. If, for a given process, the process width is fully contained within the specification width, then we deem that process to be *process capable.* That is, the process is capable of reliably producing the product to the desired specifications. One way to communicate the degree of **process capability** is by using the capability index, C_p. This index (and its associated measure, C_{pk}) are used to compare the specification width and the process width. Both C_p and C_{pk} are measures of process capability.

Determining C_p

Mathematically, the C_p is calculated as follows:

$$C_p = \frac{\text{Specification width}}{\text{Process width}} = \frac{S}{P}$$

This calculation is built on the assumption that the process width center and the specification width center are coincident (the same number). The specification width is defined by finite upper and lower limits. Most actual process output distributions are open-ended, that is, there is a possibility that any output value might be produced. So statisticians often define the effective limits of process output at three standard deviations (3σ) on each side of the mean for the process. The $\pm 3\sigma$ limit is chosen because the chance a process will produce something outside this range is very small. For example, the $\pm 3\sigma$ range encompasses over 99 percent of expected output from a normally distributed process output.

To illustrate the application of C_p, Exhibit 6 shows three different distributions of process performance data. All have the same specification width ($S = 40 - 20 = 20$). Distribution A shows process width that exceeds the limits set by the specification width. The resulting C_p value of 0.67 indicates an incapable process in that it meets specifications less than 99 percent of the time. Distribution B is barely capable with a C_p value of 1.0. While this represents an improvement over distribution A, it is only a marginal improvement. Any slight disruption or problem in the process will send its output outside acceptable limits. Finally, distribution C indicates significantly better process performance (i.e., it is a capable process). The process width is well within the limits set by the specification width, giving a C_p value of 1.67. This provides a cushion of protection or a safety margin.

EXHIBIT 6
Sample Distributions and Their Associated C_p Measures

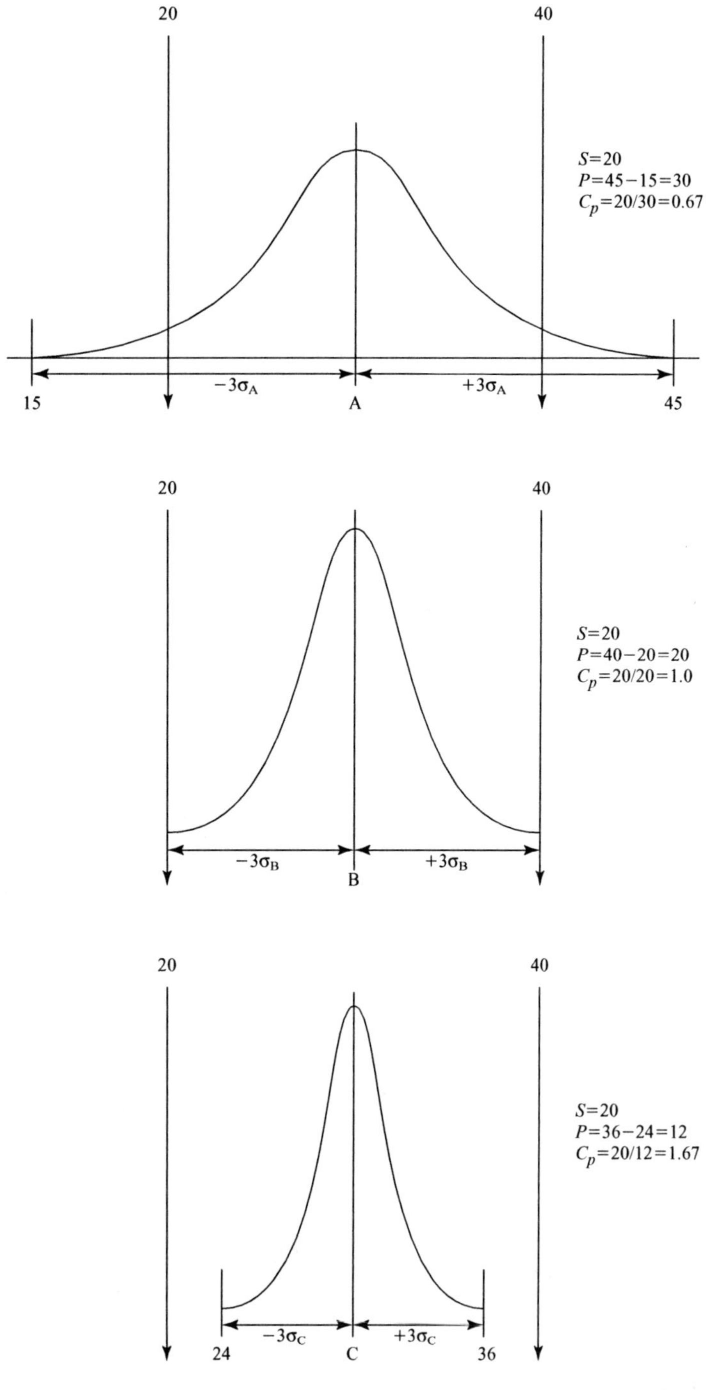

How would you interpret a C_{pk} of 1.67? How much of an increase in the process width could we tolerate before the process becomes incapable?

In general, a larger C_p value indicates a more reliable and predictable process and a higher probability that the process will satisfy or exceed customers' requirements. Some buyers use C_p values as part of their supplier-selection mechanisms. That is, they will work only with suppliers whose processes can meet or exceed some minimum C_p value (e.g., 2.0).

C_{pk}—Improving on the C_p Statistic

As noted previously, the C_p value effectively measures process capability only for those processes having a centered distribution of performance data. The distribution in Exhibit 7 shows the problems when this assumption is not met. The distribution has the same process width as Distribution C from Exhibit 6 and the specification width remains the same, so the C_p value is unchanged. However, while Distribution C showed a highly capable process, the distribution in Exhibit 7 shows a noncapable process. This distribution is centered on the lower specification limit rather than the midpoint of the specification width (30). This indicates that 50 percent of the output of this process is outside the acceptable range.

The C_{pk} is an adjusted version of the C_p. The adjustment compensates for the difference between the center of the P range and the midpoint of the S range by introducing a correction factor to the calculation. Mathematically, the C_{pk} can be written as follows:

$$C_p = \frac{S}{P}$$

$$K = \frac{D - X}{S/2}$$ (Adjustment for differences between the two centers)

$$C_{pk} = (1-K) \times C_p$$

S and P still stand for the specification width and process width, respectively. D represents the design center of the specification width, the target value for performance data, while $\bar{X}$ is the process average. When D equals $\bar{X}$, then C_{pk} equals C_p.

To calculate the C_{pk} value for the distribution in Exhibit 7, set D equal to 30 ($D = (20 + 40)/2$), the midpoint of the specification width; $\bar{X}$ equals 20 ($(14 + 26)/2$). Although the C_p value remains at 1.67, K is 1 ($|30 - 20|/(20/2)$). These figures give a C_{pk} value of 0.0 ($C_{pk} = (1 - 1) \times 1.67 = 0$), indicating an unreliable process that cannot meet customers' needs regularly.

Firms use both the C_p and C_{pk} values. If both values are the same, then the user knows that the two distributions are properly centered with each other. This allows them to focus on the task of reducing the variance by changing the process (or processes) responsible for this variance. On the other hand, if the C_{pk} is less than the C_p value, then the user knows that the process must be recentered. This **process centering** must be achieved before the problem of variances can be attacked. Finally, a high C_{pk} value (also consistent with a high C_p value) indicates a very capable process, one in which there is low variance combined with a properly centered distribution of performance data. Exhibit 8 provides another example of a non-centered process.

Why would you as a purchasing agent want a high C_{pk} value reported to you whenever you receive items from your suppliers?

EXHIBIT 7

Deceptive C_p Value—The Problem of Lack of Centering

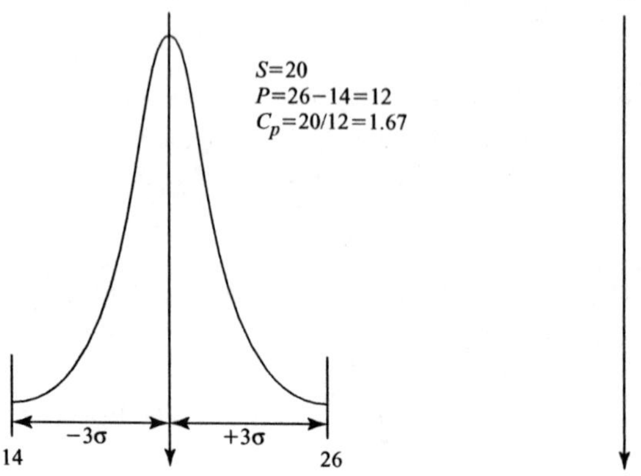

EXHIBIT 8
Example, Calculating C_{pk}

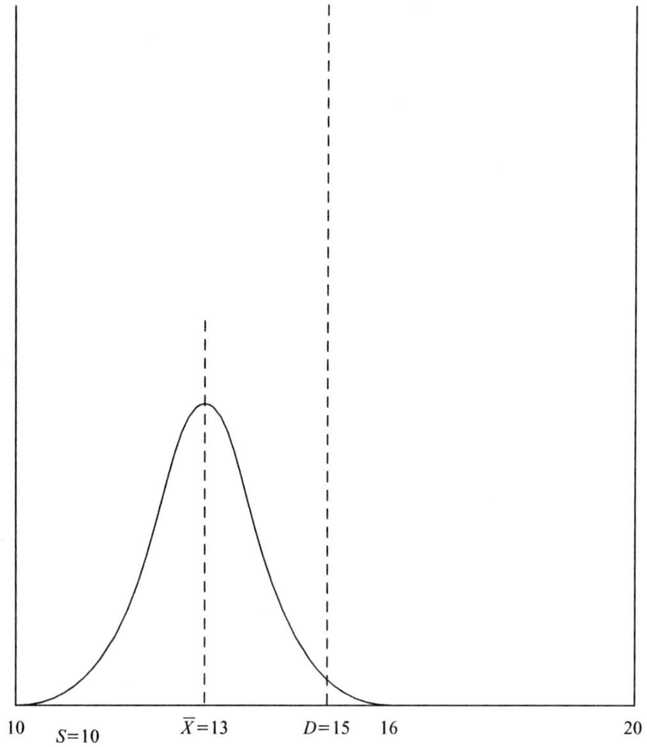

$S=10$
$S/2=5$
$C_p=10/(16-10)=1.667$
$K=2/5=.4$
$C_{pk}=(1-K)\times 1.667=1.00$

Example, Calculating C_{pk}

You can see that the process in Exhibit 8 has little margin for error since a slight shift in the process to the left will likely produce goods with the measured variable less than 10. How many? That will depend on how much the distribution has shifted to the left.

Taguchi Methods—Linking Process Capability to Product Design

One of the first researchers to recognize the importance of linking product design to process improvement was Professor Genichi Taguchi, director of the Japanese Academy of Quality and four-time recipient of the Deming Prize. He recognized that managers could eliminate the need for mass inspection by building quality into both the products and processes at the design stage.

Taguchi developed a straightforward, well-integrated system for improving the design of both a product and the process used to produce it.[3] The objective of this system—the **Taguchi methods**—is to identify easily controllable factors and their settings that can minimize variation in product features while keeping the mean values (or "response") of these features on target. Taguchi developed a methodology for designing experiments than can help managers identify the optimal settings of product specifications and process controls. One result of identifying these settings is that a product can be made robust with respect to changes in its operating and environmental conditions. Ultimately, this results in more stable and higher-quality designs. In other words, by focusing on both the product and the process and using well-developed designs, managers can develop products and processes

[3] N. Logothetis, *Managing for Total Quality* (New York: Prentice Hall, 1992), chap. 11–14.

that are properly centered and that have performance distributions with reduced spread. Using the parlance of the C_{pk} perspective, Taguchi provided a structured system for generating highly capable products and processes.[4]

Cause-and-Effect Diagrams

Objectives

While managers often can readily identify symptoms of problems (increasing costs, increasing scrap rates, decreasing quality, lengthening lead times), the root causes of the problems remain elusive. This analysis becomes especially difficult when the relationship between a cause and a symptom is not direct. For example, poor equipment maintenance may create symptoms such as poor tool adjustments, which may lead to defects. But inadequate operator training combined with insufficient spare time and too few tools may lead to poor equipment maintenance.

The **cause-and-effect diagram** (CED) is a tool used to examine complex interrelationships and identify the root causes of observed symptoms. It is also known as a fishbone diagram (because a completed diagram looks like a fish skeleton), or an Ishikawa chart, in honor of Dr. Kaoru Ishikawa, who first developed this tool.[5] CED diagrams are widely used in both service and manufacturing operations. They facilitate and structure brainstorming work, encouraging people to share ideas and providing visual images of those ideas.

Constructing a Cause and Effect Diagram

The process of building a CED consists of the following steps:[6]

1. *Identify the problem to examine.* The process begins by clearly stating the problem to examine in the diagram in a form acceptable to everyone involved. After noting the problem at the extreme right of the diagram, an arrow drawn from left to right illustrates the root effect.

2. *Identify the major categories of causes.* Next, identify the major categories of potential causes that could contribute to the effect under study. Represent them as main branches off the problem arrow, indicating the name of each category at the end of its branch. These main branches gather potential causes into groups and begin to structure the cause-and-effect relationships. The categories often reflect issues identified in an earlier study of the problem or such universal categories as labor, work methods, materials, machines, and measurement.

3. *Identify more specific causes.* On each main branch, place smaller branches, or twigs, to represent detailed causes that could contribute to the primary categories of causes. For each detailed cause, ever smaller twigs represent still more specific and detailed causes. Brainstorming methods are used to identify major categories of causes and the more detailed causes. Later analysis eliminates unlikely possibilities to focus on the more likely ones.

4. *Circle likely causes.* After the diagram has been developed with sufficient care to ensure that it shows all potential causes, the next step is to review all of the causes and circle the most likely ones. Further analysis and data collection can then focus on those causes.

5. *Verify the causes.* After identifying the most likely causes, use the other tools to ensure they really are the root cause of the problem.

The best way of understanding how to use a CED diagram is to actually develop one. Consider the following example.

[4] The Taguchi method is very much a well-developed, well-integrated, comprehensive statistical system and approach. For more information on this system, see ibid.
[5] Kaoru Ishikawa, *Guide to Quality Control* (White Plains, NY: Quality Resources, 1985), pp. 18–29.
[6] Ibid., pp. 19–20.

Suppose that Bob Feller discovered that damage to CPUs during assembly is the number one cause of defects. He constructed the cause-and-effect diagram shown in Exhibit 9 to try to pinpoint the specific causes of this damage.

Bob knew that his role as facilitator was crucial to the success of the exercise. He first invited everyone with information about the problem to develop the CED with him. This included a process engineer, a maintenance technician, a line employee, and an inspector. Bob went through one category at a time asking why that category caused CPU damage during assembly. For example, Bob asked, "Why does the CPU chip lead to CPU damage during assembly?" He received multiple answers from different participants. These are shown in Exhibit 9 as arrows coming out of the CPU category arrow (e.g., received defective, pins not aligned). Bob then went through each one of these explanations, continuing to ask why, until each logic chain answered at least five levels of why. This is illustrated in Exhibit 9 where the main problem is the first why, the CPU category is the second why, the pins not aligned is the third why, poor design is the fourth why, and, in answer to his question of "why does poor design lead to pins not being aligned?" Bob was told the fifth why, that "the specifications are not precise."

Exhibit 9 illustrates the most common type of CED diagram—the dispersion analysis diagram. A second type of CED diagram, the process classification diagram, explains the causes of problems by tracing through the activities in the production process.[7]

EXHIBIT 9
Cause-and-Effect Diagram for Pear's CPU Damage Problem

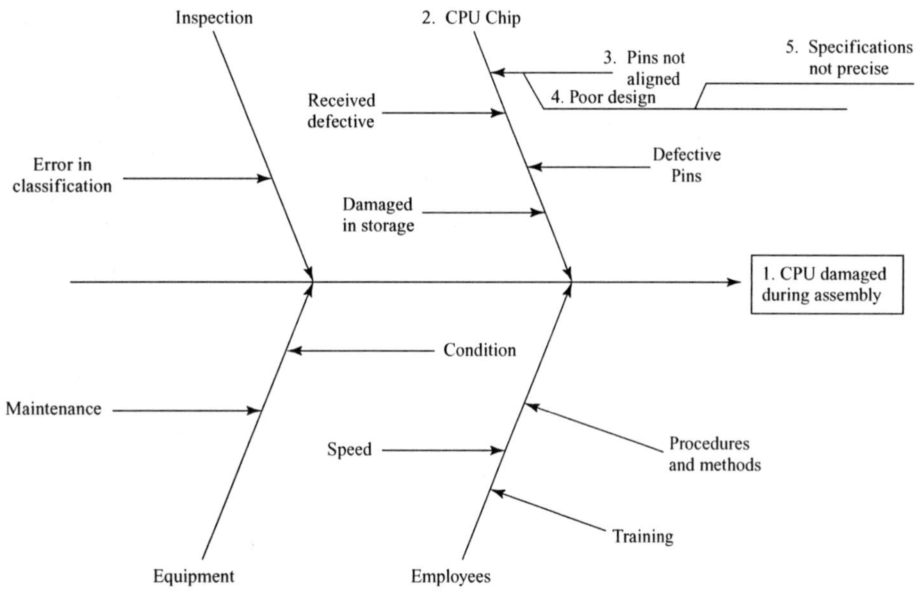

Check Sheets

Objectives

A **check sheet** is a simple, widely used tool for recording occurrences of some outcome. There two goals for using a check sheet:

- To reveal patterns and trends.
- To display data in a form that can be easily read and understood.

The three basic types of check sheets include attribute check sheets, variable check sheets, and location check sheets.[8]

[7] Ibid., pp. 20–25.
[8] For a list of other variants of check sheets, see ibid., chap. 4.

Attribute Check Sheets As the name implies, an **attribute check sheet** captures attribute data. Typically, this type of check sheet consists of categories that reflect topics such as problem types, problem categories, or the time. To understand what an attribute check sheet looks like, review the data in Exhibit 3. Let us assume that the people who examined the incoming batches, recorded the reasons why parts were rejected and then assigned each of the rejected items to one of these problem categories as shown in Exhibit 10.

This check sheet clearly shows that the largest reason for rejecting a part is that it is not marked properly. We could introduce more detail into the classification scheme found in the check sheet by noting the time of day each reject was found, if we think this affects a part's probability of being rejected.

EXHIBIT 10
Example of Attribute Check Sheet

Reason for Reject	Number Rejected
Item damaged	✓✓✓✓✓✓✓✓✓✓✓✓✓
Wrong part shipped	✓✓✓✓✓✓✓✓
Part does not work	✓✓✓✓
Component missing from part	✓✓✓✓✓✓✓✓✓✓✓✓✓✓✓✓✓✓✓✓✓✓✓✓
Not properly marked	✓✓✓✓✓✓✓✓✓✓✓✓✓✓✓✓✓✓✓✓✓✓✓✓✓✓✓✓✓✓✓✓✓✓
(no bar code on part)	✓✓✓✓✓✓✓
Rust found on part	✓✓✓✓✓✓✓✓✓✓✓✓
Other (factors not noted above)	✓✓✓✓

Variable Check Sheets **Variable check sheets** represent continuous data. This check sheet defines categories based on the variable data being tracked. For example, suppose we measured the time that a customer must wait before that customer is served for 12 customers in a row, and the data were as follows:

16.4 minutes, 1.5 minutes, 5.1 minutes, 1.8 minutes, 3.2 minutes, 6.5 minutes, 8.1 minutes, 2.3 minutes, 0.8 minute, 4.6 minutes, 6.3 minutes, 3.9 minutes

These data are not very informative. We could calculate the mean and standard deviation. However, this information does not really tell us anything about the underlying pattern. Yet, suppose we decide to use four categories for capturing waiting time: less than 5 minutes, 5 to 9.9 minutes, 10 to 14.9 minutes, and 15 minutes and above. Using these categories to organize the data, we find the following:

$<$ 5 minutes	7 observations
(5, 10] minutes	4 observations
(10, 15] minutes	0 observations
$=>$ 15 minutes	1 observation

About 58 percent (7⁄12) of the customers waited less than 5 minutes. About 33 percent waited between 5 and 10 minutes and there was one customer that had to wait over 15 minutes. This check sheet both draws our attention to the largest category of observations as well as flags a true outlier—the one customer who had to wait over 15 minutes. We also have a good idea of the shape of the distribution of waiting times.

Location Check Sheets A **location check sheet** shows the spatial concentration of defects by noting the physical locations of defects. For example, suppose we are interested in determining the location of rust spots on a part (this issue was flagged as one of the reasons for rejects in the attribute check sheet). We could note each location of rust on a drawing of a part. Over time, this would identify areas of the part where rust is most likely to occur. An example of a location check sheet is illustrated in Exhibit 11.

EXHIBIT 11
Location Check Sheet for Rust

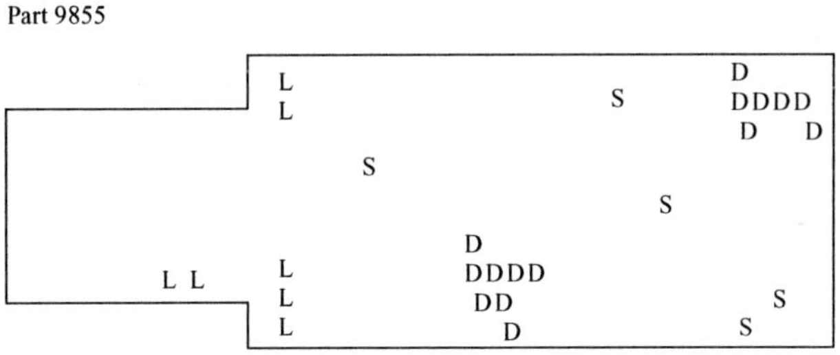

L= rust loose on surface
D= rust on design feature
S= rust in scratch

Developing a Check Sheet

The development of a check sheet is relatively straightforward.

1. *Decide on the conditions or events being observed.*
2. *Select the appropriate form of check sheet to use.*
3. *Specify the categories to be tracked.*
4. *Consult with the users who will enter the data and get input regarding the design and arrangement of the sheet.*
5. *Decide on the appropriate time period over which to collect information.*

Process Flow Diagram

Process flow diagramming is a methodology that uses symbols to represent the activities and interrelationships contained in an operating process. Diagramming a process usually leads to a better understanding of an overall process and its potential problems. For example, after Bob Feller completes a cause-and-effect diagram, he might continue with a process flow analysis of the activities involved in inserting the CPU during computer assembly. By diagramming the process, he can spot variance, or differences in times to carry out an activity. He also can look for confusion in activity flows or disruptions that force employees to spend more time than necessary on a certain task.

The basic symbols and procedures used in process flow diagramming are fully discussed in two modules: Process Management and Process Mapping and Analysis.

Pareto Analysis

Objectives

Pareto analysis sets priorities for management action based on the assumption that 80 percent of problems results from 20 percent of the possible causes. At any time, an operations manager may face many different problems, each competing for a share of time and attention. Pareto analysis separates the critical few from the trivial many. In doing so, Pareto analysis helps to focus attention on the areas with the greatest potential for a payoff. The effective operations manager concentrates attention and effort where the investment of time, effort, and money will yield the largest return. Juran first applied Pareto analysis to quality management. He referenced the work of Italian economist Vilfredo Pareto (1848–1923) among others who had observed and applied the 80-20 rule.[9]

[9] J. M. Juran, "Universals in Management Planning and Controlling," *The Management Review,* November 1954.

Using Pareto Analysis

Pareto analysis consists of a seven-step procedure:

1. *Identify categories about which to collect information.* Specify categories that describe types of defects. Once the categories are known, we can use check sheets to gather the data.

2. *Decide on the time period to cover.* This requires a trade-off between a shorter period, which would reduce the time and resources invested in gathering data, and a longer period, which would ensure that data would accurately represent the current situation. A longer data collection period produces more representative information, but at the cost of a slower, more expensive process.

3. *Gather the data and calculate total frequencies by category for the time period.* Total the observed variations in the activities under study. For example, if there are seven reasons for rejecting a part, we would sum the number of defects for each of the seven reasons for rejects. Summing these totals for all categories then gives the grand total. Dividing each category by the grand total and multiplying by 100 gives a percentage for each category.

4. *Sort the categories in descending order based on their percentages.* This places the category with the highest percentage of variation at the top of the list of categories and the one with the lowest percentage at the bottom.

5. *Identify the vital few categories that account for most of the variation.* This step separates out the vital few categories based on the 80-20 rule.

6. *Adjust the categories for any qualitative factors.* The previous steps identify a few categories of variation as vital based on quantitative data, but this type of data ignores information that cannot be counted or measured objectively. For example, a Pareto analysis of a quality problem might measure defect levels based on either frequency or the dollars involved. This would ignore such considerations as the severity of the problem or the potential costs of resolving the problem should it occur. Qualitative considerations could move a category with low frequency but high severity from near the bottom of the list up to the top.

7. *Present the data graphically.* The final step creates a bar graph. The horizontal axis of the chart represents the categories of variation identified early in the analysis, arranged in descending order; the vertical axis represents the frequencies. In addition, the graph includes the cumulative frequency of variation for each category.

Let's apply Pareto analysis to the computer manufacturer scenario identified earlier.

Pear Computers, a small midwestern manufacturer of personal computers, has built a reputation for innovation, flexible product configurations, on-time delivery, and quality. Recently, however, quality has slipped. Final inspections of the new Pear 6000 model revealed problems in an unacceptably high number of computers. Some have refused to boot up, while others have run for the first 5 hours of the 48-hour burn-in, then shut down after generating error messages. After talking with assembly workers, Bob Feller, the operations manager in charge of the assembly line, identified possible causes of these problems and gathered information about the frequency of problems. Over a four-week test period, 15,000 computers were assembled. The identified defects are shown in Exhibit 12.

A chart of the data constructed using Pareto analysis shows that the last two causes together account for about 47 percent of all defects (Exhibit 13). This chart suggests that Bob should begin his improvement efforts in these two areas. Just by eliminating the causes of damage to the CPU during assembly, he could reduce defects from 1,084 to 823.

EXHIBIT 12
Frequency of Computer Problems

Potential Problems	Number of Occurrences	Percent	Rank
Chips inserted incorrectly	43	3.97	8
CPU chip/memory chips popping out during burn-in	117	10.79	4
Traces cut on the motherboard (during assembly)	78	7.20	6
Loose power connections	150	13.84	3
Connections not made on the motherboard	34	3.14	9
Dust getting into critical areas of the computer	90	8.30	5
Wrong components put on the computer	51	4.71	7
Motherboard incorrectly seated	15	1.38	10
Motherboard damaged during installation	245	22.60	2
CPU damaged during assembly	261	24.08	1
	1,084	100.01	

EXHIBIT 13
Pareto Analysis for Pear Computer

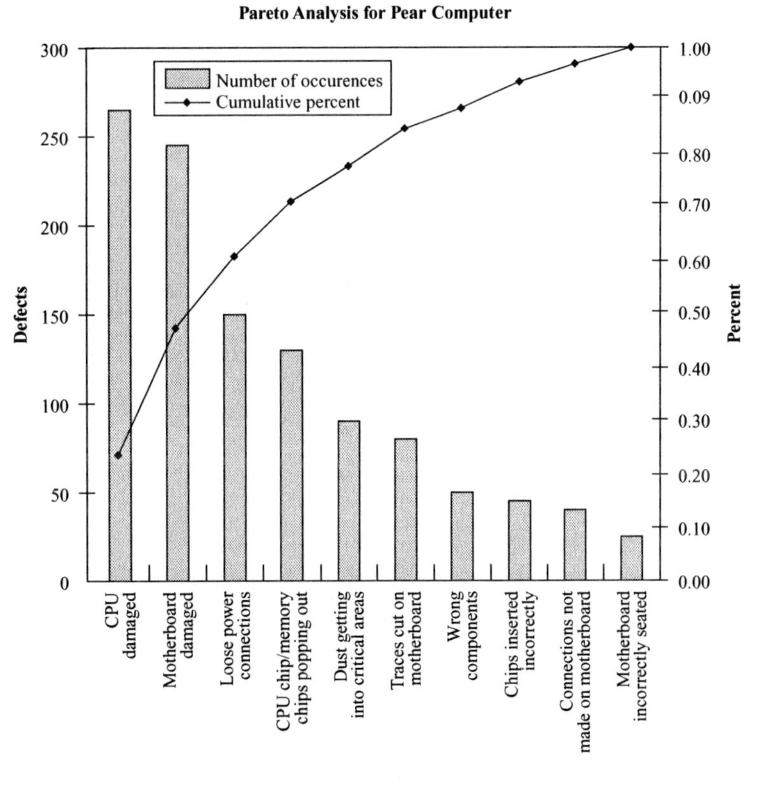

Process Control Charts

Objectives

A **control chart** (the terms "statistical process control (SPC)" and "control charts" are often used synonymously) plots data collected over time across a set of limits for the upper and lower boundaries of acceptable performance (Exhibit 14 on page 18). Process control charts identify the moment when the process is no longer giving desired results (i.e., it is "out of control"). This allows the manager to stop and correct the process. Any sample that is between the upper and lower limits as shown in Exhibit 12 indicates acceptable performance; any points that fall outside these limits indicate problems with the process that generated the performance data. Operations managers consider points outside acceptable limits as indicators of a need to intervene to improve the operation of the process. They typically set performance boundaries to correspond to a given confidence interval (usually 99 percent or

EXHIBIT 14
Limits of Acceptable Performance for Process Control

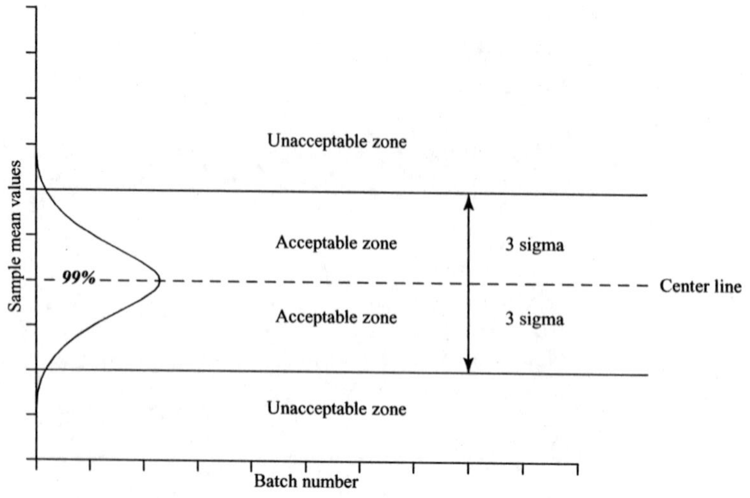

3σ). They attribute divergence from the mean of any points that fall between the upper and lower limits to random variations; points outside the limits indicate underlying systematic problems with the process.

There are five common types of control charts, listed in Exhibit 15. Each type of chart is used with a particular type of data. Continuous data can vary anywhere within a particular range (e.g., holes can be any size). Discrete data state some quantity that people can count such as the number of defective units in a batch or the fraction of defective products in a sample. In this section, we will deal primarily with continuous data and the $\bar{x} - R$ control chart, one of the most common control charts.

Constructing an $\bar{x} - R$ Chart

This control chart is used to monitor both the mean, $\bar{x}$, and range, R, of sampled process output. There is a 10-step procedure for constructing and using **$\bar{x} - R$ chart.** To illustrate this process, the data found in Exhibit 16 are used. Bob Feller of Pear Computer wants to track hard-disk seek times to make sure that the process of building the disks is under control. To make this assessment, he would follow these steps:

1. *Initialize the system and collect data to calculate performance limits.* The data from which the analyst calculates the control limits for charts should come from a process known to be under control. Managers often gather this kind of data from processes just

EXHIBIT 15
Types of Control Charts and Data Covered

Source: Ishikawa, Kaoru, *Guide to Quality Control* (White Plains, NY: Quality Resources, 1982), p. 64.

Type of Data	Control Chart Used	Examples
Variable	$\bar{x} - R$ (mean and range)	Measurement (inches, mm) Volume Product weight Power consumed
Attribute	P_n (number of defects)	Number of units with blemished label, damaged package.
Attribute	p (Fraction defective)	Proportion of sample with blemished label, damaged package
Attribute	u (number of defects per unit area where area inspected is variable)	Number of pin holes in pieces of plated sheet, differing in area
Attribute	c (total number of defects where area inspected is constant)	Number of pin holes in a specified area

EXHIBIT 16
Hard-Disk Seek Times (millisecond)

Note: Nominal mean seek time = 12 ms.

	Observations						
Sample Number	1	2	3	4	5	$\bar{X}$	R
1	12.2	12.3	12.4	11.8	12.7	12.3	0.9
2	12.3	12.1	11.8	12.2	12.3	12.1	0.5
3	12.4	12.7	12.3	12.5	12.3	12.4	0.4
4	12.5	12.3	12.3	12.1	12.1	12.3	0.4
5	12.1	12.4	11.9	12.0	12.3	12.1	0.5
6	12.6	11.8	12.2	11.9	11.9	12.1	0.8
7	11.8	12.1	12.5	12.8	12.5	12.3	1.0
8	12.5	12.8	12.0	12.5	11.9	12.3	0.9
9	12.1	12.3	12.0	11.9	12.1	12.1	0.4
10	11.2	12.3	11.8	11.7	11.9	11.8	1.1
11	11.7	12.2	12.2	11.7	12.1	12.0	0.5
12	12.4	12.2	12.1	12.1	12.1	12.2	0.3
13	11.7	12.1	11.9	11.8	11.9	11.9	0.4
14	11.8	12.2	12.2	12.1	12.2	12.1	0.4
15	11.9	12.3	11.8	11.9	12.1	12.0	0.5
16	12.3	12.4	13.0	12.3	12.2	12.4	0.8
17	11.9	12.6	12.6	12.9	12.1	12.4	0.9
18	11.9	12.0	12.7	12.7	11.9	12.2	0.8
19	11.4	11.6	12.4	11.9	11.8	11.8	1.0
20	11.6	11.8	12.4	12.3	11.2	11.9	1.2
						$\bar{\bar{X}} = 12.14$	$\bar{R} = 0.69$

after major overhauls, when they know that they can rely on smooth operations. In general, these data should include about 100 observations of the process.

2. *Group observations into samples.* Next, the analyst groups observations into coherent samples that share some common trait (e.g., data from a single production run or from one day or shift). For each sample, the control-limit calculation requires the number of observations (n). In general, a larger sample size allows the analyst to calculate tighter limits, leaving a smaller gap between the upper and lower limits. However, this increased precision comes at the cost of gathering more data. The variable k denotes the number of samples available for the control-limit calculation. Exhibit 14 groups the 100 data points into 20 samples of 5 observations, so n equals 5 and k equals 20.

3. *For each sample, find the sample mean.* For each sample, the analyst should calculate the sample mean to one-decimal-point accuracy using the following formula:

$$\bar{x} = \frac{\sum_{i=1}^{n} x_i}{n}$$

4. *For each sample, find the range,* R. The range measures the difference between the largest and smallest values.

5. *Calculate the overall mean,* $\bar{\bar{x}}$. Summing the sample means, $\bar{x}$, and dividing by the total number of samples gives the mean for the entire data set. This number defines the centerline for the control chart.

6. *Calculate the mean range,* $\bar{R}$. The R chart needs a centerline as well. To define this line, sum the R values from all of the samples and divide by the number of samples to arrive at the mean R, or $\bar{R}$. Besides defining the centerline for the R chart, $\bar{R}$ also helps the analyst to estimate the upper and lower control limits, since the range is an indicator of the variability of the process.

EXHIBIT 17
Values for Setting Control Limit Lines

Number of Observations in Each Sample, *n*	$A_2 - \bar{x}$ Limits for 99.7% (3 sigma)	$D_4 - \bar{R}$ Upper Limit	$D_3 - \bar{R}$ Lower Limit
2	1.88	3.27	0
3	1.02	2.58	0
4	0.73	2.28	0
5	0.58	2.12	0
6	0.48	2.00	0
7	0.42	1.92	0.08
8	0.37	1.86	0.14
9	0.34	1.82	0.18
10	0.31	1.78	0.22
11	0.29	1.74	0.26
12	0.27	1.72	0.28
13	0.25	1.69	0.31
14	0.24	1.67	0.33
15	0.22	1.65	0.35
16	0.21	1.64	0.36
17	0.20	1.62	0.38
18	0.19	1.60	0.39
19	0.19	1.61	0.40
20	0.18	1.59	0.41

7. *Compute control limits.* To calculate the positions of the control limit lines, the analyst enters values for A_2, D_3, and D_4 found in Exhibit 17 into the equations below:

$\bar{X}$ control chart:

Central line $= \bar{\bar{x}}$

Lower control limit $= \bar{\bar{x}} - A_2\bar{R}$

Upper control limit $= \bar{\bar{x}} + A_2\bar{R}$

R control chart:

Central line $= \bar{R}$

Lower control limit (LCL) $= D_3\,\bar{R}$

Upper control limit (UCL) $= D_4\,\bar{R}$

For the data contained in Exhibit 14, we can calculate the various control limits. These are summarized in Exhibit 18.

EXHIBIT 18
Control Limits Calculated for the Data in Exhibit 16

Data Points	$\bar{x}$ Chart	R Chart
Central line	12.14 ms	0.69
Lower control limit (LCL)	12.14 − 0.577 × 0.69 = 11.74	0
Upper control limit (UCL)	12.14 + 0.577 × 0.69 = 12.54	2.115 × 0.69 = 1.459

8. *Construct and annotate the control charts.* With this information, the user can draw the control charts. By convention, the centerline appears as a solid line and broken or dotted lines mark the control limits. The analyst notes on the charts such information as the $\bar{x}$ and R values, the n value, the numerical values for the control limits, and other information about the nature of the data. This step completes the control charts.

9. *Begin sampling and ploting the* $\bar{x}$ *and* R *values.* With the centerline and control limits established, the analyst can plot the data for future sample means and ranges on the appropriate charts. Exhibit 19 shows how the resulting charts might look using future

EXHIBIT 19
$\bar{X}$ **and** ***R*** **Charts**

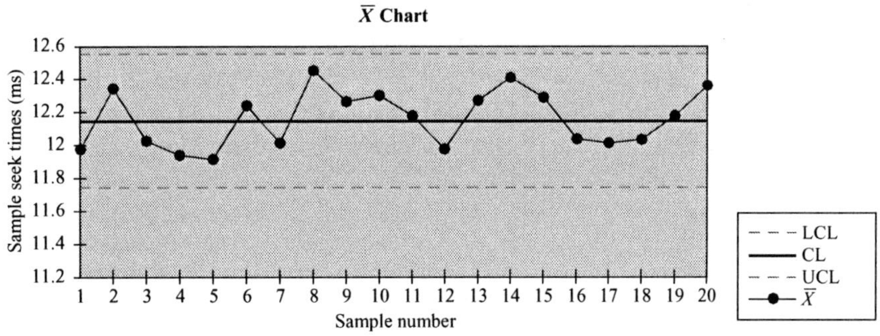

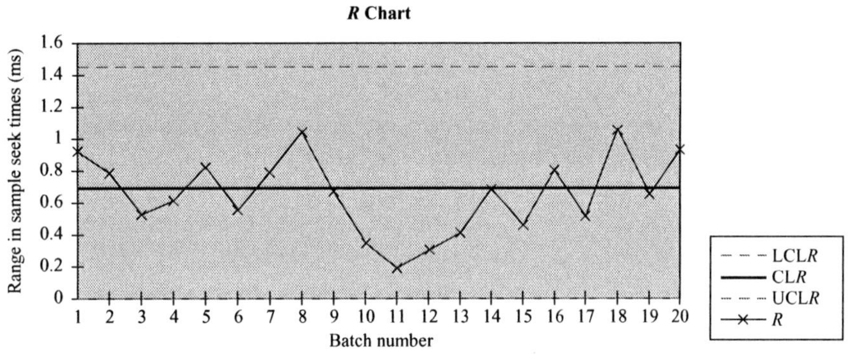

data. After plotting the data, the analyst circles any outliers, or points above or below the control limits, in either control chart. These circled points indicate unusual variance that requires intervention to improve process control.

Interpreting Control Charts

The process is out of control whenever the sample means or range values appear outside the control lines. This signals managers or workers to stop the process to identify and correct the underlying problems that caused the faulty data. Control charts also may indicate a need for intervention in the process in three other conditions: trends, runs, and hugging.

Trends A control chart indicates a **trend** when successive points seem to fall along a line moving either upward or downward. A trend in control chart data indicates some continuing change in the process. This signal may warrant intervention before the trend line crosses control limits to generate an actual defect.

Runs Truly random variations should not form any pattern in the distribution of data around the central lines. A **run** occurs when successive sample means or ranges form a trend or pattern, four increasing values in a row, for example. Such patterns or cycles indicate systematic problems in the process that require attention.

Hugging Hugging occurs when various points appear so closely grouped around the central line that they seem to show no variation in the data. **Hugging** usually indicates that some intervention has been made in the process to limit or eliminate variation. In other words, some intervention is masking the natural variation in the process. This intervention might be the action of some employee who wants the process to look good. The TQM practitioner must uncover and remove this limiting force to reveal the true operation and natural variation in the process. Hugging prevents the analyst from judging whether the process as currently constituted really operates under control or if some outside force is taking unusual measures to produce acceptable results.

Acceptance Sampling

Process control is highly effective when the process is accessible to management, that is, it is part of the internal operations system. However, there are numerous instances when managers must make a decision about a batch of products sourced from a process outside their immediate access. For example, consider the situation of a firm that buys parts from a supplier located on the other side of the world. A batch of parts arrives on their shipping dock and they must decide whether or not the parts meet the design specifications. If the supplier is not very reliable, then testing is usually done to determine the quality of the parts.

One approach is to test every single part in the batch. Often this approach is not very attractive. First, it is time-consuming, since every part must be removed and tested. Second, such testing is not really a value-adding activity. Third, it may not even be possible. We may have to destroy the part in order to evaluate it. For example, to test the thickness of a coating on a part, we may have to saw the part in half.

A more common approach is to apply **acceptance sampling.** Acceptance sampling is a statistics-based approach in which a decision (accept or reject) is made for the entire batch of parts based on the information gained from evaluating a relatively small sample of the parts. The rules used to determine the size of the sample and the conditions governing the specific decision options are a function of the acceptance sampling plan that is in place.

Objective

The objective of an acceptance sampling plan is to achieve the desired level of quality in a manner that is appropriate for the specific environment. Acceptance sampling plans are designed to balance the costs of sampling against the risk of making an incorrect decision regarding the batch. As the sample size is increased, sampling costs increase and the risks of making an incorrect decision decrease. There are two risks of incorrect decisions that must be considered: **consumer's risk,** the risk of deciding that a batch is acceptable when in fact it is unacceptable, and **producer's risk,** the risk of deciding a batch is unacceptable when in fact it is acceptable.

Types of Acceptance Sampling Plans

Many types of acceptance sampling plans have been developed, each addressing specific environmental conditions. Most of these plans fit into one of three categories: (1) lot-by-lot acceptance sampling, (2) continuous flow acceptance sampling, and (3) special cases.

Lot-by-Lot This type of sampling occurs when we have goods or services that can be conveniently grouped into lots. Lot-by-lot acceptance sampling plans can be specified for either attribute or variable data. These plans can be broken down into either acceptance/rejection plans (plans in which a sample is drawn from the lot and the lot is accepted or rejected based on the analysis of the sample) or rectifying plans (plans that call for continued sampling until a decision can be made).

Continuous Flow This type of sampling plan is used when we cannot group units into convenient lots (e.g., products on a conveyor). One commonly used plan is clear sampling. This focuses on the number of acceptable units that are observed between the occurrences of two defective units. If the number observed is greater than the critical *N*, the lot is accepted; otherwise it is rejected or subjected to 100 percent inspection.

Special Cases Specially developed sampling plans include chain sampling plans, skip-lots, variable plans, narrow limit plans, and first/last sampling. First/last sampling is interesting since it has been most used by the Japanese as part of their lean systems approaches. With this approach, the first and last items in a batch are tested. If both pass, it is assumed that the parts between these two end points are also good, and the batch is accepted. Otherwise, the batch is rejected.

Scatter Diagram

A **scatter diagram** is a plot of observed values of two variables. This plot graphically illustrates the relationship between a pair of variables, such as number of defects per batch against changes in the speed of the production line, or production time per unit against hours of training.

Objectives

Scatter diagrams provide a visual and statistical means to evaluate the strength of a potential relationship between variables. When combined with tools such as CED diagrams, scatter diagrams help determine if there is more to a relationship than simply the consensus uncovered through the CED diagrams.

Scatter diagrams can give managers a lot of information about the nature of the relationship between process performance variables. A group of points that seem to form a horizontal or vertical line indicates no relationship. Points that approximate a line from the upper left to the lower right indicate a **negative relationship,** whereas points that approximate a line from the lower left to the upper right indicate a **positive relationship**. Points that seem to fall along an arc indicate a nonlinear relationship.

In addition, tightly grouped points indicate a **strong relationship,** while loosely scattered points suggest a **weak relationship.** This information can help to confirm or deny hypothetical causes of observed effects.

Constructing a Scatter Diagram

Building a scatter diagram is relatively straightforward. In its basic form, it consists of four steps:

1. *Collect paired samples of data that may be related.* A good starting point is to collect between 50 and 100 paired samples of data.
2. *Lay out the axis lines of the diagram.*
3. *Plot the data on the diagram.* Now, the data are placed at their respective coordinates on the diagram. A commonly used convention is to circle a point as many times as its value is repeated (i.e., more than one set of paired data having the same coordinates).
4. *Interpret the data.* The final step is to study the resulting relationship. This study can be done at many levels. It can start with a simple visual assessment and include the use of statistical analysis. In addition, it can involve an assessment of linear and nonlinear relationships.

Exhibit 20 shows three different scatter diagrams. The scatter diagram for the data in Exhibit 20 B suggests a negative relationship between the production run length and the percentage of defective parts produced in each batch. Contrast this with the data in Exhibit 20 A, where the relationship does not appear to be strong. The data presented in Exhibit 20 C suggest a nonlinear relationship. To determine the significance of the relationship between two variables, further analysis might include a statistical analysis such as regression.

EXHIBIT 20 **Scatter Diagram Forms**

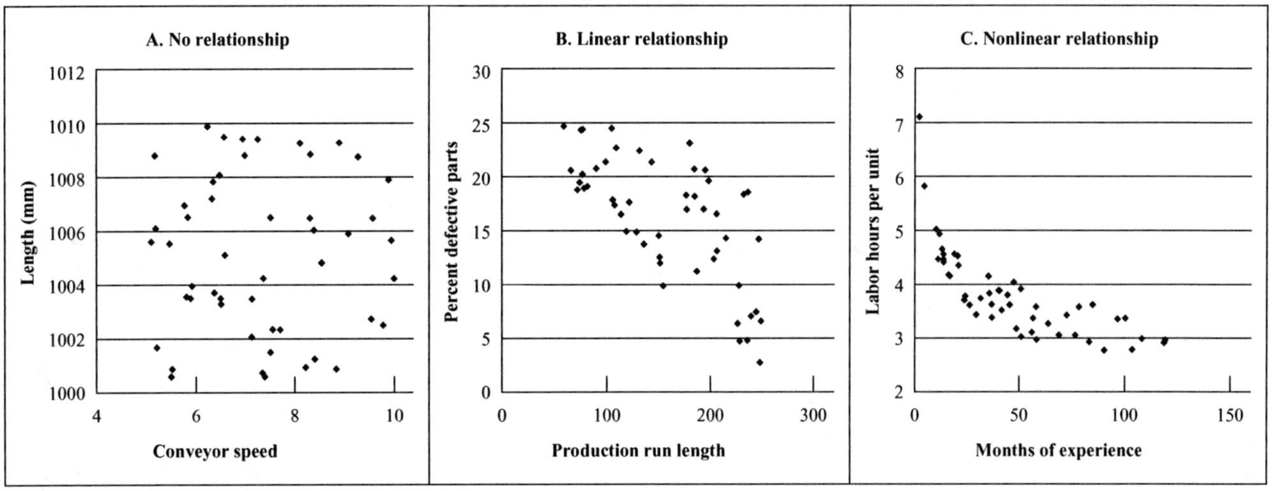

Module Summary

We began this module by looking at the experiences of Sulzer Bingham Pumps. We saw a company that had achieved significant strategic success by relying on a quality-based strategy. The success of this firm was not simply due to committed people at all levels. This factor, while important, was insufficient by itself. For Sulzer Bingham to have succeeded, it needed committed employees trained in the appropriate quality-related tools. The tools had to be applied to both the management of the process and to the design of new or revised products and processes. We explored many of the tools that are integral to value-driven management:

1. While management frameworks are important to TQM, success depends on giving people the right tools and teaching them how to use those tools. Practitioners use process tools to assess current conditions in processes, identify potential problems, and bring the processes back under control. They use design tools to ensure quality and reliable performance in new products and processes.
2. TQM tools can manipulate either attribute or variable data. Variable data can be measured and compared while attribute data describe states (pass/fail, go/no-go, good/bad) or locations. Variable data can always be converted into attribute data, but attribute data may indicate only general limits for variable data. Irrespective of the type of data, we must always remember that the effectiveness of the tools is highly dependent on the quality of the data. Poor data will always generate poor analysis and results.
3. Some important TQM process tools include Pareto analysis, check sheets, cause-and-effect diagrams, process flow analysis, histograms, measures of process capability (C_p and C_{pk}), process control charts, and scatter diagrams. While any of these tools can advance a TQM effort by itself, they are most effective when used together.

Increasingly, managers are moving beyond the task of controlling existing processes to work on understanding fundamental relationships between process elements and their ultimate impacts on quality. Managers also are becoming more proactive, working to improve processes and products through integrated efforts that join together people from marketing, engineering, purchasing, finance, and operations management. Organizational success now requires these people to deliver more than expected quality; they now must offer quality that excites the customer, so that the customer will perceive a higher value in their product/service.

Key Terms

Acceptance sampling, *22*
Attribute check sheet, *14*
Attribute data, *5*
Bell-shaped distribution, *6*
C_p, C_{pk}, *8*
Cause-and-effect diagram, *12*
Check sheet, *13*
Comb distribution, *6*
Consumer's risk, *22*
Control charts, *17*
Deming wheel, *3*
Double-peaked distribution, *6*
Histogram, *6*
Hugging, *21*
Location check sheet, *14*
Negative relationship, *23*
Pareto analysis, *15*
Plan–do–check–act (PDCA) cycle, *3*
Plateau distribution, *6*
Positive relationship, *23*
Process capability, *8*
Process centering, *10*
Process width, *8*
Producer's risk, *22*
Runs, *21*
Scatter diagram, *22*
Skewed distribution, *6*
Specification width, *8*
Strong relationship, *23*
Taguchi methods, *11*
Trend, *21*
Variable data, *4*
Variable check sheet, *14*
Weak relationship, *23*
$\bar{X}-R$ chart, *18*

Discussion Questions

1. As the quality control czar of your household, you have been asked to solve a complex problem found in most homes—the single sock gremlin. A flaw in many household processes results in either the loss of one sock or the arrival of an undeclared single sock from an unknown source.
   a. Develop a cause-and-effect diagram and use any other appropriate SPC tools that might shed light on this mystery.
   b. Prepare a list of some of the possible corrective actions.
2. In this module, it has been argued that inspections are generally not a value-adding activity. Under what conditions do inspections really add value?
3. Why is it difficult or inappropriate to apply the TQM tools discussed in this module to long-term personal relationships?

4. Given the importance placed on good data and good instrumentation (the devices used to measure and collect performance), how would you as a manager protect yourself from problems created by either bad data or incorrect instrumentation? What are the potential problems created by these two areas?
5. In the module, it was noted that inspections are not value-adding activities but that there were conditions under which inspections were needed. What conditions lead to a situation where inspections are required?

Solved Problems

Variable Versus Attribute Data

For each of the following situations, examine the data set that has been collected and determine if we are dealing with variable data or attribute data.

1. An engine arrives at a test station. First, it is connected to a power supply. Second, the tester attempts to start the engine. Third, the tester at the test station records whether or not the engine started. This record of starts represents what type of data?

   In this case, we are dealing with attribute data. The reason is that the only aspect of performance that we are recording is whether or not the engine starts.
2. You are working at a lumber mill. Trees arrive into the plant where they are trimmed and cut. After being cut, they are dried in a kiln. After they are removed from the kiln, the wood is graded in terms of its length (in millimeters), its weight (in pounds), the number of knotholes, and its moisture content. After this information is recorded, the wood is graded as to whether it is premium, grade, standard, or substandard. These grades represent what type of data?

   Here, we have to differentiate between the grades and the information used in determining the grades. While this input information is variable in nature, the grades are attribute in nature. In this problem, we see an example of how variable data can be mapped onto attribute data. We also see the problems inherent in this transformation. Once we convert variable to attribute data, we can no longer convert back, if all we have is the attribute data.
3. You work for the local Red Cross blood bank. Donors are complaining about the long waiting times to give blood. To help assess the waiting times, you have designed a form that is given to each donor upon entering the clinic. The form allows the nurses to record each person's arrival and departure times from each station in the blood-donating process. You collect these data for a three-week period. The resulting database represents what type of data?

   These data are variable in nature because the information gathered can be compared and the magnitudes have meaning. We know, for example, that a person who is in the process for 40 minutes as compared to someone else who has been in the system for 60 minutes has spent 33 percent less time in the system.
4. *Consumer's Reports* regularly evaluates cars and their performance. One of the attributes of performance that is reported is the average miles per gallon both in the city and on the highway. This statistic represents what type of data?

   Again, we are dealing with variable data. Miles per gallon can assume any value. Furthermore, meaningful information can be gained by comparing the performance of two cars—one getting 19.5 miles per gallon and another car getting 30.4 miles per gallon.

C_p and C_{pk}

You have been given the following data for a production process that is responsible for filling bags of flour. With these data, you have been asked by management to determine the answers to two questions:

1. Is the process capable?
2. If it is not, then what has to be done to bring the process back in control (i.e., make it capable again)?

Production specifications	10.00 ± 0.20 pounds
Process standard deviation (σ)	0.05 pound
Process distribution centered at	10.10 pounds
Specification width (S)	$10.20 - 9.80 = 0.40$
Process width (P)	99 percent or 3σ on each side, or $10.10 - 0.15 = 9.95$ and $10.10 + 0.15 = 10.25$ $10.25 - 9.95 = 0.30$

$C_p = S/P = 0.40/0.30 = 1.333$ (based on the C_p value alone, the process is capable . . . but barely).

$$K = |D - \bar{X}|/(S/2) = |10.00 - 10.10|/(0.40/2) = 0.10/0.20 = 0.5$$

$$C_{pk} = (1-K) \times C_p = 0.5 \times 1.333 = 0.667$$

This indicates that the process is no longer capable. The first step for management is to recenter the production process. That is, the center of the production process must be shifted from 10.10 to 10.00. This action, while improving things, is not enough. The next is to reduce the variance of the process. The two actions, when combined, should result in a process that is now capable.

Control Chart

You have been given the following data taken from 20 samples, where each sample consists of five observations. You have been asked to calculate the limits for the $\bar{X}$–R charts.

Sample Number	Sample Mean ($\bar{X}$)	Range (R)
1	12.25	4.50
2	12.75	5.00
3	10.63	0.50
4	15.88	1.00
5	12.00	4.00
6	14.75	4.00
7	13.25	3.00
8	13.48	8.00
9	15.50	3.00
10	15.25	7.00
11	15.75	5.00
12	13.13	4.50
13	11.88	3.00
14	15.00	6.00
15	14.30	4.50
16	14.50	6.00
17	17.65	9.00
18	14.88	3.50
19	12.63	4.00
20	16.88	4.00
Means	14.15	4.45

Calculating the control limits for the $\bar{X}$ chart:

Upper control limit $= \bar{X} + A_2 \times \bar{R} = 14.15 + 0.58 \times 4.45$
(0.58, taken from table where $n = 5$) $= 16.73$

Lower control limit $= \bar{X} - A_2 \times \bar{R} = 14.15 - 0.58 \times 4.45 = 11.57$

Note: As long as $\bar{X}$ remains between 11.57 and 16.73, this process is under control.

Calculating the control limits for R charts:

Upper control limit $= D_4 \times \bar{R}$ (where D_4 is taken from table) $= 2.11 \times 4.45 = 9.39$

Lower control limit $= D_2 \times \bar{R} = 0 \times 4.45 = 0.0$

Note: As long $\bar{R}$ remains between 0 and 9.39, then the process is under control.

Problems

1. The time students entered the class room of MGT 390, Introductory Operations Management, was recorded by the professor in Exhibit 21 for five class meetings. Create and analyze a histogram of these data.

EXHIBIT 21
Data for Problem 1

Minutes Arrival before Class (class starts at time 0)	Class 1	Class 2	Class 3	Class 4	Class 5
15	3	4	6	1	4
14	0	0	2	1	3
13	1	2	0	3	1
12	1	0	0	1	0
11	1	1	2	1	0
10	2	0	0	1	1
9	4	2	0	2	0
8	0	1	4	3	0
7	1	5	1	0	3
6	1	1	2	1	2
5	5	6	2	4	5
4	6	1	7	4	6
3	0	0	3	2	0
2	3	2	0	5	0
1	2	2	0	0	4
0	1	2	0	0	1
−1	0	0	0	0	1
−2	0	0	0	0	0
−3	0	0	0	1	0
−4	0	0	0	0	0
−5	0	1	0	0	0
−6	0	0	0	0	0
−7	0	0	0	0	0
−8	0	0	1	0	0
−9	0	0	0	1	0
−10	0	0	0	0	0

2. The injection-molded caps of disposable ball point pens must meet tight specifications to fit snugly on the pen. One specification that is tracked is the cap's weight, which should be 0.2 g. A sample of 100 pens is taken each day. Make a histogram of the data for one day's production, given the data in Exhibit 22.

EXHIBIT 22 **Weights of Molded Caps in Grams—Data for Problem 2**

0.225	0.243	0.239	0.231	0.228	0.215	0.161	0.161	0.207	0.177
0.190	0.186	0.203	0.230	0.228	0.180	0.230	0.194	0.243	0.177
0.210	0.210	0.185	0.225	0.204	0.152	0.245	0.231	0.152	0.150
0.161	0.171	0.208	0.208	0.170	0.204	0.250	0.178	0.205	0.236
0.159	0.229	0.173	0.228	0.184	0.223	0.240	0.193	0.170	0.241
0.161	0.193	0.165	0.154	0.192	0.214	0.189	0.208	0.227	0.169
0.163	0.196	0.181	0.197	0.248	0.238	0.205	0.207	0.244	0.208
0.200	0.207	0.225	0.162	0.229	0.151	0.224	0.169	0.220	0.182
0.214	0.233	0.194	0.181	0.208	0.249	0.220	0.197	0.204	0.247
0.216	0.160	0.210	0.222	0.157	0.174	0.173	0.240	0.203	0.247

3. The specifications for the diameter of an injection-molded part are 25 mm ± 0.5 mm. The actual average and standard deviation from 250 parts sampled are 25.01 and 0.1 mm respectively. What are the C_p and C_{pk}?
4. The specification for the weight of a box of cereal is 16.2 oz ± 0.1 oz. The actual mean and standard deviation from a sample of 200 boxes are 16.1 oz and 0.05 oz respectively. What are the C_p and C_{pk}?
5. A professor who teaches the Introduction to Management course, MGT 301, has noticed that 20 percent of the students in her sections receive a grade lower than 2.0 on a 4.0 scale. This is the

first management course that any of these students have taken. The text for the course is a standard survey text, which is used at many other colleges and universities. All of the students in the class are first-semester-junior, business students. The students work in teams to manage a simulated factory. As part of this they must use a computer spreadsheet to do simple income statements, balance sheets, and cash-flow problems. Prepare a cause-and-effect diagram to analyze the problem of "why do students in MGT 301 receive low grades?" For the main branches of the CED, use the titles of student, books, faculty, and equipment.

6. Create a check sheet to organize the data given in problem 1 above.
7. Create a check sheet to analyze the data in problem 2 above.
8. In an apparel factory, every time a sewing machine breaks, the symptom is recorded. All of the sewing machine breakdowns for the past 30 days are recorded in Exhibit 23. Create a check sheet to organize and analyze these data.

EXHIBIT 23
Data for Problem 8

Day	Machine Number	Reason for Breakdown	Day	Machine Number	Reason for Breakdown
1	217	Dull knife	6	192	Breaking needles
1	145	Skip stitch	6	165	Other
1	193	Stuck pedal	6	192	Breaking needles
1	187	Skip stitch	6	217	Thread breaks
1	234	Breaking needles	6	217	Skip stitch
2	165	Air pressure low	7	165	Skip stitch
2	192	Breaking needles	7	195	Stuck pedal
2	217	Thread breaks	7	187	Skip stitch
2	217	Skip stitch	7	234	Breaking needles
2	165	Skip stitch	7	165	Air pressure low
2	181	Breaking needles	8	192	Other
2	201	Dull knife	8	234	Breaking needles
2	172	Breaking needles	8	165	Air pressure low
2	195	Stuck pedal	9	192	Breaking needles
3	187	Skip stitch	9	217	Thread breaks
3	234	Breaking needles	9	151	Other
3	165	Air pressure low	9	187	Skip stitch
3	192	Breaking needles	9	234	Breaking needles
3	151	Skip stitch	9	151	Breaking needles
4	187	Skip stitch	10	234	Skip stitch
4	234	Breaking needles	10	165	Air pressure low
5	195	Stuck pedal	10	192	Breaking needles
5	187	Skip stitch	10	187	Skip stitch
6	165	Air pressure low	10	131	Other

9. The quality inspectors at Windows Inc. visually inspect each sheet of 4'×8' glass when it is through with the annealing process. They record all of the defects onto a form. The defects that have been found this week are given in Exhibit 24. Use these data to create a location check sheet.

EXHIBIT 24
Data for Problem 9

Corner	Body	Defect	Corner	Body	Defect
Left upper		Chipped corner		Center	Scratch
	Center	Indentation	Left upper		Chipped corner
Left upper		Chipped corner	Right upper	Chipped corner	
Right lower		Scratch	Right lower		Scratch
	Left of center	Bump		Right of center	Indentation
Left upper		Chipped corner	Left upper		Chipped corner
Left upper		Chipped corner	Left lower		Scratch
Left lower		Scratch	Left upper		Crack

10. Use the data in Exhibit 23 to create a Pareto diagram.
11. Use the data in Exhibit 24 to create a Pareto diagram.

12. For the following check sheet, assume that o indicates a surface scratch, x a blowhole, D a defective finish, * improper shape, and ? others. How would you go about analyzing the following check sheet?

	Worker	Mon AM	Mon PM	Tue AM	Tue PM	Wedn AM	Wed PM	Thur AM	Thur PM	Fri AM	Fri PM
Mach 1	1	oox*	ox	oxx	oooxxxo	oooooxxxo	ooxx	oooo	oxx	oo	oDxx
Mach 2	2	oxx*	oooxx*	oooooxx	oooxx	ooooooxx*	ooooox*	ooooxx	ooox**	ooxx*	ooooo

For this question, analyze the data using Pareto analysis. Is stratification appropriate for this type of a problem? How would you stratify the data? That is, identify those variables you think have an important effect on the observed results.

13. Construct an $\bar{X} - R$ chart for the data set in Exhibit 25.

EXHIBIT 25
Data for Problem 13

Subgroup Number	6:00	10:00	14:00	18:00	22:00	$\bar{x}$	R
1	14.0	12.6	13.2	13.1	12.1	13.00	1.9
2	13.2	13.3	12.7	13.4	12.1	12.94	1.3
3	13.5	12.8	13.0	12.8	12.4	12.90	1.1`
4	13.9	12.4	13.3	13.1	13.2	13.18	1.5
5	13.0	13.0	12.1	12.2	13.3	2.72	1.2
6	13.7	12.0	12.5	12.4	12.4	12.60	1.7
7	13.9	12.1	12.7	13.4	13.0	13.02	1.8
8	13.4	13.6	13.0	12.4	13.5	13.18	1.2
9	14.4	12.4	12.2	12.4	12.5	12.78	2.2
10	13.3	12.4	12.6	12.9	12.8	12.80	0.9
11	13.3	12.8	13.0	13.0	13.1	13.04	0.5
12	13.6	12.5	13.3	13.5	12.8	13.14	1.1
13	13.4	13.3	12.0	13.0	13.1	12.96	1.4
14	13.9	13.1	13.5	12.6	12.8	13.18	1.3
15	14.2	12.7	12.9	12.9	12.5	13.04	1.7
16	13.6	12.6	12.4	12.5	12.2	12.66	1.4
17	14.0	13.2	12.4	13.0	13.0	13.12	1.6
18	13.1	12.9	13.5	12.3	12.8	12.92	1.2
19	14.6	13.7	13.4	12.2	12.5	13.28	2.4
20	13.9	13.0	13.0	13.2	12.6	13.14	1.3
21	13.3	12.7	12.6	12.8	12.7	12.82	0.7
22	13.9	12.4	12.7	12.4	12.8	12.84	1.5
23	13.2	12.3	12.6	13.1	12.7	12.78	0.9
24	13.2	12.8	12.8	12.3	12.6	12.74	0.9
25	13.3	12.8	12.0	12.3	12.2	12.72	1.1
					$\sum$ of $\bar{x}$	323.50	33.8
					Grand mean ($\bar{\bar{x}}$)	12.94	1.35

14. You are responsible for managing a process that manufactures electronic capacitors. This process has experienced an unacceptable level of rejects. Consequently, you asked that the people responsible for the process that manufactures these products collect data regarding the defects and the reason for these defects. This information has been collected in the following table (assume that the data are representative).

Observation	Reject Cause	Observation	Reject Cause	Observation	Reject Cause
1	Corrosion	2	Oxide defect	3	Contamination
4	Oxide defect	5	Oxide defect	6	Miscellaneous
7	Oxide defect	8	Contamination	9	Metallization
10	Oxide defect	11	Contamination	12	Contamination
13	Oxide defect	14	Contamination	15	Contamination
16	Contamination	17	Corrosion	18	Silicon defect

continued on next page

continued

Observation	Reject Cause	Observation	Reject Cause	Observation	Reject Cause
19	Miscellaneous	20	Contamination	21	Contamination
22	Contamination	23	Contamination	24	Contamination
25	Miscellaneous	26	Doping	27	Oxide defect
28	Oxide defect	29	Metallization	30	Contamination
31	Contamination	32	Oxide defect	33	Contamination

What conclusions can draw from these data? What techniques would you use? How would you manage the data?

15. As a result of a TQM exercise, the process described in problem 14 has been modified. Data again have been collected and summarized in the following table. To what extent have the improvements introduced by the process modification been successful in improving the process?

Failure Cause	Number Observed
Doping	0
Corrosion	2
Metallization	4
Miscellaneous	2
Oxide defect	1
Contamination	8
Silicon defect	2

16. Big Turkey Burger Farms (BTBF) produces a large turkey burger that is world famous. This burger is known not only for its quality, but also for its size and consistency. They produce a turkey burger that on average is 12 ounces large (with a standard deviation of 0.10 ounce). Currently, it has been approached by two major restaurant chains: Monarch Burgers and Audrey's.
    a. Monarch wants a turkey burger that is between 11.77 and 12.23 ounces.
        i. For this supplier, calculate the C_p.
        ii. Calculate the C_{pk} value.
        iii. How well would BTBF's products meet the demands of Monarch Burgers?
    b. Audrey's, in contrast, wants a turkey burger that is 11.95 ounces on average with a tolerance of 0.30 ounce.
        i. For this supplier, calculate the Cp.
        ii. Calculate the Cpk value.
        iii. How well would BTBF's products meet the demands of Audrey's?
    c. If BTBF had a choice of restaurant chains to serve (it can only pick one), which one should it select? Why?
17. In an article in *Quality Engineering*, a research study presented individual measurement data on sand compactability, as follows

46	43	41	42	40	44	40	41	40	42
41	41	43	43	40	38	45	42	41	43
42	43	39	44	44	45	43	42	41	46
41	39	40	40	42	44	42	40	43	

For these data, the author reported that the lower and upper specifications for sand compactability are 38 and 46, respectively. Use this information to calculate the C_p and C_{pk} values.

18. Calculate the C_p and C_{pk} for a process characterized by the following data:

Production specifications: 1.00 +/− 0.08 cm
Process standard deviation: 0.005 cm
Process distribution centered at 0.95 cm

Cases

Bully Boy Bagging Line

The manager reviewed the production on the Firm's large bag packaging line. There seemed to be much more variation in quality than she normally noticed. After calling for a summary of data from production control, she received the following data for the last 16 work weeks.

Date	Day	Number of Workers	Number of Bags Produced	Number of Bad Bags
1	Monday	4	2997	59
2	Tuesday	5	4349	173
3	Wednesday	5	2886	114
4	Thursday	5	2772	110
5	Friday	3	1934	19
6	Saturday	3	1211	12
7	Monday	5	3761	150
8	Tuesday	5	3924	156
9	Wednesday	5	4913	196
10	Thursday	5	4049	161
11	Friday	5	3465	138
12	Saturday	4	1720	34
13	Monday	4	2201	44
14	Tuesday	5	3269	130
15	Wednesday	5	4345	173
16	Thursday	5	2454	98
17	Friday	5	3726	149
18	Saturday	4	2733	54
19	Monday	5	3934	157
20	Tuesday	5	3016	120
21	Wednesday	5	3420	136
22	Thursday	5	2727	109
23	Friday	5	3328	133
24	Saturday	0	0	0
25	Monday	4	2574	51
26	Tuesday	4	2524	50
27	Wednesday	5	3012	120
28	Thursday	5	2412	96
29	Friday	4	2291	45
30	Saturday	3	1429	14
31	Monday	4	2481	49
32	Tuesday	5	3010	120
33	Wednesday	5	4634	185
34	Thursday	5	3352	134
35	Friday	5	2274	90
36	Saturday	0	0	0
37	Monday	5	3540	141
38	Tuesday	5	3854	154
39	Wednesday	5	3163	126
40	Thursday	4	3040	60
41	Friday	4	3153	63
42	Saturday	4	1804	18
43	Monday	5	2873	114
44	Tuesday	5	3439	137
45	Wednesday	4	3352	67
46	Thursday	4	3607	72
47	Friday	4	3127	62

continued on next page

Date	Day	Number of Workers	Number of Bags Produced	Number of Bad Bags
48	Saturday	0	0	0
49	Monday	5	2399	95
50	Tuesday	5	2699	107
51	Wednesday	5	2995	119
52	Thursday	5	3115	124
53	Friday	5	3520	140
54	Saturday	3	1712	17
55	Monday	4	2611	52
56	Tuesday	5	2450	98
57	Wednesday	5	4360	174
58	Thursday	5	2491	99
59	Friday	5	3307	132
60	Saturday	0	0	0
61	Monday	4	2390	47
62	Tuesday	4	3007	60
63	Wednesday	4	2979	59
64	Thursday	4	2173	43
65	Friday	4	2346	46
66	Saturday	0	0	0
67	Monday	5	3666	146
68	Tuesday	4	3510	70
69	Wednesday	4	2032	40
70	Thursday	4	2319	46
71	Friday	3	1900	19
72	Saturday	3	1537	15
73	Monday	4	2086	41
74	Tuesday	5	3596	143
75	Wednesday	5	2418	96
76	Thursday	5	2571	102
77	Friday	3	2288	22
78	Saturday	3	1441	14
79	Monday	4	2358	47
80	Tuesday	5	3661	146
81	Wednesday	5	3449	137
82	Thursday	5	3952	158
83	Friday	5	3749	149
84	Saturday	0	0	0
85	Monday	4	2717	54
86	Tuesday	4	3069	61
87	Wednesday	4	2197	43
88	Thursday	3	1623	16
89	Friday	3	1903	19
90	Saturday	0	0	0
91	Monday	4	1824	36
92	Tuesday	4	3797	75
93	Wednesday	5	3810	152
94	Thursday	5	2767	110
95	Friday	5	2106	84
96	Saturday	3	1436	14

QUESTIONS

1. What does this date tell you?
2. Which tools did you use to determine what is happening?
3. What management actions are appropriate?

Related Modules of Interest

- Total Quality Management: Framework, Measures and Standards
- Lean Systems Tools and Procedures
- Fundamentals of Process Management
- Foundations of Value

Selected Readings

Association for Manufacturing Excellence. *Manufacturing Report 21: The Future of Japanese Manufacturing.* Ed. Robert Hall. Wheeling, IL: Association for Manufacturing Excellence, 1990.

AT&T. *Statistical Quality Control Handbook.* 11th ed. Charlotte, NC: Delmar Printing, 1985.

Bhote, Keri R. *Strategic Supplier Management: A Blueprint for Revitalizing the Manufacturer-Supplier Partnership.* New York: American Management Association, 1989.

Dean, James W., Jr., and James R. Evans. *Total Quality: Management, Organization and Strategy.* Minneapolis/St. Paul, MN: West Publishing Company, 1994.

Deming, W. Edward. *Quality, Productivity, and Competitive Position.* Cambridge, MA: Massachusetts Institute of Technology, Center for Advanced Engineering Study, 1982.

——. *Out of Crisis.* Cambridge, MA: Massachusetts Institute of Technology, Center for Advanced Engineering Study, 1986.

Garvin, David A. *Managing Quality.* New York: Free Press, 1988.

Gitlow, Howard, Shelly Gitlow, Alan Oppenheim, and Rosa Oppenheim. *Tools and Methods for the Improvement of Quality.* New York: McGraw-Hill/Irwin, 1989.

Imai, Masaaki. *Kaizen: The Key to Japan's Competitive Success.* New York: Random House, 1986.

Ishikawa, Kaoru. *Guide to Quality Control.* White Plains, NY: Quality Resources, 1982.

——. *What Is Total Quality Control? The Japanese Way.* Englewood Cliffs, NJ: Prentice Hall, 1985.

Juran, Joseph M., and Frank M. Gryna Jr. *Quality Planning and Analysis.* New York: McGraw-Hill, 1980.

Klippel, Warren H., ed. *Statistical Quality Control.* Dearborn, MI: Society of Manufacturing Engineers, 1984.

Logothetis, N. *Managing for Total Quality: From Deming to Taguchi and SPC.* Hertfordshire, UK: Prentice Hall International (UK), 1992.

Mizuno, Shigerua, and Yoji Akao, eds. *QFD: The Customer-Driven Approach to Quality Planning and Deployment.* Hong Kong: Nordica International, 1994.

National Center for Manufacturing Sciences. *21st Manufacturing Enterprise Strategy: An Industry-Led View,* Volume 1. Ann Arbor, MI: National Center for Manufacturing Sciences, November 1991.

——. *21st Manufacturing Enterprise Strategy: An Industry-Led View,* Volume 2. Ann Arbor, MI: National Center for Manufacturing Sciences, November 1991.

Palady, Paul. *Failure Modes and Effects Analysis.* West Palm Beach, FL: PT Publications, 1995.

Steudel, Harold J., and Paul Destruelle. *Manufacturing in the Nineties.* New York: Van Nostrand Reinhold, 1992.

Tribus, Myron. *Quality First: Selected Papers on Quality and Productivity Improvements.* Washington, DC: American Quality and Productivity Institute, 1988.

Appendix

Areas under the normal curve, 0 to *z*

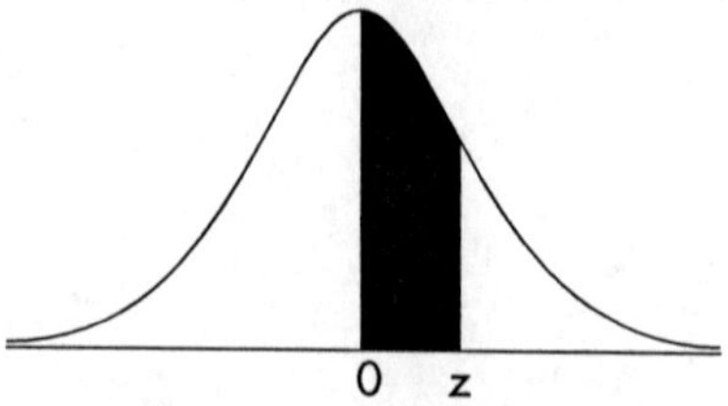

Note: The shaded area is the total area under the curve

z	0	0.01	0.02	0.03	0.04	0.05	0.06	0.07	0.08	0.09
0.0	.0000	.0040	.0080	.0120	.0160	.0199	.0239	.0279	.0319	.0359
0.1	.0398	.0438	.0478	.0517	.0557	.0596	.0636	.0675	.0714	.0753
0.2	.0793	.0832	.0871	.0910	.0948	.0987	.1026	.1064	.1103	.1141
0.3	.1179	.1217	.1255	.1293	.1331	.1368	.1406	.1443	.1480	.1517
0.4	.1554	.1591	.1628	.1664	.1700	.1736	.1772	.1808	.1844	.1879
0.5	.1915	.1950	.1985	.2019	.2054	.2088	.2123	.2157	.2190	.2224
0.6	.2257	.2291	.2324	.2357	.2389	.2422	.2454	.2486	.2517	.2549
0.7	.2580	.2611	.2642	.2673	.2703	.2734	.2764	.2794	.2823	.2852
0.8	.2881	.2910	.2939	.2967	.2995	.3023	.3051	.3078	.3106	.3133
0.9	.3159	.3186	.3212	.3238	.3264	.3289	.3315	.3340	.3365	.3389
1.0	.3413	.3438	.3461	.3485	.3508	.3531	.3554	.3577	.3599	.3621
1.1	.3643	.3665	.3686	.3708	.3729	.3749	.3770	.3790	.3810	.3830
1.2	.3849	.3869	.3888	.3907	.3925	.3944	.3962	.3980	.3997	.4015
1.3	.4032	.4049	.4066	.4082	.4099	.4115	.4131	.4147	.4162	.4177
1.4	.4192	.4207	.4222	.4236	.4251	.4265	.4279	.4292	.4306	.4319
1.5	.4332	.4345	.4357	.4370	.4382	.4394	.4406	.4418	.4429	.4441
1.6	.4452	.4463	.4474	.4484	.4495	.4505	.4515	.4525	.4535	.4545
1.7	.4554	.4564	.4573	.4582	.4591	.4599	.4608	.4616	.4625	.4633
1.8	.4641	.4649	.4656	.4664	.4671	.4678	.4686	.4693	.4699	.4706
1.9	.4713	.4719	.4726	.4732	.4738	.4744	.4750	.4756	.4761	.4767
2.0	.4772	.4778	.4783	.4788	.4793	.4798	.4803	.4808	.4812	.4817
2.1	.4821	.4826	.4830	.4834	.4838	.4842	.4846	.4850	.4854	.4857
2.2	.4861	.4864	.4868	.4871	.4875	.4878	.4881	.4884	.4887	.4890
2.3	.4893	.4896	.4898	.4901	.4904	.4906	.4909	.4911	.4913	.4916
2.4	.4918	.4920	.4922	.4925	.4927	.4929	.4939	.4932	.4934	.4936
2.5	.4938	.4940	.4941	.4943	.4945	.4946	.4948	.4949	.4951	.4952
2.6	.4953	.4955	.4956	.4957	.4959	.4960	.4961	.4962	.4963	.4964
2.7	.4965	.4966	.4967	.4968	.4969	.4970	.4971	.4972	.4973	.4974
2.8	.4974	.4975	.4976	.4977	.4977	.4978	.4979	.4979	.4980	.4981
2.9	.4981	.4982	.4982	.4983	.4984	.4984	.4985	.4985	.4986	.4986
3.0	.4987	.4987	.4987	.4988	.4988	.4989	.4989	.4989	.4990	.4990

Lean/ Just-in-Time Systems

Steven A. Melnyk
Michigan State University

Lawrence D. Fredendall
Clemson University

McGraw-Hill Irwin

Boston Burr Ridge, IL Dubuque, IA Madison, WI New York San Francisco St. Louis
Bangkok Bogotá Caracas Kuala Lumpur Lisbon London Madrid Mexico City
Milan Montreal New Delhi Santiago Seoul Singapore Sydney Taipei Toronto

Lean/JIT Systems

Module Objectives

By the end of this module, you should be able to

- Describe the philosophy and history of lean systems.
- Understand how the lean system approach improves value
- Explain the 5 steps required to implement lean systems.
- Identify opportunities for applying the lean approach across functions in the firm.

Rally of the Dolls: It Worked for Toyota. Can It Work for Toys?

For three-quarters of a century, little girls have been unwrapping Madame Alexander dolls at Christmas. The collectible dolls, which cost from $40 to $600 apiece, are modeled on figures both fictional (Cinderella) and real (Elizabeth Taylor); with their hand-painted faces and elaborate costumes, they're charming artifacts of an age before Nintendos and Furbies. But the company that makes them has had to struggle to stay alive for its 75th Christmas. That the dolls are still around is due to an unusual group of manufacturing experts, who have adapted their experience in streamlining the assembly of fenders and crankshafts to the task of turning out wigs, shoes, and all the other tiny bits that go into a doll.

"Madame" Beatrice Alexander, a daughter of Russian immigrants, was raised over her father's doll hospital in New York City. In 1923, she founded the Alexander Doll Co. Her business prospered, and in the 1950s she moved it to a six-story building in Harlem. After the company faltered in 1995, it was bought for $17.5 million by TBM Consulting.

The partners of TBM used Toyota's lean systems techniques to make Alexander Doll Co. lean and efficient. Making dolls is easier than making, say, Lexus LS400s, but not as easy as you'd think. The costumes alone contain 20 or more separate items, which go through as many as 30 production steps. Before TBM arrived, the factory was using archaic methods. It was organized according to the old-fashioned principles of batch manufacturing, so boxes of costume material and vinyl doll parts were stacked to the ceiling. Since nothing was built to order, more than 90,000 dolls were stored in partly finished condition, and customers waited up to 16 weeks for delivery.

In August 1996 TBM installed a new CEO: Herbert Brown, an earnest, fast-talking manufacturing expert. When Brown tried to fill a customer order for 300 dolls, only 117 could be completed because so many pieces were missing. So he went to work reorganizing the factory and, in true Toyota fashion, enlisted the aid of the 470 workers, mostly Dominican immigrants who spoke limited English.

First, a lean system was implemented on the production line for baby dolls by setting up a cross-functional team of 10 employees. They identified 25 operations in the process and measured the time to perform each operation. They discovered that each batch of dolls traveled 630 feet on three different floors over a 90-day period. By combining operations into one floor and processing one doll at a time, the team reduced production time to 90 minutes and distance traveled to 40 feet. Now there are only 34 pieces of work-in-process inventory instead of the 29,000 pieces before and the process occupies only 980 square feet instead of 2,010. As lean system practices have spread throughout the entire factory, the amount of work in progress has been cut by 96 percent, and orders can now be filled in one or two weeks instead of two months. Dolls now flow through the process.

Each team of seven or eight people working in a manufacturing cell is given responsibility for an entire portion of the process. For example one team is responsible for completing about 300 doll wardrobe assemblies a day. The team makes an entire dress, doing all of the sewing, assembly, and pressing in the cell. In another cell, the dolls' features are all hand painted by women sitting in lines at tables. The company now makes more than 400 types of dolls a year and more than 3,000 dolls a day for a total of more than 500,000 dolls a year.

Lean systems require change not only from production, but also from marketing. Marketing responded by encouraging collector doll shops and creating new marketing programs for home-shopping channels. The Alexander Doll Club has more than 10,000 members and its own website. Adult professional women, as well as celebrities such as Demi Moore, Cindy Crawford, and Barbara Streisand, are owners of these beautiful, luxurious dolls.

Source: Knight-Ridder/Tribune Business News, "Alexander Doll Stays in Harlem, Thanks to Kaizen Breakthrough Partnership," June 13, 1995, 6130356; Knight-Ridder/Tribune Business News, "Alexander Doll Inc.," March 11, 1997, 311B1063;

A. Taylor III, "It Worked for Toyota. Can It Work for Toys?" *Fortune* 139, no. 1 (January 11, 1999), p. 36;

J. Van Dyk, "The Magic of Madame Alexander Dolls," *Smithsonian* 3 (2001), pp. 105–109.

Lean Systems/Just-in-Time Defined

The lean systems idea may have started in a car company, but it is changing how we manufacture everything, even dolls at Alexander Doll. There have been a variety of terms that refer to what is usually called **lean systems** or **just-in-time** (JIT) manufacturing. These include lean production, stockless production, zero inventories, and the Toyota Production System (TPS). Currently the most common name is lean systems and that is how we will refer to it in the remainder of this module. APICS, the educational society for resources management, defines lean systems as "a philosophy of production that emphasizes the minimization of the amount of all the resources (including time) used in the various activities of the enterprise . . ."[1]

There are several very important aspects of this definition. First, the statement that lean systems is "a philosophy of production" means that it is a set of manufacturing principles to improve performance in all firms. While the principles remain the same, their application changes in different production environments. Second, the lean systems approach minimizes the use of resources, which means that lean systems seek to eliminate waste. It is as a direct result of eliminating waste that productivity is increased.

This module focuses on the philosophy and principles of lean systems. It creates a framework to understand lean systems and to determine when to use each of the lean systems tools. The tools used in lean systems to eliminate all forms of waste are explicitly addressed in a companion module, "Lean Systems Tools and Procedures."

The Value Concept and Lean Systems

Lean systems are a logical outgrowth of the value-driven perspective. Implementing lean systems requires a broad reorganization of operations to create a transformation system that constantly strives to increase value by eliminating waste throughout its entire design, structure, and management. Further, for lean systems to be successful, they must be implemented throughout the entire firm and indeed throughout the supply chain. We can see the reasons for this by examining the value equation:

$$Value = \frac{f(Quality,\ Timeliness)}{Cost}$$

The lean systems approach influences each term in the value equation. Lean systems reduce costs by continuously eliminating the waste of resources throughout the entire organization and throughout the entire supply chain. A common waste of resources in the supply chain occurs when one member duplicates the efforts of another member within the supply chain, thus leading to higher-than-necessary costs. Improving the supply chain is also important in lean systems because many quality problems are created at the supplier and not within a firm's own transformation process. The lean systems approach strives to continuously improve the

[1] James F. Cox and John H. Blackstone Jr., eds., *APICS Dictionary,* 9th ed. (1998).

quality characteristics that are critical to the customer. Lean systems improve timeliness by working to achieve shorter, more dependable lead times at every link in the supply chain. These improvements in quality and timeliness increase value to the customer. As cost decreases and quality and timeliness increase due to the implementation of lean systems, the value of the product as perceived by the customer should increase.

Origins of Lean Systems and Just-in-Time

Lean systems thinking was initiated and developed as the Toyota Production System (TPS) by that firm's vice president, Taiichi Ohno, beginning in 1937 when he discovered that labor at American manufacturers was nine times more productive than labor at Japanese manufacturers.[2] Pressure to improve intensified after World War II, as capital was restricted and production volumes were low. However, it was not until the 1973 oil crisis that most Japanese manufacturers became interested in TPS and it was not until the end of the 1970s that a significant number of U.S. manufacturers began to investigate TPS. The Toyota Production System became widely known in the United States in 1983 when a book of that title was published. During the 1980s, the popular term in the United States for the TPS system was *just-in-time manufacturing.* At the beginning of the 1990s, the term *lean systems* became popular because of a series of books and articles by U.S. consultants and researchers in which they referred to TPS as "lean systems," because they allow more and more to be done with less and less.

Ohno borrowed important roots of lean systems from two distinct American institutions: Henry Ford's mass production system and the supermarket.

Ford's Mass Production System

Henry Ford was only one among many competitors when he introduced his car to the market in 1886, using a standardized manufacturing system that constantly sought to reduce costs and improve performance. To control and reduce costs, Ford built large factories to produce identical cars, and he vertically integrated to manage the entire supply chain within his own organization. For example, Ford employees mined iron ore in the firm's own pits. Ford ships and tractors transported the ore to the company's docks, where Ford cranes unloaded it. Ford steel mills processed the iron ore to make steel plate from which Ford factories built the Model T. Henry Ford and his employees controlled every step. Inventory never sat unused for long. Ford boasted that iron ore unloaded at his River Rouge plant became steel components in a Ford truck rolling off the assembly line within 48 hours.

Ford recognized that uneven, fluctuating schedules caused variations in workflows that created confusion, complicated time management, and obscured opportunities for improvements. Ford instituted level schedules, building the same number of cars every day, to avoid these costly problems. Henry Ford also maximized the productivity of labor by introducing a number of innovations in worker–company relationships, including skills training, a hospital system to guarantee his workers the best possible health care, generous compensation packages, and technology to reduce the physical strain and stress on workers. Ford insisted that his systems be improved continuously. He stated, "Our own attitude is that we are charged with discovering the best way of doing everything, and that we must regard every process employed as purely experimental."[3]

Supermarkets and Lean Systems

Ohno found the retailing innovation of the American supermarkets to be a vision of the ideal operating system.

> We made a connection between supermarkets and the just-in-time system. . . . A supermarket is where a customer can get (1) what is needed, (2) at the time needed, (3) in the amount needed. From the supermarket, we got the idea of viewing the earlier processes in the pro-

[2] Yasuhiro Monden, *Toyota Production System* (Norcross, GA: Industrial Engineering and Management Press, 1983), p. v.
[3] Henry Ford, *Today and Tomorrow* (Cambridge, MA: Productivity Press, 1989), pp. 52–53.

EXHIBIT 1
Performance Characteristics for Lean Systems

Source: from Womack, James P., Daniel T. Jones, and Daniel Roos, *The Machine That Changed the World*, (New York: Rawson Associates, 1990). Reprinted with the permission of Rawson/Scribner, an imprint of Simon & Schuster.

	Japanese in Japan	Japanese in North America	Americans in North America	All Europe
Performance				
Productivity (hours/vehicle)	16.8	21.2	25.1	36.2
Quality (assembly defects/100 vehicle)	60.0	65.0	82.3	97.0
Layout				
Space (square feet/ vehicle/year)	5.7	9.1	7.8	7.8
Size of repair areas (as percent of assembly space)	4.1	4.9	12.9	14.4
Inventories (days for 8 sample parts)	0.2	1.6	2.9	2.0
Workforce				
Percent of workforce in teams	69.3	71.3	17.3	0.6
Job rotation (0 = none; 4 = frequent)	3.0	2.7	0.9	1.9
Suggestions/ employee	61.6	1.4	0.4	0.4
Number of job classes	11.9	8.7	67.1	14.8
Training of new production workers (hours)	380.3	370.0	46.4	173.3
Absenteeism	5.0	4.8	11.7	12.1
Automation				
Welding (percent of direct steps)	86.2	85.0	76.2	76.6
Painting (percent of direct steps)	54.6	40.7	33.6	38.2
Assembly (percent of direct steps)	1.7	1.1	1.2	3.1

duction line as a kind of store. The later process (the customer) goes to the earlier process (the supermarket) to acquire the required parts (the commodities) at the time and in the quantity needed. The earlier process immediately produces the quantity just taken (restocking the shelves). We hoped that this would help us approach our just-in-time goal, and . . . we actually applied the system to our machine shop at the main plant.[4]

During the 1980s, some U.S. companies successfully implemented lean systems. But many more failed or even refused to take action. Many managers felt that either TPS could not succeed in the United States or it provided no real benefits. However, the publication of a book titled *The Machine That Changed the World*[5] ended debate about whether lean systems created real, lasting benefits. The book presented the results of a three-year study of automobile manufacturing throughout the developed world. Some of these data are given in Exhibit 1. Notice that in 1990 a Japanese plant in Japan took 16.8 hours to build an auto, while a U.S plant in the United States took 25.1 hours per car. Not only did a Japanese

[4] William H. Davidow and Michael S. Malone, *The Virtual Corporation* (New York: Harper Business, 1992), pp. 119–20.

[5] James P. Womack, Daniel T. Jones, and Daniel Roos, *The Machine That Changed the World* (New York: Rawson Associates, 1990).

plant produce cars faster, its cars had fewer defects per hundred vehicles, lower space requirements, and lower inventories than their competitors. The data in Exhibit 1 also indicate that it is the management system and not the country's culture that is responsible for the success of lean companies, since Japanese plants in the United States performed better than U.S. plants on all criteria.

The Theory of Lean Systems

To help us understand the fundamental objectives and benefits of lean systems, we will examine two important functions: Little's Law and the VUT equation.

Little's Law

Little's Law[6] shows the relationship of inventory in a system (I) to the flow time (F) and to the system throughput rate (TH) in an operating system:

$$I = \text{TH} \times F \qquad \textbf{(1)}$$

Flow time is the time it takes one unit to get through the system. Little's Law suggests, but does not prove, that the key to increased throughput (e.g., units/day) is shorter flow times. If flow time is decreased, then either throughput is increased or inventory is decreased, or both changes occur. This means that by decreasing flow times we can support more sales with less inventory, thus simultaneously decreasing costs and increasing revenue!

The flow time for a unit is the result of the time that unit spends being processed plus the time that unit spends waiting to be processed. If the actual process time is shortened or if the waiting time is reduced, then Little's Law says that inventory will decrease. Since in most systems the time a unit spends waiting far exceeds the time it spends being processed, identifying the causes of waiting and reducing or eliminating them can create fundamental improvement in the system.

Processing variance is one of the key causes of waiting in production systems. So eliminating variability in the process is also central to the lean systems philosophy, since variance increases waiting time and consequently flow time. In the following section we examine how variance impacts system performance using a relationship called the variance utilization time (VUT) equation.

VUT Equation

Variance is a measure of dispersion within a distribution of outcomes. Variance can exist in the rate at which units are supplied to a system and in the rate at which they are processed. In either case, variance indicates that variability is present, and this variability creates uncertainty. Variability is often inherent in processes because of fluctuations in processing time due to differences in operators, machines (resources), and material. Variability also results when a process experiences breakdowns, setups, operator unavailability, or rework requirements. For example, if a machine randomly destroys pieces on which it is working, the processing variance increases.

The **variance utilization time (VUT) given in equation**[7], equation 2, approximates the average waiting time of a unit in the queue of a system. The equation has three terms: a variance measure, a measure of utilization, and the processing time.

$$\textit{Queue time} = \left(\frac{CV_a^2 + CV_p^2}{2}\right)\left(\frac{\rho}{1-\rho}\right)t_p$$

The variance term in the VUT equation measures system variance as the coefficient of variation squared (CV^2). The coefficient of variation (CV) is the standard deviation divided by the mean. So a work center with a mean processing time per unit of five hours and a standard deviation of one hour has a $\text{CV}_p = 1/5 = 0.20$. The variance term in equation 2 includes both the coefficient of variation in time between unit arrivals to the system (CV_a) and the coeffi-

[6] J. D. C. Little, *IIE Transactions*; Norcross; Jul 1992; Little, John D.C.; 24(3), 7-13

[7] W. J. Hopp and M. L. Spearman, *Factory Physics*, 2nd ed. (New York, NY, McGraw-Hill/Irwin, 2000).

In Practice

ALEXANDER DOLL INC. AND LITTLE'S LAW

A key outcome of establishing cells that are dedicated to producing a family of parts is that setup time is greatly reduced or eliminated. This means that batch sizes of one are practical. This in turn reduces the flow time. As stated in the introductory vignette, improving the baby doll production process at Alexander Doll resulted in a lead time of 90 minutes and a reduction of WIP inventory to 34 pieces. According to Little's Law, that means that throughput of this process is now TH = 34 dolls/90 minutes = 22.7 dolls per hour.

cient of variation in processing times (CV_p) for the system. This equation tells us that increased variance in either arrival times or processing times increases the time a unit spends in the queue.

The second term in equation 2 explains how the utilization level, ρ, influences the waiting time. Utilization is defined as the rate of arrivals divided by the processing rate (capacity) of the system. As expected, as the utilization increases, the waiting time increases. Notice that at low utilization levels, the impact of variance on waiting time in the system becomes small. For example if the system's utilization is 0.25, then the second term becomes $[0.25/(1 - 0.25)]$, which is 0.333. So the impact of variance on the waiting time in the queue of this system is reduced by one-third. At high levels of utilization (i.e., $1 - \rho < \rho$), the impact of variance on waiting time is amplified (when $\rho = 1$, queue time is unbounded!). The third term in equation 2, t_p, is the average processing time. This has a linear relationship with the waiting time. As the average processing time increases, the time in the queue increases and vice versa.

The VUT equation is applied to a single machine. But, by applying it to the bottleneck operation* in a system, we can estimate the system's performance. When the bottleneck utilization is high, the time a job is in its queue will increase dramatically with even a slight increase in variance at the bottleneck operation. For example, if the utilization is 90 percent at this bottleneck and the coefficient of variation of arrivals and processing times at the bottleneck are each one, then the time in the queue is nine times as large as the processing time

$$\textit{Queue time} = \left(\frac{1+1}{2}\right)\left(\frac{0.9}{1-0.9}\right)t_p = 9t_p$$

If the coefficient of variation of arrivals and processing times at the bottleneck increases to 1.2 each, then the time in the queue becomes $12.96t_p$. As the VUT equation suggests, variance is strongly related to wasted time waiting. In general, as variability increases, the level of corresponding waste in the system increases. This waste is usually reflected by increased flow times and increased inventory.

Most of the tools and procedures used in lean systems seek to eliminate variability from the system. As shown above, eliminating variability improves the process. The tools are discussed in detail in the "Lean Systems Tools and Procedures" module.

Implementing Lean Systems

The book *Lean Thinking*[8] lists five steps of lean thinking. As stated earlier, the lean systems approach is not just a set of techniques; it is a management philosophy. This means managers must have a different mental model or perspective of manufacturing management. The five steps or principles to develop this mental model are

1. Precisely specify value for each specific product.
2. Identify the value stream for each product.

* A bottleneck operation is the operation that requires the longest amount of processing time. Bottlenecks are discussed fully in the "Process Management" module.

[8] J.P. Womack and D.T. Jones, *Lean Thinking: Banish Waste and Create Wealth in Your Corporation* (New York: Simon and Shuster, 1996).

In Practice

ALEXANDER DOLL INC. AND LEAN THINKING

It is clear from the introduction that Alexander Doll has adopted many lean systems practices. It is also evident that they have followed the principles of lean thinking to do this.

Principle 1: Alexander Doll recognized that the value of the doll to the customer comes in part from its uniqueness. It is a collectible. To enhance its "collectibility," Alexander maintains a doll hospital where it will repair its creations that have "been loved too much" using remnants of the original cloth. This means that Alexander must save cuttings from each roll of cloth that it uses so that it can match it with dolls that enter the hospital. Other ways that the dolls' value is enhanced are by constantly developing new character dolls and by maintaining a website where it can allow adult collectors to mingle on-line with each other.

Principle 2: Alexander Doll reorganized the value stream for each doll it produces into cells. Their first step was to analyze the product flow of each doll and each wardrobe, starting with the baby doll product.

Principle 3: Alexander Doll has worked to ensure that the dolls flow through the cells without sitting in queues. The dolls and the wardrobes go from raw material to finished product quickly.

Principle 4: More work is needed to implement this principle. The customer (which is usually a retailer such as F.A.O. Schwarz and Neiman Marcus) places orders with Alexander Doll's warehouse. The customer is not fully pulling value yet, since Alexander produces many finished goods and ships them to its warehouse and not directly to customers.

Principle 5: Pursuing perfection is practiced at Alexander Doll. Management recognizes that their process still needs improvement and has outlined multiple projects for continuous improvement.

3. Make value flow without interruptions.
4. Let the customer pull value from the producer.
5. Pursue perfection.

Principle 1 fully agrees with the value concepts we discussed earlier. It is the final consumer that determines the value of a product or service, and it is the responsibility of the producer to create a product or service that the consumer will perceive as having value. This requires the firm to engage in a dialogue with the consumers of its products and services to determine which features, functions, and capabilities are valuable to the consumer. Implementing this principle means that the firm fully understands what its customers want. This provides the basis for continual improvement since it allows everyone to identify non-value-added activities and to eliminate them from its processes.

Principle 2, identify the value stream for each product, suggests that a firm must understand all of the activities involved in product development, order processing, and product creation and delivery. As a first step in understanding its value stream, companies often create process flow diagrams or value stream maps to identify value-adding steps; non-value-adding steps that are currently necessary due to technological constraints; and non-value-adding steps that are waste or ***muda*** (i.e., the Japanese word for waste). As managers and workers begin to eliminate waste from their internal processes, they typically become aware of waste throughout the external value streams as well. Methods to analyze processes in this way are explained in the "Process Mapping and Analysis" module. Internal and external wastes typically fit into one of seven basic categories of waste described in Exhibit 2.

At one company, managers involved every employee in the effort of identifying value-adding and wasteful process steps by issuing Polaroid cameras to the employees and having them take pictures of every activity they performed. These pictures were then placed on the walls, creating a pictorial flow chart. The collage surprised both the managers and employees alike, since the process involved over 1,100 steps. The employees then developed ways to eliminate the wasteful activities. As the workers eliminated a non-value-adding step, they removed the photograph from the process flow collage and pinned it to a picture of a trashcan on another bulletin board. In this way the team was able to simultaneously visually chart its progress in eliminating waste and recognize those workers who eliminated non-value-adding activities.

Principle 3 of lean systems is to make value flow without interruptions. This principle highlights the even flow associated with the just-in-time (JIT) principle. It means that we

EXHIBIT 2 **Seven Basic Types of Waste**

Waste	Symptoms	Root Causes
Waste of overproduction (building more units than are needed)	• Extra inventory • Excessive floorspace utilized • Unbalanced material flow • Complex information management • Disposal charges • Extra waste handling and treatment • High utility costs	• Misuse of automation • Long process setups • Unlevel scheduling • Poor market forecast • Overengineered equipment /capability • Lack of reuse and recycling • Product complexity
Waste of waiting time (jobs waiting to be processed)	• Underutilization of resources • Reduced productivity • Increase in investment • Idle equipment • Large waiting/storage rooms • Equipment running, not producing • Unnecessary testing	• Unbalanced work load • Unplanned maintenance • Long process setup times • Misuse of automation • Unlevel scheduling • Ineffective layout • Too much specialization
Transportation waste (jobs being unnecessarily moved)	• Extra handling equipment • Large storage areas • Overstaffing • Damaged product • Extra paperwork and handoffs • Excessive energy consumption	• Mislocated materials • Unlevel scheduling • Unfavorable facility layout • Poor organization/housekeeping • Unbalanced processes
Process waste (excessive or unnecessary operations)	• Extra equipment • Longer lead time • Reduced productivity • Extra material movement • Sorting, testing, inspection • Inappropriate use of resources • Excess energy consumption • Processing by-products	• Product changes without process changes • Just-in-case logic • Lack of communication • Redundant approvals and inspections • Undefined customer requirements • Stop-gap measures that become routine • Lack of reuse/recycling
Inventory waste (building more to protect against system problems)	• Complex tracking systems • Extra storage and handling • Extra rework/hidden problems • Paperwork/documents • Stagnated information flow • High disposal costs • In-process packaging	• Just-in-case logic • Incapable processes (poor quality) • Unbalanced workload • Unreliable supplier shipments • Inadequate measurement and reward system
Waste of motion (unnecessary or excessive human activity)	• Reduced productivity • Large reach/walk distances • Excess handling • Reduced quality • People/machines waiting	• Poor ergonomics/layout • Machine/process design • Non-standardized work methods • Poor organization/housekeeping
Waste from product defects (waste due to scrap, rework, salvage)	• Rework, repairs, and scrap • Customer returns • Loss of customer confidence • Missed shipments/deliveries • Hazardous waste generation • High disposal costs	• Lack of process control and error-proofing • Deficient planned maintenance • Poor product design • Customer needs not understood • Improper handling • Inadequate training

produce only what the customer wants, when they want it. If we produce inventory before it is needed, then it must sit and wait somewhere, so its flow is interrupted. Little's Law clearly shows that eliminating non-value-adding activities (i.e., reducing flow time) allows the system to maintain its throughput while inventory is reduced. Since the throughput remains constant while flow time decreases, Little's Law says that the inventory decreases (i.e., $I \downarrow = F \downarrow \text{TH}\rightarrow$).

How does this work in practice? The effects of inventory waste on system performance are often illustrated with a picture similar to that in Exhibit 3. Excess inventory is itself wasteful, but what is worse is that inventory allows other wastes to occur without detection. Inventory hides problems created by poor quality, long lead times, and ineffective designs. For example, if a firm keeps enough units in stock, quality problems might remain hidden. If one selected component is defective, workers can simply throw it aside and take another one. Inventory can also hide long order lead times or unreliable delivery schedules, since production can continue to draw down stock levels until new shipments arrive. The system in Exhibit 3 continues to operate because the inventory level is high enough that the system (i.e., the sailboat) floats above the problems. To truly improve flow, the problems hidden by inventory need to be eliminated.

EXHIBIT 3
Inventory Hides Operating Problems

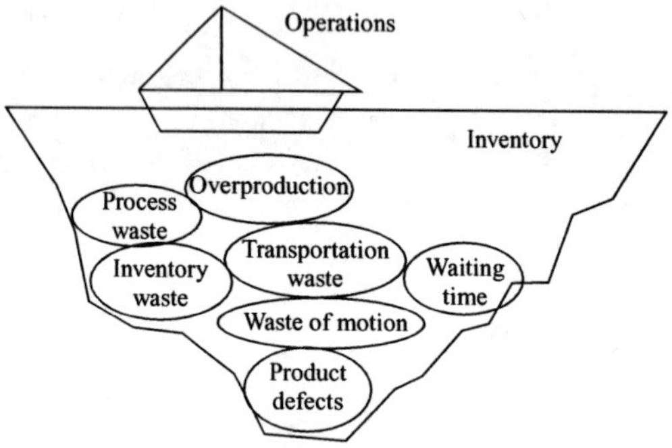

The operating problems shown in Exhibit 3 not only create waste directly, but they also are sources of variance. Since variance increases waiting times and inventory, to achieve uninterrupted flow we must eliminate these problems. So inventory serves as a measure of the health of the system just like a thermometer measures a patient's temperature. The more inventory needed for the system to work, the less healthy we perceive the system to be. As the system continually improves, it should have less and less inventory on hand. In this way, the leanness of inventories in the system is a measure of the system's improving health.

The goal in uninterrupted flow is to produce everything in a batch size of one. To many managers, this is counterintuitive. How can doing an activity multiple times instead of once improve performance? Most of us intuitively believe that the batch-and-queue model of doing work is inherently correct. In fact, most of us create batches to process the tasks of daily living. For example, we might put aside bills that come in the mail during the week and process them as a batch on the weekend. Or we will accumulate dirty dishes in the sink until it is convenient to process a batch of dishes. The trick to achieving uninterrupted flow with batches of one is to reduce setups or changeover activities that cause us to want to batch activities together in the first place. In our bill-paying example above, we would have to identify all the preparation steps required to pay bills (e.g., finding the checkbook) and determine how to eliminate these steps or make their time so insignificant that they are not a barrier to paying our bills when they arrive.

Principle 4 is to let the customer pull value from the producer. This idea is the source of the term *pull systems*. A pull system is one in which the production process is able to immediately recognize and respond to a variety of customer requests. This allows firms to avoid having to forecast customer demands. Reducing reliance on forecasts and finished goods inventories tends to reduce the lumpiness of demand. This reduces demand arrival variance, which in turn helps eliminate congestion. In the parlance of the VUT equation, reduced reliance on forecasts should reduce CV_a^2. Tools and techniques that can be used to create a pull system are discussed in the "Lean Systems Tools and Procedures" module.

Principle 5 is to pursue perfection. This principle suggests that continuous improvement is always possible. As long as we are implementing the first four principles, we will always uncover more places where we can improve and eliminate waste. This principle emphasizes the need to continuously improve and eliminate waste in our effort to achieve perfection. Further it implies that everyone in the organization must be engaged in this ongoing effort to seek perfection. Everyone in the organization must strive to do more with less every day. To accomplish this, good employees need to be hired. Perhaps more importantly, they must be empowered—given the training, tools, and authority to make improvements.

Employee Empowerment

The system at Toyota provides a good example of employee empowerment as a means for continuous improvement. Toyota empowers its employees by training them to use the scientific method to continuously improve processes. The scientific method involves four elements: theory, hypotheses, data, and verification. Spear and Bowen state that the scientific method is integrated into the Toyota Production System so that every time a job is performed, it is an experiment.[9] This creates a system where all the work processes are very specified and structured, but the system itself is very flexible and responsive. Toyota implements the scientific method as part of four unspoken rules that everyone in the organization must learn and practice:

1. All work is highly specified as to content, sequence, timing, and outcome expected.
2. Every customer–supplier connection must be direct, and there must be an unambiguous yes-or-no method to send requests and receive responses.
3. The pathway for every product and service must be simple and direct.
4. Any improvement must be made in accordance with the scientific method, under the guidance of a teacher, at the lowest possible level in the organization.

1. Highly Specified Work

Toyota's first rule requires that managers, engineers, and line workers fully understand how a job is to be done and its relationship to other jobs. By ensuring that every job has a very clearly defined set of steps, it is obvious when the correct process is not being followed and it is also obvious when more training is needed or when the job definition needs to be changed. This allows quick identification and correction of any problems that occur. This first rule reduces variance in how work is done. From the VUT equation, we know that reducing variance reduces inventory, which can increase system throughput.

By creating a highly specified sequence of steps to perform the job, Toyota is actually proposing a theory that this procedure is the best way to do the job. Given this theory, two implicit hypotheses in every standard job specification are first that each person doing the activity is capable of performing it correctly and second that performing the activity as specified actually creates the expected outcome. Each time the job is performed, data are gathered to test these two hypotheses. If the worker is unable to perform the job activities exactly as planned, then the first hypothesis is wrong and either a new job specification must be developed or the worker must receive more training. If the worker actually completes the job as specified, then the second hypothesis is tested by determining whether the worker produced the expected outcome. If either hypothesis is not supported, then a new theory about how to perform the job (i.e., a specified sequence of steps) is developed and then tested. This rule means that every employee is constantly searching for ways to improve the sequence of steps to perform his or her job.

2. Direct Connections

Toyota's second rule states that there must be direct, unambiguous communication between each customer and supplier. Direct, unambiguous communication means that each customer and each supplier know the exact form and quantity of goods and services to be provided. The theory implicit in this second rule is that the supplier has the capacity to meet the customer's needs as they are communicated. This theory leads to two hypotheses: (1) the

[9] S. Spear and H. K. Bowen, "Decoding the DNA of the Toyota Production System," *Harvard Business Review*, September–October 1999, pp. 96–106.

customers' requests will be for goods and services in a specific mix and volume and (2) the supplier can respond to the customers' requests. The production process generates data through the observation of the customer–supplier interactions. Is the supplier overwhelmed? Is the supplier idle? The data are used to verify whether the theory is correct. This leads to decisions about how to change the connection or the allocation of work. Both Little's Law and the VUT equation suggest that Toyota's second rule will reduce inventory. For example, if the supplier cannot meet a scheduled delivery, then there is variance in the supplier's delivery to the customer. This increases CV_a^2, consequently increasing congestion and flow time, which, according to Little's Law, means that inventory must increase to keep throughput the same (i.e., $I\uparrow = F\uparrow \text{TH}\rightarrow$).

3. Simple Direct Pathways

Toyota's third rule is that all pathways must be simple and direct. This means that goods and services must flow to a specific person or machine. The underlying theory in this rule is that having simple and direct pathways will quickly reveal any source of variances in the flow of goods and services. This rule suggests two hypotheses: (1) every supplier is necessary and (2) any supplier not connected to the pathway is not necessary. Each day of production provides data to analyze the hypotheses. Was there a supplier who was not connected to a pathway? Obviously any supplier or activity not connected to the flow pathway can be eliminated. This rule eliminates noise from the system and means that there are no pooled queues of completed work from suppliers waiting for the customers to use. Instead, completed work leaves one activity and goes to the next activity. If one supplier has a high variance in deliveries, their variance will not be hidden by the deliveries of the other suppliers.

4. Scientific Method

Toyota's fourth rule requires that employees be trained to formulate and test hypotheses about how they can improve their job activities. Toyota constantly encourages its workers to conduct experiments trying to identify a better method of performing their job activities. But the employees must explicitly state the logic of their proposed hypotheses before conducting the experiment. For example, suppose that workers feel that they can eliminate the average setup time for a process by 50 percent. Rule 4 requires that they state the existing setup time (e.g., mean setup time of 30 minutes with a range of 10 minutes) and then state what they intend to do to reduce the setup time (e.g., install one-turn fasteners) and describe how this change will meet their goals (e.g., currently 16 minutes are spent fastening the new die in place, a one-turn fastener will reduce this fastening time to 1 minute). To test the hypothesis, they will make the specified changes and then measure and compare the amount of time it takes to do the setups against their hypothesized results. This formalized process improves learning by forcing the documentation and systematic evaluation of improvement ideas.

Implementation Phases

Implementation of lean systems often requires a change in thinking away from the mass production mental paradigm. Consequently, it is essential that top managers actively lead the lean systems effort. Frequently, a ***sensei*** (teacher) is brought in to lead the first ***kaikaku*** campaign (i.e., radical improvement). Usually, a highly visible portion of the process flow that is in great need of improvement is selected for the first effort. A dramatic, initial success is important to demonstrate to everyone that the lean systems approach is feasible in their facility. This demonstration helps to overcome both worker and management resistance. For example, in 1992 the *sensei* hired by Porsche gave Porsche's CEO a circular saw to start cutting each rack of shelving in the Engine Assembly Department in half. This forced Porsche to reduce its inventory by 50 percent the first week. To continue producing, they had to quickly solve the problems that had been hidden by the inventory.[10]

[10] Womack and Jones, *Lean Thinking.*

In Practice

ALEXANDER DOLL INC. AND TOYOTA'S FOUR UNSPOKEN RULES

The four unspoken rules of Toyota are not fully practiced at Alexander Doll. Implementing these rules is a difficult task, which takes time and constant management vigilance.

Rule 1: Alexander Doll has specified the content, sequence, and outcome expected for each process in each cell. But there are no explicit internal timing rules. The nature of a cellular organization is such that if one person in the cell cannot perform a task, all of the members of the cell become aware of the problem and can help. So the cell design may compensate for the lack of internal timing. Workers who cannot perform the task may be given additional training, or a reassignment of tasks so that the bottleneck in the cell has less work to do.

Rule 2: Within the cell, the customer–supplier connections are direct and unambiguous. Workers pass the work they complete directly to another worker in the cell. It is clear when the worker received it, whether it was acceptable. It is not clear if the connections throughout the rest of Alexander Doll are this clear and direct. For example, is there a clear connection to the purchasing department to ensure that necessary materials and supplies are ordered?

Rule 3: Within the cell the pathway for every product and service is simple and direct. Again, this is one of the major advantages of cellular manufacturing. However, it is not clear that the pathway for every product and service is direct throughout the rest of the company. For example, Alexander Doll ships its finished products to a warehouse in Kentucky, which creates additional steps in its pathway to the customer.

Rule 4: Workers have become involved in the improvement process. It is not clear, however, that the workers actually develop hypotheses before they begin an improvement project. A clearly stated hypothesis is necessary for the implementation of the scientific method.

After the initial demonstration, it is necessary to keep the momentum going. This requires training for both the employees and the managers. And it requires constant repetition of the *kaikaku* campaign in each part of the organization. To institutionalize this change process, companies create explicit systems to encourage and support the desired changes. One example of this system at Ford Motor is shown in the In Practice box on page 14.

Performance Measurements

A lean system, like any system, is a goal-driven set of interrelated or linked activities. Managers who recognize that they are managing a system are aware of two main points: (1) the system reacts to any solution and (2) the system controls the behavior of those individuals who operate within it. The first point means that there are often unintended consequences when a solution to a problem in a system is introduced. To avoid unintended consequences, managers must fully understand the system. The second point means that managers must avoid attributing the problems in a system to the character of the individuals within the system. The manager must instead identify how the structure of the system is shaping the choices of the individuals within the system. By understanding these two points, the manager can redesign the system to increase the system's performance.

The incorrect use of performance measures can prevent the successful introduction of lean systems. For example, a performance measurement system that encourages high equipment and high labor utilization often discourages production at the rate demanded by the customer. Indeed, these performance measures actually encourage large-batch production, thus creating the waste of overproduction and decreasing the system's ability to respond to the customer.

Firms that implement lean systems often use a performance measure called **overall equipment effectiveness (OEE).** Soiichi Nakajima first formulated this performance measure to assess how effectively equipment is maintained and operated. Exhibit 4, page 14, shows six types of capacity losses in the right-hand column (breakdown losses, setup and adjustment losses, idling and minor stoppages, speed losses, quality defects, and start-up and yield losses). These capacity losses are organized into three categories: downtime losses, speed losses, and quality losses.

The OEE measure is calculated as follows. First, every machine has a scheduled block of time that it can be used for production. This scheduled loading time is shown in

In Practice

FORD PRODUCTION SYSTEM (FPS)

The Ford Production System has seven integrated processes:

1. Material flow systems: to create a pull system through the entire value chain to achieve continuous material flow.
2. In-station process control: to detect mistakes at work stations immediately.
3. Total productive maintenance (TPM): to improve equipment reliability to allow smooth flow.
4. Quality operating system: to ensure standard quality systems for all of the processes.
5. Engineering: to ensure that product development and processes support the defect-free flow of material.
6. Industrial materials: to ensure that the flow of indirect materials is smooth.
7. People: organized into empowered work groups.

The changes to fully achieve these seven processes take time and are to be accomplished in five phases called stability, continuous flow, synchronous production, pull system, and level production.

In the stability phase, the goal is to create workstations capable of consistent production. In the continuous-flow phase, the goal is to ensure that commodities arrive at the line in the sequence in which they are needed. In the synchronous-production phase, internal customers and suppliers are linked together to create an even flow. In the fourth phase, the pull phase, formal pull systems are to be established so that customers pull value through the system. In the fifth phase, level production, the production levels throughout the entire value chain are to be set so that they match customer orders.

Source: Jeffrey K. Liker, "Introduction: Bringing Lean Back to the U.S.A.," in *Becoming Lean: Inside Stories of U.S. Manufacturers*, ed. J.K. Liker (Portland, OR: Productivity Press, 1998).

Exhibit 4 as a shaded block. Availability is the ratio of the actual running time (i.e., loading time minus the downtime losses) to the loading time. (This is shown in Exhibit 4 in the block under "Availability.") By multiplying the scheduled loading time by the availability, one can estimate the net operation time, that is, the amount of the loading time that is actually available to process parts. The net operation time is shown in Exhibit 4 as a gray block that is smaller in size than the loading time block. The net operation time is further reduced by any speed losses. These speed losses are accounted for by calculating the performance rate. This rate is the product of the actual output (i.e., the actual parts produced) and the ideal **cycle time** divided by the net operation time (see the block under "Performance rate" in Exhibit 4). The numerator in this ratio represents the amount of time that ideally should have been required to make the actual output quantity. Multiplying the net operation time by the performance rate gives the valuable operation time (shown in Exhibit 4 as a shaded block that is smaller than the block for the net operation time). The valuable operation time is the actual time available on the machine to produce product. But a portion of this valuable operation time can be lost to quality losses. This is shown in Exhibit 4 in the box below "Quality rate." The quality rate is calculated simply as the percent of product produced on the machine that is defect free its first time through. The calculated value for each of these three categories of losses

EXHIBIT 4
Six Equipment Losses

Source: Adapted from Tajiri, Masaji and Fumio Gotoh, *TPM Implementation: A Japanese Approach* (New York: McGraw-Hill, 1992), p. 4.

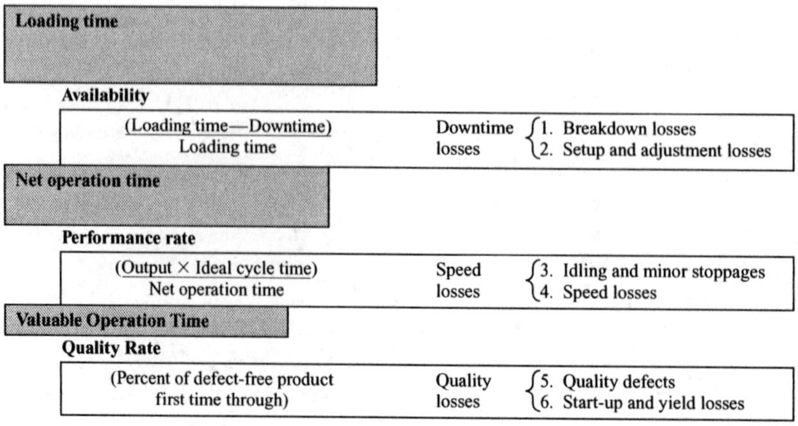

(i.e., availability, performance rate, and quality rate) is multiplied together to determine the OEE, as shown in equation 3.

$$\text{Overall equipment effectiveness} = \text{Availability} \times \text{Performance rate} \times \text{Quality rate} \times 100 \qquad \textbf{(3)}$$

Consider this simple example to illustrate the OEE calculation. A given machine has 460 minutes available for loading in a 480-minute day. For this machine, 60 minutes are lost to breakdowns and another 20 minutes are lost to retooling and readjustments during setup. The availability is therefore $\{[460 - (60 + 20)]/460\} \times 100 = 82.61$ percent, and the net operation time is $460 \times 0.8261 = 380$ minutes. The performance rate is how fast a machine actually runs compared to its ideal design speed. If the machine has an ideal cycle time of 30 seconds per item, and it processes 475 items a day within its net operation time of 380 minutes, then its performance rate is $[(475 \times 30 \text{ seconds})/380 \text{ minutes}] \times 100 = 62.5$ percent, and its valuable operation time is $380 \times 0.625 = 237.5$ minutes. Finally, if 1 percent of the product the machine produces is scrap and if it usually has start-up losses of 19 parts for each batch of 475 items, then its quality losses are 24 (i.e., $19 + 1\%(475 - 19) = 23.56 \approx 24$), which is 5 percent of production. The defect-free product the first time through is 95 percent (i.e., $1 - 5\%$ quality loss) and the machine's OEE $= 0.8261 \times 0.625 \times 0.95 \times 100 = 49.05$ percent. Typically factories try to achieve an OEE of 85 percent or greater. Thus, the machine in our example has a very low OEE.

Performance measurements are an important part of any manufacturing system. The operations manager must select the performance measurements that will encourage behaviors that lead to the desired business performance. In a lean system, the desired business performance is shorter flow time, reduced costs, and faster response to the customer. For example, Ford Motor Company has had to change how it measures its plant managers' performance. Instead of evaluating them on the basis of how well they reduce labor and overhead costs, Ford has developed measures that assess continuous improvement, overall equipment effectiveness, build to schedule (i.e., on-time delivery), and total dock-to-dock time (i.e., throughput time) as shown in Exhibit 5. This is a good example of how just a few measures can encourage the implementation of lean systems.

EXHIBIT 5
Ford's Performance Measures

Lean Performance Measure	Lean Systems Goal
Build to schedule	Reduce waste of overproduction and create level flow
Total dock-to-dock time	Reduce flow time
Overall equipment effectiveness (OEE)	Reduce flow time, increase customer responsiveness, improve quality
Continuous improvement efforts	Pursue perfection

Source: Jeffrey K. Liker, "Introduction: Bringing Lean Back to the U.S.A.," in *Becoming Lean: Inside Stories of U.S. Manufacturers*," ed. J. K. Liker (Portland, OR: Productivity Press, 1998).

Lean Systems Throughout the Firm

Lean systems cannot thrive in an organization if they are isolated to the shop floor. To support lean systems, the entire organization must become lean. This means that each function within the firm must adopt the principles of lean systems for its own operations. Consider the following examples of required changes.

Marketing

Lean systems make valuable contributions to the firm's marketing effort. Marketers find the constant stream of low-cost, high-quality products delivered consistently on time to be highly attractive. Also, reductions in order lead times through lean systems allow quick responses to market trends.

A primary task of marketing is to educate the customer about the firm's new capabilities and the concrete limits on the responsiveness of the lean system. This requires tight coordination of marketing and operations to increase communication and decrease the time from receipt of an order to the shipment of an order. One method some firms have used to accomplish this is to create product teams, who are responsible for marketing, design, production, and distribution.

As lean systems are implemented, sales/marketing must change their approach. Lean systems require the reduction of variance in order arrivals. Often this is not completely possible, but marketing can improve the situation by changing policies that encourage large swings in demand into policies that encourage steady demand. For example, marketing needs to evaluate the number of product options that the firm offers. Such options allow buyers to customize products, but this customization can introduce variance into the production system. As demonstrated earlier in this module, increasing variance increases the flow time, so marketing may limit the choice of options available to reduce the variance in demand. For example, a bicycle manufacturer can make a bike frame out of three different types of steel, and it might offer 12 different paint schemes. The customer might choose among five saddles, four types of pedals, six types of wheels, and eight packages of shifting and braking components. This creates 35,560 different combinations. It would be difficult to produce that many combinations with a lean system. One solution to this problem is to drop options with weak demand. Alternatively, the firm might group individual options together into packages. For example, a premium-performance package might include the firm's best saddle, a specific pedal type, a performance wheel set, and a choice between two packages of components rather than eight. To make the packages attractive to customers, the firm might offer price reductions on the packages as compared to purchasing options separately. Another solution is for the firm to offer some options that are installed later as modifications at the bicycle dealers.

Engineering

Lean systems also can be applied to product and process engineering. Lean systems require the ability to move machines to allow for continuous improvement. As the system eliminates non-value-adding steps, machines will need to be moved. To facilitate this, engineering must identify process methods that provide sufficient capacity without relying on "monument" machines (i.e., large, expensive machines that are difficult to move). Usually, the monument machines are cost effective only when they produce large batches, because their setup times are so long. When a machine produces large batches, it will increase inventory. Since throughput remains the same, Little's Law says that flow time must increase (i.e., $I\uparrow = F\uparrow \text{TH}\rightarrow$), so the product lead time increases, which makes it impossible for the customer to pull value through the shop.

Engineers also can ensure that product designs exploit any possible commonalities in processing methods or components. Commonalities in processing and shared component parts both can reduce setups. Since setup times can create variance in processing times, eliminating the needs for setups can reduce congestion according to the VUT equation.

Human Resources

All aspects of every organization are influenced by human resource practices. To successfully practice lean systems, human resources practices for recruitment and selection, training, and performance evaluation and compensation must reflect the needs of lean systems. Recruitment and selection must strive to hire curious, self-motivated employees who want to improve operations. Recruiters need to recruit employees who want interesting, proactive roles and will constantly ask why a system works like it does and why it does not work better. Employees need to identify and solve problems, work effectively with others in teams, and learn new skills quickly. These include skills with the tools and process of problem solving. In a lean system, training tends to continue as long as the employee keeps working in the system. For example, Japanese auto assembly plants located in the United States give new employees, on average, 370 hours, or just over nine weeks, of training. In contrast, the average American automaker gives each new employee about 46 hours of training. Until recently, Saturn, one of a few exceptions, gave its employees about 350 hours of training.

Purchasing/Supply-Chain Management

It is very difficult for one firm to be lean in isolation. The ability to operate a lean system depends on both suppliers and customers. If these two sets of partners are not also striving to operate in a lean manner, they will limit the ability of an individual firm in the supply chain to be lean itself. Ideally, a JIT system needs suppliers to supply parts with 100 percent quality levels. This standard eliminates the need for inspections of incoming shipments and it allows all inputs to move directly from the receiving dock to the process activities. High quality also reduces the need for inventory control and material handling at shipping and receiving.

In many industries, more than 50 percent of the costs are purchased parts or materials. Significant improvement requires the cooperation of the entire supply base. This means that the suppliers must develop their own lean systems.

Benefits of Lean Systems

Lean systems significantly affect the firm's break-even production quantity (i.e., the amount of output past which the firm begins to make money) in two ways: by increasing the contribution margin (the difference between price and the firm's direct costs) and by reducing overhead costs. The contribution margin grows as the firm charges a higher price to deliver a better product faster while it reduces direct costs at the same time (Exhibit 6). Together, these changes drive the break-even point downward, enhancing the firm's flexibility. It can afford to produce smaller quantities, allowing niche marketing, and it can change outputs more quickly in response to changes in customer demand. Compared with mass producers with lower contribution margins and higher fixed costs, the lean producer seems quite agile, leading some to favor the term *agile competitor* over lean producer.

EXHIBIT 6
Changes in Cost Structure under Lean Systems

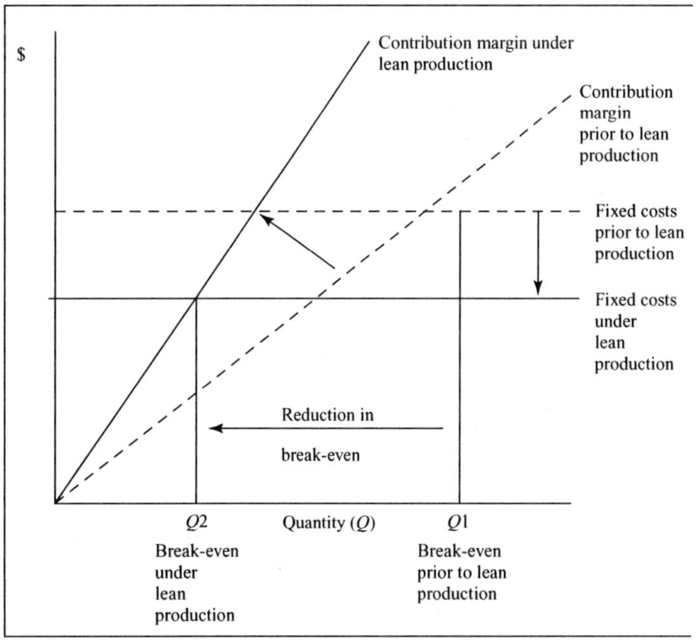

Module Summary

Despite its relatively recent emergence in North America, the lean systems approach has now become an integral element of operations management. In this module, we have examined many of the concepts, management tools, and developments associated with this system. The following are some of the major issues raised in this module:

1. Lean systems manufacturing is a corporatewide approach that works continuously to identify, control, and eliminate all sources of waste within the firm. This requires that variance at all levels of the firm be eliminated.
2. The definition of waste varies with the customers' definitions of value. Because waste is related to value, each firm implements lean systems in a way that suits its specific customers.
3. The lean systems approach continuously strives to achieve seven major objectives: produce only what customers want, produce products only at the rate that customers want them, produce with perfect quality, produce with minimum lead times, produce only the features that customers want, produce without wasting resources, and produce with methods that support people's development.
4. A lean system needs to be an organizationwide system because its implementation affects operations of functions throughout the firm, including marketing, product engineering, human resource management, cost accounting, logistics, purchasing, and corporate strategy.
5. Lean systems implementation requires flexible work standardization. All tasks must be highly specified, but the specifications must be able to change quickly in response to customers and to greater job knowledge.

Key Terms

cycle time *14*
Flow time *6*
Just-in-time *3*
Lean systems *3*
Little's Law *6*
Kaikaku 12
Muda 8
Overall equipment effectiveness (OEE) *13*
Sensei 12
Variance utilization time (VUT) equation *6*

Discussion Questions

1. What parts of the American food distribution systems inspired Toyota to develop lean systems?
2. Describe the two major things that Taichi Ohno saw at Ford's huge car manufacturing complex that led, in part, to the development of Toyota's lean system. Why were these two things unacceptable to the Japanese? Why had American manufacturers so willingly accepted them?
3. Explain what you think are the underlying principles of lean systems.
4. Exhibit 3 uses the analogy of a boat hitting rocks as the level of water falls. Why is water a good analogy for inventory? Is the sequence in which rocks are encountered a good way to prioritize inventory reduction activities? How might this prioritization scheme differ from one used in an accounting department?
5. Why is achievement of the following goals critical to the success of lean systems?
   a. Setup time and cost reduction.
   b. A relatively stable shop load.
   c. Employee empowerment.
   d. Statistical quality control.

   Give an example of how each area contributes to the success of a lean system.
6. Why is the concept of waste such an important part of the lean systems philosophy?
7. In your own words, explain each component of the OEE measurement and evaluate the types of behavior this type of performance measurement will induce and whether this behavior will support lean systems in each of the following personnel: (a) a machine operator, (b) a shop floor supervisor, and (c) a plant manager.
8. You work in the marketing department of a firm that sells mountain bicycles and related gear. Its manufacturing division has decided to wholeheartedly adopt the lean systems philosophy. Will this affect your ability to delight your customers? Make a list of the potential pluses and minuses of this lean systems decision.
9. How does the concept of system variance impact your ability to drive inventory out of a plant when a lean systems approach has been adopted? Create an electronic spreadsheet model to show how a reduction in demand variance impacts inventory in a two-stage manufacturing process.
10. Discuss how lean systems might apply to a fast-food hamburger stand. How will it have to be modified to deal with daily demand variation?

11. Differentiate between the types of waste that you would expect to see in a plant making transmissions for the Big Three (Ford, GM, and Chrysler) and a plant that makes identical transmissions for the repair or spare parts markets.
12. Can lean systems enhance a worker's quality of life? Discuss how it might or might not.
13. How could you apply lean systems principles and practices to product design?
14. Where would you most successfully apply lean systems principles during the introductory or growth stages of the product life cycle?
15. Lean systems require work standardization with flexibility. That is, all of the work activities must be highly specified, but the employees must be able to change quickly in response to customer needs. Discuss the types of relationships that management must have with their employees for standardization with flexibility to be implemented.

Problems

1. Use Little's Law to calculate the expected inventory level if the throughput is 25 jobs an hour and the processing time at an operation is 10 minutes.
2. Use Little's Law to calculate the expected flow time if the throughput of the system is 420 jobs a shift (420 minutes per shift) and the average inventory is one job.
3. If the variance of a process increased from 9 to 12 while the mean remained 4, what is the coefficient of variation after the increase? Discuss whether the coefficient of variation provides useful information compared to looking at just the mean or the variance.
4. What is the effect on queue time if the squared coefficient of variation of arrivals (CV_a^2) increases from 0.5 to 1.5, given that the utilization is 70 percent, the squared coefficient of variation of processing time is 0.5 and the processing time is 10 minutes.
5. A work center has a utilization of 80 percent, a processing time of 20 minutes, a $CV_a^2 = 0.5$, and a $CV_p^2 = 0.5$.
   a. Which increases queue time more: Increasing CV_a^2 to 1 or increasing CV_p^2 to 1 while the other is constant?
   b. Is it better to decrease both CV_a^2 and CV_p^2 to 0.4, or to reduce t_p from 20 minutes to 18 minutes?
6. Calculate the availability of a bottleneck machine given that of the 480 minutes of time it could be scheduled for production, it is actually scheduled 420 minutes. Of these 420 minutes of loading time, on average 45 minutes are lost to breakdowns, 25 minutes are spent on retooling, and another 15 minutes are spent on readjustments each day.
7. Calculate the performance rate for a bottleneck machine where the net operating time is 335 minutes, the ideal cycle time is 45 seconds, the actual cycle time is 60 seconds, and the number of parts produced each day on average is 335.
8. If the first-time-through defect-free product is 98 percent for the machine in problems 6 and 7, calculate the OEE for that machine.
9. Calculate the OEE for a bottleneck machine that has an availability of 98 percent, a performance rate of 98 percent, and a quality rate of 98 percent. Explain why the OEE can be lower than any of its individual components.

Related Modules of Interest

- Process Management
- Lean Systems Tools and Procedures
- Capacity Management
- Process Mapping and Analysis

Selected Readings

Abegglen, James C., and George Stalk Jr. *Kaisha: The Japanese Corporation.* New York: Basic Books, 1985.

Bhote, Keki R. *Strategic Supply Management: A Blue Print for Revitalizing the Manufacturer Supplier Partnership.* New York: American Management Association, 1989.

Cox, James F., and John H. Blackstone Jr., eds. *APICS Dictionary.* 9th ed. 1998. Falls Church, VA: APICS

"Designers to the Dolls." *Crain's New York Business,* January 25, 1999, p. 6.

Ford, Henry. *Today and Tomorrow.* Cambridge, MA: Productivity Press, 1989.

Goldman, Steven L., Roger N. Nagel, and Kenneth Preiss. *Agile Competitors and Virtual Organizations.* New York: Van Nostrand Reinhold, 1995.

Goldratt, E. M., and J. Cox. *The Goal.* 2nd rev. ed. Croton-on-Hudson, NY: North River Press, 1992.

Greif, Michel. *The Visual Factory: Building Participation Through Shared Information.* Portland, OR: Productivity Press, 1991.

Grieco, Peter L., Michael W. Gozzo, and Jerry W. Claunch. *Just-in-Time Purchasing: In Pursuit of Excellence.* Plantsville, CT: PT Publications, 1988.

Hall, Robert W. *Zero Inventories.* New York: McGraw-Hill/Irwin, 1983.

———. "Keeping It Simple." *Target: Innovation at Work* 14, no. 1 (1998), pp. 40–46.

———. "Timeprints and Takt Times." *Target: Innovation at Work* 14, no. 3 (1998), pp. 6–13.

Hallihan, A., P. Sackett, and G. M. Williams, "JIT Manufacturing: The Evolution to an Implementation Model Founded in Current Practice." *International Journal Production Research* 35, no. 4 (1997), pp. 901–920.

Hopp, W. J., and M. L. Spearman. *Factory Physics.* 2nd ed. New York: McGraw-Hill/Irwin, 2000.

Imai, Masaaki. *Kaizen: The Key to Japan's Competitive Success.* New York: Random House, 1986.

———. *Gemba Kaizen: A Commonsense, Low Cost Approach to Management.* New York,: McGraw-Hill, 1997.

Keller, A. Z., and A. Kazazi, "Manufacturing Systems: A Literature Review." *Industrial Management and Data Systems* 93, no. 7 (1993), pp. 1–32.

Krafcik, J. F. "Triumph of the Lean Systems System." *Sloan Management Review* 30, no. 1 (Fall 1988), pp. 41–53.

Liker, Jeffre K. "Introduction: Bringing Lean Back to the U.S.A." In *Becoming Lean: Inside Stories of U.S. Manufacturers,* ed. J. K. Liker, pp. 3–40. Portland, OR: Productivity Press, 1998.

Little, J. D. C. "A Proof for the Queuing Formula: $L = \lambda W$." *Operations Research* 9 (1961), pp. 383–87.

Maynard, R. "A Company Is Turned around through Japanese Principles." *Nation's Business* 84, no. 2 (February 1996), p. 9.

Monden, Yasuhiro. *Toyota Production System.* Norcross, GA: Industrial Engineering and Management Press, 1983.

Nakajima, Seiichi. *TPM: Introduction to TPM, Total Productive Maintenance.* Cambridge, MA: Productivity Press, 1988.

Shingo, Shigeo. *A Revolution in Manufacturing: The SMED System.* Cambridge, MA: Productivity Press, 1985.

Shirouzu, Norhiko. "Ford Has Big Problem Beyond Tire Mess: Making Quality Cars." *The Wall Street Journal,* May 25, 2001, pp. A1, A6.

Spear, S., and H. K. Bowen. "Decoding the DNA of the Toyota Production System." *Harvard Business Review,* September–October 1999, pp. 96–106.

Sugimori, Y. K., F. Cho Kusunoki, and S. Uchikawa. "Toyota Production System and Kanban System—Materialization of Just-in-Time and Respect-for-Human System." *International Journal of Production Research* 15, no. 6 (1977), pp. 553–64.

Suzaki, Kiyoshi. *The New Manufacturing Challenge: Techniques for Continuous Improvement.* New York: Free Press, 1987.

Tajiri, Masaji, and Fumio Gotoh. *TPM Implementation: A Japanese Approach.* New York: McGraw-Hill, 1992.

Wantuck, Kenneth A. *Just-in-Time for America: A Common Sense Production Strategy.* Southfield, MI: KWA Media, 1989.

Womack, J. P., and D. T. Jones. *Lean Thinking: Banish Waste and Create Wealth in Your Corporation.* New York: Simon and Schuster, 1996.

Womack, James P., Daniel T. Jones, and Daniel Roos. *The Machine That Changed the World.* New York: Rawson Associates, 1990.

Module Objectives

By the end of this module, you should be able to

- Understand and apply the major tools and procedures that the lean systems philosophy draws upon in achieving its objectives.
- Learn how to use such calculations as TAKT time to synchronize and balance flows and to achieve the objectives of one-piece part flow.
- Understand how developments such as continuous improvement can be made to generate real benefits for management and for the value-driven operations management system.

Making Lean Manufacturing Work in a Custom Environment

Are the tools, procedures, and approaches of lean systems applicable to a setting where short runs, frequent changeovers, and numerous product configurations are the rule, not the exception? This was the question faced by a 40-year manufacturer of electrical and electronic enclosures for computer and electronic equipment. Management found that the answer was an astounding and unconditional "YES."

At first glance, this should not have been the case. The manufacturer broke all of the commonly held rules for lean systems. The plant was not automotive-related; it did not make a standard product. Its product mix was highly variable. Some of its products were as small as 4″ while others were as large as 6′ × 4′. Some of its products were made of mild steel, in 100 custom colors as well as multiple colors; others were made of stainless, plated, or galvanized steel or aluminum.

The company calls some manufacturing lines "standard" and others "custom." Yet, there is very little that is standard. Even so, management learned that this company could improve its performance by implementing standardized processes—one of the major tactics of lean systems.

To eliminate overproduction and underproduction, managers had to determine customer demand so that they could calculate TAKT time and balance the lines accordingly. Managers posted visual instructions in the work area describing the specific work content for each operation based on the product being produced. Though an ideal balance was not always achieved, the goal was to ensure continuous flow of product. As the implementation proceeded, continuous improvement activities focused on refining work balance.

To achieve a desired level of predictability, managers set standards for determining the run sequence of orders. In addition, pull systems with each line were established. Yet, the real challenge for management was in selling lean principles to the employees. The implementation team decided to be creative and to simulate the concept of single-piece flow for the operators. Acting as human conveyors, the team moved the product from operation to operation without operator intervention. The demonstration showed the people working in these areas the benefits of lean systems. As they understood the benefits, they became more willing to accept the layout and process changes.

Source: John H. Allen, "Make Lean Manufacturing Work for You," *Manufacturing Engineering,* June 2001, pp. 54–64.

Conventional knowledge says that just-in-time (JIT) or lean systems are primarily appropriate for high-volume production of standard or near-standard items. To many, lean systems are something done in the automotive industry. As the opening vignette shows, this is not the case. The tools, procedures, and systems that accompany lean systems are highly versatile. They are applied to a variety of products and operating settings. Understanding these tools and procedures is critical to any attempt to reduce or eliminate waste and variance—the twin objectives of the value-driven operations management system.

Lean Systems Tools and Procedures

Steven A. Melnyk
Michigan State University

Lawrence D. Fredendall
Clemson University

McGraw-Hill Irwin

Boston Burr Ridge, IL Dubuque, IA Madison, WI New York San Francisco St. Louis
Bangkok Bogotá Caracas Kuala Lumpur Lisbon London Madrid Mexico City
Milan Montreal New Delhi Santiago Seoul Singapore Sydney Taipei Toronto

Lean Systems Tools and Procedures

JIT or Lean Systems

When it was initially introduced, the **lean systems** approach to waste and variance reduction was referred to as just-in-time manufacturing. However, over time, there has been a significant shift in how managers have come to view **just-in-time systems.** We have now come to see that it is more than just-in-time deliveries. Also, the principles, practices, philosophies, and tools of lean systems are not limited to only the automotive industry or even to manufacturing firms. The principles can be applied equally and successfully to services, banks, restaurants, hospitals, or government offices. This approach ultimately enables firms to do more with less—less resources, less overhead, less variable costs, less fixed costs, and less lead time. For these and other reasons, we will use the term "lean systems" rather than just-in-time.

Lean Systems Objectives and Tools

As we stated earlier, the twin aims of the lean systems approach are to improve value and reduce waste. These broad aims lead to seven primary objectives, given in Exhibit 1. Note that these objectives collectively address all of the elements of value: quality, timeliness, and cost, as well as aspects of waste. Further, the seventh objective identifies the key means for improvement, the development of people.

EXHIBIT 1
Lean Systems' Objectives[1]

1. Produce only the products (goods or services) that customers want.
2. Produce products only as quickly as customers want to use them.
3. Produce products with perfect quality.
4. Produce in the minimum possible lead times.
5. Produce products with features that customers want, and no others.
6. Produce with no waste of labor, materials, or equipment; designate a purpose for every movement to leave zero idle inventory.
7. Produce with methods that reinforce the occupational development of workers.

In their quest to achieve these objectives, managers, researchers, and consultants have developed many lean systems tools and procedures that are becoming increasingly widespread. These techniques can be grouped in many different ways. In this module, we have classified them according to their area of primary management impact. Exhibit 2 provides the framework that organizes our coverage of the tools and procedures addressed in this module. Keep in mind, however, that the implementation of any given tool may call for changes in many areas of operations management.

EXHIBIT 2
Lean Systems Tools and Techniques

Area of Primary Impact		
Facilities and Resources	**Scheduling and Control**	**Process Improvement**
Worker cross-training	Takt time/Flow balancing	Quality at the source
Group technology	Kanban (pull) scheduling	Poka-yoke (fool proofing)
Focused factories	Mixed model scheduling	5–S Program
Total productive maintenance	Set-up reduction	Standardization/Simplification
	Statistical process control	Kaizen/Continuous improvement
	Visual control	

Facilities and Resources Tools

Many of the important changes involved in implementing a lean systems approach have to do with the way primary resources, facilities and workers, are managed. For example, managers may change the layout of a plant to improve flow and minimize wasted movement. Similarly, policies affecting areas such as training or maintenance may be changed in order

[1] A more detailed discussion of these objectives is provided in the Lean Systems Module.

to improve the flexibility or reliability of resources (i.e., workers and machines). These types of changes are discussed in this section.

Worker Cross-Training

To produce the products that customers want at the rate that they want them, a lean system requires a new understanding of capacity. Instead of treating capacity as a certain quantity fixed by current levels of workers and equipment, lean systems assume that operations managers can quickly vary capacity to match customers' needs.[2] This, in turn, requires operations managers to change how they schedule and train the workforce.

A worker who can perform only one task does not fit well into a just-in-time environment, which requires a more flexible resource. A flexible workforce can move from an area where the firm experiences low demand to more active areas. By cross-training employees, that is, by training workers to perform more than one operation or task, a firm can more easily develop such a flexible workforce.

This move toward a flexible workforce—**flexible/cross-trained workers**—has several important implications for management and compensation of employees. It places more demands on workers, requiring them to move beyond the role of simple problem solvers to become multiskilled resources. Lean system programs hire and retain people who are interested in doing many things within the firm, so pay and job security can no longer be linked solely to seniority. Instead, they reflect the number and types of an individual employee's skills. Some firms refer to programs to pay people according to the range of their job skills as "pay for skill."

Group Technology

Many firms organize their transformation systems along functional lines. For example, the management at the electronic cabinet manufacturer discussed in the opening vignette might locate the equipment for cutting steel panels in one work center and all painting equipment in another. A cabinet in process would move from area to area to allow completion of needed operations. This arrangement makes production extremely flexible, since any work center can process any part that requires its function. However, this flexibility comes at a price. Such layouts experience a great deal of physical movement and handling. Products have to move to the centers offering the functions that the orders need. The result is often an inefficient flow of orders, with many orders moving back and forth through the system, traveling from one work center to another.

Not only is the flow inefficient, but orders in such shops spend most of their time waiting in queues. In many cases, orders can spend between 80 and 95 percent of their total lead time waiting to be processed. Finally, systems laid out along functional lines adversely affect opportunities for improvements. Because of the constantly changing product mix, people working in such systems may not see a specific product enough times to identify areas and activities where waste is present.

Group technology (GT) gathers all of the equipment necessary for complete production of a family of similar parts into one location.[3] Group technology is based on the concept of part families, or groups of similar parts. These similarities could reflect common design features or manufacturing needs. After grouping parts into families that share some important characteristics, the operations manager organizes a work cell for each family that gathers together all of the equipment and facilities needed to build that set of parts. The physical layout arranges facilities in the optimum sequence to produce the parts in the family. Typically such a layout forms a U-shaped sequence like that in Exhibit 3. From a position in the middle, the operator performs all of the operations needed to build each unit of output.

Compared to functional layouts, GT work cells shrink the physical distances between operations, so they often sharply reduce lead times. In addition, they smooth the flow of

[2] This ability to rebalance capacity quickly is the basis of the TAKT time analysis/system synchronization discussed later on in this module.

[3] Kenneth A. Wantuck, *Just in Time in America* (Southfield, MI: **KWA Media**, 1989)

EXHIBIT 3
Example of a Group Technology Layout

Source: Kenneth A. Wantuck, *Just in Time in America* (Southfield, MI: KWA Media, 1989), p. 145.

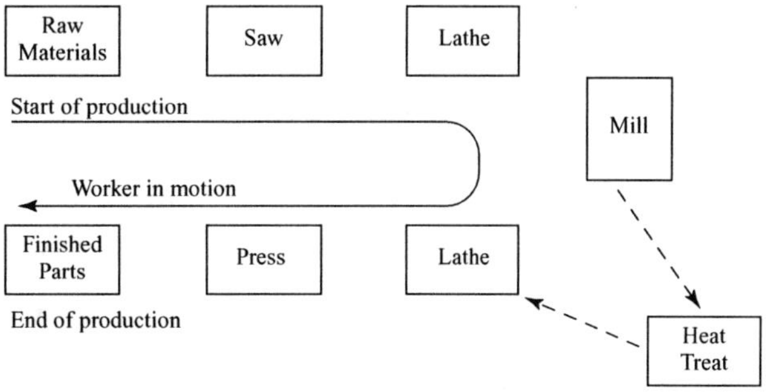

functionally organized facilities. Since the operator often can move parts between nearby operations by hand, group technology may eliminate the need for automated material-handling equipment. GT work cells also enable **visual control.** An operator standing in the middle of a GT cell can easily visually monitor the status of the equipment and work within the cell. An operator working at the center of a set of equipment arranged in a straight line cannot see the equipment at the end of the lines.

By building similar parts in a single work cell, group technology can produce orders with fewer setups than a functionally organized system. This promotes progress toward the lean systems' goal of building what customers want in the amounts they want with minimum lead times. In addition, a GT layout makes full use of cross-trained workers. Such a worker provides the GT work cell with a level of flexibility not found in the functionally laid out system.[4]

As a GT work cell builds a single set of outputs continuously, workers become intimately familiar with the system's outputs and processes, avoiding the need for expensive relearning and helping them to identify opportunities for improvement. Finally, a work cell can improve quality by providing an opportunity for visual inspection after each operation as the operator moves a part from one machine to the next. All of the benefits are consistent with the various objectives of lean systems.

The discussion of group technology shows why lean systems frequently abandon efforts to build many diverse products in single large systems. Instead, lean systems tend to organize production into a series of smaller, more focused systems.

Focused Factories

In traditional manufacturing, a large factory produces every one of a firm's products in one location to take advantage of economies of scale. However, large plants are more difficult to manage than smaller facilities. In general, managing more people requires more rigid, bureaucratic methods. Also, to achieve the volume of production it needs to justify its fixed costs, a large plant often must produce wide varieties of products that require many different types of processes. This variety complicates worker training, and it can spread confusion and increase operating variances that are detrimental to performance.

Consider a large auto components plant that produces similar parts both for auto manufacturers and for the repair and replacement part market. Car manufacturers want low-cost components delivered on time, so they provide suppliers with demand schedules for large orders several weeks in advance. In contrast, small distributors buy replacement parts only to meet their customers' repair needs. These buyers need speedy service on comparatively small orders, and demand is difficult to predict because no one knows how many of a particular part will break.

To satisfy the first group of customers, the plant needs to run large lots with few schedule variations and relatively high levels of capacity utilization. To satisfy the second group

[4] This is program or rerouting flexibility, using the categories of flexibility as described in the foundation modules.

of customers, it needs to respond quickly to changing demand, frequently shifting production from one component to another. To resolve this conflict, the plant's managers might replace the single plant with two separate plants: one dedicated to the automotive market, another dedicated to the parts replacement market. One way to do this while preserving the economies of a single facility is to create two **plants-within-a-plant.** Using this approach, managers would physically divide the plant and create separate production lines, with each line dedicated to meet the needs of its specific target market. Each *market-focused factory* would then organize its capabilities to be consistent with one market's order winners, order qualifiers, and order losers.[5]

Factories also can be focused on other dimensions. For example, what if the auto parts manufacturer in our example also does refurbishing and remanufacturing of used parts? Remanufacturing processes typically require very different types of equipment and skills than new parts manufacturing do. Another way to focus the plant would be to create two separate *process-focused factories,* one dedicated to original parts manufacturing and the other dedicated to remanufacturing.

By focusing attention on a limited set of process, product, and/or market requirements, **focused factories** reduce confusion and variance. They allow better organization of the transformation process to encourage efficient product movements through the system and consistent workforce policies. A focused factory can justify investments in special-purpose equipment, and it can make employee training simpler and less costly. The familiar stream of work also helps workers improve at a faster rate.

Firms have reaped many significant benefits by implementing focused factories. For example, Ferro Manufacturing, a supplier of door mechanisms and latching systems to the auto industry, has seen the following improvements:[6]

- Productivity increased by 46 percent.
- Scrap rates fell by 67 percent.
- Rework hours fell by 93 percent.
- The total cost of quality fell by 47 percent.
- Assembly floor space shrank by 15 percent.

Total Productive Maintenance (TPM)

Equipment breakdowns can seriously disrupt a firm's entire operations. In the early 1980s, for example, Chrysler was struggling to survive. One of their major problems was an equipment uptime ratio of 36 percent.[7] In other words, workers could use the equipment to produce output only 36 percent of the time; breakdowns, maintenance, and readjustments occupied the rest of the time.

Breakdowns create variance and costs within the OM system. In an effort to make managers aware of how poor maintenance practices waste their system's capacity, Nakajima identified six major types of losses due to maintenance problems:[8]

1. Downtime due to equipment failure.
2. Downtime for setups and adjustments such as exchanges of dies in injection molding machines, and so on.
3. Speed losses due to idling and minor stoppages caused by abnormal operations of sensors, blockages, and so forth.

[5] Terry Hill, *Manufacturing Strategy* (New York: McGraw-Hill/Irwin, 1994); and Wickham Skinner, "The Focused Factory," *Harvard Business Review,* May/June 1974, pp. 113–21.
[6] Wantuck, *Just in Time in America,* pp. 136–37.
[7] Richard E. Dauch, *Passion for Excellence* (New York: McGraw-Hill/Irwin, 1993), p. 176.
[8] Seiichi Nakajima, *TPM: Introduction to TPM, Total Productive Maintenance* (Cambridge, MA: Productivity Press, 1988), p. 14.

4. Speed losses due to discrepancies between designed and actual speeds of equipment.
5. Defect losses due to process defects that cause scrap and quality problems.
6. Defect losses due to reduced yields in the time between machine startup and stable production.

Total productive maintenance (TPM) is used in lean systems to eliminate these six losses. It is designed to identify and attack all causes of equipment breakdowns and system downtime.

TPM was originally developed in Japan. It is the latest stage in the evolution of maintenance methods. There were three other stages in the evolution of maintenance before TPM. First, there was what is referred to as breakdown maintenance or **corrective maintenance.** This maintenance practice follows the adage "If it ain't broke, don't fix it." A corrective maintenance system performs no maintenance on any piece of equipment if it can run without attention. Preventive maintenance was the second stage in the evolution of maintenance. Preventive maintenance establishes routines to take care of equipment. For example, maintenance workers regularly oil and clean equipment and perform other periodic maintenance. This is similar to car owners performing preventive maintenance by changing the oil every three months or 3,000 miles. The third stage in the evolution of maintenance was productive maintenance, or predictive maintenance. This practice uses modern monitoring and analysis techniques to diagnose the condition of the equipment during operation. The goal is to identify signs of equipment deterioration or imminent failure and to take corrective action before actual equipment failure.

TPM, the fourth stage in the evolution of maintenance techniques, works much more broadly to identify and correct all potential causes of breakdowns. TPM's ambitious goal of zero breakdowns. Five principles guide TPM programs:[9]

1. Maximize equipment effectiveness (i.e., reduce downtime to zero).
2. Establish a thorough system of preventive maintenance for the entire life span of equipment, from design and acquisition to disposition.
3. Implement maintenance programs in all organizational areas (engineering, operations, facility management, and maintenance) to spread TPM throughout the system.
4. Involve every single member of the organization, from top managers to workers on the shop floor.
5. Assign responsibility for preventive maintenance to small, autonomous groups of employees rather than managers.

TPM is a comprehensive system of equipment maintenance that encompasses all activities with any influence on equipment uptime.[10] The five major components of TPM are

1. *Regulating basic conditions:* TPM advocates keeping a well-organized shop floor. A Japanese term translates as parlor factory, suggesting that an entire shop should be so clean that workers feel they should walk around in stocking feet to avoid making messes.
2. *Adhering to proper operating procedures:* The most significant cause of chance breakdowns is a failure to follow proper operating procedures. When operators deviate from procedures, they introduce errors and variance into the process.
3. *Restoring deterioration:* TPM requires diligent effort to discover and predict deterioration in equipment and then to follow standard repair methods designed to eliminate any sources of variation in the system.
4. *Improving weaknesses in design:* TPM tries to identify and correct any defects in equipment designs that contribute to breakdowns or complicate maintenance. For example,

[9] Ibid., p. 10.
[10] Ibid., p. 40.

some computers are produced with modular designs. When a part breaks down, the computer shows a code to indicate the location of the problem. The user reports the code through a toll-free telephone support line, and a company representative identifies the defective part and sends a new one along with instructions for replacing it. The user need not resort to specialized service people or repair facilities.

5. *Improving operation and maintenance skills:* Equipment users contribute to TPM by learning and following correct operating procedures to prevent errors that may cause chance breakdowns. Also, these sharpened skills help to prevent repair errors and correct any problems on the first try. TPM enhances the skills of both users and maintenance workers through education and training.

Through these activities, TPM attacks the variance and waste that breakdowns create by preventing problems and eliminating causes of defects.

Scheduling and Control Tools

An essential component of the lean systems approach is a changed perspective on production planning and control. In this section, we discuss some of the important procedures in this area.

TAKT Time—Flow Balancing

A major objective of lean systems is to produce products at the rate wanted by the customer. To do so, we have to synchronize or balance the rate of supply with the rate of demand. In addition, we also have to ensure that capacities of the operations management system (internal and external) are organized to support this coordination. One step in balancing flows is to use **TAKT Time (T-T).**

TAKT is the German word for the beat (as in the beat in a band). This word is highly appropriate. By calculating the TAKT time, we hope to identify the rate (identified in units of time) at which we must produce to keep supply balanced with demand.

TAKT Time

The TAKT time approach is applied as a five-step process:

1. Calculate the Net Available Operating Time (NAOT).
2. Calculate the customer requirements per period.
3. Calculate the TAKT time.
4. Calculate the operator cycle time and the machine cycle time.
5. Adjust the process capacity to achieve balance between the rate of demand and the rate of supply.

Calculating NAOT The **net available operating time (NAOT)** is calculated by determining the total available production time available and adjusting it for the presence of breaks, clean-up, and lunch. In the NAOT calculation, no allowance is made for buffer capacity, setup time, or machine breakdown. These uses of capacity are ignored because we are trying to reduce the amount of time taken by them. The NAOT is the amount of time available for production.

For example, consider the following NAOT calculation:

Gross available time/shift	480	minutes (8 hours × 60 minutes/hour)
Breaks: 2 breaks, 15 minutes each	−30	minutes
Clean-up (end of shift)	−15	minutes
Lunch	−45	minutes
NAOT/shift	390	minutes

NAOT for 1 day, assuming 3 shifts a day:	
NAOT in minutes	1,170 minutes
NAOT in seconds	70,200 seconds

Calculating Customer Requirements Next, we determine the customer requirements. This is based on taking the customer requirements for a period of time, such as a month, and stating them in terms of the number needed per day. In making this conversion, we must consider the number of working days, as compared to total days. This calculation would be done as follows:

Monthly requirements:	24,000 units
Number of working days/month:	20 days
Customer requirements/day:	1,200 units per day

Calculating TAKT Time We are now ready to calculate the TAKT time. This is done by dividing the customer requirements per day by the NAOT per day (remember that this was the NAOT per shift multiplied by three). Using the numbers from our example, this would work out as follows, measured in seconds:

$$\text{TAKT time} = \begin{array}{l}3\ (\text{NAOT/shift})\\ \text{Customer requirements per day}\end{array}$$

$$= \frac{70{,}200 \text{ seconds}}{1{,}200 \text{ units per day}}$$

= 58.5 seconds per unit, or 58 seconds with rounding[11]

This tells us that if we produce one unit every 58 seconds, we will have balanced supply with demand. This calculation, while important, is not enough. We must ensure that the capacity of the process can support the TAKT time.

Calculating Operator Cycle Time and Machine Cycle Time The **operator cycle time (OCT)** is the total time required by a worker to complete one cycle of an operation. The **machine cycle time (MCT)** is the total time needed for a machine to finish one complete cycle (including unloading and loading time). In a machine/operator system, one or both of these will limit capacity of the process. In this section, we will assume that the operator is the bottleneck, or the limit in the process. As a result, our attention will be on OCT.

Returning to our example, let's assume that our process has four steps with the following OCTs.

OCT for step 1 is 10 seconds.

OCT for step 2 is 30 seconds.

OCT for step 3 is 50 seconds.

OCT for step 4 is 49 seconds.

Total process time (TPT) is 139 seconds.

The number of resources needed is TPT/TAKT time = 139/58.5 = 2.38 workers. Rounding up, we identify that we know that we need three operators. If we have four operators, then we have too much capacity and the extra employee can be released for use elsewhere within the system. To manage these three operators, we will use the following rules:

If the OCT for any activity > TAKT time, we add capacity to that step.

If the OCT for any activity = TAKT time, we do nothing.

[11] When calculating the TAKT time, we round down because if we were to use 59 seconds, the rate of supply would be slower than the rate of demand. Synchronization of flows would not be present.

> If the OCT for any activity < TAKT time, we can combine that activity with one or more other activities to bring the total cycle time for the operator up to the TAKT time.

To meet our goal of a 58.5-second TAKT time in the example above, we could initially assign one operator to steps 1 and 2, a second operator to step 3, and the third operator to step 4. This will give us a system that produces one unit every 50 seconds. If possible, we might want to subdivide or rearrange tasks to spread the work more evenly. In this way, TAKT time enables managers to balance the line to match demand.

Kanban (Pull) Scheduling

To build only what customers demand when they demand it, lean systems need a scheduling system that can immediately and clearly communicate the demands of the customer to the delivery system. The kanban or pull scheduling system does this. In its simplest meaning, the word *kanban* is the Japanese term for a card. In lean systems, **kanban** is a name for a system of signals or control cards that govern material movements through an OM system.

The kanban control system relies on visual signals such as control cards, but it can use a variety of visual signals such as empty squares on the floor or a shelf or even colored golf balls to control the withdrawal and replenishment of materials and components during processing. (Exhibit 4 gives some examples of kanban signals and their meanings.) Kanbans send urgent signals to workers to initiate specific actions immediately, perhaps beginning production of a certain part or transferring inventory from one location to another. A kanban system creates real-time links between both customers and suppliers.

EXHIBIT 4
Examples of Kanban

Golf balls: When a golf ball rolls up to a workstation, the operator builds a product indicated by the color of the golf ball.
Cards: Information might state the amount and type of item to produce, a stock location, or a process.
Taped square on the floor: When the square empties, fill it.
Metal triangle on a pile: When removed products expose the metal triangle, build more.
Carts or trucks: When an empty cart arrives, fill it.
Containers: When a container empties to a line painted inside, refill it.

Pull versus Push Scheduling

Kanbans are used to create a **pull scheduling** system that begins production only when an internal or external customer sends a signal. In contrast, a **push scheduling** system directs a worker to produce according to a schedule and to move output to the next work center on its route when it is completed. This may lead to piles of inventories waiting unproductively at various points within the system. The shop then experiences waves of work. For example, one day a work center is overloaded, while the next day it is idle. A kanban system seeks to set up a smooth flow of materials at each stage of production from raw material to customer delivery.

Toyota's Kanban System

To understand how kanban works, look at Toyota's implementation of the concept.[12] This system defines two basic types of kanbans: production kanbans and withdrawal kanbans (also known as conveyance kanbans). A **production kanban** authorizes a worker to replenish an empty bin. When an empty bin arrives at a workstation with a production kanban attached, it is a signal to build a new batch of items to fill the bin. The production kanban specifies the type of parts and the number to build, typically the amount that will fit in a kanban container. **Withdrawal kanbans** authorize someone to withdraw a

[12] Y. Monden, "What Makes the Toyota Production System Really Tick?" *Industrial Engineering* 13, no. 1 (1981), pp. 36–46.

standard lot of a specific item. This kanban is typically attached to a container of parts undergoing processing at a specific operation. If a worker processing the job runs out of a part, the withdrawal kanban that accompanied the job gives that person the authority to take an empty bin to a replenishment area to exchange for a full bin. The worker reattaches the withdrawal kanban to a filled bin, leaves the empty bin at the replenishment area, and takes the filled bin with the attached withdrawal kanban back to his or her workstation.

Exhibit 5 illustrates how the two kinds of kanbans control interactions between workstations.[13] Work center A supplies inputs for work center B. The storage area between the work centers contains one container of each type of part. In Exhibit 5(A) the storage area between the work centers is full. So work center A sits idle since work center B does not need any parts. In Exhibit 5(B) there is an empty bin at work center B with a withdrawal kanban attached. To get more parts, the operator at work center B takes the empty bin with the attached withdrawal kanban to the storage area next to work center A. The worker moves the withdrawal kanban from the empty bin to the full bin. The worker then moves the production kanban that was on the full bin to the empty bin and returns with the full bin and the withdrawal kanban to work center B.

EXHIBIT 5
Kanbans in Operation

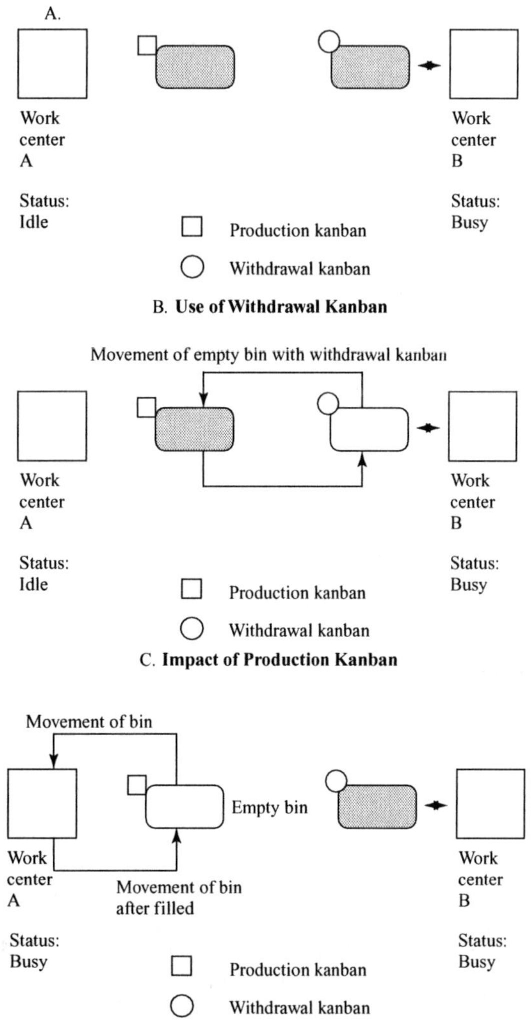

[13] Steven A. Melnyk and Phillip L. Carter, "Viewing Kanban as an (*s,Q*) System: Developing New Insights into a Japanese Method of Production and Inventory Control," in *Management by Japanese Systems,* ed. Sang M. Lee and Gary Schwendiman (New York: Praeger, 1982), pp. 165–80.

In Exhibit 5(C), the worker at work center A picks up the empty bin with the attached production kanban and begins production to refill the bin and return it to the storage area. If no empty bins await the operator at work center A at the end of this cycle, production stops.

This example illustrates why kanban is a pull system. Work center B pulls needed parts from the storage area, which effectively pulls replacement parts from work center A. This pull system responds quickly and automatically to preexisting demand and prevents inventory from growing large.

The kanban system eliminates the need for traditional paperwork such as sheaves of orders or long lists of due dates. Each worker produces whatever the kanbans dictate. Kanban is also a simple system to use and understand, eliminating the need for complex computer technology for order tracking and scheduling.

Point to Remember

In a push system, the creation of supply takes place before the demand that consumes it occurs. Push systems create inventory.

In a pull system, the demand must take place first then the supply is created in response. Pull systems eliminate the build-up of not-yet-needed inventory.

Something to Think About

Can you think of situations where pull as compared to push scheduling has been used?

Benefits of Kanban

As practiced at companies such as Hewlett-Packard and Toyota, kanban systems have resulted in significant benefits:

- Reduced inventory levels.
- Less confusion over sequences of activities.
- Less obsolescence of inventories while in storage.
- Smaller floor-space requirements for storing inventory.
- Reduced lead times.
- Improved quality.
- Higher employee productivity.
- Greater system flexibility.

Level, Mixed-Model Scheduling

To build what customers want in the desired amounts at the correct times and at the desired rates (See Exhibit 1—Lean Systems objectives 1 and 2), a firm must change how it schedules and controls operations every day. On the shop floor, this is done with Kanban or pull scheduling. However, most production systems produce multiple products. Each of these products requires different resources and materials, which must be made available and scheduled so that a bottleneck is not created. The role of the **master production schedule** (MPS) is to identify for a given period of time (e.g., a month) the number of units of each specific end product that will be built, so that the OM system can coordinate with the other systems. The MPS serves as a critical interface between the OM system and the rest of the firm. It tells people throughout the firm what they can expect to receive from the OM system and when. Based on this information, marketing can make promises to customers, purchasing can plan for material needs, finance can arrange funding for working capital needs, and so forth. The concept of master production scheduling is discussed in greater detail in the "Dependent Demand Requirements Planning Systems" module.

EXHIBIT 6
Example of Mixed Model Scheduling

Model	Sales (units)		Cycle Time
A	15,000 per month	750 per day	38.4 seconds
B	7,500 per month	375 per day	76.8 seconds
C	3,750 per month	187.5 per day	153.6 seconds
D	3,750 per month	187.5 per day	153.6 seconds
Total sales:	30,000 per month	1,500 per day	19.2 seconds
Capacity:	20 days of production planned	8 hours of production planned	

To produce only products the customer wants when they want them, a Lean Systems master production schedule produces some units of every end product every day. In a Lean System, the MPS should create an identical schedule for each day, so that the work flow is smooth and predictable. This means that one day's production is planned in detail and then this schedule is repeated every day of the month.

Load Leveling

Lean Systems develop a daily schedule through **load leveling,** a technique for balancing the rate of production with the rate at which the market wants products. For example, suppose that a firm makes four different end products, A, B, C, and D, with the sales levels given in Exhibit 6.

The number of units to be produced in a month is divided by the number of working days per month (i.e., 30,000 units/20 days-1,500 units per day). The daily load for each model is found in the same way (e.g., for Model A in Exhibit 6, 15,000/20 = 750 Model A's a day). At this point, we want to produce the various models at rates that ensure that a balance in the flows is maintained. Since this is a form of TAKT time, we will calculate the TAKT times for each model. For Model A, we should try to produce one unit every 38.4 seconds; for model B, the TAKT time is 76.8; for models C and D, the TAKT times are identical at 153.9. Furthermore, if we divide the total number of Models that we have to produce every day (1500) by time available (8 hours * 60 minutes * 60 seconds per minute = 28,800 seconds), we find that we have to produce one unit of product (irrespective of the model) every 19.2 seconds.

Something to Think About

How would the Electronic Cabinet Manufacturer described at the beginning of this module use the concept of level scheduling in its cabinet production?

Mixed-Model Scheduling

With a daily schedule that identifies how many units of each model an OM system will produce per day, operations managers must decide how to distribute this production over the day. One option is to run all units of model A in one batch, followed by three more batches for all units of model B, model C, and then model D. This schedule would create very uneven demand for components during the day, as the system would have to supply everything needed to produce each model in a single, large batch or lump. This would create waves of work moving through the shop.

Another option, referred to as mixed-model scheduling, is to create a production sequence that will repeat during the day. The detailed procedures for developing such a schedule are explained in the Operations Scheduling module. A brief example using the information in Exhibit 6 is explained here.

One way of developing such a schedule is to think in terms of how many overall TAKT times of 19.2 seconds should fall between each successive unit of the various models. For Model A, we would expect two units of 19.2 seconds to pass (the TAKT time for Model A is 38.4 seconds). What this means is that we would expect one unit of some non-Model A product to separate units of Model A. For Model B, we would plan for 4 units (76.8/19.2) of non-Model Bs to separate each unit of B. For Models C and D, we would plan for 8 units (153.6/19.2) to separate each successive unit of C and D.

With this information, we would develop the schedule found in Exhibit 7. The only difficulty in the scheduling is that we are to produce one-half unit of C and one-half unit of D each day. This is difficult to do. One solution is to build an additional C one day and an additional D another.

EXHIBIT 7
Mixed Model Scheduling Example

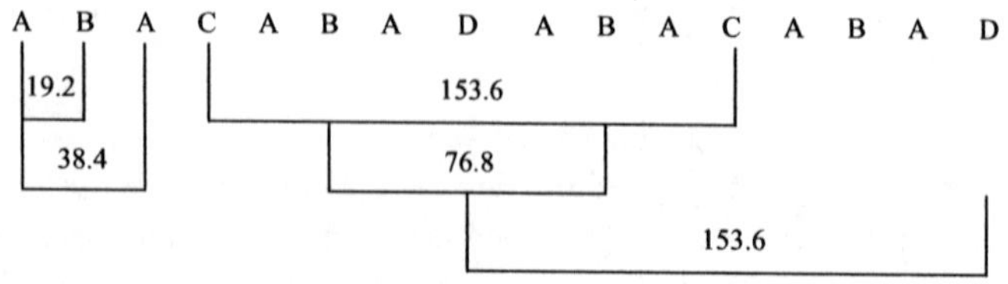

In reviewing this schedule, we find that it meets the TAKT time requirements that we had established in the preceding paragraphs. Specifically, since the time interval separating each unit of output is 19.2 seconds, we find that we produce one A every 38.4 seconds; one B every 76.8 seconds (there are four intervals separating the two units of B); one C every 153.6 seconds; and, one D every 153.6 seconds. The schedule is balanced and repeatable.

Benefits of Level, Mixed-Model Scheduling

Level, mixed-model scheduling promotes the Lean Systems goal of simple flows through relatively simple methods. The technique offers other benefits, as well:

- *Smoother response to market demand:* This scheduling system produces some units of every product every day, so customers need not wait for the completion of large batches to get the products that they want. The firm can meet customer demand without holding large finished-goods inventories.
- *Simpler coordination of supply:* Because each day's schedule is identical over the month, operations managers can coordinate the flows of supplies once and then repeat the same arrangements each day.
- *Flatter learning curves:* Because operators produce every product and component frequently, the needed techniques and skills remain fresh.
- *Less inventory:* Continuous production synchronized to demand frees the firm from storing large quantities to meet demand between runs.

Setup Reduction

To produce just what customers want in the desired amounts (objectives 1 and 2 of a lean system), an OM system must build in small lot sizes, ideally in order quantities of one unit. Long setup times make this impossible in many OM systems. The time required to prepare a system to process a job includes

1. **Process teardown time:** At the end of producing one type of job, workers must remove the tools and dies for that part to allow adjustments to the equipment to process a new job.
2. **Learning time:** Before processing a new job, the operator must find and read instructions about preparing the equipment and executing the needed tasks.
3. **Process preparation time:** This includes the time for activities such as finding needed tools and accessories, changing the equipment, and testing and adjusting the new setup to ensure that it can produce good quality consistently.

Setups cost money and consume capacity without adding value. Setups that are not managed well also introduce variation into an OM process as workers try to locate needed tools, materials, and instructions. The times required to calibrate or adjust equipment also may vary. And, finally, the time requirements for testing output to evaluate the accuracy of the setup will change each time it is done.

Reducing Setup Times

A lean system works hard to reduce setup times. An effective **setup-reduction** program should pursue four major objectives:[14]

- *Evolve toward lot sizes of one unit.* This requires setups that take no longer than the time to produce a single unit of output. This supports the policy of building to order: It allows the system to build what customers want when they want it.
- *Run every part every day.* This keeps the schedule level. It also ensures that workers are familiar with every part made (learning how to make the part "right" is time consuming and not a value adding activity).
- *Make the first piece right every time.* Effective setup reduction not only must reduce the time it takes to change over from one part to another, it also ensures that even the first part to emerge from the process is perfect.
- *Keep setup times to 10 minutes.* A typical goal is to reduce the time it takes to change over equipment to 10 minutes or less. This may seem ambitious, but it has proven to be a very feasible goal in many situations. (See Exhibit 8.)

EXHIBIT 8
Auto Hood and Fender Setups for an 800-Ton Press

Source: Kenneth A. Wantuck, *Just in Time in America* (Southfield, MI: KWA Media, 1989), pp. 186–88.

	Toyota	USA	Sweden	Germany
Setup time	10 minutes	6 hours	4 hours	4 hours
Setups/day	3	1	—	1/2
Lot size	1 day	10 days	1 month	—

There are four common techniques that managers use to reduce setup times: process flow analysis, housekeeping, practiced teamwork, and single-minute exchange of dies.

Process Flow Analysis of Setup Times

Creating a process flowchart is a first step in understanding the current setup procedures. Managers also sometimes videotape the setup procedures and study the tapes to understand what is being done.

Housekeeping

Good housekeeping and careful organization help to smooth the setup process. Good housekeeping means that every tool and container is in a specified place at all times. Good housekeeping also means that cleanliness is stressed and that clutter is avoided. Clutter causes unplanned delays and variance. An efficient setup should look like a pit stop at the Indianapolis Speedway.

Practiced Teamwork

An efficient setup requires people to work together as a team in which each member knows and carries out certain responsibilities and tasks. Workers must practice setups so that the members can carry out their tasks quickly, almost without thinking, and without error.

Single-Minute Exchange of Dies (SMED)

Single-minute exchange of dies (SMED) is a systematic procedure for reducing long setups developed by Shigeo Shingo.[15] This technique traces the origins of long setups to several causes:

[14] Wantuck, *Just in Time in America*, p. 188.
[15] Shigeo Shingo, *A Revolution in Manufacturing: The SMED System* (Cambridge, MA: Productivity Press, 1985).

- Preparation, after-process adjustment, checking of material, and so forth.
- Mounting and removal of tools and fittings.
- Measurements, settings, and calibrations.
- Trial runs and adjustments.

SMED tries to reduce the impact of these causes by using a three-stage process. Stage 1 separates internal and external setups. An **internal setup** includes any setup procedure that occurs while the equipment sits idle. For example, if a pancake cook were to wait for the griddle to heat up before mixing the batter, the mixing step would represent an internal setup. In contrast, an **external setup** is any setup activity that workers complete while the equipment operates. In an external setup the cook would mix the batter while waiting for the griddle to heat. Decisions about what is an internal setup and what is an external setup are often made using the process flowchart or the video tape of the process.

Stage 2 converts internal setups to external setups. Again, this is done by examining the flow process chart and developing a new process.

Stage 3 works to streamline all activities in a setup. This stage tries to eliminate any activities performed to make adjustments, calibrations, elaborate positioning, unnecessary tightening, or trial runs. This is done by setting up mounts and guides or back plates so that tools slide into the correct position. Standardizing setups can flatten learning curves by eliminating the need for relearning. Or technology can reduce setup time. For example, a laser level can help workers judge the alignment of dies. Or a pancake griddle could include a light that turns green when it reaches the right temperature.

Benefits of Reduced Setups

Reducing setups can bring many benefits. Quicker setups increase capital turnover rates, earning a higher return on the firm's investment in equipment by maximizing its productive time. Smaller inventory requirements use plant space more efficiently and reduce non-value-adding operations such as stock handling, further enhancing productivity. Also, low inventory requirements minimize losses due to unusable stock after model changes or demand forecast errors. Eliminating setup errors improves both quality and safety. Less complicated setups simplify housekeeping and lower operating expenses as well.

Statistical Process Control

To generate output with perfect quality, a lean system needs to apply analytical tools to monitor process performance and evaluate their control of the process. Many of these tools form the basis of **statistical process control.**[16] Techniques such as run charts, control charts, and scatterplots enable employees to measure their control of a process and identify any need for intervention. Traditional manufacturing might assign specialists to apply these tools, but lean systems place them in the hands of employees to move decision-making authority to the lowest levels and achieve quality at the source. The tools are discussed more fully in the "Quality Improvement Tools and Techniques" module.

Visual Control

Many of the tools and procedures discussed in this module (e.g., andon, kanban [pull] scheduling, the 5-S program) make use of an approach to shop floor management broadly known as *visual control.* The goal of visual control is to make known immediately and clearly the needs and condition of the execution system at any point in time. For example, when a kanban signal appears, the worker immediately knows the type and the amount of production that is needed.

Visual control ultimately replaces tracking using computer systems with tracking using the eyes. Visual control emphasizes an intimacy and familiarity with those areas in the shop

[16] These and other tools are discussed in greater detail in the module "Total Quality Management: Frameworks, Measures, and Standards" by Steven A. Melnyk and Lawrence D. Fredendall (New York: McGraw-Hill/Irwin 2002).

floor where the "action" takes place. These places could be the shop floor of a manufacturing facility or the operating room of a hospital. Visual control is based on the view that the computer systems are not as informative as visual cues.

For visual control to work effectively and efficiently, the areas of interest must be organized to facilitate visual management. For example, no structure or floor stocks are allowed to be over four feet. Why four feet? If above four feet, the manager has difficulty seeing over the pile. Similarly, visual control strives to reduce the clutter on the floor that hides problems and reduces the urgency to respond. Visual control works to reduce waste by reducing reaction time by maintaining that sense of urgency found in any lean system.

Process Improvement Tools

This final set of lean systems tools provides means for identifying and solving problems in the different areas of system management.

Quality at the Source

To achieve the objectives of lean systems, a firm must develop new ways to identify and solve problems. It can no longer merely catch problems after they occur through inspections. Instead, improvement must focus on the sources of problems. The quality of a product is determined when it is made, and no amount of inspection will ever make it any better.[17]

An emphasis on **quality at the source (*Q@S*)** forces every person involved in a transformation process to recognize his or her role as a supplier to one or more internal or external customers. The quality of the outputs of later stages of production depends substantially on the quality of their inputs. Quality at the source also means that problems are addressed at the appropriate level and location. Problems due to poor material coming from our suppliers cannot be effectively solved by people on the shop floor. Rather, our personnel, working closely with the appropriate supplier's personnel, should address the problems at the supplier's location.

Human input is the key to successful implementation of quality at the source. Human workers must study, identify, analyze, uncover, and correct quality problems in the process. The operations manager, in turn, must support these human activities by providing sufficient training (e.g., in the problem-solving tools) and by implementing technology to help support human contributions. Quality at the source reinforces the major principle of lean systems that promotes respect for humans through three techniques: jidoka (autonomation), stop-and-fix/line-stop systems, and andons (trouble lights).

Jidoka

Jidoka, Japanese for autonomation, describes technological features of equipment and processes that detect problems while the systems run and flag these problems to operators.[18] A jidoka system tries to eliminate the need for the operator to spend time monitoring routine activities of a process. For example, a limit switch on a machine might monitor the contents of a feeding bin and light a signal or sound a tone when the bin becomes nearly empty to alert the operator to refill it. A counter might track the number of parts produced and light a signal or sound a tone when this number equals the amount needed.

Stop-and-Fix/Line-Stop Systems

A **stop-and-fix** or **line-stop system** works on the simple premise that an operator should stop the process and immediately fix any significant problem that arises rather than allowing it to continue making poor-quality output. Besides guarding against low quality, such a system causes serious discomfort at the source of the problem since its failure has shut down the process in a highly visible and immediate way, perhaps disrupting other operations that depend on the problem activity. This discomfort motivates employees to find a solution.

[17] Wantuck, *Just in Time in America,* p. 39.
[18] Suzaki, *New Manufacturing Challenge,* pp. 91–93.

In Practice

STOP-AND-FIX AT CHEVROLET

Implementing a stop-and-fix system can be a very cost-effective move. On the first day such a system was installed in a Chevrolet engine plant, an operator stopped the line because a piston-and-ring assembly had scored the cylinder wall on one of the engines. This old, recurring problem resulted from sharp edges and burrs left on the rings during manufacturing. The people on the shop floor could identify no quick fix, so they called the product engineer at another building across town. The engineer immediately saw the reasons for the problem and offered to write a change order to add a little chamfer (sloped shoulder) to eliminate the sharp edges. This pleased the plant workers, but they wondered why engineering had not addressed their earlier complaints about the same problem. The product engineer replied that, "I didn't know you had the problem." The old system suffered due to lack of a needed communication link between the plant, where the problem surfaced, and engineering, which held authority to make the necessary changes.

Source: Kenneth A. Wantuck, *Just in Time in America* (Southfield, MI: KWA Media, 1989), pp. 57–58.

Stop-and-fix systems differ from jidoka, in which the equipment sends the signal and stops itself. In contrast, stop-and-fix empowers the operator to stop the system as needed, as the In Practice box shows.

Andons/Trouble Lights

Programs to enhance quality at the source may rely on visual signals to identify the exact locations of problems in OM systems. Lean systems often combine these **andons,** or **trouble lights,** with jidoka and stop-and-fix systems to make problems highly visible, allowing workers to develop visual control of a process. For example, the Chevrolet engine plant might have placed a light over the workstation where the piston was inserted to act as an andon and shine when the worker noticed the problem. This light would communicate the problem to everyone on the shop floor, and it would identify the exact location of the problem. This would allow supervisors and engineers to go to the right place without wasting time finding it.

Poka-Yoke (Foolproofing)

One of the objectives of a lean system is to produce output with perfect quality every time. Unfortunately, within any process or system, there are many opportunities for error and confusion, and these arise for many reasons. Assembly workers may insert components upside down, or the setup workers may mount dies onto machines incorrectly. An incomplete process may force workers to supply missing information. Poor markings may allow confusion about how to combine parts. Poor communication about the exact sequence of activities may lead to variance when workers follow conflicting procedures. OM systems rely on the experience and accumulated knowledge of employees, but it is expensive if the workers gain this knowledge and experience by making errors.

To produce perfect quality the first time and every time, operations managers must identify these opportunities for error and eliminate them. They must design parts and processes that make the desired results inevitable. This goal design activity is known as **poka-yoke** or **foolproofing.**[19]

Some poka-yoke methods include

- Color code similar parts to help workers distinguish them (e.g., right is red, left is green).
- Set up counters to detect the number of welding operations on an assembly and compare this number with the standard. A warning signal sounds whenever the two numbers do not match.
- Place templates over an assembled component to show operators the differences between parts and how to insert them.

[19] Kiyoshi Suzaki, *The New Manufacturing Challenge: Techniques for Continuous Improvement* (New York: Free Press, 1987), pp. 98–101; Shigeo Shingo, *Zero Quality Control: Source, Inspection, and the Poka-Yoke System* (Norwalk, CT: Productivity Press, 1986).

Examples of poka-yoke abound in everyday life. For example, a standard electrical plug fits into an outlet in only one way because one of the two prongs is larger than the other. This ensures that people will insert the plug properly to create a grounded circuit.

Poka-yoke can yield a number of important benefits for an OM system. It reduces the cost of relearning and simplifies production scheduling. By strictly limiting the opportunity for worker errors, and the associated frustration, it often helps to improve employee morale.

Something to Think About

What poka-yokes are present in a video cassette?

Poka-Yoke and Human Discretion

Humans like to use some skills more than others. People, in general, do not perform especially well in tasks that involve monitoring, data recording, and checking. These are the tasks that poka-yoke tries to eliminate by replacing them with foolproof mechanisms. In contrast, people excel at recognizing patterns and differences and at problem solving. By eliminating the need for people to monitor data and check operations, poka-yoke frees employees to focus on solving more stubborn problems.

The 5-S Program

Effective housekeeping is an important and integral element of any lean system. It ensures that the workspace is clean and in order. It instills a sense of discipline in the operators. Finally, it helps to reduce the possibility of breakdowns by having the operators regularly check on the status of the equipment in their area. Companies using the lean systems approach often implement effective housekeeping using the **5-S program.**

The term "5-S" refers to the first letters of the five Japanese words that describe the major activities of this program. In some American companies, this program has been modified with the Japanese words being replaced by their American counterparts. In these cases, it is more commonly referred to as the 5-S campaign or the 5-C campaign. These terms and their intent are summarized in Exhibit 9.

EXHIBIT 9
Defining the Major Activities of the 5-S Program (and Its Variants

The 5-S Program	The 5-S Campaign	The 5-C Campaign	Intent
Seiri	Sort	Clear out	Separate all that is unnecessary and eliminate it.
Seiton	Straighten	Configure	Put everything in an orderly fashion so that it can be located—"a place for everything and everything in its place."
Seiso	Scrub	Clean and check	Clean everything and eliminate the sources of dirt.
Seiketsu	Systematize	Conform	Make cleaning and checking routine. Set the standard, train, and maintain.
Shitsuke	Standardize	Custom and practice	Standardize the previous four steps into one process and emphasize the concept of continuous improvement.

In Practice

THE 5-S PROGRAM APPLIED

Recently, the international purchasing manager for a large automotive company implemented the 5-S program in the support area of his department. This area was responsible for maintaining and providing the paperwork needed by the department. It was also responsible for ordering and delivering supplies. The problem was that these tasks were not being done well. Complaints were heard about supplies not being delivered when wanted (or even being lost), needed forms not being available, and too many forms being stocked.

The manager worked with the staff in this area (six secretaries), teaching them the 5-S program. They immediately applied the tools. They sorted through the forms and identified those that were no longer needed (segregate and discard). The forms that were not needed were put in a room down the hall. These forms were monitored to determine which could be discarded. The remaining forms were standardized to a smaller number. These forms were then moved to a closet where each form had its own area. The intent was to achieve the 30-second rule: any form could be found within 30 seconds. Ordering was simplified, with the items often immediately going to the person who placed the order. The results have been impressive: inventory is down, costs are down, speed is up. All of these benefits were achieved within less than six weeks, with very little capital investment (creativity before capital).

This program, while developed in Japan, has been used successfully in such American firms as GM, Masco, Lear, and Metaldyne. It also has been used for both manufacturing and support activities such as the filling out of purchase orders and the maintenance and management of office stores supplies.

The 5-S's Described

The 5-S program attempts to create a method and a process to maintain an organized, clean, focused, and high-performance workplace. It does this through a series of steps where each step builds on what has taken place before:

Step 1: **Seiri**—*Segregate and discard.* That is, review the workplace and identify those items (tools, parts, fixtures, and so on) that you use on a regular basis and those that you use infrequently. The ones that you use infrequently, you must discard. They only serve to create clutter and confusion. They hide problems and difficulties. The basic rule for this step is a simple one: "When in doubt, throw it out." Often, a procedure known as **red tagging** is used to visually label (with a red tag) all unnecessary items.

Step 2: **Seiton**—*Arrange and identify for ease of use.* This step is based on a simple but critical principle. Everything that we use should have its place and everything that we use should be in its place. This reduces the waste created by having to look for parts and tools because they are not "where they should be." A tool that aids this process is **footprinting,** where workers identify and outline with paint all the areas occupied by machines, workstations, bins, material, and carts. Each item is required to be in that spot. No item is allowed to occupy any other space.

Step 3: **Seiso**—*Clean daily.* This step is familiar to most people who have worked with total productive maintenance and just-in-time. This is the notion that housekeeping is a daily discipline. Why this emphasis? A clean workplace enhances quality, safety, and pride. It highlights problems. It encourages the employee to examine the work area regularly and to identify potential problems (and correct them) before they become serious.

Step 4: **Seiketsu**—*Revisit frequently.* It is not enough to go through the first three steps once. Rather, the first three steps are a continuous cycle. Each time we go through the cycle, we identify new opportunities for improvement. We also move from a remedial mindset (what do I have to do to correct the immediate problem) to a preventive mindset. That is, we try to develop and implement countermeasures to prevent dirt and problems from occurring in the first place.

Step 5: **Shitsuke**—*Motivate to sustain.* Here, we work at promoting a shop floor–wide adherence to maintaining a high-performance, high-quality, safe, and innovative workplace. We work at getting committed top management support. We encourage the implementation and use of visual performance measures such as **performance boards** that contain checklists, graphs, and status reports. Area supervisors, for example, must check that the workshop areas meet the 5-S principles before allowing people to leave work.

Benefits of the 5-S Program

The 5-S program has gained a great deal of attention because of the benefits that it offers management, employees, and the firm. Experiences have shown that when successfully implemented, the 5-S program leads to

- *An environment that encourages standard work.* This is a setting where the same task is done identically by everyone in the shop. With standard methods and procedures, an important and often overlooked source of variance—variances due to differences in method—is eliminated.
- *Creation of the conditions for perfect quality.*
- *Visual control.* Problems quickly become evident because they depart from the normal. For example, we know a tool is missing because it is not on the board where it should be and the outline filled by the tool is empty.
- *An intolerance for waste.*
- *A high value on safety.*
- *Increased employee satisfaction.*

5-S tools attempt to make these results inevitable, as illustrated by the In Practice box below.

Standardization/Simplification

Within the lean systems' perspective, waste and variance are closely linked. As variance increases, so does the opportunity for waste. Variance often occurs as a result of unnecessary complexity or a lack of standardization. Thus, **standardization** and **simplification** activities are integral to lean system implementation.

Consider the following example: Suppose that a workstation receives six containers of parts with 41, 38, 42 45, 40, and 48 units inside, respectively. The differences in unit counts may seem more of an annoyance or inconvenience than a major problem, but consider how they would complicate an inventory count. If every container holds a different number of parts, workers would have to physically count every part in every container. This time-consuming activity bores workers, and it creates no value.

To reduce the amount of time spent in such routine tasks, a lean systems' practitioner relies on process analysis techniques to identify and eliminate any unnecessary process steps. A related practice, standardization, replaces inconsistent or unstandardized methods with standard routines for process tasks. By defining a single method for all workers who perform any activity, operations managers can identify problems with equipment, materials, or worker capabilities. Also, employees can spend less time learning how to carry out an activity so they can spend more time identifying and correcting problems. The result is a **cycle of improvement,** as illustrated in Exhibit 10. This technique promotes continuous improvement in much the same way as the plan–do–check–act cycle or Deming wheel.

This emphasis on standardization can carry beyond individual tasks to address the overall layout of the workplace. A common or standard layout can reduce the amount of time

EXHIBIT 10
Cycle of Improvement

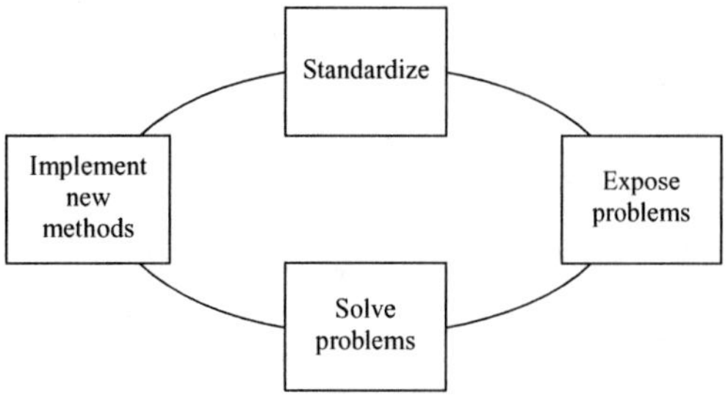

In Practice

STANDARDIZATION AT TOYOTA'S CAMRY PLANT

If you were to visit Toyota's Camry Plant in Kentucky, you would find a fierce devotion to the concept of standardization. This devotion even extends to the task of fastening seats into a Camry. There is a specific sequence in which the bolts are to be tightened. No deviation from this standard sequence is tolerated. Why such a fierce devotion? The answer is that the benefits far outweigh the costs. Management can monitor this activity and be able to predict the chances that the employee will be finished in the allotted time. Management knows when the first, second, third and fourth bolts are to be tightened. If the employee is lagging by the time that he or she gets to the second bolt, there is a good chance that he or she will not be able to get the seat fastened in time. Consequently, corrective actions can be taken immediately. Since there is only one way of doing the tasks, training is simplified. Third, when a problem occurs, the variation introduced by the employee because each employee has his or her own way of doing this task is eliminated. It is now easier to identify the root causes of problems. Standardization is now seen by everyone as providing a rich soil for continuous improvement.

Source: Steven Spear and H. Kent Bowen, "Decoding the DNA of the Toyota Production System," *Harvard Business Review,* Vol. 77, No. 5 (Sept/Oct 1999), pp. 96–106.

that workers spend looking for tools and inputs in unfamiliar surroundings. This also reduces the burden of training workers who move from one work center to another.

Standardization of shipping and storage containers could vastly simplify the task of maintaining accurate inventory records in the earlier example by filling every container with 40 units arranged in five layers of eight units each. To evaluate inventory, workers could then count the full containers and multiply the number by 40 to arrive at the number of units inside. They could then count the number of full layers in any partially full containers and multiply by 8, then add the few units in any partial layers. As shown in the In Practice box, standardization also can be used to facilitate problem solving and can become a predictive metric.

Something to Think About

There can be no continuous improvement where there is no standardization.

Kaizen/Continuous Improvement

Kaizen is a Japanese term that conveys the idea of never-ending improvement. The discipline of Kaizen unites everyone within the organization from top managers and operations managers to operating workers in pursuit of the goal of ongoing improvement.[20] A goal of kaizen is to inspire everyone in the company to improve one aspect of the operations management system, major or minor, every day.

Continuous improvement makes a lot of sense in theory, a lot less in practice. The reason is that if you are required to try to do something better each day, then after a while, the only types of improvements that you focus on are small and inconsequential. Increasingly, practitioners are moving from emphasizing constant Kaizen (which some describe as continuous pressure) to periodic events known as **Kaizen Events.** A Kaizen event is a group-based improvement effort that is short, intense, process-focused, inexpensive to implement, and highly successful.

This approach is being extensively used by companies such as General Motors, Chrysler, Honda, Toyota (where it was first developed), Donnelly (a major printer), Lear Corporation (a major supplier of automotive interiors), Masco/MascoTech, and the U.S. Navy.[21] Kaizen Events have been used to reduce office clutter in the purchasing department of a large company, to reduce the investment lead time (i.e., the time from the moment that money is withdrawn from an employee's check until that money is invested) for a 401(k) program of a large firm (at an annual real savings of $6.5 million), and to improve the efficiency of medical systems being used to treat patients. In each case, the Kaizen Event was a three- to four-day effort.

A Kaizen Event is characterized by the following traits:

[20] Masaaki Imai, *Kaizen: The Key to Japan's Competitive Success* (New York: Random House, 1986), p. xxix.

[21] T. McNicholas, R. Hassinger, and G. Bapst, "Quick and Continuous Improvement through Kaizen Blitz," *1997 APICS Conference,* Washington, DC (forthcoming); and J. P. Womack and D. T. Jones, *Lean Thinking: Banish Waste and Create Wealth in Your Corporation* (New York: Simon and Schuster, 1996).

In Practice

AN AMERICAN FIRM'S EXPERIENCES WITH KAIZEN EVENTS

The genesis of the Kaizen process at a major automotive supplier came when the chief operations officer and group presidents attended a Kaizen Event at another firm in a related industry. They were impressed enough to plan twenty-four Kaizen Events for their own firm in the following year. The firm hired a consulting firm to assist, and general managers attended Kaizen Events at other companies in order to gain a better understanding of the Kaizen approach.

Personnel from the firm's other sites observed the first Kaizen Event. It would be an understatement to say that things went well. Not only did the firm achieve quickly realized productivity gains, it found the Kaizen Event process very easy to use. So easy, in fact, that it held 51 Kaizen Events at various sites, more than double the planned 24.

In the next year, the firm continued and expanded the Kaizen approach. Customers and suppliers were included in Event teams. This showed the workers the deep commitment that the firm had made to the technique. In addition, including these groups extended the learning and improvement process beyond the firm's own organization to impact supply chain partners.

As the next step, the firm began developing its own Kaizen Event training materials, and trained its own Kaizen Event facilitators. By the end of the year, 77 Kaizen Events had been held. Examples of the benefits achieved through the use of Kaizen Events are summarized below.

Impact of 77 Kaizen Events in a 12-month period

Improvement Measurable	Before Kaizen	Achievement	Improvement
Floor Space (ft^2)	56,000	39,000	30%
Operators/Day	165	125	24%
Distance Traveled	91,000 ft.	15,000 ft.	84%
Inventory (WIP pieces)	4,760,000	2,570,000	46%
Setup Time Reduction	1,660 minutes	460 minutes	72%
Safety Improvements		200 improvements implemented	

- *Short term:* Kaizen events usually take between one and four days from start to finish. During this time period, the teams are introduced to the process analysis tools they will use. They then study the process, identify opportunities for improvement, implement them, assess the impact, redo the cycle, and present their results to management. Tools such as the process flow analysis procedures, the 5-S program, and TAKT time are used.
- *Team-oriented:* The responsibility for an event is placed in the hands of a cross-functional team that consists of employees from the process being studied, employees outside of the process, management and, in some cases, supplier representatives. It is responsible for studying, implementing, assessing, and improving the process. As a result, there is ownership by the employees of these changes.
- *Highly focused:* One specific process is identified and all the attention of the team is focused on studying, documenting, analyzing, and improving the performance of that process.
- *Action-oriented:* An interesting feature of this process is the immediacy of action. That is, any change that has been identified and approved by the group is immediately implemented. The only major constraint is that the changes not require any major funding or capital requests. Equipment layout is changed as required (this does dictate the involvement of facilities management). After the changes have been implemented, the new system is run and the resulting performance documented and compared with the old system.
- *Verifiable metrics:* Improvements in the process must be verified. Typically this is done using metrics such as floor space occupied by the process, operators required per day, distance traveled by an order within the process, work-in-process inventory (in piece count), setup time (measured in minutes), quality recommendations generated, and safety improvements implemented.
- *Repetitive:* Once begun, Kaizen events are regularly repeated. Each event generates an action list or a list of opportunities for improvement identified by the team in areas that they could address within their event. These items, in turn, become the focal point for future Kaizen Events.

These characteristics are illustrated in In Practice box.

Module Summary

To achieve the various objectives of lean systems, managers must draw on a large number of tools and procedures. This module has identified and examined several of these tools and procedures. In reviewing this module, several major observations can be made:

1. There are a large number of tactical tools such as pull scheduling, setup reduction, foolproofing, and quality at the source. These tools tend to be very focused and deal with one area involving variance and waste.
2. The attainment of lean system goals also involves the use of several broad-based tools and procedures such as synchronized flows, the 5-S program, group technology, visual control, and the focused factory. These tools affect multiple areas in the pursuit of waste and variance reduction.
3. Critical to the success of lean systems is the pursuit of continuous improvement. Increasingly, this concept has been implemented using the vehicle of the Kaizen Event. This approach is attractive because it is a proven procedure that generates real results very quickly at very low costs.
4. The various lean systems' tools are highly versatile: They can be applied in manufacturing and service settings, to standard and to nonstandard products, and in any setting where waste and variance are present.

Key Terms

Andons/trouble lights, *18*
Continuous improvement, *22*
Corrective maintenance, *7*
Cycle of improvement, *21*
External setup, *16*
5-S program, *19*
Flexible/cross-trained workers, *4*
Focused factory, *6*
Footprinting, *20*
Group technology, *4*
Internal setup, *16*
Jidoka, *17*
Just-in-time systems, *3*
Kaizen, *22*
Kaizen Event, *22*
Kanban, *10*
Lean systems, *3*
Learning time, *14*
Level, mixed-model scheduling, *14*
Load leveling, *13*
Machine cycle time (MCT), *9*
Master production schedule, *12*
Net available operating time (NAOT), *8*
Operator cycle time (OCT), *9*
Performance boards, *20*
Plants-within-a-plant, *6*
Poka-yoke (foolproofing), *18*
Process preparation time, *14*
Process teardown time, *14*
Production kanban, *10*
Pull scheduling, *10*
Push scheduling, *10*
Quality at the source (Q@S), *17*
Red tagging, *20*
Seiketsu, *20*
Seiri, *20*
Seiso, *20*
Seiton, *20*
Setup reduction, *15*
Shitsuke, *20*
Single-minute exchange of dies (SMED), *15*
Standardization/simplification, *21*
Statistical process control, *16*
Stop-and-fix/line-stop systems, *17*
TAKT time (T-T), *8*
Total productive maintenance, *7*
Visual control, *5*
Withdrawal kanban, *10*

Discussion Questions

1. Explain what you think are the underlying principles of lean systems.
2. Relate the objectives of lean systems to the lean systems' various tools described within the module.
3. Why is achievement of the following goals critical to the success of lean systems?
   a. Setup time and cost reduction.
   b. A relatively stable shop load.
   c. Employee empowerment.
   d. Statistical quality control.

   Give an example of how each area contributes to the success of a Lean System program.
4. You are given the following information about a plant:

   2 shifts per day
   20 days of production per month
   8 hours per shift
   2 breaks per shift of 15 minutes each
   lunch time per shift–30 minutes
   clean up time–15 minutes
   26,000 units required per month

Operation	Cycle Time
1	15 seconds
2	60 seconds
3	20 seconds

a. What is the TAKT time for this operation?
b. How many operators do you need? How would you assign them?

5. How would a restaurant use the 5-S program? How would an operating room using this program?
6. To what extent does the 5-S program draw on Visual Control approaches? Look at the five elements and identify those elements that provide the strongest examples of 5-S in action. Also provide examples of 5-S procedures that are essentially implementations of Visual Control.
7. Your boss asks you how many kanban cards each location within your plant needs. What factors should go into your answer? Create a formula to answer this question.
8. How does the concept of system variance impact your ability to drive inventory out of a plant when a lean systems' approach has been adopted? Create an electronic spreadsheet model to show how a reduction in demand variance impacts inventory in a two-stage manufacturing process.
9. Discuss how lead time reduction impacts a kanban system.
10. Under what conditions are the use of kanbans and pull scheduling least appropriate?
11. Why should you include setup times when calculating the TAKT times?
12. How do the first three steps of the 5-S program contribute to our ability to identify and eliminate waste and variance?
13. Apply the 5-S program to your work or studio area. To what extent was it applicable?
14. What is the relationship between bottlenecks and TAKT time?
15. Why do we need flexible/cross-trained employees and easily moved equipment to realize the objectives of Synchronized Flow (and TAKT Time)?
16. Our goal is to develop and encourage the growth of a flexible/cross trained work force? How would this goal affect the following activities that you as an operations manager may be involved in:
    a. recruiting of employees;
    b. employee assignment (i.e., to what extent are the employees assigned to work positions or work groups);
    c. job compensation; and,
    d. performance evaluation.
17. Your objective is to reduce setup times at a particular work center. As a first step, you decide to study the current setup procedures. What quality tools might you draw on to evaluate the setup process and to describe its various attributes?
18. In setup reduction, one of the major objectives is to convert internal setup times to external setup times? Why? What is the rationale underlying this goal?
19. As setup times fall, we can expect that the minimum order quantities (the minimum number of items that we have to make the order economically viable) should also fall. As these minimum order quantities fall, what are the potential strategic implications for the firm? That is, how does an improved ability to run smaller order quantities more frequently affect how the firm competes in the marketplace?
20. You are evaluating a work station for a potential setup reduction program. Your initial assessment has identified the following about the current setup:

Number of parts scrapped during setup	8 (10 minutes of labor per part and $2.50 of material costs per part)
Setup time required	1 hour 30 minutes
Requires one setup person @ $25.00 per hour (a constrained resource)	
Requires one tool kit (which contains $30.00 of consumables)	
Operator cost	$14.00 per hour
Physical machine downtime	1 hour 30 minutes

Given this information:

a. What is the internal setup time? What is the external setup time?
b. Cost accounting evaluates the setup cost at $50. Is this an accurate assessment of the setup costs?

   c. The equipment that you have studied is considered to be a bottleneck. Cost accounting is concerned about the extent to which this setup reduction project is really economically justifiable. How would you justify the need for setup reduction in this work center?

21. What features of a Kaizen Event make it very attractive to
   a. Management.
   b. Employees.
   c. Shareholders.
22. In the Foundations module, you were told that problems could arise in one of four areas: products, process, metrics, and customers. To which of these four is the Kaizen Event approach most appropriate? Why? What would you expect to see occur if we were to apply the Kaizen Event approach to a problem area for which it was not appropriate?
23. Many practitioners of the Kaizen Event recommend that it not be done more than once a month. Would you expect to occur if we were to apply it more frequently? Consider the following real situation: A firm carried out some 277 Kaizen Events within one year at one location. Management came to the conclusion that this approach did not work. Why? What went wrong?
24. One Lean Systems' consultant has stated that "without standardization, there can be no improvement." Why? What does standardization offer that enables improvement and waste elimination to take place?
25. Can we apply these lean system tools in a supply chain environment?

Cases

GOOD GUY HOSPITAL $UPPLY

Good Guy Hospital $upply (GGH$) was founded in the 1960s to serve the hospital and nursing home industry. Over the past 35 years, its sales have grown an average 26 percent per year, through both geographical expansion and increased existing-market penetration. Key to GGH$'s success is service. It prides itself that it is able to fill 99.4 percent of all requests within 24 hours and many requests actually are delivered more quickly.

In 1996, GGH$'s quality service coordinator developed a plan to improve service levels. The new system uses a just-in-time approach to the medical supply needs of GGH$'s clients.

GGH$'s clients had been using personal computers in their hospital medical supply stockrooms to place GGH$ orders. While these clients could still purchase from other supply houses, the GGH$ order entry system made it much easier for the clerical staff to place an order with GGH$.

The new JIT plan, however, eliminates supplies going through GGH$'s clients' medical supply stockroom. Now the medical facility's staff and GGH$ would determine the type and desired level of supplies at each stocking point. GGH$ plans to place supplies at each of these stocking points; and a GGH$ sales representative will tour the medical facility, identify items that have been used, and immediately restock them using inventory in the sales representative's van. Using barcoded stock and a mobile sales register, GGH$ will give the hospital a detailed invoice for the items consumed each day. These reports will be designed to support each facility's medical cost control system.

GGH$'s quality service coordinator argues that the increased distribution costs of this proposed system will be offset by increased product and service pricing and by the increased share of each hospital's business, and GGH$ will become the vendor of choice for all items covered by its system. She argues that the hospitals will find this system attractive because it will greatly reduce their costs for stocking, ordering, and distributing medical supplies within the medical facility.

QUESTIONS

1. Is Good Guy's plan an appropriate application of JIT? Why or why not?
2. Identify each of the stakeholders in this situation. What will each give up and get if the proposed system is accepted by GGH$'s clients?

ROBOWORKS, INC.

An engineering student at MIT, Roberta Reese created an all-purpose household robot for her senior project. Her project attracted a venture capitalist's interest.

The initial product line included three battery-powered robots code-named Red, Blue, and Yellow. Red uses vacuum technology to clean carpets and dust shelves. Blue uses water-jet technology to clean dishes, toilet bowls, bath tubs, and the like. Yellow can do Red's work and Blue's work.

The material used for these three models is shown below.

I. Red
  A. Vacuum system
    1. Sensing system
    2. Vacuum kit
  B. Mobile platform R
    1. Wheel set
    2. R batteries

II. Blue
  A. Cleaning system
    1. Sensing system
    2. Washer/dryer kit
  B. Mobile platform B
    1. Wheel set
    2. B Batteries

III. Yellow
  A. Vacuum system
    1. Sensing system
    2. Vacuum kit
  B. Cleaning system
    1. Sensing system
    2. Washer/dryer kit
  C. Mobile platform C
    1. Wheel set
    2. R batteries
    3. B batteries

Reese has hired Taiichi O'Brien as the production manager to design the production system. O'Brien has extensive experience with just-in-time. JIT appeals to Reese because she has limited capital. Taiichi decided on a two-stage system. The cleaning, vacuum, and mobile platforms would be assembled in the first stage. The second stage consists of the final assembly and testing.

O'Brien sets up the following manufacturing floor plan:

Finished Goods	Subassembly Units	Raw Materials
Red	Vacuum systems	Vacuum kit
	Cleaning systems	Cleaning kit
		R Base
Blue	Red base	B Base
		Wheels
	Blue base	R batteries
Yellow	Yellow base	B batteries

Production moves from raw materials through the subassembly department to finished goods. Reese estimates the daily demand for each product to have the following distributions:

Red	Discrete uniform	Range: 1 thru 6
Blue	Discrete uniform	Range: 1 thru 6
Yellow	Unsure	

Yellow has a strange demand distribution. Reese estimates demand for Yellow as the difference between the demand for Red and Blue—the demand for Yellow is the larger of the demands for Red and Blue minus the smaller of the demands for Red and Blue.

O'Brien needs to determine the number of kanban cards for each stocking point. Given the plant's ample capacity, both the finished goods and the subassembly unit departments can live with a one-day lead time. Reese's suppliers all demand five days to deliver goods (goods ordered on day 1 are delivered at the start of day 6). Vacuum and cleaning kits can be ordered individually, whereas all other products must be ordered in quantities of 10.

QUESTION

How many kanban cards does Roboworks need to avoid stockouts?

Selected Readings

Abegglen, James C., and George Stalk, Jr. *Kaisha: The Japanese Corporation.* New York: Basic Books, 1985.

Bhote, Keki R. *Strategic Supply Management: A Blueprint for Revitalizing the Manufacturer-Supplier Partnership.* New York: American Management Association, 1989.

Ford, Henry. *Today and Tomorrow.* Cambridge, Mass.: Productivity Press, 1989.

Grieco, Peter L., Michael W. Gozzo, and Jerry W. Claunch. *Just-in-Time Purchasing: In Pursuit of Excellence.* Plantsville, Conn.: PT Publications, 1988.

Hall, Robert W. *Zero Inventories,* New York: McGraw-Hill/Irwin, 1983.

Nakajima, Seiichi. *TPM: Introduction to TPM, Total Productive Maintenance.* Cambridge, Mass.: Productivity Press, 1988.

Shingo, Shigeo. *A Revolution in Manufacturing: The SMED System.* Cambridge, Mass.: Productivity Press, 1985.

Stewart, Douglas M., and Melnyk, Steven A. "Effective Process Management: Developing Poka-Yoke Processes." *Production and Inventory Management,* Vol. 41 (2000), No. 4, pp. 48–55.

Suzaki, Kiyoshi. *The New Manufacturing Challenge: Techniques for Continuous Improvement.* New York: Free Press, 1987.

Womack, James P., and Jones, Daniel T. *Lean Thinking: Banish Waste and Create Wealth in your Corporation.* New York, NY: Simon & Schuster, 1996.

Supply Chain Structure and Strategy

Steven A. Melnyk
Michigan State University

Morgan Swink
Michigan State University

McGraw-Hill Irwin

Boston Burr Ridge, IL Dubuque, IA Madison, WI New York San Francisco St. Louis
Bangkok Bogotá Caracas Kuala Lumpur Lisbon London Madrid Mexico City
Milan Montreal New Delhi Santiago Seoul Singapore Sydney Taipei Toronto

Supply Chain Structure and Strategy

Module objectives

By the end of this module, you should be able to

- Describe the key elements of a supply chain and the supply-chain paradigm.
- Understand the roles of upstream and downstream players in the supply chain and be able to explain how these players add value in a value-driven operations management system.
- State the pros and cons of vertical integration.
- Understand strategic supply-chain design issues including trade-offs in supply-chain structure, supply-base segmentation, and global supply.
- Understand the dynamic nature of the supply chain and the factors that drive inefficiency in supply-chain relationships.
- Understand the purpose and objectives of major policy and technological initiatives that are being applied at various stages across the supply chain today.
- Apply important metrics for evaluating the performance of the supply chain.

Souping up the Supply Chain

Even in this "just-in-time" age, the production line that churns out Hewlett-Packard ink-jet printers in Newark, California, is impressive. In response to electronic orders from customers around the country, parts trucked in moments earlier are loaded onto a 110-foot assembly line. Finished printers fly off the other end and soon are aboard another truck headed to a distributor. The operation is seamless and speedy. But then, what would you expect from one of America's premier high-tech corporations?

You might think that the factory belongs to Hewlett-Packard Co., but you would be wrong. It is owned by Solectron Corporation, a contract manufacturer. What's more, even as Milpitas, California–based Solectron pumps out HP's printers, its 24 production lines are simultaneously assembling everything from pagers to television decoding boxes for some of the biggest brand names in electronics.

Solectron is part of a new breed of U.S. supercontractors that promise to revolutionize operations management well into the next century. It commands dozens of factories and supply networks around the world. Increasingly, it also manages its customers' entire product lines, offering an array of services from design to inventory management to delivery and after-sales service. Its unusually flexible operations are surprisingly profitable, producing returns on assets in the range of 20 percent.

In place of traditional contracting relationships between client and supplier, arrangements with companies such as Solectron represent a sort of extended enterprise—a set of partnerships between product developers and specialists in components, distribution, retailing, and manufacturing.

The resulting organization can be so tight as to behave like a single, closely knit company —only better. Its strategies can slash time and costs out of the supply chain, the process between the invention of a new product and the time it reaches the consumer. Customers say they have achieved cost efficiencies of 15 to 25 percent already. And that, says James E. Morehouse, a logistics expert at A.T. Kearny, Inc., is only 5 to 10 percent of U.S. industries' potential. This is the closest thing to a real win-win situation ever encountered.

Source: Pete Engardio, "Souping Up the Supply Chain," *Business Week,* August 31, 1998, pp. 110, 112.

Growth of the Supply Chain Paradigm and Its Relationship to Value

A major change is taking place in how companies define, build, and manage operations management systems. Increasingly, operations managers are seeking to coordinate activities inside and outside their corporate boundaries. The partnership experience of Hewlett-Packard,

EXHIBIT 1

Conceptual View of the Supply Chain

Source: Supply chain faculty, Michigan State University, Lansing, MI.

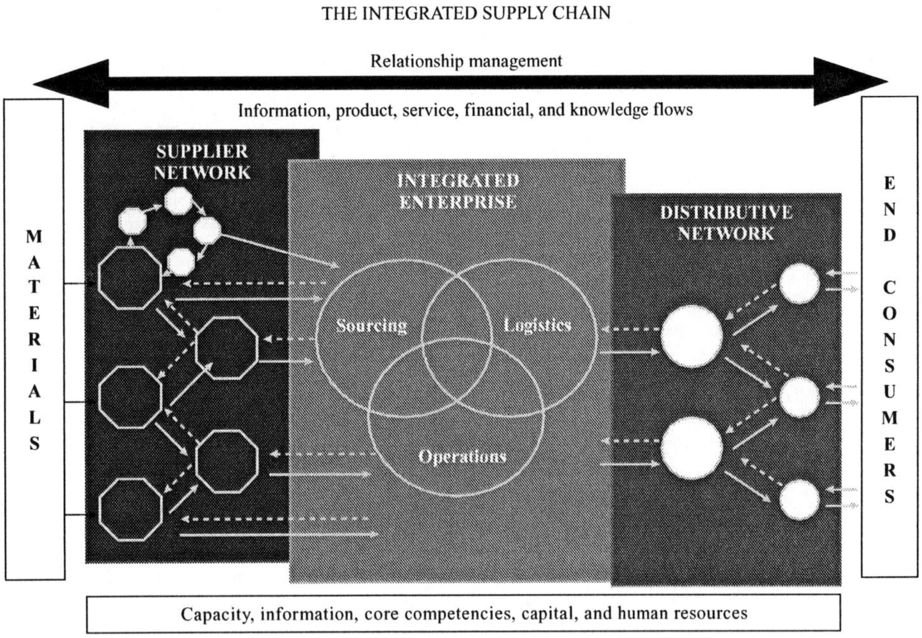

as described above, has been duplicated by Kodak, Chrysler, Wal-Mart, Procter & Gamble, Nintendo, Ford, Marriott Hotels, and a host of other firms. These firms are redefining their operations management systems because it is the best way of providing the types of value that their customers now want. Managers are finding that they must blur the boundaries between their own operations, that is, the **internal factories,** and those of their suppliers and customers, the so-called **external factories.** The result is a broader and more responsive operations management system, a system that comprises many organizations. Exhibit 1 illustrates this system, which we call the integrated supply chain.

"The boundaries between companies will blur as they view themselves as part of an ecosystem, supply chain, or value chain."

Hasso Plattner, co-founder and vice chairman, SAP

"Supply Chain Management will be the major and continued source of value as we move into the 21st century."

Ralph Drayer, vice president, Procter & Gamble

If you asked three persons in different businesses to define the term *supply chain,* you would probably receive three different definitions. For some, the phrase *supply chain* conjures thoughts of purchasing, procurement, and other activities needed to acquire raw materials and components for production. For others, supply chain means warehousing and distribution, transportation, and retail channels. For still others, supply chain refers to sources of capital or human resources. In this text we will adopt a very holistic definition of the supply chain.

Supply chain: The entire network of organizations involved in (1) converting raw materials and information into products and services, (2) consuming the products and services, and (3) disposing of the products and services.

This definition treats the supply chain as a product cradle-to-grave concept, including all value-added activities required to plan, source, make, and deliver products and services that meet customer needs.

The emergence and growth of **supply-chain management** as a dominant paradigm in the operations management system is a value-driven response to certain forces now present in the marketplace. Following are a few of the reasons for this fundamental shift:

Demands for the Flexibility of Partnership

In today's marketplace, customers' expectations are continually rising, and their desires, needs, and preferences are constantly changing. Globalization, improved communications networks, and technological changes now offer customers more choices and greater ability to make comparisons. Due to these dynamics, organizations today must be flexible—able to respond quickly to changing needs and opportunities. Value in this environment is a moving target, making it very difficult for a single organization to possess all the capabilities required to deliver value today and tomorrow. Integrated supply chains are better suited to meet the demands of this new environment. Instead of going through the costly and time-consuming process of acquiring the resources and knowledge required to meet a new demand, firms now look for **suppliers** that offer needed skills, systems, and capabilities. A firm can easily form partnerships with appropriately skilled suppliers that last as long as the need exists. As demands change, the firm can quickly respond by changing suppliers and forming new partnerships.

Advances in Technology

Recent advances in communications, computers, and graphics technologies have facilitated the growth of supply-chain partnerships by enabling extensive connectivity. Earlier, computer power was limited and people passed information either by telephone or by mail, creating disjointed information flows. Today's computer networks, electronic data interchange (EDI) systems, graphics standards, and the Internet enable people working in different areas of the country or around the world to maintain constant contact. Since information transactions have become so easy, there is less of a need to include all operations within one organizational boundary.

These new information capabilities offer a variety of opportunities to increase value. Constant information sharing between supply-chain partners improves efficiencies in planning, in material movements, and in the transfer of funds. For example, EDI systems link computers, allowing suppliers and buyers to exchange all forms of information instantly. A buyer's computer system can release a schedule to the supplier's computer system without human intervention. In turn, a supplier can routinely access production schedule updates by browsing through the buyer's computer system, reserving important communications for problems that require everyone's attention. EDI facilitates real-time scheduling, monitoring, and payment systems. As a result, the partnering firms hold lower inventories and they incur fewer transaction costs. These lower costs are passed on to the customer in the form of lower prices and better value.

Collaborative Networks

Firms have come to realize that great improvements in value can be realized by coordinating the efforts of partners along the supply chain. When firms concentrate only on their internal operations, they are uncertain about decisions suppliers and customers are making. Consequently, they tend to react to external changes in demand or supply without knowing the cause or severity of the changes. Firms that operate in isolation quickly find that by following such an approach, the overall performance across the supply chain deteriorates. The symptoms are clear: inventory is too high, replenishment lead times are too long, and too many items are not available when they are needed. These problems can be remedied when partners in a supply chain share plans and other information.

Recognition of Core Competencies

In the past, firms based their decisions on markets and products. For example, RCA saw itself as a manufacturer of televisions for the mass market; General Motors viewed itself as a car manufacturer for style-conscious buyers. Recently, there has been a shift away from thinking only about markets and products toward considering core competencies.

A focus on core competencies leads a firm to concentrate on those few skills and areas of knowledge that make the firm distinct and competitive. A **core competency** is a unique set of skills that confer a competitive advantage because rival firms cannot easily duplicate them. Recognizing that some internal processes are core competencies and that some are not has led many firms to consider outsourcing noncore activities. For example, Honda was one of the first companies to exploit its core competencies in the production of engines and motors, concentrating on products—lawn mowers, automobiles, generators—in which success depended on reliable motors. Honda outsourced noncore competencies such as component manufacturing, logistics, and certain services. This rationalization of activities produces supply chains where each of the partnering organizations focuses on what it does best. The overall effect is to produce greater value through higher quality and greater efficiencies.

The combined effects of more dynamic markets, technological innovations, collaborative networks, and a focus on core competencies have promoted the growth of supply-chain management as a central focus of operations management. The ultimate objective of the supply-chain approach is the seamless integration of the various supply-chain partners. As we saw with Hewlett-Packard and Solectron, seamless integration creates a situation where we cannot easily tell where one firm's responsibilities begin and where the other firm's responsibilities end. These integrated capabilities offer several value-based benefits:[1]

- A faster response to shifts in market demand, enabling an increase in market share or the avoidance of obsolete inventories.
- Improved linkages with suppliers that maximize suppliers' value-added activities.
- Quick-response manufacturing capable of mass customization if necessary and directly driven by actual customer demands.
- An order fulfillment process that integrates all of a customer's needs and provides service levels that are a competitive strength.

In the following sections, we look at the elements of the supply chain more closely as we examine important strategies and tactics for managing relationships among customers, suppliers, and the firm.

The Structure of the Supply Chain

As we noted earlier, the supply chain in its broadest form consists of all the parties involved in the planning, sourcing, making, delivery, consumption, and disposal of a product. This process begins ultimately with the extraction of resources from the earth. It ends with the return, reclamation, or disposal of any associated residuals (waste). The supply chain brings together and integrates the activities of all the parties involved.

Exhibit 2 on page 6 identifies important groups of partners in the supply chain. From a single firm's perspective, there are upstream suppliers, downstream suppliers, technology/resource suppliers, aftermarket suppliers, and customers. Upstream suppliers typically provide raw materials, components, and services, for example, warehousing. Downstream suppliers typically provide enhancements to the firm's finished goods, for example, assembly, packaging, or other value-added activities, storage, and transportation services. Technology/resource suppliers provide equipment, labor, process design, and other resources needed to enable and improve production processes. Aftermarket suppliers provide product service and support such as maintenance, repair, disposal, or recycling.

The **upstream supply chain** brings together four major sets of partners: (1) production planning, (2) suppliers, (3) purchasing, and (4) logistics. Schedules produced by production planning activities drive the upstream supply chain. Suppliers are held accountable for meeting scheduled needs. Purchasing, the third partner, is the functional group within the firm that is responsible for managing the interface between the firm and its suppliers. Finally, logistics is responsible for managing the flows of materials and information between the various elements of the supply chain.

[1] Supply Chain Council, *Integrated Supply Chain Performance Measurement: A Multi-Industry Consortium Recommendation,* Supply Chain Council Report #5566, p. 1.

EXHIBIT 2
Important Partners and Players in the Supply Chain

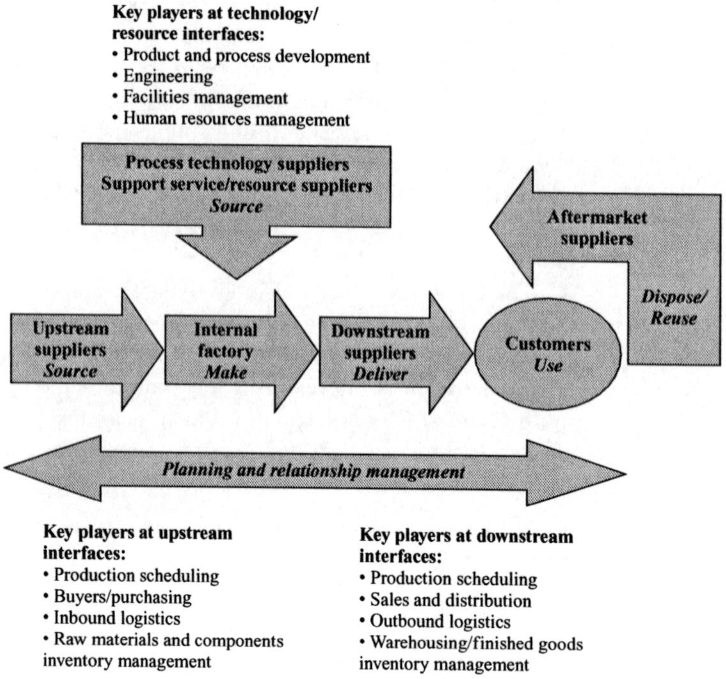

The **downstream supply chain** also involves production planning, suppliers, and logistics functions. Sales and distribution functions manage the interface between the firm and its downstream suppliers and customers. Sales personnel work with distribution and inventory management personnel to generate demand forecasts that generate production plans.

The horizontal dimension of Exhibit 2 illustrates the flow of materials, information, and money related to the sourcing, making, and delivery of primary *products.* The vertical dimension of Exhibit 2 depicts suppliers of technologies and support services. These suppliers are involved in the procurement and installation of *resources* necessary to execute production. For example, these include suppliers of production equipment, maintenance, repair, and operating items; facility cleaning; food preparation; and security services. Technology and resource suppliers interface with product and process designers, engineers, and internal resource managers such as those that manage facilities and human resources. As we will see, each partner in the supply chain performs a set of important activities necessary to deliver superior value.

Actual supply chains usually involve many stages of sourcing, making, and delivery, and these stages are not always sequential. For example, consider the supply chain for a manufacturer of high-end, mechanical watches depicted in Exhibit 3. There are several stages of supply involved in the upstream supply chain. In supply chain parlance, each stage is known as a **tier.** The tier number (first, second, and third) refers to how closely the supplier works with the firm. A first-tier supplier provides components and services directly to the firm. A second-tier supplier provides components to the first-tier supplier, and so on.

Each tier of the upstream supply chain could involve multiple suppliers for the same items or services. Also, a single supplier might provide materials for multiple stages of the supply process. (Note that suppliers of fabricated metal parts provide parts for movement subassemblies and wristbands as well as for final assemblies.) In addition to suppliers of components that are assembled into watches, there are also suppliers of indirect materials and goods used in production processes. For example, in order to run a watch assembly factory, the factory must purchase machine tools, light bulbs, fire extinguishers, and so forth.

There are also multiple levels making up the downstream side of the supply chain. These levels are commonly referred to as **echelons.** A single echelon might contain partners in locations all over the world. Furthermore, the downstream supply chain can be broken into different channels of distribution. Different channels might appeal to specific customer

EXHIBIT 3
Supply Chain for a Mechanical Watch Manufacturer

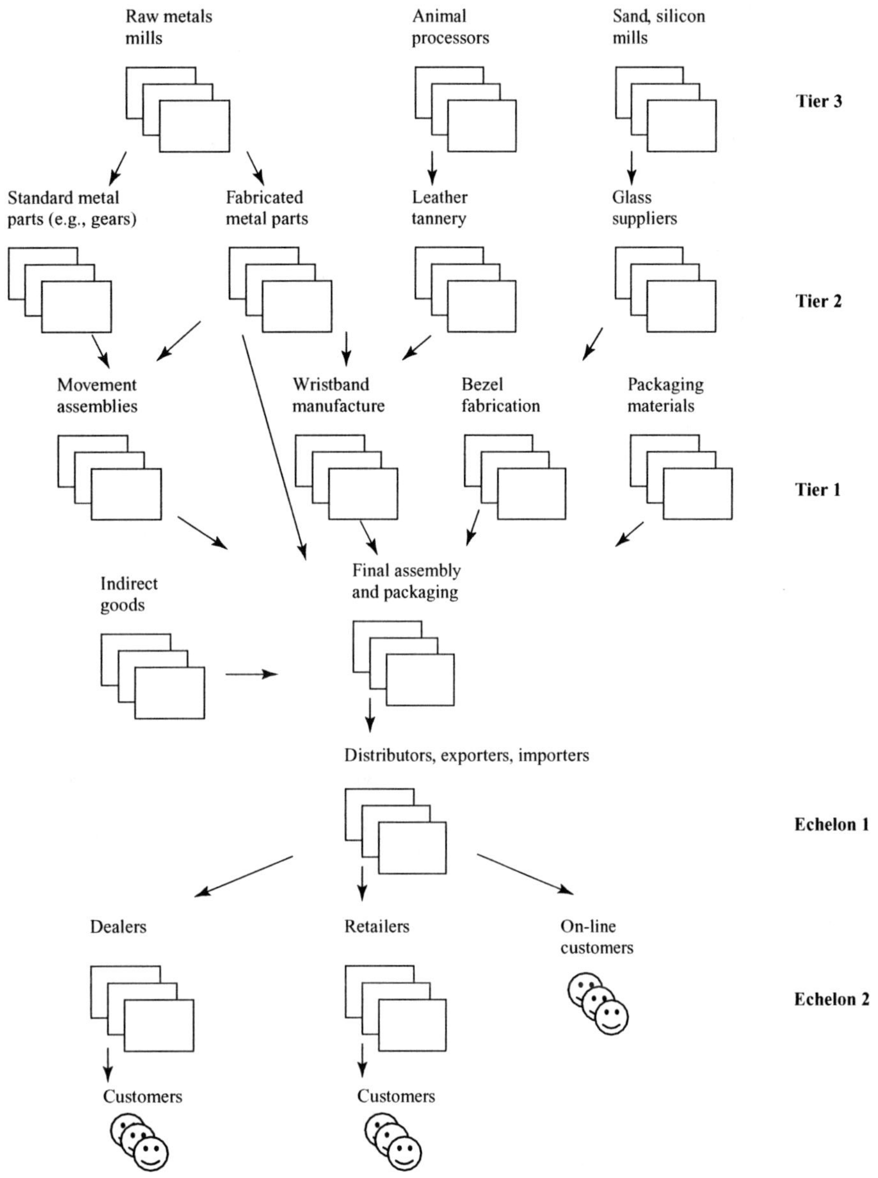

groups that value certain aspects of the purchase experience. For example, Exhibit 3 indicates three separate channels linking distributors to customers.

Not shown in Exhibit 3 are a host of other suppliers who make up a part of the total chain. First, there are many service providers that transport goods, maintain equipment, operate food or cleaning services, or supply other necessary activities. Second, there are frequently a number of "middlemen" organizations that serve as mediators between stages of the supply chain. Instead of dealing directly with suppliers of standard parts and components, the watch manufacturer may buy from manufacturers' representatives, distributors, or wholesalers. Finally, there are suppliers of energy and natural resources; suppliers of process equipment, labor, and materials; and suppliers of information and expertise. For example, engineering firms supply expertise for product design and technical decisions.

As one can see, the entire supply chain for even a relatively simple product can be quite complex. For most products, there are literally hundreds of firms involved in the harvesting, manufacturing, assembly, distribution, and sales processes. Moreover, each supplier shown in Exhibit 3 produces other products and has connections with suppliers and customers in other markets. Thus, all firms in an industry are ultimately connected to one another through links of sourcing, making, and delivery for different products and services in various markets.

Supply-Chain Strategy

Managers are rarely presented with the opportunity to design a supply chain from scratch. Instead, the structure of supply chains evolves over time as many individual decisions and supplier choices are made. This makes it very important that an overall strategy for the supply chain is well articulated and well understood by all decision makers in purchasing, logistics, manufacturing, product development, and other relevant functions. Many issues are relevant to supply-chain strategy decisions. In this module we will address only a few of the major ones, including sourcing decisions, required performance characteristics, supply-base segmentation, and globalization.

Insourcing, Outsourcing, and Vertical Integration

One of the key decisions a firm faces is deciding which operations it will accomplish internally, that is, **insourced,** and which operations and items it will purchase from suppliers, that is, **outsourced.** All business firms depend on at least some suppliers for support, ranging from the supply of paper clips to major subsystems. Even if a company could feasibly generate all of the inputs it needs to make its products internally, it would still choose to buy from suppliers for several compelling reasons:

Better cost and quality: Suppliers have specialized resources, facilities, economies of scale, and expertise to produce items and services at low costs and high quality. Firms that attempt to do too many things lose the focus needed to achieve superior performance.

Greater flexibility: Purchasing goods from suppliers enables a firm to avoid making investments in equipment and other capital resources that would limit the firm's ability to adapt to changes in market demands, technologies, or economic conditions.

Enhanced market reputation: By purchasing inputs from suppliers with strong reputations for quality, a firm can enhance its own product's quality image.

Easier availability of capacity: By subcontracting, a firm can quickly acquire additional production capacity in times of strong demand without bearing the burden of paying for wasted capacity when demand declines.

Broader access to technical expertise: Evaluating and choosing from multiple suppliers enables a firm to find and tap into the best technical expertise available.

Better market information: Suppliers often serve multiple customers in many markets, enabling them to share valuable intelligence with buying firms regarding new technological developments, competitors' actions, labor–management relations, and customer behavior.

The spectrum in Exhibit 4 illustrates how the benefits offered by suppliers tend to be viewed by purchasing firms. At one end, through **product (capacity) buys,** firms seek to augment their own production capabilities by finding suppliers that provide low-cost, high-quality inputs that enhance the firm's name recognition while furnishing flexible excess production capacity. These purchases outsource production that could be done internally but not as well. At this end of the spectrum, economic considerations drive the purchase decision;

EXHIBIT 4
Spectrum of Supplier Activities/Functions

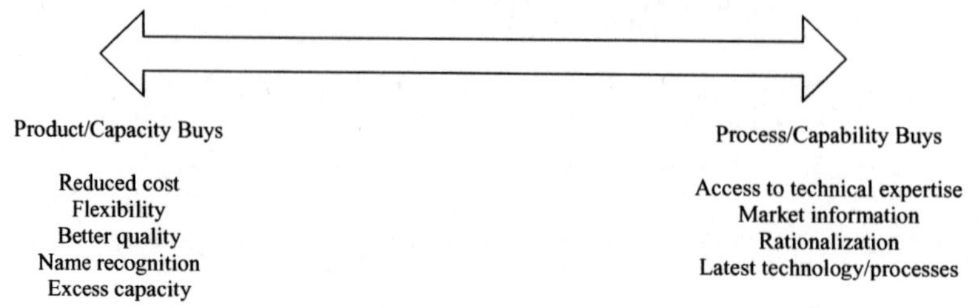

In Practice

VERTICAL INTEGRATION FOR SUPPLY CHAIN AT FORD MOTOR COMPANY

In his 1926 book entitled *Today and Tomorrow,* Henry Ford summarized many of the lessons he learned in managing the Ford Motor Company. One of these lessons involved the importance of the supply chain and the need to control it. By the early 1910s, Ford had developed a transformation process that ran like clockwork. In Ford's system, every form and source of variance had been identified, analyzed, and eliminated or controlled. Yet, Ford was still unable to create a system that was totally under control. Why? Because the system was still susceptible to the problems originating with the various suppliers.

Ford assigned managers to study the problem of his suppliers. What they found greatly bothered him. Although Ford's factories were models of efficiency, in which housekeeping was emphasized and employees well paid, the factories of the suppliers were often poorly organized, poorly run, and chaotic. Worse yet, workers were frequently poorly paid, poorly trained, and overworked.

To solve this problem, Ford took the radical step of acquiring all suppliers in the supply chain between his factories and the raw materials. By the mid 1920s, the supply chain linking Ford to the sources of raw material was almost totally owned by Ford and managed by Ford-appointed managers.

The result was total control. Iron ore was mined from Ford mines. It was then hauled by Ford's own tractors to Ford-owned docks. There, it was loaded onto Ford ships and delivered to River Rouge, Michigan. At River Rouge, the ore was unloaded by Ford equipment and moved to a Ford steel plant, where it was converted into iron and steel. From the steel plant, the steel sheets were moved into the Ford assembly plants, where they were used to build Ford cars and trucks. The finished cars were then shipped to Ford dealers for final delivery. Ultimately, the entire supply chain was controlled by decisions made at Ford headquarters in Dearborn, Michigan. Ford used to boast that it would take no more than 48 hours from the time iron ore was unloaded at the River Rouge docks for it to find its way into a car rolling off the assembly line.

Source: Henry Ford, *Today and Tomorrow* (Cambridge, MA: Productivity Press, 1988; reprint of 1926 edition).

the firm buys from suppliers when they can provide inputs more cheaply and reliably than it could produce them through internal processes.

At the other end, **process (capability) buys** seek to provide a technical capability that the firm lacks. Process/capability buys bring newer technology, broader technical expertise, better market information, and a sharper focus on the firm's own core competencies. Process/capability buys often involve intimate relationships between the buyer and the supplier as they share highly technical information and make many process connections. These relationships are far more complex and difficult to manage than a simple product buy.

It sometimes becomes attractive for a firm to try and gain direct control over a supplier either by purchasing the supplier outright or by securing a controlling financial interest in the firm. Both options are examples of **vertical integration.** *Forward vertical integration* occurs when a firm decides to acquire downstream suppliers or customers. For example, a television manufacturer might acquire one of its distributors or a logistics service provider. *Backward vertical integration* occurs when a firm acquires one or more of its upstream suppliers. As can be seen in the In Practice box, the old Ford Motor Company offers an extreme example of both forward and backward vertical integration.

Vertical integration offers some important advantages and disadvantages (these are summarized in Exhibit 5 on page 10). An important advantage is greater control. As was the case with Ford, a firm that owns its suppliers can ensure that proper and consistent management policies are followed at supplier locations. Owning a controlling interest in suppliers also gives the firm greater priority and control of the suppliers' production planning and scheduling. If the supplier's capabilities are in high demand, the acquiring firm can ensure that its needs will be met first. A second major advantage of vertical integration is related to competition. In some industries, synergies of improved market information, product design, and development result from having many stages of the supply chain under a single firm's control. For example, a large pharmaceutical manufacturer such as Eli Lilly owns its own product research and development organization, base chemical manufacturing, finished goods and packaging operations, and marketing organization.

A start-up firm seeking to obtain the same synergies from operations enjoyed by Eli Lilly would have to invest huge amounts of money and time to build a similar organization, which is a large barrier to entry for new competitors. Finally, vertical integration allows a firm to avoid transaction costs and risk premiums that result when two separate firms do business.

EXHIBIT 5
Advantages and Disadvantages of Vertical Integration

Advantages	Disadvantages
Control • Insulates scarce resources • More comprehensive planning and coordinated scheduling • More direct influence on delivery and quality • Closer linkages/materials movement efficiencies	Compatibility • Incompatible strategies and infrastructures • Diverts attention away from core capabilities and markets • Breakeven volume of production may rise • Imbalance of capacity across stages; inability to sell/use excess capacity
Competition • Creates barriers to entry • Improved market information, which may open new opportunities	Competition • Creates exit barriers • Reduced flexibility to technological and market changes
Costs • More complete use of resources • Avoid transaction (middleman) costs • Reduce supplier risk premiums	Costs • Increased overhead, planning, and logistics costs • May integrate into low rate-of-return activities

Since a supplier experiences demand uncertainty, it must seek higher profit margins to buffer itself from cycles and variations in demand. A wholly owned supplier does not experience as much uncertainty, so the buying firm can purchase goods at intrafirm transfer prices reflecting thinner profit margins.

The major disadvantages of vertical integration can be serious. If the vertically integrating firm is not careful, it might find itself strapped to a business that is incompatible with its core business. For example, consider a high-tech medical instruments manufacturer that buys metal castings for its products from a large supplier. The medical instruments firm operates in a highly dynamic, science-driven environment. The castings supplier, on the other hand, operates in a relatively stable and lower-tech environment. It might appear attractive to the medical instruments firm to acquire the castings firm in order to secure a steady supply. However, these two firms are likely to have—and to require—vastly different management styles. Furthermore, their differing production technologies probably have different scale economies, organizational structures, and investment requirements. Thus, the castings firm might not be a good fit as a candidate for vertical integration. Another major problem that vertically integrated firms often experience is that they are less flexible. That is, they are unable to quickly respond to changes in market or technological conditions because they carry the weight of large investments in multiple stages of the supply chain. Highly vertically integrated firms typically have large corporate overhead costs associated with the management and coordination of various supplier organizations. If one of these suppliers becomes obsolete due to technological advancements, the vertically integrated firm is saddled with the costs of disposing of the supplier or with the costs of living with an unprofitable business.

Virtual Organizations

Recently, firms have sought partnerships with suppliers that allow many of the advantages of vertical integration while avoiding the disadvantages. In such a partnership, the firms recognize their mutual interdependence and encourage shared risks and shared knowledge. At the extreme, close partnerships create **virtual organizations.** This relationship becomes close enough to obscure the boundaries between the supplier's responsibilities and those of the buyer. Over the life of such a relationship, the two partners commit to integrating their information systems, policies and procedures, and metrics systems.

The buyers and suppliers in a virtual corporation offer important complementary skills and capabilities. Each firm focuses on developing and meshing its core competencies with its partners. The strength of these relationships depends on the needs of ultimate customers and the specific requirements of the product. As these requirements change, certain relationships become more important, while others lose importance.

Supply-Base Segmentation

Suppliers interact with a firm's operations management system in different ways, depending on the circumstances. Often, suppliers have primarily **transaction-based relationships** with the firm. They work through relatively formal, structured procedures, and the scope of their activities is limited to simply receiving and filling orders. Other times suppliers develop collaborative relationships with a firm. In such cases, their interactions may include close involvement with the firm in initial product or process design along with routine deliveries of standing orders. When managed strategically, both transaction-based and collaborative supplier relationships can produce advantages. Transaction-based relationships preserve the benefits of competition among suppliers and flexibility for the buying firm. Collaborative relationships reap the rewards of mutual commitments, shared knowledge, and better coordination. Instead of using a single management model to deal with all suppliers, leading firms are developing segmentation approaches that identify different roles and management approaches for the suppliers making up the total supply base. Exhibit 6 provides an example of such a segmentation scheme.

The first step in developing a supply-base segmentation strategy is to analyze parts, components, and systems provided by suppliers in order to identify those items and suppliers that are highly strategic versus those that are less so. Strategic items include high value, highly customized systems that differentiate products from the competition. These items justify long-term, exclusive commitments between supplier–buyer partners—a **full partnership.** The buyer and supplier work closely together in all aspects of the design, development, production, and assembly of these systems. In some cases, buyers have established *modular consortia* relationships with suppliers of these types of systems. In a modular consortia arrangement, the supplier is responsible for designing and developing an entire module that fits the functional and dimensional specifications of the buyer. Further, the supplier locates final assembly operations for the module near the buyer's product assembly operations, and the supplier builds modules and assembles them onto the product in a just-in-time fashion. For example, a supplier of an entire control panel system builds and assembles the modules into the cockpits of cars as they move down the automaker's assembly line.

EXHIBIT 6 Segmented Supplier Management, an Example

Transaction-Based Relationships	Arm's-Length Relationships with Mutual Goals	Full Partnerships
Commodities and off-the-shelf components and parts, e.g., tires, batteries, nuts, and bolts	Tailored, proprietary components, e.g., engine parts, radiators	Highly customized, high-value systems and components, e.g., instrument panel, entire transmission system
Annual contracts	Three-year contracts, within model	Five-plus-year contract, several model changeovers
Source individual commodities or look for "one-stop shops"	Source families of components	Source systems and families
Open market plus a few key suppliers of multiple items	Three to five suppliers per family	One to two suppliers per system or family
Work together to establish service/ delivery requirements	Monitor suppliers' operations	Close involvement with suppliers' operations
Issue specifications for bidding	Hold product and process design	Joint engineering and design reviews
Cost reductions through competitive bidding	Flat rate cost reduction goal each year	Mutually designed cost reduction programs, goals, and rewards
10% of product value 50% of total part numbers	20% of product value 30% of total part numbers	70% of product value 20% of total part numbers
50% of suppliers	35% of suppliers	15% of suppliers

In Practice

INTEGRATED SUPPLY OF MRO ITEMS

One of the bright spots in the relatively brief life of integrated supply-chain management is the area of maintenance, repair, and operating (MRO) goods. "Integrated supply," as it is sometimes called by industrial distributors, has been delivering a degree of buyer–supplier integration that is not often approached by the few integrated supply-chain management programs that are up and running. Behind the integrated supply movement are four drivers:

1. Deliberate reductions that buyers are making in the size of their distribution supplier bases.
2. The growing insistence by buyers that distributor suppliers add greater value to each transaction.
3. Greater competitiveness in the distribution industry and greater emphasis on competition across wider product groups, resulting from supplier-base reductions and the insistence by purchasing departments on reduced transaction costs.
4. A deliberate effort by the distribution industry and the manufacturers who supply them to concentrate more efforts on jointly selling their products.

In an integrated supply agreement, a distributor offers to provide a high level of service in supplying an entire line of products at agreed-upon prices. This is pure systems contracting. Integrated supply, however, goes beyond the traditional systems contract and offers a much wider range of products—often multiple lines of products—for which the distributor assumes most of the responsibility for stocking, reordering, and forecasting future needs. A growing number of integrated supply agreements also provide for physical distribution of products within the customer's plant and for performing a specified number of logistics services.

Under integrated supply agreements, distributors work closely with MRO buyers to eliminate and/or streamline non-value-added activities in the process of acquiring and disbursing indirect items. To a great extent, integrated supply agreements can vary widely, depending on what the contracting parties include in them. For some buyers and their distributor partners, integrated supply can mean having a distributor manage a storeroom. For others, the emphasis may be on having several distributors locate branches nearby in some sort of grouping arrangement. For still others, an integrated supply agreement may entail outsourcing the entire MRO buying activity to a distributor or consortium of distributors and/or manufacturers. In some cases they even maintain onsite offices.

Integrated supply agreements have experienced their most enthusiastic reception in process industries, where the volume of MRO goods is high and the cost reduction opportunities on raw materials and capital equipment are relatively low. For some distributors, opportunities for showing huge cost savings were like walking through an orchard picking low-hanging fruit. Many large process operations in the past often were burdened with excessively large supplier bases for their MRO requirements and saddled with transaction processing systems—paper and electronic—that were hopelessly work intensive. On top of that, many large process industries were carrying years' worth of MRO inventory.

Source: This material is taken from an article by James Morgan, "MRO Report: Integrated Supply Offers Opportunities, Limits," *Purchasing,* June 3, 1999.

Modular consortia: An arrangement in which suppliers design, develop, manufacture, and assemble an entire module or subsystem that fits the functional and dimensional specifications of the buyer. The supplier typically locates operations on or near the buyer's assembly site so that the supplier can feed or assemble systems immediately into the buyer's product flow.

Other proprietary, but less strategic items can be managed with **arm's-length relationships** in which mutual goals are identified and pursued. These items involve less complexity and strategic value, and, thus, require close involvement but less commitment than a full partnership. Suppliers and buyers still work closely on the design of parts and components through electronic information exchange and design review meetings, but **co-location** may not be justified. A buyer may purchase an entire family of related or similar parts from a single supplier in order to reduce the total number of suppliers in the supply base. This approach allows the buyer to spend more time with each supplier. It also creates greater levels of commitment since the buyer demands a greater portion of the supplier's production capacity.

Finally, many products involve a large number of common, off-the-shelf parts and components. These items are offered by numerous suppliers and are found in a variety of product uses, for example, batteries; therefore, they provide little strategic value. Suppliers of these items can be managed with transaction-based relationships, allowing the buying firm to gain cost reductions through competitive bidding. However, this approach does not necessarily require that interactions be adversarial. Even commodity-type products often have unique aspects requiring cooperation. For example, a buying firm might have unusual service and delivery requirements. Furthermore, transaction cost savings can result when buyers are able to supply a large number of different items from a single supplier, that is, one-stop shopping. Thus, establishing good working relationships with relatively fewer suppliers can yield benefits even for nonstrategic, but necessary, items. An example of this kind of relationship is given in the In Practice box on page 12.

Pursuing a supply-base segmentation strategy allows a buying firm to concentrate its supplier development and partnership efforts where they are needed most. It also forces the buying firm to think strategically about all the parts and components that make up its product. Inevitably, the buying firm must consider its core competencies, the strategic positioning of its products, and future operations and technological developments when it seeks to rationalize its supply base.

Efficient versus Market-Responsive Supply Chains

An important consideration in supply-chain design is how performance characteristics should relate to the characteristics of product demand. An article by Marshall Fisher addresses this issue.[2] Fisher maintains that supply-chain design choices tend to emphasize efficiency or market-responsiveness; it is difficult, if not impossible, to achieve excellent performance in both dimensions simultaneously. Fisher suggests that managers need to recognize this substantial trade-off when they make choices that govern the structure of supply chains. Exhibit 7 shows how supply-chain design choices should be linked to aspects of demand. Choices that emphasize physical efficiency should be made for functional products, that is, products that have stable, predictable demands and that contribute low margins. Conversely, managers should make choices that emphasize flexibility and market-responsiveness in supply chains for "innovative" products; that is, products that have highly volatile demands, involve high levels of variety, and contribute to relatively high profit margins.

EXHIBIT 7

Efficient versus Market-Responsive Supply Chains

Source: Marshall Fisher, "What Is the Right Supply Chain for Your Product?" *Harvard Business Review,* March–April 1997, pp. 105–16.

Aspects of Demand	**Functional (Predictable Demand)**	**Innovative (Unpredictable Demand)**
Product life cycle	> 2 years	< 1 year
Contribution margin	5–20 %	20–60 %
Product variety	Low (10–20 variants/category)	High (large number of variants/category)
Average forecast error	10%	40–100%
Average stockout rate	1–2%	10–40%
Average end-of-season markdown	0%	10–25%
Lead time for MTO products	6–12 months	1–2 days
Supply Chain Design Choices	**Physically Efficient Process**	**Market-Responsive Process**
Primary purpose	Supply predictable demand efficiently	Respond quickly to unpredictable demand to maximize service
Manufacturing focus	Maintain high average utilization rate	Deploy excess buffer capacity
Inventory strategy	Generate high turns and minimize inventory	Deploy significant buffer stocks
Lead time focus	Shorten lead time while not increasing cost	Invest in ways to reduce lead time
Approach to choosing suppliers	Select primarily for cost and quality	Select primarily for speed, flexibility, and quality
Product-design strategy	Maximize performance and minimize cost	Use modular design to postpone differentiation

[2] Marshall Fisher, "What Is the Right Supply Chain for your Product?" *Harvard Business Review,* March–April 1997, pp. 105–16.

Most supply-chain managers understand these key differences. Unfortunately, decision makers in various areas rarely make individual decisions in an integrated manner. Incremental decisions made over long periods of time may cause a firm to gravitate toward one type of supply chain or another without clear regard for the alignment that is needed. More commonly, the resulting supply chain is a mish-mash of performance characteristics. This situation is exacerbated by the typically simplistic goals and incentives communicated to different functional areas (e.g., sales representatives emphasize service while logistics personnel emphasize cost). Fisher suggests that achieving alignment between supply and product strategies is difficult. However, there appear to be large advantages and profits in doing so.

Global Supply-Chain Management

Increasingly, supply chains involve relationships that cross international boundaries. Hewlett-Packard, for example, obtains components from suppliers located in Malaysia, Singapore, Taipei, Japan, and Canada. Some of its products are assembled in Mexico. Similarly, numerous firms are developing global supply chains in order to capture advantages offered by offshore suppliers.

Reasons for Global Supply Chains

There are some very important reasons for going global:

- *Lower costs.* Foreign suppliers frequently offer less expensive products because they enjoy cost advantages. For example, companies such as Mattel and Hasbro produce most of their toys in low-cost labor countries such as Malaysia, Taipei, and the People's Republic of China (PRC). Besides labor, global sources also can provide low-cost materials and other inputs, attractive currency exchange rates, and low value-added taxes.
- *Superior quality.* Suppliers located outside of the United States often offer unique levels of product quality. For example, Shimano (from Japan) and Campagnolo (from Italy) are recognized around the world as the market and technological leaders in bicycle components design.
- *Incentives.* Countries that are keen to attract foreign investment will offer tax advantages or other financial incentives. For example, many automotive manufacturers have located facilities in Mexico because the Mexican government offers a unique manufacturing situation, known as a *maquiladora.*[3] This arrangement relaxes taxes, import/export duties, and environmental and other regulations.
- *Unique product or service.* Sometimes very specialized products or services may be found in only a few places around the world, for example, diamonds. A foreign supplier may be the only capable source, or it may hold patents that prevent other producers from supplying the product.
- *Increased capacity and availability of supply.* Due to differences in economic conditions, suppliers in foreign countries may have excess capacity when domestic suppliers are unable to keep pace with demands.
- *Need to meet the local requirements or demands.* Foreign governments often require firms selling products in their country to produce or buy a portion of the product locally. Laws requiring this are called **local content laws.** In other cases firms use local suppliers in order to increase the attractiveness of products to the target market, for example Japanese auto manufacturers using U.S. suppliers.

[3] A *maquiladora* is a manufacturing facility located in Mexico that charges no import or export duty as long as the user agrees to build the product in Mexico using relatively cheap Mexican labor and then to immediately export the product out of the country.

- *Requirement to fulfill current marketing commitments.* As part of the terms of foreign trade, a firm may be required to reinvest a portion of its sales to a foreign country by purchasing goods and services from companies in that country. This practice is commonly referred to as **countertrade.**

Challenges of Going Global

While strong and compelling reasons for going global exist, supply-chain managers must recognize the presence of significant challenges and costs. The following are some of the most significant:

- *Time differences.* At least seven time zones separate a buyer in California from a potential supplier in Germany. The buyer may dislike having to make phone calls at 5 A.M. to reach the German supplier at 2 P.M. local time.
- *Cultural differences.* Most firms feel most comfortable dealing with firms with which they share many cultural characteristics. And basic cultural norms may vary. For example, representatives of North American firms may routinely drink wine or beer during a business lunch, potentially offending people from Malaysia, a Muslim country that does not tolerate the consumption of alcohol.
- *Lead time.* Due to distance; geographic obstacles, for example, oceans; and customs delays, order shipments take longer to travel from foreign suppliers than from domestic ones. Increased lead time can decrease flexibility because orders have to be placed earlier, and more inventory fills the transportation pipeline. For example, in the recession of the mid-1980s, one American buyer of steel suffered a setback when demand declined after the firm committed to purchase from Japanese suppliers that had lead times of six months and longer. American steel makers were quoting lead times of weeks or days, so the buyer could have avoided the long-term commitment.
- *Hidden costs.* Costs for transactions with foreign suppliers may change due to exchange-rate fluctuations, tariffs, duties, and high inventories to compensate for long lead times.
- *Language differences.* Language differences can complicate communication. For example, foreign suppliers may have trouble providing essential training and technical support to distant buyers.
- *Returns and repairs of defective products.* If a batch of inputs from a foreign supplier fails to meet quality standards, the buyer may have greater difficulty in documenting problems and returning shipments because it must deal with customs and accommodate long lead times.
- *Political risks.* Doing business with foreign suppliers can expose a firm to risks associated with unstable or uncooperative governments. Furthermore, business practices in foreign locations may reflect badly on the buying firm—for example, the use of child or slave labor by a supplier.
- *Differences in units of measurement.* American firms deal with measurements based on pounds, inches, and ounces. For the most part, the rest of the world deals with the metric system.

Increasingly, global supply-chain management is becoming a fact of life. If managed correctly, a global supply base can greatly enhance the competitive position of the firm. However, the costs and complexities associated with such a supply chain should not be overlooked.

Centralized versus Regionalized Global Sourcing

Part of a global sourcing strategy involves the decision of whether to pursue **centralized sourcing** or **regionalized sourcing.** In a centralized strategy, a central purchasing group manages a few suppliers for each commodity, and these few suppliers provide all the company's

EXHIBIT 8
Advantages of Centralized versus Regionalized Global Sourcing

Arguments for Centralized Sourcing	Arguments for Regionalized Sourcing
The best vendor should supply the whole company	Each plant knows its own needs best
Transportation costs are decreasing	Shorter distance means more reliable delivery and less transit inventory
Inventory tracking and management capabilities are increasing	Better inventory coordination and scheduling from onsite/nearby vendors
Centralization gives critical mass—can build expertise in each commodity area	Avoids corporate procurement empire-builing
Increases purchasing clout—quantity discounts	Helps satisfy local content laws
Encourages supplier to commit dedicated investments in technology, service, etc.	Local vendors provide more responsive engineering expertise

requirements worldwide for that commodity. In a regionalized strategy, purchasing activities are divided within the firm by region of the world. Each regional group is allowed to identify local suppliers and procure items according to their specialized needs. Some of the advantages of each strategy are listed in Exhibit 8. Firms today are increasingly seeking mixed strategies that simultaneously provide the economies of centralized sourcing for some commodities, while preserving the flexibility associated with regionalized sourcing for other commodities.

Dynamics and Change within the Supply Chain

The modern supply chain is largely a creation of, and a response to, today's dynamic environment. The dynamic nature of the supply chain is evident in its changing structure. Over time new partnerships and relationships are created while others are terminated. Moreover, the nature of supply-chain relationships changes. Some relationships become more closely coupled while others become more arm's length in nature.

The dynamic nature of the supply chain is also evident in the day-to-day activities of the supply-chain participants. In a typical supply chain, each participant can create disturbances, either independently or in response to actions taken elsewhere, within the supply chain. These disturbances frequently create a chain of reaction consisting of three major elements: *cause, response* (reaction), and *effect.*

Cause

Most disturbances in the smooth operation of supply chains stem from variability and delay in the flow of materials or information. Variability and delay create uncertainty in the minds of decision makers, who then react to triggering events or actions that they must interpret. A triggering event could take one of many forms: a change in the quantity, timing, or mix of orders (either placed by a downstream customer or orders shipped by an upstream supplier); cost/price fluctuations; incomplete orders (either placed or delivered); forecast inaccuracies; product/process designs that fail to recognize supply chain considerations; and so on. A list of the underlying root sources of triggering events is provided in Exhibit 9.

Response

The uncertainty surrounding triggering events causes responses that are often detrimental to supply-chain performance. Responses are based on how the firm processes the information from the event, the inventory policies it has in place, its planning and scheduling system, and the types and levels of buffers it uses for coping with these events. Suppose a firm receives an unexpected order for 50 units of a component from a major customer (a potential triggering event). It currently has 42 units in stock, not enough to meet its customer's needs. Suppose the firm's purchasing system mandates a minimum order quantity of 250 for the item. Even though only eight additional units are needed, an order of 250 is placed. The result is an increase in inventory (242 units now) due to the combination of the unexpected customer's order with the firm's simplistic purchasing rule.

EXHIBIT 9 **Deficiencies in Supply-Chain Management and Their Symptoms**

Root Deficiency	Examples	Symptoms
Internal focus lacking deep understanding of customers	There is no clear, shared definition of who the critical customers are or how various groups should respond to them.	• Line-item fill-rate measures are the only metrics used. • No measures for response time, lateness, or backorder profile.
	Priority is given to external customers, thus causing delays, backorders, and order expediting for internal customers.	• No service measures for internal customers. • Inappropriate incentive systems. • Jockeying for priority between different internal divisions.
	The structure of the supply chain addresses only the internal factory or first-tier suppliers and customers.	• Focus on internal operations only. • Inadequate understanding of operational environment and needs of immediate and ultimate customers.
Inadequate information systems	Systems are unable to provide customers with timely and accurate order status. System incompatibilities cause delays in information retrieval and transmission, making it difficult to quote accurate shipment dates to customers.	• Delays in providing delivery information. • Inaccurate delivery information. • Inadequate linkage among databases at different sites. • Use of different systems to do the same function at different locations. • Delays and inaccuracies of data transfer.
Lack of organizational integration leading to local optimization	Independent groups manage joint activities, each group according to its own objectives and mission. Metrics may conflict and not be best overall.	• Independent and disconnected individual sites. • Incomplete metrics. • Performance measures not tracked or not given attention.
	Transport mode decisions concentrate on freight costs, ignoring impacts on inventory and service.	• Transportation managers are graded only on transportation cost per period.
	Evaluations of the opportunity costs of inventory rework do not take into account obsolescence and required due to short product life and design changes.	• No quantitative basis for inventory holding cost assessments.
	Internal functional barriers and external organizational barriers frustrate efforts to coordinate information, resource, service, and product flows.	• Conflicting performance measure and incentive systems at different sites. • Barriers between manufacturing and distribution (as one example).
	Products and processes are designed without considering the capabilities and expertise of suppliers, manufacturing, sales support, etc.	• Excessive product variety. • Organizational barriers between R&D and the supply chain.
	Changes in supply network structure are evaluated from a limited—fixed and logistical costs—perspective.	• Chain decisions are modeled without consideration of operating, inventory, and response time efficiencies
Ignoring the impact of variability and uncertainties	There is high variability in material quality, processing times, transit times, and demands.	• No documentation or tracking key sources of variability. • Partial information on sources of uncertainties.
	Inventory stocking policies ignore uncertainties or make limited usage of information in managing inventories by part and by location.	• Stocking policies are independent of magnitudes of uncertainties. • Static stocking policies. • Generic and subjective stocking policies.
Poor scheduling and coordination	Items to be assembled arrive from different areas at different times, causing delays, poor customer service, and expedited orders.	• Supplying divisions schedule deliveries independently. • No system information from multiple supplying divisions.

Source: Adapted from H. L. Lee and C. Billington, "Managing Supply Chain Inventory: Pitfalls and Opportunities," *Sloan Management Review 3*, no. 33, Spring 1992, p. 65.

Now, consider how this firm's supplier might react to the unexpected order of 250 units placed on it. Triggering events do not always precipitate responses. When they do, however, the response of one firm can become a triggering event to another firm in the supply chain. Thus, as our example suggests, another round of cause–response–effect is triggered. The cumulative reactions of all the participants in the supply chain result in an overall effect.

Effect

Effect describes the impact of the cause and the response on the supply chain as a whole. In general, disturbances in the supply chain can be dampened, passed on, or amplified. For example, suppose a firm that happens to have lots of excess inventory receives an unexpected order from a customer. Because the firm has excess stock, it is able to meet the order and the disturbance proceeds no further. In this lucky instance, the firm has completely negated the disturbance. Unfortunately, supply-chain effects are frequently amplified or worsened. This phenomenon is often referred to as the *bullwhip effect.*

The Bullwhip Effect

The **bullwhip effect** occurs when a small disturbance generated by a customer produces successively larger disturbances at each upstream stage in the supply chain. Bullwhip effects are of great concern because they incite excessive expediting (moving certain orders ahead of others), increased levels of inventory, uneven levels of capacity utilization (where plants go from being idle to working overtime), and, ultimately, increased costs.

To understand how a bullwhip effect is created, consider a hypothetical four-tiered supply chain. In this chain, a customer orders finished products from the tier-one supplier, who in turn orders components from the tier-two supplier, and so on. Now, suppose that the tier-one supplier decides to run an advertising promotion. In order to stock up for anticipated increases in sales, the tier-one supplier temporarily boosts orders to the tier-two supplier, which is indicated by an increase in order size in weeks two and three depicted in Exhibit 10. How should the tier-two supplier react? If he knows nothing about the promotion, he might be surprised by the increased orders from the tier-one supplier and worried that he won't be able to fill orders of this magnitude in the future. A natural response would be for the tier-two supplier to place even larger orders with the tier-three supplier. After all, as far as the tier-two supplier knows, his customer—the tier-one supplier—might place even larger orders in the future. Thus, the tier-two supplier places an order that is larger than his immediate need in order to hedge against the uncertainty of future demand. This phenomenon is replicated upstream, until finally the orders placed by the tier-four supplier are quite large indeed. Once the tier-one supplier's promotion campaign is over, he returns to placing normal smaller orders. How might the tier-two supplier react? By now he has lots of excess inventory sitting around. As a result he will probably decide to reduce future orders drastically. And so this opposite effect cascades up the supply chain.

EXHIBIT 10
The Bullwhip Effect, an Example

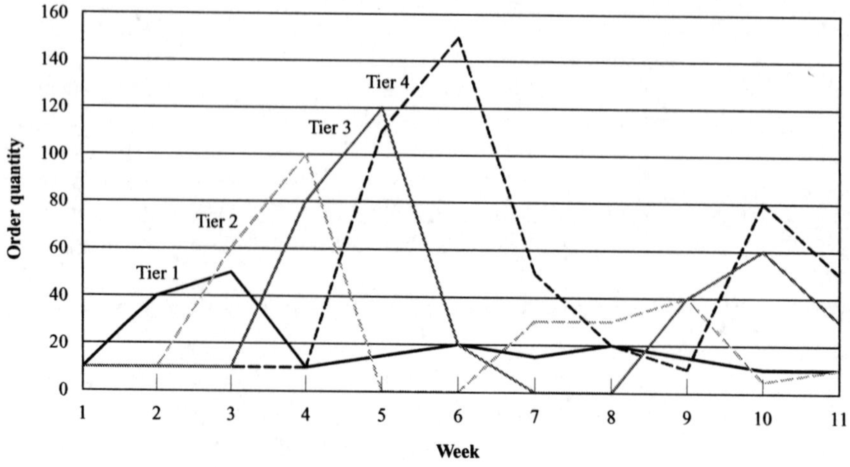

As Exhibit 10 indicates, small variations in demand at the customer end of the supply chain can produce massive variations in orders upstream. Why? In the absence of information, suppliers are likely to overreact to changes in order sizes, whether upward or downward. This amplification of variations through the stages of the supply chain is the bullwhip effect.

The bullwhip effect is shaped by numerous factors. First, it could reflect the impact of planning factors such as lot sizing rules or marketing promotions used at each supply chain stage. Second, it could reflect the speed or delay with which each stage reacts. Other factors include process variability and failures, demand cycles and seasonality, and product design changes and introductions. Overall, these factors and the others listed in Exhibit 9 create system nervousness throughout the supply chain.

Tactics for Reducing the Bullwhip Effect

Firms typically deal with bullwhip triggering events in one of four basic ways: (1) buffering, (2) postponement, (3) information sharing, and (4) coordination.

Buffering Firms insulate their operations against uncertain events by using one or more of three basic types of **buffers: safety stock, safety lead time,** and **safety capacity.**

- Safety stock refers to the use of extra inventory to protect the firm from unexpected variations in demand or supply quantities, timing, or product mix.
- Safety lead time increases the delivery lead time that is promised to customers in order to allow a firm to reschedule work or to otherwise cope with unexpected internal delays. The problem with safety lead time is that there is a tendency for the actual lead times to expand and to consume all of the allotted safety lead time. Personnel become accustomed to the extra time and begin to use safety lead time as part of their regular schedule.
- Safety capacity is unused, excess production capacity—machines and/or labor—that is intended to accommodate unplanned changes in orders. This includes the ability to quickly subcontract work to suppliers, sometimes called *virtual capacity.*

Postponement In its simplest terms, **postponement** involves delaying an action until associated uncertainties are resolved. There are three types of postponement strategies:[4] (1) **production** (or form) **postponement,** (2) **logistics** (or place) **postponement,** and (3) **full postponement.** Production postponement involves keeping the product in as neutral or noncommittal a form as possible until an order is placed. The product is not made, configured, labeled, or packaged until necessary. For example, Herman Miller Corp. postpones the final assembly of chairs since they can be configured in hundreds of thousands of different combinations based on fabric choices alone. Instead of stocking each possible type of chair, the company makes only the frames for all of its chairs, which are then knocked down and shipped as ready-to-assemble kits to warehouses located around the world. When an order comes in, the manager of the warehouse nearest to the customer adds the appropriate cloth-based components to the chair and the entire order is quickly shipped to the customer. Suppose that Herman Miller decided to eliminate its warehouses and instead build and ship chairs from one central location. Such a strategy would add the element of logistics postponement to create a full postponement approach where all orders are shipped from a centralized plant directly to the customer. The advantage of this strategy is that no inventories are stored in regional locations, and the firm does not need to speculate about the type or location of demand. Disadvantages associated with postponement are the loss of scale economies and protracted order fulfillment lead times. To reap the rewards of postponement strategies, a firm usually must reduce its production and logistics cycle times.

[4]Janus D. Pagh and Martha C. Cooper, "Supply Chain Postponement and Speculation Strategies: How to Choose the Right Strategy," *Journal of Business Logistics* 19, no. 2, 1998, pp. 13–33.

Information Sharing Uncertainty in the supply chain is largely the product of a lack of **information sharing** across supply stages. Customers reduce uncertainty when they share their forecasts, sales data, production schedules, and future plans with suppliers more frequently, more rapidly, and more comprehensively. In turn, suppliers reduce uncertainty by sharing production schedules, available capacity, and future capacity plans with their customers. It sounds simple, but information sharing can be quite difficult. Imagine the systems required for a supplier to share information with thousands of customers. What's more, information is power, and suppliers and their customers are often reticent to share information that is perceived to be proprietary or important to their competitive advantages.

Coordination Going beyond simple information sharing to achieve greater **coordination** requires supply-chain partners to commit themselves to certain actions. Consider the following example. A buyer provides the supplier with a set of forecasts, and the supplier gives a buyer a schedule of production runs and available capacity levels. Suppose then the buyer agrees to commit to a certain level of purchases from the supplier during the next month, irrespective of what happens to its demand. In turn, the supplier agrees to set aside capacity to fill these orders. With these agreements, the supplier can plan production with greater certainty, and the buyer has greater certainty regarding the availability of supply. Information sharing and coordination are fundamental to new supply-chain management initiatives such as collaborative planning, forecasting, and replenishment (CPFR).

The tactics described above differ in the degree to which they are reactive or proactive (see Exhibit 11). Reactive tactics are designed to position a firm to deal with uncertainty in the supply chain. Such tactics are appropriate when a firm cannot influence its customers or other firms that might initiate changes. Alternatively, proactive strategies seek to reduce uncertainty and make sense when other parties' actions can be influenced.

Initiatives for Supply-Chain Integration

Every day, supply-chain managers uncover new ways of improving performance by more thoroughly integrating decision making and execution. The power of integration is illustrated in the Wal-Mart case. The following sections discuss some of the more important and recent developments in the practice of integrating supply-chain management.

Vendor-Managed Inventories

In the past, it was standard practice for operations managers to own and manage all the inventories on their property. They were responsible for the storage, control, replenishment, and overall management of the inventory. A materials planner and a purchasing agent—or buyer—typically worked together with vendors to ensure that enough inventory (but not too much) was on hand at all times.

Recently, an increasing number of firms have implemented **vendor-managed-inventory (VMI)** arrangements, also known as continuous replenishment systems. As the name suggests, the vendor is responsible for managing the inventory located at the operations management facility, including stocking the inventory, controlling its flow in and out of the stockroom, and placing replenishment orders. Often the vendor owns the inventory until the customer uses it and a vendor representative often is located at the inventory-stocking site.

EXHIBIT 11
Classifying the Uncertainty Response Tactics along the Passive/Active Spectrum

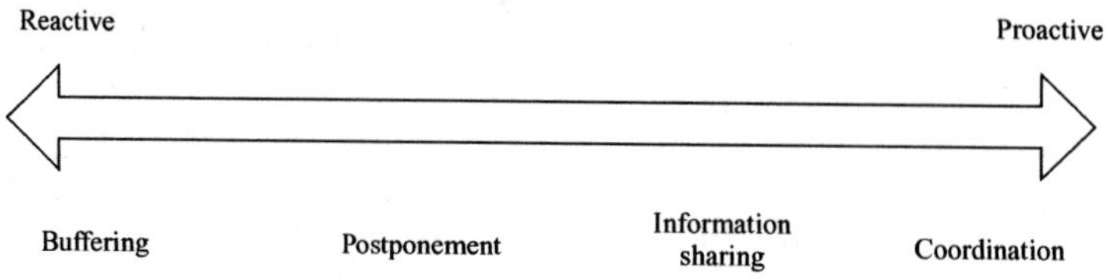

In Practice

SUPPLY CHAIN INTEGRATION AS THE ROAD TO IMPROVEMENT

Firms are coming to recognize that great improvements in value can be realized by coordinating the efforts of partners along the supply chain. When firms concentrate only on their internal operations, they are uncertain about the decisions suppliers and customers are making. Furthermore, they tend to maximize their own objectives, often to the detriment of the supply chain as a whole. Sam Walton, the founder of Wal-Mart, was one of the first business leaders to recognize this principle. In the early 1990s, Wal-Mart began to share its product forecasts and long-term purchase requirements with its suppliers and eventually with the suppliers of its suppliers. In turn, suppliers shared capacity and production information with Wal-Mart. As a result, second-guessing and forecasting forecasts, which is what the suppliers essentially did, were replaced with data analysis. To reduce uncertainty further, Wal-Mart began to make commitments to purchase inventory. Suppliers used these commitments instead of speculation to drive their production planning processes. Over time, all parties realized a reduction in inventories, lower costs, better schedules, and higher levels of product availability. Collaborative networks are now common in retail markets, health services, food, and even the automotive industry.

This approach offers several important advantages to both the customer and the vendor. The customer saves the costs associated with managing inventories, including the labor costs usually incurred by both the materials and purchasing managers. The customer also receives more responsive service from the vendor since the onsite vendor representative works directly with production schedulers and other production personnel, thereby gaining a better understanding of the customer's schedule and quality needs. The vendor gains better insights into the customer's operations, and, surprisingly, often does a better job of scheduling inventory replenishment orders than the customer does. By controlling the order schedule, the vendor also can accommodate the needs of his/her own internal operations. For example, the vendor has the liberty to batch orders together to reduce costly production set-ups. In addition, the production personnel at the vendor site receive higher quality and more timely information since the person generating the information has the vendor's interests at heart.

VMI approaches often blur the boundaries between the vendor's and the customer's operations management systems. This lack of separation sometimes poses a threat to the customer or vendor if secrecy is a high priority. Successful VMI arrangements require a fairly long-term commitment from both parties. Consequently, most VMI partnerships are reserved for only a few, important vendor relationships.

Efficient Consumer Response

Efficient consumer response (ECR) was first developed and implemented by the grocery industry. It has since been implemented by the retail industry, the health services and supply sector, and now by firms such as Toyota in the automotive industry. ECR is a process-based system in which distributors and suppliers work closely together to improve the overall efficiency of the complete supply chain by sharing information, reducing paper flows, cooperating, and improving the overall product flow from the source to the customer.

Systems developed using ECR principles (see Exhibit 12 on page 22) make extensive use of tools and procedures found in just-in-time (JIT) systems, total quality management (TQM), and business process reengineering/redesign. They also make extensive use of information technology via the Internet, electronic data interchange (EDI) systems, and automated data-capturing systems such as bar coding.

ECR systems deal with all aspects of product flow, touching on store assortments (how products are placed and located), replenishment (how orders are placed and replenishment time managed), promotion (how trade and consumer promotions are managed), and product introductions (how new product development and introductions are managed). When Procter & Gamble introduced ECR into its system, they replaced promotions and trade discounts with value pricing, that is, setting a price that is low on average and not influenced by promotions such as sales. Its second action was to reduce its range of packaging sizes and assortments by 25 percent. The third was to drop marginal brands that contributed to

EXHIBIT 12
Guiding Principles of Efficient Consumer Response

1. Constantly focus on providing better value to the consumer by offering better product, quality, assortment, in-stock service, and convenience with less cost throughout the total supply chain.
2. ECR must be driven by committed business leaders determined to achieve profit by replacing old paradigms of win–lose trading relationships with mutually profitable win–win business alliances.
3. Accurate and timely information must be used to support effective marketing, production, and logistic decisions. This information will flow externally between partners through EDI or the Internet using conventional standards.
4. Product flow must maximize value-adding processes from the end of product/packaging to the consumer's basket to ensure the right product is available at the right time.
5. A common and consistent performance measurement and reward system must focus on the effectiveness of the total system, that is, better value through reduced costs, lower inventory, and better asset utilization; clearly identify the potential rewards, that is, increased revenue and profit; and promote equitable sharing of those rewards.

customer confusion in the marketplace. For example Bain de Soleil, a sun-tanning product, was dropped. These actions ultimately reduced cost and improved Proctor & Gambles' market efficiency.

Since its introduction in 1993, ECR has worked well. It has saved the grocery industry some $30 billion; inventory has fallen by 41 percent (from 104 days to 61 days). Customers have benefited from lower prices, higher quality (fresher product), greater system responsiveness, and shorter lead times. ECR has shown managers in all industries the need for and benefits of total supply-chain cooperation.

What are the advantages of replacing promotions with value pricing? Why does this make sense from an operations management perspective? Go to a grocery store and try to identify other companies that have followed this approach.

Collaborative Planning, Forecasting, and Production Replenishment (CPFR)

Managing the supply chain presents a paradox of self-interest. By acting in its own interests, each party involved in the supply chain takes actions that reduce the effectiveness and efficiency of the overall system. The reason is that each party, acting on its own, makes assumptions about the actions of every other party in the supply chain. Further, each supplier is faced by the need to forecast the demands of its customers, and forecasts are typically filled with uncertainty.

During the early 1990s, supply-chain partner firms in the retail marketing industry began to work together, sharing information and insights so better plans and forecasts could be generated. The results were better service with less inventory and lower costs. This approach gave rise to a methodology known as **collaborative planning, forecasting, and replenishment (CPFR),** pronounced C-P-FAR.

CPFR requires the involvement of parties willing to make commitments to the plans generated by the planning process. It also requires an emphasis on continuous planning and replanning. Exhibit 13 illustrates the basic activities involved in CPFR. The process begins when the major players in the supply chain come together to generate replenishment plans for products. The customers, companies such as Wal-Mart that serve the end consumer, provide their suppliers with forecasts of product demands. Included in these forecasts are information regarding product promotions (timing and type) and other factors that can influence demand. The suppliers, in turn, share production planning information: what items they will be building, the order quantities, and when these items will be built. They also inform customers about any critical bottlenecks or capacity limitations. For example, the suppliers might tell the customers that their plants are typically shut down for two weeks during the Christmas holidays for maintenance. Customers' demands are compared with production plans to determine the extent to which supply is sufficient to meet demand. When demand

EXHIBIT 13 **CPFR Activities and Responsibilities**

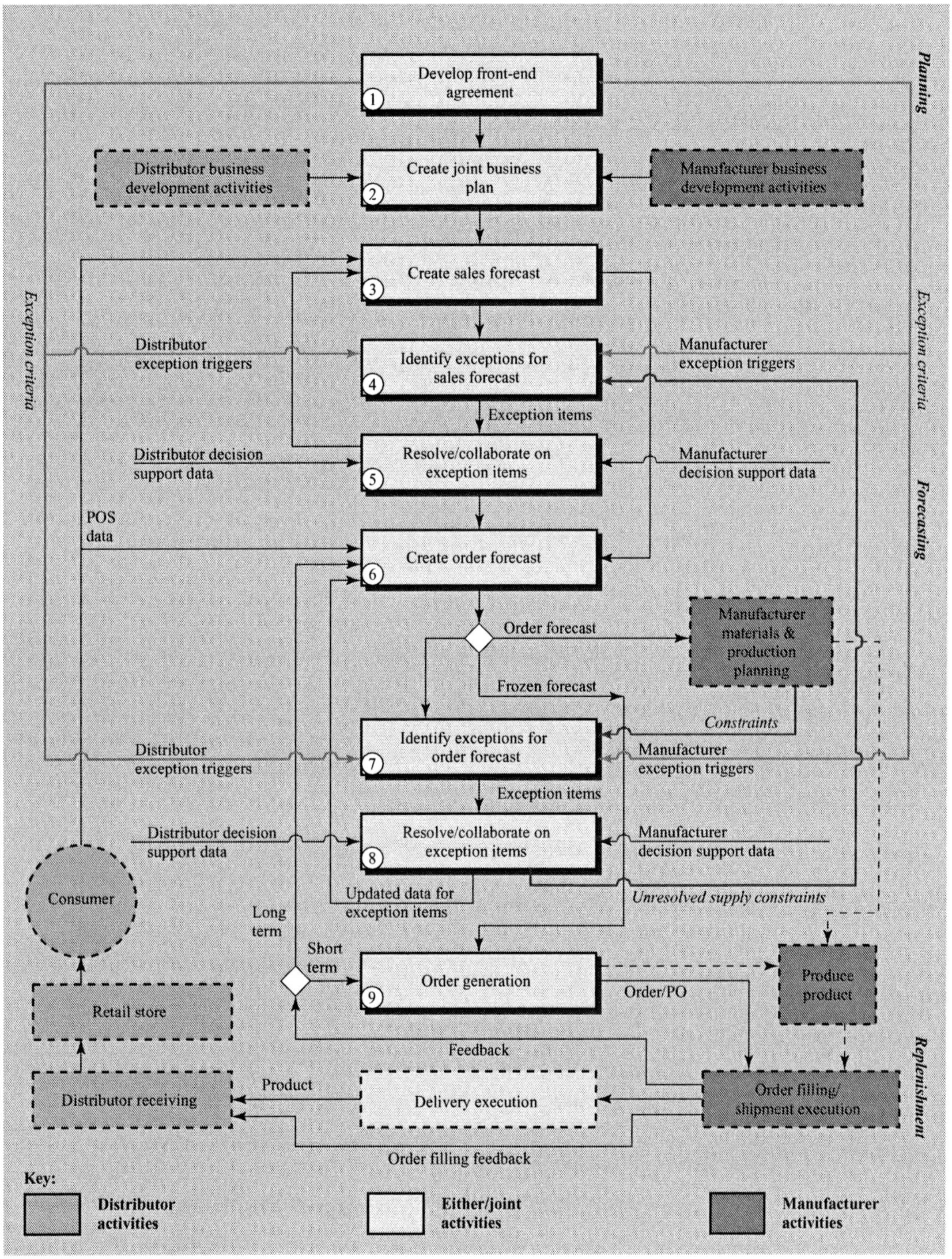

Source: www.cpfr.org/processmodel.html

and supply are not closely matched, the partners work on ways to resolve these gaps. This may require changing demand; it also could require shifting production from one product to another.

Once an acceptable plan has been collaboratively established, the plan is finalized when customers along the supply chain commit to orders with suppliers. These commitments enable suppliers to begin producing items with little risk. The parties then meet on a regular basis, for example, once a month, to review progress and to make appropriate adjustments. Commitments are reevaluated and new commitments are generated. All the major parties involved in the supply chain must agree upon changes made to the plan. This process is described in greater detail at www.cpfr.org/process model.html.

The use of CPFR approaches has grown since the early 1990s, and it has worked quite well for companies such as Wal-Mart and Procter & Gamble. Both firms have found that fill rates—the rate at which customer orders are filled on time—have improved from 60 percent to 80 percent and above, while inventories and lead times have remained constant or have fallen.

Customer Relationship Management (CRM)

The objective of **customer relationship management (CRM)** is to develop a customer-centered organization that utilizes every opportunity to delight customers, foster their loyalty, and build long-term, mutually beneficial relationships. CRM involves the science of first gathering and analyzing data that describe individual customer needs and purchasing habits, and second building systems that enable workers to meet those individual needs more completely. CRM has grown rapidly over recent years as a tool for improving the overall performance of a business by better understanding and anticipating the wants and needs of customers.

CRM systems ensure rapid responses to customer inquiries and past purchases. One such application provides field representatives with a timely and accurate tool for information gathering and reporting. A salesperson can now identify a customer's past orders and preferences and see what products are available for immediate delivery, all while sitting in a client's office. Amazon.com has taken this approach one step further by automating its CRM functionality. For example, every time repeat customers log onto Amazon.com, they get tips on new books and other products they might like based on their previous purchases. Companies that have embraced CRM technology do so because of their overwhelming belief that the customer is the sole driver for the entire business.

CRM's relevance to the overall supply chain lies in its need for cross-functional transparency, which can be enhanced through execution and planning systems. Companies need to organize their entire enterprise around processes that drive value, such as product and market planning, closing sales, fulfilling orders, and retaining customers. The CRM system can provide a business with the information necessary to achieve these tasks through applications for account management and instant access to historical purchasing habits as well as forecast, order, and contract generation. Much of the information available from a CRM system begins and ends with the company's warehouse management systems and enterprise resource planning applications. As the need for supply-chain transparency increases, businesses are consistently looking to the Internet as a viable channel to communicate their value-added information.

E-business and the Supply Chain

In recent years, the Internet has had an enormous impact on the emergence and growth of supply-chain management as a discipline. Increasingly, people are using the Internet to search for new products and services, place and pay for orders, check on the status of existing orders, and deliver information-intensive products and services. The Internet offers a very effective mechanism for coordinating the flow of information between the various parties of the supply chain.

If one thinks of the supply chain as a body with many interdependent parts, the Internet is fast becoming this body's nervous system—it facilitates quick, low-cost, and accurate flow of information. As such, the Internet provides the means to reduce uncertainty in planning and execution activities throughout the supply chain. For example, when a company such as Wal-Mart gives one of its suppliers a large order, the supplier can immediately distribute information about the order to all its upstream suppliers. Using this information, these suppliers can inform the first-tier supplier of their ability to support the order. By reducing uncertainty, greater information availability via the Internet helps reduce uncertainty-driven costs, including costs of inventory, forecasting, scheduling, and expediting. By speeding up the transfer of information, the Internet enables richer, more timely, and more interactive communication between supply-chain parties, including most forms of information: voice, data, text, and graphics.

This greater connectivity enables supply-chain firms and customers to operate in wider scopes than previously possible. Today, a firm can have instant, low-cost access to hundreds of suppliers located around the world. In the same way, individual customers have easy access to many firms as well as access to other customers who have similar interests. This capability enables aggregation economies, savings, or discounts that result from pooling product orders. The Internet also provides a means for low-cost mediation of purchasing transactions. These two benefits are primary reasons for the growth of electronic markets (e-markets) and Internet-based exchanges. eBay, Echemicals, and Monster.com are all examples of these types of businesses.

Explore the websites of E-bay.com, E-chemicals.com, Monster.com, and Covisint.com. What are the basic value-added functions that are provided by these companies? How would these activities be accomplished without the Internet?

Beyond the simple exchange of information, e-business software that resides on the Internet serves to automate many information-intensive processes, such as order transactions, product searches, product specification, and billing. Automated processes are usually executed faster and more reliably that manual processes. In addition, automated online processes are available to be used continuously at the user's convenience. Finally, automated processes are usually cheaper to operate.

Many of the opportunities offered by the Internet and associated resident software programs are just now being uncovered and explored. Most analysts expect that in the coming years, many firms will experience increasing levels of supply chain integration and efficiency through innovative uses of the Internet. The "E-commerce" module discusses E-business issues more thoroughly.

Supply-Chain Metrics

Effective value delivery requires the presence of a comprehensive set of metrics, especially when it comes to supply-chain management. If one's goal is to deliver superior value through an integrated supply chain, then one must be able to determine the extent to which the current supply chain is able to meet or exceed the objective. However, developing effective supply-chain performance metrics can be quite a challenge due to the scope and complexity of the activities involved.

The Supply Chain Council (SCC)[5] has proposed a metrics system now being using by many of its member companies. At the heart of this system are four areas of focus: (1) customer satisfaction/quality, (2) time, (3) cost, and (4) assets. Each of these four areas contains both outcome metrics and predictive metrics such as those summarized in Exhibit 14 on page 26. We will examine three of these metrics in detail: (1) the perfect order, (2) cash-to-cash cycle time (C-to-C), and (3) supply-chain response time (SCRT).

[5] The SCC is an independent not-for-profit trade organization dedicated to the development, promotion, and support of cross-industry standards for supply-chain management. The SCC was organized in 1996 by Pittiglio Rabin Todd & McGrath (PRTM) and Advanced Manufacturing Research (AMR) and originally consisted of 73 founding member companies. It currently consists of more than 200 firms.

EXHIBIT 14
Supply-Chain Metrics

Metric Type	Outcome	Predictive
Customer satisfaction/ quality	Perfect order fulfillment Customer satisfaction Product quality	Delivery-to-commit date Customer inquiry response time
Time	Order fulfillment lead time	Source/make cycle time Supply-chain response time Production plan achievement
Costs	Warranty costs, returns, and allowances Total supply-chain costs	Value-added productivity, e.g., sales per labor hour input
Assets	Cash-to-cash cycle time Inventory days of supply Net asset turns (working capital)	Forecast accuracy Inventory obsolescence Capacity utilization

Source: Adapted from Supply Chain Council, *Integrated Supply Chain Performance Measurement: A Multi-Industry Consortium Recommendation,* Supply Chain Council Report #5566, (1996) p. 6.

To learn about the Supply Chain Council and its activities, read about it at www.supply-chain.org.

Perfect Order Fulfillment

The concept of a perfect order forces management to look at how it ultimately meets the customer's expectations. A **perfect order** meets all of the following standards:

- Delivered complete; all items on order are delivered in the quantities requested.
- Delivered to the customer's request date, with one-day tolerance.
- Documentation supporting the order, including packing slips, bills of lading, invoices, and so on, is complete and accurate.
- Perfect condition: Faultlessly installed (as applicable), correct configuration, customer-ready, no damage.

For each of these four standards, a 0 to 1 rating is used (0, if you did not achieve the standard; 1 if you did). To have a perfect order, all four standards must be met. Perfect order fulfillment is defined as

$$\frac{\text{Number of perfect orders}}{\text{Total number of orders}}$$

This metric is now being used by numerous best-in-class firms, and measuring perfect orders has been very revealing. Procter & Gamble found that when it started measuring perfect order fulfillment in the mid 1990s, it was at about 60 percent. Now, it is operating in excess of 90 percent. Experience with firms has shown that there is a direct positive correlation between performance on this dimension and corporate profitability.

Cash-to-Cash Cycle Time

If a firm is managing its supply chain efficiently, it should be able to reduce the average time that it needs to convert a dollar spent to acquire raw materials into a dollar collected for finished products. This is the reasoning underlying the **cash-to-cash cycle time (C-to-C)** measure, which is defined operationally as follows:

$$\text{Cash-to-cash cycle time} = \text{Total inventory days of supply} + \text{Days sales receivables outstanding} - \text{Days payables outstanding}$$

In order to reduce cash-to-cash cycle time, a firm must reduce the total inventory days of supply, reduce the days of sales receivables outstanding, or increase the days of payables outstanding. Again, good performance on this metric is positively correlated with corporate performance. For example, Kmart found out that it took some 60 days to sell a product after it had ordered it. Yet, its payment cycle for its vendors was 45 days, standard for the industry. This meant that Kmart had to support its inventory for some 15 days. In contrast, Wal-Mart took only 22 days to sell a product after it had been first ordered. Like Kmart, the payment cycle for its vendors was 45 days. While Kmart was struggling, Wal-Mart was prospering and growing.

What does a negative cash-to-cash cycle time indicate?

Supply-Chain Response Time

Supply-chain response time (SCRT) is a measure of the time, in cumulative calendar days, required to recognize a major shift in the marketplace demand, internalize that finding, reevaluate demand, and increase production by 20 percent. Operationally, SCRT can be defined as

$$\text{SCRT} = \text{Forecast cycle} + \text{Reevaluate cycle} + \text{Time to increase production by } 20\%$$

For new products, one would add in ramp up cycle time—the time needed from the production of the first unit until full production is achieved. With SCRT, the lower the number, the more responsive the supply-chain system is.

Module Summary

In recent years, operations management systems have expanded beyond the walls of the internal factory to include the skills and capacities of suppliers and the insights of customers. This expanded system is now referred to as the supply chain. This transformation has occurred because of the needs of firms to enhance their competitiveness and to deliver superior value to their customers. This new approach to operations management has created a more complex and dynamic environment. As we have seen in this module, supply-chain management demands that we coordinate the plans and efforts of such groups as purchasing (representing the firm as buyer), our suppliers, our customers, and logistics (responsible for managing the flows of goods and services within the supply chain). All elements must be considered when managing the supply chain.

From this module, we identified a number of critical lessons and points:

1. Every operations management system combines two components: the internal factory, over which the operations manager has responsibility, and the external factories of suppliers. Operations managers can extend many of the same principles and practices for managing the internal factory to control the activities of suppliers.

2. The entire supply chain can be broken into two major subsystems. The first is the upstream supply chain, which begins with internal operations, extends through first-tier suppliers, and ends with the ultimate producers of raw materials. The second is the downstream supply chain, which starts at the internal operation and ends with the ultimate consumption and/or disposal of goods and services. A firm must manage both ends of the supply chain effectively if it is to be ultimately successful in generating superior value for its customers.

3. The increased interest in supply chains is a result of the increasing needs of "never satisfied" customers, advances in information technology, the emergence of collaborative networks, and the recognition of the need to focus on core competencies.

4. Insourcing–outsourcing and vertical integration decisions should address a wide range of issues including core competencies, quantitative costs, and qualitative advantages and risks.

5. Supply-chain management relationships fall along a spectrum from transaction-based relationships to full partnerships. Transaction-based relationships suit purchases of mature, off-the-shelf products in stable markets. Partnerships intertwine elements of both internal and external factories. At its logical extreme, a partnership creates a virtual corporation, blurring the boundaries between the responsibilities and decisions of a buying firm and its suppliers.

6. Strategic decisions affecting the structure of the supply chain include vertical integration, major objectives (efficiency vs. flexibility), supply-base segmentation and rationalization, and the extent of globalization.

7. The supply chain is dynamic and subject to uncertainties and disturbances that can be detrimental to overall performance. Firms deal with these issues by buffering their internal operations, using postponement strategies; increasing information sharing with supply-chain partners; and increasing integration and coordination of operating systems.

8. A number of innovative approaches and tools are being developed to improve collaborative work among various players in the supply chain. As partners develop procedures and use technologies such as the Internet to improve planning and information sharing, they tend to see large improvements in supply-chain efficiency and customer value.

9. A number of specialized metrics for evaluating supply chain management performance are now in development. Those discussed in this module include the perfect order, cash-to-cash cycle time (C-to-C), and supply-chain response time (SCRT).

Key Terms

Arm's-length relationships, *12*
Buffering, *19*
Bullwhip effect, *18*
Cash-to-cash cycle time (C-to-C), *26*
Centralized sourcing, *15*
Collaborative planning, forecasting, and replenishment (CPFR), *22*
Co-location, *12*
Coordination, *20*
Core competency, *4*
Countertrade, *15*
Customer relationship management (CRM), *24*
Downstream supply chain, *6*
Echelon, *6*
Efficient consumer response (ECR), *21*
External factory, *3*
Full partnerships, *11*
Full postponement, *19*
Information sharing, *20*
Insourcing, *8*
Internal factory, *3*
Local content laws, *14*
Logistics postponement, *19*
Modular consortia, *12*
Outsourcing, *8*
Perfect order, *26*
Postponement, *19*
Process (capability) buy, *9*
Product (capacity) buy, *8*
Production postponement, *19*
Regionalized sourcing, *15*
Safety capacity, *19*
Safety lead time, *19*
Safety stock, *19*
Supplier, *4*
Supply chain, *3*
Supply-chain management, *3*
Supply-chain response time (SCRT), *27*
Tier, *6*
Transaction-based relationships, *11*
Upstream supply chain, *5*
Vendor-managed inventory (VMI), *20*
Vertical integration, *9*
Virtual organizations, *10*

Discussion Questions

1. Identify the core competencies of the following companies:
   a. McDonald's
   b. Hewlett-Packard
   c. Wal-Mart
   d. Taco Bell
2. Discuss how supply-chain management contributes to each element of the value equation:
   a. Timeliness
   b. Quality
   c. Cost
3. "Upstream supply-chain management is considered with efficiency, while the downstream supply-chain management deals more with effectiveness." Discuss this statement and the rationale underlying it.
4. List three firms you think have achieved a competitive advantage through vertical integration. Then cite five firms you think are at a competitive disadvantage because of vertical integration. Compare and contrast the end-product market and raw material sourcing conditions of each. What can you infer?
5. Given the attractiveness of virtual corporations, under what conditions does it make sense to vertically integrate, that is, buy our suppliers?
6. Many firms have moved their manufacturing operations offshore in recent years in favor of lower labor costs. What are the long-term implications of such a strategy?
7. Suppose you manage a small supply firm in an industry in which modular consortia and family-based sourcing are becoming popular. What might you want to do to remain viable in this environment?

8. Discuss the linkages between a firm's demand management and demand forecasting activities and its supply-chain management function. Cite instances in which a firm caused problems for its suppliers because it was unable to provide reasonably accurate demand projections.
9. Consider the supply-chain integration initiatives discussed in this module. What are the fundamental ideas behind the practices that are being implemented? What problems are being addressed?
10. What issues might make a firm unwilling to collaborate with other firms in its supply chain?

Cases

TOY MAKERS 'R' SCARED[6]

Say Hello to Furby. It's here to save Christmas for Hasbro. A five-inch ball of fluffy fur, Furby looks like an Olympic mascot gone mutant. It blinks its eyes fervently before emitting a squawky "cock-a-doodle-doo," followed by mutterings in a nonsensical language called "furbish." Then Furby flaps its pointy little pink ears and giggles. A lot. Then it burps. Toy stores began promoting the $30 toy in late September, and Hasbro is launching a splashy ad and public relations campaign that has landed the ugly critter everywhere from morning talk shows to CNBC and *Fortune* magazine.

The reason Hasbro seems so determined to shove Furby under your tree is that it, along with the other toy titan, Mattel, is heading into one of the most uncertain holiday seasons in a long time. The companies are facing grinches on two fronts. First, the global economic meltdown—particularly in Latin America, which accounts for as much as 10 percent of American toy makers' sales—may crimp revenues this year. Sales of high-end collectible and electronic toys in the United States also may drop as parents spend more carefully in the slowing economy.

But the economy pales next to the manufacturers' second problem: Toys 'R' Us, the toy industry's largest single distributor. Toys 'R' Us has been desperately trying to compete with discount retailers such as Kmart and Wal-Mart, both of which have sliced deeply into its market share. In addition to closing or selling 59 stores worldwide and slashing its existing inventory, it is belatedly adopting the same kind of just-in-time inventory system as its competitors'—which means havoc for toy manufacturers.

Just-in-time toys make perfect sense for Toys 'R' Us; it's an attempt by the company to avoid getting stuck with mounds of unsold merchandise come January 2. But for Hasbro and Mattel, it makes life a lot more complicated. It places the onus of inventory management squarely on the toy manufacturers, complicating their already tricky timing exercise during the holiday season. Most toys are manufactured in Asia, so orders and production for the holiday season usually begin in February, with delivery traditionally scheduled for the third quarter. But the retailers do not pay the manufacturers until they accept the shipment of toys—that is, if they do. Now that the last toy mega-retailer is cleaning up its logistical act, even more shipments and payments are pushed back into the fourth quarter. "The manufacturers will have to make the decisions and produce accordingly," says Kevin Grant, an industry analysis at Harris Associates in Chicago.

Publicly, the toy companies are downplaying the impact of the Toys 'R' Us shift. But despite its recent woes, Toys 'R' Us remains a very significant customer. (Last year, Toys 'R' Us accounted for about 18 percent of Mattel's sales; that number should shrink to about 14 percent this year.) Shortly after Toys 'R' Us announced its restructuring, Mattel and Hasbro each slashed their expected sales by as much as $200 million for the year. Wall Street responded by cutting earnings expectations for the toy companies for this year and next. Analysts' 1999 consensus estimates for Mattel, as reported by First Call, dropped from $2.24 to $2.10; for Hasbro, they dipped from $2.21 to $2.03.

Children may have to cut their expectations, too. If you thought Tickle Me Elmo was hard to get, just wait. "Sometimes you don't quite satisfy the demand. It's probably better than erring in the other direction," says Glenn Bozarth, a spokesman at Mattel. Your kid wants Furby? Run.

QUESTIONS

1. What types of metrics could the management of Mattel and Hasbro have used to help them identify potential problems in their supply chains?

[6]Julier Creswell, "Toymakers 'R' Scared," *Fortune,* November 9, 1998, pp. 36, 38.

2. What can the management of these toy companies do in the short term to deal with the action taken by Toys 'R' Us?

3. What can the management of these toy companies do in the long term to improve the performance of their system? On what management principles can they draw to improve the performance of the supply chain? What incentive(s) can they provide Toys 'R' Us so that it would cooperate?

Related Modules of Interest

- Logistics Management
- Purchasing and Supplier Management
- E-Commerce

Selected Readings

"The Bullwhip Effect in Supply Chain." *Sloan Management Review,* Spring 1997, pp. 93–102.

Davidow, William H., and Michael S. Malone. *The Virtual Corporation: Structuring and Revitalizing the Corporation for the 21st Century.* New York: Harper Business, 1992.

Dobler, Donald, David Burt, and Lamar Lee. *Purchasing and Materials Management,* 5th ed. New York: McGraw-Hill, 1990.

Dyer, J. H., D. S. Cho, and W. Chu. "Strategic Supplier Segmentation: The Next 'Best Practice' in Supply Chain Management." *California Management Review* 40, no. 2, (1998), pp. 57–77.

"Dynamic Demand Management: Striking a Profitable Balance." *Supply Chain Management Review.* Summer 1997, pp. 68–75.

"E-Fulfillment: The Critical Success Factors in e-Commerce." *Supply Chain Management Review,* Global Supplement, Fall 1999.

Fine, Charles H. *Clock Speed: Winning Industry Control in the Age of Temporary Advantage.* Reading, MA: Perseus Books, 1998.

Hamel, Gary, and C. K. Prahalad. "Corporate Imagination and Expeditionary Marketing." *Harvard Business Review,* July–August 1991.

———*Competing for the Future: Breakthrough Strategies for Seizing Control of Your Industry and Creating the Markets of Tomorrow.* Cambridge, MA: Harvard Business School Press, 1994.

"How to Design an Optimum Worldwide Supply Chain." *Supply Chain Management Review,* Spring 1997.

Lee, Hau L. "Creating Value through Supply Chain Integration." *Supply Chain Management Review,* September/October 2000.

McKenna, Regis. *Real Time: Preparing for the Age of the Never Satisfied Customer.* Boston, MA: Harvard Business School Press, 1997.

"A New Framework for Integrated Supply-Chain Management." *Insight* 8, No. 3, pp. 1–4.

"The Power of Virtual Integration: An Interview with Dell Computer's Michael Dell." *Harvard Business Review,* March–April 1998, pp. 72–84.

Pyke, David F., M. Eric Johnson, and Phil Desmond. "eFulfillment—It's Harder Than It Looks!" Supply Chain Management Review, Jan-Feb, 2001.

Prahalad, C. K., and Gary Hamel. "The Core Competence of the Corporation." *Harvard Business Review,* May–June 1990, pp. 79–91.

Quinn, James Brian, and Frederick G. Hilmer. "Strategic Outsourcing." *Sloan Management Review,* Summer 1994, pp. 43–55.

Schorr, J. E., and T. F. Wallace. *High Performance Purchasing.* Brattleboro, VT: Oliver Wight, 1986.

Supply Chain Council. *Integrated Supply Chain Performance Measurement: A Multi-Industry Consortium Recommendation.* Supply Chain Council, Report #5566.

"Supply Chain Postponement and Speculation Strategies: How to Choose the Right Strategy." *Journal of Business Logistics* 19, no. 2 (1998), pp. 13–33.

Womack, James P., Daniel T. Jones, and Daniel Roos. *The Machine That Changed the World.* New York: Rawson Associates, 1990.

Inventory Management

J. Douglas Blocher
Indiana University

McGraw-Hill Irwin

Boston Burr Ridge, IL Dubuque, IA Madison, WI New York San Francisco St. Louis
Bangkok Bogotá Caracas Kuala Lumpur Lisbon London Madrid Mexico City
Milan Montreal New Delhi Santiago Seoul Singapore Sydney Taipei Toronto

Inventory Management

Module objectives

By the end of this module, you should be able to

- Understand the basic components of an inventory system and how it should be managed to create value for the customer.
- Understand the difference between dependent demand and independent demand, and how each requires a different management system.
- Explain the different uses for inventory and the value of the inventory for each of these managerial uses.
- Identify the key metrics for effectively managing inventory performance.
- Identify the different types of inventory.
- Be able to apply an ABC inventory categorization and understand its use.
- Understand the importance of inventory accuracy and how record accuracy can be maintained.

Inventory Management at Welch's, Inc.

Welch's is one of those brands that American consumers have been fond of for years. The company is the largest processor of Concord and Niagara grapes and now distributes a variety of products to both United States and international markets. Its sales in 1999 were just shy of $650 million. Headquartered in Concord, Massachusetts, Welch's is the production, marketing, and distribution arm of the National Grape Cooperative Association representing growers in Michigan, New York, Ohio, Pennsylvania, Washington, and Ontario, Canada.

Like many other agricultural products, the Welch's raw materials are produced in a very seasonal manner requiring Welch's to hold this raw material inventory the rest of the year. Inventory investment at Welch's has averaged 20 percent of its asset base for the last two years, with most of this inventory being raw materials stored as grape juice in refrigerated tanks. These tanks are located at the various production facilities based on upcoming demand forecasts for various products. Transporting the juice between plants is very expensive and is only done when a plant runs short of its requirement; thus, having the right inventory at the right location is an important inventory planning issue for Welch's operations managers.

Welch's produces a variety of end products from its grapes in hundreds of different stockkeeping units. This includes canned, bottled, and frozen juices in sizes from single-serve to half-gallon milk-carton-style containers, jellies and jams in a number of configurations, and other products such as frozen fruit juice bars. Some of these products include other fruits and ingredients as well as the grapes. Due to the volatility in customer demand at the store level, Welch's does hold finished goods to ensure good customer service.

Welch's also sells juice in bulk form to other companies needing it as a raw material. A part of the decision of how much to sell in this raw-material form depends on projected demand for its various end products and the amount of juice required for these products. Welch's uses an MRP (materials requirement planning) system to find the time-phased component requirements for each of its products in their prefinished forms. The MRP system is tied to the accounting systems so that cost and profit projections can be made based on the many possible production plans available to the company. When extra juice is left over from one year, it can be carried into the following year if needed, but of course this increases the company's overall costs as well as its investment needs.

Source: Information from www.welchs.com and E. W. Schuster and S. S. Allen, "Raw Material Management at Welch's, Inc.," *Interfaces*, September–October 1998, pp. 13–24.

As this vignette clearly shows, managers at Welch's are faced with a complex set of challenges and trade-offs. Inputs for their base product are highly seasonal, while the demand for the products made from these inputs (e.g., jams, jellies, and juice) is year round. Furthermore, the customers who buy Welch's jams, jellies, and juices want to have the products available on the shelf when they walk into the grocery store. If the products are not there, then the customers may decide to buy a product made by one of Welch's many competitors—and Welch's could forever lose that customer. Customers also want products that are "fresh"—products that have not been sitting around for a long time somewhere in the supply channel (e.g., in the warehouse or on the store shelves). Finally, Welch's must deal with the ever-present pressure from its corporate customers and distributors for reduced lead times, improved quality, reduced costs, and enhanced flexibility.

Inventory plays critical roles in the tactics Welch's managers are using to deal with these various challenges. Inventory is defined in the *APICS Dictionary* as

> Those stocks or items used to support production (raw materials and work-in-process items), supporting activities (maintenance, report, and operating supplies), and customer service (finished goods and spare parts).[1]

There is certainly a need for finished goods inventories to cover the randomness of daily customer demand. But, in addition, Welch's is faced with an interesting raw material problem. All of its grape raw material must be bought in the summer in a period of a month or two and then stored throughout the rest of the year. Not only does this inventory represent a significant investment for the company, but the storage facilities for the juice require a significant investment as well. In addition, there is an operating expense to keep the product under constant refrigeration so that it doesn't spoil.

Of course, the company has a choice: it could transform the juice into its products as it is brought to the plant. However, much of this finished product—finished goods inventory—would then need to be stored in special facilities. Transforming the juice as it arrives from the farmers also means that larger production capacities would be needed. Storing the raw material adds flexibility as the juice can be used to make a number of different products at the time these products are needed. Thus, decisions about how much inventory to hold, and the form in which it should be held, are key management decisions.

Unfortunately, managers often misunderstand the proper uses of inventory and the ease with which inventory can be abused. Many managers look at inventory as a necessary evil: it is necessary to run a business yet is expensive to hold. In today's customer-oriented environment, having product when the customer wants it can be the difference between a profitable business and one that is bankrupt. Holding inventory can be costly—finding the right level is an important management goal.

In this module we present concepts that should help managers develop a better understanding of inventory within the value-driven operations management system by addressing the following questions:

- What is inventory?
- How does the use of inventory affect the ability of the firm to deliver value to its customers?
- What are the major forms and functions provided by inventory?
- What types of inventory exist (independent versus dependent) and what are the implications of these types for the inventory management function?
- What costs and metrics are most appropriate when dealing with inventory management?

[1] James F. Cox III and John H. Blackstone Jr. (eds.), *APICS Dictionary,* 9th ed. (Falls Church, VA: APICS, 1998), p. 45.

Inventory and Value

Inventory is a corporate asset. That is, it is an investment made by the firm and the operations management system in goods and products. Inventory is created when, over a given period of time, the amount supplied is greater than the amount that is demanded. Inventory can be generated as a result of unforeseen events. For example, Welch's forecasts a high demand for a new product—Concord grape jam that has been tinted pink. To ensure that the product is successfully launched, Welch's has to make sure that sufficient inventory is in the supply chain (at the warehouses and in the stores). However, when released to the market, the customers are not excited. The result is that Welch's now has a lot of unintended inventory in the system.

Alternatively, inventory can be intentional and "valuable" if it enables quality, timeliness, or cost improvements. For example, some inventory exists because the costs of not having it (lost sales, backorders, expedited orders, unplanned disruptions in production) are greater than the costs of having it (e.g., investments, storage costs, holding costs, need for personnel to monitor it). In this case, inventory enhances value through cost avoidance. Inventory also improves value by providing availability (i.e., timeliness) to customers and users. By keeping grapes in processed form (work-in-process inventory), Welch's does not have to halt and start operations with each harvest. Similarly, by Welch's placing jars of its jellies and jams on the shelves of the grocery stores, customers do not have to wait until these items are delivered from the factory.

While inventory often contributes to value, it also can be wasteful, or it can serve as an enabler of waste. Having too much inventory at the wrong place or in the wrong form is wasteful. This is because, ultimately, inventory enhances value only if it is consumed. To put jars of jelly on the shelf of a grocery store, Welch's had to invest resources in making the glass jars, the tops, the labels, and the jelly ingredients. These resources are wasted if the product is not consumed. Why wouldn't the product be consumed? In the case of unsold product languishing on a shelf, it is probably due to inaccurate demand forecasts, or inability to deliver the product in a timely fashion (i.e., a missed sale). This example raises an important point. While inventory is sometimes wasted, the *root cause* of the waste is always somewhere else. Wasted inventory is always an outcome of a deficiency in some other process (e.g., forecasting or delivery).

Looking at it another way, inventory is wasteful when it enables or hides problems. For example, suppose Welch's has quality problems that produce high scrap rates. These quality problems lead to an uncertain production rate. With this uncertainty, one way to still fill product demand reliably would be for Welch's to build large buffer stocks of inventory. Products from the buffer stocks could be used to quickly replace unacceptable product outputs. However, if this solution is seen to be satisfactory, the root causes of the scrap are likely never to be addressed. If the buffer stocks disappeared, then Welch's would be forced to deal with the quality problem. As long as the buffer stocks remain, the quality problem remains. In this way, inventory is an enabler of waste.

In the past, and still too often today, inventory is wasteful, or at least an enabler of waste. Why? First, inventory is often seen as a quick and painless solution. Creating inventory simply requires the production operation to produce more than it needs. Second, inventory is treated positively by the accounting system. It is recorded as an asset—something that is fundamentally "good." Third, inventory is attractive as a type of "security blanket." When we see ourselves surrounded by inventory, we feel that we will not have customer demand problems. These are very powerful motivators that help us to understand why inventory has to be managed carefully.

Economic Importance of Inventory

According to the president's *Economic Report,* the U.S. economy held \$1.4 trillion in inventories in 1999.[2] This represents a decline in the amount of inventory as a percentage of sales over the past 10 years. Exhibit 1 shows that there also has been a shift in where the

[2] *Economic Report of the President* (Washington, DC: Government Printing Office, 2000).

EXHIBIT 1
Inventory in the Economy - By Sector

Source: *Economic Report of the President* (Washington, DC: Government Printing Office, 2000).

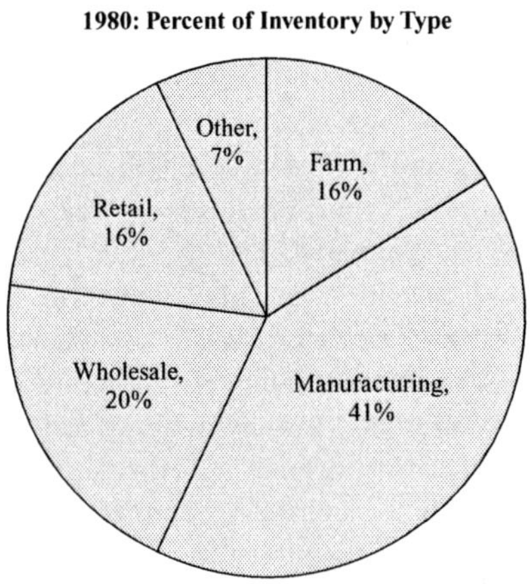

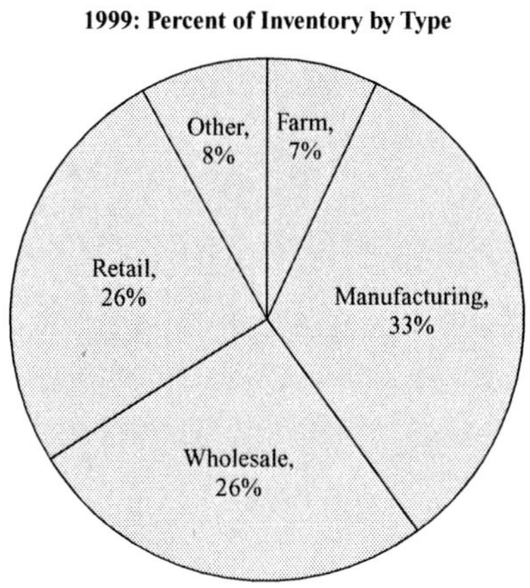

inventories are held. Notice that inventories in manufacturing are declining as an overall percentage while inventories in the retail and wholesale sectors—businesses predominately in the service sector—are increasing as a percentage of the overall amount. It is also interesting to notice that the retail and wholesale inventories combined now make up a larger part of the inventories than that of the manufacturing sector.

While it is hard to characterize the importance of inventories on a firm-by-firm basis, suffice it to say that almost all firms have them, and they can have a significant cost and investment importance. Inventory data as well as other important information on a number of leading business firms are given in Exhibit 2. These firms were picked from three different industries. Some are "old economy" firms from the auto sector, some are "newer economy" high-tech firms, and some are common service-sector firms that use physical product as a "supporting good" to the service transaction.

While services are not directly "inventoried," most service business managers must still understand the role of inventory as many of them use physical products as supporting goods to the service transaction. As the data suggest, understanding inventory and the systems to manage that inventory are important for managers in both service businesses and manufacturing businesses. The notion that controlling inventory is very important for manufacturing firms, but less so for service firms, can't be farther from the truth. The firms shown in Exhibit 2 may not be representative of all types of service firms, but the exhibit does show how important holding costs can be for key retailers. This also should make clear that inventory management is not just a discipline for manufacturing managers.

Wal-Mart has such a keen understanding of what drives inventory costs that it has pushed the manufacturing industries that supply Wal-Mart to new levels of inventory efficiency. Some of these manufacturers are even responsible for the inventory in Wal-Mart stores, getting paid for the item only when it sells. Notice that Wal-Mart has about 30 percent of their

EXHIBIT 2 **1999 Selected Corporate Financial Highlights ($ Billions)**

Company	Assets	Sales	Cost of Goods Sold	Net Income	Inventory Investment	Turns	Investments/ Assets	Holding Cost*	Holding/ Net Income
Ford	276	162	118	7.2	6.4	4.9	2.3%	1.9	27%
GM	275	177	127	6.0	10.6	2.8	3.9	3.2	53
Toyota	131	106	76	3.7	6.4	3.2	4.8	1.9	51
IBM	87	88	49	7.7	4.9	2.4	5.6	1.5	19
HP	35	42	28	3.5	4.9	1.3	13.8	1.5	42
Dell	11	25	20	7.3	0.4	15.0	3.4	0.1	7
Intel	44	29	9	1.7	1.5	1.4	3.4	0.4	27
Wal-Mart	70	165	127	5.4	19.8	1.7	28	5.9	110
Kmart	15	36	27	0.4	7.1	1.0	47	2.1	530
Sears	37	41	27	1.5	5.1	1.4	14	1.5	105

*Holding cost is estimated at 30 percent of inventory investment.

assets in inventory and their holding costs can be as large as their net income! This is true for their competition as well.

While manufacturing firms do not have the relative magnitude of inventories as a percent of assets, the impact of inventories on the bottom line still can be staggering. Elimination of these holding costs could increase the bottom line on the order of 50 percent and, at the same time, reduce the asset burden of the company as well. Manufacturing firms, in general, have been working on reducing inventories for years now under the banners of just-in-time and lean production, concepts that view inventory as waste and therefore fodder for elimination. Now with the focus on supply-chain management, manufacturers, their distributors, and the retailers are all working together to reduce inventory along the whole supply chain.

With all of the emphasis on reducing inventory in the supply chain, it is imperative that managers understand how to manage and control inventory. It may seem at first thought that since there is less inventory to manage, inventory management is less important. However, upon further reflection, the opposite is the case. Inventory can be a substitute for management attention: less inventory implies more management attention. The real important issue to understand is that inventory must be held only for reasons of value: reducing costs and increasing customer satisfaction.

Part of the goal of this chapter is to show how inventory can add value. When inventory is removed from a system, the associated costs of holding the inventory decline, but at the same time, other costs can increase. These increases can show up most noticeably in the cost of customer service: if inventory is reduced too much, customers can't find the product they want when they want it and can become dissatisfied with the company making the product or the retailer selling it.

In addition, the productivity of the workforce and the utilization of equipment can be affected as well. Without proper buffers, if something goes wrong with one step in a production process with no inventory available to buffer the problem, the whole process may stop, idling the plant and reducing its overall capacity.

Finally, when inventory is reduced, something else must take its place. Information and control systems must improve to make up for the lack of the inventory. More management attention may be required, at least in the short run, to create processes and systems that lead to the best use of the inventory investment. Thus, as inventory is reduced, its management becomes even more critical.

Inventory Metrics

There are two basic categories of inventory performance metrics: one category addresses cost; the other, delivery timeliness. Note that cost and timeliness are two basic elements of value. Regarding cost, **inventory turnover** is the ratio of the cost of annual sales to the average inventory level. The higher the inventory turns, the better the firm uses its inventory assets. Another common measure is **days of supply.** If no more shipments are received, this measure indicates how long the current inventory would last.

As an example of these measures, assume a firm has an annual cost of sales of $180 million and an average inventory level for the year of $20 million, then

$$\text{Inventory turns} = \text{Cost of sales/Average inventory level} = \$180/\$20 = 9 \text{ turns}$$

The cost of sales for a day is $180 million/360 days = $0.5 million.

$$\text{Days of supply} = \text{Average inventory/Cost of a day's sales} = \$20/\$0.5 = 40 \text{ days' supply}$$

Regarding delivery timeliness, the key inventory performance metrics indicate the degree to which customers receive what they order on time. These percent-met measures are commonly referred to as **fill rates,** of which there are a number of different kinds. The *item fill rate* is the ratio of the total number of items shipped divided by the total number of items ordered. The *line-item fill rate* measures the percentage of line items shipped as a function of the total line items ordered. Finally, the *order fill rate* is a measure of the percentage of orders shipped completely.

EXHIBIT 3
Sample Order

Item Number	Item Description	Quantity Ordered	Quantity Shipped
A3550	Step signal	90	90
J9333	Indicator lamp	200	100
L2433-a		5	0
P1943	3-pole switch—12 amp, r1	4000	3900
P1944	3-pole switch—14 amp, r1	600	600
P3007	3-pole switch—22 amp, r8	100	90
R1220	Double capacitor	10	10
S5762	Switch board	25	25
S5763	Switch board	4	0
X8019	Conductor plate	2	2

To illustrate these fill rate measures, consider the order displayed in Exhibit 3. First, there are a total of 5,036 items (i.e., units ordered) on this order. Since 4,817 of the items were shipped, the item fill rate is

$$\text{Item fill rate} = 4{,}817/5{,}036 = 95.6\ \%$$

A stricter measure is the line-item fill rate. There are 10 lines of items ordered, and of these 10 line items, only 5 of them were filled in their entirety; thus the line-item fill rate is

$$\text{Line-item fill rate} = 5/10 = 50\%$$

An even stricter measure is the order fill rate, that is, the percentage of orders filled completely. Clearly, the order shown in Exhibit 3 counts in the unfilled category. This measure is the strictest of the three measures of customer service, but it also might be the one that is the most relevant in keeping customers happy in the long run.

Fill rates can sometimes be manipulated to make them look as good as one wants to make them look. Not only are there three different fill rates one can use, but the timing of how quickly the order is filled can be manipulated as well. For instance, if an order is shipped within a week of being placed, that may satisfy the supplying firm's measurement of fill. However, if the customer is counting on the product in three days, there is obviously a disconnect between the firm and its customer. Whatever the fill metric used, it should be used for improvement in customer perception—the metric needs to be based on the voice of the customer. Designing a metric that, when computed, makes the firm sound like a winner every period doesn't add value for anyone. An appropriate measure tracked through time and based on customer expectations will get everyone moving toward the right goal. As customer expectations change over time, these metrics may need to be changed as well.

Inventory Types

Most of us tend to think about three main types of inventories: raw material, work-in-process, and finished goods. Accounting texts and tax forms have made these terms fairly common. Raw material inventory is that material that one buys from suppliers to use in the making of a product. Once raw material enters the production process, it becomes classified as work-in-process inventory. Finally, when the product is completed and put in a warehouse or on a dock to move to the customer, it becomes finished goods inventory.

Two comments are needed relative to these three inventory types. First, it is important to recognize that raw material is generally less costly to hold than WIP, and WIP is generally less costly to hold than finished goods. Second, one has to be careful with the terminology when discussions involve multiple firms: what leaves one firm as a finished good enters the next firm down the supply chain as raw material.

The three types of inventory discussed above apply mainly to **productive material**—material that is a direct component of the product the company sells. Another type of inventory is nonproductive—that is, material that is not used directly as a component of a product, but is instead used indirectly in the production of the product or used in the more general operation of the firm. This nonproductive material is generally referred to as **maintenance, repair, and operating supplies,** or **MRO** for short, and includes office paper and forms, toilet paper and cleaning supplies, and tools and parts to repair equipment.

From an operations management perspective, this typology provides limited help in conversing about inventories. For productive material, a different breakdown can be even more helpful for understanding how inventory impacts customer value. What is required is a way of understanding why inventory is needed—understanding its value to the customer and the firm.

The Functions of Inventory

Inventory, when used properly, adds value to the firm; otherwise, no firm would have any. Understanding how inventory adds value, along with understanding the costs, should be a part of most managers' training. There are a number of different functions that inventory provides to add value. Understanding each function is essential to improving the value of a firm's inventory assets. Furthermore, to reduce inventories, it is difficult to "attack" inventory directly. Rather, you must attack the relevant inventory driver, the function provided by the inventory. Each inventory function requires a unique management perspective as well as a different management planning and control methodology. So a more useful inventory typology for those managing and controlling inventories (as opposed to an accounting classification of raw, WIP, and finished) is one that classifies inventory by its function or role. In the following sections, we define the primary inventory functions.

Production Smoothing

When demand for a product is **seasonal,** inventory may be accumulated during low-demand periods for use in high-demand periods. This allows managers to produce with a lower overall plant capacity and to maintain a more stable workforce and production material flow. An opposite policy can be used to deal with seasonality in supply (accumulate inventory in high-supply periods for use in low-supply periods).

The decisions about these **production-smoothing inventories** are made as a part of the aggregate production plan, a medium- to long-term planning decision. This inventory is usually held in the form of finished goods or as almost-complete work-in-process inventory when dealing with demand seasonality. The inventory is held as raw materials or work-in-process if supply seasonality is the issue, as was the case in the opening story about Welch's.

Obviously, the more seasonal or cyclical demand is, the more need there is for this type of inventory. The higher the costs of changing production rates (e.g., by hiring or firing workers) and the more restrictions placed on these rates (work contracts), the higher the smoothing inventories. If plant and equipment capacity is very expensive, then it is more likely a firm will use this kind of inventory to smooth production so that peak capacity needs are kept to a minimum. High capacity utilization would be important throughout the year.

Lot Size

The **lot size** determines the number of units of an item that will be produced or purchased each time the item is ordered. In many cases, production resources are deployed to produce more than one product; thus, the equipment must undergo a changeover when production is switched from one product to another. For instance, suppose a machine produces four products, each of which is run during one week of every month. During a production run, the process must produce enough product to meet demand over the one-month period; therefore, the production lot size is one month's worth of inventory. The average inventory of the four products would be about two weeks' worth.

The smaller the lot size, the smaller the average lot-size inventory, an important concept for JIT environments. Lot-size choices at some stage of the manufacturing process can impact every other stage producing components for that stage. Suppose Cannondale assembles a particular bicycle in batches of 100. Then frames likely will be produced in batch

In Practice

BIGGER AND BETTER CLEARANCE SALES?

Retail chains that conduct clearance sales can increase profits by millions of dollars by taking markdowns sooner and giving steeper discounts or even donating excess merchandise to charities, according to a study in the current edition of *Management Science.*

Authors Stephen A. Smith and Dale D. Achabal of the Leavey School of Business at Santa Clara University have created a mathematical model that can be applied by computers at each of a chain's individual stores.

It sets an optimal price and adjusts inventories during end-of-season clearance—the last phase of a product's life after regular and promotional sales. The researchers designed their model to draw on data from point-of-sale (POS) databases that retailers use to retain and track product sales.

The model is incorporated into a retailer's decision support system for ease of use. It determines a table of recommended clearance markdowns as a function of store inventory level and projected sales for the remainder of the season for which the model is applied.

Clearance markdowns often total several hundred million dollars annually for major retail chains. Given thin margins of many retailers, the effectiveness of clearance markdown policies can make the difference between a profitable and unprofitable season.

Setting clearance pricing and inventory policies, though, is a challenge when individual stores in a large chain have different levels of demand for individual products. There is an advantage to setting clearance prices at the store level to account for variations in inventory levels and sales rates across stores. But existing systems often apply the same markdown regionally or nationwide due to the complexity and time-consuming nature of the decision.

That analysis applies when the rate of sale is sensitive to inventory level—when sales rates drop as inventory falls below a certain level. In general, the authors conclude, the initial clearance markdowns should be deeper than buyers are accustomed to taking, while excessive markdowns at the end of the season should be avoided in favor of donating products to charities, or even discarding unsold merchandise.

Source: "Clearance pricing and inventory policies for retail chains," *MS/OR Today,* March 1988, v. 44, No. 3, p. 285–300

sizes of at least 100 and the tubing for the frames will need to be purchased with these same lot sizes in mind. In addition, lot-size choices may be made at lower levels independent of what happens at the master-scheduling level. High setup and changeover costs can increase lot sizes for fabricated components and high shipping and order-related costs can increase purchasing lot sizes. Lot-size inventories therefore can occur as finished goods, as work in process, and as raw material.

Purchasing decisions also impact inventories. Suppliers may offer price discounts when larger quantities are purchased. Part of this price discount comes from shipping economies while part comes from longer production runs at the supplier's plants. Part of Wal-Mart's cost advantage is its ability to buy large volumes, divide it among its distribution centers, and then ship to its stores in small quantities as the product is demanded.

Customer Service Safety Stock

Demand uncertainties cause a firm to hold inventory in case demand is higher than expected in a given period. This *safety stock inventory,* as it is usually called, is a direct result of the order fill-rate policy (also referred to as safety stock policy, stockout policy, or service level policy) derived from the business's marketing strategy. If demand varies significantly and this variation cannot be reliably forecast, then firms wishing to support a high order fill rate may need a lot of customer service inventory. Since safety stock inventories buffer the firm from demand fluctuations, they are sometimes referred to as demand buffer inventories.

Safety stock inventories are usually held in finished goods or almost-complete work in process, although this is highly dependent on the response speed of a plant or the amount of customization required. Dell is primarily an assemble-to-order firm, making hundreds of different possible computer configurations. However, the number of components they carry is significantly less than the number of configurations they sell, so they are better off holding customer service inventory in components—raw materials for the most part. This means that Dell must be able to assemble a finished computer very quickly so that the customer doesn't have to wait very long when an order is placed. If Dell had to hold all possible end-item configurations in inventory, its inventory would be massive. Obviously, in a make-to-order firm where customer requirements are not known in advance, it is very difficult to have any safety stock inventory.

The higher the **customer service level,** the higher the need for safety stock inventories. Some firms create this high service expectation with their advertisements. Others are required to have high service levels because of the competition. The more variable the demand, the higher the level of safety stock required. Finally, long lead times also increase the need for customer service inventories. Customer service inventories can be thought of as inventory that decouples the variation of market demand from the more desired constant production rate of a manufacturer. This has some similarities to process decoupling inventory, the kind of inventory that is discussed next.

Process Decoupling

As a product is produced, it moves through a series of production stages. Keeping inventories between production stages acts as a **decoupling** buffer, allowing the two stages to operate independently. This is especially important if the two stages naturally operate at significantly different output rates, or if they are required to. Even when two stages can operate at the same output rate, if no inventory is maintained between successive stages, then an equipment failure or quality problem in one stage can cause the other stage to be shut down as well. Carried to an extreme, if no inventory is maintained at any stage of a process, then a breakdown or quality problem at any stage of the process can shut a whole plant down.

On the other hand, if quality problems are very rare, machines are maintained so that they are dependable, and lot sizes can be matched from stage to stage, then these decoupling inventories are less necessary and product can be moved "just in time" from one process to the next. Process decoupling inventories by definition are work in process.

Supply Decoupling

Supply decoupling inventories, or sometimes supply safety stock or supply **buffer,** are held to guard against raw material shortages. This extra inventory may be held to decouple the firm from its supplier due to an unreliable supplier, a strike at a supplier's plant, or a problem with the transportation system. The degree to which this is important depends on the firm's supply strategy and the nature of the industry in which it operates. These inventories are generally held as raw materials although some preliminary processing may occur in certain cases.

Economic Incentive

Suppliers often offer discounts when products are purchased in large quantities. Firms make decisions about balancing this **quantity discount** with the cost of holding the extra inventory. A firm may set guidelines on how this is handled, but most often it is a purchasing decision. These inventories, like the supply decoupling inventories, are generally held as raw material inventories.

Pipeline

When goods must be transported long distances, a firm may have a substantial amount of inventory "rolling" from one location to another. Rail shipments from a plant in Pittsburgh to a market location such as Los Angeles, for example, may take on average eight days to complete. If the daily demand in the LA area is 10,000 units per day, then 80,000 units of inventory are needed to "fill the pipeline." This in-transit inventory is a result of the firm's plant location strategy and distribution transport mode. Pipeline inventories generally are finished goods; however, an argument can be made that transportation between any two stages of a process can cause this kind of inventory as well. In general, the amount of this **in-transit inventory** is a function of three factors: (1) the distance covered, (2) the quantity shipped, and (3) the mode of transportation used (e.g., truck, rail, air, water, pipeline).

Speculative

A firm that uses gold, platinum, or any commodity that can have high price volatility may buy large volumes at certain times betting that the market price will go up and therefore give it an advantage over its competitors. There should be little value in doing this if there is a well-developed futures market for the particular material. Care should be taken that purchasing managers aren't making these decisions, which should be made by financial market experts. After all, the price also can drop and thus the firm is open to higher costs when buying up front. Firms that choose to do this speculating and consistently make money doing so should probably consider changing businesses.

Purchasing managers also may make "speculative buys" if they suspect that shortages or supply disruptions will occur in the near future. For example, they might invest in this function of inventory if they suspect a strike is eminent at a key supplier, or if they think that the supplier is about to reduce the allotment of a key component. **Speculative inventories** are generally held as raw materials.

Summary of Inventory Functions

For each of these eight functions of inventory we can identify ways to reduce the functional need, and thereby reduce the associated inventory levels. Some exemplar methods are summarized in Exhibit 4. This table reinforces the message previously noted, inventory is a symptom, not necessarily the problem. Note that none of the "solutions" offered in Exhibit 4 are "free." Many involve replacing inventory with another type of cost, or another type of inventory. Frequently, however, inventory reductions that come as a result of reducing uncertainties or inefficiencies are almost always cost effective.

EXHIBIT 4
Methods for Reducing the Functional Needs for Inventory

Inventory Function	Possible Means for Reducing the Need for Inventory
Production smoothing	Demand seasonality: Offer incentives to customers to increase the demand period, to smooth demand quantities, or to accept back-orders. Supply seasonality: Source supplies that are available year round (e.g., Welch's buys grapes in South America as well as in California/Florida).
Lot size	Reduce setup/ordering costs or time. Improve master production scheduling.
Customer service	Learn more about customers in order to develop better forecasting procedures. Offer incentives to customers to accept backorders.
Process decoupling	Balance production rates of the equipment. Reduce breakdowns, quality problems, or other disruptions.
Supply decoupling	Reduce uncertainties at the supplier through certification, joint development programs, or better supplier selection.
Economic incentive	Negotiate large volume purchases with phased deliveries and payment on receipt.
Pipeline	Find closer locations and/or faster transport modes. Shift ownership of the inventories to the shipper or receiver.
Speculative	Develop alternative suppliers or substitutes. Lock suppliers into long-term agreements. Vertically integrate.

Inventory Costs

Inventory decisions are affected by a number of different cost factors. These factors include the costs of ordering and holding inventory, costs related to the purchase price of an item, and the costs of the inventory policy being used, and the costs of transporting items between suppliers and buyers. Some of these costs can be difficult to quantify, so specific awareness and implicit management consideration are often the only way to incorporate them into the decision process. Examples of these cost categories are given below.

Ordering

Any costs that are a function of the number of orders placed are grouped under ordering costs. These include

- Order placement costs.
- Quote management costs.

- Order-dependent shipment costs.
- Shipment-dependent receiving and inspection costs.
- Accounts payable transaction costs.

Holding

The costs most often associated with inventory are grouped under the broad heading of inventory holding. These costs are a function of the number of units held in inventory and are generally stated in terms of some percentage of the value of the average inventory. They include

- Cost of capital.
- Floor or warehouse space.
- Obsolescence, spoilage, and pilferage.
- Utilities and insurance.
- Movement to/from storage.
- Record accuracy (see section below).

Stockout

A shortage of inventory, or **stockout,** can lead to a number of customer-service-related costs because there is no inventory to meet demand. Some of these costs are quite difficult to quantify, but include

- In-plant expediting.
- Expedited shipments.
- Substitution of higher-cost item.
- Customer goodwill on lost sales and backorders.

From an inventory management standpoint, keeping track of lost sales and backorders is important so that service can be improved. Backorders are easier to track than lost sales and are probably less expensive. Manufacturers who get calls from their customers and then can't deliver (lost sale) or can't deliver on time (backorder) have an advantage over service businesses. Many service businesses don't have the luxury of even knowing if they miss a sale. Unless a customer specifically makes a request or inquiry about a product, in which case the customer might be given a "rain check," which creates a backorder, service companies may never know that a sale was lost. Expediting, substitution, and to some degree other backorder costs can be reasonably estimated, but lost sales costs are very difficult to quantify. In fact, in many cases, management may not even try to estimate a cost but instead opt for some kind of service fill-rate policy.

Product Price

Suppliers sometimes induce their customers to buy in larger quantities than they would otherwise by offering discounts that are a function of the quantity purchased. In addition, prices are sometimes a function of the time of the year an item is purchased, and thus lot sizes may be influenced by when prices are expected to rise or fall. These product-price costs include

- Quantity discounts.
- Time-dependent prices.

Management System

Firms must make choices about how to manage their various assets—inventory is no exception. The type of inventory policy used for an item determines how much effort and cost are required while the level of forecast sophistication impacts costs as well. While both of these costs are difficult to quantify, they do have an impact on overall cost and an attempt to quantify the costs is better management practice than simply ignoring the costs.

Computerized inventory management systems can require large investments in hardware and software, not to mention the internal and external costs to keep these systems going and to keep them current. Just keeping the databases on which these systems operate up to date can require significant levels of resources. Engineering changes must constantly be fed into the product database and inventory levels and lead times must be accurate for each component.

Inventory Management

The basic management decisions about inventories involve determining (*i*) how much of it should be held, (*ii*) in which form or where it should be held, and (*iii*) how much effort should be put into its management system. These decisions must be made while keeping in mind the key trade-offs of the situation. Inventory provides value in terms of customer service and cost efficiency, but there also is a cost to maintain and manage the asset. To a large degree, this is determined by the cost of not having enough versus the cost of having too much; however, it also may be based on the strategy of the firm and the firm's overall philosophy about inventory, especially as related to lean manufacturing and JIT.

How Much?

The decision about how much to hold depends on a number of things, one of which is the level of customer service desired. Both service and manufacturing firms must decide how much finished goods (and, in some cases, almost-finished goods) to hold as these decisions affect customer service. If customers value being able to pick up an item, pay for it, and leave with the product in hand, then inventory must be available.

Inventory investment also impacts the workforce strategy employed. Building inventory in advance of peak selling seasons allows workers to be employed year round rather than being laid off during slow selling times.

For manufacturing firms, keeping inventory between stages of the production process can help the process run more efficiently and more effectively. Picking the correct amount, however, is not an easy decision. For years, many firms had tremendous amounts of inventory between stages because of lot size choices and just in case something went wrong. While the level of inventory investment should have been a policy decision, many times the level was set based on how much the system seemed to need. When policies set these levels, many times the levels are based on static assumptions rather than with the thinking that things can be improved over time. The just-in-time philosophy pushes companies to eliminate those things in the production process that lead to large lot sizes or add uncertainty. Thus, the amount of between-process inventory can be reduced significantly when the proper steps are taken to make the production environment simple, flexible, and stable.

Which Form or Where?

Decisions also must be made about whether to hold inventory as raw material, work-in-process, or finished goods. These decisions are in large part dependent on the function of the inventory. Still, it is almost always cheaper to hold inventory before value is added: the closer to the raw material state the better. For instance, **safety stock** is often held to guard against demand variability; thus, it may seem appropriate to hold this safety stock inventory in a finished form. However, if customers can purchase the final product with an almost unlimited number of options, then it might make more sense to stock the basic components (work-in-process) and then assemble the product from these components at the last minute, or very quickly after an order is received. A good example of a product that fits this category is the personal computer. The closer a firm can come to assembling on demand, the better the chances of holding safety stock in a cheaper form. A thorough understanding of the complete value chain aids this decision process.

Determining which form of inventory to hold is really the same as determining where in the value chain inventory should be held. For instance, inventory to be held in raw material form should be held at the very beginning of the process. When product is moving from the manufacturer through some kind of distribution network, determining where in the network to hold the inventory is as important as how much to hold. As a distributor commits inventory by moving it downstream from the manufacturer toward the customer, the distributor gives up flexibility. In other words, it can be difficult and expensive to move inventory back up the chain so that it can be reassigned to some other location.

How Much Management Effort?

There are a number of classical inventory management systems as well as many hybrids and derivatives. Each of these systems requires varying amounts of information and resources. As one might imagine, the more complex a system is, or the more information a system requires, the more expensive the system is to operate.

Inventory systems are often divided into two classes: those for dependent-demand items and those for independent-demand items. For every bicycle Cannondale plans to build, it needs two tires. Demand for tires is *dependent* on the number of bicycles produced—producing 10 bicycles requires 20 tires. However, the demand for bicycles is unknown since it is impossible to predict what or if consumers will buy on any given day or in any given week. It doesn't depend on the demand for any other product. Therefore, demand for the finished bicycle is termed *independent.* Independent demand can be estimated, but demand forecasts always have some uncertainty in them.

Managing the demand for tires requires requirements planning–type models, often referred to as **materials requirement planning (MRP)** systems. On the other hand, the demand for bicycles is better handled with replenishment-type models, or independent-demand models. Systems for dependent items and those for independent items are discussed next.

Dependent-Demand Systems

Dependent-demand systems, or requirement planning systems, use a bill of materials for an end item (like a bicycle) to determine not only the component quantities (such as two tires per bicycle) but also the timing of the delivery of the tires. For instance, assume a firm makes and sells four models of bicycles, each requiring different tires. Average weekly sales for these models are shown in Exhibit 5.

EXHIBIT 5
Average Sales Data for Bicycles

Model	A	B	C	D
Average sales/Week	300	100	50	50

This bicycle manufacturer might have a master schedule that looks something like that in Exhibit 6, where the plan is to assemble 100 units per day with the same production pattern each week. To look at the issue of timing, note that model B has demand of 100 per week, or an average of 20 per day. But average sales data in this case are not what we are interested in for ordering tires. The average sales of 20 per day is aggregated for the week and produced on Thursday. Thus, if the tires for Model B take two days to get to the plant from the supplier, an order needs to be placed on Tuesday for 200 tires so that they will arrive just as needed for Thursday's production. This of course assumes that there is no inventory available. If there were some tires in inventory, the requirement planning

EXHIBIT 6
Master Production Schedule for Bicycle Manufacturer

Day of Week	Monday	Tuesday	Wednesday	Thursday	Friday
Model	A	A	A	B	C, D

system would need to net out the available inventory and order the 200 less what is in current inventory.

In some sense, dependent-demand items should be easy to control because of this dependency. Certainly the logic behind such a system is relatively straightforward. Even though these systems are logically simple, they can be quite expensive to put in place, maintain, and operate.

Inventory accuracy is important in these systems because they are designed to have very little extra stock. After all, if you plan to make 100 bicycles and this requires 400 axle nuts, what is the purpose of buying 450? On the other hand, keeping the inventory records accurate for a small, inexpensive item such as an axle nut might be more expensive than simply managing the axle nut as if it were an independent-demand item. For this reason, some low-value items with demand that is clearly dependent are managed with a simple independent-demand system such as a min-max system or a two-bin system. These independent-demand systems are discussed next.

Independent-Demand Systems

Independent-demand inventory systems are designed to replenish inventory based on some period of time, some inventory level, or some combination of both. **Periodic inventory review** systems trigger inventory replenishment when some particular time point is reached. **Continuous inventory review** systems trigger orders when the on-hand inventory level reaches a prespecified level and thus require continuous monitoring to decide when this trigger point has been reached. Below are some common inventory management systems that are variations and hybrids of these periodic and continuous review policies.

The **base stock inventory system** attempts to keep inventory at a constant level. In its purest form, each time there is a withdrawal from inventory, an order is placed to replenish the amount removed. This kind of system is most appropriate for expensive items that involve fairly infrequent demand, where holding costs greatly dominate ordering costs. In this form, the base stock system is a continuous review system.

A variation of the base stock system, the **period base stock system,** is much more common. At the end of each day (or this could be done each week), everything that was sold that day is replenished the next day. This variant is more akin to a periodic review system. Some large retailers that have trucks arriving daily from a warehouse might choose to replenish the amount used daily. Still, in this environment it is necessary to keep inventory-ordering costs low, so automatic electronic reordering based on point-of-sale (POS) data drives such a system's orders.

A **min-max system** is another common simple inventory system that is a hybrid of the continuous and periodic concepts. Some also refer to this as an *s,S* system or an optional replenishment system. Two levels of inventory, a minimum level and a maximum level, are needed for this system. Inventory is checked periodically, say at the end of each day, to see if it has fallen below the minimum level. If it has, then it is replenished to its maximum level.

The **two-bin system,** as its name implies, uses two containers. Inventory is taken from one container, usually the larger of the two, until that container is empty. When the first container is empty, an order for replenishment is sent and the second container is used while the replenishment order is being shipped. This is one of the most common implementations of a continuous review system as inventory is replenished each time it reaches a certain level. The **one-bin system** is like a period base stock system. A single container holds some desired amount of inventory, and after some period of usage, the bin is refilled to its original level.

Controlling the inventory of independent-demand items is difficult due to the uncertainty inherent in the timing and size of customer orders. Even the best forecasting methods, if one can afford them, still involve uncertainty. While the above systems can be easy to use when the parameters are set in an ad hoc manner, they can be much more difficult to use when these parameters are set based on statistically derived reasoning. Implementation, on the other hand, is generally rather cheap when compared to MRP systems.

Many service firms, such as retailers selling goods to consumers, have little if any dependent-demand items—they aren't producing a product and therefore aren't concerned with components. Thus, they have almost all independent-demand items. They need some way to divide items into different categories, as some are more important than others in terms of cost or priority. Manufacturers are faced with the same set of issues in managing their MRO items.

To help establish priorities about individual inventory items, an ABC Pareto analysis can be used to divide inventories into categories of relative importance. In general, those items that are expensive to hold, because of large volumes, high costs, or both, generally deserve more resources. The investment in those items can be used to justify more expensive inventory management systems. On the other hand, less expensive or low-volume items can be managed with a minimum amount of effort and simple inventory systems. The next section discusses this ABC categorization in more depth.

ABC Inventory Categorization

Managing inventories, like anything else, requires resources. Just as the line manager must decide which subordinates will require the closest supervision, so must the materials manager decide which inventory items will be given the most attention. The materials manager must decide which item to order, when to order it, and how much to order. For some distribution firms with tens if not hundreds of thousands of items to manage, this task cannot be done efficiently without automating a large part of the work.

The **ABC classification** concept is based on the Pareto principle of simply classifying the various inventory items based on their relative importance. Often there are three classes—labeled A, B, and C—although this varies from firm to firm. The process of assigning items to classes (i.e., determining relative importance) is sometimes a contentious subject. One can argue that the Pareto logic for inventory translates into the following statement.

> There are a few items that are vitally important to the firm (the A items) and thus should be managed with great attention. In addition, there are many items that are trivial (the C items) and thus warrant little attention. Items between these two classifications (the B items) are generally not trivial nor of vital importance and thus are given a moderate amount of attention.

This statement can lead to some serious management concerns such as "if an item is not important, why should it even be carried" or "all of our items are important so we have all A items." Of course, eliminating all but the A items is, in most cases, not a reasonable business decision; and categorizing everything as an A doesn't help us manage things any better.

The most common measure used for classification in an ABC system is that of total annual dollar volume for each inventory item. Although this is certainly not the only measure available, it is in most cases correlated with the percentage of profit the company makes on an SKU, correlated with the cost of holding the inventory, and it is a readily available measure from the firm's database. The example in Exhibit 7 of 10 SKUs (stockkeeping units, or inventory items) should help illustrate the ABC concept with the annual value measure determining the rank.

After ranking the various items, the next step is assigning them to classes so that the appropriate amount of management resources can be allocated to each class. For this example, a

EXHIBIT 7
Sample Ranking of Inventory Items

SKU	Item Cost	Annual Usage	Annual Value	Rank
G-507-aa	$0.45	50,000	$ 22,500	2
G-680-va	0.80	600	480	10
K-100-ls	1.70	2,000	3,400	4
K-300-lt	2.20	250	550	9
K-303-lv	0.90	8,000	7,200	3
K-601-lt	0.50	4,000	2,000	5
N-005-sa	8.50	80	680	8
N-035-dx	4.00	24,000	96,000	1
P-440-va	1.20	900	1,080	7
Z-212-rs	0.02	100,000	2,000	6
Total			$135,890	

starting point can be obtained by assigning the top 20 percent of items to the A group and the bottom 50 percent to the C group. After closer inspection, one might revise this and put the two SKUs with the same annual dollar volumes, ranked fifth and sixth, into the same group, say the C group. Thus, the A group would have two items making up 87 percent of the total annual inventory value, the B group two items making up 8 percent, and the C group six items making up 5 percent. A visual illustration of the values for these items is shown in Exhibit 8.

EXHIBIT 8
Pareto Distribution of Inventory Items

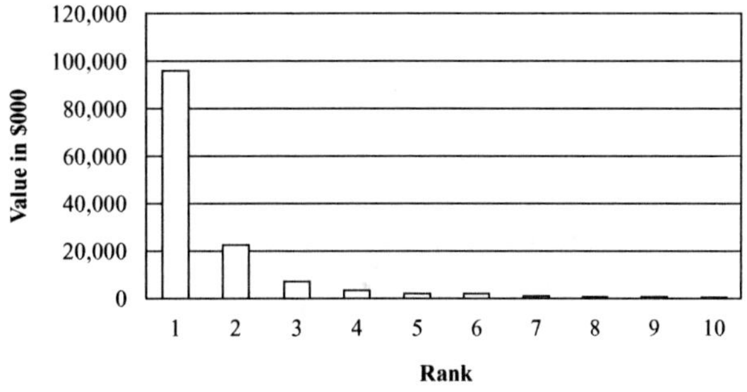

Managing the A items is something that probably will be done with human intervention while the C items likely will be put on automatic pilot. With brainpower allocated to the A items, less safety stock, in general, will be needed as market issues affecting forecasts can be used to update planned purchases and shipments. Since high volumes of these products will be used on a daily basis, special shipments can be brought in with fairly low extra cost per item.

Likewise, since C items are relatively inexpensive to hold, a higher level of safety stock might be required to avoid the use of valuable management time tracking them. Managers running out of C items spend too much time chasing thousands of items worth very little to the bottom line.

This is somewhat counter to the intuitive thinking that "important items should have the most safety stock." Keep in mind, however, that every item requires some level of forecasting and each item missed on a shipment will cause some kind of extraordinary effort. Better these efforts be concentrated on the same small set of items—the A items—than spread over every item the firm holds.

It is hard to imagine a production control person responsible for ensuring an adequate supply of a C item such as screws to an assembly plant shutting that plant down because of schedule changes that led to a slightly higher-than-expected usage of screws. That person would quickly be looking for a job elsewhere. Note that the car couldn't be shipped without the screws any more than it could be shipped without a tire. But the cost of holding screws is so low that extra screw inventory wouldn't be as big of a deal as holding extra tires.

There will be some cases where dollar value is not the only criterion for establishing the classification, but too many exceptions to the classification methods might well defeat the purpose of the system. Still, there may be a C item, while not of much aggregate value, that may require a very high level of warehousing space. Thus, the actual cost of holding the item may be much higher than its annual sales volume indicates. Maybe it is a candidate for being reslotted to the A category to avoid using up valuable space. Hopefully this extra-space issue also is recognized when pricing this item to the customer. The Cs to avoid moving are those like a vital field repair item that could cause considerable customer bad will. More management time is not necessarily needed, but a higher level of safety stock would be warranted.

Some firms have very-slow-moving items that are not stocked and only available on order. If customers are aware of these items and know the policy, this is not necessarily a problem. These would generally fall out as C items but could be moved to a new classification—say D—to avoid confusion.

There is no reason that every item in a given classification needs to be managed the same. Some B items may require different levels of safety stock and different reorder policies than other B items. The reason for the classification is to ascertain which items will be managed closely with human intervention and which items will be handled primarily with a computer system.

Costing Inventory Policies

To compare different inventory management policies, it is helpful to be able to determine the cost of a given policy. The total cost of a policy is the sum of the five primary inventory-related costs presented earlier. For convenience, these total costs are usually presented as annual costs. The concept of costing a policy is presented next in an example.

> Suppose Foodtown, a local supermarket, orders juices, jams and other products from Welch's on a weekly basis. One of these products, a 16 ounce jar of strawberry jam has an average weekly demand of 25 units. The cost of this jam is \$2.90 and Foodtown assumes inventory holding costs are 20% of this cost on an annual basis. The per-order costs related to purchasing, receiving, and paying for these orders is assumed to be \$30 per order.
>
> Foodtown has its inventory policy set so that there is a 1% chance of stocking out in each order cycle. If there is a stockout, they assume that the lost profit and customer bad will cost averages \$40. To ensure this 99% cycle fill rate (100%-1%), Foodtown keeps an average 10 units of safety stock inventory.

To analyze the total cost of this policy, it is beneficial to organize the costs into the categories presented earlier: ordering, holding, stockout, product-price, and management system costs.

Order Each order placed has a cost of S=\$30, and because there is an order placed each week, N=52 orders are placed each year. Thus,

$$\text{Ordering Costs} = S \times N = \$30 \times 52 = \$1560.$$

Holding The cost of holding a unit of inventory, H, is found using the estimated annual holding rate, r=0.20, multiplied by the value of a unit of inventory, p=\$2.90. This yields an annual per-unit holding cost of

$$H = r \times p = 0.20 \times \$2.9 = \$0.58/\text{year}.$$

To find the annual cost of holding the inventory defined in the policy for the 16-ounce jar of Welch's strawberry jam, it is often helpful to break the inventory costs into two pieces based on the function of the inventory: cycle inventory and safety stock inventory, as shown in Exhibit 9.

If one thinks about the inventory policy described for this example, when inventory arrives at the Foodtown, on average, there are 10 units of inventory in stock (by definition, the safety stock). After the arrival of the order, the inventory increases by the size of the order, q = 25 units, so that there is a total of 35 units in stock. As the week progresses, the inventory drops until the next order arrives–thus, inventory fluctuates from the average 35 units after an order arrives to the average 10 units of safety stock just before the next order arrives. The 10 units of safety stock (SS = 10) will, on average, remain constant over the year so that

$$\text{Safety Stock Holding Cost} = H \times SS = \$0.58 \times 10 = \$5.80$$

EXHIBIT 9
Inventory Replenishment Cycle

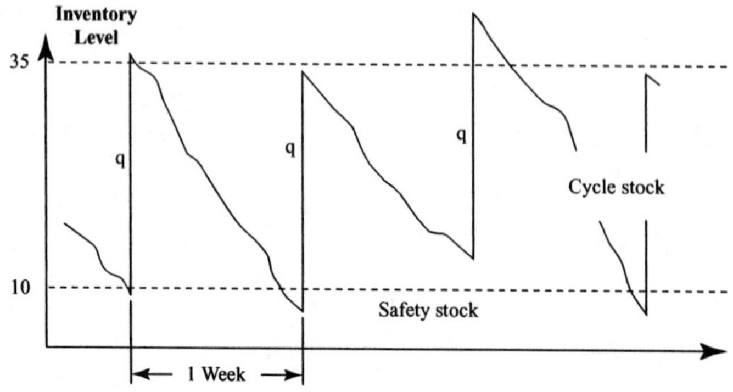

The part that fluctuates is the *cycle stock,* which on average is q = 25 units–on average, there is q/2 units of cycle inventory over the year

$$\text{Cycle Stock Holding Cost} = H \times q/2 = \$0.58 \times 25 = \$14.50$$

Stockout The example puts the chance of a stockout for any given order period at 1%. When there is a stockout, or an understock, the cost is C_{us} = \$40. Since the probability of being understocked, P_{us}, is 1%, the expected stockout cost each week is $C_{us} \times P_{us} = \$40 \times 1\% = \$0.40$. Because there are 52 weeks in a year, or in other words N = 52 orders or cycles when this understock situation can occur, the annual stockout costs are

$$\text{Stockout Costs} = C_{us} \times P_{us} \times N = \$40 \times 1\% \times 52 = \$20.80$$

Product-Price In this example, because price is not a function of the quantity ordered, product-price is not really relevant. Product-price is relevant when comparing two inventory plans, usually where there is a price discount when an order is placed for some large quantity. This cost, though, is simply the annual demand, D, multiplied by the cost of a unit of inventory, p: D×P.

System The type of inventory system used can determine certain costs related to managing that inventory. It is usually not easily quantified. For this example, these costs will be ignored.

Total Ignoring the product-price and inventory management system costs, the total annual inventory policy related costs (TAC) for the Welch's example is

$$TAC = \text{Ordering} + \text{Holding} + \text{Stockout}$$

$$TAC = S \times N + H \times (SS + q/2) + N \times P_{us} \times C_{us}$$

$$TAC = \$30 \times 52 + \$0.58 \times (10 + 25/2) + 52 \times 0.01 \times \$40$$

$$TAC = \$1560 + \$20.30 + \$20.80 = \$1601.10.$$

Inventory Record Accuracy

Any system is only as good as the data that it contains, and inventory systems are no different. The more accurate inventory records are, the less inventories are needed. Inaccurate inventory records that employees and managers don't trust cause inventories to be created because of the uncertainty in the information. As firms attempt to reduce inventory, it is even more imperative that the records can be trusted.

Record accuracy is affected by a number of things. Purchased products and components, as they are received or produced, must be logged into the system correctly and in a timely fashion so that the organization knows they are available. This implies, for example, that there is a good method for identifying parts, netting out scrap, and ensuring inventory is in its correct location. Technologies such as bar coding and the more recent electronic identification tags can help in this effort. Point-of-sale scanning systems help with accuracy and up-to-date information as well.

Inventory audits are important to ensure that entry and count errors are found and corrected. Annual physical inventories can help, but these are expensive and lack the kind of frequency that most systems need. A common audit approach is cycle counting, where each item in inventory is checked every so many periods. An easy way to set these audit cycles is to use the ABC classification discussed earlier. For example, A item inventories might be checked every month, B items checked every quarter, and C items checked once each year. These checks are then spread out over the audit cycle so that a few are checked each day. This not only breaks a large job into manageable pieces, but it also sets up a daily routine around which personnel assignments can be made. For example, a firm working 20 days a month with 200 A items, 400 B items, and 1,000 C items using the check frequency above might check approximately 10 A items, 27 B items, and 54 C items a day. These checks can be used to fill in nonbusy times of the day.

Inventory Record Analysis

An inventory record for an item sold by a medical supplies distributor is shown in Exhibit 10. The inventory record shows the amount of inventory removed each day in which there is demand for the item. For instance, on 1/31/00, 3 units were shipped from inventory so that at the end of the day, 73 units were left. Notice on 2/25/00 an order was placed with the supplier of this item for 250 units. These units arrived on 3/1/00, after a five-day lead time. Evidently, there also was demand for 20 units on 3/1, as inventory increased by only 230 units instead of the ordered amount of 250. An alternative explanation would be that the supplier only shipped the distributor 230 units rather than the 250 ordered—detailed records would need to be consulted to determine exactly what happened that day. In interpreting and analyzing this record, some assumptions may be required as this record does not indicate each detailed withdrawal and addition, nor does it tell us where some policy parameter might have been changed.

EXHIBIT 10
Sample Inventory Record

Inventory Record — 3" × 3" Gauze Pads
Unit of measure: Box of 25

Date	Order Placed	Units Sold	Inventory On Hand
			76
1/31/00		3	73
2/1/00		8	65
2/2/00		6	59
2/3/00		2	57
2/4/00	150	24	33
2/7/00		6	27
2/8/00		10	17
2/9/00		−150	167
2/10/00		14	153
2/11/00		14	139
2/12/00		6	133
2/14/00		30	103
2/15/00		2	101
2/17/00		5	96
2/18/00		16	80
2/19/00		1	79
2/21/00		8	71
2/22/00		4	67
2/23/00		14	53
2/25/00	250	31	22
2/26/00		12	10
2/28/00		8	2
2/29/00		15	−13
3/1/00		−230	217
3/2/00		3	214
3/3/00		37	177
3/4/00		12	165
3/6/00		7	158
3/7/00		10	148
3/8/00		25	123
3/9/00		20	103
3/10/00	200	42	61
3/11/00		6	55
3/14/00		9	46
3/15/00		−188	234
3/16/00		6	228
3/17/00		12	216

EXHIBIT 10
continued

Date	Order Placed	Units Sold	Inventory On Hand
			76
3/18/00		5	211
3/20/00		1	210
3/21/00		3	207
3/22/00		4	203
3/23/00		8	195
3/24/00		18	177
3/25/00		2	175
3/27/00		9	166
3/28/00		9	157
3/30/00		3	154
3/31/00	150	36	118
4/1/00		11	107
4/3/00		10	97
4/4/00		7	90
4/5/00		−145	235
4/6/00		9	226
4/7/00		42	184
4/8/00		1	183
4/11/00		15	168
4/12/00		10	158
4/13/00		4	154
4/14/00		28	126
4/15/00		2	124

A plot of the on-hand inventory by day is shown in Exhibit 11. One can see from this graph how inventory gradually decreases until an order arrives, at which time inventory increases with a sudden jump. Note that inventory drops below 0 on 2/29, and this is also shown in the inventory record of Exhibit 10. This drop below zero indicates a backorder situation where the customer (or customers) is (are) waiting until the next order arrives from the supplier. If the customer(s) had decided not to wait, then the order(s) would have been removed and the inventory would have stayed above 0.

EXHIBIT 11 **Graph of Inventory Position**

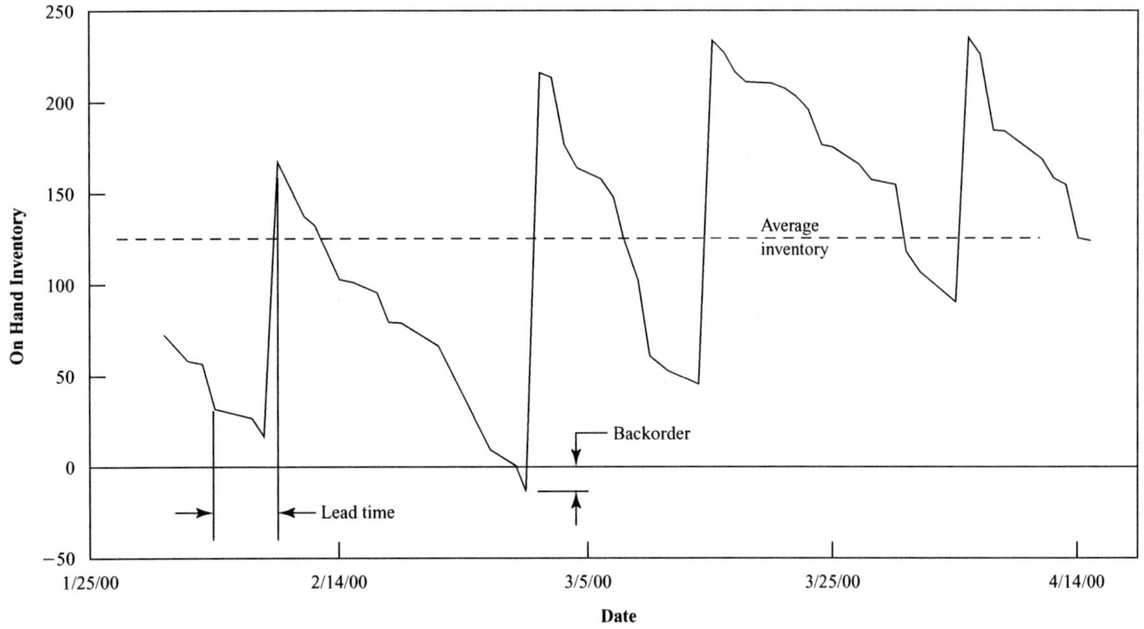

The plot of inventory over time has a cyclical nature to it—about every three weeks (two weeks in one case) an order arrives to increase the inventory level. This would seem to indicate that this firm is using some type of hybrid inventory system, a combination of ordering periodically every three weeks but at the same time reviewing inventory every two weeks to ensure that adequate inventory is brought in when needed. While it looks like the standard policy is to order every three weeks, when the company sees demand to be higher than expected during the first two weeks, an order is placed earlier than normal. In addition, it seems that there must be a constraint on how much is ordered at one time—each order is for some multiple of 50 units.

While the average inventory is shown in Exhibit 11 with a dashed line at a level of 125 units, it should be apparent from the graph that inventory is increasing. Each inventory cycle (from the peak point to the next low point) is ending at a higher inventory level. This may be a result of the stockout on 2/29—someone may have increased the safety stock to reduce the chances of stocking out again in the future, but it also could be a result of careless ordering actions.

Module Summary

Inventory may be a necessary evil, and even though it may be expensive to hold, it is also essential for providing value to the customer. Thus, the need to understand it and its uses is imperative for most businesses.

Inventory adds value in a number of ways:

1. It provides a way of decoupling the production process from the immediate and unpredictable nature of customer demand.
2. It provides for the more efficient use of plant and equipment assets by allowing multiple products to be produced with the same assets.
3. It provides for a way of leveling the need for productive labor when faced with seasonal and cyclical demand patterns.
4. It provides a way of decoupling one firm from another so that they can operate independently and in different geographical locations.

Key Terms

ABC classification, *16*
base stock inventory system, *15*
buffer, *10*
continuous inventory review, *15*
customer service level, *10*
days of supply, *6*
decoupling, *10*
fill rate, *6*
functions of inventory, *8*
in-transit inventory, *10*
inventory turnover, *6*
lot-size, *8*
maintenance, repair, and operating (MRO) supplies, *8*
materials requirement planning (MRP), *14*
min-max system, *15*
one-bin system, *15*
period base stock system, *15*
periodic inventory policy, *15*
production-smoothing inventory, *8*
productive material, *7*
quantity discount, *10*
safety stock, *13*
stockout, *12*
seasonal, *8*
speculative inventory, *11*
two-bin system, *15*

Discussion Questions

1. Explain the difference between independent-demand and dependent-demand components.
2. Why isn't the inventory-form typology of raw material, work-in-process, and finished goods as good as one that breaks inventory into its function?
3. List five functions for inventory and briefly explain why each is needed.
4. Service businesses, since they don't manufacture goods, have no need for inventory systems. Comment.
5. Why would one use an independent-demand inventory policy for a dependent-demand item?
6. Which functional area(s) of the business should probably have very heavy input into setting safety stocks? Why?
7. Safety stock sometimes referred to as customer service inventories, are generally held as finished goods. What factors could cause a firm not to want to hold safety stock as finished goods, but rather as work-in-process or perhaps raw material? What might such a firm need to do to compensate for holding safety stock in this unfinished form?
8. Which definition of fill rate would likely make a firm look better, the order fill rate or item fill rate? Why?
9. We refer to the basic inventory policy decisions made by operations managers as the operating doctrine. Which of the following options best captures the critical decisions, embedded in the operating doctrine, as presented in this module.
   a) why and when
   b) why, which kind, and where
   c) how much, what form, and how much effort
   d) how much, the purpose, and where
10. Which of the following is *not* a reason for carrying inventory?
    a) Inventory can act as a buffer against uncertainty.
    b) Inventory can decouple operations.
    c) Inventory can allow for larger lot-sizes.
    d) Inventory can help smooth out production levels.
    e) None of the above. (All of the above are reasons for carrying inventory.)

Problems

1. Given the order shown below, what is the item fill rate? The line-item fill rate?

Item Number	Quantity Ordered	Quantity Shipped
1	45	40
2	10	10
3	2,200	2,100
4	60	40
5	400	390
6	10	9
7	30	25
8	1,000	1,000

2. A firm has a policy of ordering 100 units of a certain item each time it places an order for that item. Holding cost for this item is $4.00 per unit per year. Demand for the product is 2000 per year and each time an order is placed the firm incurs a $45 ordering cost. The firm maintains a safety stock of 30 units of this item which is enough to maintain a cycle fill rate of 95% (there is a 5% chance of stocking out in any inventory order cycle. A stockout costs the firm $90. What is the total annual inventory policy costs for this item?
3. In Exhibit 12, a demand history and inventory position data are given for two products that are ordered from the same supplier. Analyze this history and explain the firm's apparent ordering policy for getting these products. Construct a graph of the inventory position as a function of the time period. What are the approximate order quantities? What is the average inventory level of the products? What is the approximate cycle stock inventory? What is the approximate safety stock inventory? Are there any patterns to the data that one should be aware of to better understand the situation?
4. For problem 3, what is the approximate total annual inventory ordering and holding costs for items W5X and Y4T? Assume that item W5X has a cost of $180 and that item Y4T has a cost of $120. When an order is placed for either product, the order-related costs are $20. Inventory costs are assumed to be 30% of the item's cost on an annual basis.

EXHIBIT 12
Data for Problem 3.

	Product Y4T		Product W5X	
Date Hand	Sold	On Hand	Sold	On
		417		245
2/10/00 R	98	319	31	214
2/11/00 F	109	210	27	187
2/12/00 S	28	182	7	180
2/14/00 M	89	93	42	138
2/15/00 T	110	−17	26	112
2/16/00 W	115	468	42	70
2/17/00 R	97	371	31	39
2/18/00 F	111	260	40	−1
2/19/00 S	27	233	6	376
2/21/00 M	115	118	29	347
2/22/00 T	105	613	36	311
2/23/00 W	108	505	43	268
2/24/00 R	93	412	26	242
2/25/00 F	85	327	37	205
2/26/00 S	35	292	15	190
2/28/00 M	91	201	27	163
2/29/00 T	91	110	38	125
3/1/00 W	101	609	40	85
3/2/00 R	88	521	32	53

continued

EXHIBIT 12
continued

		Product Y4T		Product W5X	
Date Hand		Sold	On Hand	Sold	On
3/3/00	F	113	408	26	27
3/4/00	S	34	374	15	382
3/6/00	M	109	265	40	342
3/7/00	T	87	178	34	308
3/8/00	W	96	82	37	271
3/9/00	R	97	685	31	240
3/10/00	F	95	590	32	208
3/11/00	S	33	557	9	199
3/13/00	M	102	455	31	168
3/14/00	T	90	365	32	136
3/15/00	W	95	270	29	107
3/16/00	R	100	170	30	77
3/17/00	F	88	82	25	52
3/18/00	S	27	655	7	395
3/20/00	M	94	561	33	362
3/21/00	T	94	467	33	329
3/22/00	W	91	376	33	296
3/23/00	R	100	276	30	266
3/24/00	F	85	191	39	227
3/25/00	S	28	763	12	215
3/27/00	M	109	654	26	189
3/28/00	T	107	547	29	160
3/29/00	W	89	458	37	123
3/30/00	R	98	360	36	87
3/31/00	F	107	253	43	44
4/1/00	S	28	625	13	381
4/3/00	M	92	533	40	341
4/4/00	T	112	421	32	309
4/5/00	W	99	322	34	275
4/6/00	R	102	220	32	243
4/7/00	F	92	128	35	208
4/8/00	S	26	102	15	193
4/10/00	M	112	490	45	148
4/11/00	T	88	402	43	105
4/12/00	W	111	291	38	67
4/13/00	R	112	179	37	30

Cases

CHAMPION ELECTRIC

Champion Electric, a regional supplier of electrical and electronic components, keeps thousands of SKUs (stockkeeping units) of various products on hand for its customers. A new operations manager, Barb Patterson, has just been hired to replace Bob, who resigned because of customer complaints and management pressure to keep inventories in check.

Gil, a longtime warehouse manager reporting to Barb, has been filling her in on past performance. "Bob was a good manager who always did what the bosses wanted him to do. He just couldn't do everything. Management was upset with Bob about customer service, the number of people we have working in this area, and, more recently, the overall level of inventory."

"Barb, I think you need to put some pressure on marketing to stop adding products, and while you're at it, we should get rid of many of the items that sell so infrequently that you have to dust the box off to read the label. We always have the higher-volume, more-profitable items in stock—we keep lots of safety stock so we never run out."

"We are always getting hammered because of customer complaints, and yet our records show that we have a fill rate of 99.9 percent. With over 30,000 SKUs, you can't get much better than that. None of our competition has that kind of service. At the same time, every other order has a request for some piddley item that we don't have in stock. Sometimes our system even shows we should have stock but we don't. When we don't have an item, we have to reorder it or expedite it or do something extraordinary to make sure the customer gets the product—and many times it's late. That takes people and time. It drives us crazy. We shouldn't sell all of these things. You just can't keep enough inventory."

Gil continues, "But adding products every day just makes it worse. Marketing always makes the case that it is our strategy to supply customers a 'full line' of supplies—that means we have to add a product if there is demand for it. Customers often decide they want a new and improved version of what we are stocking and we almost always try to get them what they need."

Barb questions, "How do we add these items—what's the process?"

"Sales makes an estimate of what they think they can sell and then we place an order. We try to determine the best 'economical' volume to buy of that item when we place the order. The problem is that even though customers say they want these new items, many times these things are never ordered after the first time. Would you believe that we have some 20 percent of our inventory classified as dead—it hasn't moved in over three months."

Later that day in President Campos's office, Barb gets some more information on her new mandate. "I have continued to invest money in inventory, but there is a limit to how much we can afford. Customers are still complaining. I know that our inventories are higher than our competitors'—I have backed that idea so that we could get a higher customer service rating than our competitors. But I'm not sure our service is any better, and I know our inventory is higher. You have to get this thing under control."

QUESTIONS

1. Champion Electric has made a decision to be a full service supplier with high customer service. What is the impact of this strategic decision?
2. Why do you think Champion Electric has a high customer fill rate service (99.9%) and yet has a significant number of complaints.
3. What do you think of the way Champion Electric adds new products? What are the inventory risks of adding new products? How should this be done to minimize the inventory impact?

Related Modules of Interest

- Aggregate Planning
- Inventory Modeling
- Lean Systems
- Materials Requirement Planning
- Supply Chain Management

Selected Readings

Cox, James F., III, and John H. Blackstone Jr. (eds.). *APICS Dictionary,* 9th ed. Falls Church, VA: APICS, 1998.

Hadley, G., and T. M. Whiten. *Analysis of Inventory Systems.* Englewood Cliffs, NJ: Prentice Hall, 1963.

Independent Demand Inventory Management Systems

J. Douglas Blocher
Indiana University

McGraw-Hill Irwin

Boston Burr Ridge, IL Dubuque, IA Madison, WI New York San Francisco St. Louis
Bangkok Bogotá Caracas Kuala Lumpur Lisbon London Madrid Mexico City
Milan Montreal New Delhi Santiago Seoul Singapore Sydney Taipei Toronto

Independent Demand Inventory Management Systems

Module Objectives

By the end of this module, you should be able to

- Understand basic inventory models for managing independent-demand inventory.
- Explain the concept of marginal analysis and its application to inventory management.
- Understand the differences between continuous and periodic review policies.
- Articulate the different ways of defining service levels for a single inventory item.
- Identify ways to "optimize" inventory policies.
- Explain the trade-off between customer service and inventory investment.
- Explain the effect of order frequency on inventory levels and customer service.

The Power of Inventory Modeling at HP

Recently, the Integrated Circuit Manufacturing Division of Hewlett-Packard was able to reduce $1.6 million of finished goods inventory while at the same time bringing on-time deliveries from 93 percent to 97 percent. In a period of about three weeks, another division of HP was able to eliminate all of its backorders. What was behind this improvement? An inventory-modeling tool developed by a group of internal consultants.

Previous to this development, decisions were made using simple inventory control techniques such as the ABC technique to set inventory levels. These simple models were not able to take into account the variability inherent in inventory control problems nor were they able to balance the costs of stocking out with the costs of holding inventory. The sources of variability included poor supplier performance in meeting promised delivery dates, fluctuating internal manufacturing lead times, unpredictable customer deliveries, and randomness in customer demand.

Over the last 10 years, a group of internal consultants at HP, known as the Strategic Planning and Modeling team, has developed a number of models for supply-chain costs. One of those models was based on a statistical inventory model known as the periodic review model. The model is capable of handling uncertainty in both supply and demand so that safety stock levels are set for the proper customer service while keeping inventory costs at a reasonable level. Indeed, when managers decide that service levels should be higher, the model allows decision makers to understand exactly how much of an increase in inventory will be required.

Inventory-driven costs at HP "are now the biggest control lever that the manufacturing organization has on business performance, measured in terms of ROA (return on assets) or EVA (economic value added)." Having a model that can accurately assess the service available for this inventory or provide a basis for reducing it where possible has added value to the bottom line.

Source: Drawn from "Part Tool, Part Process: Inventory Optimization at Hewlett-Packard Co.," *MS/OR Today,* October 1999, pp. 18–24; and "Effective Supply Chain Management," *Sloan Management Review,* Summer 1993, pp. 35–46.

Understanding how inventory system models add value to the customer in terms of product availability and to the company in terms of the correct inventory investment is important for many of today's managers dealing with supply-chain issues. While a general knowledge of inventory management and system concepts is important, this may not be sufficient. Some understanding of how the parameters of a system are set is needed to understand how to make inventory systems more efficient and effective. This is not only important for operations managers, who likely must implement these systems to meet the organization's needs, but for other managers as well. This is especially important for marketing managers who need to understand customer service issues at as deep a level as possible. Operations managers may be pushed by the financial managers to reduce investments in inventory, but this inventory may impact customer perceptions of product availability. The model developed at HP is able to show the financial impact of marketing's desire for higher customer service levels and to give operations managers a good picture of where inventory should be held to add the most value for the organization.

Inventory Systems Framework

Two basic types of inventory systems are used to manage inventories: dependent-demand systems and independent-demand systems. Demand for an item is *dependent* if its demand is derived from some other item's demand. For instance, the demand for radio speakers in a Bose radio plant is dependent on the number of radios produced. If Bose plans to make 2,000 radios next week, it needs 4,000 speakers. In some sense, dependent-demand items should be easy to control because of this dependency, although in many cases, the systems required to help in this control can be quite expensive to put in place, maintain, and operate.

On the other hand, the demand for radios isn't derived from the production of any other product at the plant and therefore is referred to as *independent* demand. Instead, demand for radios can be highly unpredictable as consumer demand fluctuates based on a variety of issues. Controlling the inventory of independent-demand inventory items is difficult due to the uncertainty inherent in the timing and size of customer orders. Even the best forecasting methods, if one can afford them, still involve uncertainty. Thus, one of the biggest values of holding inventory is that of making sure the company has enough inventory when faced with uncertainty about demand.

Independent-demand models are the focus of this module while dependent demand is discussed in another module on material requirements planning. These independent models can be broken into two types. First there is the periodic review model, where the management system is built around checking and ordering inventory at some regular interval. Second, there is the continuous review model, where inventory is constantly monitored to decide when an order needs to be placed.

These models generally require two basic control decisions, when to order and how much to order. A company's "when" decision might be based on a particular period of time or when inventory reaches a certain level. A company's "how-much" decision might involve ordering enough to bring inventory back to some desired stock level or might involve ordering the same quantity each time an order is placed. These different models and decisions are shown in Exhibit 1.

EXHIBIT 1
Independent-Demand Inventory Models—Review Method Framework

Basic Model	Special Case	When	How Much
Continuous review	Regular demand	Inventory reaches a certain level	Fixed quantity to order each time an order is placed
Periodic review	Regular demand	Weekly or monthly or on some periodic basis	Enough to cover demand over the next period
	One-time buys	Prior to an event	Enough to cover demand for the one-time event

In this two-type categorization, a special case of the periodic review model is the single-period model, where one purchase is made to cover some period of time, with the assumption that more purchases of the same item won't be made any time in the near future. For instance, some stores make a one-time buy of fresh-cut Christmas trees each year with the assumption that they are buying for this Christmas season only. Another example is where event programs must be produced in advance of the Super Bowl—these programs are sold during that event but have no value for future events. In both cases, only demand for the current event is used to decide the amount of product to be purchased—generally, any leftover inventory is of little or no value, or perhaps of negative value if there is a cost to dispose of the unsold goods.

There are some who view the modeling ideas for the periodic review, one-time buy case as different from the other two; thus, this module presents the models as three types: single period (which covers the one-time buy for the periodic review case), continuous review, and periodic review (which covers the regular-demand periodic review case). Thus, one also can think of the models in the framework presented in Exhibit 2, where alternative names also are given for each model.

EXHIBIT 2
Independent-Demand Inventory Models—Time Framework

Time Periods	Review Method	Model	Alternative Name
Single	Periodic based on events	Single period	Newsboy model
Multiple	Continuous	Continuous review	Reorder point model
	Periodic based on the calendar	Periodic review	Fixed-period model

Before presenting these models, it is helpful first to look at some key inventory metrics so that some evaluation of the models can be made. Then, the models for these independent-demand inventory systems are introduced by looking first at the single-period model. Marginal analysis, a powerful technique because it has such general applicability to many problems, can be applied to this problem and then extended to other problems. After this introduction to single-period modeling, models for multiperiod problems are presented, one of which is the periodic review system model mentioned above for helping HP manage its supply-chain inventory assets.

Key Inventory Modeling Metrics

Inventory model performance is measured with two basic kinds of metrics: cost and service. While service, in some ways, can be represented as a cost, managers usually talk about these two metrics in different ways. Thus, the two are presented as different measures.

Measuring Inventory Policy Costs

Inventory decisions are affected by a number of different cost factors. These include the costs of ordering and holding inventory, the impact of inventory on customer service, cost related to the purchase price of an item, and the costs of the inventory policy being used. Some of these costs can be difficult to quantify, so specific awareness and implicit management consideration are often the only way to incorporate them into the decision process. These cost categories are described below.

Ordering

Any costs that are a function of the number of orders placed are grouped under ordering costs. These include

- The cost of placing orders and managing quotes.
- Order-dependent shipment costs.
- Shipment-dependent receiving and inspection costs.
- Accounts payable transactions.

The first item in this list, that of placing a cost on the actual order and/or quote process, can be very difficult to quantify accurately. The difficulty is due in part to the many people involved in the process. It is extremely important to approximate this cost, rather than ignoring it.

Holding

The costs most often associated with inventory are grouped under the broad heading of inventory holding. These costs are a function of the number of units held in inventory, a variable cost, and include

- The cost of capital.
- Floor or warehouse space.
- Obsolescence, spoilage, and pilferage.
- Utilities and insurance.
- Movement to or from storage.
- Record accuracy (see section below).

The cost of capital generally can be estimated fairly accurately, but some of the others are more difficult. Still, this cost is usually stated in terms of some percentage of the value of the average inventory.

Stockout

A shortage of inventory, or **stockout,** can lead to a number of customer-service-related costs. These costs are based on how the firm measures customer service. Some can be quite difficult to quantify, but they include

- In-plant expediting.
- Expedited shipments.
- Substitution of higher cost item.
- Customer goodwill on lost sales and backorders.

In many cases it is difficult to quantify the cost to a customer of having to wait for a product or not getting a product from us and having to go to a competitor. Consequently, there is often a desire to understand the level of customer service that the company maintains. This will be described in more detail in the section "Measuring Customer Service."

Product-Price

Suppliers sometimes induce their customers to buy in larger quantities than they would otherwise. In addition, prices are sometimes a function of the time of the year an item is purchased. Thus, product-price costs include

- Quantity discounts.
- Time-dependent prices.

These costs are generally easy to calculate but are not always relevant to the decision.

Management System

Firms must make choices about how to manage their various assets, and managing inventory is no exception. The type of inventory policy used for an item determines how much effort and cost are required, while the level of forecast sophistication impacts costs as well. While both of these costs are difficult to quantify, they do have an impact on overall cost and an attempt to quantify the costs is better management practice than ignoring the costs as though they didn't exist.

Measuring Customer Service

The value of holding inventory for independent-demand situations is having product on hand when customers ask for it rather than having to produce it after an order is placed. Demand might occur when the customer arrives to make a purchase in a retail store or it might occur when a customer calls a manufacturer wanting an immediate shipment. The safety stock quantity in particular, and the inventory policy more generally, determine the **customer service level.** The higher the safety stock, the less chance there is of running out of inventory—a *stockout* situation—and the better the customer service.

Two common metrics for measuring customer service levels for inventory modeling are *cycle fill rate* and *unit fill rate.* **Cycle fill rates** are based on the probability of a stockout during an inventory replenishment cycle, while **unit fill rates** are based on the expected percentage of units short. Some swear by one measure, some by the other. However, both are good measures, and the choice of which to use should be guided by the nature of the possible stockout situation. Both can be referred to as "fill rates" even though they mean different things. Therefore, the astute manager asks the proper questions so that the implied definition is understood, rather than the incorrect one being assumed.

One also must be aware that the unit fill rate discussed above is most accurately thought of as an *item fill rate.* The item fill rate is the ratio of the total number of items shipped divided by the total number of items ordered. Alternatively, the *line-item fill rate* measures the percentage of line items shipped as a function of the total line items on an order. Finally, the *order fill rate* is a measure of the percentage of orders shipped completely.

Cycle Fill Rate

In certain situations, managers are worried about the need for a rush shipment to ensure adequate inventory. In this situation, it doesn't matter how many units of demand are "missed" when there is going to be a stockout since some extraordinary effort will be made to ensure that no demand is really missed. For these situations, managers have a method to get inventory and what matters is not by how many units it is short, but if a shortage will happen. Note that this rush shipment requires a special activity to get more inventory and, in fact, is in many cases not a shortage to the customer, but would be if no extraordinary effort were made. The estimation of the cycle fill performance metric is based on the probability of a stockout during any one inventory cycle, P_{us}:

$$\text{Cycle fill rate, cfr} = (1 - P_{us}) \times 100\%$$

Unit Fill Rate

In other situations, a shortage implies that a customer has to wait for a product (there is a backorder), go to a competitor to find the product (there is a lost sale), or buy a closely related product rather than the one that was desired (substitution). Managers need to measure customer service as a percentage of demand missed, since each occurrence costs the firm or the customer some amount for each unit not in stock. This may be an expediting and shipping cost and some customer bad will when a backorder occurs, just bad will in the case of a customer leaving because of the lack of stock, or a substitution cost if the firm is forced to substitute some more expensive item for the one not in stock. In any case, the manager needs to know the number of units short, so this measure is based on the expected percentage of demand missed:

$$\text{Unit fill rate, ufr} = 100\% - \text{Expected percentage of demand missed}$$

The Single-Period Inventory Model

When managers are faced with one-time inventory buys, the single period, or so-called newsboy model can be an important tool for analysis. The name comes from the classical problem faced by newspaper vendors on a daily basis. These vendors must place a one-time order for the next day's papers with no chance of reordering—setting up the presses again would be cost prohibitive. Since the exact demand for a particular day's paper is unknown, the newspaper vendor may order "too much" or "not enough." If this vendor orders too much, then he or she will be faced with the cost of being *overstocked.* Likewise, if too few papers are ordered, then the vendor will incur the cost of being *understocked.* The vendor should be interested in balancing these two costs so that expected profit is maximized.

The cost of being overstocked, C_{os}, includes the cost of the leftover product net of any salvage value. This salvage value might be negative in the case of having to dispose of excess, useless product. The cost of being understocked, C_{us}, includes the lost profit from sales not made and the cost of the loss of customer goodwill. Although the amount of goodwill lost is difficult to estimate, it needs to be accounted for in some manner.

There are many similar situations under which managers face this same kind of dilemma, where what is purchased for the one-time event is perishable and can't be carried into the next period. These situations are modeled many times with the newsboy model. When a specialized piece of equipment is purchased, a one-time spare-parts order may be placed at the same time. When capacity is perishable, the same kind of problem occurs. For instance, airlines must decide how many reservations to take for a given flight—they may overbook since they don't know how many people actually will show up and use their reservation and if not enough show up, the plane takes off without all of the seats filled.

Discrete Demand Analysis

Aladea Medical is in the business of servicing heart monitoring devices for hospitals in the Denver metropolitan area. An older model monitor requires a certain $80 electrical component for repairs and the manufacturer has just announced it will no longer sell that component after the beginning of next month. Instead, a more expensive replacement component, with a cost of $100, will need to be used for future repairs. Aladea's best guess is that hospitals will continue to use this monitor for about two more years and any excess inventory of this component will then need to be sold to a salvage company for an estimated $10. This component has failed a number of times in the past; therefore, Aladea must decide how many replacement components it should order.

If Aladea knew the exact number of failures there would be for this component over the next two-year period, the inventory decision would be a simple one: buy that number of units in the next order. However, failures of this component have varied considerably for Aladea and other businesses that service this monitor. The data in Exhibit 3 show the failure rate of this component over the last two years for Aladea and several of its competitors in other regions. Aladea management feels that these past failure data are probably a good representation of the failure variation it is likely to see in the future, and since it believes its current customer base has about 1,000 units in use, the data are a good projection of the next two years of demand.

EXHIBIT 3
Replacement Part History for Aladea and Other Firms (per 1,000 monitors)

46	62	53	71	60	51
58	75	58	69	64	61

Since the parts must be bought in multiples of 10, we use the data in Exhibit 3 to construct a frequency distribution, shown in Exhibit 4, page 8, around the midpoints, 50, 60, and 70. This exhibit indicates that there is a .25 probability (3 times out of 12 in Exhibit 3) that demand will be between 46 and 55, a .50 probability that demand will be between 56 and 65, and so on. If future demand mirrors the past, then an order should be placed for either 50, 60, or 70 units.

The decision tree in Exhibit 5, page 8, can help in the analysis of this inventory decision. For the major branch representing the decision to order 50 units, there are three possible outcomes: demands of 50, 60, or 70 units. If demand is 50, then the cost is 50($80) = $4,000. If demand is 60, then the cost is 50($80) for buying the 50 units and 10($100) for buying 10 on special order for a total of $5,000. Finally, if demand is 70, then the cost is 50($80) + 20($100) = $6,000. Multiplying these by their respective probabilities of occurrence, the expected cost of the "order 50" decision is 4,000(.25) + 5,000(.50) + 6,000(.25) = 5,000. Exploring the other two possible decisions, those of ordering 60 or 70 units, is done in a similar manner.

EXHIBIT 4
Frequency Distribution of Demand

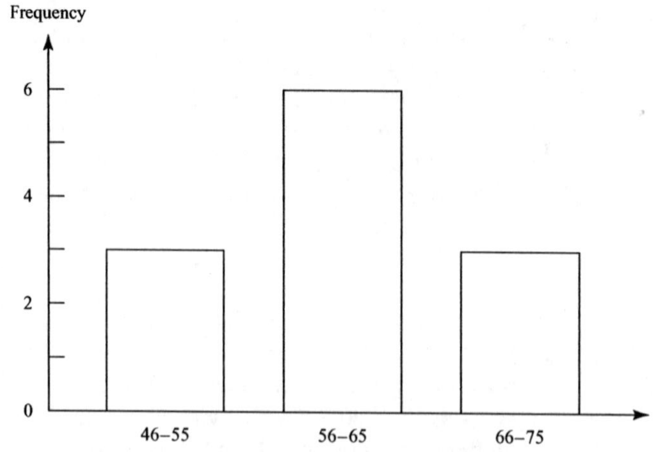

EXHIBIT 5
Aladea Inventory Decision Tree

Decision	Outcomes	Situation Cost	Probability	Expected Cost
	$d = 50$	50($80) = $4,000	.25	$1,000
Order 50	$d = 60$	50($80) + 10($100) = $5,000	.50	2,500
	$d = 70$	50($80) + 20($100) = $6,000	.25	1,500
				$5,000
	$d = 50$	60($80) − 10($10) = $4,700	.25	$1,175
Order 60	$d = 60$	60($80) = $4,800	.50	2,400
	$d = 70$	60($80) + 10($100) = $5,800	.25	1,450
				$5,025
	$d = 50$	70($80) − 20($10) = $5,400	.25	$1,350
Order 70	$d = 60$	70($80) − 10($10) = $5,500	.50	$2,750
	$d = 70$	70($80) = $5,600	.25	$1,400
				$5,500

From this analysis, it should be clear that ordering 50 units is the lowest expected cost decision. Notice that if one averages the 12 demand occurrences in Exhibit 3, the expected demand is actually 61 units; yet the analysis shows that it is best to order something less than this expected amount. The intuition is that the $20 cost of substituting the higher-value component is outweighed by the $70 loss from buying an item that isn't used. Aladea, therefore, wants to be able to use what it buys with a high probability and then wants to substitute the higher-cost item when demand is above the 50-unit level.

Numerous examples of this type of problem exist. Consumer electronic devices are sometimes closely modeled as one-time buys because by the time an order is placed for more units, the device is in the next generation of production so the old items are of much less value. Many times in the fashion industry, orders are placed one time for a particular item without the chance to reorder. This does not occur because reordering is impossible but because a reorder is economically infeasible due to the setup cost at the manufacturer or the expense of a rushed air shipment.

Marginal Analysis Approach

The decision tree approach can become quite tedious when there are large numbers of outcomes or decisions. When continuous distributions are used (instead of the discrete one used above), it is even more inconvenient to use such an approach. Luckily, there is an easier approach based on the concept of marginal cost analysis. A **marginal cost analysis** approach compares the marginal profit of selling one more unit with the marginal loss associated with holding an additional unit of inventory, and tries to find a level where these two amounts are "balanced" on an expected-cost basis. The marginal profit is the same as the cost of understocking, C_{us}, introduced earlier; and the marginal loss is the same as the cost of overstocking, C_{os}.

If P_{us} is the probability of understocking, then the decision rule is

$$\text{If } (P_{us})C_{us} \geq (1 - P_{us})C_{os}, \text{ then stock one more unit.}$$

That is, if the expected cost of understocking is greater than or equal to the expected cost of overstocking, then we should stock one more unit.

With some algebra,

$$(P_{us})C_{us} \geq C_{os} - (P_{us})C_{os}$$

$$(P_{us})C_{us} + P_{us}(C_{os}) \geq C_{os}$$

$$P_{us}(C_{us} + C_{os}) \geq C_{os}$$

$$P_{us} \geq \frac{C_{os}}{C_{us} + C_{os}}$$

As an equation, this formula defines the probability of a stockout for which the total expected costs of overstocking and understocking are minimized. This can be interpreted as a desirable cycle fill rate as

$$\text{cfr} = \frac{C_{us}}{C_{us} + C_{os}}$$

We would want to stock an amount that provides this cycle fill rate.

Continuous Demand Analysis

Korner Hardware makes a once-a-year buy of fresh-cut Christmas trees. The trees are purchased at a cost of \$10 each and sell for \$38 each. Managers of the store estimate demand to average 400 units and to vary between 300 and 500 trees, with any amount in that range equally likely. The demand distribution is shown in Exhibit 6. For every tree left over at the end of the season, the store pays a \$1 disposal fee, while for every tree short, it estimates that it loses \$2 in lost customer goodwill.

EXHIBIT 6
Christmas Tree Demand Distribution

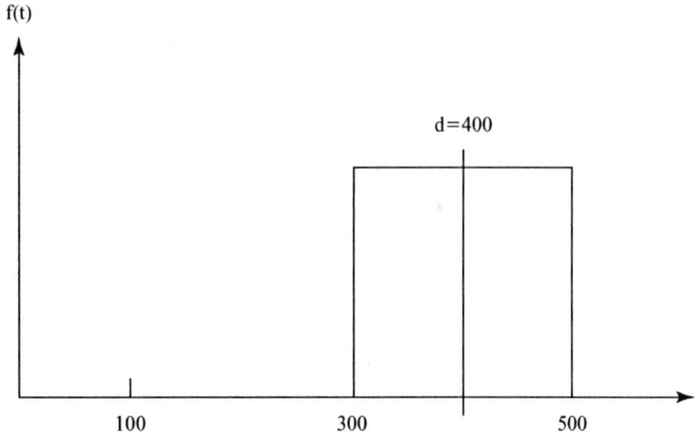

To find the best quantity to stock, the function for P_{us} is used.

$$P_{us} \geq \frac{C_{os}}{C_{us} + C_{os}}$$

The cost of overstocking (or the cost of having too much) is the cost of buying the tree plus the disposal cost. The cost of understocking (or the cost of not having enough) is the cost of lost goodwill and lost profit. Therefore, $C_{os} = \$10 + \$1 = \$11$ and $C_{us} = \$28 + \$2 = \$30$.

EXHIBIT 7
Demand Distribution—Probability of Meeting Demand

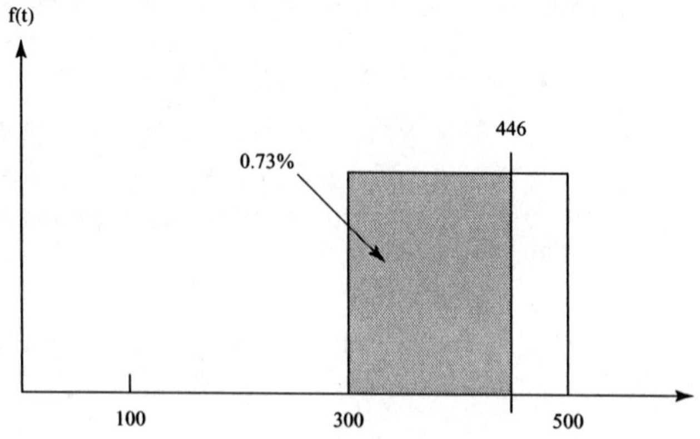

$$P_{us} \geq \frac{11}{30 + 11} = 0.27$$

$P_{us} = .27$ is the desired probability of a stockout, corresponding to the right-hand tail of the distribution. Thus, the desired probability of meeting demand is $1 - P_{us}$, or cfr = .73, corresponding to the left-hand tail of the distribution. For the uniform distribution, the target inventory level is .73(500 − 300) + 300 = 446, as shown in Exhibit 7. In the language of the current situation, the hardware store wants to cover 73 percent of the possible demand situations. Notice in this situation that the cost of being understocked, C_{us}, is significantly higher than the cost of being overstocked, C_{os}. Therefore, the preference would be for overstocking, or stocking more than the expected demand of 400 units. This matches the calculation.

Customer Service Measures

Earlier, we presented two metrics for customer service, the cycle fill rate and item fill rate. For the example situation of Korner Hardware, one of the two measures of customer service, the cycle fill rate, can be determined easily:

$$\text{cfr} = (1 - P_{us}) \times 100\% = (1 - .27) \times 100\% = 73\%$$

This comes directly from the marginal analysis methodology for the single-period model presented above.

However, if a customer arrives to purchase a tree and there is no inventory available, the store incurs the bad will cost of the customer dissatisfaction and also loses the profit of the tree that could have been sold. The store incurs these losses for every customer coming to the store. Thus, Korner Hardware might be more interested in the expected percentage of demand met, the item fill rate, because each unit short impacts their customer service costs.

If Korner Hardware stocks 446 Christmas trees and demand is 450, then the store incurs a shortage of 4 units. Since the demand distribution is continuous, the probability of demand being exactly 450 is 1/200. Thus, the probability that demand will be in the range of 447 to 450 is 4 × 1/200 = 4/200. By summing the probabilities of occurrence over all possible demand quantities above 446, the expected units short, $E[\text{us}]$, can be found.

$$E[\text{us}] = \frac{1}{200} + \frac{2}{200} + \frac{3}{200} + \cdots + \frac{54}{200} = \frac{54}{2} \times \frac{55}{200} = 7.4 \text{ units}$$

Since expected demand is 400 units and the expected number of units short is 7.4, the unit fill rate is computed as

$$\text{ufr} = 100\% - \text{Expected percentage of demand missed}$$

$$= 100\% - \frac{7.4}{400} = 98\%$$

Korner Hardware expects to meet 98 percent of its demand for trees by stocking 446 units. This looks considerably better than the 73 percent cycle fill rate calculated earlier, yet both fill rates are customer service measures for the same inventory level decision!

Value of Forecast Information

Forecasts are often used to get a more accurate assessment of demand so that high inventories do not have to be kept for the uncertainties in demand. Forecasting data, though, can be quite expensive if the forecasting process uses much more than historical sales data. If Aladea could forecast exactly what the demand would be, it would know which of the three demand situations to expect and the decision of how much to order would be easy. Suppose forecast information is available; how much should Aladea be willing to pay to get this information. This question is hard to answer since even if forecast information were available, it still would not be completely accurate. Even so, it would be interesting to know what *the value of perfect information* would be worth so that Aladea would have an upper limit on how much they should be willing to pay for the forecast information.

If it were known that demand was going to be 50, Aladea would order 50 units at a total cost of \$4,000. Similarly, for demands of 60 or 70, the costs would be \$4,800 and \$5,600, respectively. Thus, the expected cost if Aladea knew the outcome prior to it happening would be \$4,000(.25) + \$4,800(.50) + \$5,600(.25) = \$4,800. The difference between the expected cost without any information (the expected value given that the best decision is made—\$5000) and the expected cost with perfect information is the value of perfect information:

$$\text{Value of perfect information, Vpi} = \$5{,}000 - \$4{,}800 = \$200$$

Thus, Aladea shouldn't spend more than \$200 for additional forecast information, and it should probably spend something less since even forecasts will have some uncertainty.

Multiperiod Models

A more complicated modeling situation is encountered when inventory items must be ordered on a regular basis. The decision becomes not only one of how much to order but involves the decision of when to order or reorder as well. In the single-period model just presented, the decision of when to reorder is often set by the firm offering the goods and therefore is generally out of the hands of the purchaser. But, when orders must be placed over and over for the same item over some period of time, the decision is not so straightforward.

A common inventory replenishment problem the average person faces on a regular basis is that of buying food, beverages, personal care products, and the like. The consumer must make a decision of how much of each item to buy and when to buy each item. Some shoppers choose to buy on a regular basis, say weekly, and some choose to buy whenever the inventory of a given item reaches a "reorder point," or some level of inventory. The person using the weekly replenishments is using a periodic review policy while the person buying when inventory reaches a certain level is using a continuous review policy. In reality, consumers use a mix of these systems, choosing to buy such staples as milk and bread when stocks get low and buying canned goods and the like on a more periodic basis. Built into these decisions about how much to buy and how long to wait between buys is a recognition of the time, effort, and transportation expense required to make the trip to the store, that is, the ordering cost. This must be balanced with the amount of funds that are invested in the inventory, the likelihood of the product spoiling, and the space available to hold the inventory.

In a similar manner to these personal decisions, corporate managers must make much larger-scale business decisions. While it is unlikely to be worth the time and expense to conduct detailed analyses of decisions about personal inventories, the expense of such an analysis is usually justified for firms managing the types of inventory that are necessary to remain competitive.

Introduction to the Continuous Review Model

Consider the situation at Btown Dentistry where latex gloves, at a cost of $14.25 per box, are used at an average rate of 10 boxes per week. The standard deviation of demand has been calculated to be 1.4 boxes per week. Btown orders 100 boxes of these gloves from its supplier in Mexico when its inventory on-hand reaches 25 boxes. It takes two weeks for the gloves to arrive after they are ordered.

Btown Dentistry uses a **continuous review (CR) policy** a policy where inventory is continuously monitored until it reaches some level, the ROP, after which an order is placed. The inventory is continuously monitored until it reaches the **reorder point (ROP),** the level of inventory that, when reached, triggers an order. *Average demand* (d) is 10 boxes per week. The *reorder quantity* (Q) in this kind of policy is the same amount each time an order is placed. The order arrives after some supply **lead time** (L) has passed, which in this case is two weeks. This policy is shown in Exhibit 8. Note that the time between each order with this policy varies with each inventory cycle.

EXHIBIT 8
Continuous Review Policy

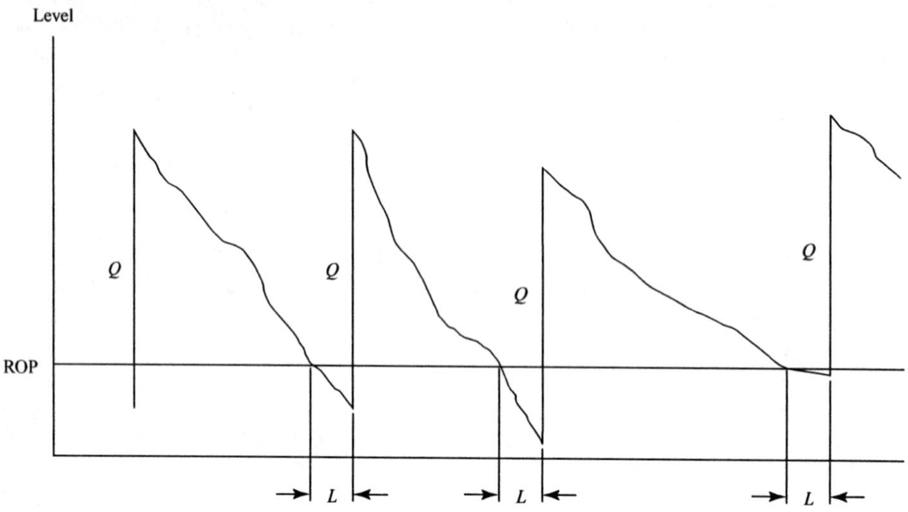

At first glance, it might seem that Btown could improve its inventory situation by reordering the latex gloves when the inventory level reaches 20 boxes, instead of ordering at a level of 25 boxes. After all, the **demand during the lead time,** $d(L)$, is 20 boxes:

$$d(L) = d \times L = 10 \text{ units/week} \times 2 \text{ weeks} = 20 \text{ units}$$

But this logic ignores the fact that demand is uncertain and may vary. If the reorder point were 20 units instead of the actual 25, then the dentist office would stockout, on average, 50 percent of the time. This may not be an acceptable outcome. Thus, the office places its order when inventory reaches 25, and therefore expects an average of 5 units of inventory to be available when the order arrives. These 5 units of inventory are referred to as **safety stock** (SS), the amount of inventory above expected demand. Thus, the ROP is

$$\text{ROP} = d(L) + \text{SS}$$

or, for this example,

$$\text{ROP} = d(L) + \text{SS} = 20 \text{ units} + 5 \text{ units} = 25 \text{ units}$$

The inventory status diagram in Exhibit 9 shows what the continuous policy looks like graphically for the latex gloves.

Introduction to the Periodic Review Model

Another basic multiperiod model is the **periodic review (PR) policy.** With this kind of policy, the inventory is reviewed and replenished at specified points in time (time-triggered

EXHIBIT 9
Continuous Review Policy Example

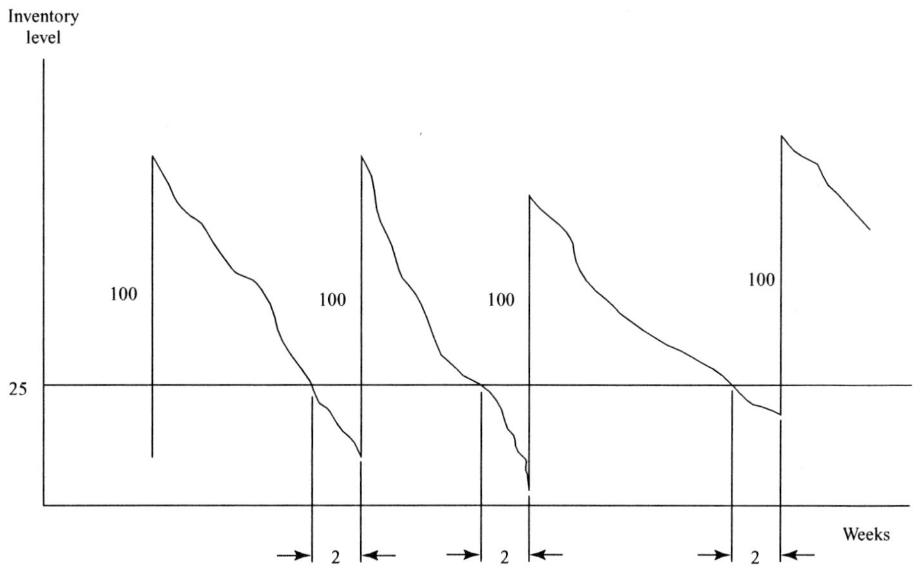

replenishment). In a periodic review system, the inventory is reviewed at some point in time and then subsequently at regular intervals of T units of time (or T periods). At the time of the review, a decision must be made about how much to order. After T more periods, another review is made to decide what must be ordered for the next T periods.

For this policy, the orders will generally be different each time an order is placed, as the level of inventory on hand when the order is placed will be different each cycle. A graphical depiction of this inventory–time relationship is shown in Exhibit 10. Note in this graph that the order quantity is depicted as q (as opposed to Q for the fixed quantity in the continuous review model) to indicate that the order size must be computed each time an order is placed.

With a PR policy, there is no control over the inventory level on hand when an order is placed—an order is placed at some point in time, not when a particular inventory level is reached. The inventory level can be measured when a decision has been made to place an order, but unlike the CR system, the amount on hand is unknown until the review time is reached. What is known is that it is *time* to place an order. Therefore, the decision to place an order has no impact on whether or not the inventory is depleted after L more periods. The current inventory plus the current order must be sufficient to meet demand over the lead time and the following inventory cycle as well. Thus, the **uncertainty period** is $T + L$ periods, the time between when an order is placed and when the next order arrives. This is certainly different from the CR policy, which has a much shorter uncertainty period of length L.

EXHIBIT 10
Periodic Review Policy

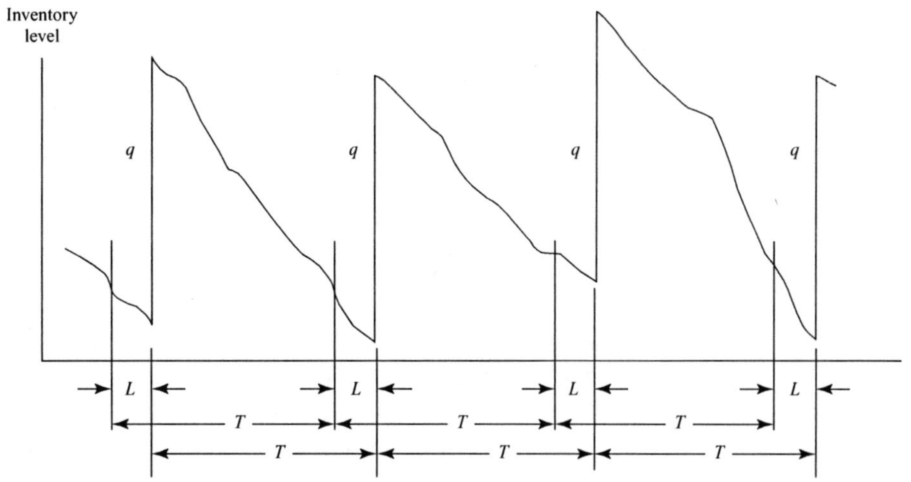

Although T represents the time between orders, when the lead time L is constant, T also is the length of time between the arrivals of orders. Thus, in Exhibit 10, both of these time periods are labeled with a T.

Returning to our example, Btown Dentistry is considering moving to a periodic review policy for its latex gloves, and several other items that it orders, so that orders can be placed on a more regular basis and in conjunction with orders for other items. It is currently considering ordering the gloves every 10 weeks (to stay consistent with the current CR policy of ordering 100 boxes, or 10 weeks' worth) and wants to continue to keep 5 units of safety stock to guard against demand uncertainty.

The periodic review policy requires a little more thought because the order quantity is different each time an order is placed. When it is time to place an order, someone must check the inventory level (I) to determine the current inventory status. Notice from Exhibit 10, that after the order is placed, demand occurs each period for L periods. At the end of this lead time, q units of inventory are added, and then demand occurs for T more periods before the SS level is met. Thus, letting $d(L)$ and $d(T)$ be the expected demand over the period L and over the period T, respectively,

$$I - d(L) + q - d(T) = \text{SS}$$

so that q is found algebraically by

$$q = \text{SS} + d(L) + d(T) - I = \text{SS} + d(T + L) - I$$

Suppose Btown Dentistry has reached the reorder period for the latex gloves. A check of the inventory of that item shows the current inventory level to be 32 units. Assuming that Btown wants 5 units of safety stock, an order should be placed for

$$q = \text{SS} + d(T + L) - I = 5 + 120 - 32 = 93 \text{ units.}$$

Similarity of the CR and PR Policies

One might argue that the continuous review and periodic review models should behave similarly. In fact, they are identical when there is no uncertainty. With no uncertainty, demand is exactly 10 per week and orders will be placed every 10 weeks under both policies. For the PR policy, the 10 week cycle is a choice, but for the CR policy, it is a result. It will take exactly 10 weeks to use up the 100 units ordered each time an order is needed. For the CR policy, $Q = 100$ was defined, but with no uncertainty, the PR policy should be $q = 100$ as well. Thus, if there is no variation, inventory pictures such as those shown in Exhibits 8 and 10 will be identical.

To go a step further, then, the PR and CR policies will perform similarly, *on average*. Using this logic, the inventory level for the PR policy should be, on average, 25 units when an order is placed. Notice how this logic can be used to find q in the PR policy. If at the time of the reorder, the inventory level is found to be 32 units ($I = 32$), the inventory level is 7 units above ($32 - 25$) where it would be on average. Therefore, an order should be placed for 7 units less than what is needed for an average order. Because an average order is 100 units, and there are 7 units more inventory than expected at the time of the reorder, only 93 units should be ordered ($100 - 7 = 93$). Note that this is exactly the same number of units determined for q in the earlier example calculation for the PR policy.

Measuring Customer Service

Earlier, two different methods of determining customer service levels were discussed. For the multiperiod models, the easiest to understand in terms of mathematical modeling is the cycle fill approach, which is illustrated here. The unit fill approach is not difficult conceptually, and the manager who understands the cycle fill approach can, with some effort, successfully use the unit fill approach. The unit fill method is presented in detail in the appendix 1.

Consider the situation of Btown Dentistry, where there is a possibility of running out of latex gloves. The dentist office cannot operate without them. They are not going to go to the expense of shutting down the office until the gloves arrive. Therefore, before they run out (or immediately after they run out), someone will have to make a special trip to a local supply store and buy the gloves at a higher price than Btown normally pays to their regular source. They will also incur the lost time and trip cost because of this nonnormal replenishment method. Alternatively, Btown might choose to call a supply store in some neighboring city and have a couple of boxes shipped overnight to its office. Either way, there is an extra one-time expense for handling this in a nonnormal way. For this situation, Btown is not worried about how many units it expects to stockout, but whether or not it will stockout. Thus, the cycle fill rate is the customer service metric that should be used to determine safety stock service levels.

When Btown uses the continuous review policy with ROP = 25, their P_{us} is determined by looking at the demand distribution over the uncertainty period—the two-week lead time—and then determining the probability that they will need more than 25 units. This probability is a function of the expected demand during lead time, 20 units, the standard deviation of demand, $\sigma_d = 1.4$ units per week, and the lead time, $L = 2$ weeks. If the demand each week is assumed to be normally distributed and independent, the standard deviation of the demand during lead time can be found by

$$\sigma_{dL} = \sqrt{\sigma_d^2 L} = \sqrt{1.4^2 \times 2} = 2$$

This formula simply sums the demand variances across L periods to get a total variance for the lead time. Finding P_{us} requires finding the z value (the number of standard deviations from the mean), which is

$$z = \frac{25 - 20}{2} = 2.5$$

This z of 2.5 yields a right-tail probability value of .0062, shown graphically in Exhibit 11. A standard normal table such as that in Exhibit 12, page 16, or a spreadsheet can be used to find this value. Thus, the probability that demand is greater than 2.5 standard deviations is .0062 and the cycle fill rate is thus cfr = 99.4 percent.

EXHIBIT 11
Normal Probability Distribution of Demand During Lead Time Showing P_{us} = .0062

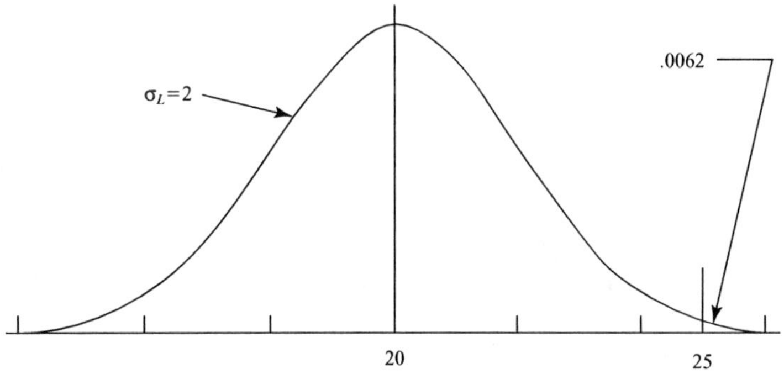

Mathematically, the relationship between the safety stock level and the variability of demand that we used above is

$$SS = z\ \sigma_{dL}$$

where $\sqrt{\sigma_d^2 L}$ and σ_d is the standard deviation of daily demand.

When Btown uses the periodic review policy with SS = 5, their P_{us} is again determined by looking at the uncertainty period, but in this case the uncertainty period is $T + L$ periods. The standard deviation of the demand over this time period, assuming a normal and independent daily demand stream, can be found by taking the square root of the sum of $T + L$ weekly variances

$$\sqrt{d(L+T)} = \sqrt{\sigma_d^2 \times (L+T)} = \sqrt{1.4^2 \times (10+2)} = 4.9$$

which yields

$$z = \frac{(5 - 0)}{4.9} = 1.02$$

EXHIBIT 12
Standard Normal Probabilities

$F(z)$ is the standard normal cumulative probability from the left tail to the value of z.

z	$F(z)$	$1 - F(z)$	z	$F(z)$	$1 - F(z)$
0.0	.5000	.5000	1.9	.9713	.0287
0.1	.5398	.4602	2.0	.9772	.0228
0.2	.5793	.4207	2.1	.9821	.0179
0.3	.6179	.3821	2.2	.9861	.0139
0.4	.6554	.3446	2.3	.9893	.0107
0.5	.6915	.3085	2.4	.9918	.0082
0.6	.7257	.2743	**2.5**	**.9938**	**.0062**
0.7	.7580	.2420	2.6	.9953	.0047
0.8	.7881	.2119	2.7	.9965	.0035
0.9	.8159	.0026	2.8	.1841	.9974
1.0	.8413	.1587	2.9	.9981	.0019
1.1	.8643	.1357	3.0	.9987	.0013
1.2	.8849	.1151	3.1	.9990	.0010
1.3	.9032	.0968	3.2	.9993	.0007
1.4	.9192	.0808	3.3	.9995	.0005
1.5	.9332	.0668	3.4	.9997	.0003
1.6	.9452	.0548	3.5	.9998	.0002
1.7	.9554	.0446	3.6	.9998	.0002
1.8	.9641	.0359	3.7	.9999	.0001

A z value of 1.02 corresponds to P_{us} = .154, considerably worse than the continuous review system, for a cycle fill rate of 84.6 percent. Continuous review policies, all other things being equal, are subject to less uncertainty and therefore better customer service: the period of uncertainty for CR systems is L while the period of uncertainty for PR systems is $T + L$.

Costing Multiperiod Policies

To compare different inventory policies, it is helpful to be able to determine the cost of a given policy, just as it is important to be able to determine the customer service level. The total cost of a policy is the sum of the five primary inventory-related costs: holding, ordering, customer service, product-volume, and system costs. For convenience, these total costs are presented as annual costs.

Returning to our earlier example, Btown Dentistry would like to compare the relevant costs of the current continuous review policy with those of the proposed periodic review policy and, in addition, would like to know if there are differences in the likelihood of stocking out. The relevant cost to place an order is S = \$50 and it is believed that holding costs are 18 percent per year of the value of the inventory being held, which is p = \$14.25 per box. If there is a stockout, Btown can expedite an order locally, but they estimate that this costs them an average of \$100 every time it is done, or C_s = \$100.

Continuous Review Policy Cost

For the continuous review policy at Btown (ROP = 25, Q = 100), the annual costs are

Order: Each order placed has a cost of S = \$50. If d = 10 units per week, then D = 520 units per year, (a capital D is generally used to denote annual demand). If each order placed is for Q = 100 units, then there are d/Q = 520/100 = 5.2 orders per year on average. Thus,

$$\text{Ordering costs} = S \times D/Q = \$50 \times 5.2 = \$260$$

Holding: The cost of holding a unit of inventory, H, is found using the estimated annual holding rate, r = 0.18, multiplied by the value of a unit of inventory, p = \$14.25. This yields an annual per-unit holding cost of

$$H = r \times p = 0.18 \times \$14.25 = \$2.565\text{/unit/year}$$

It is often helpful to break inventory costs into two pieces, based on the function of the inventory. Inventory fluctuates, on average, between SS and SS + Q, so the average level of inventory is SS + $Q/2$. The $Q/2$ amount represents the *cycle stock* component.

$$\text{Cycle stock holding cost} = H \times Q/2 = \$2.565 \times 100/2 = \$128.25$$

$$\text{Safety stock holding cost} = H \times \text{SS} = \$2.565 \times 5 = \$12.83$$

Stockout: As suggested earlier, customer service for this policy is measured by the cycle fill rate, which from earlier calculations was determined to be 99.4 percent. This fill rate was computed based on $P_{\text{us}} = .0062$. Since stockouts can occur at the end of each inventory cycle, and there are $d/Q = 5.2$ of these cycles per year, the stockout cost is

$$\text{Stockout cost} = D/Q \times P_{\text{us}} \times C_s = 5.2 \times .0062 \times \$100 = \$3.22$$

Product: In this case, because price is not a function of the quantity ordered, there are no relevant product-volume costs to consider.

System: The CR system is generally a higher-cost system than the periodic system, but determining an actual cost is very difficult. Thus, this cost is usually one that is considered in a nonquantifiable manner.

Total: Ignoring the inventory management system costs, the total annual inventory policy–related costs (TAC) for the latex glove example at Btown Dentistry is

$$\text{TAC} = \text{Ordering} + \text{Holding} + \text{Stockout}$$

$$\text{TAC} = S \times D/Q + H \times (\text{SS} + Q/2) + D/Q \times P_{\text{us}} \times C_s$$

$$\text{TAC} = \$50 \times 5.2 + \$2.565 \times (5 + 50) + 5.2 \times .0062 \times \$100$$

$$\text{TAC} = \$260 + \$141.08 + \$3.22 = \$404.30$$

Periodic Review Policy Cost

For the periodic review policy at Btown ($T = 10$ weeks, SS = 5), notice that since the same average quantity is purchased and the same safety stock is used, the ordering and holding costs are the same as those for the continuous review policy. Notice also that the product-related costs are still irrelevant in this scenario. The periodic system costs are lower than the system costs for the continuous case, but are still hard to quantify. The only quantifiable difference is the service cost component.

Stockout: If the same safety stock is held, then the probability of a stockout is considerably higher for the PR policy as compared to the CR policy due to the much longer uncertainty period of $T + L$. Thus we would expect this cost to be higher than the stockout cost of the continuous policy. Recall from the example calculations for service above that $P_{\text{us}} = .1539$ for this periodic policy. The annual stockout cost is then

$$\text{Stockout cost} = D/Q \times P_{\text{us}} \times C_s = 5.2 \times .1539 \times \$100 = \$80.03$$

Total: The total annual cost for the periodic review policy is then

$$\text{TAC} = \text{Ordering} + \text{Holding} + \text{Stockout}$$

$$\text{TAC} = S \times D/Q + H \times (\text{SS} + Q/2) + D/Q \times P_{\text{us}} \times C_s$$

$$\text{TAC} = \$50 \times 5.2 + \$2.565 \times (5 + 50) + 5.2 \times .154 \times \$100$$

$$\text{TAC} = \$260 + \$141.08 + \$80.08 = \$481.16$$

If Btown Dentistry wanted a periodic policy with a service level similar to that of the CR policy, then the safety stock would need to be enough to yield a probability of stockout in a cycle of .0062. This simply means that 2.5 standard deviations of safety stock would be needed instead of the 1.02 that were assumed. These 2.5 standard deviations would then yield 2.5(4.9) = 12.25 boxes. Using a higher safety stock level would increase their inventory cost but decrease their service cost. This revised periodic policy (T = 10 weeks, SS = 12.5), again ignoring the system costs, would have a total annual cost of

$$\text{TAC} = \text{Ordering} + \text{Holding} + \text{Stockout}$$

$$\text{TAC} = S \times D/Q + H \times (\text{SS} + Q/2) + D/Q \times P_{\text{us}} \times C_s$$

$$\text{TAC} = \$50 \times 5.2 + \$2.565 \times (12.5 + 50) + 5.2 \times .0062 \times \$100$$

$$\text{TAC} = \$260 + \$160.31 + \$3.22 = \$423.53$$

Notice that the periodic policy with SS = 12.5 dominates the periodic policy with SS = 5 because the first policy's cost is lower ($423.53 compared to $481.16) and its service is higher (cycle fill rate = 99.4 percent compared to a cycle fill rate of 84.6 percent).

Costs and Customer Service

Although, in the above cases, estimates were available for most of the costs, estimating the cost of using a continuous review system over a periodic one is almost impossible. Thus, a manager must be willing to compare the policies and make a judgment:

CR (ROP = 25, Q = 100) : Cost of $404.30

or

PR (T = 10 weeks, SS = 12.5) : Cost of $423.53

In addition, there are situations where managers find that estimating the customer service cost is too difficult to do. These managers argue that they are better able to determine the correct policy by setting customer service levels based on probabilities or fill rates. In these cases, three parameters—cost, customer service level, and policy type—must be considered. Suppose no value was available for C_s in the three example scenarios for Btown above; then one might present the scenarios to a manager in the following way (where Order cycle fill = 1 − P_{us}):

Policy	Annual Ordering and Holding Cost	Service Level
CR (ROP = 25, Q = 100)	$260 + $141.08 = $401.08	Order cycle fill = 99.4 percent
PR (T = 10 weeks, SS = 5)	$260 + $141.08 = $401.08	Order cycle fill = 84.6 percent
PR (T = 10 weeks, SS = 12.5)	$260 + $161.31 = $420.31	Order cycle fill = 99.4 percent

It would then be left to the manager to make a qualitative trade-off of inventory costs versus service levels.

Optimizing Multiperiod Policies

Now that the basic ideas of finding good decisions for these models has been presented, determining an optimal policy, or a "close-to-optimal" one, is the next step. To be able to find a minimum-cost policy, or one that is optimal, a manager must understand the tradeoffs between the different costs. It should be apparent that to lower ordering costs, fewer orders should be made. However, fewer orders increase holding costs because larger quantities are purchased when each order is placed. Likewise, increasing the frequency of orders lowers cycle holding cost. Lowering safety stock levels can reduce safety stock holding costs, but this increases stockout costs. Also as the frequency of orders increases there are more opportunities for stockouts.

Btown could iteratively evaluate the costs associated with different policy parameters, but the possible combinations are numerous. There are three key managerial decisions that determine a policy's cost: the quantity ordered, the safety stock desired (which implies a certain level of customer service), and the type of policy used. It is often difficult to estimate the relative cost of using either a periodic or continuous policy. Consequently the type of policy decision is often based on managerial judgment, or it is dictated by information systems already in place. Optimal order quantity and safety stock decisions are discussed in turn below.

Order Quantity

As a first step toward determining the best order quantity for Btown, we will assume that demand is constant over time, that holding and order cost rates are constant, and that product price and therefore the holding cost rate are not a function of the quantity ordered. Under these conditions, the relevant total cost for both the CR and PR polices, assuming that they both have the same fixed safety stock, is

$$\text{TAC} = \text{Cycle inventory holding} + \text{Ordering}$$

$$\text{TAC} = \frac{HQ}{2} + \frac{SD}{Q}$$

For the CR policy, we would like to find the order quantity, Q^*, that minimizes the TAC. A plot of $HQ/2 + Sd/Q$ as a function of Q is given in Exhibit 13. This function is continuous and differentiable. Differentiating TAC with respect to Q and setting it equal to 0 yields

$$\frac{H}{2} - \frac{SD}{Q^2} = 0 \Rightarrow Q^2 = \frac{2DS}{H} \Rightarrow Q^* = \left(\frac{2DS}{H}\right)^{1/2}$$

EXHIBIT 13
Order Quantity Cost Trade-Offs

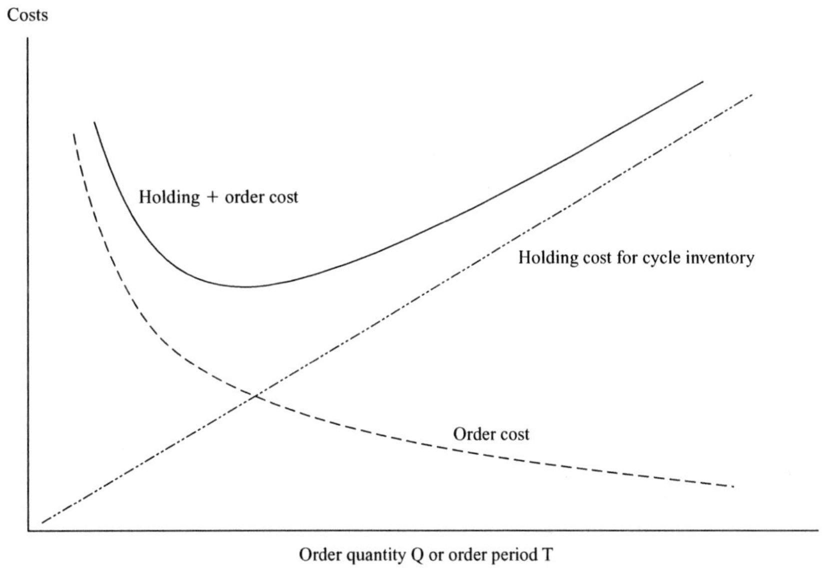

The quantity Q^* is known as the **economic order quantity,** EOQ.

For Btown, the EOQ is

$$Q^* = \sqrt{\frac{2DS}{H}}$$

$$= \sqrt{\frac{2 \times 520 \times \$50}{\$2.565}}$$

$$= 142.38 \text{ units}$$

This is an order quantity of either 142 units or 143 units. The best value cannot be found by simple rounding. Values above and below must be tested because the shape of the cost curve is not symmetrical, as seen in Exhibit 13. The exact calculation is shown on the following page.

Insight: Rounding Q^*

$Q = 142$

$SD/Q = \$50 \times 520/142 = \$183.10$

$HQ/2 = 142/2 \times \$2.565 = 182.12$

Total cost = \$365.22

$Q = 143$

$SD/Q = \$50 \times 520/143 = \$181.82$

$HQ/2 = 143/2 \times \$2.565 = 183.40$

Total cost = \$365.22

In this case, the total cost is the same when Q is rounded up or down.

The EOQ for the CR system can be translated easily into an **economic order period,** EOP, for the PR system by noting that d/Q is the number of cycles per year; thus, $T^* = Q^*/d$ is the economic order period:

$$T^* = \frac{Q^*}{D} = \frac{142}{520} = 0.273 \text{ year} \cong 100 \text{ days}$$

The order and holding costs are

$$\text{Annual order cost} = \frac{SD}{Q} = \$50 \times \frac{520}{142} \cong \$183$$

$$\text{Annual cycle inventory holding cost} = \frac{HQ}{2} = \frac{142}{2} \times \$2.565 \cong \$182$$

Observe that the two costs are equal except for rounding. This is not an accident but a result of the location of the minimum on the total cost curve in Exhibit 13, which happens to be at the point where the order cost curve and the cycle inventory holding cost curve intersect.

Although we calculated Q^* under the special assumption of a constant demand rate, it serves as a good starting point in a nonconstant-demand environment. In addition, when price is a function of the quantity ordered, Q, a slightly different methodology must be used to find Q^*. This is shown next using the example from Btown.

Price Discounts

When the purchase price of an item is a function of the quantity ordered, some additional work is needed to find the optimal order quantity. If a company decides to buy a certain quantity based on the EOQ model and the minimum order quantity required to get the price discount is less than Q^*, then the decision is easy: one orders Q^* and also gets the price discount. The real decision comes when the price break requires one to buy more than the Q^* found by an EOQ calculation. The decision rests on balancing the costs of holding more inventory than desired against the savings incurred by getting a price break for buying a larger lot.

Returning to our example, Btown Dentistry has been offered a discount by a sales representative from another paper company. They are offering to provide latex gloves at \$14 per box if orders are placed for at least 200 boxes at a time. Some analysis needs to be done to see if buying in quantities of 200 boxes is worth it when all expenses are included. Although there is probably space in the storeroom, Btown would incur some additional inventory costs.

Another part of the TAC equation has now entered the picture, the product-related costs, since price is now a function of the order quantity Q. This situation is best handled by solving the problem multiple times, once for each price offered. This is due to the stepwise nature of the price change. (If price changes were continuous with respect to Q, the price as a function of Q could be added easily to the total cost equation and differentiated to find the optimal Q.) Recall that Btown currently pays \$14.25 per box of gloves, and the Q^* is 142 units. The cost of the current policy, excluding safety stock and stockout cost, is approximately

$$\text{TAC}_{14.25} = \$50\left(\frac{520}{142}\right) + \$2.565\left(\frac{142}{2}\right) \cong \$183 + \$182 = \$365$$

To find the cost of the policy if the price were $14.00 per box, a value of Q would be needed such that the cycle holding and ordering costs are balanced, or $Q = (2dS/H)^{1/2} = (2 \times 520 \times 50/2.52)^{1/2} = 144$, where H has decreased to 18 percent of $14.00 (obviously a very minor change). However, to get the $14.00 price, 200 boxes must be purchased at a time. This is higher than the EOQ of 144, but the closest feasible amount to it. The total annual cost of this policy would be

$$\text{TAC} = \frac{SD}{Q} + \frac{HQ}{2}$$

$$\text{TAC}_{14.00} = \left(\frac{520}{200}\right) + 2.52\left(\frac{200}{2}\right)$$

$$= 130 + 252 = \$382$$

This TAC is slightly higher than the TAC for $Q^*_{14.25} = 142$. However, we must also consider the price discount:

$$\text{TAC}_{14.00\text{ with discount}} = \$382 - D \times \text{price discount}$$

$$= \$382 - 520 \times \$0.25$$

$$= \$382 - \$130 = \$252$$

Notice that the inventory holding and ordering costs went up by only $17 (382 − 365) while the savings from the quantity discount was $130. Plus, there is an additional bonus: the service level has improved because the frequency of possible stockouts has decreased. Thus, the decision, assuming there is enough space to hold it, should be to pursue the quantity discount and purchase the additional units so that 200 units are purchased at a time.

Setting Safety Stock Levels

The primary trade-off in deciding the level of safety stock is the cost of holding versus the cost of shortage, as can be viewed in Exhibit 14. At low levels of safety stock, shortage costs can be high and at high levels of safety stock, holding costs can be high. In this section, these cost trade-offs are explored using the cycle fill rate service level method.

Customer service costs are affected primarily by the safety stock, but they also are affected by the order size: The more frequently orders are made, the more chances for stockouts. In

EXHIBIT 14
Cost Trade-Offs for Safety Stocks

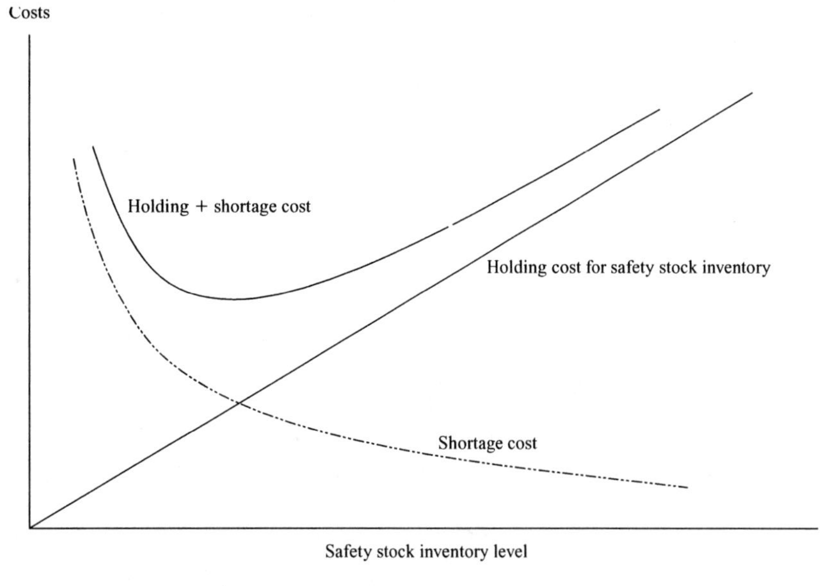

this section, the focus is on setting the safety stock level while trying to balance shortage and holding costs with the assumption that a good order size was found via EOQ logic. In the next section, the interaction between the order size, shortage costs, and safety stock levels is analyzed.

For the Btown Dentistry example, the relevant annual holding and shortage costs are shown in Exhibit 15, as a function of the level of safety stock held. Due to the mathematical nature of the probability function associated with the normal distribution, finding the minimum on this curve must be done numerically as opposed to the closed-form solution derived for the EOQ. Exhibit 15 is taken from a spreadsheet enumeration of different levels of safety stocks and the associated cost for both holding and shortages. The highlighted numbers show the lowest-cost alternative of all possible safety stock levels, assuming an EOQ of 142.

EXHIBIT 15
Costs for Various SS Levels with $Q = 142$

			Annual Costs		
			Component Costs		
z	SS	P_{us}	Holding	Shortage	Total Cost
0.0	0	.5000	0.000	182.606	182.606
0.5	1	.3085	2.565	112.668	115.233
1.0	2	.1587	5.130	57.959	63.089
1.5	3	.0668	7.695	24.396	32.091
2.0	4	.0228	10.260	8.327	18.587
2.5	**5**	**.0062**	**12.825**	**2.264**	**15.089**
3.0	6	.0014	15.390	0.493	15.883
3.5	7	.0002	17.955	0.085	18.040
4.0	8	3.2E−05	20.520	0.012	20.532
4.5	9	3.4E−06	23.085	0.001	23.086
5.0	10	2.9E−07	25.650	0.000	25.650

Exhibit 16 shows the cost curves as a function of safety stock level for the example situation. Just as the table shows, the lowest-cost safety stock level is five units.

EXHIBIT 16
Detailed Trade-off Example

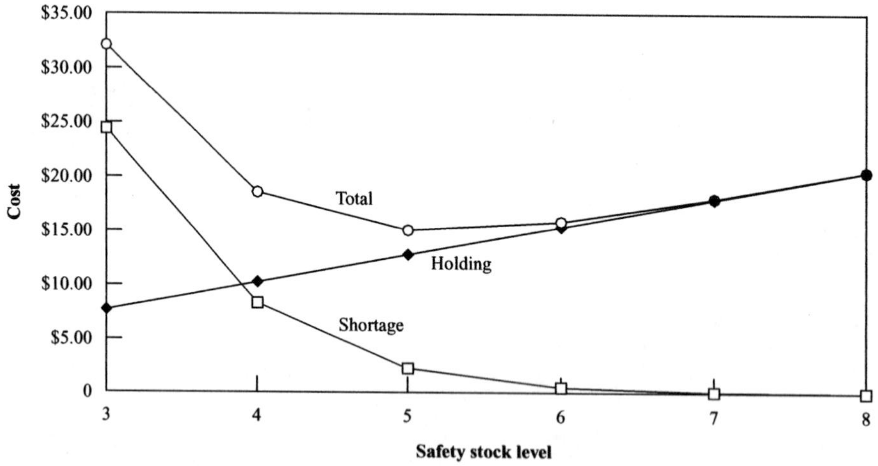

Combining Order Quantity and Safety Stock Decisions

The fact that service costs are a function of both safety stock levels and order frequency should prompt one to question whether, when combined, one has the optimal policy. Inventory policies based on the two independent calculations above are, for all practical purposes, close to optimal. Indeed, when policy parameters are adjusted to fit normal management practices, which include some "ease-of-implementation" policy parameter values, there is no real reason to find *the* optimal policy.

While we advocate the simple two-step heuristic procedure of first finding the EOQ and then the safety stock level, independent of one another, it is instructive here to show that the procedure generally gives good results and that the optimal will be very close to the suggested heuristic.

As an illustration, consider the Btown Dentistry example. Again, because of the nature of the normal distribution, numerical methods must be used, the starting point being the two parameter values obtained above, EOQ = 142 and SS = 5. Exhibit 17 contains different values of EOQ and SS and the associated costs, where the best solution is highlighted. It can be seen from this table that changing the safety stock only increases costs—any policy with four or six units of safety stock is clearly inferior to a policy with five units of safety stock. Notice that increasing the order quantity from 142 to 143 made a slight improvement, but remember that there was indifference between these two order quantities as they had the same total order and holding cost. Still, moves toward slightly higher order quantities at this step are not uncommon and make some intuitive sense. Recall that when the EOQ was computed, the service costs were not included. Yet we know that as we raise the order quantity, there are fewer possible stockouts and thus overall service costs are lower.

EXHIBIT 17
Combining Order Quantity and SS Decisions

Policy			Annual Component Costs				Total Annual
Q	SS	P_{us}	Order	Cycle	SS	Service	Cost
140	4	.0228	185.714	179.550	10.260	8.469	383.993
141	4	.0228	184.397	180.833	10.260	8.409	383.898
142	4	.0228	183.099	182.115	10.260	8.349	383.823
143	4	.0228	181.818	183.398	10.260	8.291	383.767
144	4	.0228	180.556	184.680	10.260	8.233	383.729
145	4	.0228	179.310	185.963	10.260	8.177	383.709
140	5	.0062	185.714	179.550	12.825	2.303	380.392
141	5	.0062	184.397	180.833	12.825	2.287	380.341
142	5	.0062	183.099	182.115	12.825	2.270	380.309
143	**5**	**.0062**	**181.818**	**183.398**	**12.825**	**2.255**	**380.295**
144	5	.0062	180.556	184.680	12.825	2.239	380.299
145	5	.0062	179.310	185.963	12.825	2.223	380.321
140	6	.0014	185.714	179.550	15.390	0.501	381.156
141	6	.0014	184.397	180.833	15.390	0.498	381.118
142	6	.0014	183.099	182.115	15.390	0.494	381.098
143	6	.0014	181.818	183.398	15.390	0.491	381.097
144	6	.0014	180.556	184.680	15.390	0.488	381.113
145	6	.0014	179.310	185.963	15.390	0.484	381.147

Other Modeling Decisions

Marginal Analysis to Set Safety Stocks

Rather than set the service level based on some manager's intuition (i.e., the corporate goal is to have safety stocks yielding a 99 percent fill rate), the marginal approach of the single-period inventory model can be adapted to work for the multiperiod problem. The trick is to note that instead of selling or discarding an item at the end of a period, the item can be carried into the next period with a holding penalty.

Korner Hardware also sells small propane tanks for grills and campers. These tanks sell for \$35 each. Korner buys these tanks for \$15 each and places the annual cost of holding these tanks at 30 percent of this value. Demand for tanks averages seven per day, with a standard deviation σ_d = 1.15 per day. The lead time for getting more tanks is three days. Korner Hardware currently uses a continuous review policy with ROP = 24 and an order quantity Q of 70 units. For each unit short, the lost sale causes a \$20 lost profit and they estimate \$10 more in customer goodwill.

Thus, the marginal profit, or the cost of not having enough, is the \$30 shortage cost. Likewise, the marginal loss, or the cost of having too much, is the per-unit holding cost for one order cycle. The annual holding cost is $0.30 \times \$15 = \$4.50$, but the per-cycle holding cost is computed as

$$\text{Per-cycle holding cost} = \$4.50 \times 70/(365 \times 7) = \$0.123$$

Using the marginal analysis equation,

$$P_{\text{us}} \geq \frac{C_{\text{os}}}{C_{\text{us}} + C_{\text{os}}}$$

$$P_{\text{us}} \geq \frac{0.123}{30 + 0.123}$$

$$P_{\text{us}} \geq .0041$$

From the standard normal probability table, a probability of .0041 corresponds to $z = 2.64$. Thus, the safety stock should be set, with these economics, at

$$\text{SS} = \sigma_{dL} \times z = 2 \times 2.64 = 5.3 \cong 5 \text{ units}$$

This compares to Korner Hardware's current safety stock of

$$\text{SS} = \text{ROP} - d(L) = 24 - 3(7) = 3 \text{ units}$$

From the standard normal table, $P_{\text{us}} = 0.067$, which yeilds a

$$\text{cfr} = 93.3\%$$

Production Order Quantities

The ideas behind the EOQ model can be used in production environments where the desire is to determine the quantity to produce in a production run before changing over to another product. The primary costs involved in the decision—changeover and holding—are similar to their counterparts when making an ordering decision when buying from a supplier. The only difference is that the inventory available to meet demand does not arrive instantaneously as it was assumed in the ordering situation above. This is shown graphically in Exhibit 18. Notice that although Q units are produced, they arrive gradually over the period of time denoted as t and when production ends after this time period t, the inventory is used up over the remainder of the complete inventory cycle T.

EXHIBIT 18
Inventory Graph for Production Situation

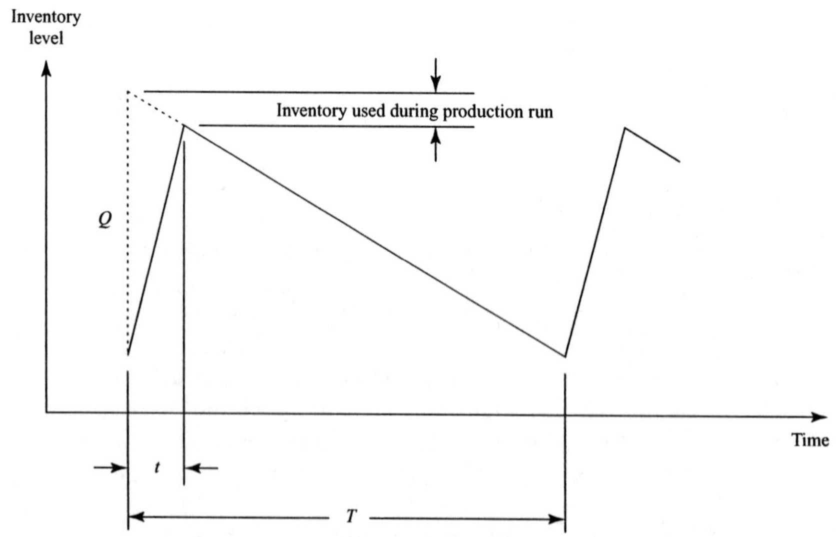

If R is the production rate and d the demand rate, then the **production order quantity**, POQ*, is

$$\text{POQ*} = \sqrt{\frac{2DS}{H(1 - D/R)}}$$

and it can be seen from this that the optimal order quantity in a production environment is very similar to the optimal order quantity in a purchasing environment, with the only difference being the $(1 - d/R)$ multiplier on the holding cost to adjust for the lower amount of inventory that is held during the production run over the time period t.

Lead Time Variation

In the above analysis of the multiperiod inventory models, the assumption was made that lead times are constant. In fact, there may be variation in the lead time. This can be accommodated easily in the various models by making a simple adjustment to the calculation of demand variance during uncertainty period. For normally distributed demand and lead time variation, the average demand over the lead time is the product of the average demand and the average lead time. The total variance of demand during lead time, σ_{dL}^2, is a function of the demand variance, σ_d^2 and the lead time variance, σ_L^2.

$$\sigma_{dL}^2 = L\sigma_d^2 + d^2\sigma_L^2$$

The lack of a square on the average lead time, L, may not look correct to those using intuitive reasoning but the equation above can be developed from an analysis of the variance function.

Module Summary

This module has provided an introduction to modeling independent-demand inventory items. Three basic models were motivated, presented, and illustrated:

1. The single-period "newsboy" model.
2. The multiperiod continuous review model.
3. The multiperiod periodic review model.

The concept of marginal analysis was used to determine the order quantity for situations were a order is placed to cover some one-time demand. The best order quantity was determined by balancing the expected costs related to overstocking the item with the expected costs of understocking the item. this concept was later used as a way to set safety stocks for the multiperiod models.

For the continuous review model, not only was the EOQ method introduced to determine the amount to order, but the ROP concept was discussed to determine when to order. The EOQ was developed based on balancing two types of costs: inventory holding and ordering. The ROP was constructed based on expected demand over the lead time and some safety stock determined by a desired customer service level.

The periodic review model was presented as an alternative to the continuous model, with the major differences being that it is simpler to use, provides for ordering on a more regular basis, and requires more safety stock because of its longer uncertainty period. In addition, the EOP idea, something very similar to the EOQ, was introduced as a way to set a constant order interval for this model.

Two primary categories of metrics were discussed relative to these models: customer service and inventory management costs. Five primary inventory-related costs were presented as well as two different ways of looking at customer service. To compare different inventory policies, a method was shown to calculate costs and service levels for so that managerial decisions about policies and decisions parameters could be made. Examples were used to illustrate the computational methods of finding lowest cost policies.

Key Terms

Continuous review (CR) policy, *12*
Customer service level, *6*
Cycle fill rates, *6*
Demand during lead time, *12*
Economic order period, *19*
Economic order quantity, *19*
Lead time, *12*
Marginal cost analysis, *8*
Periodic review (PR) policy, *12*
Production order quantity, *24*
Reorder point (ROP), *12*
Safety stock, *12*
Stockout, *5*
Uncertainty period, *13*
Unit fill rates, *6*

Discussion Questions

1. Explain the difference between the two different types of customer service levels, the cycle fill rate and the unit fill rate. Explain the circumstances under which one or the other would be appropriate.

2. For each of the following issues, what are the key differences between the continuous and periodic review inventory policies?
   a. Safety stock inventory.
   b. Cycle stock inventory.
   c. When to place order.
   d. Operating the system.
   e. Order quantity.
3. Given that the same service level is required (in terms of the cycle fill rate), which inventory system—periodic or continuous—requires more safety stock? Why?
4. Explain two ways in which product price can impact the inventory decision.
5. Give a situation from your experience as a consumer, where you believe the unit fill rate was the proper customer service measure. Explain.
6. A firm currently using a periodic review inventory system wants to reduce its level of safety stock. List at least three ways this can be accomplished without affecting the percentage of demand met on time.
7. The reorder point is
   a. Equal to the safety stock plus the lead time.
   b. Equal to the expected demand during lead time plus safety stock.
   c. Equal to the economic order quantity plus safety stock.
   d. Equal to the expected demand during the lead time.
   e. None of the above.
8. Which of the following statements is true about the EOQ with quantity discounts model?
   a. Annual ordering costs will always equal annual carrying costs.
   b. The lowest cost order quantity will be one of the EOQ amounts calculated at the various price discounts.
   c. Annual ordering costs will always exceed annual holding costs.
   d. The lowest cost order quantity will be the quantity that generates the least amount of carrying costs.
   e. None of the above is true.

Problems

1. Healthrite Distribution Inc. uses a periodic inventory system to stock many of its bandages. One such product, 4×4 gauze pads, has a six-week review period, a two-week lead time for replenishment, and a safety stock equivalent to one week's demand. Demand averages 20 boxes/week with a standard deviation of 8 boxes/week.
   a. What is the service level based on the cycle fill rate?
   b. What will be the *average* size of the orders?
   c. What is the ROP?
2. Reliable Drug places an order for Gatorade every four weeks. Once the order is placed, delivery to the store occurs in one week. Average demand is 200 cases/week with a standard deviation of 50 cases/week. The store policy is to stock an amount of inventory that allows for an average stockout condition of 50 percent (on average, every other order cycle) due to the ability to get additional inventory from its sister stores.
   a. What kind of inventory system is the store using?
   b. It is time to place an order and current inventory is 320. How much should the store order?
3. Consider the Christmas tree inventory example at Korner Hardware. What level of inventory should be held if the firm wants to have a 95 percent cycle fill rate?
4. Korner Hardware manager Emerson Jones is interested in determining how many nativity scenes to order for the 10-day holiday season. Past experience indicates that demand for these nativity scenes averages five per day during this 10-day period, with a standard deviation of two per day. Demand is approximately normal. Emerson purchases the nativity scenes for $5 per unit and sells them for $10 each during the season. After Christmas, they are marked down as sale items for $3 each.
   a. How many nativity scenes should Emerson order for the coming holiday season?
   b. Assume it is currently December 21st and there are three more days left in the holiday shopping season. There are now 12 nativity scenes in stock. What is the chance of selling all of these before Christmas?
5. The Bloomfield Office Supply Store uses a continuous review inventory system to reorder items. One line of pens experiences demand of five units per day, normally distributed with a standard deviation of two units per day. Bloomfield orders in quantities of 180, has established a reorder point for this pen of 24, and experiences a four-day replenishment time for the pens. The stockout cost is estimated to be $35 per occurrence. What is the expected annual stockout cost?

6. Suppose a continuous review inventory policy is established so that 100 units are ordered when a reorder point of 12 units of inventory is reached. Suppose further that the lead time is one week and demand is 10 units per week. Ordering costs are $100 per order and holding costs are $10 per unit per week. What is the annual cost of this policy using only the data above? What other costs should be considered?
7. Suppose you use a continuous review inventory policy where the reorder point is 100 units. Daily demand is 20 units and the lead time is four days. Two days after placing an order, you have sold 60 of the 100 units. What is the probability that you will run out of inventory before the order arrives?
8. The E.O. Queue Company manufactures magazine racks for supermarket checkout lines. The demand for the racks is a constant 200 racks per week, and the company operates 50 weeks per year. Racks can be manufactured at a cost of approximately $10 per unit, and annual carrying costs are 10 percent of the manufacturing cost. It costs $8 to set up the process each time a production run is initiated. Racks can be produced at a rate of 400 units per week. What is the production order quantity that comes closest to minimizing total annual ordering (setup) and carrying costs?
9. A firm is presently using the basic EOQ model and is considering switching to the production order quantity model (i.e., receiving gradual deliveries over time). If all the cost and demand parameters stay the same, what changes should the firm expect?
10. Suppose you are a corporate buyer. One of your suppliers delivers a particular part in five days on average, with a lead time variance of three. The daily usage averages 10 units per day with a variance of four. What is the variance of demand during lead time? If you use a continuous review policy, how much safety stock would you want on hand to ensure at least 90 percent availability of the part?
11. General Candle Co., a produce-to-stock firm, uses an average of 30 kilos of wax per day to make candles. The procurement lead time is a constant 10 days. Given the demand during lead time and associated occurrence data, what is the lowest safety stock level given below which will provide a "guaranteed" 80% service level? (Choose the most correct response.)

Demand During Lead Time	**251–270**	**271–290**	**291–310**	**311–330**	**331–350**
Occurrences (frequency):	2	5	6	4	3

12. As a part of determining the optimal inventory management and control policy, an analyst has developed the following information on a popular kitchen table set. What is the optimal order point that minimizes the expected costs?

Cost of being short by one unit during lead time = $10

Cost of carrying one extra unit during lead time = $30

Demand During Lead Time	**3**	**4**	**5**	**6**
Relative Frequency	0.1	0.3	0.4	0.2

13. A bookstore estimates annual demand for a new bestseller to be 250 units. The cost of this book to the bookstore is $10.00 per book. The publisher of the book is located in the East, but delivery is known for certain to be two weeks. The cost of placing an order is $20.00, and the annual carrying cost is 10 percent of the cost of the book. Given this information, what is the economic order quantity for this book.
14. Given the following information:

    Average daily demand for a product is 100 units, with the range being 85 to 115 units.
    Lead time for reorders is a constant 5 days.

    At the time an order is placed, how much safety stock should be on hand to *completely eliminate* the chance of a stockout during the lead time (100% cycle fill rate)? What should be the ROP?
15. The operations manager at J. Hansen Enterprises, Inc. has a historical sample of demand during the lead time that is normally distributed. She found that the average daily demand is 70 units and the standard deviation of daily demand is 20 units. Lead time is a constant three days. What is the optimal ROP to meet a 95 percent cycle fill rate?
16. The management of Star Co has reviewed the current policy of ordering 500 units of item C3P when an order is placed. They found this ordering policy resulted in a total annual ordering cost of $2000 and a total annual carrying cost of $1800. Which of the following actions can management take to lower the total annual cost?

a. Increase the order quantity for C3P.
b. Order C3P more often.
c. Order C3P less than once a year.
d. Switch to internal production of C3P.
e. Decrease the order quantity for C3P.

17. A company has been employing the basic EOQ model to manage the inventories of item R2D. The current EOQ covers two-month's demand requirements. What will be the total annual carrying cost if the cost to place an order is $50?
18. Perry's Pizza uses cheese at a fairly constant rate of 200,000 pounds per year. The holding cost rate is 10 percent per year for each 10-pound can of cheese held in inventory. The per-order costs are $100 for each order placed. Currently, the prices offered are as follows: $4.15 per can for an order of 0–699 cans, $4.00 for an order of 700–1299 cans, and $3.85 for an order of 1300 or more cans. How many cans should be ordered at a time to minimize total costs?
19. Underwood's Furnishings stocks a multitude of home improvement items sold to regional showrooms and department stores. Eeg R. Beaver, the firm's manager, is curious if the EQO model can be used to save money. She decides to analyze one item, the Snazzy Cleaner, for which she has gathered the following information:
Daily demand: 40 units
Acquisition cost of Snazzy Cleaner: $2.00
Carrying cost per unit per year: 20% of acquisition cost
Ordering cost: $5.50 per order
Underwood's is open five days per week, 50 weeks a year. They experience demand only on the days that they are open.
a. If Underwood's is currently purchasing the Snazzy Cleaner in quantities of 300, how much annual savings (if any) could they realize by switching to EOQ?
b. The supplier of the Snazzy Cleaner has decided to offer Underwood's the following quantity discounts:

Range of Order Quantity	Acquisition Cost per Cleaner
0–399	$2.20
400–699	$2.00
700+	$1.80

Under the quantity discount system, what should be the new order quantity?

20. Herb and Ersel's Herb Emporium (HEHE) is open 12 months out of the year. At HEHE, the demand for Cayenne pepper is a very consistent four pounds per month. HEHE orders the pepper from an outlet in Louisiana at a cost of $12 per order. Cayenne pepper costs $20 per pound, and the annual carrying charge is 10 percent of the purchase price. What is the order quantity (in pounds) that comes closes to minimizing total annual ordering and carrying costs?
21. Pam's warehouse operates five days per week 52 weeks per year. Only when it is open can demand be experienced or orders received. Pam has decided to analyze one of her warehouse's products, *family size caviar* (the caviar is purchased and sold in five kilogram cans). The following data has been accumulated for these cans of family size caviar:
Average daily demand: 100 cans
Standard deviation of daily demand: 30 cans
Lead time: 3 days
Holding cost, per unit, per year: 15% of acquisition cost
Ordering cost: $85 per order
Acquisition cost: $60 per can
a. What is the EOQ for the family size caviar?
b. How often (in days) should an order for family size caviar be placed?
c. If daily demand for family size caviar is normally distributed with a standard deviation of 30 cans, what is the ROP if an 86 percent cycle fill rate is desired?

Related Modules of Interest

- Inventory Management
- Supply Chain Structure and Strategy
- Dependent Demand Requirements Planning Systems

Appendix 1

Calculated Expected Units Short When Demand is Normally Distributed

Under the "Customer Service Measures" section, the unit fill rate was found for the inventory decision in the Korner Hardware Christmas tree example. Finding this was relatively straightforward because demand was uniformly distributed. The problem is a little more difficult when demand follows a normal distribution. Using the Korner Hardware propane tanks example given earlier, the unit fill rate concept is illustrated for a continuous demand distribution. Recall that $\sigma d = 1.15$, $L = 3$, and $SS = 3$ in the Korner example.

Thus, the standard deviation over the uncertainty period is

$$\sigma_{dL} = \sqrt{1.15^2 \times 3} = 2$$

and the current safety stock coverage is $z = SS/\sigma_{dL} = 3/2 = 1.5$ standard units.

The expected number of units short, $E(\text{us})$, is found by summing the probability of being one unit short times one unit, the probability of being two units short times two units, and so on. This is tedious for the normal distribution, so these numbers have been computed for a standard normal distribution and are presented in Exhibit A1.

From this exhibit, when $z = 1.5$, $E(z) = 0.029$. The 0.029 represents the standard number of units short, or the units short if $\sigma_{dL} = 1$. Because in this example $\sigma_{dL} = 2$, the 0.029 must be "unstandardized" by multiplying it by 2. Algebraically,

$$E(\text{us}) = E(z) \times \sigma_{dL} = 0.029 \times 2 = .058$$

Therefore, Korner can expect to be 0.058 units short per inventory cycle. Since the expected demand for a cycle is $Q = 70$ units, the expected percentage short is $0.058 \times 100\%/70 = 0.083\%$ for a unit fill rate of

$$\text{ufr} = 99.92\%$$

Suppose Korner was interested in setting its safety stock so that, on average, 99 percent of unit demand would be met. This is the same as saying that $E(\text{us}) = 0.01 \times 70 = 0.7$ units short per cycle. This number must be standardized to use Exhibit A1.

EXHIBIT A1
Expected Units Short Table

$E(z)$ represents the expected number of units short when $SS = z$ and $\sigma_{dL} = 1$

z	E(z)	z	E(z)	z	E(z)
−4.5	4.500	−2.0	2.008	0.5	0.198
−4.4	4.400	−1.9	1.911	0.6	0.169
−4.3	4.300	−1.8	1.814	0.7	0.143
−4.2	4.200	−1.7	1.718	0.8	0.120
−4.1	4.100	−1.6	1.623	0.9	0.100
−4.0	4.000	−1.5	1.529	1.0	0.083
−3.9	3.900	−1.4	1.437	1.1	0.069
−3.8	3.800	−1.3	1.346	1.2	0.056
−3.7	3.700	−1.2	1.256	1.3	0.046
−3.6	3.600	−1.1	1.169	1.4	0.037
−3.5	3.500	−1.0	1.083	1.5	0.029
−3.4	3.400	−0.9	1.000	1.6	0.023
−3.3	3.300	−0.8	0.920	1.7	0.018
−3.2	3.200	−0.7	0.843	1.8	0.014
−3.1	3.100	−0.6	0.769	1.9	0.011
−3.0	3.000	−0.5	0.698	2.0	0.008
−2.9	2.901	−0.4	0.630	2.1	0.006
−2.8	2.801	−0.3	0.567	2.2	0.005
−2.7	2.701	−0.2	0.507	2.3	0.004
−2.6	2.601	−0.1	0.451	2.4	0.003
−2.5	2.502	0.0	0.399	2.5	0.002
−2.4	2.403	0.1	0.351	2.6	0.001
−2.3	2.303	0.2	0.307	2.7	0.001
−2.2	2.205	0.3	0.267	2.8	0.001
−2.1	2.106	0.4	0.230	2.9	0.001

$$E(z) = \frac{E(\text{us})}{\sigma_{dL}} = \frac{0.7}{2} = 0.35$$

From Exhibit A1, this refers to a z value of about 0.1, representing a need for 0.1 standard deviations of safety stock coverage.

$$\text{SS} = z \times \sigma_{dL} = 0.1 \times 2 = 0.2 \cong 0 \text{ units}$$

Thus,

$$\text{ROP} = d(L) + \text{SS} = 21 + 0 = 21$$

This tells us that if we hold zero safety stock we will expect a 99 percent unit fill rate.

Appendix 2

Areas under the normal curve, 0 to *z*

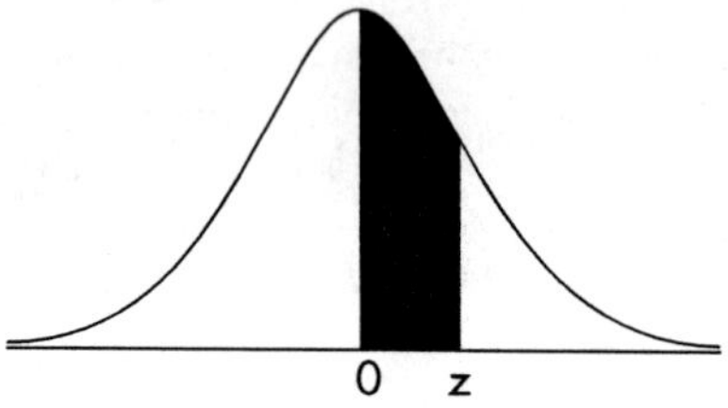

Note: The shaded area is the total area under the curve

z	0	0.01	0.02	0.03	0.04	0.05	0.06	0.07	0.08	0.09
0.0	.0000	.0040	.0080	.0120	.0160	.0199	.0239	.0279	.0319	.0359
0.1	.0398	.0438	.0478	.0517	.0557	.0596	.0636	.0675	.0714	.0753
0.2	.0793	.0832	.0871	.0910	.0948	.0987	.1026	.1064	.1103	.1141
0.3	.1179	.1217	.1255	.1293	.1331	.1368	.1406	.1443	.1480	.1517
0.4	.1554	.1591	.1628	.1664	.1700	.1736	.1772	.1808	.1844	.1879
0.5	.1915	.1950	.1985	.2019	.2054	.2088	.2123	.2157	.2190	.2224
0.6	.2257	.2291	.2324	.2357	.2389	.2422	.2454	.2486	.2517	.2549
0.7	.2580	.2611	.2642	.2673	.2703	.2734	.2764	.2794	.2823	.2852
0.8	.2881	.2910	.2939	.2967	.2995	.3023	.3051	.3078	.3106	.3133
0.9	.3159	.3186	.3212	.3238	.3264	.3289	.3315	.3340	.3365	.3389
1.0	.3413	.3438	.3461	.3485	.3508	.3531	.3554	.3577	.3599	.3621
1.1	.3643	.3665	.3686	.3708	.3729	.3749	.3770	.3790	.3810	.3830
1.2	.3849	.3869	.3888	.3907	.3925	.3944	.3962	.3980	.3997	.4015
1.3	.4032	.4049	.4066	.4082	.4099	.4115	.4131	.4147	.4162	.4177
1.4	.4192	.4207	.4222	.4236	.4251	.4265	.4279	.4292	.4306	.4319
1.5	.4332	.4345	.4357	.4370	.4382	.4394	.4406	.4418	.4429	.4441
1.6	.4452	.4463	.4474	.4484	.4495	.4505	.4515	.4525	.4535	.4545
1.7	.4554	.4564	.4573	.4582	.4591	.4599	.4608	.4616	.4625	.4633
1.8	.4641	.4649	.4656	.4664	.4671	.4678	.4686	.4693	.4699	.4706
1.9	.4713	.4719	.4726	.4732	.4738	.4744	.4750	.4756	.4761	.4767
2.0	.4772	.4778	.4783	.4788	.4793	.4798	.4803	.4808	.4812	.4817
2.1	.4821	.4826	.4830	.4834	.4838	.4842	.4846	.4850	.4854	.4857
2.2	.4861	.4864	.4868	.4871	.4875	.4878	.4881	.4884	.4887	.4890
2.3	.4893	.4896	.4898	.4901	.4904	.4906	.4909	.4911	.4913	.4916
2.4	.4918	.4920	.4922	.4925	.4927	.4929	.4939	.4932	.4934	.4936
2.5	.4938	.4940	.4941	.4943	.4945	.4946	.4948	.4949	.4951	.4952
2.6	.4953	.4955	.4956	.4957	.4959	.4960	.4961	.4962	.4963	.4964
2.7	.4965	.4966	.4967	.4968	.4969	.4970	.4971	.4972	.4973	.4974
2.8	.4974	.4975	.4976	.4977	.4977	.4978	.4979	.4979	.4980	.4981
2.9	.4981	.4982	.4982	.4983	.4984	.4984	.4985	.4985	.4986	.4986
3.0	.4987	.4987	.4987	.4988	.4988	.4989	.4989	.4989	.4990	.4990

Dependent Demand Requirements Planning Systems

J. Douglas Blocher
Indiana University

McGraw-Hill Irwin

Boston Burr Ridge, IL Dubuque, IA Madison, WI New York San Francisco St. Louis
Bangkok Bogotá Caracas Kuala Lumpur Lisbon London Madrid Mexico City
Milan Montreal New Delhi Santiago Seoul Singapore Sydney Taipei Toronto

Dependent Demand Requirements Planning Systems

Module Objectives

By the end of this module, you should be able to

- Know why requirements planning systems are used.
- Know how MRP, DRP, and CRP systems interact.
- Understand the logic behind requirements planning and be able to compute future inventory needs for a product.
- Be able to read and understand an MRP record (or a DRP record).
- Be able to compute the capacity requirements for a plan given a set of MRP records and know how to adjust a plan if capacity is not sufficient in some period.

MRP for $20,000?

Material Requirements Planning (MRP) systems traditionally have been used by large manufacturers to manage complex products with numerous components and assemblies. It was not uncommon to have a million dollars invested in the software and hardware needed to run such a system. MRP systems can be valuable for small companies as well, but these companies can't afford investments of this magnitude.

On-Demand Solutions Inc., a manufacturer of CD-ROMs and computer disks and a provider of e-business services, was struggling to meet demand in early 1997. The company didn't understand its capacity needs and was constantly chasing paper work, and its employees didn't know what to promise their customers in terms of product availability and order delivery.

In the early years, the business was run with the help of a word processor, some spreadsheets, and an accounting program running in a DOS environment. But company managers knew they needed to update their systems if they were to position the company for growth. The problem was that the company couldn't afford to spend the historical amounts paid for MRP software packages and the supporting hardware.

The solution was provided by Bild LLC, a consulting organization that helps small manufacturers with their MRP and Enterprise Resource Planning (ERP) applications. Bild used an off-the-shelf MRP II software package from Alliance Manufacturing Software Inc. enhanced with their own Bild Reporter for generating management reports on things such as backorders or margin per customer.

The installation, along with employee training, was completed in three weeks for $20,000, a price that was less than half what On-Demand had budgeted for the implementation. Chad Huemme, On-Demand's VP in charge of operations, estimated that the investment payback period was around two months. Not only did this MRP system improve efficiency in the manufacturing operations, its information helped the company grow from a $0.5 million company to a $4 million company in an 18-month period. Says Huemme, "If we had not invested in the MRP software when we did, I'm positive we would never have grown the way we have."

Source: "VAR MRP Solution Pays Off for Client in Revenue Growth," *Computer Reseller News,* October 5, 1998, pp. 95–96.

Requirements Planning Systems

Controlling component part inventories as well as finished good inventories is an important management activity for any size company. As On-Demand found, without a proper inventory management system, communication with customers and suppliers was limited by the poor quality of information from the manufacturing process, and this limited communication hindered growth.

For companies such as On-Demand, a **materials requirements planning (MRP)** system offers an easy way to communicate the requirements for component parts to manufacturing operations and suppliers, keeping the inventory to a minimum based on the planned sales of end items. While the end-item demand is considered "independent" because it must be forecast, the demand for the component parts is "dependent" on the production plan for the end item. MRP systems are used for planning for dependent demand items, the subject of this module.

MRP systems have been around for years. MRP logic was present during World War II in the Quarterly Order System, which was essentially a manual MRP system. However, four developments helped to bring MRP to its present widespread use. The first was the increase in the cost of holding inventory. Prior to MRP, firms used independent-demand inventory management systems to manage dependent-demand environments. These systems worked because they did not require a great deal of information—inventory was used in place of information. When the cost of holding inventory went up, the costs due to the inefficiency of using simple independent-demand systems also went up. Second was a dramatic growth in computer power that continues today—a key requirement since MRP systems are most efficiently implemented on computer systems. Third, computational cost has decreased enormously. One wag once noted that if cars had followed the price curve observed in computers, everyone could buy a Rolls Royce for less than a dollar. Fourth, there was an explosion of MRP software running on all types of platforms from the mainframe to the mini (e.g., the AS 400) to the PC—this continues to this day as MRP logic is now embedded in the new **enterprise resource planning (ERP)** systems and many of the supply-chain management software packages as well.

Just as MRP systems are used in a manufacturing operation, **distribution requirements planning (DRP)** systems are used in service and distribution businesses. When they are used together within the same company, MRP systems are used on the supply (upstream) side of the business while DRP systems are used on the demand (downstream) side. DRP systems gather requirements from retailers, consolidate requirements at the wholesale level, and then consolidate the wholesale level needs back to the manufacturer's central distribution facility.

While MRP systems were first implemented to control component inventory in large manufacturing companies, these systems eventually grew and evolved to include all of the financial information needed to go through the planning and budgeting processes. These more advanced systems became known as MRP II (manufacturing resource planning) systems. Today, these systems have evolved even further into what are known as ERP systems, which tie all of the areas of the company together using one common database of information. These systems are generally composed of modules. Material Control is the module that contains the MRP logic. Another module having to do with sales and distribution includes the DRP logic. In addition, other modules are available for quality, maintenance, finance and accounting, and human resources. While ERP systems haven't necessarily replaced MRP and MRPII systems, certainly the logic of MRP and MRPII is available in almost every ERP system available today.

Exploiting Dependent Demand

Requirements planning systems were conceived to exploit the dependent nature of one item's requirements on those of another. When National Bicycle makes a batch of 100 XT bikes, their MRP system ensures that they order 100 XT frames, 200 tires, and so on. In other words, their inventory policy for tires and frames is based on—is dependent on—their plan to produce **end items,** or bicycles. The demand for tires and frames, the bicycle component parts, is **dependent demand.** The demand for bicycles at retail outlets, the end-item customer demand, is **independent demand.**

Since MRP systems exploit the dependent nature of one item's demand on that of another, these systems are most valuable in industries involving product assembly, rather than discrete part manufacturing. Thus, machine shops are likely to have little use for MRP systems unless they are actually assembling components that they fabricate in house. Auto companies, on the other hand, assemble very complex products, requiring coordination of thousands of components coming from internal fabrication processes and numerous suppliers. It is these complex assembly environments that benefit the most from MRP systems since the systems make planning and control much easier than it would be without such a system.

The following pages first present a general discussion of MRP systems. This discussion will show how a requirements planning system exploits the hierarchical product assembly structure to plan the needs for component parts and assemblies. Next, DRP systems are discussed, the logic of which is very much the same as that of an MRP system. While MRP and DRP systems show the end product and components needs, period by period, they do not by themselves consider the capacity of the manufacturing plant (in the case of the fabricated or assembled components of MRP) or of the shipping and warehousing activities (in the case of the finished goods of DRP). Thus, a discussion of capacity requirements planning (CRP) is presented next, with attention paid to how the MRP and DRP systems provide valuable inputs to the capacity planning process. Finally, a comprehensive example tying the whole planning process together is discussed in the last section.

Materials Requirements Planning (MRP)

An MRP system is designed to keep inventory low by getting the right part to the right place at the right time, given the plan to produce some end item. An MRP system computes the quantity and timing of the needs for component parts required to make an end item.

The MRP system is a part of an overall production planning system, shown graphically in Exhibit 1. It uses as inputs the master schedule, the bill of materials, and the item master file. The basics of each of these three inputs will be discussed next, while a more detailed explanation will be presented with examples in the following sections.

First, the **master production schedule (MPS)**, sometimes shortened to master schedule, is a schedule of when and how much of each end item a firm plans to produce. This plan is constructed based on external information from customer orders and forecasts, including information from the firm's DRP system; internal information on available inventories; internal constraints from the firm's aggregate production plan; and internal cost information on changing production from one product to another.

Second, a **bill of materials (BOM)** is needed. The BOM lists all of the components, assemblies, subassemblies, parts, and raw materials required to make the end item. The BOM comes from the engineering database specifying each part needed to make a particular product.

Finally, an **inventory records file** is necessary for each component of the BOM. These records keep track of the current inventory position of an item, the standard lead time to

EXHIBIT 1
Production Planning System

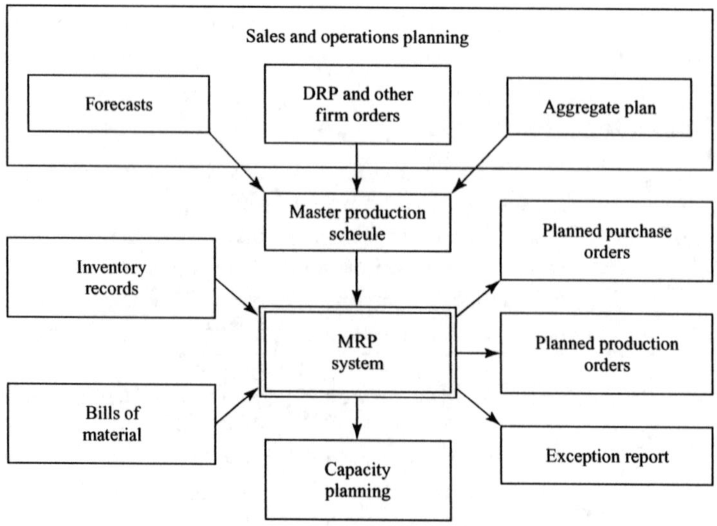

In Practice

CAN I REPLENISH YOUR COFFEE?

Starbucks uses an MRP system from Oracle to automate the roasting and packing of some 85 million pounds of coffee each year.

Source: *Forbes,* August 24, 1998.

get the part, any lot-sizing information, and, for purchased items, information about the supplier. These files can contain other information, such as the safety stock or preferred lot sizes.

An MRP system "explodes" the master schedule using the BOM. The result of this explosion is the requirements for subassemblies and component parts for each unit in the MPS. These requirements translate into shop orders when the components are made internally, and purchase orders when the components are purchased as raw material. Next, a simple example is used to show this explosion process and to illustrate the logic contained in a set of MRP transactions.

The Logic Behind Requirements Planning: An MRP Example

Cumberland Cutlery specializes in making high-end knives. One product it offers includes a hand-carved wooden handle that can be engraved with a laser to the customer's wishes. These knives come in a gift-boxed set, each containing four knives. Each of the four knives is made up of a blade, a hand-carved handle, and three rivets to hold the blade to the handle.

For illustrative purposes, the MRP computations are shown in three stages: BOM explosion, inventory netting, and lead time offsetting.

Stage 1: BOM Explosion

The exploded view schematic in Exhibit 2 illustrates the knife as a set of parts. The first diagram of Exhibit 3, on the next page, depicts how these parts come together in the assembly process. This diagram is often referred to as a **product structure diagram,** a "pictorial view" of the bill of materials for the product. Also in Exhibit 3, this same product structure is shown in an **indented bill of materials,** a more computer-friendly representation.

The MRP calculations start with the quantity of end items to be shipped, in this case a set of knives. Suppose Cumberland Cutlery has orders for 40 boxed knife sets. To make these 40 sets, the requirements for parts and assemblies would be as shown in Exhibit 4 on the next page. These component requirements are a result of the **bill of materials explosion,** where the requirement for 40 boxed knife sets is exploded to find the total number required of each component. Thus, if the company is to produce the 40 sets, it needs to buy the proper components—40 boxes, 160 blades, 160 handles, and 480 rivets—so that it can assemble the 160 knives and package them 4 to a box.

EXHIBIT 2
Exploded Schematic Knife

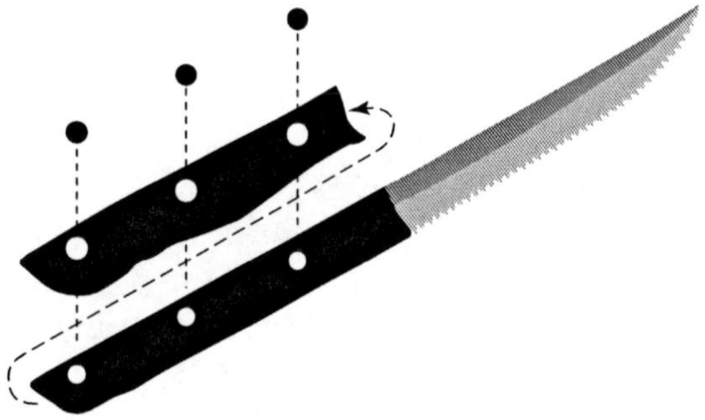

EXHIBIT 3
Product Structure Diagram and Indented BOM for Knife Set

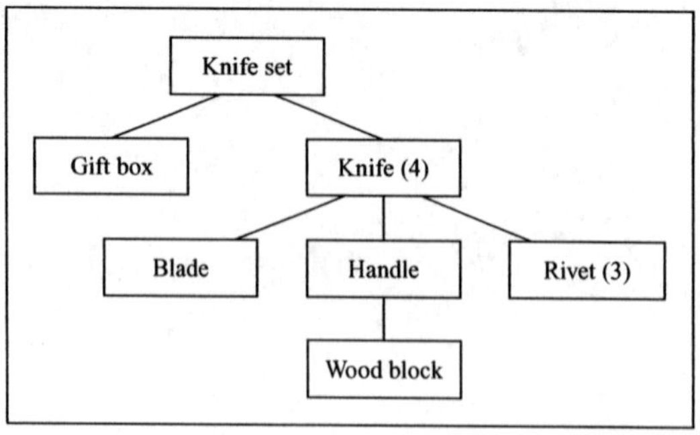

Knife set
• Knife (4)
•• Blade (1)
•• Rivets (3)
•• Handle (1)
••• Wood block (1)
• Gift box (1)

EXHIBIT 4
Exploded Requirements for Knife Set

Part Name	Level	Quantity	Calculation	Explanation
Knife set	0	40		Number needed
• Gift box	1	40	40 × 1	1 box per set
• Knife	1	160	40 × 4	4 knives per set
•• Blade	2	160	160 × 1	1 blade per knife
•• Rivet	2	480	160 × 3	3 rivets per knife
•• Handle	2	160	160 × 1	1 handle per knife
••• Wood block	3	160	160 × 1	1 block per handle

The BOM explosion is done one level at a time. The boxed knife set, the end item in this case, is coded as level 0 and is the starting point of the explosion process. Level 1 components of the boxed knife set—the gift box and the knife—are derived from the Level 0 item. Level 2 components—those with the two bullets to their left—are derived from the level 1 requirements, in this case the knife requirements. Finally, the level 3 component, the wood block (having 3 bullets), is derived from a level 2 item.

Stage 2: On-Hand Inventory Netting

If the company has some finished goods inventory and some component inventory on hand, then it would want to take this inventory into account before producing more. In finished goods, there are 10 boxed sets while in component or raw material inventory there are 100 rivets and 20 blades. If the company's goal is to order only what is needed, thereby keeping inventory to a minimum, then there is no need to order all of the components required from the BOM explosion. To find the net amount needed, on-hand inventory should be netted with the exploded requirements. The inventory-netting calculations are shown below in Exhibit 5. Notice that these computations are done on a level-by-level basis, starting with level 0 and then progressing down the product structure diagram to lower-level components. This is important because the higher a part's level in the product structure, the more lower level components it contains.

For instance, note that there are 20 blades in inventory. In the BOM explosion of Exhibit 4, the total number of blades required is 160 (40 boxed sets × 4 knives per box × 1 blade per knife). If the inventory of 20 blades is subtracted from the 160 required, the net number of blades needed is 140. However, this number is too high. Why? Because the 10 boxed knife sets in inventory have knives with blades in them as well–40 knives with 40 blades. Thus, there is a need for only 100 blades, as was found in the computations in Exhibit 5.

Stage 3: Offsetting the Lead time

Finally, since the company making these boxed knife sets must purchase or make the components, there must be some allowance for the time it takes to obtain the purchased parts from a vendor or for the time it takes to make the component parts. For purposes of illustration, assume the **lead times** shown in Exhibit 6 are those required to make parts or obtain them from some source.

EXHIBIT 5 **Inventory Netting for Knife Set**

Part name		Quantity	Calculation required
Boxed sets	Gross requirement	40	
	Less on-hand inventory	10	
	Net requirement	30	
• Gift boxes	Gross requirement	30	30 × 1
	Less on-hand inventory	0	
	Net requirement	30	
• Knives	Gross requirement	120	30 × 4
	Less on-hand inventory	0	
	Net requirement	120	
•• Blades	Gross requirement	120	120 × 1
	Less on-hand inventory	20	
	Net requirement	100	
•• Rivets	Gross requirement	360	120 × 3
	Less on-hand inventory	100	
	Net requirement	260	
•• Handles	Gross requirement	120	120 × 1
	Less on-hand inventory	0	
	Net requirement	120	

EXHIBIT 6
Lead times for Knife Set Components

Part Name	Lead Time	Explanation
Knife sets	0	Can engrave and assemble quickly, on demand
• Gift boxes	1 week	Requires 1 week to obtain
• Knives	1 week	Requires 1 week to assemble the knives
•• Blades	2 weeks	Requires 2 weeks to obtain this component
•• Rivets	1 week	Requires 1 week to obtain this component
•• Handles	1 week	Requires 1 week to make the handle
••• Wood	1 week	Requires 1 week to obtain this material

Assuming the 40 boxed sets discussed earlier are needed in week 5, not only must the quantities be computed, but the time period in which the part is needed must be found as well. This is done by *offsetting the lead time* at each stage, as shown in Exhibit 7 on the next page.

Thus, MRP calculations are made up of three basic sets of calculations: (1) exploding the BOM to get the gross requirement for parts, (2) netting out the on-hand inventory to find the net number of parts needed, and (3) offsetting the lead time to know when to order the required components.

Time Buckets

Many MRP and DRP systems are bucketed. In other words, the systems group requirements into some time period, usually a week. Once a requirement is put into a particular period, or **time bucket,** the requirements planning system makes no other distinction about sequencing or scheduling of parts within that bucket.

Suppose an MRP system shows planned orders for two particular parts in week 7, and these two parts are both produced on the same piece of equipment. While the system may be able to check via capacity planning logic whether there is sufficient capacity in the department to make the two parts in week 7, it will not indicate which should be produced on Monday, which on Tuesday, and so on. The MRP system just indicates that both must be produced in week 7. The detailed sequencing is done either manually by a scheduler or through systems usually referred to as *shop floor control* systems.

There are "bucketless" MRP systems that work in continuous time, but these systems aren't as pervasive as bucketed systems and can be somewhat difficult to use. Of course, bucket size can be changed to some other appropriate time period such as one day or one

EXHIBIT 7 **Lead Time Offsets for Knife Set**

		Period (week)				
Part name		1	2	3	4	5
Knife sets	Gross requirement					40
	Less on-hand inventory					10
	Net requirement					30
• Gift boxes	Gross requirement				30	
	Less on-hand inventory				0	
	Net requirement				30	
• Knives	Gross requirement				120	
	Less on-hand inventory				0	
	Net requirement				120	
•• Blades	Gross requirement		120			
	Less on-hand inventory		20			
	Net requirement		100			
•• Rivets	Gross requirement			360		
	Less on-hand inventory			100		
	Net requirement			260		
•• Handles	Gross requirement			120		
	Less on-hand inventory			0		
	Net requirement			120		
••• Wood	Gross requirement		120			
	Less on-hand inventory		0			
	Net requirement		120			

month, depending on the company's needs, but the most common tends to be one week. Even if a system does not use time buckets, the basic logic presented here is still useful for understanding how these systems work.

Low-Level Coding

To properly explode the BOM into its component parts, the computations are done one level of the BOM at a time as explained earlier. When a common component part appears in multiple places in the BOM, the component should be coded with the lowest level of all of the occurrences. This ensures that the component's requirements are calculated only once and that they are calculated only after all of their parent requirements have been determined as well.

In Exhibit 8, a sample product diagram is shown with component X **low-level coded** to level 2. Notice that component X exists as a level 1 component, feeding directly into the final product, but since it also appears at level 2 as a component of Assembly A, it gets coded as a level 2 part.

EXHIBIT 8
Low Level Coding Example

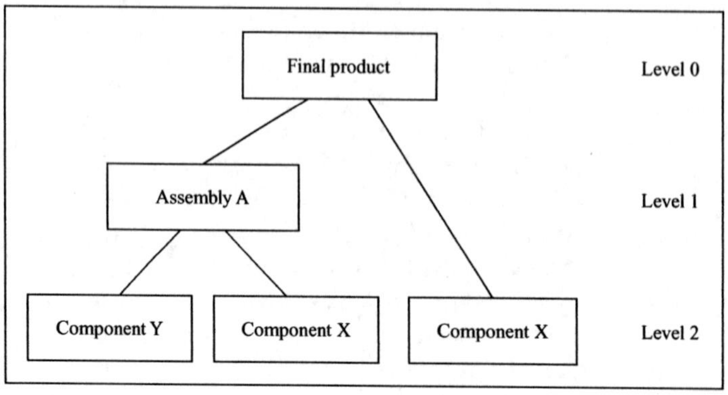

MRP Records

While the logic can be shown easily with the simple knife example above, keeping track of all of the information in most complex situations is more difficult to follow without more detail. The table in Exhibit 7 can be broken into seven separate MRP records, one for each component and assembly. While these records can be configured in a variety of ways, a typical one for the rivet is shown in Exhibit 9 with more detail. Each line in the inventory-planning portion of the record is defined and then explained below. While conventions can vary, on-hand inventory is assumed here to represent inventory available at the end of the period.

EXHIBIT 9
Inventory Record for Rivet

Part Name: Rivet								
Part Number:		Lead Time: 2				Order Quantity: 1,020		
Supplier: PH Fasteners Buyer:	Past Due	Period 1	2	3	4	5	6	7
Gross requirement		240	360	300	360	420	300	360
Scheduled receipts		1,020						
On-hand inventory	220	1,000	640	340	1,000	580	280	940
Net requirement					20			80
Planned order receipts					1,020			1,020
Planned order releases			1,020			1,020		

Gross requirement: The gross amount required by the item's parent or parents. This information comes from the planned order releases of the parent item, or, in this case, the planned order releases for the knife. Assume the knife releases are

	1	2	3	4	5	6	7
Planned order releases	80	120	100	120	140	100	120

This means that there should be enough rivets available in period 1 to make 80 knives. Thus, since each knife requires 3 rivets, the gross requirement for rivets in period 1 is $3 \times 80 = 240$.

Scheduled receipts: Orders placed for an item in a period prior to the current one but not yet delivered. An order has already been placed with the vendor for 1,020 parts. These parts are due to arrive by the end of period 1 but have not arrived yet.

On-hand inventory: Inventory available to meet the gross requirement, plus safety stock. There are currently 220 rivets in stock, which appears in the Past Due column. Since 1,020 rivets are to arrive in period 1 and 240 are needed to produce knives, the stock remaining at the end of period 1 should be $220 + 1{,}020 - 240 = 1{,}000$ (recall that an end-of-period inventory convention is being used—this could just as easily be shown as beginning of period). For period 2, planned production requires 360 more rivets, which will reduce the on-hand inventory to 640. For period 3, stock is again reduced by the requirement to use another 300 units, so on-hand inventory is reduced to 340. Finally, in period 4, since the 340 rivets are less than the required 360, no inventory remains. Instead, a deficit of 20 rivets will occur unless something is done to bring in more rivets. Thus, an order needs to be received, and since the lot size is 1,020 units, that is the number that must be received in period 4.

Net requirement: If there is not sufficient on-hand inventory or pipeline inventory (scheduled receipts), then this is the amount needed to meet the gross requirement.

Note in the first three periods that there is no net requirement. In other words, there should be enough inventory from previous actions to meet demand in these periods. In period 4, there is a net requirement of 20 rivets (360–340).

Planned order receipts: Amount of an item that is planned to arrive in the period. The first period when rivets need to arrive is the first period in which there is an amount showing in the net requirements row. This occurs in period 4, when there is a need for 20 rivets. Thus, an order needs to be received in period 4 for at least 20 rivets. But note that there is a **lot-size** requirement in the top-right corner of the MRP record—there are 1,020 pieces contained in a box. Thus, when an order is placed, it is placed for 1,020 rivets. If things go as planned, no rivets need be delivered in periods 5 and 6 as the 1,020 will be available to cover these requirements. The second planned order receipt occurs in period 7 because the requirements of periods 4 to 7 are 1,100 (20 + 420 + 300 + 360), which is 80 more than the 1,020 that are to arrive in period 4.

Planned order releases: Amount of an item to be ordered in the period. The figures appearing in this row are identical to those of the planned order receipt row, but they are moved back in time by their two-period lead time (the lead time for the part as shown at the top center of the MRP record). Thus, if an order for 1,020 units is placed in period 3, it will arrive in period 5 when it is needed.

Lot-Sizing in MRP Systems

In the example just presented for rivets, a lot-size requirement of 1,020 pieces was used when an order was needed for rivets. There are a number of lot-sizing rules that are used in MRP systems, each of which has its advantages and disadvantages. Some of the most common are discussed below and illustrated with a partial MRP record using the rivet as an example.

Fixed quantity: When order sizes are constrained because of shipping carton size, this method is common. This is the method that was illustrated in the rivet example in Exhibit 9.

Lot-for-lot: When inventory is to be minimized, the planned order receipts should be the same as the net requirement—only the amount needed is ordered each period (Exhibit 10).

Economic lot size: The EOQ (economic order quantity) model is used to balance the cost of ordering with the cost of holding. Suppose that the EOQ for the rivet is 700, then the quantity ordered, whenever an order is needed, is 700 (Exhibit 11). This is similar to the fixed-quantity rule.

Period order quantity: This quantity is computed in a method similar to the economic lot size, but in this case, the EOQ is converted to the average number of periods of demand.

EXHIBIT 10

Example of Lot-for-Lot Lot-Size Rule for Rivets

Part Name: Rivet								
Part Number:		Lead Time: 2				Order Quantity: Lot-for-Lot		
Supplier: PH Fasteners Buyer:	Past Due	Period						
		1	2	3	4	5	6	7
Gross requirement		240	360	300	360	420	300	360
Scheduled receipts		1,020						
On-hand inventory	220	1,000	640	340				
Net requirement					20	420	300	360
Planned order receipts					20	420	300	360
Planned order releases			20	420	300	360		

EXHIBIT 11
Example of EOQ Lot-Size Rule for Rivets

Part Name: Rivet								
Part Number:		Lead Time: 2			Order Quantity: Lot-for-Lot			
Supplier: PH Fasteners		Period						
Buyer:	Past Due	1	2	3	4	5	6	7
Gross requirement		240	360	300	360	420	300	360
Scheduled receipts		1,020						
On-hand inventory	220	1,000	640	340	680	260	660	300
Net requirement					20		40	
Planned order receipts					700		700	
Planned order releases			700		700			

The average demand over periods 1 to 7 is (240 + 360 + 300 + 360 + 420 + 300 + 360)/7 = 334. Thus, the period order quantity (POQ) is 700/334, which is approximately two periods. Whenever an order is needed, the next two periods of demand are ordered. As can be seen in Exhibit 12, when an order is needed in period 4, the order quantity should be the next two periods' needs, or 20 + 420 = 440. This method tends to keep inventory lower than the EOQ method because there is no provision to carry inventory into period t from period $t-1$ if there is to be an order arriving in period t.

As a convenience to the reader, Exhibit 13, page 12, contains a list of the key terms introduced above with a short description.

Advantages and Disadvantages of MRP Systems

MRP has its critics, but then so do a lot of useful tools. The past decade has seen much discussion about the demise of MRP systems with arguments that JIT and lean systems* are what is needed to help manufacturing firms. But like any other tool, MRP has its place and, when used properly, can provide tremendous benefits. On the other hand, when it is used incorrectly or used for the wrong application, it can create significant problems.

Some hybrid systems use a combination of JIT and MRP, combining the simplicity of JIT with the information content of an MRP system. The MRP system might use the first level or two of the BOM to set final order quantities for major assemblies and subassemblies and to order key components from suppliers. Rather than have the MRP system explode the needs for lower-level components, JIT systems are then used to bring the remaining fabrications and components through the manufacturing process.

EXHIBIT 12
Example of POQ Lot-Size Rule for Rivets

Part Name: Rivet								
Part Number:		Lead Time: 2			Order Quantity: Lot-for-Lot			
Supplier: PH Fasteners		Period						
Buyer:	Past Due	1	2	3	4	5	6	7
Gross requirement		240	360	300	360	420	300	360
Scheduled receipts		1,020						
On-hand inventory	220	1,000	640	340	420		360	
Net requirement					20		300	
Planned order receipts					440		660	
Planned order releases			440		660			

* JIT (Just in Time) and lean systems approaches attempt to simplify scheduling by making operations more flexible. The approaches are discussed fully in the "Lean/Just-in-Time Systems" module by Steven A. Melnyk and Lawrence D. Fredendall (New York: McGraw-Hill/Irwin 2002).

EXHIBIT 13
Summary of Commonly Used MRP Terminology

Term	Description
Bill of materials (BOM)	List of all components, assemblies, subassemblies, parts, and raw materials required to make the end item.
BOM explosion	End-item requirements are translated into component-by-component requirements for each level of the BOM.
Master production schedule (MPS)	A schedule of when and how much of each end item a firm plans to produce.
Gross requirement	The gross amount required by the item's parent part or parts.
Net requirement	If there is not sufficient on-hand inventory or pipeline inventory (scheduled receipts), then this is the amount needed to meet the gross requirement.
Scheduled receipts	Amount of an item that will arrive in the period due to a past order.
Planned order receipts	Amount of an item that is planned to arrive in the period if an order is placed.
Planned order releases	Amount of an item to be ordered in the period.
On-hand inventory	Inventory available to meet the gross requirement.
Lead time	The required amount of time, from when an order is placed until that order is delivered, to get a component from a supplier or internal department.
Lot-size rule	A rule about the quantity to order given that some quantity needs to be ordered.

High-volume "batch" plants that fabricate parts for a number of different products are the ideal candidates for MRP systems, especially when the final products have some similarity with each other. On the other hand, plants that make few product variants that require little assembly aren't likely to see much advantage in such a system.

MRP systems basically ignore capacity constraints (they are "infinite planning" systems as they assume infinite capacity) and thus rely on other planning mechanisms to ensure that the MPS can indeed be met with the available plant capacity. Thus an MRP system can compute a plan that is infeasible in terms of the capacity of the plant's resources. JIT systems don't do any better with capacity issues. There are "finite planning" packages available, and, to some degree, aggregate production planning approaches minimize the impact of cyclical and seasonal demand changes. Some advanced planning and scheduling (APS) systems contain good finite capacity approaches. Capacity planning as it relates to MRP is discussed in a later section on capacity requirements planning (CRP).

There are those who argue that JIT systems do a much better job than MRP systems of keeping inventory low. In practice, this may be the case for many applications, due in large part to the simplicity of such JIT systems and the discipline that can be instilled by using JIT. However, MRP systems should lead to as low or lower inventories, and should theoretically do so at lower cost, because MRP systems are forward looking, not reactionary like JIT systems. MRP makes use of dependency information and using this information should improve performance. The problem with many ad hoc comparisons of MRP and JIT systems, where supposedly JIT systems come out looking better, is that the MRP systems being compared are not being used correctly—in other words, MRP is being used without *discipline.* This is discussed in more detail in the next section. JIT systems used without discipline could result in the same problems.

Some Pitfalls in the Use of MRP Systems

There are a number of reasons why MRP systems may not result in lower inventories in practice, when compared to other systems, and especially JIT. User trust is one reason, especially since it usually leads to buffering, which is a second reason. Finally, system nervousness, caused primarily from changes in the schedule, can lead to significant inventories as well.

MRP System Trust

Users that don't trust a system may not use the system to its potential. There can be a number of reasons for this lack of trust. One is just the lack of confidence that the system can really do what it is supposed to do. Users who understand a system but feel the system is not being administered and implemented correctly also will not trust the system. Finally, since systems generally require some kind of input, if the information being fed into the system can't be trusted, then neither can the output of the system. For an MRP system, this includes inaccurate bills of materials from the engineering department, inaccurate inventory levels from production control, and inaccurate lead times from suppliers or other internal departments. All of these factors lead to personnel making sure the system won't cause them problems and thus each user starts "buffering" his or her part of the process just in case something goes wrong.

Buffers in MRP Systems

Two of the most common types of buffers in MRP systems, as well as in processing systems in general, are inventory and time. Inventory can be increased directly by simply inserting safety stock at any of the MRP levels. In other words, the system never plans for the inventory to fall below a certain level. Consider the MRP record in Exhibit 14 for the rivets used in the earlier example. This record is revised to include a safety stock of 100 units and a lot-for-lot ordering policy. Note the difference between this record and the record shown in Exhibit 11 where on-hand inventory was 0 in periods 4 through 7. The period 4 net requirements for the SS = 100 scenario are 100 units higher since all of the inventory on hand can't be used to meet ordinary demand requirements. The 100 units of inventory specified to be safety stock must be reserved for unforeseen need that the firm hasn't anticipated.

Inserting safety stock at every level of the BOM for those "just-in-case" situations works counter to what MRP is supposed to achieve. If, instead, the firm should decide to keep inventory at the finished goods level, or at some appropriate level, then whenever something goes wrong, demand can be met from this inventory, which has been set aside for this purpose, even though the problem may have occurred at some other level with some other part.

While inserting safety stock into the MRP system is immediately interpreted as inventory, another way to buffer the system is to increase the lead time from what is really needed. This might be done because of the uncertainty of the lead time estimate—a point estimate in MRP—so that when the lead time for a component is longer than expected, more time is available in the plan to make the assemblies using that component. Suppose a supervisor really needs a week to move things through his or her department; however, the supervisor enters a two-week lead time in the MRP system "just in case" things don't go as planned. Essentially what the supervisor has done is add one week's worth of inventory to the system. The additional week of lead time is the same as holding an extra week of inventory, and if everyone in the supply chain pads his or her lead times, lots of excess inventory is the result.

EXHIBIT 14
Revised Rivet Record—SS = 100 Units

Part Name: Rivet								
Part Number:		Lead Time: 2				Order Quantity: Lot-for-Lot		
Supplier: PH Fasteners						Safety Stock: 100		
Buyer:		Period						
	Past Due	1	2	3	4	5	6	7
Gross requirement		240	360	300	360	420	300	360
Scheduled receipts		1,020						
On-hand inventory	220	1,000	640	340	100	100	100	100
Net requirement					120	420	300	360
Planned order receipts					120	420	300	360
Planned order releases			120	420	300	360		

System Nervousness and Time Fences

The starting point of an MRP system is the master schedule. If the master schedule is changed, then so are the requirements for every component part. If the master schedule is changed from week to week, then managers responsible for items at lower levels in the product code see changes in their requirements as well. This constant changing of the master schedule and the resulting changes in the requirements for components is referred to as **system nervousness.**

System nervousness can make planning for the future very difficult. The lack of any constancy in future requirements can lead to a lack of trust in the system as well as a perceived need for inventory buffers just in case something changes to which one can't react. These problems can be severe at the lowest level of the product structure because of the lead time offsetting required by the MRP system.

As the master schedule is exploded into its component part requirements, layer by layer, lead times are offset for each layer of the explosion. Thus, for the knife set illustration of Exhibit 7, notice that a requirement for final product in week 5 results in a requirement for wood in week 2. This three-week difference can be thought of as the **MRP reaction time.** Changes made to the MPS within this reaction time will result in "past due" changes at lower levels of the product structure.

Consider the knife set example shown in Exhibit 15, where MRP information for some of the components is not shown—only the information for getting from the master schedule to the requirement for wood is shown. Note the requirement in week 3 for 50 units of the final product results in a need for wood in the period prior to the current planning period, period 1. Thus, changes to the week 3 requirement for a finished product creates changes in the requirement for some lower-level components to which it may be impossible to react because of the lead time offsets.

To help minimize the effect of system nervousness, **time fences** can be used to ensure that at least certain portions of the requirements plan are not affected by changes to the master schedule. A three-week *firm time fence* for the knife example would block any changes to the MPS in the first three weeks. In other words, any changes to the MPS would only be allowed in weeks 4 and beyond. That doesn't mean that changes in week 4 and beyond won't still result in system nervousness. A manager responsible for the wood component would still see changes in future periods (an MPS change in week 4 would change the requirement for wood in period 1), but at least it would be possible to react to those changes by changing future plans. In addition, the firm making the knives may have a five-week *semi-firm time fence* allowing changes to be made in weeks 4 and 5, but only if the changes are within, say, 15 percent of the previous plan. This ensures that adequate future capacity plans can be made while still allowing for small short-term changes in the requirements.

EXHIBIT 15 **MRP Reaction Time Illustration for Knife Set**

			Period (week)				
Part name			1	2	3	4	5
Boxed sets	Gross requirement				50		
	Less on-hand inventory				5		
	Net requirement				45		
• Knives	Gross requirement			180			
	Less on-hand inventory			0			
	Net requirement			180			
•• Handles	Gross requirement		180				
	Less on-hand inventory		20				
	Net requirement		160				
••• Wood	Gross requirement	160					
	Less on-hand inventory	0					
	Net requirement	160					

Running the MRP System

With the increases in computing power and data storage, MRP systems are no longer something that only large firms can afford. While up through the 1990s, most applications were hosted on mainframe and mini computers, systems are now available that run on networked PCs, a solution that puts these systems within the grasp of even small firms. In fact, with the growth of Internet solutions, software service providers such as mySAP offer MRP solutions that do not require the user to purchase and run the software in house. Instead, users run their system via the Internet and thus don't need to maintain an in-house expert on the MRP system.

Large MRP calculations can require significant computing resources. There are two primary ways of making these calculations. The first is known as regenerative, where an MPS is used to generate a complete set of MRP records. The regenerative approach can take a day or more of computing time for some large companies. Thus, these types of calculations can't be done in real time and are normally done at the end of every week.

So that information can be kept more current, another way of running an MRP system is known as net change. This approach only changes those records that are impacted by events such as the completion of a day's production or changes in raw material availability. With this method, only those reports necessary for action are generated. In other words, if the production and shipment of everything on the master schedule have been completed for a particular day, inventory records and the like would be updated for on-line access, but no reporting would be necessary since everything occurred as planned.

Distribution Requirements Planning (DRP)

Just as component requirements are exploded through the various levels of the BOM in MRP, the levels of the various distribution steps in the supply chain must be combined—imploded—to determine the total requirements for end items for the master schedule. Forecasts and firm orders at each of the points of contact with the customer—those points farthest down the supply chain—must be rolled up to the next level in the supply chain, many times a local warehouse. Demand at each of the warehouses is then combined and rolled up as demand on some regional distribution center and finally the regional centers are combined to find the demand at the central distribution center. The information from the central distribution center is then passed to the factory to put together the MPS.

Not only does a DRP system gather and consolidate orders from all of the various distribution points for the central distribution facility, but the information that is contained within the DRP database is valuable for planning truck capacity and routing, for planning warehouse transactions and labor, and for understanding customer purchasing patterns.

The DRP system works with the same logic as the MRP system, with a slight difference in the DRP records closest to the customer. Rather than use "gross requirement" in line 1, that line is referred to as "forecast requirement." Forecast requirement could include firm orders already received as well as forecasts of orders not yet received. In addition, rather than use scheduled receipts in line 2, the DRP record uses "in transit."

Exhibit 16 provides an example showing one product for a distributor with a central distribution center (CDC) that supplies two warehouses. The lead time for replenishment at the CDC is one week to obtain the item from the manufacturer, and this item must be ordered in lot sizes of 400 units. Shipment to warehouse #1 requires one week of transit time while shipment to warehouse #2 requires two weeks. Both of the warehouses require 10 units of safety stock—their on-hand inventory should never fall below 10 units—so that unexpected demand can be met without delay. Both warehouses use lot-for-lot lot sizing, so whatever is needed in a period is shipped in that period.

For warehouse #1, on-hand inventory begins at 60 units and decreases to 20 at the end of the first period due to the projected usage of 40 units from the forecast. In period 2, the expected demand is 50 units, but while on-hand inventory is 20 units, only 10 units of

In Practice

A GIANT DRP SYSTEM

Giant Food, an East Cost supermarket chain, uses a DRP system to make its supply-chain initiatives in the area of efficient consumer response (ECR) and continuous replenishment work as well as possible. The system helps keep inventory costs low but at the same time ensure good customer service.

The key is being able to respond quickly to consumer orders, and the DRP system supplies the information about where the inventories are in the supply chain and passes this information to the various distribution levels involved. The DRP system allows point-of-sale transactions to pull inventory through the chain all the way back to the manufacturers. Giant managers believe that the DRP system helps them maintain control over their inventory and customer service rather than putting it all in their vendors' hands.

Source: *Progressive Grocer*, September 1994, pp. 73–78.

inventory are available because of the desired safety stock of 10 units. This leaves a net requirement of 40 units. Since a lot-for-lot lot-sizing rule is being used, planned order receipts are the same as the net requirement and planned order releases then mirror these but are offset by the one-week lead time.

The CDC ships this product to the two warehouses so that the gross requirement at the CDC is the sum of the time-period requirements at the two warehouses. In week 2, the gross requirement of 110 at the CDC is a result of planned order releases in week 2 for 100 units from warehouse #1 and 10 units from warehouse #2. The company must buy this particular item from a company that sells the product in 400-unit lots, thus the planned receipts and planned orders for 400 units at a time. The first planned receipt comes in week 2 when the inventory is able to cover 55 units of the 110 units required to ship to the warehouses. The remaining 55 units must be covered by sending an order to the supplier in week 1 (the planned order release) so that 400 units arrive in week 2. Again, even though only 55 units appear as a net requirement, 400 units are ordered since that is the required lot size.

Capacity Requirements Planning (CRP)

The goal of any good planning system is to make credible promises about what can be delivered–a credible promise for a production planning system has to do with production output. While an MRP system gives information about the timing and quantity of purchased

EXHIBIT 16
Distribution Company Example Illustrating DRP for One Item

	Item: Supplier:	Past Due	Period 1	2	3	4	5	6	7	8
Warehouse #1	Forecast requirement		40	50	100	60	60	100	70	80
	In transit									
LT= 1	On-hand inventory	60	20	10	10	10	10	10	10	10
SS= 10	Net requirement			40	100	60	60	100	70	80
Lot for lot	Planned order receipts			40	100	60	60	100	70	80
	Planned order releases		40	100	60	60	100	70	80	
Warehouse #2	Forecast requirement		10	10	5	15	20	20	15	10
	In transit		15							
LT= 2	On-hand inventory	25	30	20	15	10	10	10	10	10
SS= 10	Net requirement					10	20	20	15	10
Lot for lot	Planned order receipts					10	20	20	15	10
	Planned order releases			10	20	20	15	10		
CDC	Gross requirement		40	110	80	80	115	80	80	
	In transit									
LT= 1	On-hand inventory	95	55	345	265	185	70	390	310	
SS= 0	Net requirement			55				10		
Lot= 400	Planned order receipts			400				400		
	Planned order releases		400				400			

EXHIBIT 17
MRP Table for Knife Handle

Part Name: Handle								
Part Number:		**Lead Time: 1**				**Order Quantity: Lot for Lot**		
Supplier: PH Fasteners		**Week**						
Buyer:	**Past Due**	**1**	**2**	**3**	**4**	**5**	**6**	**7**
Gross requirement		120	120	120	160	160	200	120
Scheduled receipts		100						
On-hand inventory	40	20						
Net requirement			100	120	160	160	200	120
Planned order receipts			100	120	160	160	200	120
Planned order releases		100	120	160	160	200	120	

components from suppliers and fabricated components, assemblies, and subassemblies from manufacturing facilities, the system really has no way to ensure that these quantities can be delivered. The projected needs are based on a desired master production schedule without regard to whether there is sufficient capacity to build the desired quantities. Thus, some kind of capacity planning is needed—**capacity requirements planning (CRP)** is the term used for this activity.

Fortunately, the logic of requirements planning already presented extends to CRP as well. Since the quantity and timing of each component are known, an estimate of the capacity requirement for each period can be derived easily from the planned orders. The time required to produce an item is multiplied by the number of units in the planned order releases, period by period, to find the needed capacity in each period. This period-by-period capacity requirement can then be checked against available capacity to determine if the plan is feasible.

This approach—where work is assigned to work centers and then capacity is checked to see if what has been assigned can be made—is often referred to as *infinite loading,* or infinite capacity planning. This is the approach taken here. An alternative is finite loading, where work is only assigned if there is capacity. Both of these planning methods have the same goal, but the difference is in how the objective is reached. Infinite loading is certainly an easy approach and one that shows projected loads as they are needed. Managers then can make decisions about whether, for instance, they want to use overtime to make what is needed; or they might decide to build units ahead (make inventory) to smooth out the capacity requirements. Finite loading—more of an optimization approach—is sometimes plagued by proper problem definition and even lack of any possible feasible solution. It also can be more complex to understand.

The CRP concept is illustrated for the knife handle of the Cumberland Cutlery example used earlier. Each knife requires a wooden handle that is shaped in Cumberland Cutlery's plant from a block of wood. The handles are hand carved by one of three carvers in the shaping production area. Each handle requires 42 minutes of carving time. Exhibit 17 provides the MRP table for the knife handle showing the planned order releases for the shaping area.

The MRP table indicates that 100 handles must be completed in period 1. In the CRP table in Exhibit 18, the 100 handles needed during period 1 are converted to the number of production hours required to produce the 100 handles. The 42-minute production time for

EXHIBIT 18
CRP Table for Knife Handle

Capacity Requirements: Shaping Department								
Part Number:		**Week**						
Processing Time: 42 minutes	**Past Due**	**1**	**2**	**3**	**4**	**5**	**6**	**7**
Handle requirements		100	120	160	160	200	120	
Time required (hours)		70	84	112	112	140	84	
Planned capacity available		80	120	120	120	120	120	

EXHIBIT 19
CRP Load Profile for Shaping Department

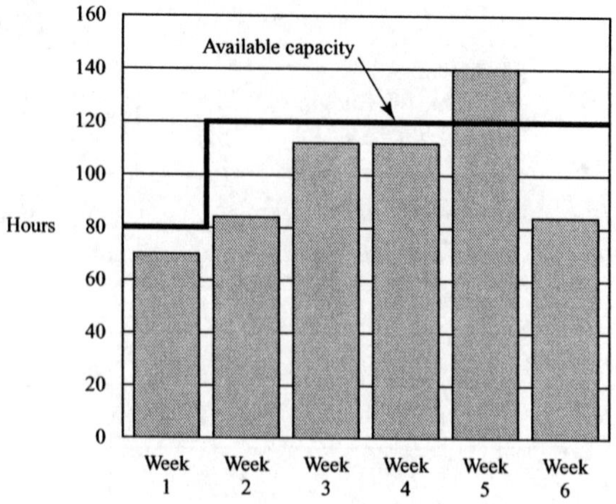

a knife is 0.7 hour and thus 70 hours are required in week 1. While the shaping department normally has three carvers working 40 hours per week for a total capacity of 120 hours, one of the carvers is on vacation during week 1, leaving production capacity at 80 hours, as indicated in the last line of the table.

This CRP information can be presented in a department **load profile graph** so that managers can see visually what the capacity situation is for their departments. A load profile for the shaping department is presented in Exhibit 19 showing available capacity and required capacity under the current plans.

Both the CRP table and the load profile show a problem in week 5 with insufficient capacity for the required workload. There are a number of ways this can be rectified.

The first alternative is to simply use the excess capacity of the four previous weeks to build inventory in anticipation of week 5. Second, overtime or subcontracting could be used to increase capacity in week 5. Third, the production requirements might be routed through another department where the same kind of capacity is available. Fourth, the planners might decide to change the MPS for the boxed sets to more evenly spread the production across the various weeks. Finally, although it isn't a problem in this particular case, the lot-size rules for the knife handle, the knife, or the boxed sets could be changed so that demand doesn't get lumped together. The alternatives discussed above are shown in Exhibit 20.

EXHIBIT 20
Capacity Requirements Planning

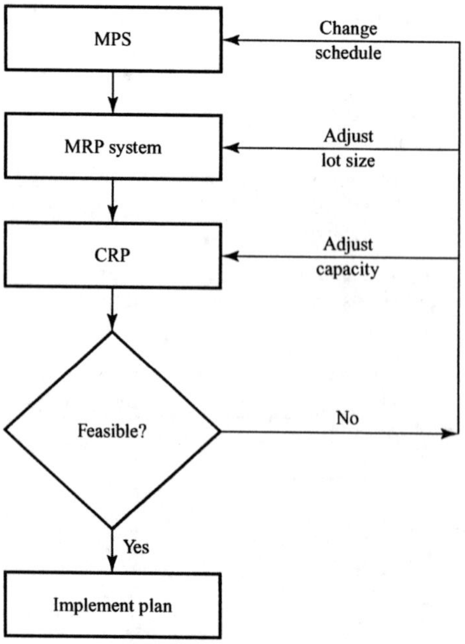

The diagram illustrates the basic decision flow and adjustments at each level of the planning process. Once a feasible plan is found by the capacity checks of the systems, the plan can be firmed up for implementation.

Eaton Furniture Company: A Comprehensive Example

The case example from Eaton Furniture Company illustrates more comprehensively the individual issues discussed in the preceding pages. In addition, the example shows how MRP and DRP work together and how capacity decisions can be made from the requirements planning system.

Case Example: The Eaton Furniture Company

The Eaton Furniture Company (EFC) makes book-shelving units for homes and businesses in a variety of models. These shelving units are stored in a central distribution center (CDC) adjacent to EFC's Eaton, Ohio, manufacturing facility. From the CDC, product is shipped to one of four regional distribution centers (RDCs), three in the United States and one in Kobe, Japan. The U.S. RDCs are located in Atlanta, Dallas, and Monterrey, California. The CDC acts as a fifth RDC as it also is set up to ship product directly to customers.

The shelving units come in various heights, widths, material, and finish, making the planning and movement of material and finished product an essential management task. With the variety of parts and orders moving into and through its plant, EFC uses an MRP system to determine raw material needs from the inbound side of its supply network and component requirements and timing within its factory. To keep inventory costs low and customer service high, EFC also uses a DRP system to move finished product through the distribution portion of its supply chain.

As an example of how these systems work, the MRP and DRP tables are shown for one of EFC's products, part number 3X3-O1, a 3-foot-high, 3-foot-wide, standard-depth oak book shelf. A picture of this product and its indented BOM are shown in Exhibit 21. Low-level coding, discussed in an earlier section, is illustrated in this example as well. Note that oak sheet is a component of both level 2 components (back, side, and end) and a level 1 component (shelf); therefore, it is coded as a level 3 component.

Planning meetings are held each Friday morning to look at forecasts and firm orders for the following week and the weeks that follow. This one-week planning pattern calls for the company's MRP and DRP systems to use one-week planning buckets. Forecasts and production, purchasing, and shipping requirements are stated and planned in these weekly amounts.

Moving product from the plant to the CDC can be done very quickly as it is adjacent to the plant. Moving material from the CDC to the three U.S. RDCs requires a week of transportation time, while the trip to Kobe requires three weeks. Seven-week forecasts are used for each of the regular U.S. RDCs, six-week forecasts are used for the Eaton CDC, and, because

EXHIBIT 21
Book Shelf Schematic and BOM

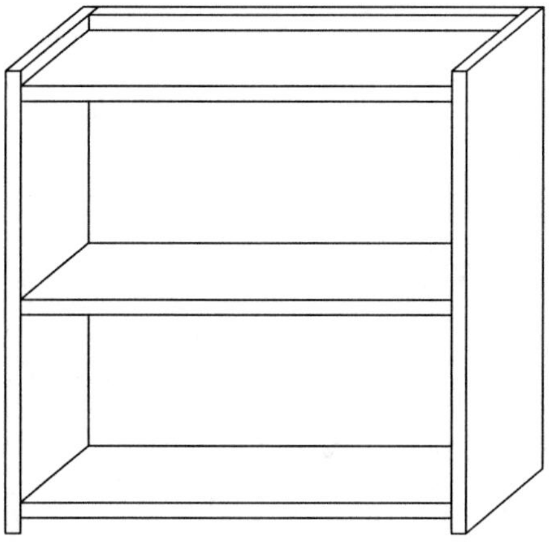

Book shelf 3X3-01
- • Cabinet
  - •• Back
    - ••• Oak sheet $\left(\frac{9}{32}\right)$
  - •• Side (2)
    - ••• Oak sheet $\left(\frac{4}{32}\right)$
  - •• End (2)
    - ••• Oak sheet $\left(\frac{3}{32}\right)$
- • Shelf
    - ••• Oak sheet $\left(\frac{3}{32}\right)$
- • Bracket (4)

EXHIBIT 22
Demand Forecasts for 3X3-O1 Shelf

Shipping Point	Lead Time	SS	Lot Size	Inventory on Hand	Demand Forecast by Week 1	2	3	4	5	6	7	8
Atlanta	1	10	20	12	9	10	11	11	10	10	10	
Dallas	1	10	10	15	10	10	8	8	8	8	8	
Kobe	3	40	40	55	11	12	25	12	12	12	12	12
Monterrey	1	10	20	20	15	13	15	12	15	13	13	
Eaton	0	0	10	0	30	20	40	20	30	30		

of the long lead time, an eight-week forecast is used for Kobe. The first three weeks of a forecast are firm orders from customers while orders farther out than three weeks contain estimates of demand. This three-week time fence is used by the firm to limit the amount of changes that would occur in the production area if orders could be changed constantly. Because of its access to the plant, the CDC carries no safety stock inventory. The three U.S. RDCs carry 10 units of safety stock inventory, while the Kobe RDC carries 40 units. This information, along with current shipping lot size and inventory information, is summarized in Exhibit 22.

The DRP system rolls the requirements at each RDC into one set of demand numbers, time phased to account for the different shipping times. The planned order releases from the DRP table are key inputs for the master scheduling activity. The DRP tables for the current plan are given in Exhibit 23.

EXHIBIT 23
DRP Tables for 3X3-O1 Shelf

		Past Due	Period 1	2	3	4	5	6	7	8
Atlanta	Forecast requirement		9	10	11	11	10	10	10	
	In transit		20							
LT = 1	On-hand inventory	12	23	13	22	11	21	11	21	
SS = 10	Net requirement				8		9		9	
Lot = 20	Planned order receipts				20		20		20	
	Planned order releases			20		20		20		
Dallas	Forecast requirement		10	10	8	8	8	8	8	
	In transit		10							
LT = 1	On-hand inventory	15	15	15	17	19	11	13	15	
SS = 10	Net requirement			5	3	1		7	5	
Lot = 10	Planned order receipts			10	10	10		10	10	
	Planned order releases		10	10	10		10	10		
Kobe	Forecast requirement		11	12	25	12	12	12	12	12
	In transit			40						
LT = 3	On-hand inventory	55	44	72	47	75	63	51	79	67
SS = 40	Net requirement					5			1	
Lot = 40	Planned order receipts					40			40	
	Planned order releases		40			40				
Monterrey	Forecast requirement		15	13	15	12	15	13	13	
	In transit		20							
LT = 1	On-hand inventory	20	25	12	17	25	10	17	24	
SS = 10	Net requirement				13	5		13	6	
Lot = 20	Planned order receipts				20	20		20	20	
	Planned order releases			20	20		20	20		
Eaton	Forecast Requirement		30	20	40	20	30	30		
Eaton CDC	Gross requirement		80	70	70	80	60	80		
	In transit									
LT = 0	On-hand inventory	0	0							
SS = 0	Net requirement		80	70	70	80	60	80		
Lot = 10	Planned order receipts		80	70	70	80	60	80		
	Planned order releases		80	70	70	80	60	80		

EXHIBIT 24
Master Schedule for 3X3-O1 Shelf

MPS and Final Assembly: 3X3-01 Shelf										
		Past	Period							
		Due	1	2	3	4	5	6	7	8
	From DRP system		80	70	70	80	60	80		
	Adjustments for AP				10	10				
3X3-01	Gross requirement		80	70	80	90	60	80		
	Scheduled receipts									
LT= 0	On-hand inventory	10	0							
SS= 0	Net requirement		70	70	80	90	60	80		
Lot= LFL	Planned order receipts		70	70	80	90	60	80		
	Planned order releases		70	70	80	90	60	80		

Each Friday afternoon, a meeting is planned to review the following weeks' production plans, using the forecast information from the morning meeting. The largest part of this discussion has to do with whether or not to build exactly what the rolled-up forecasts indicate. In particular, week-to-week forecast information gives some indication as to whether the longer-term aggregate plan can be maintained or whether adjustments should be made. In addition, if the aggregate plan calls for building inventory now for the peak season, the committee must decide which products to use for building this production-smoothing inventory, and these quantities must be added to the MPS.

The MPS for the 3X3-O1 shelf is shown in Exhibit 24 along with the MRP record for the final assembly of this product. The MPS was adjusted in the third and fourth periods—evidently the planning committee has decided that 20 units of the 3X3-O1 shelf should be built to meet the aggregate planning targets. The planned order releases basically mirror the gross requirement, except that the 10 units in inventory are netted out of the first week's requirement.

Notice that the final assembly of the 3X3-O1 shelf requires no lead time offset for building the required product. The final assembly area is set up to respond very quickly to demand so that product can be built to order when necessary, as long as the MRP system has ensured that all of the required components are ready. This short lead time, and the lack of any lot-sizing requirement, indicates that there is very little setup required to get ready to make this product. In fact, changeovers in this area are limited to the type of wood being used, and this has little effect on setups.

The MRP system then uses the planned order releases from the final assembly to explode the BOM, net out the current inventories, and offset the lead times. The cabinets are built in a second department and the shelves, backs, sides, and ends are fabricated in a third. The resulting MRP records are shown in Exhibit 25.

Since there are currently 120 cabinets in inventory and only 70 units are needed to build the 3X3-O1 in the first period, no planned receipts for cabinets are needed in period 1. Likewise, since there will still be 50 units of inventory left for period 2 and since 40 more units are scheduled to arrive in period 2 (some order for these has already been placed and the order is currently being processed), there are no planned receipts needed in period 2. Finally, in period 3, there is a need to have 60 units available ($70 + 70 + 80 - 120 - 40$) to send to final assembly for the production of the 3X3-O1. These 60 show up as planned receipts in period 3 and, with the two-week lead time, must be started in period 1 (thus they show up there as a planned order release).

The requirements for brackets are obtained by multiplying the final assembly planned releases by four because there are four brackets per final unit. While there is no inventory of brackets currently in stock, an order has been placed for these brackets sometime in the past and 600 are scheduled to arrive this coming period. The first net requirement for brackets occurs in period 3, as there is a need for 280 units. To cover this, there must be a planned order receipt. The order size is two periods' worth, so the order is placed for the net requirements of periods 3 and 4, for a total of 640 units ($280 + 360$).

EXHIBIT 25
MRP Tables for 3X3-O1 Shelf

		Past Due	Period 1	2	3	4	5	6	7	8
3X3-01	MPS order releases		70	70	80	90	60	**80**		
• Cabinet	Gross requirement		70	70	80	90	60	**80**		
	Scheduled receipts			40						
LT= 2	On-hand inventory	120	50	20	0					
SS= 0	Net requirement				60	90	60	**80**		
Lot= LFL	Planned order receipts				60	90	60	**80**		
	Planned order releases		60	90	60	**80**				
• Shelf	Gross requirement		70	70	80	90	60	**80**		
	Scheduled Receipts									
LT= 1	On-hand inventory	70	0							
SS= 0	Net requirement			70	80	90	60	**80**		
Lot= LFL	Planned order receipts			70	80	90	60	**80**		
Level 1	Planned order releases		70	80	90	60	**80**			
• Bracket	Gross requirement		280	280	320	360	240	**320**		
	Scheduled receipts		600							
LT= 1	On-hand inventory	0	320	40	360		320			
SS= 0	Net requirement				280		240	**320**		
Lot= 2 periods	Planned order receipts				640		**560**			
	Planned order releases			640		**560**				
•• Back	Gross requirement		60	90	60	**80**				
	Scheduled receipts									
LT= 1	On-hand inventory	100	40	0						
SS= 0	Net requirement			50	60	**80**				
Lot= LFL	Planned order receipts			50	60	**80**				
	Planned order releases		50	60	**80**					
•• Side	Gross requirement		120	180	120	**160**				
	Scheduled receipts									
LT= 1	On-hand inventory	200	80	0						
SS= 0	Net requirement			100	120	**160**				
Lot= LFL	Planned order receipts			100	120	**160**				
	Planned order releases		100	120	**160**					
•• End	Gross requirement		120	180	120	**160**				
	Scheduled receipts									
LT= 1	On-hand inventory	200	80	0						
SS= 0	Net requirement			100	120	**160**				
Lot= LFL	Planned order receipts			100	120	**160**				
	Planned order releases		100	120	**160**					
••• Oak Sheet	Gross requirement		42	51	**66**	6	**8**			
	Scheduled receipts			50						
LT= 2	On-hand inventory	144	102	101	35	229	221			
SS= 30	Net requirement					1				
Lot=200	Planned order receipts					**200**				
	Planned order releases			**200**						

The requirements for oak sheets deserve some discussion as they are slightly more complicated to illustrate because of the fractional usage and the number of parent items requiring the sheets. The period 1 gross requirement is found by multiplying the shelf requirement by $\frac{3}{32}$, the back requirement by $\frac{9}{32}$, the side requirement by $\frac{4}{32}$, and the end requirement by $\frac{3}{32}$ to get 42 units ($70 \times \frac{3}{32} + 50 \times \frac{9}{32} + 100 \times \frac{4}{32} + 100 \times \frac{3}{32} = 42$). These fractions are those found for each part in the BOM.

To add further understanding to what the MRP computations do for a company and how these transactions flow through the various product and component levels, we will look in more detail at the MPS quantity of 80 units in period 6. The bold figures in both the DRP and MRP records (Exhibits 23 and 25) are the units being discussed.

Where did the quantity come from? The 80 units can be traced to the 80 units of gross requirement of the CDC and then to the 40 units forecast for the Eaton CDC in period 6 and the 20 units of planned order releases in period 7 for the Atlanta and Monterrey RDCs. The Atlanta and Monterrey releases correspond to the period 7 forecasts in those two RDCs for 10 and 13 units respectively, but since these warehouses use 20-unit lot sizes, more than the 10 and 13 units are ordered.

How are the materials brought together for these 80 units? The 80-units gross requirement in period 6 of the MPS gets translated into units of order releases in period 6 because of the zero lead time. These, in turn, are translated into gross requirement for 80 cabinets, 80 shelves, and 320 brackets, all in period 6. Following the bold numbers in the tables, note how the requirement for these 80 units require shelves to be made in one period (period 5), while the backs, sides, and ends for these units are made in another (period 3). Thus, capacity in the fabrication area is affected in two different time periods by the same order. Note also that this MPS order of 80 units requires raw material sheeting to arrive at two separate times. While one might be tempted to order all of the sheeting for a given order at the same time when not using an MRP system, this shows how an MRP system is designed to keep inventories low.

One further explanation is needed. Notice that as one progresses down the records, the number of periods of information gets smaller and smaller. This is due to the lead time offsetting as one goes deeper and deeper in the product structure. In addition, the gross requirement for sheeting in periods 4 and 5 look peculiarly low as one looks at an MPS that seems to be somewhat constant. If the six and eight units of periods 4 and 5 are **pegged** to the components that require them, then it can be seen that they come from shelving requirements of 60 and 80 units in periods 5 and 6 ($60 \times \frac{3}{32} = 5.6$, which rounds to 6, and $80 \times \frac{3}{32} = 7.5$, which rounds to 8). But notice that there are no backs, sides, and ends used to compute the sheeting requirements. There isn't sufficient information in the forecasts to find these requirements.

Checking Capacity Requirements

There are three primary departments involved in the production of the 3X3-O1 shelves: final assembly, cabinet assembly, and component fabrication. Tables showing the projected capacity needs for the above plan are presented in Exhibit 26. These capacity projections show excess capacity in the final assembly area. The tables show a capacity shortage in the cabinet assembly area in period 2, but if some of the period-2 production can be moved into period 1,

EXHIBIT 26
Departmental Capacity Requirements

Capacity Requirements

Department	Part	Unit Time	Quantity	Period 1	2	3	4	5	6
Final assembly	3X3-01		Units	70	70	80	90	60	80
		0.42	Hours	29	29	34	38	25	33
	Total hours required			29	29	34	38	25	33
	Capacity available hours			40	40	40	40	40	40
Cabinet assembly	Cabinet		Units	60	90	60	80		
		1.2	Hours	72	108	72	96		
	Total hours required			72	108	72	96		
	Capacity available hours			100	100	100	100	100	100
Component fabrication	Shelf		Units	70	80	90	60	80	
		0.22	Hours	18	20	23	15	20	
	Side		Units	100	120	160			
		0.25	Hours	25	30	40			
	End		Units	100	120	160			
		0.25	Hours	25	30	40			
	Back		Units	50	60	80			
		0.6	Hours	30	36	48			
	Total hours required			98	116	151			
	Capacity available hours			120	120	120			

EXHIBIT 27
Restated MRP Record for Bracket—Supplier Problem

• Bracket	Gross requirement		280	280	320	360	240	**320**
	Scheduled receipts		300	300				
LT= 1	On-hand inventory	0	20	40	360	0	320	
SS= 0	Net requirement				280		240	**320**
Lot= 2 periods	Planned order receipts				640		**560**	
	Planned order releases			640		**560**		

assuming that the components can be made available, then this shouldn't be a problem. Since cabinet assembly has a two-week time period to complete its orders before shipping to final assembly, and the numbers presented in the table are releases of orders into the department in any given week, two-week averages should lead to sufficient capacity in this area.

The component fabrication area has enough capacity over the first two weeks but not enough by a larger margin in period 3. If raw material can be brought in early, moving some of period-3 fabrication into the first two periods would help but would not completely alleviate the problem. This might be a starting point but it looks like the plant needs to plan for more capacity, perhaps some overtime, in period 3. If something is not done now, though, there could be a serious problem in period 3.

Moving Forward in Time—Using Requirements Planning for Decisions

Suppose during week 1 of the plan just presented managers at EFC are told by the supplier of the bracket that the order for 600 units will not arrive as planned. Instead, 300 will arrive this week and 300 will arrive next week, instead of all 600 arriving at the same time. EFC managers must decide if this will affect production, and if so, to what extent. By looking at the restated record in Exhibit 27 above, it can be seen that splitting the scheduled receipt into two receipts for 300 each has no effect on the plan as only 280 units of the 600 were needed in the first period. This record indicates that no changes need to be made.

Suppose now that time has advanced so that EFS management is meeting at the end of period 1 making plans for period 2 and beyond. The following has occurred since last week's meeting.

Actual demand: Atlanta demand is 13 in period 1, instead of 9 as earlier forecast.

Bracket supply: 300 arrive in period 1; 300 more to arrive in period 2.

Quality problem: Of the 200 sides in inventory at the beginning of the week, 50 had to be scrapped due to an incorrect dimensional issue.

First, the DRP records are updated. Atlanta had 12 units of inventory and another 20 on the way from a schedule receipt to be delivered in period 1, for a total available of 32 units in period 1. Demand during period 1 was 13, so this means inventory should be 19 units at the end of the period 1. This is the inventory shown in the updated set of DRP records in Exhibit 28. The DRP records for the other demand sites should reflect the plan. For instance, for Dallas, there was a planned order release in period 1 for 10 units, which now shows as a scheduled receipt in period 2. Projected end-of-period inventory for period 1 was 15, and this is reflected in the updated tables as the current inventory on hand. Demand forecasts for all of the locations move left one column to reflect the advance of time by one period.

The new MPS is shown in Exhibit 29 and the updated MRP tables in Exhibit 30, where the period 6 figures represent new forecasts of demand and an adjustment for more aggregate planning inventory. The updated MRP tables are shown below in Exhibit 30, where the period 6 figures represent new forecasts of demand and an adjustment for more aggregate

EXHIBIT 28
Updated DRP Tables for 3X3-O1 Shelf

		Past Due	Period 2	3	4	5	6	7	8	9
Atlanta	Forecast requirement		10	11	11	10	10	10	12	
	In transit									
LT= 1	On-hand inventory	19	29	18	27	17	27	17	25	
SS= 10	Net requirement		1		3		3		5	
Lot=20	Planned order receipts		20		20		20		20	
	Planned order releases	20		20		20		20		
Dallas	Forecast requirement		10	8	8	8	8	8	8	
	In transit		10							
LT= 1	On-hand inventory	15	15	17	19	11	13	15	17	
SS= 10	Net requirement			3	1		7	5	3	
Lot= 10	Planned order receipts			10	10		10	10	10	
	Planned order releases		10	10		10	10	10		
Kobe	Forecast requirement	11	12	25	12	12	12	12	12	12
	In transit		40							
LT= 3	On-hand inventory	44	72	47	75	63	51	79	67	55
SS= 40	Net requirement				5			1		
Lot=40	Planned order receipts				40			40		
	Planned order releases				40					
Monterrey	Forecast requirement		13	15	12	15	13	13	14	
	In transit									
LT= 1	On-hand inventory	25	12	17	25	10	17	24	10	
SS= 10	Net requirement			13	5		13	6		
Lot=20	Planned order receipts			20	20		20	20		
	Planned order releases		20	20		20	20			
Eaton	Forecast requirement		20	40	20	30	30	30		
Eaton CDC	Gross requirement		70	70	80	60	80	60		
	In transit									
LT= 0	On-hand inventory	0	0							
SS= 0	Net requirement		70	70	80	60	80	60		
Lot= 10	Planned order receipts		70	70	80	60	80	60		
	Planned order releases		70	70	80	60	80	60		

EXHIBIT 29
Updated Master Schedule for 3X3-O1 Shelf

MPS and Final Assembly: 3X3-01 Shelf

		Past Due	Period 1	2	3	4	5	6	7	8
	From DRP system		70	70	80	60	80	60		
	Adjustments for AP		0	10	10	0	0	20		
3X3-01	Gross requirement		70	80	90	60	80	80		
	Scheduled receipts									
LT= 0	On-hand inventory	0								
SS= 0	Net requirement		70	80	90	60	80	80		
Lot= LFL	Planned order receipts		70	80	90	60	80	80		
	Planned order releases		70	80	90	60	80	80		

EXHIBIT 30
Updated MRP Records for 3X3-O1 Shelf

		Past Due	Period 1	2	3	4	5	6	7	8
3X3-01	MPS Order Releases		70	80	90	60	80	80		
• Cabinet	Gross requirement		70	80	90	60	80	80		
	Scheduled receipts		40	60						
LT= 2	On-hand inventory	50	20	0						
SS= 0	Net requirement				90	60	80	80		
Lot= LFL	Planned order receipts				90	60	80	80		
	Planned order releases		90	60	80	80				
• Shelf	Gross requirement		70	80	90	60	80	80		
	Scheduled receipts		70							
LT= 1	On-hand inventory	0								
SS= 0	Net requirement			80	90	60	80	80		
Lot= LFL	Planned order receipts			80	90	60	80	80		
Level 1	Planned order releases		80	90	60	80	80			
• Bracket	Gross requirement		280	320	360	240	320	320		
	Scheduled receipts		300							
LT= 1	On-hand inventory	20	40	360		320				
SS= 0	Net requirement			280	360	240	320	320		
Lot= 2 periods	Planned order receipts			640		560		320		
	Planned order releases		640		560		320			
•• Back	Gross requirement		90	60	80	80				
	Scheduled receipts		50							
LT= 1	On-hand inventory	40	0							
SS= 0	Net requirement			60	80	80				
Lot= LFL	Planned order receipts			60	80	80				
	Planned order releases		60	80	80					
•• Side	Gross requirement		180	120	160	160				
	Scheduled receipts		100							
LT= 1	On-hand inventory	30	0							
SS= 0	Net requirement		50	120	160	160				
Lot= LFL	Planned order receipts		50	120	160	160				
	Planned order releases	50	120	160	160					
•• End	Gross requirement		180	120	160	160				
	Scheduled Receipts		100							
LT= 1	On-hand inventory	80	0							
SS= 0	Net requirement			120	160	160				
Lot= LFL	Planned order receipts			120	160	160				
	Planned order releases		120	160	160					
••• Oak sheet	Gross requirement	6	51	66	63	8	8			
	Scheduled receipts		50							
LT= 2	On-hand inventory	96	95	29	166	158	150			
SS= 30	Net requirement				64					
Lot=200	Planned order receipts				200					
	Planned order releases		200							

Module Summary

Requirements planning systems are useful in situations where demand for one item is dependent on the demand for some other item, or in the case of distribution systems, where the demand for an item at one level of the supply chain is dependent on the demand of the item at some other level. These systems help plan inventory levels based on the demand of the product from the customer. While a customer could be any firm along the supply chain, the closer this customer is to being the end consumer, the better the information for inventory control and production planning.

Materials requirements planning (MRP) systems are used primarily to plan and control inventory in the production facilities of companies assembling products that are made in substantial volumes. Distribution requirements planning (DRP) systems are used in wholesale and retail firms, or in the distribution arms of manufacturing firms, to maintain control of inventories at the various locations and levels of the supply chain. Production, warehousing, and shipping capacities can all be managed more effectively with the use of capacity requirements planning (CRP) tools that use the information from the MRP and DRP systems.

Most requirements planning initiatives require the manipulation of large databases of information that would be next to impossible to do without computers and the necessary software. With the advances in computing power, these software solutions are now available to a wide variety of small firms in both the manufacturing and service sectors. The Internet even makes it possible to use one of these systems without worrying about maintaining hardware, software, and internal experts.

Key Terms

bill of materials (BOM), *4*
bill of materials explosion, *5*
capacity requirements planning (CRP), *17*
dependent demand, *3*
distribution requirements planning (DRP), *3*
end item, *3*
enterprise resource planning (ERP), *3*
indented bill of materials, *5*
independent demand, *3*
inventory records file, *4*
lead time, *6*
load profile graph, *18*
lot size, *10*
low-level coding, *8*
master production schedule (MPS), *4*
materials requirements planning (MRP), *3*
MRP reaction time, *14*
pegging, *23*
product structure diagram, *5*
system nervousness, *14*
time bucket, *7*
time fence, *14*

Discussion Questions

1. How would you, in just a few nontechnical sentences, explain the basic ideas behind MRP systems and DRP systems?
2. One complaint of lot sizing in MRP systems is that it leads to large lumps of demand for assemblies and component parts. Explain.
3. How do lot-sizing rules in MRP and DRP systems contribute to a "shortage of capacity" in a particular planning period?
4. How can an MRP system that is designed to keep inventories low actually cause an increase in inventories?
5. Explain the impact (costs and benefits) of time fences/frozen schedule (freezing part of the master schedule) in terms of the master schedule and MRP.
6. Explain how the output from an MRP system could be used to check short-term capacity requirements.
7. Describe the type of companies that could greatly benefit from implementing an MRP system and explain why?

Problems

1. Door Package SZ-30 is comprised of a Z-30 door assembly and six screws so that the customer can attach the door to the doorframe. The Z-30 door assembly is comprised of (1) a 30-inch door slab, (2) two hinges and six screws to attach these hinges to the door slab, and (3) a handle assembly and two screws to attach it to the slab.

   The packaging department has no SZ-30 packages in stock. The door assembly department has 40 door assemblies in inventory and 20 more almost finished from a previous work order. The current inventory of raw materials is 800 screws, 40 hinges, 25 handle assemblies, and 15 slabs. Forty more hinges are due to be received in week 1. The lead time for an SZ-30 door package is very small and assumed to be 0. The lead time for the Z-30 door assembly is one day and for the other parts, the lead time is two days.

a. Draw a diagram or make an indented BOM to represent the product structure.
b. The next four weeks of production requirements for the SZ-30 are 60, 50, 60, and 50. When should the next order be placed for screws and what should the quantity be (at a minimum)? Feel free to use the tables below or any method you desire—BUT show your work. [*Hint:* Be careful that you don't do a lot more work than you need to.]
c. The MRP inventory of screws always seems to be inaccurate and thus requires constant attention in updating the inventory files (which is $$). What would you suggest this company do about maintaining adequate inventories of this low-cost item?

		Period			
Item		**1**	**2**	**3**	**4**
SZ-30 package	Gross requirement	60	50	60	50
	Scheduled receipts				
	On-hand Inventory				
	Planned order receipts				
	Planned order releases				
Z-30 assembly	Gross requirement				
	Scheduled receipts				
	On-hand Inventory				
	Planned order receipts				
	Planned order releases				
Slab	Gross requirement				
	Scheduled receipts				
	On-hand Inventory				
	Planned order receipts				
	Planned order releases				
Handle	Gross requirement				
	Scheduled receipts				
	On-hand Inventory				
	Planned order receipts				
	Planned order releases				
Hinges	Gross requirement				
	Scheduled receipts				
	On-hand Inventory				
	Planned order receipts				
	Planned order releases				
Screws	Gross requirement				
	Scheduled receipts				
	On-hand Inventory				
	Planned order receipts				
	Planned order releases				

2. The X4050 assembly required in a new computer being produced by the American Computer Company requires two A-boards and four B-boards. Each A-board requires two X92 processors and two Z85 memory chips and each B-board requires one X90 processor and two Z85 memory chips. The lead times for all items are one week. In addition, the table and information below are part of the MRP scheduling and inventory control system for this assembly. When should orders be released (or planned to be released) for the Z85 and X90?

Part	On Hand	Scheduled Receipts
X4050	120	80 in week 1
A-Board	0	140 in week 1
B-Board	0	360 in week 1
X92	200	0
Z85	200	0
X90	100	150 in week 1

Item			1	2	3	4
X4050 assembly	Gross requirement		100	100	90	100
	Scheduled receipts		80			
	On-hand inventory		100		90	100
	Planned order receipts	120			90	100
	Planned order releases			90	100	
A-Board	Gross requirement			180	200	
	Scheduled receipts		140			
	On-hand inventory		140			
	Planned order receipts			40	200	
	Planned order releases		40	200		
B-Board	Gross requirement			360		
	Scheduled receipts		360		400	
	On-hand inventory		360			
	Planned order receipts				400	
	Planned order releases			400		
X92	Gross requirement		80	400		
	Scheduled receipts					
	On-hand inventory		120			
	Planned order receipts	200		280		
	Planned order releases		280			
Z85	Gross requirement					
	Scheduled receipts					
	On-hand inventory					
	Planned order receipts					
	Planned order releases					
X90	Gross requirements					
	Scheduled receipts					
	On-hand inventory					
	Planned order receipt					
	Planned order release					

3. Yovirio has a distribution system made up of a central distribution center (CDC) and three regional distribution centers (RDC). It uses a DRP system to ensure inventory remains as low as possible while still meeting demand. Each RDC serves several retailers in its area and all RDCs get their material from the CDC. The lead times to get material from the CDC for each of these RDCs are given in a table below. The CDC, in addition to supplying the RDCs, also serves a few retailers.

All of the RDCs and the CDC use a lot-for-lot lot-sizing rule to decide how much to order when an order is required. It takes orders two weeks to move from the CDC to RDC 1, one week to move from the CDC to RDCs 2 and 3, and one week to move from the factory to the CDC. What orders should be placed on the factory for the next five weeks?

	Lead Time	On-Hand Inventory	Lot-Size Rule
RDC 1	2	950	Lot-for-lot
RDC 2	1	270	Lot-for-lot
RDC 3	1	200	Lot-for-lot
CDC	1	10	Lot-for-lot

	8	9	10	11	12	13	14	15	16	17
RDC 1 demand	230	450	400	360	290	410	440	370	390	370
RDC 2 demand	130	100	110	150	100	90	140	160	130	100
RDC 3 demand	190	250	230	270	200	270	260	240	180	240
CDC retail demand	40	80	60	40	50	40	70	70	60	50

Note: An order for 60 units was shipped from the factory in period 7 and is to arrive at the CDC in period 8. These 60 units are not accounted for in any of the inventories above.

Related Modules of Interest

- Aggregate Capacity Planning
- Inventory Management
- Independent Demand Inventory Management Systems
- Lean/Just-in-Time Systems
- Supply Chain Structure and Strategy
- Purchasing and Supplier Management

Selected Readings

Miller, J. G., and L. G. Sprague. "Behind the Growth in Material Requirements Planning." *Harvard Business Review,* September–October 1975, pp. 83–91.

Orlicky, J. *Material Requirements Planning.* New York: McGraw-Hill, 1975.

Vollmann, T. E.; W. L. Berry; and D. C. Whybark. *Manufacturing Planning and Control Systems.* 4th ed. New York: McGraw-Hill/Irwin, 1997.

Wight, O. *MRPII: Making It Happen.* 2nd ed. Essex Junction, VT: Oliver Wight, 1990.

Project Management

Karen A. Brown
University of Washington, Bothell

McGraw-Hill Irwin

Boston Burr Ridge, IL Dubuque, IA Madison, WI New York San Francisco St. Louis
Bangkok Bogotá Caracas Kuala Lumpur Lisbon London Madrid Mexico City
Milan Montreal New Delhi Santiago Seoul Singapore Sydney Taipei Toronto

Project Management

Module Objectives

By the end of this module, you should be able to

- Differentiate projects from routine operations and describe the role of projects in organizations.
- Understand the ways in which projects can deliver value in the form of timeliness, cost, scope, and quality.
- Identify the elements of a comprehensive project plan.
- Recognize the risks associated with projects in their various stages.
- Develop a work breakdown structure (WBS).
- Create a project schedule with a network planning model and identify the critical path and slack (float).

Managing Routine and Project Operations at Boston Scientific

Boston Scientific's Northwest Technology Center (NWTC) in Redmond, Washington, was recognized as a leader in implementing many of the tools and concepts described in this module series: JIT, cellular manufacturing, systematic use of metrics, skill-based pay, kaizen, and quality control, to name a few examples. Although routine operations were central to its success, the facility also managed numerous research and development projects to create a continuing stream of advanced products for customers. This required careful coordination with routine activities on the shop floor, especially during production ramp up for new products.

This symbiotic balance of routine operations and project operations was seriously interrupted in July 2000 when corporate officials in Boston announced a decision to close the Seattle-area facility as part of a supply-chain consolidation effort. The energies of all team members were suddenly refocused toward the implementation of a well-constructed plant closure plan. Public announcements, phase-out schedules, and transfer of product lines to Cork, Ireland, and Miami were carefully scheduled and communicated on a special website. Employees were offered attractive financial incentives to stay with NWTC until pre-arranged separations dates. Top management used Microsoft Project software to coordinate parallel and sequential activities. Although there were a few unexpected challenges, the project appears to have been a success. Employees were committed to staying at NWTC until the phase-out was complete, product quality was sustained, and handoffs to other facilities came off relatively smoothly. Keys to the success of this project appear to have been clear objectives, regular and honest communication with all stakeholders, a well-planned schedule, and the creation of incentives that aligned employee interests with project goals.

In Practice

PROJECT FAILURES

Worldwide, many projects are focused on information technology (IT)—development of new IT products, installation of new IT systems, implementation of e-commerce solutions, and so forth. Research published by the Standish Group (www.standishgroup.com) indicates that in 1995 the average cost for an IT development project in a large U.S. company was $2,322,000. In medium and small companies, the figures were $1,331,00 and $434,000, respectively. The results of their study indicate that 31.1 percent of these projects were cancelled before completion, but after considerable funds already had been expended. The majority of completed IT projects exceeded their budgets by nearly 200 percent. At the time of the study, the Standish Group estimated that only 16 percent of IT projects were completed on time and within budget. These results indicate a need for better project management—from project selection, to definition of customer requirements, to planning and control systems.

Projects and Project Management Defined

A **project** is a one-time or infrequently occurring set of activities that uses resources to transform inputs into specified outputs that are valuable to its customers. A project's customers may reside either inside (e.g., the users of a new computer system installation) or outside the organization (e.g., the users of a new product). A project is constrained by a designated end date and limited resources. Most projects involve coordination across multiple functions in an organization, and many projects rely on resources, such as subcontractors, outside of the organization.

Projects may be of any duration (from a few hours to several years) and the scope in size and expenditure can vary widely. Note that an endeavor does not have to be big to qualify as a project. Examples of projects include development of a new product, a marketing campaign, a merger or acquisition, construction of a new warehouse, installation of a new computer system, improvement of a manufacturing process, development of a corporate emergency plan, organization of a temporary plant shut down for maintenance, a new business start up, and special events—from a company picnic to the Olympic Games. The Boston Scientific story illustrates two examples of project types—new product development and a plant closure—and distinguishes them from the routine manufacturing operations that repeatedly deliver customer value on a day-to-day basis. In contrast, projects create value for customers by doing something unique, such as creating something new, solving a problem, or repairing something. Oftentimes, projects are executed in concert with routine operations. For example, continuous improvement (kaizen) project activities make possible an evolution toward world-class status for production operations.

Projects do not carry with them the same degree of certainty or repeatability that routine operations (a.k.a., "processes") do. In a project, the manager and team must anticipate as many potential problems as possible, finding ways to solve, avoid, or mitigate them before they happen. Although many operations management concepts may be applied in project environments, the unique nature of a project necessitates the use of special tools for planning, coordinating, and controlling the value delivery process.

Value Delivery in Project Management

The value concepts that serve as the basis for this module series are magnified in many project environments. Organizations initiate projects to meet very specific customer needs. Because of the intensity and limited duration associated with projects, team members may need to be more attuned to customer requirements in project situations than they are in routine operations. The customer for each project will have slightly different expectations, and it will be the project manager's role to determine what these expectations are, communicate them to team members, and create mechanisms to ensure that they do not take a back seat as the project evolves. (See Exhibit 1.)

Value to a particular customer may fall into three general categories: time, cost, and performance, where performance is a function of the scope and quality of project outcomes.

EXHIBIT 1
Value Delivery—The Cattle Drive

"Say . . . Wait just a dang minute, here . . . We forgot the cattle."

During the life of a project, the project manager and team members must keep in mind the customer value specifications that drive the project. In this case, we see a humorous depiction of a project team that has become so wrapped up in its process that it has forgotten the central purpose of the project—to deliver cattle to the customer.

Some customers want to receive project outcomes quickly and are willing to compromise on cost in exchange for speed. For example, if a contractor is required to rapidly complete a roof repair before an impending storm arrives, it may require extra resources and extra cost to complete the necessary work at a specified quality level. Sometimes customers care more about the project being completed on time, and they are willing to accept higher cost or reduced function. Such was the case in the time-sensitive efforts to find survivors after the tragic destruction of the World Trade Center towers in New York in 2001. Other customers may have very serious needs for high-performance project outcomes, and therefore may be willing to wait a little longer or to accept a smaller number of project deliverables. For example, in a complex information technology installation where performance quality is essential to the system's operation, the project manager and the customer may need to accept that these constraints will lead to a somewhat longer schedule or limitations in scope.

The three value categories (time, cost, performance) and the trade-offs among them are known as the **triple constraint** in project management (see Exhibit 2). Although all three of these criteria may be important, most project management experts would agree that it is unrealistic for a project team to attempt to excel in all three value categories. Some world-class organizations have found ways to simultaneously optimize all three of these criteria in their routine operations, but this sort of synergy requires the kind of repetition that projects simply don't offer. Therefore, it is important for the project manager to firmly establish early in the planning process the dimensions of value most critical to the customer. In

EXHIBIT 2
The Project Management Triple Constraint

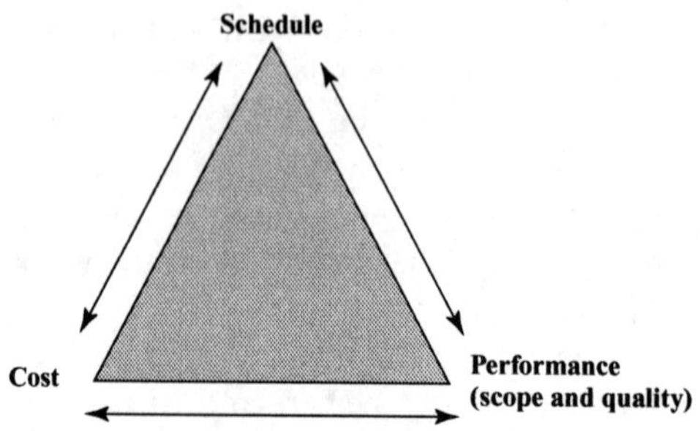

In Practice

BALANCING VISION AND ANALYSIS: THE 1990 EVEREST EARTH DAY CLIMB

In April of 1990 an international team of 20 climbers from China, Russia, and the United States reached the summit of Mount Everest in what has been lauded as the most successful climbing expedition in world history (*Guinness Book of World Records*, 1999). Many factors (including good fortune and good weather) contributed to the success of the project. The leadership structure was particularly noteworthy, however. Jim Whitaker, who in 1963 became the first American to reach the summit of Everest, served as the primary project leader. Whitaker was held in high regard by members of the international climbing community and his visionary leadership provided the glue that held the diverse team together. Warren Thompson, a corporate tax attorney by trade, was deputy leader of the team—his role was to plan and monitor the schedule and handle the logistics of the expedition. Between the two of them, they represented the combined roles so necessary for successful project execution. This is an example of a situation in which the visionary and analytical roles were effectively distributed across two individuals, but in most projects the project manager must embody both of these.

addition, the manager must remain sensitive and responsive to ways that the customer's perceptions of value might change as the project progresses. By doing so, the project manager increases the chances that overall value—the right combination of time, performance, and cost from the customer's perspective—will be maximized.

What Does It Take to Be a Project Manager?

Project management requires a somewhat different skill set and orientation than those generally needed for managing day-to-day operations. The project manager must play a leadership role—conveying a project vision, sustaining team member motivation, communicating objectives, persuading stakeholders of the project's importance, and seeing "big picture" links with broader organizational objectives. Additionally, he or she must pay attention to managerial details such as schedule monitoring, making sure materials and resources arrive when they are needed, and ensuring that quality standards are met. The first set of roles is more creative or right brain in nature, and the second set of roles is more analytical or left brain in nature. The effective project manager balances both of these roles; if this is not possible, he or she should know when to enlist the help of others who possess complementary skills.

Traits and Functions of Project Managers

What does it take to be an effective project manager? You might expect there is a personality style best suited to project management, but research suggests that certain attributes, which anyone may develop through training, experience, and discipline, characterize the best project managers:[1]

1. *Systems thinker:* Able to take a holistic view of the entire project.
2. *Personal integrity:* Displays by words and deeds the credibility to sustain the trust and confidence of others.
3. *Proactive:* Savvy enough to foresee problems and take action before it is necessary.
4. *High tolerance for stress:* Able to cope with schedule deadlines, technical uncertainties, and competing stakeholder agendas.
5. *General business perspective:* Understands the role of the project in meeting higher-level business objectives, and sufficiently familiar with all of the functions involved in project delivery.
6. *Good communicator:* Capable of listening to, and hearing, the voices of all project stakeholders, and skilled in conveying clear, concise, persuasive written and oral communication.

[1] List adapted from Clifford F. Gray and Erik W. Larson, *Project Management* (New York: McGraw-Hill/Irwin, 1999).
[2] CH2MHILL, *Project Delivery* (Denver, Co. CH2MHILL, 1996).

7. *Effective time management:* Uses time effectively, according to project priorities.
8. *Skillful politician:* Able to sell project ideas to a wide variety of people and skilled at resolving cross-disciplinary conflicts that may potentially hinder project progress.
9. *Optimist:* Displays a "can-do" attitude consistently through the ups and downs of a project.

The combined set of these traits is useful because project managers frequently play multiple roles that they must juggle and manage with great care. CH2MHILL, an international engineering consulting firm, classifies these roles as follows:[2]

- *Focusing on the client:* Understanding the customer's needs and expectations, gaining client endorsement, and maintaining regular communication with the client.
- *Creating the project vision:* Conveying to stakeholders an image or understanding of what the project will accomplish and what will be different when it is completed.
- *Building and maintaining the project team:* Selecting the right team members and helping them to become, collectively, an effective working unit.
- *Planning the project:* Through stakeholder involvement, developing a comprehensive plan that ensures the achievement of project objectives.
- *Managing resources:* Developing a plan for resource (people, money, materials, technology, equipment) deployment during the life of the project, maintaining knowledge about progress and resource utilization, and altering plans to meet contingencies as they arise.
- *Ensuring quality:* Establishing quality criteria based on customer needs, developing a plan that provides for maximum likelihood of quality, and monitoring quality during the life of the project.

Our focus here will be on project planning and managing resources. The Selected Readings listed at the end of this module offer resources that provide more comprehensive coverage of the other functions of project managers.

Project Success Factors

Anyone reading this module has probably lived through an unsuccessful project. Less-than-perfect projects, especially if they are not of great consequence to a person's career, can provide valuable learning experiences if participants are savvy enough to capture lessons learned. A project may be characterized as successful if it is completed on or before its due date, if its expenditures stay within budget, if it meets the expectations of the client, if it does not cause unexpected damage to the environment or society, and if team members and other stakeholders are satisfied at its conclusion. It is difficult to achieve all of these criteria, and even the most successful projects have their flaws. For example, the 2000 Olympic Games in Sydney were generally considered a big success, but television viewership in the northern hemisphere did not give advertisers the product exposure they had hoped to achieve through their sponsorship. Moreover, multiple incidents of positive drug tests for Olympic athletes caused some damage to the public image of the Olympic Games. Overall, though, most people would agree that the games were a success.

Think about a successful project in which you have been involved. It may be work-related, community service, family, or a school project. What factors contributed to the success of the project. Are these universal?

When experienced project managers are asked to identify factors that characterize successful projects in which they have been involved, the lists they generate are often nearly identical. A typical list would include

- "The project had top management support."
- "Everyone involved understood the project's mission."
- "The right people were assigned to the team."
- "Team members were involved in creating the plan."
- "Team members' roles were clear."

These are just a few examples from much longer lists that have been generated during these kinds of discussions. Perhaps your own list would be similar. Research has demonstrated that the two most important features are *top management support* and a *clear mission or purpose.*[3] These and other factors that contribute to project success fall into three categories: systems, structure, and spirit. (See Exhibit 3.)

Project systems include metrics, rewards, communication, planning, and integrating technologies. Structure includes organizational hierarchy, team structure, team location, interfaces among project entities, authority of participants and stakeholders, designation of roles and responsibilities, and facility design. Spirit, the least tangible but possibly the most important of these elements, suggests an enthusiasm for the project that is shared by the sponsor, team members, customers, suppliers, the larger organization, and the project manager. Some projects will be stronger in spirit, others may be stronger in structure. But, in every case, these three elements are intertwined with each other. For example, unclear specification of the project manager's authority to solve problems (a *structure* component) may lead to conflicts and a reduction in team morale (*spirit*). If team members are not co-located (*structure*) they may not be able to develop a good *system* of communication. The symbiosis among these three elements is paramount in project management. As you read the remainder of this module, keep in mind that each project management tool influences one or more of these elements.

EXHIBIT 3
Critical Success Factors in Project Management

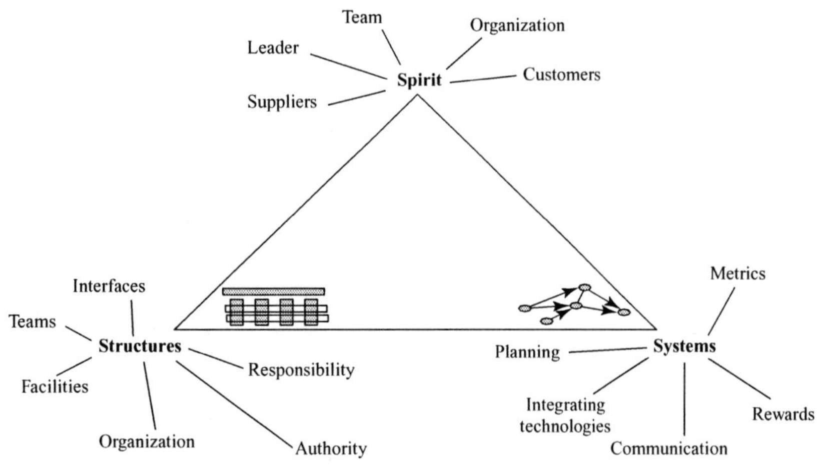

[3] J. Pinto and D. Slevin, "Critical Success Factors across the Project Life Cycle," *Project Management Journal* 19, no. 3 (1988), pp. 67–75.

The Project Management Process

The nature of the project management process will vary from situation to situation and from organization to organization. Small projects will not require the level of sophistication that large ones will. Some organizations specify a set of steps that every project must follow, and others take a more flexible approach. An increasing number of organizations have recognized the need to codify certain procedures and standardize project management terminology.[4] This unifying function may be addressed through a centralized project management office.[5]

Regardless of the extent to which the project management process is formalized, nearly all projects seem to go through the same phases:

- Selection.
- Initiation.
- Planning.
- Delivering and controlling.
- Closing.

Imagine you are planning a high school class reunion. Can you envision the tasks that would be included in each of the phases shown in the list above?

Although these five phases generally occur in the sequence presented, they will overlap to some extent. Exhibit 4 shows the typical level of activity associated with each stage. Although projects are subject to risk throughout their life cycles, the stages that generally present the highest risk are selection, initiation, and closing. First, it is not uncommon for an organization to select the wrong project—one that does not meet its goals. For example, a company might institute an expensive advertising campaign in order to turn around a declining market share trend. However, if the decline were actually caused by poor customer service or low quality products, the money allocated to increase sales through advertising may have been poorly spent.

During the initiation stage, unclear definition of customer expectations may result in a project plan that ultimately does not produce the value the customer wanted. According to

EXHIBIT 4
Project Phases

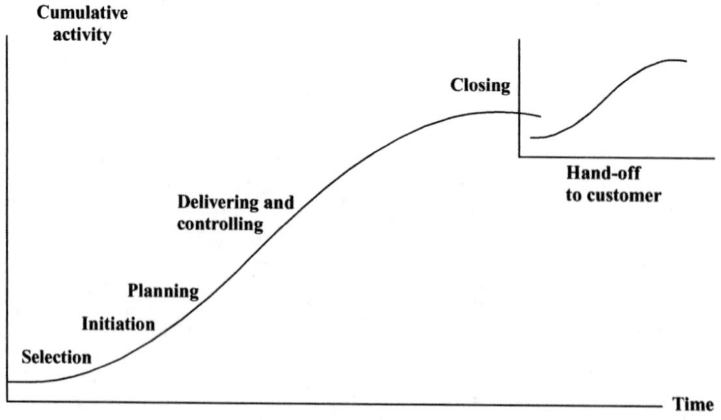

[4] The Project Management Institute has helped to make this possible by developing worldwide standards for procedures and terminology. A good reference on this subject is PMI's *Project Management Body of Knowledge.* Also see H. Kerzner, *Strategic Planning for Project Management: Using a Project Management Maturity Model* (New York: John Wiley & Sons, 2001).

[5] M. Sriram, "Developing a Proposal for a Project Management Office," *PM Network,* August 2000, pp. 44–48.

In Practice

THE STORY OF THE WRONG PROJECT

A project manager in a European auto manufacturing company was assigned the role of building a new spare parts distribution center in London. He was told that it was to be a modern, efficient facility that would deliver parts to the British market. Instead of rolling up his sleeves and beginning work on the project plan, he asked the project sponsor: "Why are we doing this? What problem will this distribution center solve?" He learned that the purpose of the project was to create conditions that allowed a 24-hour turnaround on spare parts ordered. This supported a corporate objective related to rapid customer service. Was the distribution center really the best way to address the purpose?

As it turned out, there was a less expensive and more effective solution that would meet higher-level corporate needs. The project manager investigated the possibility of developing closer relationships with air cargo and ground transportation providers. The result was a system whereby ordered parts were air-shipped daily to London then transferred in a cross-docking fashion directly from the plane to a delivery truck. This cross-docking, combined with a simple ordering system, allowed the company to avoid building the warehouse. Additionally, they actually achieved a faster response time than they would have if the parts had had to stop in a warehouse. The original project definition did not meet corporate objectives to the extent that an alternative plan could. The bottom line: The project manager must always understand the project's purpose and how it fits with corporate objectives.

Source: F. T. Hartman, *Don't Park Your Brain Outside* (Newtown Square, PA: Project Management Institute, 2000).

the Standish Group, unclear definition of requirements and lack of user input are highly predictive of IT project failure. This is a common problem in many new product development efforts, as well.

At the point of project closure, deliverables are handed over to the customer. This can be a time of conflict and unexpected rework, particularly if there was poor communication with the client throughout the project. Additionally, in complex technical projects, the closure period may represent the first time that all system elements are brought together to function as a whole. As systems increase in complexity, the risk of failure at the point of integration will escalate dramatically.[6]

The elements included within the project management process are shown in Exhibit 5. Although a sequential relationship is shown, keep in mind that the process is very iterative. So, for example, financial risks may be assessed as part of the business case analysis, but they may be re-assessed during the development of the work breakdown structure (WBS). The elements displayed in Exhibit 5, page 10, are discussed in more detail below.

Project Selection and Initiation

Organizations and individuals initiate projects for a variety of reasons: solving problems, improving performance, seeking business opportunities, enhancing public image, making contributions to society, responding to external mandates such as new regulations, or resolving crises. Most projects require some analysis prior to their adoption by the organization. Three categories of factors must be considered when an organization makes a decision to initiate a project: (1) the project's fit with overall organizational strategy, (2) the availability of resources to execute the project, and (3) the business justification for investing in the project. A look inside many organizations will reveal a host of projects that were started with good intentions but are lying fallow because the organization was already overwhelmed by a glut of projects, all of which are competing for the same resources. A careful analysis also may reveal that some projects even conflict with the organization's central mission. For example, a project to cut costs may interfere with an organization's central mission of customer service or product safety.

[6] C. Perrow, *Normal Accidents: Living with High Risk Technologies* (New York: Basic Books, 1984).

EXHIBIT 5 Key Elements of Project Planning

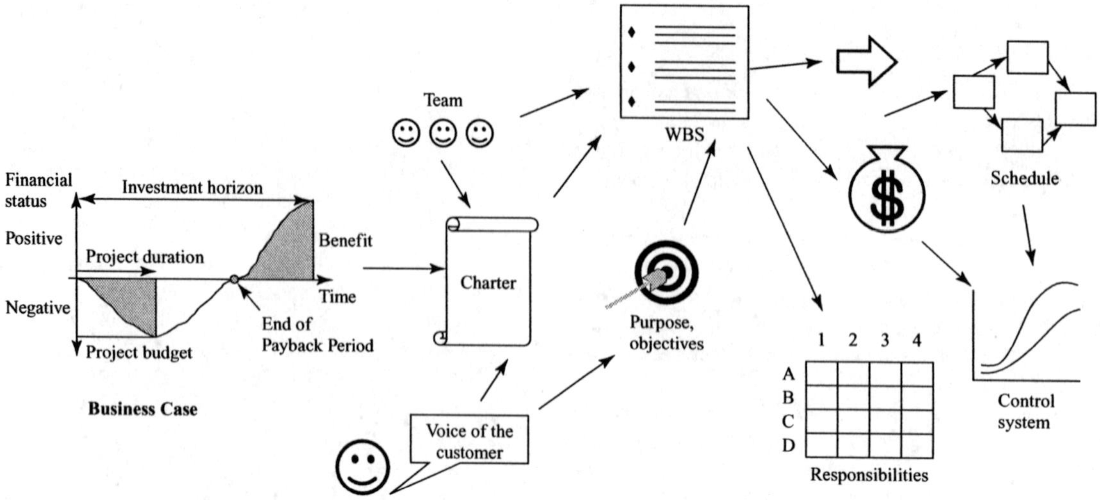

The Business Case

Business justification, or the **business case,** is an important early step in a project's life.[7] Those who champion the project, or those who have been assigned to examine its feasibility, must develop a persuasive document and accompanying presentations if the project is to receive funding and authority to proceed from a corporate sponsor. An effective business case will include a full financial analysis, presentation of assumptions, disclosure of possible risks, highlighting of potential benefits, and information about how its outcomes will support the corporate mission. Outcome projections may be based on a spreadsheet analysis, or they may involve simulation models that explore risks and reveal outcome probabilities. Financial measures used in project selection may include internal rate of return, return on investment, net present value, risk-assessed return, payback period, and so on. Some organizations use specific cutoff points for accepting or rejecting a business case—for example, a 20 percent internal rate of return is a frequently used hurdle.

Financial benefits may not be the only criteria for project selection. For example, an organization may be interested in establishing market share or gaining expertise with a new technology, even though it means that the project at hand may not be a fiscal winner.

Be Realistic/Objective

Presentation of the business case is not unlike the process one would follow to present a new business funding proposal to a venture capitalist. As such, there may be a tendency on the part of the project champion to be as persuasive as possible in order to "win" project approval. One must be cautious, though, about overselling a project that represents high risk to the organization.

The Project Charter

Once funding and corporate commitment have been established, the project is ready to move to the initiation stage. At this point, a project manager (who may have prepared the business case), along with a small planning team, should be assigned to take the project through its early stages. In large organizations, the sponsor may issue a **project charter** that establishes the authority of the project manager to proceed, specifies the project's purpose, identifies key stakeholders, establishes a preliminary budget, highlights major deliverables and specifications, and specifies an end date. Charters for larger projects may include additional detail.

[7] Of course, not all projects will require this degree of formality in the acceptance process. A shop floor improvement effort, a departmental party, or a small community service effort may not require a business case analysis.

In Practice

THE COAT HOOK

Legend has it that during the product definition stage, an aircraft manufacturer assigned a team to interview pilots about their preferences for cockpit design. Among other issues, the pilots specified a need for a coat hook, and the team went to work in earnest to design a coat hook that fit the pilots' requirements. After considerable analysis and design work, one team member asked a simple question: "Why is it that you need the coat hook, anyway?" The pilots then informed the team that the coat hook was necessary because the cockpit got too hot during flights. Finally, after much wasted effort, the team had discovered the latent need driving the request for a coat hook. This led to a discussion of ways in which to improve temperature control and ventilation in the cockpit. The moral of the story is to always ask "why?" in order to discover latent needs.

Although funding and deadlines may be modified as the detailed project plan unfolds, the baseline data provided in the project charter give the project team a general sense of the scope of its task. Unfortunately, many projects are initiated without adequate charters, and they are highly likely to fail. An example of a charter for a customer survey project appears in Exhibit 6.

The Planning Phase

The project charter signals the start of the project and commissions the core team to begin the planning process. Although the charter may have specified objectives, customer requirements, a preliminary budget, and other project attributes, these do not constitute a complete project plan. The next step is to flesh out the details of a comprehensive plan. The most

EXHIBIT 6
Sample Project Charter

Warmest Window Company

Company Mission: To produce high-quality custom vinyl insulated windows in the moderate to upper price categories to meet the needs of small to medium sized window dealers in the western United States and their homeowner customers.

Project Charter
Customer Survey Project

Purpose of Project: To conduct a mailed customer survey to all of Warmest Window Company's dealer customers in the Pacific Northwest to assess their satisfaction and suggestions for improvement in our window quality, window designs, ordering system, delivery system and financing. The results of the survey will guide the strategic planning team in setting priorities for the next fiscal year.

Project Sponsor: Claus Martin, President
Project Manager: Hugh Stevenson, Marketing Vice President
Project Customers: Charlene York, V.P. Operations and Logistics; Mac Thomas, V.P. Finance; Donna Kelly, Manager, Customer Service

Preliminary Project Budget: $5,000 in outside cost, plus 400 hours of internal staff and management time.

Timeline: Project to be completed by June 2003.

Note from Claus Martin, President
I am pleased that Hugh Stevenson has agreed to spearhead this project, knowing that his experience will enable him and his team to deliver useful information. The results of this survey will be critical to our strategic planning process for 2003, so timing is the most important priority here. Assuming we don't face any market-related or capacity-related crises in the next six months, I would like everyone in the company to give Hugh the support he needs to finish this project on time. That may mean that other projects, such as the order-streamlining and supply-chain-strategy projects, may need to be delayed a bit if necessary.

successful project managers engage team members early, taking advantage of their collective ideas and increasing their commitment to the project. Elements of this process are described below.

Clarifying Customer Needs

Although the charter may have highlighted some customer requirements, the project team will need to ensure that it understands customer expectations in full detail. Too often, project personnel assume they know what the customer wants. Even when they do ask the customer, they may not dig deep enough to uncover latent needs that are at the heart of a customer's requirements.

A tool known as quality function deployment (QFD)[8] can be very effective in helping a team to capture customer needs and translate them into design specifications. QFD involves a series of matrices and reveals points of conflict or areas where customer needs have not been addressed. The module, "New Product and Process Development," provides more detail about this popular and effective tool.

Deciding on the Course of Action

Early in the planning process the core team should take a careful look at the project's purpose and its links with corporate objectives. The example of the European auto manufacturer that improved its logistics system instead of building a warehouse provides good evidence for the importance of recognizing that there may be more than one way to achieve a project's goals. Before project plans become very well developed, the project manager may want to ask: "Is there more than one way to achieve our desired outcomes?" This can lead to a brainstorming approach, or, if more structure is desired, a decision tree might be appropriate. Decision trees are examined in depth in the decision analysis module in this series. Although that module's treatment of the decision tree subject is shown in a structured format emphasizing financial outcomes, the concept may be applied in a less formal way and could include subjective outcomes. Its advantage in a project environment is that it encourages team members to articulate their assumptions about outcomes and likelihoods for various scenarios.

Developing the Work Breakdown Structure

The **work breakdown structure,** or WBS, is one of the most important elements of a project plan. The WBS is a hierarchical listing of all project elements. The hierarchy may include many levels, depending on the complexity of the project, but the lowest level will display detailed tasks. An example of a WBS outline for the survey project discussed in Exhibit 6 is displayed in Exhibit 7.

Tasks, subtasks, and work packages represent hierarchical levels. Two levels are probably sufficient for this project, but larger projects may require many more levels of detail. At the lowest level, subtasks or work packages should identify work that can be assigned relatively easily to an individual or group. Each work package should have a measurable outcome. So, for example, if you were planning a children's party and had specified a work package entitled "Have fun," it would be difficult to measure the outcome. However, if you specified a work package entitled "Play BINGO," you would be able to determine if this task had been completed. Having fun was the *purpose;* the game was the *work package.* Here are a few things to keep in mind when developing a WBS:

- The project team should be involved in developing the WBS. This will instill ownership and provide useful creativity at the beginning of the project.
- At the lowest level of the hierarchy, each work package should include a noun and a verb to imply action (e.g., "meet with customers" rather than "customers").
- Tasks that are not defined at a sufficient level of detail will be difficult to manage, but too little detail will provide insufficient information to team members. A commonly cited

[8] J. R. Hauser and D. Clausing, "The House of Quality" *Harvard Business Review,* 63–67, May-June, 1988.

EXHIBIT 7
WBS Outline for Phase I of Customer Survey

Tasks	Subtasks	Work Packages (sample)
Survey	Design survey draft	
	Finalize survey design	
	Print surveys	
Subjects	Create client database	
	Select pretest subjects	
	Pretest survey →	**Assemble surveys** **Mail surveys** **Analyze pretest data** **Report results** **Recommend changes**
Mailing	Create/print personalized cover letters	
	Prepare mailing labels	
	Attach labels to envelopes	
	Assemble materials	
	Mail survey packages	

rule of thumb is that low-level tasks should be no shorter in duration than 8 work hours and no more than 80 hours.[9]

- Try to use a consistent level of detail throughout the WBS.
- The WBS stage provides an opportunity for considering possible project risks. As the team is brainstorming about project content, the facilitator can ask members to step back from time to time and consider possible risks. "As you look at this WBS, what thoughts come to mind about things that could go wrong?"
- It is important to remember that project management activities, in themselves, should be part of the WBS. After all, they will consume resources and take time in the schedule.
- Avoid asking the question "What should we do first?" This pushes the team into an analytical scheduling mode and out of a creative state—the schedule can come later. The key is to make sure that all important activities are included, not to decide on sequencing.
- In outlining terminology, if there is an "A" there should be a "B." Given an outline or indented WBS format, let us say that we have a task called Site Work that includes two work packages: Bulldozing the site to level it and Landscaping to add grass and shrubs. But if, for some reason, the Landscaping task is omitted, we will be left with Bulldozing as the only work package. This is an example of an "A" without a "B." In this case, Bulldozing and Site Work would be one and the same, and the lower level of detail would be unnecessary.
- Brainstorming tools such as **mind mapping**[10] can be very useful for getting a group to consider all of the possible activities in a project. An example of a WBS mind map for the survey project appears in Exhibit 8 on page 14. Note that a mind map displays the same information that an outline does, but it also includes images. Group members gather around a large (at least 1 meter by 2 meters) wall-mounted sheet of butcher paper and brainstorm about project activities. The mind map can later be "cleaned up" and converted to an outline. This method encourages group involvement, ensures team member buy-in, and increases the chance that the group will not overlook important tasks.

[9] E. Verzuh, *The Fast Forward MBA in Project Management* (New York: John Wiley & Sons, 1999).
[10] K. A. Brown & N. L. Hyer, Whole Brain Thinking for Project Management, *Business Horizons,* May/June, 2002 (in press).

EXHIBIT 8
WBS in Mind Map Form—Customer Survey Phase I

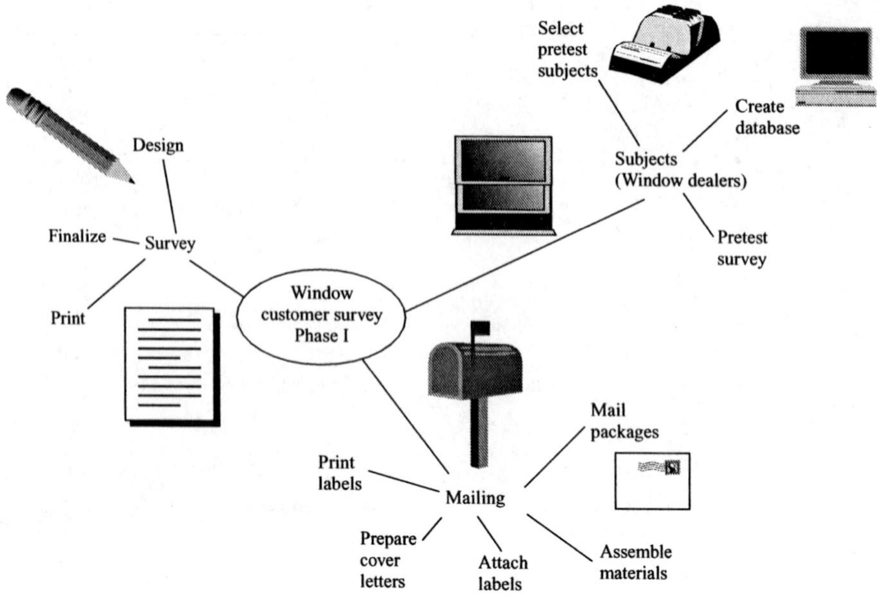

Risk Assessment Although some financial and other risks will have been considered as part of the project justification step, a good project manager knows that he or she must perpetually keep an eye out for risks. When the WBS is nearly complete, the planning team should step back and ask the questions: "Given all of these tasks, what could go wrong? What might we add, delete, or modify in the WBS to reduce the chance of this risk occurring?" There are numerous tools available for assessing project risk. Two examples are failure modes and effects analysis (FMEA) and fault tree analysis. Both of these tools come out of the reliability engineering field and involve a hierarchical or sequential analysis of causes that may underlie an undesirable project outcome. These are especially useful for analyzing risks in projects involving complex systems.

For most projects, the best guideline may be to keep it simple and not allow risk assessment to become a project in itself. If a group uses a brainstorming approach, it should identify the following:

- What are the potential risks?
- What is the approximate likelihood of each risk?
- What is the potential impact of each risk? (consider all stakeholders)
- What are the causes of these risks and outcomes? To what extent do we control the causes?
- What strategies and tactics should we use to avoid risks, mitigate the possibility of their occurrence, or deal with them if they arise?
- What will these strategies cost?

Depending on the size and complexity of the project, the team may decide to create a risk table as a way of recording the results of a risk analysis. An example of a risk table is shown in Exhibit 9.

Time Estimation

Time estimation can be quite straightforward in industries where historical records and similarity across projects allow for cross-referencing. For example, in the construction industry, an experienced estimator can forecast relatively accurately the time and the cost required

In Practice

TIME ESTIMATION FOR CREATIVE TASKS

Bryan Cline, an industrial engineering manager at a Fortune 500 company, was responsible for scheduling the production of drawings for industrial tooling as part of a new product design project. Many of the engineers complained that task precedences had not been considered in the schedule. As a consequence, the drawings they wanted to see before they produced theirs were not available. They would proceed with their work, even though they did not have the information that they required. However, rework was often necessary when the information did become available.

Although Bryan knew that the drawing tasks were behind schedule, he didn't have a good method for measuring progress. He met with the engineers and asked them to estimate the amount of time required for a typical drawing. The initial response was strong resistance: "Our work is creative; you can't put a number on it." "Each drawing is unique—there is no typical drawing." Bryan recognized the real reason for resistance: people do not like to be measured, especially if they believe the measurement outcomes will be used against them. Thus, he had to persuade them that if everyone's tasks were subjected to estimation, the entire team would benefit because they would be able to get the information they needed when they needed it, and the excessive rework would be diminished. The engineers ultimately, but still reluctantly, agreed to provide time estimates.

Through an analysis of historical records and their own experience, they estimated that a typical drawing took about 30 workdays. They then added conditional variations—drawings that had certain characteristics might take slightly less time. Drawings with other characteristics might require more time. Each drawing estimate started with the "typical" time as its baseline, then the estimator made adjustments based on factors such as complexity, interfaces with other tools or parts, need for input from an outside contractor, and so forth. These estimates became the basis for task times entered into a network schedule, which team members developed by consensus and updated regularly.

The new system resulted in a smoother schedule, less work-in-process inventory of drawings, reduced rework, and a more satisfied team. Project teams in other parts of the organization received word of this success, and the tools that Bryan had applied were exported to several other work units. If Bryan had allowed the initial resistance to time estimation stop him, this success story would not have materialized.

EXHIBIT 9
Risk Management Table for Phase I of Market Survey Project

*Note that costs do not necessarily have to be in monetary terms.

Risk	Outcome/ Impact	Likelihood	Strategies/ Responses	Cost*
Low response rate	• Invalid results • Strategic planning process impeded	• 80% under current plan	1. Delay survey until after holidays. 2. Offer gift as incentive.	1. Delayed ability to respond to customer needs (est.: $1,000,000 in lost sales). 2. Estimated cost of gifts; for 200 dealer/customers = $2,000.

to construct a building just by knowing the type of construction and the number of square feet of floor space. In projects with less tangible products, or in new industries that have not yet developed databases, estimating is more difficult. Here are a few tips for increasing the likelihood of estimation accuracy:

- *Those who will be responsible* for performing the work should *take part* in the time estimation process. This will ensure more accurate estimates, and the estimates will serve as self-set goals, carrying with them greater team member commitment.
- Use *historical data* whenever possible. Even if a previous project was not identical to the current ones, it may have included similar activities.
- Consider the *assumptions* that underlie the estimates. For example:
  - How many people will be working on the task?
  - What will be the skill level of those involved?
  - Will people be assigned 100 percent to the project, or something less than that?
- Estimate at a *detailed level*—experience has shown that estimates at the detail level are more accurate than estimates that attempt to capture the time required for a macro-level task. For example, you could probably more accurately estimate how long it would take

In Practice

GETTING THE RIGHT TEAM

After five years of employment in her company, Barbara Zhu had been given the opportunity to manage her first major project. She and her core team had developed a project charter, a work breakdown structure, and preliminary time and cost estimates. The plan called for the addition of four engineers who had experience and expertise in Web-based business-to-business purchasing systems. She had four specific engineers in mind, so she asked the engineering department head if these individuals could be allocated full-time for the next year to her project. The engineering department head indicated that he needed all four of these people for other activities and could not release them. He did offer four other people, but Barbara knew that they did not have the skill, experience, or motivation that she required. If you were Barbara, what would you do next?

you to drive from your house to your workplace than you could estimate the time required to drive across the country. As another example, the scheduling staff at Puget Sound Naval Shipyard recently began developing time estimates for ship overhauls at a much more detailed level than they had in the past. Detailed estimates were summed to produce estimates for higher level tasks. The result was a phenomenal increase in estimating accuracy.

- Consider applying *probabilistic concepts*. Most time estimates are recorded as single points in time rather than as ranges. Some experts suggest that project managers should attempt to find a range of times, from most pessimistic to most optimistic, and then apply statistical concepts to determine a confidence interval for each task.[11] Some tasks will have more risks, and therefore a wider confidence interval. A specific method for creating probabilistic estimates is presented in the project management module entitled "Managing and Controlling Project Resources."

Project Budgeting

The project charter typically will include a preliminary budget. This will have been based on rough "ball park" figures. Once the core project team has created the WBS and determined time estimates, more detailed budgeting is possible. To the extent possible, project budgets should be tied to the WBS to ensure accountability for project expenditures. Some project costs, such as overhead allocations for space and equipment rental, may need to appear as line items separate from the WBS, however. Exhibit 10 shows a costed WBS for Phase I of the survey project. Note from the exhibit that costs of lower-level elements are rolled up and summed to form budget allocations for higher levels.

When developing the budget, the team should consider human resource costs derived from time estimates, materials, equipment, subcontracting payments, interest on loans, fees

EXHIBIT 10
Costed WBS for Market Survey Project Phase I

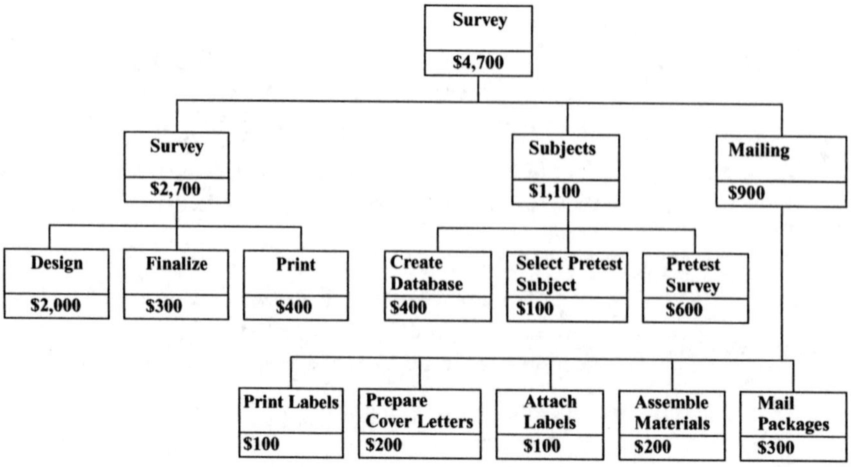

[11] E. M. Goldratt, *Critical Chain* (New York: North River Press, 1997); and F. Hartman, *Don't Park Your Brain Outside* (Newtown Square, PA: Project Management Institute, 2000).

to public agencies, insurance, reserves for expected and unexpected future circumstances, and other relevant factors.

Forming the Project Team

So far, we have discussed the core team and its role in developing the project plan. Once a more detailed plan is available, the project manager will be able to determine if additional human resources will be needed to carry out the project. Depending on the scope and duration of the project, additional team members may be assigned full-time or they may be "borrowed" on a part-time basis from functional units within the organization. In either case, the project manager will need to negotiate with functional managers to acquire the people who have the necessary skills. Because most project team members retain "home" affiliations within their functional units, their loyalties will be split between project work and ongoing work. Additionally, each team member may be assigned to more than one project, further diluting commitment. Managing dispersed team members is one of the greatest challenges of the project manager. These issues are discussed in more depth in the module entitled "Achieving Operational Excellence through People," but the scenario in the In Practice box highlights some of the challenges.

The Responsibility Matrix A helpful tool for making team assignments is known as a **responsibility matrix.** The matrix links team member names to specific project deliverables or tasks. An example of a responsibility matrix for a small portion of the survey project appears in Exhibit 11. As shown in the exhibit, project tasks are listed along the vertical axis on the left side of the chart, and team member names appear across the top. The simplest responsibility matrix might involve the use of check marks in the boxes to show which person would perform which task. The sample matrix is somewhat more detailed in that it highlights the nature of each person's role: Participant, Accountable, Review required, Input required, and Signoff required. The matrix may look relatively simple, but negotiating team member roles will require time and patience.

EXHIBIT 11
Responsibility Matrix for Survey Project Phase I

P=Participant, A=Accountable, R=Review required, I=Input required, S=Signoff required.

	Project Team Members				
Project Task	**Hugh**	**Charlene**	**Mac**	**Donna**	**Claus**
Survey	A/S	P	I	I	R
Data	I	I	I	A/P	R
Mailing	A/P	I	P	P	R

Have you ever been involved in a project where people's roles were unclear? How did this affect the project's outcome?

Project Scheduling

When some technically oriented people think about project management, the first thing that may come to their minds is the development of a network type of project schedule. As you can see from our discussion so far, there is a great deal of work that must be done before we can even consider how a project schedule will look. In fact, for some projects a formal schedule may be unnecessary—a simple check list could very well be sufficient. For many projects, however, a special set of scheduling tools can be very helpful for ensuring that tasks are completed in the proper sequence.

There are many stories in the business news about projects with schedule overruns. In information technology projects, it is not unusual for total durations to be double their original estimates. Although these overruns may be caused by a variety of factors (e.g., poor definition of requirements), a well-devised project schedule can ensure that task sequences are handled efficiently and provide the basis for effective control systems. There are several formats for presenting project schedules. Those included in this module will be network diagrams, bar charts, and time-based networks.

Network Diagrams A **network diagram** is a tool that graphically depicts the parallel and sequential relationships among tasks identified in the WBS. A parallel relationship between two tasks means that they can be performed simultaneously. For example, if you were building a house, one crew could landscape the yard at the same time that another crew was installing the light fixtures indoors. On the other hand, sequential activities are tasks that depend on each other—that is, one must be completed before the other can start. Following the house example, pouring the concrete for the foundation would depend on the prior completion of necessary site excavation work. A simple project network for the first phase of a customer survey is shown in Exhibit 12. Note that the items in this schedule are drawn from the WBS subtasks displayed in Exhibits 7 and 8.

EXHIBIT 12
AON Project Network for Survey Design and Mailing Project

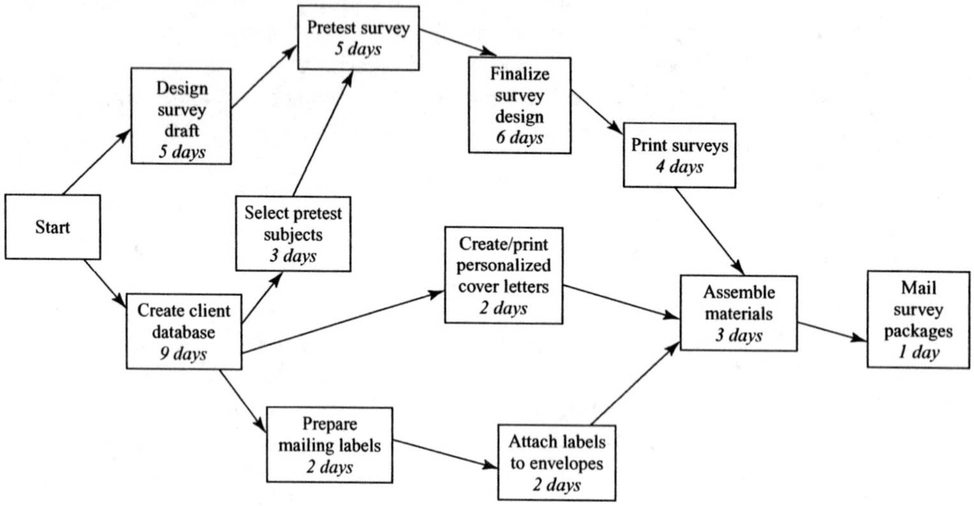

The presentation format shown in Exhibit 12 is called an **activity on node (AON)** diagram. It is given this name because the activities appear inside the boxes or nodes of the network. The same project may be shown as an **activity on arrow (AOA)** diagram, as depicted in Exhibit 13.

In both network formats, neither the line lengths nor their compass directions necessarily convey meaning. The arrows are intended to show logical relationships only. Note that in both cases, however, the two initial tasks are joined on the left side by a starting node. It is important for every project to have a single starting point and a single ending point. In AON diagrams, this may require the use of a node labeled "Start" at the beginning of the project and a node labeled as "Finish" at the end of the project.

EXHIBIT 13
AOA Project Network for Survey Design and Mailing Project

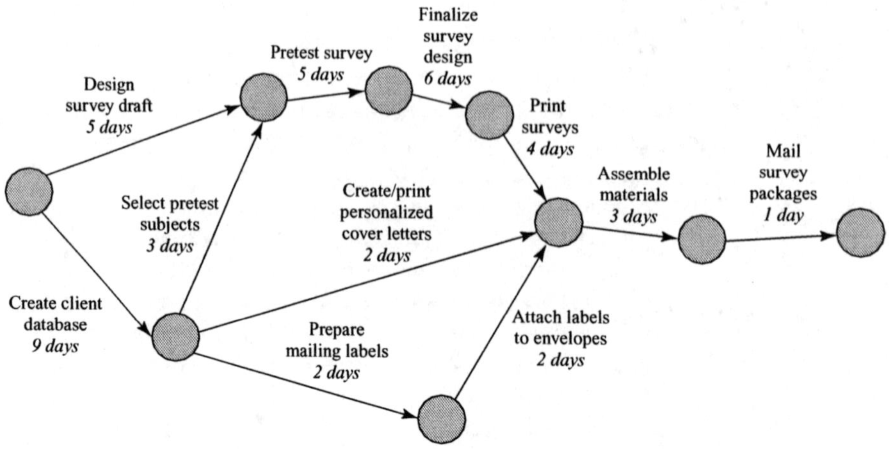

In Practice

OUT-OF-THE-BOX SEQUENCING

The Quinault Nation, a Native American tribe, built a luxury resort and casino on the Pacific shores of Washington state in 2000. Because of the difficulties associated with labor shortages at the remote site, along with construction challenges in the high winds and wet weather conditions of the coastal region, the tribe decided to use a modular approach to building the facility. They hired BFC Frontier of British Columbia to pre-fabricate the structure in modules, barge them to the construction site, and hoist them into place using large cranes. This approach violated traditional scheduling sequences and led to a highly successful outcome. A photo taken during the module assembly process is displayed in Exhibit 14.

Some people intuitively prefer AOA diagrams and others favor AON diagrams. Although AOA has been popular in the past, AON has more recently overtaken it in usage. AOA diagrams may require a complexity known as a dummy activity that can make them difficult to use (see below for details), so most project management software producers have shifted their allegiances to the AON approach.

Although the AON format is currently the most commonly used, the AOA format still has value because it allows one to use a time-based network, a useful tool that is described below.

Deciding on the Level of Detail The first step in developing a project network diagram is to determine the level of detail needed for the schedule. A project manager for a multiyear mega-project is not likely to want to see every work package in a network schedule—this could literally involve thousands of activities and require meters and meters of paper to display. Instead, the project manager is probably going to want a high-level network that shows summary tasks or deliverables in parallel and sequential relationships. The managers of subprojects within this mega-project are likely to have detailed schedules for their parts of the project.

For example, when the state of Washington built a convention center in Seattle, the project manager, Mr. Chub Foster, monitored 75 summary tasks on a daily basis. Each of these summary tasks was composed of several layers of component tasks performed by a multitude of subcontractors. All told, there were well over 10,000 work packages in the project—far too many for Foster to manage at a detailed level.

Teamwork Tip

This activity should involve no more than three people. Creative tasks such as WBS development can involve more people, but analytical tasks are best done with smaller groups. To involve more team members in scheduling, use a rotation system whereby one group creates an initial schedule and subsequent groups help to refine it. Team involvement in scheduling increases the likelihood that they will be committed to the schedule.

Developing the Network The selected level of the WBS serves as the basis for the project schedule. The project manager, with help from the project team, arranges the tasks or work packages into sequential and parallel relationships. A helpful method for doing this is as follows:

1. Place a large sheet of butcher paper (about two meters across by one meter high) on the wall at eye level.
2. Write the names of all tasks, subtasks, or work packages (depending on chosen level of detail) on Post-it Notes®.
3. Initially, arrange the notes into three groups: early, middle, and late, according to their approximate timing during the project. Attempt to reach group consensus on these clusters.
4. Determine detailed sequential and parallel relationships. For example, which task absolutely must precede task A? Could these two tasks progress in parallel without interfering with each other? Take care in making unnecessary assumptions about sequential relationships. Some of the most innovative and successful projects have broken ingrained rules and traditions to find new ways to sequence activities (see Exhibit 14 on page 20).

EXHIBIT 14
Modular Design Changes Project Sequence for Quinault Tribe

This photo shows the modules being set into place on the structure. Each module is a completely finished luxury room, including carpeting, wall paneling, and bathroom fixtures. Photo by Larry Workman, Quinault Nation. Permission granted.

5. Be open to adding elements to the WBS. During the scheduling process, team members often discover WBS elements that they previously overlooked. This does not necessarily mean that the WBS was done poorly; it is just that once the team sees tasks in sequence, members may reach new insights about what needs to be done.

Using Dummy Activities in AOA Networks

Under some circumstances, an AOA network will require a special feature known as a **dummy activity.** Dummy activities help to clarify precedence relationships and remove false dependencies. Those who wish to stick with AON networks needn't worry about these. However, because we will need to examine time-based networks later in this module, it is important to briefly introduce dummy activities. Consider the following example:

Activity	Immediate Predecessor	Time
A	—	3 days
B	—	2 days
C	A	1 day
D	B, C	4 days
E	B	3 days

Sample Problem

A project's tasks, their immediate predecessors, and their durations are displayed in the table in Exhibit 15. Use the table to draw a network diagram in AOA and AON form. The solutions appear in the appendix to this module in Exhibits A and B.

EXHIBIT 15
Sample Network Problem

Task	Immediate Predecessor(s)	Duration
A	—	2
B	—	4
C	—	4
D	A	5
E	B	6
F	B	8
G	C	4
H	D, E	7
I	F	7
J	F	6
K	G	4
L	I	10
M	J, K	5

Your AOA Diagram

Your AON Diagram

AON and AOA diagrams of this project network are shown in Exhibit 16. The AON network is straightforward. However, the AOA diagram requires some special logic. A dummy activity is needed to correctly depict the relationships among C, D, B, and E. A dummy requires no time and uses no resources. In this case, it shows that B and C precede D, but C does not precede E. If we showed the network without the dummy, it would appear as it does in the lower right side of the exhibit. Note that in this case we would imply that C precedes E, which is incorrect and would be considered a false dependency. Although dummy activities might appear complex to the uninitiated, once you become comfortable with network logic, they should come quite naturally to you.

EXHIBIT 16
Dummy Activity Example

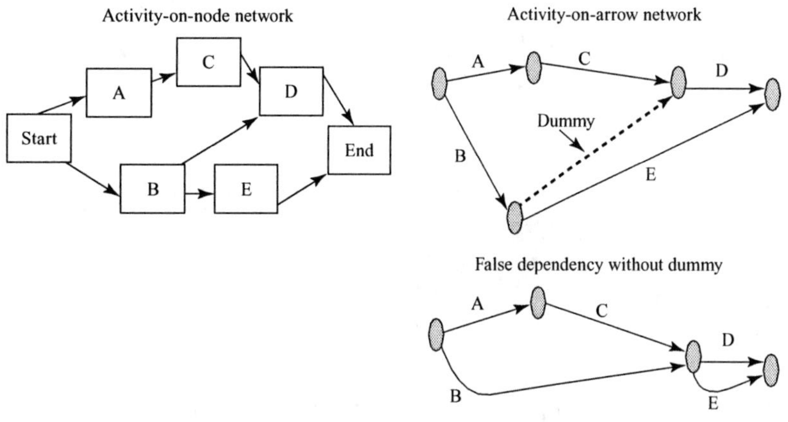

Network Calculations The completed network, inclusive of time estimates, serves as the information source for calculating several key project attributes and metrics, including the critical path and float. The **critical path** is the network path that has the longest duration, and it determines the total amount of calendar time that the project will consume. Referring back to Exhibits 12 and 13, we can calculate the length of each path as follows:

Path 1: Design (5), Pretest (5), Finalize design (6), Print (4), Assemble (3), Mail (1) = 24 days

Path 2: Database (9), Select pretest subjects (3), Pretest (5), Finalize design (6), Print (4), Assemble (3), Mail (1) = 31 days

Path 3: Database (9), Cover letters (2), Assemble (3), Mail (1) = 15 days

Path 4: Database (9), Mailing labels (2), Attach labels (2), Assemble (3), Mail (1) = 17 days

The second path is the critical path because it is the longest in duration. If any task on this path becomes delayed, the project will be completed after its anticipated finish date. All noncritical activities have what is known as **float** or **slack.** These two terms mean the same thing and refer to the amount by which a noncritical activity may be delayed without delaying the project's anticipated completion date, or the amount by which it may be delayed without holding up any other activity. Exhibit 17 shows another presentation format for the survey project. This format, known as a **time-based network,** provides a visual illustration of critical path and float concepts. In a time-based network, the span of each activity arrow corresponds to the time required for the task. In this example, each task is scheduled at its earliest possible start time.The dashed lines represent the float in the schedule, revealing where the tasks may be delayed without interference. (Although dashed lines also may represent dummy activities, they do not in this instance.) The critical path, which we identified previously, does not include float and is highlighted with double lines.

The project manager must be aware of the two different types of project float: free float and total float. **Free float** is the amount by which an activity may be delayed without delaying the earliest possible start time of any other activity. **Total float** is the amount by which an activity may be delayed without delaying the project.

In Exhibit 17 Design Survey Draft, Create Letters, and Attach Labels to Envelopes all have dashed float lines immediately following them. These dashed lines represent free float for these activities—for example, we could delay the start of Design Survey Draft by seven days and not interfere with the start of its successor, Pretest Survey. Thus, it has seven days of free float. In contrast, Prepare Mailing Labels is an example of an activity that has no

EXHIBIT 17

Time-Based Network for Survey Project (Early Start Schedule)

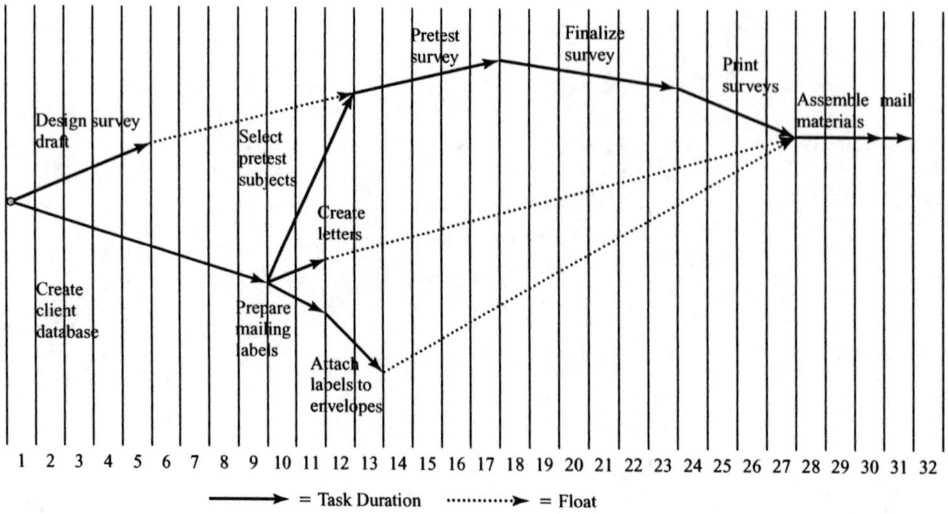

free float, but it does have total float. We can see that if we delay this task, we will, by necessity, also delay the early start time for Attach Labels to Envelopes. However, these two tasks together can be delayed by 14 days without delaying the project. Thus, in combination, they have 14 days of *shared* total float.

Warning: It is important to recognize that float along a path may be shared by several activities.

A visual analysis of the sort just described can be effective for a small project, but for larger projects it becomes necessary to use a mathematical algorithm to calculate float and identify the critical path. Details of this algorithm are presented in a later section of this module.

The Bar or Gantt Chart The **bar chart,** or **Gantt chart,** is another presentation format for project schedule information. This format is very popular because of its simplicity, but it does *not* reveal sequential relationships, the critical path, or float. A bar chart example of the survey project is presented in Exhibit 18. These are often used for displaying schedule progress in project meetings. However, if it becomes necessary to discuss schedule changes, the project team will need to consult the network schedule to assess the effects of these changes.

EXHIBIT 18
Bar or Gantt Chart for Survey Project

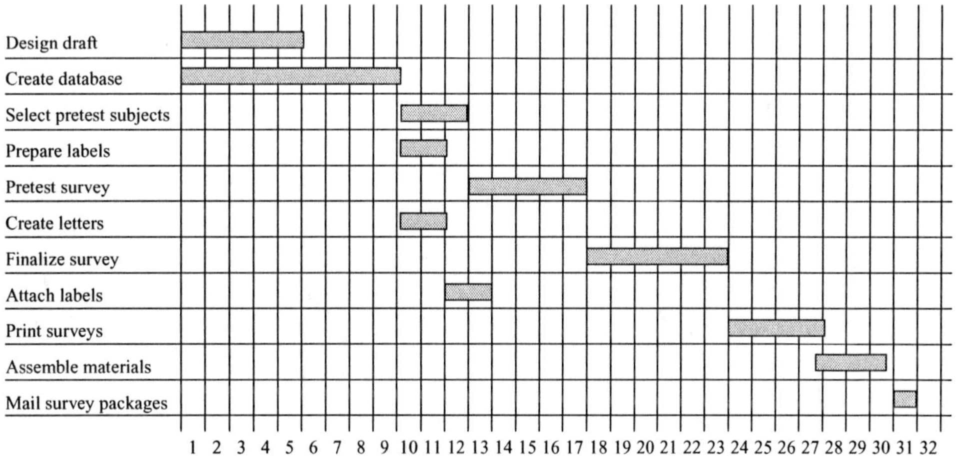

Examine Exhibits 12, 13, 17, and 18. Can you see that these are all depicting the same project information, but in different ways?

Project Scheduling Software There are dozens of software programs available for project scheduling. Examples of popular desktop packages include CA-Superproject, Timeline, Project Scheduler, TurboProject Professional, SureTrak Project Manager, and Microsoft Project.[12] Some of the advantages of using these programs include ease of updating, availability of multiple report formats, opportunity for file sharing among geographically dispersed team members, and standardization of schedule displays.

In spite of the potential benefits of project management software, project managers and team members should be aware that there are risks as well. For example, people may attach too much credibility to a computer-generated schedule, reducing the likelihood that they will ask important questions about assumptions, time estimates, and the like. Moreover, there is a tendency for people who are starting out with software to believe that it will "manage" a project for them. Consequently, they sometimes jump right into the software without completing all of the important components (e.g., agreeing on objectives, brainstorming the WBS) that should precede the scheduling step.

[12] N. H. King, "Project Management According to Plan," *PC Magazine,* June 30, 1998, pp. 209–22.

EXHIBIT 19 MS Project Output for Survey Project

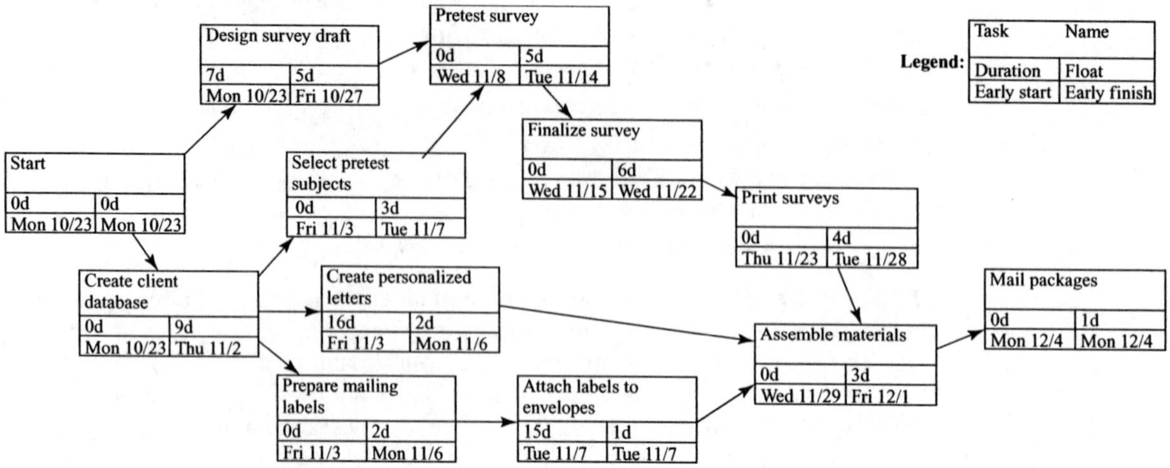

An MS Project network schedule printout for the survey project is shown in Exhibit 19. MS Project is one of many software programs available, but it is currently the most widely used desktop scheduler. Although other display formats are possible, Exhibit 19 shows the network view of the survey project that has served as our example. The legend identifies the information available in each task box, including Task Name, Early Start, Early Finish, and Free Float. (Many other display options are available for the task boxes.) Calendar dates reflect the passage of non-working days such as weekends and holidays during the project's life. The examples shown in this module are based on Microsoft Project 98, which has been chosen because it actually allows more presentation flexibility than newer versions.[13]

The Critical Path Algorithm So far, this module has explained the conceptual differences between free float and total float. These conceptual differences are important because a task manager will be in error if he or she presumes ownership of total float that may be shared with another task on the same path. In a large network, it may be difficult to visually identify all network float. However, there is a simple mathematical algorithm for assessing early start and finish times, late start and finish times, the location of the critical path, free float, and total float. It is highlighted in Exhibit 20.

EXHIBIT 20
Critical Path Algorithm

Forward Pass: Calculating Early Start and Early Finish Times

1. Time for starting node = 0
2. Early start (ES) for all beginning jobs = S
3. ES for all other jobs = Maximum or latest early finish (EF) for all tasks immediately preceding.
4. EF for task A = (ES of task A + Duration of task A)
5. Total project time = Maximum or latest EF for all jobs.

Backward Pass: Calculating Late Start and Late Finish Times

1. Total project time = Latest early finish (EF) for all ending jobs
2. Late finish (task A) = Earliest LS for all tasks following task A
3. LS task A = (LF task A − Duration of task A)

Using ES, EF, LS, LF to Calculate Float

1. Total float for task A = LS (A) − ES (A), which is equivalent to LF (A) − EF(A)
2. Free float for task A = Find the minimum (earliest) ES for all task that follow task A, then subtract the EF of task A.

[13] Author's bias!

EXHIBIT 21
Critical Path Algorithm Applied to Survey Design and Mailing Project

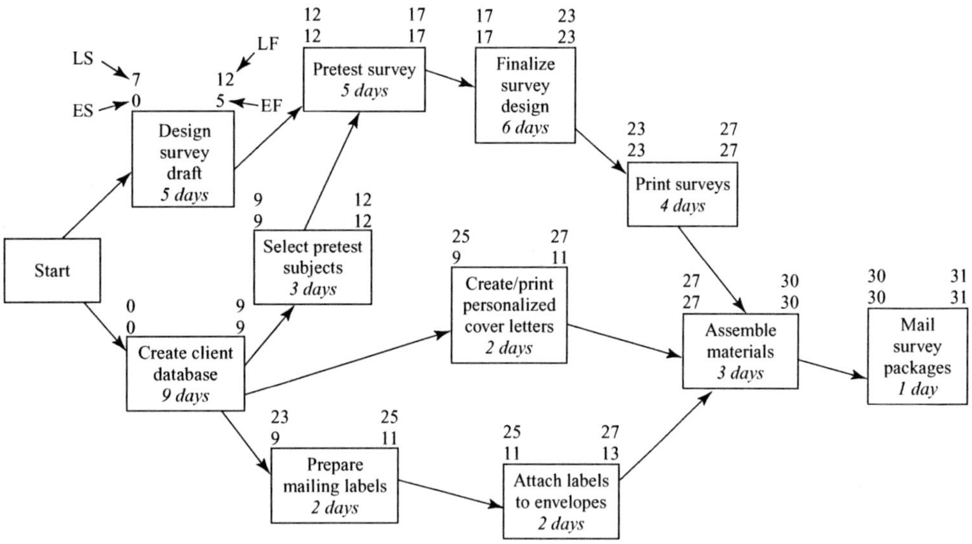

The **critical path algorithm** is applied to the survey project in Exhibit 21. Forward and backward pass calculations are displayed in the first text line above each activity box. The general procedure for the *forward pass* involves calculating the earliest possible start and finish times for each activity, beginning with all starting activities and working toward the end of the project. (For the sake of simplicity, the example uses sequential numbers rather than calendar dates, and weekends and holidays are ignored.) Assume that the start date for the project is Time 0. This becomes the early start (ES) for the activity Design Survey Draft, and the early finish (EF) will be the early start plus the task time—in this case, 5. The early start for any subsequent activity will be the latest EF for all of its predecessors. This decision rule has special relevance at merge points, where there is more than one predecessor. For example, the task Pretest Survey cannot begin until after Design Survey Draft *and* Select Pretest Subjects are complete. But Select Pretest Subjects does not end until time 12, so that is the soonest that Pretest survey may start.

The *backward pass* involves calculating the late finish and late start for each activity. The *latest* EF time for any project activity becomes the late finish (LF) for all ending activities (in this case, time 31 for the completion of phase I of the survey project). We then subtract the task time from the LF to determine the late start (LS) time. The earliest LS for any following activity becomes the LF for a predecessor. This rule has special relevance at burst points where an activity has multiple successors. For example, to determine the LF for the activity Create Client Database, we must consider the late start times for its three successor or following tasks. The earliest of these LS times is 9 for Select Pretest Subjects, so 9 becomes the LF for Create Client Database. Note that if this task ended any later, it would delay Select Pretest Subjects beyond its LS date, thereby delaying the project.

The combination of information about ES, EF, LS, and LF provides the data needed for calculating total float and free float. As discussed previously, total float (or total slack) is the amount by which we may delay a task without delaying the project. It may be shared by several activities on a noncritical path. Total float is simply the difference between the ES and LS or the EF and LF for a task (either function should produce the same number). For example, the task Prepare Mailing Labels has 14 ($23 - 9$ or $25 - 11$) days of total float. Free float or free slack is the amount by which we may delay an activity without delaying the ES of any of its successors (followers). Based on the algorithm, it is the difference between the EF of one task and the earliest ES of all successors (followers). Free float will occur when shorter paths merge with longer paths such as the critical path. For example, Create/Print Personalized Cover Letters has an EF of 11. Its successor, Assemble Materials has an ES of 27. The difference, 16, tells us the amount of free float that Assemble Materials has. We can confirm this visually by referring to Exhibit 17.

Although it is unlikely that you will perform these types of calculations yourself if you are managing a project, it is very important that you understand the critical path algorithm if you are to understand and interpret project network schedules.

Solved Problem

This is an opportunity for you to practice the critical path algorithm. Exhibit 22 presents an AON diagram for the problem data presented in Exhibit 15. Perform the forward and backward pass procedures, and identify the ES, EF, LS, LF and the critical path, total float, and free float.

EXHIBIT 22
Network Schedule for Critical Path Algorithm Practice Problem

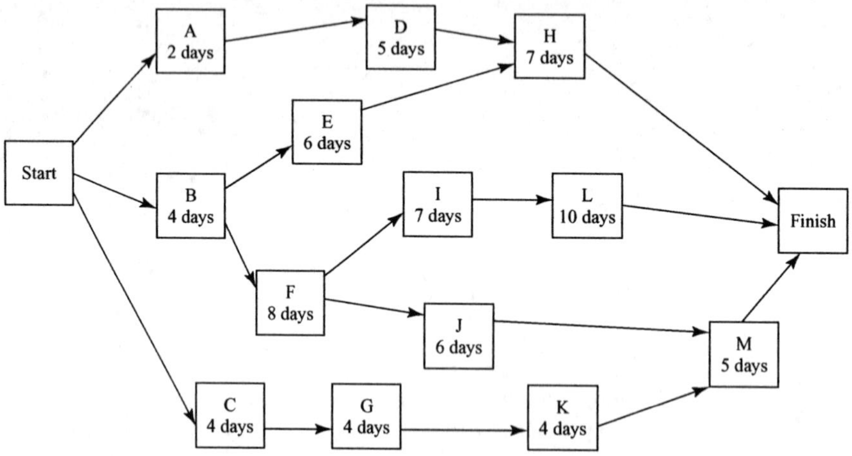

Instructions: Use the critical path algorithm to calculate ES, EF, LS, and LF for each task. Then, calculate total float and free float for each activity

Using Project Schedules for Resource Allocation Decisions

As discussed in the introduction to this module, managing resources is an important role of the project manager. Project resources include team member time, staff support, equipment, materials, space, cash, and other entities. A major challenge for the project manager is juggling scheduling priorities with the availability of team members. For example, an initial project schedule, with all tasks set at their early start times, may require more than the available number of team members. Or a specialist in a particular area may be scheduled to work on two tasks at the same time. Both of these possible scenarios are depicted in Exhibit 23.

EXHIBIT 23
Resource Allocation Scenarios

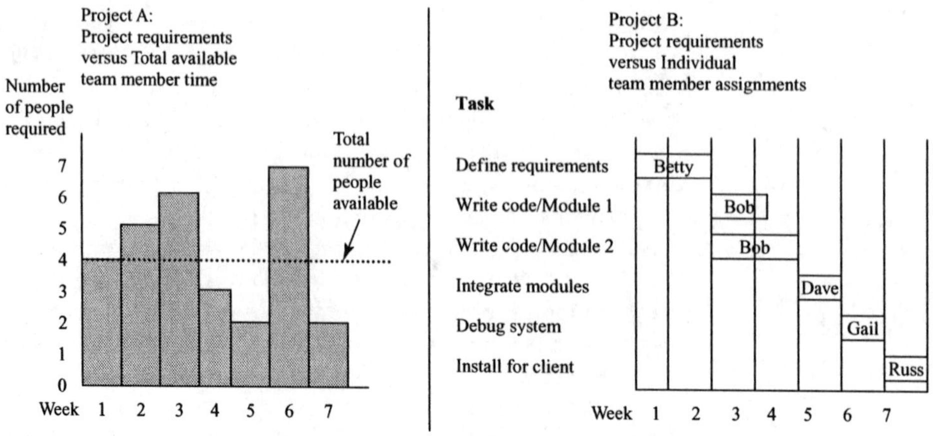

Note: These two images depict different projects. Project A represents a major project with a large, relatively interchangeable project team. Project B represents a smaller endeavor with a five-person team. Each team member in Project B is a specialist and interchange is not possible.

In Practice

RECOVERING WHEN THE CRITICAL PATH SLIPS

A group of MBA students was working on a two-weekend project to renovate a house for a low-income senior citizen. This activity was the central element of a project management elective course. The student teams had meticulously developed their plans, including elaborate network schedules. Indoor painting activities were clearly on the critical path, so all involved paid close attention to painting progress. A big issue was drying time—subsequent tasks such as drapery installation, replacing furniture, and hanging pictures had to wait until the paint was dry.

As the project unfolded, it became evident that the painting would take longer than expected. If things were allowed to continue as they were, the project would extend beyond its completion deadline at the end of the second weekend. A meeting of the leadership group was called to determine what actions to take. They noted that there were several alternatives: omit one room from the painting plan, use one coat of paint instead of two, use fans and heaters to speed drying, work overtime during the week between the two project weekends, and/or assign more people to painting. The team decided to use a combination of some of these alternatives, and the project schedule recovered.

Note that in Project A, the number of people *available* is only four, but the actual number *required* varies from two to seven. In weeks two, three, and six, project requirements exceed capacity. The project manager may be able to use activity float to delay some noncritical activities and smooth out resource requirements. In some circumstances, it may be necessary to delay the project in order to stay within resource availability boundaries. In Project B, a completely different endeavor and situation, a five-person team is scheduled to complete a software installation in seven weeks. However, team member Bob is double-booked in week three and in half of week four. If both of these tasks are on the critical path, the project will have to be delayed to remove the conflict. However, if one or both of these tasks have float available, it may be possible to complete the project on time by delaying noncritical tasks. The types of resource displays shown in Exhibit 23 can be very helpful to the project manager who needs to make a decision about resource allocation; they are also excellent communication devices. For example, a project manager might use a chart such as the one presented in Project A to convince a project sponsor of the need for more project team members.

Details about making schedule modifications to accommodate resource conflicts, overloads, or variability are presented in the module entitled "Managing and Controlling Project Resources."

Project Delivery and Control

At some point, the planning phase ends and the work of the project begins. The plans will be of no real value unless their content becomes the basis of a monitoring and control system. Monitoring refers to activities for measuring plans for expenditures, schedule performance, quality, scope, resource utilization, and so forth against the realities of the project as it unfolds. Control refers to the actions a project team takes in response to discrepancies between actual and planned performance, or in response to proposals for changing the original plan. An example of a monitoring and control scenario is presented in the In Practice box, above.

In this community service project scenario, a critical task took longer than expected and the project management team followed a **change order process** to develop a new plan. Two important success factors are important in this kind of situation. First, decision makers must consider the risks associated with leaving the plan the way it is and weigh them against the risks and costs associated with the proposed modifications. Second, they must consider which stakeholders will be affected by the change and how it will affect them. Third, they must effectively communicate the new plan to all involved, most notably the customer.

In the FCG Doghouse scenario described in the Practice box, on page 28, the project grew in size because the customer realized midstream the need for additional features. The ubiquitous tendency for projects to grow in this way is known as **scope creep.** Note that a formal change order procedure was important in this case, as well.

In Practice

CHANGES IN PROJECT SCOPE

FCG Doghouse, a website development company with 50 employees, based in Seattle, signed a $300,000 contract with a client to develop an e-commerce website for selling commercial electronic products. Several team members were assigned to the project on a part-time basis, and the duration of the project was estimated at six months. Initially, work progressed smoothly, but the customer contacted the project manager in the third month, requesting several additional website features. For example, the customer wanted the website to display customer-specific pricing based on business volume history. Additionally, the client wanted the website to accommodate product returns as well as sales.

These requests would require major design changes, adding features that had not been considered at the time the project was originally bid. The Doghouse project team had to reevaluate the WBS, reestimate task times, assess impacts on all project elements, develop a new network schedule, and inform the client of a revised contract price estimate and end date. This assessment and rebidding were conducted in the context of the company's standard change order process. As the project evolved, other change requests from the client were subjected to the same sort of careful analysis. The total project budget was increased to about $1 million, and the duration was reestimated at one year. A documented change order procedure, such as the one employed by Doghouse, can protect the project organization from succumbing to the pitfalls of *scope creep* without adequate compensation. It also allowed Doghouse to demonstrate its logic and communicate realistic expectations to the client.

Designing a Monitoring System

The project team must begin to think about monitoring systems prior to project execution, deciding on the degree of formality, frequency of reporting, and systems for approving changes. Degree of formality may range from a simple WBS checklist to a bar chart showing percentage completion for each activity, to an earned value chart. An example of an MS Project bar chart showing percent complete information is displayed in Exhibit 24.

The MS Project bar chart shown in Exhibit 24 displays percent complete information for each individual activity, providing a graphical image of what remains to be accomplished. However, it does not show cost data, which must be displayed separately. A tool known as earned value analysis provides a widely used mechanism for displaying schedule and cost data on the same graph. Earned value analysis and related concepts are addressed in the module entitled "Managing and Controlling Project Resources."

Monitoring and control are serious activities and should begin as soon as project work begins. Performance in the early stages of a project will be highly predictive of performance

EXHIBIT 24 MS Project Gantt Chart (or Bar Chart) with Percent Complete Display Option

ID	Task Name	Duration
1	Start	0d
2	Design survey draft	5d
3	Pretest survey	5d
4	Finalize survey	6d
5	Print surveys	4d
6	Create personalized letters	2d
7	Prepare mailing labels	2d
8	Attach labels to envelopes	1d
9	Assemble materials	3d
10	Mail packages	1d
11	Create client database	9d
12	Select pretest subjects	3d

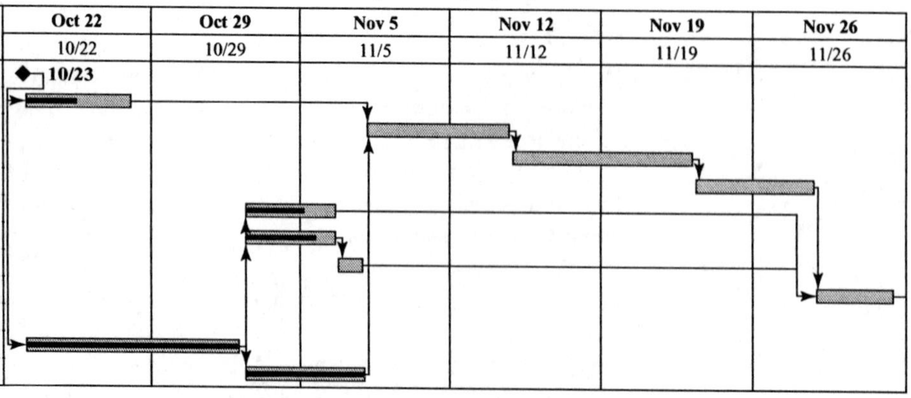

Note that the dark line through the center of any task bar indicates the percent complete. Task 1, Design Survey Draft, is 50% complete. Although Select Pretest Subjects has been completed (Task 12), Pretest Survey (Task 3) awaits the completion of Design Survey Draft before it can start.

during the remainder of a project's duration. For example, in studies of hundreds of projects, the U.S. Department of Defense has demonstrated that cost and schedule overruns at the 20 percent completion point seldom recover later in the project.[14] Early data about overruns and other problems should raise a red flag for the project manager, inspiring action to communicate with sponsors, clients, and other stakeholders; managing their expectations, seeking additional resources; reconfiguring project activities; reducing scope; and/or stopping the progress of damage. It is very difficult to recover from early poor performance, so the project manager not only must monitor progress, he or she must be on guard to anticipate potential problems before they arise.

Project Closeout

Project closeout occurs when all project deliverables have been completed to the satisfaction of the client, sponsor, and other decision makers with acceptance authority. This is a difficult project phase because team members may have turned their attentions toward the next project to which they have been assigned. It is difficult to remain focused on a project for a long period of time, and as the level of activity diminishes in a project's waning days, people may feel they can finally relax.

Project closure is the time when system components are merged to create a final product. For example, in an information technology project, different teams may have completed various deliverables. Just before project closure, when team members are feeling the effects of burnout and looking toward their next assignments, a high level of attention is needed. This is also the time when the client sits in anticipation of an idealized end product, perhaps expecting more than it will actually deliver. The collision of these two phenomena at the point of handoff creates the potential for conflict. Successful project managers know that they must finish well, or they will expose themselves to client dissatisfaction, endless rework, high cost, and loss of future business. A key to successful project handoff is to view it as a continuing process throughout the project life cycle—frequently seeking client approval for completed deliverables.

Key tasks for project closure include

- Review of deliverables completed.
- Resolution of open items (deliverables that are incomplete or do not meet client specifications or expectations).
- Transitional activities to facilitate the handoff (e.g., client training in the use of a new system.)
- Client contractual sign-off.
- **Post-project review** of time, cost, and performance data.
- Celebration.
- Redeployment of team members to new project or functional activities.
- Reconvening of team members after the dust has settled to review and record lessons learned.

Although a complete discussion of all of these elements is beyond the scope of this module, the importance of celebration is noteworthy. Any project should end with a fun event that recognizes team members for their contributions. The size of the celebration will obviously be a function of the size of the project.

[14] Q. W. Fleming and J. M. Koppelman, *Earned Value Project Management* (Newtown Square, PA: Project Management Institute, 1996).

Project Metrics

Key performance variables and their relevance to project management have been emphasized throughout this module. This section revisits those metrics and shows how they are interrelated. Three types of metrics have been addressed: strategic, objective operational, and subjective operational measures. These are summarized in Exhibit 25. **Strategic measures** capture information about a project's success in meeting its objectives. In other words, did the project do what it set out to do? For example, an organization would want to assess if market share had increased, or if process throughput time had decreased, if these were project objectives. Other strategic measures focus on financial performance. For example, did the project meet its forecasted return on investment?

EXHIBIT 25
Examples of Project Metrics

Strategic Metrics	Objective Operational Metrics	Subjective Operational Metrics
• Internal rate of return • Net present value • Payback period • Market share • Organizational learning • Cost reduction • Profit increase • Public image	• Schedule • Budget • Specifications met • WBS elements complete	• Client satisfaction • Team member satisfaction • Social responsibility of project activities (safety, environmental management)

Objective operational measures include schedule, cost, and quality/scope performance. Schedule and cost may be measured separately with progress tracking methods such as percent complete Gantt or bar charts and accounting records. Or they may be tracked simultaneously with tools such as earned value, a topic covered in the module entitled "Managing and Controlling Project Resources." It is important not to forget quality and scope performance. Here, we ask the questions: "Did we complete every deliverable in the WBS?" "Did all deliverables meet predetermined specifications or expectations of the client?" These three metrics form the basis of the triple constraint discussed in the beginning of this module.

Subjective operational measures include team satisfaction, client satisfaction, and social responsibility. Team satisfaction is seldom measured in any objective way (e.g., through surveys) during the life of a project, but an effective project manager makes observations about team morale on a continuing basis. Unhappy team members will not give the project their best efforts, and they will be disinterested in future projects. This can be a liability for an organization that thrives on continuing project activities.

One might think that client satisfaction will be fine if specifications are met. Experience with thousands of projects suggests otherwise, however. This is because clients don't always have a complete picture of what they want before a project starts. The FCG Doghouse story depicted previously provides a good example. Or, in many cases, clients do not clearly articulate their needs to the project team. In either case, the client may not be happy with project outcomes. The extent of customer satisfaction is an important, albeit subjective, metric. An unhappy client may not accept (or pay for) the project. There may be considerable rework required. The client may not seek repeat business and may spread the word of his or her disappointment to other potential clients.

Module Summary

A project is a one-time or infrequently occurring operation that is designed to deliver specified value to its customers and is constrained by a designated end date and limited resources. Most projects involve coordination across multiple functions in an organization, and many projects rely on resources, such as subcontractors, outside of the organization. Anyone who works in an organizational setting is likely to be involved in a project role of some kind. Many will be project managers. The concepts, tools, and terms presented in this module provide the basics that every business person should understand, regardless of the nature of his or her future project roles. Well-conceived projects should support organizational strategies, have clear goals, and be carefully planned. Team members must be involved in this process. The necessary degree of formality in the project plan will be a function of the size and complexity of the job. Project planning will be nearly useless if it is not paired with a monitoring and control system that measures progress and identifies variances from the plan. Project closure is an essential phase in a project's life cycle and handoff to the customer can be a challenge when the project team is preparing to end its work and disperse. However, no project is truly complete until team members conduct a post project review and identify lessons that may be applied to future projects.

Key Terms

activity on node (AON), *18*
activity on arrow (AOA), *18*
business case, *10*
change order process, *27*
critical path, *22*
critical path algorithm, *25*
dummy activity, *20*
float, *22*
free float, *22*
Gantt (or bar) chart, *23*
mind mapping, *13*
network diagram, *18*
objective operational measures, *30*
post-project review, *29*
project, *3*
project charter, *10*
responsibility matrix, *17*
scope creep, *27*
slack, *22*
strategic measures, *30*
subjective operational measures, *30*
time-based network, *22*
total float, *22*
triple constraint, *4*
work breakdown structure, *12*

Discussion Questions

1. Imagine that you work for an international telecommunications conglomerate that has just acquired a 300-person family-owned telephone service provider. You have been asked to plan and manage a corporate offsite meeting in which 50 of the top-level people from the acquired company will meet for an entire day with 50 key people from the acquiring company. The purpose of the meeting will be to disseminate information, ease people's fears, obtain input, and gain buy-in. You have only *one week* to put this together. Should you use the tools presented in this module, or, given the short time horizon, should you just get right to work? Explain your answer. If you did use any of the tools from this module, which ones would you use? Why?
2. You are managing the development of a new business-to-business sales website for a key customer. Your team includes five programmers as well as two representatives from the client company and a website interfaces expert. The project's mission and goals have been clearly defined and you have five months to complete it. Two months into the project, one of the programmers comes to you with an idea: "I think we could really add value to the customer if we extended the program to include a customized pricing feature. This part of the program is not on the critical path, and I think it would take two people a week or two to make this addition." How would you respond? Explain your rationale.
3. Imagine that you work for a Fortune 500 company that produces Class 8 trucks. You have been assigned to work on process improvement efforts as part of a larger "lean manufacturing" program. Your current focus is on the final assembly line, where there have been considerable problems with quality—the resulting need for rework has shut the line down on several occasions. A recent benchmarking visit to another company has led you to realize that automation at three major points on the line could improve first-time quality performance. However, the equipment is very expensive ($1,000,000 for each of the three stations). You present the idea to the plant manager, and she asks you to prepare a business case. What will this entail? What methods might you use? What will you want to keep in mind?
4. As a project management consultant, you have been asked to assist a local organization in assessing the lessons learned from a recently completed MRP (material requirements planning) installation project. In your meetings with the key stakeholders, you learn that the project was over budget (almost double the original plan of $500,000), and that it took six months longer than the initial schedule had specified. Additionally, system users still do not trust the accuracy of the system's output, and they continue to maintain their own records to be sure they have correct information about inventory levels, customer orders, and so on. Given what you know about the most common contributors to project success and failure, what do you think might have caused the disappointing project outcomes? Explain your conclusions and describe likely scenarios.

Problems

1. You have just been named chair of your (pick a year) high school reunion. How would you describe the mission or purpose of this project? Develop a WBS for the project, with at least three levels of detail. Use a mind map approach, then translate the mind map into an indented outline, following the guidelines presented in this module. Write a few sentences describing how the elements in the WBS support the project mission.
2. Imagine that you work for Boston Scientific, a manufacturer of surgical equipment with assembly plants around the world. The company has decided to close the 500-employee plant where you work, and you have been named manager of the 15-month phase-out project. Identify the key stakeholders for this project. Develop a WBS using a mind map, indented outline, or both.

3. Somewhere in the United States, committee members in a voting precinct have decided to conduct a vote recount following an election. They have developed a preliminary WBS and have asked you to critique it. What are the weaknesses of this WBS?

Vote Recount Project

Task	Subtask	Work Package
1. Personnel		
	1.1 Establish criteria for selection	
		1.1.1 Screen criteria for redundancy
	1.2 Bipartisan	
	1.3 Select Democratic Party representatives	
		1.3.1 Contact party
		1.3.2 Ask for nominees
		1.3.3 Select nominees
	1.4 Contact Republican Party	
	1.5 Training	
2. Process		
		2.1 Local and state requirements/history
	2.1.1 Examine local historical practices	
	2.1.2 Determine state legal requirements	
	2.2 Procedures	
	2.2.1 Benchmark procedures in other states	
	2.2.2 Select best procedures	
	2.2.3 Make modifications to best procedures selected	
	2.2.4 Document procedures	
	2.2.5 Test procedures	
	2.2.6 Modify procedures as needed	
	2.3 Maintain objectivity	
3. Facilities		
	3.1 Nice work environment	
	3.2 Search for available space	
		3.2.1 Contact real estate agents
		3.2.2 Contact government agencies
		3.2.3 Scan real estate websites
		3.2.4 Contact failed dot-coms
	3.3 Prepare rental agreement	
		3.3.1 Install utilities
	3.4 Contract for support services	
		3.4.1 Janitorial service
4. Budget		
	4.1 Determine budget needs	
		4.1.1 Prepare formal budget proposal
		4.1.2 Request budget allocation from county
5. Media and public relations		

4. Given the following information about a small project,

Task	Duration Estimates	Immediate Predecessors
A	2 days	None
B	5 days	A
C	1 day	B
D	2 days	A
E	3 days	B & D
F	12 days	E

a. Draw an activity-on-node (AON) network.
b. Identify the ES, EF, LS, LF, critical path, total float, and free float using the critical path algorithm.
c. Which of these activities should the project manager track most closely?
d. What would happen if a new estimate for task D increases its expected duration from two days to six days? Would the project take longer? Would anything else change?

5. What errors do you see in the AON diagram shown below?

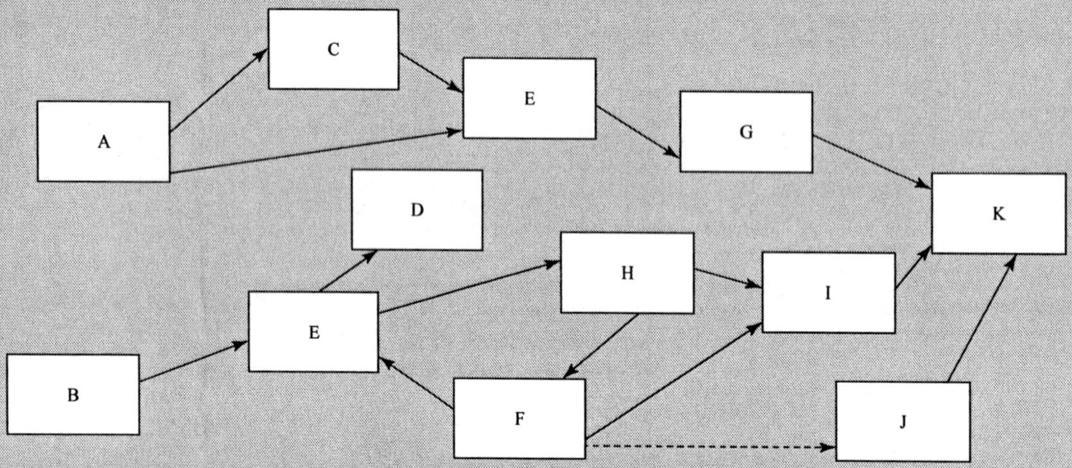

6. Given the following table of precedence relationships for a portion of a house-building project:

Task	Duration Estimates	Immediate Predecessor(s)
Prepare site	4 days	None
Install rough plumbing	3 days	Prepare site
Pour concrete foundation	2 days	Install rough plumbing
Cure concrete	3 days	Pour concrete foundation
Pre-assemble wall frames	8 days	None
Erect wall frames	4 days	Pre-assemble wall frames, cure concrete
Install roof	4 days	Erect wall frames
Install wiring	3 days	Install roof
Install exterior siding	4 days	Install roof
Install insulation	2 days	Install exterior siding
Hang drywall	3 days	Install insulation, install wiring
Install windows	1 day	Hang dry wall
Paint interior	6 days	Install windows
Paint exterior	5 days	Install exterior siding
Level yard	2 days	Cure concrete
Landscape yard	4 days	Level yard

a. Draw an activity-on-node diagram for this project and identify the critical path.
b. Draw a schedule graph (time-based network) for this project. Note that at least one dummy activity will be required. Be sure to distinguish dummy arcs from float.
c. What are some examples of assumptions may have been made in the development of the time estimates?
d. What will happen to the project if the materials needed for the frame pre-assembly are not available until the second day of the project? What if the materials were delayed until the 10th day?
e. Do you see any potential conflicts in this schedule? Will there be any incompatible tasks occurring simultaneously?

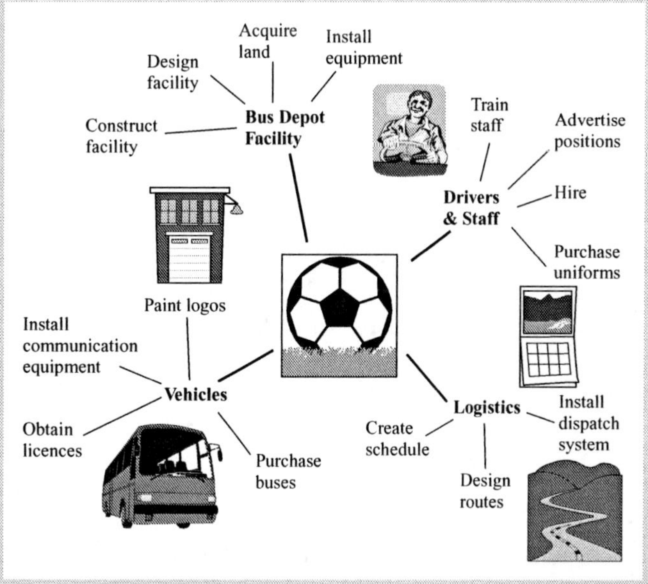

7 . Imagine that you have been selected as a project management consultant for the 2008 Olympic Games in China. Your task is to develop time estimates and a network schedule for one component of the project: Transportation of Olympic Athletes to competitive venues in Shanghai. Shanghai has been selected as the site of all soccer matches and your system must transport the athletes from the Shanghai Olympic Village to soccer stadia, venues for ceremonial events, and sight-seeing. The work breakdown structure for this project has been completed and appears in mind map form below:

Estimate the total person-days that will be required for each of the subtasks (e.g., create schedule). Do this by deciding on the number of people who will be needed and multiply this figure by the number of days these people will need for each subtask. Then, sum them hierarchically to derive a total person-days estimate for the project. Show your work. Compare your estimate with that of at least one other classmate. Write a paragraph discussing why you believe your estimate differed from that of your classmate.

8. Based on the precedence table below, draw an AOA and an AON network diagram for this project. Identify the ES, EF, LS, LF, critical path, and float using the critical path algorithm.

Activity	Duration (Days)	Immediate Predecessor
A	2	None
B	3	None
C	4	None
D	5	A
E	3	B
F	7	C
G	2	D, E
H	4	F
I	3	F
J	1	H
K	3	I

9. Given the following project network:

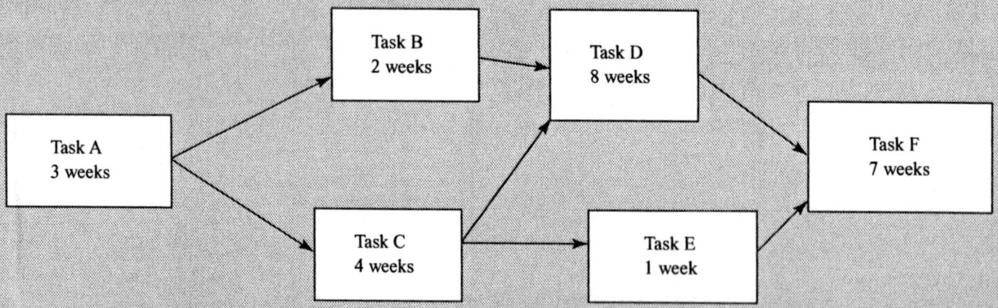

a. Use the critical path algorithm to determine ES, EF, LS, and LF times for all project activities.
b. Calculate total float and free float for every project activity.
c. Draw this network as a bar or Gantt chart.

10. Given the network in problem 9, enter project data into a project management software program such as MS Project. Print a network and a bar chart (Gantt) view. Interpret the results.

Internet Activities

1. Find the Project Management Institute's website (www.pmi.org). What is the mission of PMI? What services do they provide to support their mission? What is a PMP?
2. Locate the website for the Standish Group (www.standishgroup.com). What is the mission of this organization? What industry do they support? Describe the research that the Standish Group has conducted. Click on the link to Sample Research and then to the CHAOS Report. What were some of the key findings of this study? What do you believe are the implications of these findings for project managers? Also check the Unfinished Voyages link to view a useful diagnostic tool for project risk factors. What do they believe to be the top three risk factors for IT projects?
3. Locate the website for the Management Roundtable (www.managementroundtable.com). If you are interested in new product development and related project management issues, you may wish to sign up for the organization's monthly electronic newsletter, *The Critical Path.*

Related Modules of Interest

- Advanced Tools for Project Scheduling
- Managing and Controlling Project Resources
- Achieving Operational Excellence Through People
- Decision Analysis
- New Product and Process Development
- Purchasing and Supplier Management
- Financial Analysis

Selected Readings

CH2MHILL. *Project Delivery.* Denver: CH2Mhill, 1996.

DeMarco, T. *The Deadline.* New York: Dorset House, 1997.

Fleming, Q. W., and J. M. Koppelman. *Earned Value Project Management.* Newtown Square, PA: Project Management Institute, 1996.

Goal/QPC. *The Project Management Memory Jogger.* Salem, NH

Goldratt, E. *Critical Chain.* Great Barrington, MA: North River Press, 1997.

Gray, Clifford F. and Erik W. Larson, *Project Management.* New York: McGraw-Hill/Irwin, 1999.

Hartman, F. T. *Don't Park Your Brain Outside.* Newtown Square, PA: Project Management Institute, 2000.

Kerzner, H. *Strategic Planning for Project Management: Using a Project Management Maturity Model.* New York: John Wiley & Sons, 2001.

Meredith, J. R., and S. J. Mantell. *Project Management.* New York: John Wiley & Sons, 1999.

Verzuh, E. *The Fast Forward MBA in Project Management.* New York: John Wiley & Sons, 1999.

Appendix

Solutions to Example Problems

EXHIBIT A
AOA Solution to Network Diagramming Practice Problem in Exhibit 15

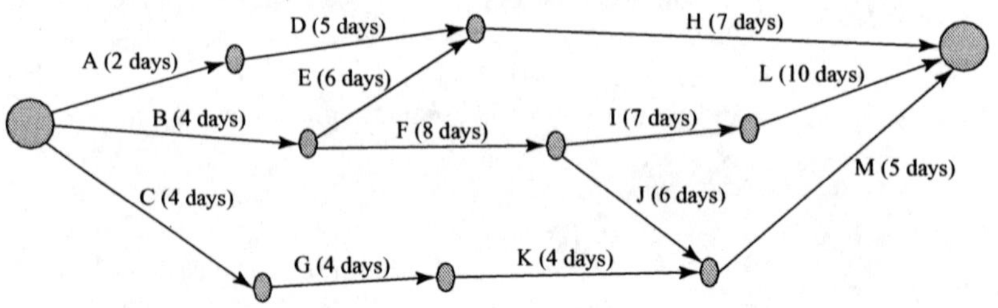

EXHIBIT B
AON Solution to Network Diagramming Practice Problem in Exhibit 15

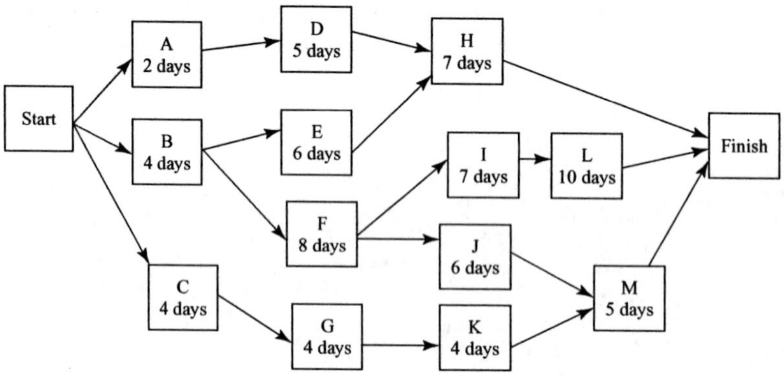

EXHIBIT C
Solution for Critical Path Algorithm Practice Problem in Exhibit 22

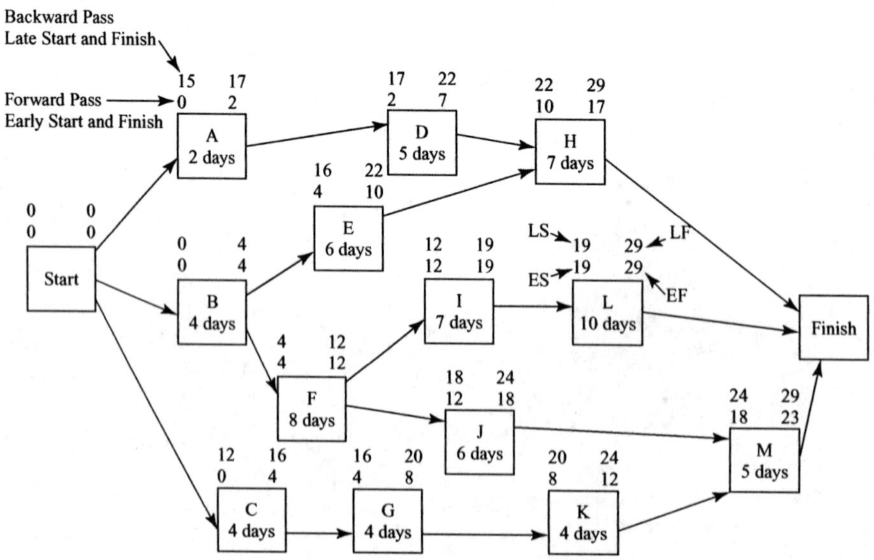